6TH EDITION

KINESIOLOGY

SCIENTIFIC BASIS OF HUMAN MOTION

KATHARINE F. WELLS, Ph.D.

Formerly Associate Professor
Wellesley College and Visiting Associate Professor
Mary Washington College

KATHRYN LUTTGENS, Ph.D.

Professor
Boston-Bouvé College
Northeastern University

W. B. SAUNDERS COMPANY
Philadelphia, London, Toronto

W. B. Saunders Company: West Washington Square
Philadelphia, PA 19105

1 St. Anne's Road
Eastbourne, East Sussex BN21 3UN, England

1 Goldthorne Avenue
Toronto, Ontario M8Z 5T9, Canada

Library of Congress Cataloging in Publication Data

Wells, Katharine F

Kinesiology: scientific basis of human motion.

Includes bibliographies.

1. Kinesiology.   I. Luttgens, Kathryn, 1926–
joint author.   II. Title. [DNLM: 1. Movement.
2. Musculoskeletal system.   3. Physical education and
training. WE103 W454k]

QP303.W43 1976   612'.76   75-8191

ISBN 0-7216-9218-4

Listed here is the latest translated edition of this
book together with the language of the translation
and the publisher.

Japanese (3rd edition) – Baseball Magazine Sha,
                Tokyo, Japan

Kinesiology   ISBN 0-7216-9218-4

Last digit is the print number: 9   8   7   6   5   4   3

PREFACE
to the Sixth Edition

Since the publication of the first edition of this text twenty-six years ago, courses in Kinesiology have undergone many changes both in content and in emphasis. Each subsequent edition has reflected these changes and the sixth edition, likewise, continues to reflect them. The greater emphasis placed upon the mechanical analysis of human motion in current kinesiology courses is provided for in a greatly expanded section on the fundamentals of mechanical analysis. Extensive revisions have been made in the section on anatomic fundamentals in order to stress applications to the analysis of human motion.

This textbook is designed as a basic resource to introduce the undergraduate student to the fundamentals of kinesiology. As such it presents the material in an elementary fashion and presupposes little background knowledge of anatomy or physics. On the other hand, it does not shy away from the presentation of materials related to the analysis of human motion which requires an understanding of principles of anatomy, physics and mathematics. Although at one time it was possible to avoid much scientific terminology and mathematical formulae, this is no longer the case. Yet the student should not be alarmed. Whatever background is needed for understanding the various applications is supplied, and numerous examples and exercises are provided.

This text is divided into three parts as follows:

I. Anatomic and Physiologic Fundamentals of Human Motion.

II. Fundamentals of Biomechanics.

III. Motor Skills: Principles and Applications.

Part One consists of nine chapters, all of which discuss the anatomic background essential for understanding human movement. The emphasis throughout is on the relation of anatomic structure to function, not on anatomy, as such. The chapters on the joint and muscular analysis of the movements of the major segments include two new features. The first of these is an application to selected common movements, either from sports and gymnastics or from daily life activities. The reason for introducing such applications early is to encourage students to start immediately putting theory into practice, rather than waiting until their knowledge of anatomy is more complete. It is hoped that this practice will sharpen their awareness of the factors that contribute to skillful movement.

The second new feature in this section is the inclusion of brief discussions of several common athletic injuries at the end of each anatomic region studied. The emphasis in these discussions is on the exact nature of each injury, the probable cause of each and the means of prevention. The purpose of this feature is to develop in the student an appreciation of the need for a thorough understanding of the functions of the bones, joints and muscles in the movements concerned, and of the potential harmfulness of the misuse of these structures.

Part Two presents the fundamentals of mechanics as they apply to movement analysis. The first chapter introduces the student to terminology and to the units of measure which are used when one studies motion analysis in quantitative terms. This chapter is followed by those that cover principles of motion and force as they apply to the body in action and in equilibrium. Throughout this section efforts have been made to maintain an elementary approach to the material without oversimplifying to the point where misconceptions could occur. In many instances the student is shown the "proof" of a principle through experimental examples or through mathematical derivation. This approach is used in the belief that greater understanding will result, and that greater comprehension of the reasons "why" optimum movement patterns occur as they do will be the reward.

Part Three opens with a chapter that discusses approaches to kinesiologic analysis of human movements and includes a classification of motor skills, the major divisions of which are Maintaining Erect Posture, Giving Impetus (to one's own body and to external objects) and Receiving Impetus (from one's own body and from external objects). This classification forms the basis for the organization of the six chapters that follow. In each of these chapters the basic principles of anatomy and mechanics are identified and applied to specific motor skills. Sample analyses are included.

Part Three concludes with a chapter on exercises for special purposes, namely, exercises for increasing range of motion, for strengthening muscles and for correcting postural faults and weaknesses (a revision of Chapter Twenty-One in the 5th edition); and a summary chapter is included on the implications that a knowledge of kinesiology has for the teaching of physical education (essentially the same as Chapter Twenty-Six in the 5th edition).

There are seven Appendices, as follows:

    A. Outline for Studying the Joints and Their Movements.
    B. Classification of Joints and Their Movements.
    C. Muscular Attachments.

D. Check Lists for the Muscular Analysis of Movements of the Major Body Segments.
E. Mathematics Review.
F. Table of Trigonometric Functions.
G. Exercises for Kinesiologic Analysis.

The authors wish to express grateful appreciation to Jeanne Rowlands for photographs taken especially for this text, to Northeastern University's Sports Information Office for providing additional photographs, to Marilyn Cairns and Kathryn J. Shaffer for critical review of certain chapters and to Betsy Bakstran, Barbara Holden and Mary Nicholson for their typing of the manuscript.

Appreciation is also expressed to the authors and publishers who graciously gave permission to quote passages and reproduce illustrations from their publications. They also wish to acknowledge their indebtedness to the many students whose stimulus has been a vital reason for the existence of this book. Finally, they would like to express their sincere thanks to the editorial and production staffs of the W. B. Saunders Company for their helpfulness throughout the preparation of this edition.

KATHARINE F. WELLS, Needham, Massachusetts
KATHRYN LUTTGENS, Wellesley, Massachusetts

PREFACE
to the First Edition
Abridged

This book is intended as a kinesiology text both for the teacher and for the student. It is believed that there is enough material to use it as a text for a full year's course, yet, at the same time, by judicious selection of the subject matter, by omission of the supplementary material and by the substitution of classroom demonstrations for some of the laboratory exercises, the book should serve equally well as a text for a one semester course in kinesiology. It is left to the discretion of the instructor to select the material that meets his particular needs.

In its original form this textbook was an unpublished handbook-laboratory manual. It was used by the author in her kinesiology classes for three years before it was expanded to its present form. The original manual did not serve as an independent textbook. It was intended to be used as a companion book to a kinesiology or anatomy text. Since this limited its usefulness, however, it was decided to expand it to what is intended as a complete and independent textbook. For those who like to use a single textbook for a course it should suffice. To help the student (and the instructor) in his collateral reading, most chapters in this text contain a comprehensive bibliography. In many cases there is also a list of readings which are particularly recommended. These bibliographies and reading lists provide a rich source of information for the inquiring student.

In regard to the value of laboratory exercises and projects as a means of learning, James B. Stroud, in his book *Psychology in Education*, points out that "Effectiveness of instruction is not determined so much by what the teacher does, as by what he leads the pupils to do. . . ." Again, "Perhaps one of the most successful procedures for infusing learning with significance has been the [educational method known as] constructive activities. . . . The activity is thus a means of making learning meaningful and of giving it a purpose." In accord with this point of view numerous laboratory exercises are suggested. In conformity to the same principle, only a few complete analyses of skills are presented, for it is the writer's contention that the student will gain far more from making one complete analysis himself than from reading a dozen or more ready-made analyses.

As a further means of enriching the kinesiology course a number of the chapters include supplementary material in the form of brief descriptions of research projects in the field of anatomy and kinesiology. A few of these were carried out by the author, but the majority were conducted by other investigators and reported in the professional journals. The purpose of including this material is to broaden the instructor's background and to provide supplementary reading assignments for advanced students.

It has been the intention of the author to write simply and to use nontechnical terminology whenever this conveyed the meaning as clearly and specifically as technical terms. The latter have been used, however, whenever they served to avoid ambiguity. While it is desirable for the kinesiology student to enlarge his scientific vocabulary, a text which confronts him with a staggering list of new and strange words defeats its purpose. Textbooks should stimulate the curiosity of their readers, not frighten them with a forbidding vocabulary.

The author acknowledges her indebtedness to many individuals without whose help it is doubtful if this book could have been written. She wishes to express her grateful appreciation particularly to Professor C. H. McCloy of the State University of Iowa for his continued guidance, encouragement and criticism, also for his generous permission to use material from his course in The Mechanical Analysis of Motor Skills, and to the students in her kinesiology classes of the last three years who served patiently as "guinea pigs" and who made many constructive suggestions concerning the laboratory exercises.

For the illustrations, which add immeasurably to the usefulness of the text, grateful acknowledgment is made to Miss Mildred Codding, who made the anatomic drawings.

The author is under obligation to a number of individuals for the use of photographs and to several publishers for permission to reproduce copyrighted materials. To all writers and teachers from whom the author, either wittingly or unwittingly, has derived ideas which have provided the necessary background for the writing of this book she humbly acknowledges her indebtedness.

KATHARINE F. WELLS

CONTENTS

INTRODUCTION TO THE STUDY OF KINESIOLOGY

Kinesiology, as it is known in physical education, orthopedics and physical medicine, is the study of human movement from the point of view of the physical sciences. The study of the human body as a machine for the performance of work has its foundations in three major areas of study, namely, mechanics, anatomy and physiology; more specifically, biomechanics, musculoskeletal anatomy and neuromuscular physiology. The majority of courses in kinesiology are based primarily on the first two of these and a separate course, physiology of muscular activity, covers much of the third. There is some overlapping, however, as there are certain physiologic concepts which even the most elementary course in kinesiology cannot afford to ignore.

In the early days of physical education, when few activities were taught other than gymnastics and the dance, the content of a course in kinesiology was confined chiefly to functional anatomy. Gradually, as sports assumed a more important place in the curriculum, the concept of kinesiology was broadened to include the study of the mechanical principles which apply to sport techniques. The principles were applied not only to the movements of the body itself, but also to the movements of the implements, balls and other equipment used for the sport in question. In like manner, the development of the kinesiology course in schools of physical therapy and occupational therapy has kept pace with the development of their expanded curricula. Having started as "muscle reeducation," it has come to include the application of mechanical principles to postural adjustments, to the gait, to the use of tools and household implements, and to the modifications of vocational and homemaking activities necessitated by limitations in neuromuscular capacity and skeletal structure.

Some authorities refer to kinesiology as a science in its own right; others claim that it should be called a study rather than a true science because the principles on which it is based are derived from basic sciences such as anatomy, physiology and physics. In any event, its unique contribution is that it selects from many sciences those principles which are pertinent to human motion and systematizes their application. However it may be categorized, to the inquiring student it is a door opening into a whole new world of discovery and appreciation. Human motion, which most of us have taken for granted all our lives, is seen through new eyes. One who gives it any thought whatever cannot help being impressed not only by the beauty of human motion, but also by its apparently infinite possibilities, its meaningfulness, its orderliness, its adaptability to the surrounding environment. Nothing is haphazard; nothing is left to chance. Every structure that participates in the movements of the body does so in obedience to physical and physiologic principles. The student of kinesiology, like the student of anatomy, physiology, psychology, genetics and other biological sciences, can only look with reverent wonder at the intricate mechanism of the body and in the words of the psalmist exclaim to his creator, "I will praise thee, for I am fearfully and wonderfully made."

But kinesiology is not studied merely for the purpose of inciting our interest in a fascinating and mysterious subject. It has a useful purpose. We study kinesiology in order to learn how to analyze the movements of the human body and to discover their underlying principles. The study of kinesiology is an essential part of the educational experience of students of physical education and physical medicine. For the physical educator it has a dual purpose: on the one hand, the purpose of perfecting performance in motor skills, and on the other, the purpose of perfecting the performer, himself. Kinesiology helps to prepare the physical educator to teach effective performance in both fundamental and specialized motor skills. Furthermore, it enables him to evaluate exercises and activities from the point of view of their effect on the human structure. As Dr. William Skarstrom used to say to his kinesiology students, the human machine has this advantage over the manufactured machine: Whereas the latter wears out with use, the former improves with use (within limits), *provided it is used in accordance with the principles of efficient human motion.* The function of kinesiology, therefore, is to contribute not only to *successful participation* in various physical activities, but also to the *improvement* of the human structure through the intelligent selection of activities and the efficient use of the body.

For the physical therapist and the occupational therapist the purpose of studying kinesiology (whether called by that name or by some other) is not unlike that of the physical education teacher. The difference is in emphasis, rather than in purpose. The therapist is primarily concerned with the effect that exercises and other techniques of physical medicine have upon the body. He—or she—is concerned particularly with the restoration of impaired function and with methods of compensating for lost function. Effective performance is a goal for the therapist as it is for the physical educator, but to the therapist "effective performance" refers not so much to *skillful* performance in athletic activities, as to *adequate* performance in the activities associated with daily living. Whereas the educator applies his knowledge of kinesiology chiefly to the movements of the normal body, the therapist is concerned with the movements of a body which has suffered an impairment in function.

The educator and the therapist have at least one purpose in common in studying kinesiology. Both are concerned with posture and body mechanics, hence both are interested in discovering the anatomic and mechanical bases for training in this area. Both apply their knowledge of kinesiology to analyzing the postural needs of others, to the intelligent selection of posture exercises based on individual need and to the mechanically efficient methods of using the body in daily life skills.

The most satisfactory way of studying kinesiology is by supplementing book study with laboratory experimentation. It is a truism that we learn best by doing. When time must be conserved, demonstration may be substituted for some of the experimental work, but it should never replace it entirely.

The use of motion picture films is another good device for supplementing book study. It is particularly helpful if a hand projector is used, or a projector which can be stopped at will, thus making it possible to analyze positions and body relationships.

Whatever method of teaching or of study is employed it is well for the student to keep in mind the aims of a kinesiology course and the applications he intends to make of what he learns. He must remember that the analysis of motion is not an end in itself, but rather a means to the learning of new movement patterns and the improvement of old ones. This is as true for the physical therapist teaching amputees and paraplegics to walk again as it is for the physical educator teaching a sport technique. Finally, he must remember that the skill itself is of less importance than the one who practices it. Kinesiology serves only half its purpose when it provides the background for learning or teaching motor skills. It must also serve to lay the foundation for perfecting, repairing and keeping in good condition that incomparable mechanism — the human body.

ANATOMIC AND PHYSIOLOGIC FUNDAMENTALS OF HUMAN MOTION

INTRODUCTION
TO PART ONE

Where does anatomy end and kinesiology begin? This is a question frequently argued by kinesiologists. Yet, in truth, there is no answer because the question itself is not a valid one. One might as well ask, "Where does the study of words end and the writing of compositions (or articles, or books) begin?" Or, "Where does the study of building materials end and the designing and erecting of buildings begin?" Just as words are the elements used in all writing, whether creative, factual or expository, and just as bricks, wood, cement, metal and glass are some of the elements used in building, so bones, joints, muscles, connective tissue, blood vessels and nerves are the vital elements of human motion. They are the essential elements used in batting a baseball, passing and carrying a football, shooting a basketball into the basket, in fact, in all running, walking, jumping, throwing, striking, catching and swimming; likewise one finds them in typewriting, manual labor, picture painting, sewing, knitting, and so forth, almost without end.

The physical education instructor and the athletic coach have two major concerns in fulfilling their responsibilities. These are, first, the learning and improvement of performance in motor skills, and second, the prevention of injury. One aim of Part One, therefore, is to prepare the physical education major student and, to a certain extent, the students of physical therapy, occupational therapy and recreational therapy for analyzing human movements in terms of joint and muscular action. This section should not be looked upon merely as a review of anatomy but as the very foundation for analysis of human motion. It demonstrates the close relationships between anatomic structure and function, and it provides a body of knowledge which can be utilized in the learning and perfecting of various motor skills. It aims to demonstrate how the bones, joints and muscles serve as elements in anatomic levers, which act in accord with the laws of mechanics. It also aims to make clear the influences of gravitational and other external forces on muscular actions. For instance, under certain circumstances, these forces may cause an action to be the exact opposite from what one would expect in view of the movement which is being performed. It should be obvious, therefore, that memorizing the actions of muscles will not prepare the student for making accurate analyses. He must be armed with a true understanding of all the conditions that influence the functions of the muscles.

A second aim of Part One is to equip the future physical education instructor and coach with the anatomic knowledge essential for understanding the nature of common athletic injuries and their prevention. For this reason considerable emphasis is placed upon the structure of each joint, the factors which contribute to its stability and the factors which influence the range of motion of each joint. One factor of which many sports instructors and coaches seem to be in ignorance is the timetable of ages at which the epiphyseal cartilages become ossified. It should be of interest because it marks the turning point between the period of bone growth and the period of bone maturity. Because of the significance of this information a schedule of the maturation age of each bone which participates in common activities has been included in the first chapter.

There are nine chapters in Part One—two on the musculoskeletal system and its movements, one on the neuromuscular aspects of motion, and six on the anatomy and the fundamental movements of specific segments of the body. The order in which these chapters are studied is entirely optional. The authors appreciate the fact that the students who use this text may differ widely in their educational backgrounds. Some may already have completed courses in anatomy, possibly even including the experience of human dissection. Others may have had only brief courses and will feel the need of receiving more detailed information. Still others may have had no anatomic instruction whatsoever and may expect none other than what is included in the kinesiology course. This situation obviously leaves authors of kinesiology texts with a dilemma. In an attempt to meet the needs of all students, whatever their backgrounds, the authors of this text have presented in Part One what they consider to be a fairly complete coverage of the aspects of anatomy that relate to movement, and at the same time have omitted details whose relation to movement seems less significant. Hence, specific muscle attachments are not included in the main body of the text but may be found in chart form in an appendix at the end of the book for those who want to refer to them. On the other hand, the muscle's line of pull and its relation to the joint at which the motion is occurring are emphasized as these are considered essential elements of movement.

In the light of the aforementioned aims of Part One—to provide the future physical education instructor and athletic coach with the knowledge necessary for analyzing human motion and applying such an analysis to the learning and improvement of performance in motor skills, and to equip both the instructor and the coach with the anatomic background for preventing athletic injuries—it might seem that the student should wait until he has completed the entire anatomic section before attempting to analyze movement. On the contrary, the earlier he can start to apply his knowledge, the better. In fact, attempting to analyze basic movements as soon as possible serves as a stimulus to the study of anatomy. An example of this situation is given below.

Let us consider starting with the arm in its anatomic position and flexing the forearm at the elbow against the stabilized upper arm. Note that we have already defined the starting position and the movement. We could be even more specific if we wished and state whether the movement was executed quickly or slowly, and whether the movement was performed against resistance as though lifting a weight.

The next step would be to consider the joint itself. The structure of the elbow joint should be reviewed. Since it was stipulated that the movement was made from the anatomic position, it would be advisable to review the radioulnar articulations also, especially the proximal joint because of its close relationship to the elbow joint. It would be helpful to refer to Chapter 2 or Appendix C to check on the types and characteristics of these joints.

The muscles performing the movement should be considered next and an attempt made to answer such questions as the following: What muscles flex the elbow joint? How are they affected by the starting position and the position of the forearm throughout the movement? Try to discover whether there is a clear-cut difference in the importance of the participating muscles in this particular movement, but do not overstress this point. Include all of the muscles that unquestionably contribute to flexion in this position without being overly concerned as to whether they are "principal movers" or "assistant movers." Review the section on the coordination of the muscular system (see page 39) and try to identify muscles serving in the capacity of stabilizers or of neutralizers.

Following the above procedure throughout the study of Part I will pave the way for the later analysis of more complex movements. Procedural steps for analyzing fitness exercises, sport skills, and other physical activities, are presented in Appendix D. For the present, however, it is suggested that the student make simple joint and muscle analyses until he is thoroughly familiar with this process.

Chapter One

THE MUSCULOSKELETAL SYSTEM

I. The Skeletal Framework and its Movements

It is customary — especially for physical education major students — to begin the study of anatomy with a detailed study of the bones, then to proceed to the joints, and then to the muscles. This path of investigation sometimes dampens the enthusiasm of the students whose chief focus of interest is movement. Therefore, the first two chapters of this text emphasize the concept of the total musculoskeletal system as a mechanism for motion. It is hoped that by using this concept, the student will find the study of the structural elements of this system to be more meaningful.

The musculoskeletal framework, as the phrase implies, is an arrangement of bones and muscles. Adjacent bones are attached to one another by joints, which provide for the motion of the articulating bones, and the muscles which span the joints provide the force for moving the bones to which they are attached. Mechanically speaking, the total bone-joint-muscle structure is an intricate combination of levers which makes possible a great number of coordinated movements, ranging from the small hand and finger motions used in assembling a television set or playing the piano, to the total body movements of a swimmer or a pole vaulter. Any single one of the levers involved in such movements is relatively simple. Physics tells us that a lever is defined as a rigid bar which turns about a fulcrum (fixed axis or pivot) when force is applied to it at some specific point. An anatomic lever, therefore, is simply a bone which engages in an angular or turning type of movement when a muscle which is attached to it contracts and thus applies force to it. This force is always a *pulling* force because muscles, being flexible, are unable to push; they can only pull.

THE BONES

Although the anatomy texts give the number of bones in the human skeleton as 206, only 177 of them engage in voluntary movement.* The skeleton consists of two major parts, the axial skeleton and the appendicular skeleton. The axial section comprises the skull, spinal column, sternum and ribs, and the appendicular section includes the bones of the upper and lower extremities. The bones of the upper extremity include the scapula, clavicle, humerus, ulna, radius, carpal bones, metacarpals and phalanges, and those of the lower extremity include the three fused bones of the pelvis, the femur, tibia, fibula, tarsal bones, metatarsals and phalanges. Although the pelvis may be classified with either the axial or the appendicular skeleton, it is actually a link between the axial skeleton and the lower extremity branch of the appendicular skeleton and is functionally as important to one as to the other.

Types of Bones.   In spite of the great variety of shapes and sizes of bones, there are only four major categories of them, namely, long, short, flat and irregular.

LONG BONES.   Characterized by a cylindrical shaft with relatively broad, knobby ends. The shaft or body has thick walls and contains a central cavity known as a medullary canal. The bones belonging in this category are the clavicle, humerus, ulna, radius, metacarpals and phalanges of the upper extremity, and the femur, tibia, fibula, metatarsals and phalanges of the lower extremity.

SHORT BONES.   Relatively small, chunky, solid bones. The carpals and tarsals (wrist and ankle bones) belong to this category.

FLAT BONES.   These include the sternum, scapulae, ribs, pelvic bones and patellas.

IRREGULAR BONES.   The bones of the spinal column, i.e., the 24 vertebrae, the sacrum and the coccyx, are found in this category.

Mechanical Axis of a Bone.   It has already been stated that bones serve as levers. When one undertakes the mechanical analysis of muscular action he needs to know what is meant by the mechanical axis of the bone, or the body segment, that is serving as the lever. The student will find it to his advantage, therefore, to learn what this term is now while he is studying the bones. *The mechanical axis of a bone or segment is a straight line which connects the midpoint of the joint at one end with the midpoint of the joint at the other end, or in the case of a terminal segment, with the midpoint of its distal end.* This axis does not necessarily pass lengthwise through the shaft of the bony lever. If the shaft is curved or if the articulating process projects at an angle from the shaft, the greater part of the axis may lie outside of the shaft, as in the case of he femur (Fig. 1–1).

The Epiphyses.   An epiphysis is a layer of cartilage whose presence in the bone is an indication that the bone has not completed its growth. In the long bones the shaft is separated from the ends and from articulating knobs by

---

*The bones not included are the hyoid, the coccyx (the sacrum and coccyx are treated as a single bone as there is no voluntary motion of one on the other), 6 ossicles, and 21 skull bones, the skull being treated as a single bone with reference to the spinal column.

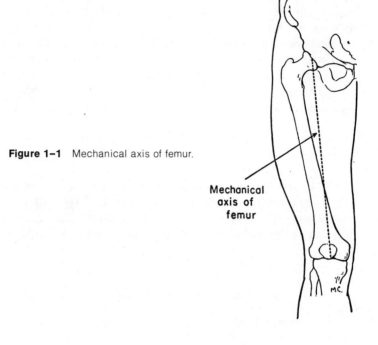

Figure 1-1 Mechanical axis of femur.

Mechanical
axis of
femur

epiphyseal cartilages. This is where growth takes place. As growth ceases, the cartilages gradually become ossified, and when closure is complete, no more growth can occur. Surprisingly, several epiphyses do not completely ossify until the twentieth, or even the twenty-fifth, year. Hence, most high school boys and many college men are engaging in vigorous sports before their bones are fully matured. Physical education instructors and coaches need to be aware of this fact. Although this is not usually harmful in the case of noncontact sports, in violent contact sports like football and boxing, the consequences may be extremely serious.[9] Protective devices are helpful, but many of the ones in current use have been judged inadequate. High standards for these devices must be insisted upon. Even more important, coaches, especially those of young adolescents, must be both knowledgeable and conscientious. They must accept their responsibility for the health and safety of each individual player as being of far greater importance than the development of a winning team. The coach who tells a high school boy to aim the top of his helmet at the numeral on his opponent's shirt and run full force into him (known as "sticking") is either grossly ignorant or callously indifferent.

There is also danger to elementary and junior high school youngsters who are permitted to bear weights that are too heavy for them. "Husky looking" boys and girls are often mistakenly permitted to be in the base of a pyramid because they give the impression of being strong. If they are on their hands and knees supporting a second and perhaps a third row of youngsters, the weight may be too much for them. This is especially likely to be the case if the individuals in the upper rows are careless about where they place their hands and knees. If these are not placed in line with the supporting individuals' arms and thighs, the vertebrae and possibly the arms and thighs will be subjected to rotatory stress which may result in serious injury to the epiphyses of these bones. Dr. Charles L. Lowman was a pioneer in warning of such dangers. In spite of the early dates of their publication, his writings are strongly recommended to today's instructors and coaches.

The approximate ages at which the ossification of the epiphyseal cartilages is completed are presented in Tables 1–1 and 1–2.[1]

ARTICULATIONS

The structure and function of joints are so interrelated that it is difficult to discuss them separately. Hence, in the discussion of structure there is much that relates to function and, conversely, much that relates to structure when function is discussed. Careful inspection of the joints depicted in Figure 1–2

TABLE 1–1 Approximate Ages of Epiphyseal Closures*

	AGE
SPINAL COLUMN	
Vertebrae and sacrum	25
THORAX	
Sternum	25
Ribs	25
UPPER EXTREMITY	
Clavicle	25
Scapula	15–17
Humerus	
Head fused with shaft	20
Lateral epicondyle	16–17
Medial epicondyle	18
Ulna	
Olecranon	16
Lower end	20
Radius	
Head and shaft	18–19
Lower end of shaft	20
LOWER EXTREMITY	
Pelvic bone	
Inferior rami of pubis and ischium (almost complete)	7–8
Acetabulum	20–25
Femur	
Greater and lesser trochanters	18
Head	18
Lower end	20
Tibia	
Upper end	20
Lower end	18
Fibula	
Upper end	25
Lower end	20

*Listed by body section.

will give an idea of the relationship between the shape of the joint and the movements that it permits. In much the same way that railroad tracks determine the route available to the train, the configuration of the bones that form an articulation, together with the reinforcing ligaments, both determine and limit the movements that the involved segment can make.

STRUCTURE

Classification.   There are many different patterns of joint structure and these form the basis for their classification. The classifications in two well-known anatomy texts[1, 2] are based on the presence or absence of a joint cavity, i.e., a space between the articulating surfaces of the bones. Each type of joint is further classified either according to shape or according to the nature of the tissues which connect the bones. These classifications, with their subdivisions, may be grasped more readily if presented in outline form.

I. Diarthrosis (from the Greek, meaning a joint in which there is a separation or articular cavity) (Figs. 1–2, 1–3 and 1–4)
   A. Characteristics
   1. An articular cavity is present.
   2. The joint is encased within a sleevelike ligamentous capsule.
   3. The capsule is lined with synovial membrane which secretes synovial fluid for lubricating the joint.
   4. The articular surfaces are smooth.
   5. The articular surfaces are covered with cartilage, usually hyaline, but occasionally fibrocartilage.

TABLE 1–2   Approximate Ages of Epiphyseal Closures*

APPROXIMATE AGE

7–8
   Inferior rami of pubis and ischium almost complete

15–17
   Upper extremity: scapula, lateral epicondyle of humerus, olecranon process of ulna

18–19
   Upper extremity: medial epicondyle of humerus, head and shaft of radius
   Lower extremity: femoral head and greater and lesser trochanters, lower end of tibia

About 20
   Upper extremity: humeral head, lower ends of radius and ulna
   Lower extremity: lower ends of femur and fibula, upper end of tibia

20–25
   Lower extremity: acetabulum in pelvis

25
   Spine: vertebrae and sacrum
   Upper extremity: clavicle
   Lower extremity: upper end of fibula
   Thorax: sternum and ribs

*Listed by age.

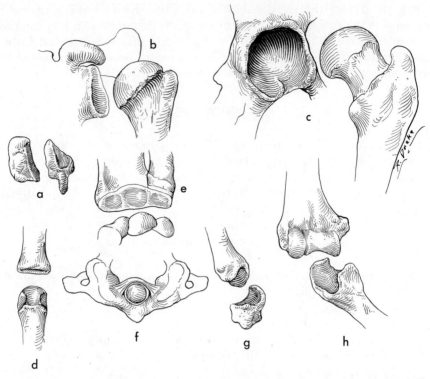

Figure 1-2   Major types of diarthrodial joints. *a*, Plane; *b*, ball-and-socket (shoulder); *c*, ball-and-socket (hip); *d*, condyloid (metacarpophalangeal); *e*, condyloid (radiocarpal); *f*, pivot (atlantoaxial); *g*, saddle (thumb or carpometacarpal); *h*, hinge (elbow or humero-ulnar). (From Hollinshead, W. H.: *Functional Anatomy of the Limbs and Back*, 3rd Ed. Philadelphia: W. B. Saunders Company, 1969.)

B. Classification*
   1. Irregular (arthrodial; plane) (Fig. 1–2, *A*). The joint surfaces are irregularly shaped, usually flat or slightly curved. The only movement permitted is of a gliding nature, hence it is nonaxial. Example: the carpal joints (Fig. 5–10).
   2. Hinge (ginglymus). One surface is spool-like; the other is concave. The concave surface fits over the spool-like process and glides partially around it in a hinge type of movement. This constitutes movement in one plane about a single axis of motion; hence it is uniaxial. The movements that occur are flexion and extension. Example: elbow joint (Figs. 1–2, *H* and 5–1).
   3. Pivot (trochoid; screw). This kind of joint may be characterized by a peglike pivot, as in the joint between atlas and axis, or by two long bones fitting against each other near each end in such a way that one bone can roll around the other one, as do the radius and ulna of the forearm. In the latter type a small concave notch on one bone fits against the rounded surface of the other. The rounded surface may

---

*This classification is based on the one in Morris' *Human Anatomy*.[2]

either be the edge of a disk (like the head of the radius), or it may be a rounded knob (like the head of the ulna). The only movement permitted in either kind of pivot joint is rotation. It is a movement in one plane about a single axis; hence the joint is uniaxial. Examples: atlanto-axial and radioulnar joints (Figs. 1–2, *F*, 5–1 and 8–10).

4. Condyloid (ovoid; ellipsoidal). An oval or egg-shaped convex surface fits into a reciprocally shaped concave surface. Movement can occur in two planes, forward and backward, and from side to side. The former movement is flexion and extension, and the latter abduction and adduction or lateral flexion. The joint is biaxial. When these movements are performed sequentially, they constitute circumduction. Example: wrist joint (Fig. 5–10).

5. Saddle (sellar; reciprocal reception). This may be thought of as a modification of a condyloid joint. Both ends of the convex surface are tipped up, making the surface concave in the other direction, like a western saddle. Fitting over this is a reciprocally concave-convex surface. Like the condyloid joint, this is a biaxial joint, permitting flexion and extension, abduction and adduction, and circumduction. The difference between the two is that the saddle joint has greater freedom of motion. Example: carpometacarpal joint of thumb (Fig. 5–11).

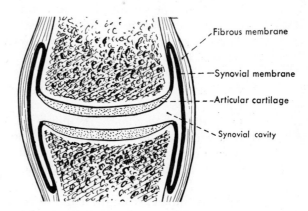

Figure 1–3 Frontal section of a diarthrodial joint. (From Hollinshead.)

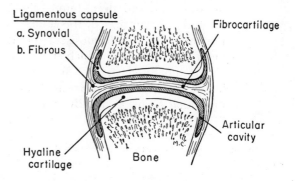

Figure 1–4 Frontal section of a diarthrodial joint having fibrocartilage.

6. Ball-and-socket (spheroidal; enarthrodial). In this type of joint the spherical head of one bone fits into the cup or saucerlike cavity of the other bone (Figs. 1–2, *B*, 1–2, *C*, 4–1, 4–2, 6–1 and 6–2). It is very like the swivel joint on top of a camera tripod. It permits flexion and extension, abduction and adduction, circumduction (the sequential combination of the preceding), horizontal flexion and extension, and rotation. It is a triaxial joint since it permits movement about three axes.

C. Summary classification of diarthrodial joints

Number of Axes:	0	1	2	3
	Nonaxial	Uniaxial	Biaxial	Triaxial
Classification:	Irregular	Hinge Pivot	Condyloid Saddle	Ball-and- socket

(See Appendix B for a more complete chart of diarthrodial joints and their motions.)

II. Synarthrosis (from the Greek, meaning literally "with joint" or, according to our usage, a joint in which there is no separation or articular cavity)
  A. Characteristics
    1. In two of the types (cartilaginous and fibrous) the two bones are united by means of an intervening substance, such as cartilage or fibrous tissue, which is continuous with the joint surfaces.
    2. The third type (ligamentous) is not a true joint but is a ligamentous connection between two bones which may or may not be contiguous.
    3. There is no articular cavity, hence no capsule, synovial membrane or synovial fluid.
  B. Classification
    1. Cartilaginous (synchondrosis; from the Greek, meaning "with cartilage")
      Only the joints which are united by fibrocartilage permit motion of a bending and twisting nature. Those united by hyaline cartilage permit only a slight compression. Example of hyaline type: epiphyseal unions. Example of fibrocartilaginous type: articulations between the bodies of the vertebrae (Fig. 8–2).*
    2. Fibrous (suture, from the Latin word for "seam"). The edges of bone are united by means of a thin layer of fibrous tissue which is continuous with the periosteum. No movements are permitted. Only example: the sutures of the skull.
    3. Ligamentous (syndesmosis; from the Greek, meaning "with ligament"). Two bones, which may be adjacent or which may be quite widely separated, are tied together by one or more ligaments. These ligaments may be in the form of cords, bands or flat sheets. The movement that occurs is usually limited and of no specific type. Examples:

---

*In some anatomy texts these are classified in a separate major category as amphiarthrodial joints.

coracoacromial union (Fig. 4–3); midunion of radius and ulna (Figs. 5–2 and 5–3).

C. Summary

The synarthrodial joints of greatest concern to the kinesiologist are those of the vertebral bodies. Owing to the thickness of the intervertebral disks, these permit a moderate amount of motion simulating that of ball-and-socket joints. The movements are flexion and extension, lateral flexion, circumduction and rotation.

Suggestions for Studying Joint Structure.   In order to understand thoroughly the structure of a joint and especially the relation of structure to function, the student should supplement his book study with firsthand study of a skeleton or of the disarticulated bones which enter into the formation of each major joint. Following this preliminary study, the student may find it helpful to "construct" a joint by taking the two bones (in some cases, three) and fastening them together with pieces of adhesive or masking tape, carefully placed to represent the specific ligaments of the joint. Pieces of thick felt, cut in the proper shape, may be used to represent the fibrocartilage. This technique is particularly helpful for studying the knee, hip and shoulder joints.

FUNCTION

The function of the joints is obviously to provide the bones with a means of moving, or rather, of being moved. But because such provisions bring with them a threat of instability, the joints have what might be called a secondary function of providing for stability without interfering with the desired motions.

Joint Stability.   By joint stability we mean resistance to displacement. Steindler uses the term *cohesion* and suggests four factors which are responsible for this stability: the joint ligaments such as the lateral ligaments of hinge joints, muscle tension (see stabilizing components of muscular force), fascia and atmospheric pressure.[4] The latter is particularly effective at the hip joint. A fifth factor is suggested here, namely, the shape of the bony structure.

SHAPE OF BONY STRUCTURE.   This may refer to the kind of joint, such as hinge, condyloid or ball-and-socket, but it is even more likely to refer to specific characteristics of the particular joint in question. The shoulder and the hip joints, for instance, are both ball-and-socket joints, yet they differ markedly in their stability. The depth of the cup-like acetabulum of the hip joint, in contrast to the small size and shallowness of the glenoid fossa of the shoulder joint, is a case in point. The bony structure of the hip joint obviously gives greater protection against displacement.

LIGAMENTOUS ARRANGEMENT.   Ligaments are strong, flexible, stress-resistant, somewhat elastic, fibrous tissues which may be in the form of strap-like bands or of round cords. They attach the ends of the bones which form a movable joint and help to maintain them in the right relationship to each other. They also check the movement when it reaches its normal limits, and they resist movements for which the joint is not constructed. For instance, the collateral ligaments of the knee help to prevent any tendency there might be for this joint to ab- or adduct. Likewise, the ulnar and radial collateral ligaments of the elbow prevent ab- and adduction. The ligaments do not always succeed in preventing abnormal or excessive movements because collisions and violent motions may cause them to be torn. Also, if they are subjected to prolonged periods of stress they become abnormally stretched. So long as the ligaments remain undamaged, they are an important factor in contributing to joint stability, but once stretched, their usefulness is permanently affected and stability is diminished.

FASCIA.   Fascia consists of fibrous connective tissue which forms sheaths for individual muscles, partitions which lie between muscles, and smaller partitions which separate bundles of muscle fibers within a single muscle. According to their location and function they may vary from thin membranes to tough, fibrous sheets. In composition they are similar to ligaments in that they are flexible and elastic within limits but are susceptible to permanent stretch if subjected to too intense or too prolonged stress.

ATMOSPHERIC PRESSURE.   The importance of atmospheric pressure as a factor in resisting dislocation of a joint was demonstrated many years ago in a unique experiment. First, all the muscles and then the ligaments of a hip joint (including the teres femoris ligament) were severed, but surprisingly the head of the femur remained in place. Then a hole was drilled through the acetabulum of another hip joint whose ligaments were intact, and immediately the femoral head separated from the socket.[4]

MUSCULAR ARRANGEMENT.   The muscles also play a part in the stability of joints, especially in those joints whose bony structure contributes little to stability. The shoulder joint is a notable example. Furthermore, the atmospheric pressure is too slight here to be of help. Of the six muscles that act on the shoulder joint, four of them, known as the rotator cuff (subscapularis, supraspinatus, infraspinatus and teres minor) are particularly important as stabilizers of this joint. One of their chief functions is protection of the shoulder joint and prevention of displacement of the humeral head. Figure 4–6 on page 78 shows that all four of these muscles have a strong inward pull on the humeral head toward the glenoid fossa. There is further discussion in the next chapter concerning the role of muscles as stabilizers as opposed to that of movers or neutralizers.

Joint Motion.   The types of motion of which the different kinds of joints are capable have already been mentioned in the Joint Classification outline, and the fundamental movements of the major body segments, described in terms of the orientation planes of the body and axes of motion, are presented at the end of this chapter. The present discussion is concerned mainly with the range of motion at the various joints and factors related to this, such as those which account for an individual's range of motion, methods of studying and measuring the ROM (range of motion), techniques for increasing the ROM and suggestions for research projects concerning ROM.

Factors Affecting the Range of Motion.   Three of the factors that affect the stability of a joint are also related to its range of motion. These are the shape of the articular surfaces, the restraining effect of the ligaments and the controlling action of the muscles. The muscles and their tendons also act as restraining agents in some movements. Many persons have been aware of the tightness of the hamstring tendons (behind the knees) when attempting to touch the floor without bending the knees. Many have also discovered that continued practice will stretch these tendons and improve the joint's range of motion appreciably.

Additional factors in the range of motion include body build (both the mesomorph and the ectomorph usually have greater flexibility than the endomorph), heredity (in addition to the body build factor), personal exercise habits, current state of physical fitness and eventually, age.

The movements of each joint should be studied both on the skeleton and on the living subject. When using the latter method, it is important to consider all the joints involved in the movement in question. For instance, in studying the movements of the elbow joint, the articulation between the humerus and the radius must not be overlooked. The close relationship that exists between certain joints should be noted, as for example, the relationship between the elbow joint and the proximal radioulnar articulation. The tilting of the pelvis which accompanies many movements of the lower extremity should be recognized; likewise the movements of the shoulder girdle which accompany those of the shoulder joint. There is a particular pitfall awaiting those who study the movements of the shoulder joint only by observing the living subject. If not forewarned, they are likely to overlook the part played by the shoulder girdle. The movements of the latter may be detected by palpating the scapula and the clavicle in all movements of the upper arm. To follow the movements of the scapula the thumb should be placed at the inferior angle, one finger on the root of the scapular spine and another on the acromion process. Firm contact should be maintained as the scapula moves.

The x-ray also affords a valuable method of studying the structure and function of the joints. Of even greater value would be the x-ray motion picture or possibly the fluoroscope, if they were readily available for such purposes.

Methods of Assessing a Joint's Range of Motion.   The usual way of assessing a joint's range of motion is to measure the number of degrees from the starting position of the segment to its position at the end of its maximal movement. This would be the way of measuring flexion. Extension is usually the return movement from flexion. If the movement continues beyond the starting position, that constitutes hyperextension. Abduction and adduction are either measured separately from the starting position, or, if desired, the total range from maximal abduction to maximal adduction is measured. There are various ways of measuring rotation depending upon the joint being measured. The instrument commonly used by physical and occupational therapists for this method of measuring is the double armed goniometer, one arm being stationary and the other movable (Fig. 1–5). The pin or axis of the movable arm is placed directly over the center of the joint whose range is to be measured. The stationary arm is held in line with the stationary segment and the movable arm is either held against the segment as it moves, or is placed in line with the segment after its limit of motion has been reached. (See pages 27ff. for material on measuring motions of specific joints from a manual published by the American Academy of Orthopaedic Surgeons.)

Another instrument frequently used by physical educators and designed by a physical educator is the Leighton Flexometer. This is a highly accurate 360-degree gravity type goniometer which is strapped to the moving segment (Fig. 1–6).[10]

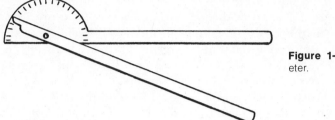

Figure 1–5   Double armed goniometer.

An electronic instrument for the continuous recording of the movements of body segments, known as an electrogoniometer or "elgon," was developed by Karpovich and his associates (Figs. 1–7 and 1–8).[5] This instrument is increasingly being used, not only in physical education laboratories, but in orthopedic treatment centers as well.

ROM Research Projects.   There are a number of projects that lend themselves both to classroom use and to graduate theses, depending upon the scope and the handling of the data. A few comparison studies are suggested here: a group of athletically active persons and a group of habitually sedentary persons; "athletic specialists" representing different activities, such as tennis players vs. golfers and swimmers vs. basketball players; contrasting age groups, e.g., 20–30 vs. 50–60; same group before and after a series of special flexibility exercises. (See the study by Wells on p. 25.)

Techniques for Increasing Joint Flexibility.   This is discussed at length in Chapter 22. In brief, joint flexibility or range of joint motion can be increased through the judicious use of the force of gravity, of momentum, of force applied by another person or by self-administered force. One example of using gravity is hanging by the hands in order to stretch the pectoral muscles as well as the anterior shoulder joint ligaments and fascia. Another example is kneeling and sitting on the heels, and then bouncing gently up and down for the purpose

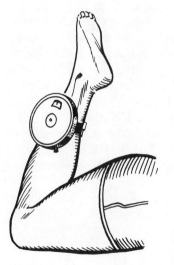

Figure 1–6   Measuring knee flexion with a Leighton Flexometer.

SIDE   VIEW

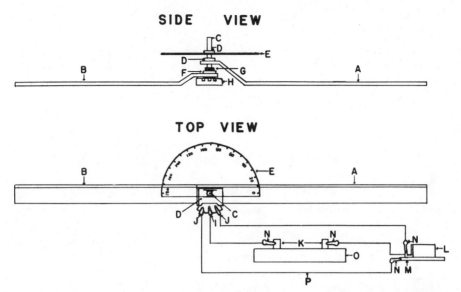

TOP   VIEW

Figure 1-7   Laboratory elgon with protractor, meter and battery. (From Adrian, M.: An introduction to electrogoniometry. *In* Kinesiology Review 1968. Washington, D. C.: Am. Assn. Health, Phys. Ed. & Recrn., 1968.)

of stretching the anterior tissues of the ankle joint, thereby increasing the range of plantar flexion. A way of using momentum is exemplified by standing in stride position with the trunk doubled over and the arms hanging down in a relaxed manner, and then bouncing down forcefully and rhythmically in an effort to touch the floor for the purpose of stretching the hamstring tendons behind the knees, along with the joints of the lumbar spine. Another use of momentum, this time for stretching the pectoral muscles and anterior tissues of

Figure 1-8   Elbow and wrist elgons on right arm; index finger and forearm elgons on left arm. (From Adrian, M.: An introduction to electrogoniometry. *In* Kinesiology Review 1968. Washington, D. C.: Am. Assn. Health, Phys. Ed. and Recrn., 1968.)

the shoulder joint, entails starting from the stride standing position with the arms relaxed down in front of the body and then flinging the arms vigorously diagonally upward and backward with the palms forward and the thumbs uppermost. A method of stretching the same tissues by external force is seen in the passive chest lifting exercise depicted in Figure 22–13 on page 510. Self-administered force might be used for stretching smaller segments of the body, such as wrist or finger joints.

MOVEMENTS OF THE SKELETAL UNITS

In preparation for defining the fundamental movements of the major segments of the body and for the analysis of these movements, certain orientation concepts and points of reference need to be established. The essential ones are the center of gravity, the line of gravity, the orientation planes of the body and axes of motion, and the standard starting positions from which the fundamental movements are made.

The Center of Gravity.   The center of gravity is defined as "an imaginary point representing the weight center of an object"; it is also "that point in a body about which all the parts exactly balance each other," and can be viewed as "the point at which the entire weight of the body may be considered as concentrated." In a perfect sphere or cube the weight center coincides with the geometric center. Its precise location in the human body depends upon the individual's anatomic structure, habitual standing posture, current position and whether he is supporting external weights. In a person of average build standing erect with the arms hanging at the sides, the center of gravity is located in the pelvis in front of the upper part of the sacrum. It is usually lower in women than in men because of their heavier pelves and thighs and shorter legs.

The Line of Gravity.   The line of gravity is an imaginary vertical line which, by definition, passes through the center of gravity. Hence, its location depends upon the position of the center of gravity which changes with every shift of the body's position.

Orientation Planes of the Body and Axes of Motion.   There are three planes corresponding to the three dimensions of space. Each plane is perpendicular to each of the other two. There are likewise three axes of motion, each perpendicular to the plane in which the motion occurs. The planes and axes of the body are defined as follows (Fig. 1–9,*A, B, C*):

Planes.

1. The sagittal, anteroposterior or median plane is a vertical plane passing through the body from front to back, dividing it into right and left halves.

2. The frontal, lateral or coronal plane is a vertical plane passing through the body from side to side, dividing it into anterior and posterior halves.

3. The horizontal or transverse plane is a horizontal plane which passes through the body, dividing it into upper and lower halves.

Since each plane bisects the body, it follows that each plane must pass through the center of gravity. Hence the center of gravity may be defined as the point at which the three planes of the body intersect one another, and the line of gravity as the vertical line at which the two vertical planes intersect each

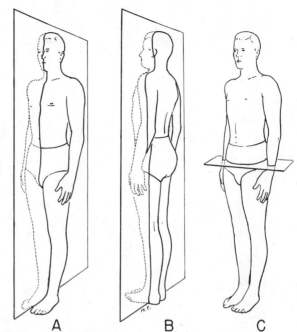

Figure 1–9 The planes of the body. *A*, Sagittal or anteroposterior plane; *B*, frontal or lateral plane; *C*, horizontal or transverse plane.

A   B   C

other. When describing a movement in terms of a plane, such as "a movement of the forearm in the sagittal plane," we mean that the movement occurs in a plane parallel to the sagittal plane. It does not necessarily imply that the movement occurs in a plane passing through the center of gravity. If the latter is intended, the term "cardinal plane" is used. Thus nodding the head is a movement occurring in the cardinal sagittal plane.

AXES.

1. The frontal-horizontal (lateral) axis passes horizontally from side to side.

2. The sagittal-horizontal (anteroposterior) axis passes horizontally from front to back.

3. The vertical axis is perpendicular to the ground.

A rotatory (axial, angular) movement of a segment of the body occurs *in* a plane and *around* an axis. The axis around which the movement takes place is always at right angles to the plane in which it occurs.

Standard Starting Positions

FUNDAMENTAL STANDING POSITION.   In this position the individual stands erect with the feet slightly separated and parallel, the arms hanging easily at the sides with palms facing the body (Fig. 1–10,*A*). This is the position usually accepted as the point of reference for analyzing all of the movements of the body's segments, *except those of the forearm.*

ANATOMIC STANDING POSITION.   This is the position usually depicted in anatomy textbooks. The individual is erect with the elbows fully extended and the palms facing forward. The legs and feet are the same as for the fundamental standing position (Fig. 1–10,*B*). It is usually accepted as the point of reference for the movements of the forearm, hand and fingers.

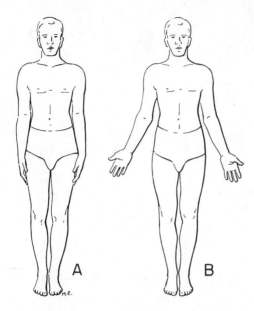

Figure 1–10 Standing positions. *A,* Fundamental standing position. *B,* Anatomic standing position.

FUNDAMENTAL MOVEMENTS OF THE MAJOR SEGMENTS OF THE BODY

Being a multijointed structure, the human body consists of many movable segments. When we watch a skillful acrobat, dancer or basketball player, it might seem like a hopeless task to try to organize their movements into a meaningful classification. The task is greatly simplified, however, when we consider one segment at a time and visualize each movement as though it were performed from the anatomic standing position. This may take a bit of imagination, but knowing ahead of time the movements of which each joint in the body is capable is nine tenths of the battle. These are described in Chapters Four through Nine in the systematic discussions of the regions of the body. The information given below is basic to understanding the movements of specific joints and segments. *Note:* The anatomic standing position is the point of reference for these movements.

Movements in the Sagittal Plane About a Frontal-Horizontal Axis. (Fig. 1–11, *A.*) Viewed from the side.

FLEXION. The angle at the joint diminishes.

Examples:

1. The forward and backward tipping of the head.
2. Lifting the foot and leg backward from the knee.
3. Raising the entire lower extremity forward-upward as though kicking.
4. With the upper arm remaining at the side, raising the forearm straight forward (Fig. 1–11,*A*).
5. With the elbow straight, raising the entire upper extremity forward-upward. The "diminishing angle" is hard to see in this movement until one views the raising of the arm from the shoulder in the same way that he views the raising of the thigh from the hip joint. In the

latter, one automatically notices the angle that appears between the top of the thigh (i.e., the anterior surface) and the trunk, or the part of the body that lies above the hip joint. Similarly, when raising the arm, the angle to look for is the angle between the top of the arm and the neck-head segment, not the angle between the underside of the raised arm and the trunk. It is necessary to train oneself to view the sagittal plane movements of the arm at the shoulder as being similar to those of the thigh at the hip joint.

For general purposes the upper arm may be considered fully flexed when it has reached the overhead vertical position. Later, when the role of the shoulder girdle in arm movements has been studied, it will be seen that the elevation of the arm does not take place solely at the shoulder joint. The movements of the scapula and clavicle are an important part of the total arm movement. Strictly speaking, the shoulder joint is in a fully flexed position when the humerus is raised until it is parallel with the long axis of the scapula (i.e., when it is in the same plane as the scapula). For the present, however, the upper arm will be considered fully flexed when it has been raised forward-upward until it has reached the vertical position and hyperflexed when it passes beyond this.

EXTENSION.   The return movement from flexion.

HYPERFLEXION.   This term refers only to the movement of the upper arm. When the arm is flexed beyond the vertical, it is considered to be hyperflexed. In other joints of the body flexion is terminated by contact of the moving segment with another part of the body, e.g., the forearm against the upper arm, the lower leg against the thigh or by structural limitations of the joints themselves (e.g., flexion of the thoracic and lumbar spine).

HYPEREXTENSION.   The continuation of extension beyond the starting position or beyond the straight line.

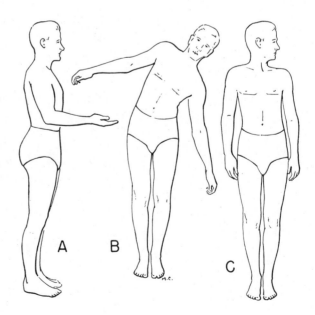

Figure 1–11 Movements of the body in the three planes. *A*, Movement of the forearm in the sagittal plane around a frontal-horizontal axis. *B*, Movement of the trunk in the frontal plane around a sagittal-horizontal axis. *C*, Movement of the head in the horizontal plane around a vertical axis.

A   B   C

Examples:

1. Hyperextension of the upper arm is said to occur when the arm is extended backward beyond the body.
2. The forearm is considered to be hyperextended when the angle at the elbow joint has exceeded 180 degrees.

REDUCTION OF HYPEREXTENSION.   Return movement from hyperextension. This could also be called flexion to the starting position, i.e., the fundamental or the anatomic starting position, as the case may be.

Movements in the Frontal Plane about a Sagittal-Horizontal Axis. (Fig. 1–11, *B*.)   Viewed from the front or back.

ABDUCTION.   Sideward movement away from the midline or sagittal plane or, in the case of the fingers, away from the midline of the hand. This term is used most commonly for sideward movements of the upper arm away from the trunk—in other words, sideward elevation of the arm—and for sideward elevation of the lower extremity. The jumping jack exercise involves both of these.

ADDUCTION.   The return movement from abduction.

LATERAL FLEXION.   This refers to the lateral bending of the head or trunk. It may also be used for sideward movements of the middle finger, but the more specific terms, radial or ulnar flexion, are usually used for these.

HYPERABDUCTION.   Like hyperflexion, this term usually refers to the upper arm when the latter is abducted beyond the vertical, as seen from the front or back.

HYPERADDUCTION.   The trunk blocks hyperadduction of the upper extremity and the presence of the supporting lower extremity blocks hyperadduction of the other lower extremity. By combining slight flexion with hyperadduction, the upper extremities can move across the front of the body and one lower extremity can move across in front of the supporting one.

REDUCTION OF HYPERADDUCTION.   The return movement from hyperadduction.

REDUCTION OF LATERAL FLEXION.   The return movement from lateral flexion.

Movements in the Horizontal Plane About a Vertical Axis. (Fig. 1–11, *C*.) Viewed or visualized from overhead or from directly beneath, e.g., through a glass platform. The point of reference for all rotations of the upper extremities is the midposition as in the fundamental (not anatomic) standing position.

ROTATION LEFT AND RIGHT.   Applies to rotation of the head or neck in such a way that the anterior aspect turns respectively to the left or to the right.

OUTWARD (LATERAL) AND INWARD (MEDIAL) ROTATION.   Applies to rotation of the thigh, the upper arm or to the upper or lower extremity as a whole in such a way that the anterior aspect of the segment turns laterally or medially.

SUPINATION AND PRONATION.   Apply respectively to outward (lateral) and inward (medial) rotation of the forearm.

REDUCTION OF OUTWARD ROTATION, INWARD ROTATION, SUPINATION OR PRONATION.   Rotation of the segment back to the midposition.

Movements in an Oblique Plane About an Oblique Axis.   Many movements take place in planes between the sagittal and frontal planes, the sagittal and horizontal planes, and the frontal and horizontal planes. These are oblique planes and the axes about which the movements occur are oblique axes. Whatever the degree of obliquity of the plane, the axis for a movement in that plane is always perpendicular to it. Although it is possible to define the obliquity precisely in terms of the number of degrees that it deviates from the fundamental planes, descriptive terms are adequate for general purposes.

A familiar example of an oblique plane movement is raising the arm between the straight forward and straight sideward directions. A golf swing and a tennis serve are also examples of arm movements that take place in oblique planes. Lower extremity examples include the frog kick in swimming and a deep knee bend performed with the heels together and the knees separated.

CIRCUMDUCTION.   An orderly sequence of the movements which occur in the sagittal, frontal and intermediate oblique planes so that the segment as a whole describes a cone.

SUPPLEMENTARY MATERIAL

Comparison of Shoulder Flexibility Before and After Corrective Exercises. In a class in corrective physical education Wells made several pertinent measurements at the beginning and end of the season of instruction. Among these was the measurement of forward elevation of the arm on the body. This primarily involves flexion at the shoulder joint but also includes some movement of the scapula, especially upward rotation. Individuals with resistant forward shoulders have limited motion in the shoulder joint. It is particularly difficult for them to raise their arms to the vertical or beyond when the arms are held just shoulder distance apart. The measurements were made on 30 girls, aged 16 to 18, in the following manner. The subject presented her left side to the examiner and raised both arms forward, upward and backward as far as possible without bending the elbows. Using a large semicircular protractor with a movable arm, the examiner held the protractor with its center opposite the center of motion at the shoulder joint and with the base line parallel with the axis of the subject's upper trunk. She then moved the arm of the protractor until it was in line with the subject's arm and read the anterior angle between the subject's arm and trunk. The results of the two sets of measurements were as follows:

	Range	*Median*
Measurements made in November	129° –170°	142.5°
Measurements made the following March	141.5°–175°	162.5°

Comparison of Measurements of Forward Elevation of the Arm Made by Different Investigators.   A comparison of measurements of a selected joint movement may be of interest to the reader. It should be noted, however, that the techniques used were not standardized and that the measurements were based on relatively small samples not selected at random. Forward elevation of the arm is the movement selected. The techniques of the three investigators were different but had this in common: they used either the vertical or the horizontal as a point of reference rather than the long axis of the trunk.

1. Experimenter: Van Horn[11]
   Number, age and sex of subjects: 165 women, aged 16 to 18 inclusive.
   Technique: The subject lay on a narrow board with the knees drawn up
     and the back kept in contact with the board. The angle between the
     horizontal surface of the board and the subject's arm was measured
     with a protractor.
   Measurements:

	Range	Median
R:	159°–196°	178°
L:	155°–198°	177°

2. Experimenters: Glanville and Kreezer[8]
   Number, age and sex of subjects: 10 men, aged 20 to 40 inclusive.
   Technique: The subject lay on his back on a table with the shoulder over
     the edge of the table. The measurement was made with an arthrometer
     having a circular scale and a weighted metal pendulum type of indi-
     cator. This instrument was strapped to the lateral surface of the
     subject's arm, just proximal to the elbow.
   Measurements:

	Range	Mean
R:	164°–191°	179°
L:	165°–187°	180°

3. Experimenter: Wells
   Number, age and sex of subjects: 24 young women, aged 17 to 20.
   Technique: The subject sat on a gymnasium bench with the head and
     back braced against the edge of an open door and raised both arms
     forward-upward as far as possible, keeping them shoulder distance
     apart with the palms facing and the elbows fully extended. The
     anterior angle between the upper arm and the plumb line was meas-
     ured with a plumb line protractor.
   Measurements:

	Range	Median
L:	161°–186°	172.5°

It is interesting to see that, despite the small number of subjects and
in spite of the differences in techniques, the results are fairly consistent. It is also interesting to note the contrast between the results
of these three investigations and the one made by Wells on the students
in the corrective class. The fact that the latter group was selected on
the basis of poor posture would undoubtedly account in part for their
lower scores. An additional factor might well be the difference in the
technique used. For this Wells used the Kraus and Weber technique
of taking the subject's own trunk as the point of reference, with the
subject standing erect.[8] Although the technique requires the use of
subjective judgment in aligning the protractor with the individual's
trunk, it is probably a more valid measure of the range of joint motion.

*Method of Measuring Joint Motion with a Protractor Type of Goniometer.**

USE OF THE GONIOMETER.   Many of the goniometers in use today are made with double lines of figures, one from zero to 180 degrees, and the other from 180 to zero degrees. A straight line may therefore be read either as zero or as 180. In using the goniometer the dial is centered against the joint at which the motion occurs, the stationary arm is placed in line with the stationary body segment and the movable arm is held in line with the moving segment. At the completion of the movement, the indicator shows the number of degrees through which the segment has moved. See Figure 1–12.

When the anatomic landmarks are definite, the use of the goniometer may be considered accurate, but when the bony landmarks are not definite due to excess soft tissue coverage or other causes, the goniometer may give inaccurate information. In these instances, an experienced surgeon may estimate the angle of motion more accurately without the use of a goniometer.

Therefore, the use of the goniometer should be elective and used according to the surgeon's discretion.

THE ELBOW.   The elbow is a typical hinge joint. Natural motion is present in *flexion.* The opposite motion to flexion, to the Zero Starting Position (the extended straight arm, i.e., zero degrees), is *extension.* As the motion beyond the Zero Starting Position is an unnatural one, it is referred to as *hyperextension.*

In Figure 1–13, flexion is measured from zero to 150 degrees, while extension is measured from 150 degrees to zero (from the angle of greatest flexion to the zero position).

THE SHOULDER.   It is important to differentiate true glenohumeral motion in relation to scapulothoracic motion. The total upward motion of the arm at the shoulder from zero degrees to 180 degrees is a smooth rhythmic combination of true glenohumeral motion, plus the upward and forward rotation of the scapula on the chest wall or scapulothoracic motion.

As the shoulder has an almost 360 degree range of motion, the individual should be examined in the standing position. (If the shoulder is examined with the individual lying down, only 180 degrees of motion are available). Thus, in the Zero Starting Position the person stands erect, with the arm at the side of the body.

In Figure 1–14, *A* illustrates vertical or upward motion of the shoulder in which abduction and adduction occurs. *Abduction* is the upward motion of the arm away from the side of the body in the coronal plane, from 0 degrees to 180 degrees. *Adduction* is the opposite motion of the arm toward the midline of the body, or beyond it in an upward plane.

In Figure 1–14, *B* illustrates forward flexion (or forward elevation) and backward extension of the shoulder. *Forward flexion* is the forward upward motion of the arm in the anterior sagittal plane of the body, from zero to 180 degrees. The opposite motion to the zero position may be termed "depression"

---

*The material in this section is adapted from the booklet *Joint Motion: Method of Measuring and Recording.* This manual is published by the American Academy of Orthopaedic Surgeons and is used by physical therapists as well as by orthopedic surgeons. It is suggested that kinesiologists and instructors in corrective physical education familiarize themselves with the technique described. The Leighton flexometer technique is also recommended.[11]

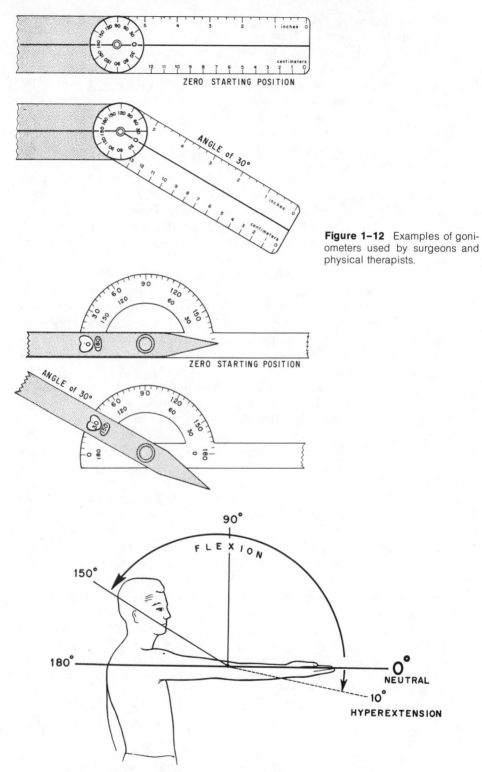

Figure 1–12 Examples of goniometers used by surgeons and physical therapists.

Figure 1–13 Range of elbow joint motion: flexion-extension and hyperextension.

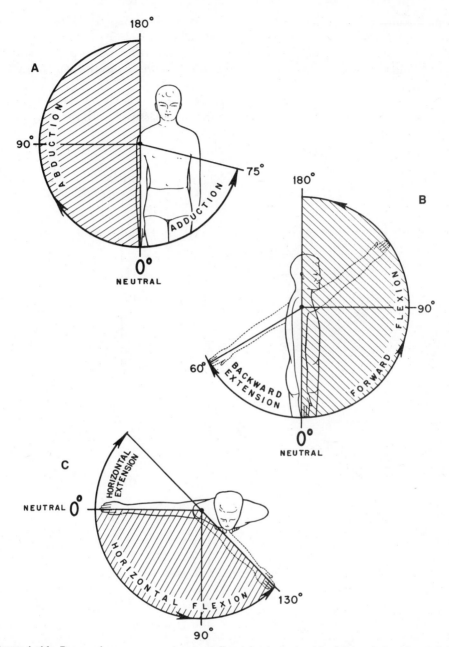

Figure 1–14 Range of arm movement on trunk (involving both shoulder joint and shoulder girdle): *A*, Sideward-upward elevation; *B*, Forward-upward elevation and backward elevation; *C*, Horizontal flexion and extension.

of the arm. *Backward extension* is the upward motion of the arm in the posterior sagittal plane of the body from zero degrees to approximately 60 degrees.

In Figure 1–14, *C* illustrates the horizontal motion of the shoulder in both flexion and extension. *Horizontal flexion* is the motion of the arm in the horizontal plane anterior to the coronal plane across the body. This motion is measured from zero degrees to approximately 130–135 degrees. *Horizontal extension* is the horizontal motion posterior to the coronal plane of the body.

In Figure 1–15, *A* shows the *neutral starting position* with the arm at the side of the body.

In Figure 1–15, *B* shows that *true glenohumeral motion* is estimated by fixing the scapula with the hand and elevating the arm passively with the other hand.

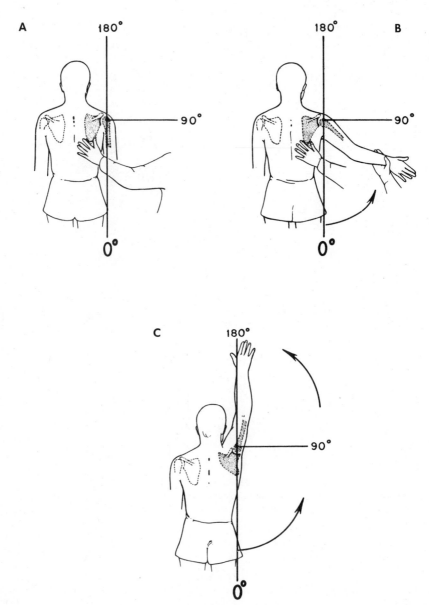

Figure 1–15 Range of shoulder joint (glenohumeral) motion: *A*, Starting position; *B*, Abduction; *C*, Sideward-upward elevation of arm (combining abduction of arm and upward rotation of scapula).

A

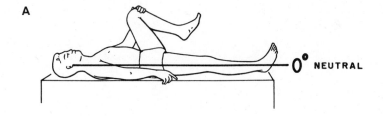

B

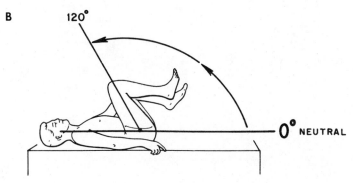

Figure 1–16 Range of hip joint flexion *A*, Starting position; *B*, Maximal flexion without rotating pelvis.

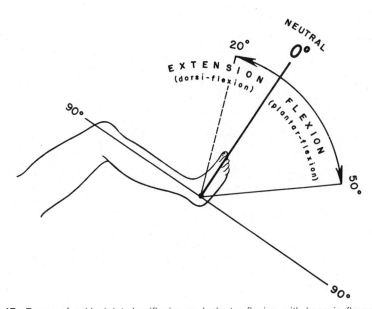

Figure 1–17 Range of ankle joint dorsiflexion and plantar flexion with knee in flexed position.

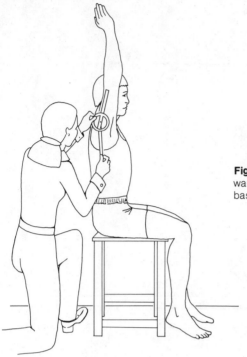

Figure 1–18 Use of goniometer to measure for-ward-upward elevation of arm on trunk. (Sketch based on photograph taken by Wells.)

Figure 1–19 Use of goniometer to measure plantar flexion of ankle. (Sketch based on photo-graph taken by Wells.)

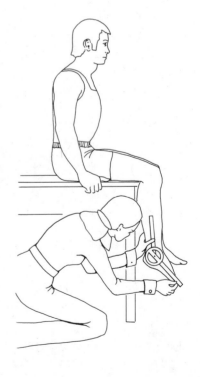

In Figure 1–15, *C* shows the *"combined" glenohumeral with scapulothoracic motion.* The rotation of the scapula upward and forward over the chest wall allows the arm to reach further upward. Normally, the range is 180 degrees.

THE HIP.   The hip is a "ball and socket" joint. Due to its deeper socket, the range of motion is less than that of the shoulder. Motions of the hip are measured with the individual lying either supine or prone. This simplifies terminology, as compared to the shoulder, as only one hemisphere of motion is measured at a time. Errors in hip motion occur when pelvis rotation is not noticed.

In Figure 1–16, *A* illustrates the *Zero Starting Position* of the right hip. The individual lies supine on a firm, flat surface with the opposite hip held in full flexion. This flattens the lumbar spine and demonstrates a flexion deformity of the hip if it is present.

In Figure 1–16, *B* indicates the *motion of the hip in flexion.* The motion in flexion is recorded from zero to 110 or 120 degrees. The examiner should place one hand on the iliac crest to note the point at which the pelvis begins to rotate.

THE ANKLE.   The ankle is a modified hinge joint, with its primary motion of flexion and extension at the tibiotalar joint. There is a slight degree of lateral motion present with the ankle in plantar flexion. This cannot be accurately estimated. Motions of the ankles should be measured with the knee in flexion in order to relax the heel cord.

The *Zero Starting Position* for the ankle has the leg at right angles to the thigh and the foot at right angles to the leg.

Figure 1–17 illustrates extension (dorsiflexion) and flexion (plantar flexion). These motions are measured in degrees from the right angle neutral position, or in percentages of motion, as compared to the opposite ankle.

LABORATORY EXPERIENCES

1. By studying a skeleton and observing a living subject, classify the following joints without referring to a textbook: hip, elbow, knee, ankle, wrist, radioulnar, metacarpophalangeal joint of finger, shoulder joint. (Do not confuse the motion at the elbow or wrist joints with that of the radioulnar joints.)

2. Take turns with a partner performing simple movements of the head, trunk, upper extremity and lower extremity and identify the planes and axes concerned.

3. Construct a simple device to illustrate the planes and axes in relation to the human body.

4. Using any of the joint-measuring instruments mentioned, measure the range of motion of the same joint movements that were described in the Supplementary Material in this chapter. (See Figs. 1–18 and 1–19.)

REFERENCES .

Joint Structure and Function

1. Goss, C. M. (Ed.): Gray's Anatomy of the Human Body, 29th Ed. Philadelphia: Lea & Febiger, 1973.
2. Schaeffer, J. P. (Ed.): Morris' Human Anatomy, 11th Ed. New York: McGraw Hill, Inc., 1953.

3. Sobotta, J.: Atlas of Human Anatomy, trans. by E. Uhlenhuth. New York: Hafner Publishing Co., 1967.
4. Steindler, A.: Kinesiology of the Human Body. Springfield, Ill.: Charles C Thomas, Publisher, 1970.

Range of Joint Motion and its Measurement

5. Adrian, M. J.: An introduction to electrogoniometry, *In* Kinesiology Review 1968. Washington, D.C.: Am. Assn. Health, Phys. Ed., and Recrn., 1968.
6. Glanville, A. D., and Kreezer, B.: Maximum amplitude and velocity of joint movement in normal male human adults. Hum. Biol., *9*:197–211, 1937.
7. American Academy of Orthopaedic Surgeons: Joint Motion: Method of Measuring and Recording. Chicago: The Academy, 1965.
8. Kraus, H., and Eisenmenger-Weber, S.: Evaluation of posture based on structural and functional measurements. Physiotherapy Rev., *25*:267–271, 1945.
9. Larson, R. L., and McMahan, R. D.: The epiphyses and the childhood athlete. J. Am. Med. Assn., *196*:607, 1966.
10. Leighton, J. R.: An instrument and technic for the measurement of range of joint motion. Arch. Phys. Med., *36*:571–578, 1955.
11. Van Horn, E. C.: Preliminary work toward the development of a table of norms of the range of motion in the shoulder joint. Unpublished seminar study, Wellesley College, 1947.

RECOMMENDED READINGS

Harris, M. L.: Flexibility (Review of the literature). J. Am. Phys. Assn., *49*:591–601, 1969.
Holland, G. J.: The physiology of flexibility; a review of the literature. *In* Kinesiology Review 1968. Washington, D.C.: Am. Assn. Health, Phys. Ed., and Rcrn., 1968.
Lowman, C. L.: The vulnerable age. J. Health & Phys. Ed., *18*:635–636, 693 (Nov.), 1947.

Chapter Two

THE MUSCULOSKELETAL SYSTEM

II. The Musculature

The muscles responsible for the movement and positioning of the bony segments of the body are known as skeletal muscles. They are constructed of bundles of striated muscle fibers which differ in both structure and function from the highly specialized cardiac muscle and from the smooth muscle of blood vessels, digestive organs, urogenital organs and so forth.

SKELETAL MUSCLES

Internal Structure. A single muscle cell is a threadlike fiber about one to three inches in length. Microscopic examination reveals that the fiber consists of many myofibrils embedded in sarcoplasm and that it is held together by a delicate membrane known as sarcolemma. Each fiber is enclosed within a thin connective tissue sheath called *endomysium.* The microscopic myofibrils, which are arranged in parallel formation within the fiber, are made up of alternating dark and light bands which give the muscle fibers their striated appearance. The electron microscope has revealed the striations to be a repeating pattern of bands and lines due to an interdigitating arrangement of two sets of filaments. It is postulated that these are filaments of the contractile proteins, mainly actin and myosin, and that when stimulated they slide past each other.[10] This explanation is a condensed and highly simplified one of contraction, a function which is the unique property of muscle tissue.

The muscle fibers are bound into bundles within bundles (Fig. 2–1). Each individual bundle of muscle fibers is enclosed in a fibrous tissue sheath called *perimysium*; the group of bundles that constitutes a complete muscle is in turn encased within a tougher connective tissue sheath called *epimysium.* In long muscles whose fibers run parallel to the long axis of the muscle, the bundles form "chains" which function as though the individual fibers ran the entire length of the muscle.[11]

Properties of Muscular Tissue. The properties of striated muscle tissue are *extensibility, elasticity* and *contractility.* The first two of these enable a

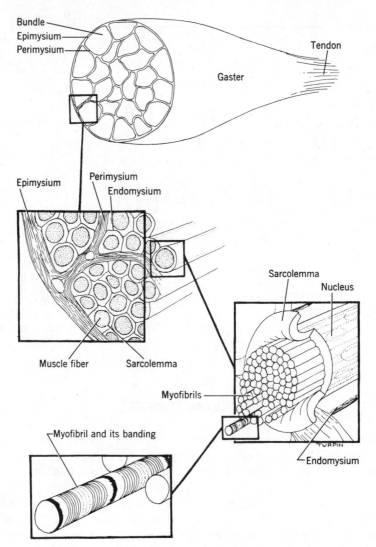

Figure 2–1   The architecture of a skeletal muscle and its fibers. (From Torrey, T. W.: Morphogenesis of the Vertebrates. New York: John Wiley & Sons, 1962.)

muscle to be stretched like an elastic band and, when the stretching force is discontinued, to return again to its normal resting length. Tendons, which are simply continuations of the muscle's connective tissue, also possess these properties. Ligaments likewise possess them. The unique property of contractility is possessed by muscle tissue alone. Experimenters have found that the average muscle fiber can shorten to approximately one-half its resting length.[1, 10] It can also be stretched until it is approximately one-half again as long as its resting length. The range between the maximal and minimal lengths of a muscle fiber is known as the amplitude of its action. The elongation varies proportionately with the length of the fiber and inversely with its cross section.

Muscular Attachments.   Muscles are attached to bone by means of their connective tissue which continues beyond the muscle belly in the form either of a tendon (a round cord or a flat band) or of an aponeurosis (a fibrous sheet). It is customary for anatomy texts to designate the attachments of the two ends of a muscle as "origin" and "insertion." The origin is usually characterized by stability and by closeness of the muscle fibers to the bone. It is usually the more proximal of the two attachments. The insertion, on the other hand, is usually the distal attachment; it frequently involves a relatively long tendon and the bone into which the muscle's tendon inserts is ordinarily the one that moves. It should be understood, however, that the muscle does not pull in one direction or the other. When it contracts it exerts equal force on the two attachments and attempts to pull them toward each other. Which bone is to remain stationary and which one is to move depends upon the purpose of the movement. A muscle spanning the inside of a hinge joint, for instance, tends to draw the two bones toward one another. But most precision movements require that the proximal bone be stabilized while the distal bone performs the movement. The stabilization of the proximal bone is achieved by the action of other muscles. Sometimes the greater weight or the more limited mobility of the proximal structure is sufficient to stabilize it against the pull of the contracting muscles.

Students often receive the impression that there is some physiologic reason for a muscle to pull in a single direction. They fail to grasp the concept of a muscle merely contracting and do not realize that it cannot pull in a predetermined direction. This misconception makes it difficult for them to understand seeming exceptions. Actually there are many movements in which the insertion or distal attachment of the muscle is stationary and the origin or proximal attachment is the one that moves. Such is the case in the familiar act of chinning oneself. The movement of the elbow joint is flexion, but it is the upper arm that moves toward the forearm, just the reverse of what happens when one lifts a book from the table. The grasp of the hands on the bar serves to immobilize the forearm and thus it provides a stable base for the contracting muscles. In order to avoid the erroneous idea of a muscle always pulling from its insertion toward its origin the following terminology for muscular attachments is used in this text.

TERMINOLOGY FOR MUSCULAR ATTACHMENTS.

Attachments of muscles of the extremities:
 Proximal attachment.
 Distal attachment.

Attachments of muscles of the head, neck and trunk:
 Upper attachment⎫
       ⎬ for muscles whose line of pull is more or less vertical, that is, parallel with the long axis of the body.
 Lower attachment⎭

 Medial attachment⎫
       ⎬ for muscles whose line of pull is more or less horizontal.
 Lateral attachment⎭

Attachments of the diaphragm:
 Peripheral attachment.
 Central attachment.

Structural Classification of Muscles on Basis of Fiber Arrangement. The arrangement of the fibers and the method of attachment vary considerably among the different muscles. These structural variations form the basis for a classification of the skeletal muscles.

LONGITUDINAL. This is a long straplike muscle whose fibers lie parallel to its long axis. Two examples are the rectus abdominis on the front of the abdomen, and the sartorius which slants across the front of the thigh.

QUADRATE OR QUADRILATERAL. (Fig. 2–2, *E* and *F*). Muscles of this type are foursided and are usually flat. They consist of parallel fibers. Examples include the pronator quadratus on the front of the wrist and the rhomboid muscle between the spine and the scapula.

TRIANGULAR OR FAN-SHAPED. (Fig. 2–2, *D*.) This is a relatively flat type of muscle whose fibers radiate from a narrow attachment at one end to a broad attachment at the other. The pectoralis major on the front of the chest is an excellent example.

FUSIFORM OR SPINDLE-SHAPED. (Fig. 2–2, *A*.) This is usually a rounded muscle which tapers at either end. It may be long or short, large or small. Good examples are the brachialis and the brachioradialis muscles of the upper extremity.

PENNIFORM OR FEATHER-LIKE. (Fig. 2–2, *B*.) In this type of muscle a series of short parallel fibers extends diagonally from the side of a long tendon, giving the muscle as a whole the appearance of a wing feather. Examples: extensor digitorum longus and tibialis posterior muscles of the leg.

BIPENNIFORM. (Fig. 2–2, *C*.) This is a double penniform muscle. It is characterized by a long central tendon with the fibers extending diagonally in pairs from either side of the tendon. It resembles a symmetrical tail feather. Examples: flexor hallucis longus and rectus femoris of the leg and thigh respectively.

MULTIPENNIFORM. In this type of muscle there are several tendons present, with the muscle fibers running diagonally between them. The middle portion of the deltoid muscle of the shoulder and upper arm is a prime example of a multipenniform muscle. (See Figs. 4–5 and 4–7.)

FUNCTION

The basis for all muscle function is the ability of muscular tissue to contract. This should be kept in mind as various aspects of muscular function are considered.

Relation of the Muscle's Line of Pull to the Joint Structure. The movement that the contracting muscle produces—flexion, extension, abduction, adduction, or rotation—is determined by two factors, namely, the type of joint that it spans and the relation of the muscle's line of pull to the joint. For instance, the contraction of a muscle whose line of pull is directly anterior to the knee joint will cause the joint to extend, whereas a muscle whose line of pull is anterior to the elbow joint will cause this joint to flex. The possible axes of motion are of course determined by the structure of the joint itself. It will be recalled that hinge joints have only a frontal horizontal axis and condyloid (ovoid) joints

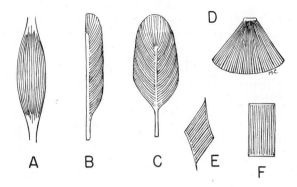

Figure 2–2 Examples of muscles of different shapes and internal structure. *A,* Fusiform or spindle; *B,* penniform; *C,* bipenniform; *D,* triangular or fan-shaped; *E,* rhomboidal; *F,* rectangular.

both a frontal horizontal and a sagittal horizontal axis; ball-and-socket joints have three axes, frontal and sagittal horizontal and vertical, while pivot joints have a vertical axis only. A muscle whose line of pull is lateral to the hip joint is a potential abductor of the thigh, but muscles whose lines of pull are lateral to the elbow joint cannot cause abduction of the forearm because the construction of the elbow joint is such that no provision is made for ab- or adduction. Being a hinge joint, its only axis of motion is a frontal horizontal one and the only movements possible are flexion and extension.

The importance of the relation of a muscle's action line to the joint's axis of motion is especially seen in some of the muscles that act on triaxial joints. Occasionally it happens that a muscle's line of pull for one of its secondary movements shifts from one side of the joint's center of motion to the other during the course of the movement. For instance, the clavicular portion of the pectoralis major is primarily a flexor, but it also adducts the humerus. When the arm is elevated sideward to a position slightly above shoulder level, however, the line of pull of some of the fibers of the clavicular portion shifts from below to above the sagittal horizontal axis of the shoulder joint (Fig. 2–3). Contraction of these fibers in this position contributes to abduction of the humerus, rather than to adduction. Similarly, several muscles or parts of muscles of the hip joint appear to reverse their customary function. Steindler pointed out that as the adductor longus adducts the hip joint it also flexes it until the flexion exceeds 70 degrees. Beyond this point the adductor longus helps to extend the hip. (See Table 2–1 for muscle classification based on joint structure.)

THE COORDINATION OF THE MUSCULAR SYSTEM

An effective, purposeful movement of the body or any of its parts involves considerable muscular activity in addition to that of the muscles which are directly responsible for the movement itself. To begin with, the muscles causing the movement must have a stable base. This means that the bone (or bones) not engaged in the movement but providing attachment for one end of such muscles must be stabilized by other muscles. In some movements, such as those

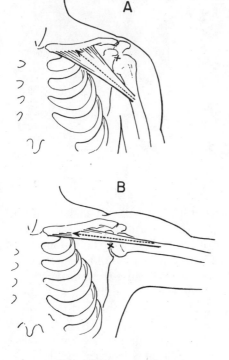

Figure 2–3 The clavicular portion of the pectoralis major muscle reversing its customary function. *A*, The line of pull is below the center of the shoulder joint. *B*, The line of pull is above the center of the shoulder joint.

in which the hands are used at a high level, the upper arms may need to be maintained in an elevated position. This necessitates contraction of the shoulder muscles to support the weight of the arms. Many muscles, especially those of biaxial and triaxial joints, can cause movements involving more than one axis, yet it may be that only one of their actions is needed for the movement in question. A similar situation exists in regard to the muscles of the scapula. A muscle cannot voluntarily choose to effect one of its movements and not another; it must depend upon other muscles to contract and prevent the unwanted movement.

TABLE 2–1 Muscle Classification Based on Joint Structure

DIARTHRODIAL AXIAL JOINTS	MUSCLES
Uniaxial	
Hinge	Flexors and extensors.
Pivot	Rotators.
Biaxial	
Condyloid (ovoid)	Flexors; extensors; abductors; adductors.
Saddle	Same as for condyloid joints.
*Triaxial**	
Ball-and-socket	Flexors; extensors; abductors; adductors; rotators.

*Although the joints between the bodies of the vertebrae are cartilaginous synarthrodial joints and those between the articular processes of the vertebrae are non-axial diarthrodial joints, the movements of the spinal column resemble those of triaxial joints. This is because of the ball-and-socket nature of the nucleus pulposus in the intervertebral disks.

Thus even a simple movement like threading a needle or hammering a nail may require the cooperative action of a relatively large number of muscles, each performing its own particular task in producing a single well-coordinated movement. It is seen then that muscles have various roles and that what their particular role is in a given movement depends upon the requirements of that movement. In summary, these roles are designated as movers, stabilizers, supporting muscles and neutralizers. Furthermore, if one concedes that the negative function of remaining relaxed can be looked upon as a role, then the muscles that are antagonistic to the movers may also be included as participants in the total cooperative effort. The definitions of these roles are as follows:

Movers.   A mover is a muscle which is directly responsible for effecting a movement. In the majority of movements there are several movers, some of them of greater importance than others. These are the principal movers. The muscles which help to perform the movement but which seem to be of less importance, or which contract only under certain circumstances, are the assistant movers. Muscles which help only when an extra amount of force is needed, as when a movement is performed against resistance, are sometimes called emergency muscles. This distinction between the various muscles which contribute to a movement is an arbitrary one. There may well be some difference of opinion as to whether a muscle is a principal or an assistant mover in a given movement.

Fixator, Stabilizing and Supporting Muscles.   This group includes the muscles which contract statically to steady or to support some part of the body against the pull of the contracting muscles, against the pull of gravity or against the effect of momentum and recoil in certain vigorous movements. One of the most common functions of these muscles is steadying or fixating the bone to which a contracting muscle is attached. It is only by the stabilizing of one of its attachments that the muscle is able to cause an effective movement of the bone at which it has its other attachment (Fig. 2–4). The term "supporting" is used when a limb or the trunk must be supported against the pull of gravity while a distal segment such as the hand, foot or head is engaging in the essential movement.

Neutralizers.   A neutralizer is a muscle which acts to prevent an undesired action of one of the movers. Thus if a muscle both flexes and abducts, but only flexion is desired in the movement, an adductor contracts to neutralize the abductory action of the mover.

Occasionally two of the movers have one action in common but can also perform second actions which are antagonistic to each other. For instance, one muscle may upward rotate and adduct while the other may downward rotate and adduct. When they contract together to cause adduction, their rotatory functions counteract each other (Fig. 2–5). Muscles which behave this way in a movement are mutual neutralizers as well as movers. Some writers use the term "synergist" for muscles which have this neutralizing function.[12] The term is used by others for muscles that stabilize bones, and by still others for any muscles that work together to contribute to a movement, regardless of the specific function of each.[10] Because of this inconsistency, the use of the term has purposely been avoided in this text.

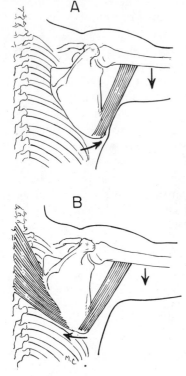

Figure 2–4 If the scapula were not stabilized, the teres major would increase the upward rotation of the scapula as it adducted the humerus. This dual action on the humerus and scapula is shown in *A*. In *B*, the scapula is stabilized by the scapular adductors and downward rotators. This permits the teres major to concentrate its force on the adduction of the humerus.

Antagonists. An antagonist is a muscle which causes the opposite movement from that of the muscle acting as a mover. Thus in a movement of flexion, the flexors are the movers and the extensors are the antagonists. In accordance with the physiologic principle known as reciprocal innervation, when a muscle contracts, its antagonist automatically relaxes (see p. 69).

Having stated the general rule, it is now necessary to describe what may at first appear to be a contradiction. If a movement performed with great force and rapidity is not checked, it will subject the ligamentous reinforcements of the joint to sudden strain. The tissues would probably be severely damaged. This is particularly true of quick movements of the arm or leg because of the tremendous momentum that can be developed in a long lever. To prevent such injury the muscles that are antagonistic to the movers contract momentarily to check the movement. As they contract, the movers relax, if indeed they have not already relaxed, allowing momentum to complete the movement. The situation is a little like taking the foot off the accelerator in order to put it on the brake. At the moment when the movement is being checked, the so-called antagonistic muscles are not truly antagonistic. In a vigorous movement, the antagonistic muscles may be said to perform two functions. Their first function is to relax in order to permit the movement to be made without hindrance; their second function is to act as a brake at the completion of the movement and, by doing so, to protect the joint.

Summary of Muscle Classification Based on Role in Total Movement

Mover: A muscle which is directly responsible for effecting a movement.

Fixator, stabilizer, supporting muscle: Muscles which contract statically to steady or to support some part of the body against the pull of contracting muscles, the pull of gravity or any other force which interferes with the desired movement.

Neutralizer: A muscle which acts to prevent an undesired action of one of the movers.

Antagonist: A muscle which causes the opposite movement from that of the movers.

Example of the Different Roles of Muscles in a Total Movement.   Let us consider the movement of the right upper arm when using a hand snow pusher or when playing shuffle-board (pushing the disk with a cue). The movement of

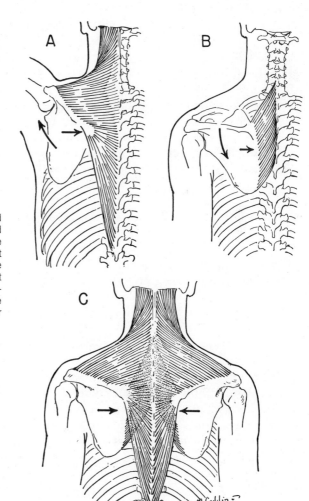

Figure 2–5 The trapezius and rhomboids as mutual movers and neutralizers. *A,* The trapezius alone adducts the scapula and rotates it upward. *B,* The rhomboids alone adduct the scapula and rotate it downward. *C,* Together the trapezius and rhomboids adduct the scapula without rotating it either upward or downward.

the humerus at the shoulder joint is flexion and this is accompanied by slight upward rotation and abduction of the scapula. The *movers of the humerus* are the anterior deltoid, clavicular portion of the pectoralis major and the coracobrachialis. (Look these up if not yet familiar with them.) The two former muscles are also inward (medial) rotators of the humerus, but as this movement is not desired it must be prevented. The infraspinatus and the teres minor take care of this. Therefore, they are serving as *neutralizers* in this pushing action. Meanwhile, the scapula is rotating upward through the action of the serratus anterior and trapezius II and IV which are serving as *shoulder girdle movers.* Trapezius II, which is an elevator as well as an upward rotator of the scapula, and trapezius IV, which is a depressor as well as an upward rotator, mutually neutralize each other with respect to elevation and depression while they are cooperating in rotating the scapula upward. Hence they are both *movers* and *mutual neutralizers.*

Consider the movers of the humerus once again, keeping in mind that muscles tend to pull both their distal and proximal ends toward each other. Note that the proximal attachments of both the anterior deltoid and the pectoralis major are side by side on the anterior border of the clavicle. As they contract they not only raise the humerus forward, they also tend to pull the clavicle laterally, a movement which would put a strain on the sternoclavicular joint. They are prevented from doing this by the action of the subclavius muscle, which pulls the clavicle medially and thus serves as a *stabilizer.* So in this simple pushing movement we see that we have muscles acting as movers, neutralizers and stabilizers which, by their cooperative action, assure an efficient movement.

Muscular Force.   Like all forces, muscular force may be described in terms of the site of its application, its direction and its magnitude. A more complete discussion of this will be found in Chapter 12.

TYPES OF MUSCULAR ACTION

The muscle classifications given earlier are but two of several classifications of muscles related to function. There are several others which are based on the nature of their composition, types of movements or other factors. A few of the more useful and widely accepted classifications are presented below. Others may be found in the literature.

Concentric, Eccentric, Static Contraction

CONCENTRIC OR SHORTENING CONTRACTION.   The muscle actually shortens, and when one end is stabilized, the other pulls the bone to which it is attached and turns it about the joint axis. The bone thus serves as a lever and the joint as its fulcrum. This is the usual type of contraction seen in physical activities.

ECCENTRIC OR LENGTHENING CONTRACTION.   This is a gradual releasing of the contraction, as when one lowers a weight slowly or gives in to an external force which is greater than that of the contracting muscle. The term "lengthening" is misleading, as in most instances the muscle does not actually lengthen. It merely returns from its shortened condition to its normal resting length (Fig. 2–6, *A*).

STATIC CONTRACTION.   The muscle remains in partial or complete contraction without changing its length. There are two different conditions under which this type of contraction is likely to occur.

1. Muscles which are antagonistic to each other contract with equal strength, thus balancing or counteracting each other. The part affected is held tensely in place without moving. Tensing the biceps to show off its bulge is an example of this. The contraction of the triceps prevents the elbow from further flexing.

2. A muscle is held in either partial or maximal contraction against another force such as the pull of gravity or an external mechanical or muscular force. Examples of this are holding a book with outstretched arm, a tug of war between two equally matched opponents and attempting to move an object which is too heavy to move.

Isotonic and Isometric Contraction. These terms come from the Greek and mean respectively "equal tension" and "equal length."

ISOTONIC CONTRACTION. This is a contraction in which the tension remains constant as the muscle shortens. It is commonly, although erroneously, used as a synonym for concentric contraction. The latter term, however, does not indicate the degree of tension; it merely indicates a decrease in length.

ISOMETRIC CONTRACTION. This is contraction without any appreciable change in length. According to this definition the term would seem to be synonymous with "static contraction," but according to current usage the muscle is unable to shorten because of the magnitude of the resistance. This is very different from merely counter-balancing the pull of gravity. The terms are synonymous only when the static contraction involves maximal contraction.

PHASIC AND TONIC CONTRACTION. These terms are used less now than formerly. They appear to have been replaced by isotonic and isometric although they are not exactly comparable. In general, the term "phasic" appears to be used for shortening contraction, but there are instances in the literature in which it seems to mean any change in length, either shortening or lengthening. The term "tonic contraction" appears to have exactly the same meaning as "static contraction." Inasmuch as the use of these terms seems to be waning, the student need not be too concerned about their exact meanings.

The Influence of Gravity and Other External Forces on Muscular Action. It may surprise the student to learn that when he replaces a book on a low table, or a suitcase on the floor, he is using the same muscles that he used for lifting it, not the opposite group as he might have thought. He uses them in a different way, however. When he lifts the book or the suitcase, the lifting muscles contract in the "normal" way. That is, they gradually shorten and their action is called shortening or concentric contraction. This is also the action that occurs when an object is moved against a resistance, regardless of the direction of movement (Fig. 2–6, C). When he slowly lowers the object, the same muscles are now gradually returning to their resting length. Although the term is paradoxical this action is known as lengthening or eccentric contraction (Fig. 2–6, A). A similar action is experienced in reverse by the lower extremity muscles when one lowers the body weight by bending the knees to assume a squat or semi-squat position, and then returns to the erect position. As he stoops, the extensor muscles of the hips and knees are undergoing eccentric contraction. They are indeed lengthening in this instance, yet their tension is increasing as they assume the burden of the body weight and gradually lower it in a controlled manner. When the joint action is reversed and the body weight is lifted, the extensor muscles are contracting concentrically until the hips and knees are straight

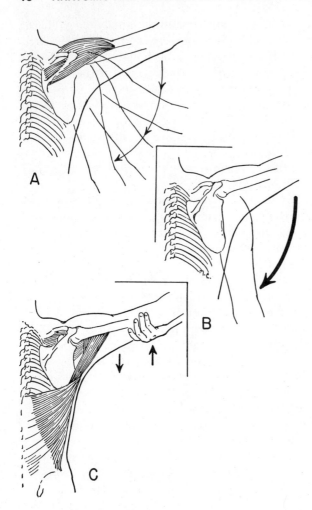

Figure 2–6 Influence of gravitational force on muscular action in sideward depression of the arm (adduction of the humerus). *A,* Eccentric contraction of the abductors in slow lowering of the arm. *B,* Absence of muscular action when the arm is dropped to the side. *C,* Concentric contraction of the adductors when the movement is performed against resistance.

and the body is erect. In the normal standing position the weight-bearing joints are stabilized as the result of the relationship between the gravitational force and the center of motion of the joints.

Similar muscular action is seen when one is opposing an external force which proves too strong for him. In a tug of war, for instance, he may pull with all his strength, but if his opponent is stronger than he is, he (the former) will find his elbows being pulled out straight in spite of himself. This is another example of eccentric contraction. When the muscles contract in this manner they are said to perform negative work.

Red and White Muscles and Their Functions.   On the basis of their muscle hemoglobin (myoglobin) content, the fibers of striated muscles are classified as red or white. The two types are roughly comparable to the dark and white meat of chicken. Red muscle fibers, which contain a rich supply of hemoglobin, tend to be more plentiful in the muscles which are responsible for long-continued contractions such as those engaged in by the antigravity muscles and also in muscles like the diaphragm which participate in regularly repeated contractions. White muscle fibers, on the other hand, tend to predominate in the flexor muscles, the muscles which in general are responsible for relatively brief, but often extremely forceful, contractions. In man, however, the distinction between red and white fibers is not nearly so clear-cut as these statements might lead one to think.

Spurt and Shunt Muscles and Their Functions. These terms are used by MacConaill, a Professor of Anatomy from Ireland, to represent two opposing types of muscular action based on the relative distance of each attachment from the center of motion of the joint between them.[2] As the terms are not very meaningful to us in this country it is best simply to learn his interpretation.

A *spurt muscle* is one in which the distance from its attachment to the stationary bone (usually the proximal attachment) to the joint is greater than the distance from its attachment to the moving bone (usually the distal attachment) to the joint. This means that the muscle's pull has a greater rotatory component than stabilizing. The brachialis and biceps brachii are good examples of this. (See Figs. 5–4 and 5–6).

A *shunt muscle* is one in which the distance from its attachment to the moving bone (usually the distal attachment) to the joint is greater than the distance from its attachment to the stationary bone (usually the proximal attachment) to the joint. This means that the muscle's line of pull has a greater stabilizing component than rotatory component. The brachioradialis is a prime example. (See Fig. 5–7.) Furthermore, it comes into action especially during quick movements which would otherwise have a centrifugal effect and would thus endanger the joint structure. (Rotatory and stabilizing components of force are discussed in Chapter 12 of this text.)

In other words, a spurt muscle is chiefly rotatory in its effect on the moving bone since it provides the force that initiates and sustains the latter's movements. On the other hand, a shunt muscle is primarily stabilizing. By pulling lengthwise along the moving bone in the direction of the joint, it provides centripetal force which serves to protect the joint structures.

Tendon Action of Two-Joint Muscles.[3, 4, 7, 9, 10] Another type of coordination of the muscular system is seen in the so-called tendon action of the two-joint muscles, that is, the muscles that pass over and act upon two joints. Examples of these are the hamstrings. (semitendinosus, semimembranosus and biceps femoris), which flex the leg at the knee and extend the thigh at the hip; the rectus femoris, which flexes the thigh and extends the leg; the sartorius, which flexes both the thigh and the leg; the gastrocnemius, which helps to flex the leg in addition to its primary function of extending the foot; and the long flexors and extensors of the fingers. The latter are actually multijoint muscles, since they cross the wrist and at least two of the joints of the fingers. A characteristic of all these muscles, whether they act on joints that flex in the same direction, as in the case of the wrist and fingers, or in the opposite direction, as in the case of the knee and hip, is that they are not long enough to permit complete movement in both joints at the same time. This results in the tension of one muscle being transmitted to the other, in much the same manner that a downward pull on a rope which passes through an overhead pulley is transmitted in the form of a pull in the reverse direction to the rope on the other side of the pulley. Thus if the hamstrings contract to help extend the hip, tension is transmitted to the rectus femoris, causing it to extend the knee. Or if the rectus femoris contracts to help flex the hip, tension is transmitted to the hamstrings, causing them to flex the knee. This is a simplified version of what in actuality is a rather complex coordination.

When one-joint muscles contract, their shortening is accompanied by a corresponding loss of tension. In quick movements of the limbs, one-joint muscles rapidly lose their tension. The advantage of two-joint muscles is that they can continue to exert tension without shortening. The two-joint muscles have two different patterns of action. These have been described by Fenn, Steindler and others as concurrent and countercurrent movements.

An example of concurrent movement is seen in the simultaneous extension of the hip and knee and also in the simultaneous flexion of these joints. As the muscles contract they act on each other in such a way that they do not lose length; therefore their tension is retained. It is as though the pull traveled up one muscle and down the other in a continuous circuit. In simultaneous extension of the hip and knee, for instance, the rectus femoris' loss of tension at the distal or knee end is balanced by a gain in tension at the proximal or hip end. Similarly, the hamstrings, which are losing tension at their proximal end, are gaining it at their distal end.

The countercurrent pattern presents a different picture. In this type of movement, while one of the two-joint muscles shortens rapidly at both joints, its antagonist lengthens correspondingly and thereby gains tension at both ends. An example of this action is seen in the rapid loss of tension in the rectus femoris and corresponding gain of tension in the hamstrings when the hip is flexed and the knee is extended simultaneously. A vigorous kick is a dramatic illustration of this kind of muscle action. The backward swing of the lower extremity preparatory to kicking is a less spectacular but equally valid example. The forward swing in walking is another. In both patterns of movement the one- and two-joint muscles appear to supplement each other, and thus, by their cooperative action, produce smooth, coordinated, efficient movements.

TYPES OF BODILY MOVEMENTS

Movements may be passive or active, and if active they may be slow or rapid. They may involve the constant application of force or, after the initial impetus has been given, they may continue without further muscular effort.

A *passive* movement requires no effort on the part of the person involved. It is performed by another person such as a physical therapist giving a treatment or an instructor or a partner stretching tight ligaments, fascia and muscles in an attempt to increase the range of motion of a particular joint. In some cases it is a movement which has been started by the subject's own effort but is continued by momentum. It might also be caused by the force of gravity if the subject remained relaxed and used no muscular effort to aid, restrain or guide the moving part.

An *active* movement is effected by the subject's muscular activity. It is usually performed volitionally, but it may be a reflex reaction to an external or internal stimulus. It may be rapid or slow. The slow movements have been called "moving fixations" because tension is maintained throughout. Pushing a heavy piece of furniture across the room would be an example of this type of movement.

Rapid movements could also be performed as *moving fixations,* but this would be an inefficient way of performing them. For efficiency, rapid movements should be performed ballistically. The concept of *ballistic movement* was introduced a number of years ago by psychologists. They used the term for movements that were initiated by vigorous muscular contraction and completed by momentum. This type of movement is characteristic of throwing, striking and kicking. It is also seen in the finger movements used for typing and piano playing. When such movements are performed nonballistically, that is, with constant muscular contraction, they are uneconomical and hence, not skillful. In fact, they are characteristic of the way in which beginners tend to attempt new coordinations, especially if they are concentrating on accuracy of aim rather than on a ballistic type of motion. They need to be encouraged in the early stages of learning a skill to concentrate on form rather than accuracy if they are to master the skill of moving ballistically.

Ballistic movements may be terminated by one of three methods: (1) by contracting antagonistic muscles, as in the forehand drive in tennis; (2) by allowing the moving part to reach the limit of motion, in which case it will be stopped by the passive resistance of ligaments or muscles, as in the case of a high kick; or (3) by the interference of an obstacle, as when chopping wood.

In many movements found in both sports and in skilled labor, three types of muscular action cooperate to produce a single act. This kind of cooperation is seen especially in striking activities which require the use of an implement, such as a tennis racket, golf club or ax. Movements such as these involve (1) fixation to support the moving part and to maintain the necessary position, (2) ballistic movement of the active limb and (3) fixation in the fingers as they grasp the implement. Hartson suggested that the purpose of the "follow through" in throwing and striking movements in sports is to assure a ballistic type of movement.[5] It would seem that there may be some sport movements which cannot be categorized as either tension or ballistic movements. When maximum speed or force is desired, it would seem that there are more factors in the "follow through" than are suggested by Hartson's hypothesis.

Cocontraction.   This is usually defined as the simultaneous contraction of movers and antagonists. This sounds simple and straightforward, but nevertheless it requires interpretation. Earlier in this chapter the various roles of muscles were discussed. In any given movement, even the simplest movement, several muscles other than the movers are likely to be involved. There are neutralizers and mutual neutralizers whose function it is to counteract an additional function of a mover which is not desired in the present movement. (See Figure 2–5.) There are also many movements that require the action of stabilizers.[8] These may be for stabilizing a weight-bearing segment against gravity, or for the stabilization of a freely movable bone which provides for the proximal attachment of one of the movers. (See Fig. 2–4.)

There are other situations which may be erroneously interpreted as examples of cocontraction. For instance, in movements that involve an interplay between movers and antagonists as a means of maintaining postural balance. Some believe that the alternation between contractions of these muscles may be so quick that the muscles appear to be contracting simultaneously and that there may actually be a slight amount of overlap, one muscle tapering off in eccentric contraction as the other begins. Even if this does happen it is not true cocontraction.

There is also the type of movement, exemplified by vigorous arm flinging, in which the opposing muscles come into quick action at the end of the movement, apparently for the protection of the ligaments and other tissues which would otherwise be subjected to violent stretching with possible tearing. This situation usually occurs in a ballistic type movement, a movement which is initiated by strong muscular action but is carried on by momentum alone, the movers having relaxed. Basmajian cites an example of this type of movement, describing it as a whip-like motion in which there is a sudden burst of activity of the antagonists at the finish. He suggests that this motion serves the purpose of protecting the joint and preventing injury.[2]

Genuine cocontraction means the simultaneous contraction of movers and their antagonists. Opinions differ concerning bona fide examples of cocontraction. Some believe that it occurs only in early attempts to master a difficult skill, especially one in which the emphasis is on accuracy rather than on speed. To those who hold this opinion cocontraction is characteristic of unskillful performance. Basmajian cites several EMG investigations which indicate that one effect of training is the progressive reduction of cocontraction.[2]

Others are convinced that there are circumstances when cocontraction occurs apart from those related to early learning, lack of skill, stabilization of skeletal segments, or neutralization of unwanted functions of the mover muscles. Watkins, a defender of the latter point of view, bases her stand on original research concerning cocontraction and the relationship between opposing muscles.[12] Her findings suggest the need for further research which will corroborate one position or the other.

METHODS OF STUDYING THE ACTIONS OF MUSCLES

In addition to the obvious method of studying these in a textbook there are a number of procedures which may be more meaningful to the student.

Conjecture and reasoning, based on a knowledge of the location and attachments of a muscle and the nature of the joint or joints it spans, is a method that has long been used in conjunction with other methods. A careful study of the muscles from this point of view will enable one to see for himself what movements a muscle is capable of causing.

Dissection is an excellent way of studying the location and attachments of a muscle and its relation to the joint it spans. This method provides a more meaningful basis for visualizing the muscle's potential movements, but it sometimes leads to misinterpretations and erroneous conclusions.

Inspection and palpation of normal, living subjects constitutes a method which can be easily used by students. Even though its use is limited to superficial muscles it is a valuable method as far as it goes. Much of the information in the early textbooks of anatomy was based on the combination of dissection of the cadaver and inspection and palpation of living subjects. Before the days of electromyography these were the chief methods of determining the actions of the muscles. There is a possibility of misinterpretation, however, against which students should be warned. When attempting to palpate a muscle, one is not sure sometimes whether he is feeling it contract. He is then likely to have the subject do the movement against resistance, often quite strong resistance. If he succeeds in feeling the muscle contract, he may conclude that the muscle is a principal mover, whereas it may be a muscle that comes into action *only* when the movement is strongly resisted. Hence it would actually be an *assistant*, or *emergency*, mover.

Inspection and Palpation of Subjects Some of Whose Muscles are Known to Be Paralyzed. The student is not likely to have the opportunity of using this method, but it has been used extensively by experienced investigators and physical therapists such as Wilhelmine G. Wright and Signe Brunnstrom. Miss Wright, who was an outstanding physical therapist and author during the twenties, found that by observing with great care the movements which a patient was unable to perform, she could judge the normal action of the muscle that she knew was paralyzed. Written before the days of electromyography, her book is well worth reading because of her meticulous observations.[14] The preface of her book, with its careful description of her technique of palpation, is especially helpful.

Models and Gadgets. There are numerous devices, both commercial and homemade, which can be used for demonstrating and studying the actions of muscles. Probably the most commonly used device is the simplest of all — a long rubber band (or chain of short ones) held against the bones of a skeleton in such a way as to represent a single muscle. The movement is demonstrated by holding the elastic on a stretch with one end representing the proximal attachment and the other the distal attachment. The tendency of both bones to move toward each other can easily be demonstrated, as well as the necessity for stabilizing one bone for the muscle to be effective in moving the other bone.

Muscle Stimulation. To most kinesiologists the term "muscle stimulation" means G. B. Duchenne, the pioneer in the use of electrical stimulation as a means of studying the actions of the muscles and the author of *Physiologie des Mouvements.* This classic work was translated into English and published in 1949. It made a tremendous contribution to the science of kinesiology, yet its limitations must be recognized. It demonstrates the contraction of individual muscles when these are stimulated electrically. Unfortunately, it cannot analyze the sequence of muscular actions that occur in an everyday act such as walking, lifting a package or working with a common tool of workshop or kitchen. Neither can it reveal the complex combinations of muscular actions in ordinary sport techniques.

In spite of its limitations, muscle stimulation is being used in many modern kinesiology laboratories as a device for studying the responses of individual muscles to electrical stimulation. For those who are interested in knowing more about this technique two articles from the Kinesiology section of J.O.H.P.E.R. are recommended. (See Recommended Readings: Hoffman; Jokl.)

Electromyography. While not many undergraduate students may have the opportunity of personal experience with this technique, all may benefit by reading the reports of EMG investigations. A wealth of information concerning muscular action is available in such reports. Electromyography is based on the fact that contracting muscles generate electrical impulses. It is a technique of recording such impulses or action currents, as they are also called. It provides specific information about muscular actions that we have only been able to guess at in the past, information which has proved much of our guessing to be inaccurate. The unique advantages of EMG are that it reveals both the intensity and the duration of a muscle's action and, in fact, discloses the precise time sequences of muscular activity in a movement. Furthermore, it reveals the actions not only of the movers, but also of the muscles serving as stabilizers and neutralizers. Perhaps its greatest contribution to our knowledge of muscular action is its ability to record the impulses of deep as well as superficial muscles. Basmajian, the apostle of electromyography, says that it surpasses all the older methods of studying muscular action in that it reveals what the individual muscles are actually doing, not just what they *"can* do," or *"probably* do."[2, 13]

SUPPLEMENTARY MATERIAL

In an article on the mechanics of muscular contraction Fenn described a simple experiment that demonstrates the influence of muscle length on the force which the muscle can exert. The strength of the rectus femoris and of the biceps femoris was tested in two positions by means of the Martin breaking-point test. The rectus femoris is situated on the front of the thigh and attaches to the pelvis just above the hip joint, and, by means of the patellar ligament, exerts its pull on the front of the tibia just below the knee joint. Hence it is a flexor of the hip and an extensor of the knee. The biceps femoris is situated on the back of the thigh and attaches above the hip and below the knee. It therefore is an extensor of the hip and a flexor of the knee.

For the first test the subject lay on his back on a table with his knees at the edge and his legs hanging down. For the second test he sat on the end of the table with his trunk flexed well forward from the hips. Clearly the rectus femoris was put on a greater stretch in the first position, and the biceps femoris in the second position. The results showed that the rectus femoris exerted greater force in the first position than in the second, but the biceps femoris exerted greater force in the second position. These experiments may easily be duplicated in the classroom.[4]

LABORATORY EXPERIENCES

1. Take two sticks which are joined at one end by a hinge. Attach a single piece of elastic or a long rubber band to the opposite ends of the two sticks.
   a. Separate the ends of the sticks as far as the elastic will permit and then demonstrate the way the elastic will pull both sticks together.
   b. Demonstrate the way the elastic will move only one of the sticks if the other one is stabilized.
   c. Repeat both a and b, using the arm of the skeleton instead of the sticks.

2. Get a subject to hold a heavy dumbbell in his right hand and slowly raise his arm sideward-upward without bending the elbow. Keep your fingers on the clavicular portion of the pectoralis major. Does it contract? If so, at what position of the arm does it begin?

3. Flex the fingers hard. Keep them flexed and flex the hand at the wrist as far as possible. What happens to the fingers? Explain.

4. Extend the fingers, then hyperextend the hand at the wrist as far as possible. What happens to the fingers? Explain.

5. Get a subject to lie on the left side with the hip and knee in a partly flexed position and the right leg fully extended. The right thigh should now be flexed passively by an operator. The subject should attempt to keep the knee straight but not to the point of interfering with the hip flexion. What happens? Where does the subject feel discomfort? Explain.

6. With the subject in the same starting position as in 5, have him flex both his right thigh and leg completely. The right thigh should now be passively extended by an operator, the subject attempting to keep the leg flexed at the knee. As the thigh becomes fully extended, what happens to the knee? Where does the subject feel discomfort? Explain. (Caution: Do not use an acrobat or acrobatic dancer as a subject for 5 or 6, or the experiments may not work. Why?)

Note: Laboratory exercises on the action of muscles as movers, stabilizers and neutralizers are not included here because, in order to do them, it is necessary to know the individual muscles. They will be found in the laboratory sections of Chapters Four through Nine.

REFERENCES

1. Arkin, A. M.: Absolute muscle power; internal kinesiology of muscle. Arch. Surg., *42*:395–410, 1941.
2. Basmajian, J. V.: Muscle mechanics. *In* Muscles Alive, 3rd Ed. Baltimore: The Williams & Wilkins Company, 1974.
3. Brunnstrom, S.: Clinical Kinesiology, 3rd Ed. Philadelphia: F. A. Davis Company, 1972.
4. Fenn, W. O.: The mechanics of muscular contraction in man. J. Appl. Physics, *9*:165–177, 1938.
5. Hartson, L. D.: Analysis of skilled movements. Personnel J., *11*:28–43, 1932.
6. Hartson, L. D.: Contrasting approaches to the analysis of skilled movements. J. Gen. Psychol., *20*:263–293, 1939.
7. Lombard, W. P.: The action of two-joint muscles. Am. Phys. Ed. Rev., *8*:141–145, 1903.
8. O'Connell, A. L., and Gardner, E. B.: Understanding the Scientific Bases of Human Movement. Baltimore: The Williams & Wilkins Company, 1972.
9. Rasch, P. J., and Burke, R. K.: Kinesiology and Applied Anatomy, 5th Ed. Philadelphia: Lea & Febiger, 1974.
10. Steindler, A.: Kinesiology of the Human Body. Springfield, Ill.: Charles C Thomas, Publisher, 1970.
11. Stetson, R. H., and McDill, J. A.: Mechanism of the different types of movement. Psychol. Monogr., *32*(3):18–40, 1923.
12. Watkins, M. P.: Co-contraction and the Relationship Between Opposing Muscles. Unpublished Master's Thesis, Sargent College of Allied Health Professions, Boston University, 1974.
13. Waterland, J. C., and Shambes, G. M.: Electromyography: one link in the experimental chain of kinesiological research. J. Am. Phys. Ther. Assn., *49*:1351–1356, 1969.
14. Wright, W. G.: Muscle Function. New York: Hafner Publishing Co., 1962.

RECOMMENDED READINGS

Craig, A. S.: Elements of kinesiology from the clinician. J. Am. Phys. Ther. Assn., *44*:470–473, 1964. A brief but comprehensive article as valuable for physical educators as for physical therapists.
Elftman, H.: The action of muscles in the body. *In* Fenn, W. O. (Ed.): Biological Symposia. Lancaster, Pa.: The Jacques Cattell Press, 1941, Vol. 3, pp. 191–209.
Hoffman, F. P.: The use of electrical stimulation as a teaching aid in kinesiology. J. Health, Phys. Ed. Rcrn., *39*:79–82, 1968.
Hubbard, A. W.: Homokinetics: muscular function in human movement. *In* Johnson, W. R., and Buskirk, E. (Eds.): Science and Medicine of Exercise and Sports, 2nd Ed. New York: Harper & Row, 1973, Chap. 1.
Jokl, E.: G. B. Duchenne's physiology of motion. J. Health, Phys. Ed. & Rcrn., *38*:67–68, 1967.
McCloy, C. H.: Some notes on differential actions of partite muscles. Res. Quart. Am. Assn. Health, Phys. Ed. & Recrn., *17*:254–262, 1946.

Chapter Three

THE NEUROMUSCULAR BASIS OF HUMAN MOVEMENT

The roles of the bones, joints and muscles in human movement were presented in the first two chapters. This chapter takes up the role of the nervous system in initiating, modifying and coordinating muscular action.

Loofbourrow, in his chapter on neuromuscular integration in the book *Science and Medicine of Exercise and Sports,* presents this topic so succinctly and vividly that his introductory paragraph is quoted here in full as an introduction to the present chapter.

The forces which move the supporting framework of the body are unleashed within skeletal muscles on receipt of signals by way of their motor nerves. In the absence of such signals, the muscles normally are relaxed. Movement is almost always the result of the combined action of a group of muscles which pull in somewhat different directions, so the control of movement involves a distribution of signals within the central nervous system (CNS) to appropriate motor nerves with precise timing and in appropriate number. In order for movements to be useful in making adjustments to external situations, it is necessary for the central nervous system to be appraised of these situations, which are continually changing. A means of providing this information promptly exists in a variety of receptors sensitive to changes in temperature, light, pressure, etc. These receptors are signal generators which dispatch signals (nerve impulses) to the CNS over afferent nerve fibers. The CNS receives these signals together with identical ones from within the muscles, joints, tendons, and other body structures and is led thereby to generate and distribute in fantastically orderly array myriads of signals to various muscles. This, despite the enormous complexity of the machinery involved, enables the individual to do one main thing at a time. This is integration. It is what Sir Charles Sherrington meant by "the integrative action of the nervous system."[12]

The following discussion does not presume to be an exhaustive treatise on neuromuscular mechanisms. It attempts rather to present as simply as possible those mechanisms which are pertinent to the study of kinesiology. Because of the newer techniques made possible by electronic devices during the past two or three decades, great strides have been made in acquiring more accurate information concerning the intricacies of muscular function.

THE NERVOUS SYSTEM AND BASIC NERVE STRUCTURES

It is assumed that the kinesiology student is already familiar with the general plan of the nervous system; hence, it will not be described in full here.

Only a brief outline of the major divisions is presented below, the purpose being to give the reader an orientation framework for the topics which have been selected for discussion.

I. Central Nervous System
    A. Brain
    B. Spinal cord
II. Peripheral Nervous System
    A. Cranial nerves (12 pairs)
    B. Spinal nerves (31 pairs)
III. Autonomic Nervous System

The autonomic nervous system is not a distinct system based on structure and geographic location, as are the central and peripheral systems, but is rather a functional division which overlaps with those in specific areas. It includes those portions of the brain, spinal cord and peripheral nervous system that supply cardiac muscle, smooth muscle and gland cells.

Neurons.   A neuron, which is the structural unit of the nervous system, is a single nerve cell consisting of a cell body and one or more projections. There are two kinds of neurons whose long fibers constitute the peripheral nervous system. These are sensory or afferent and motor or efferent (Fig. 3–1). In addition to these there are numerous connector (internuncial) neurons within the central nervous system.

The cell bodies of the majority of efferent or motor neurons are situated within the anterior horns of the spinal cord. (There are also some in the brain stem and sympathetic ganglia.) Many short threadlike extensions of the cell body, known as dendrites, make contact, i.e., synapse, with the axons of other cells, the latter being either sensory or connector neurons.

Each motor and connector neuron has a specialized process termed an axon. The axon of the motor neuron emerges from the spinal cord in a ventral root. It then travels by way of a peripheral nerve to the muscle that it helps to

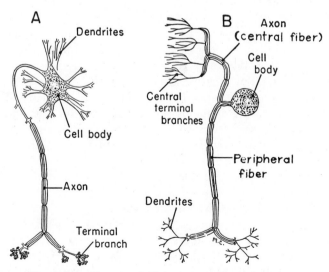

Figure 3–1   Neurons. *A*, Motor neuron; *B*, sensory neuron.

innervate. There it divides and subdivides into smaller and smaller branches, the most distal being known as the terminal branches. Each terminal branch ends within a single muscle fiber in the structure called the motor end-plate.

The cell body of a spinal afferent or sensory neuron, unlike that of a motor neuron, is situated in a dorsal root ganglion just outside of the spinal cord. (The cell bodies of cranial sensory neurons are in cranial nerve ganglia.) The neuron has a single short process that projects from the cell body and then bifurcates into two branches which go in opposite directions. One, the so-called central fiber, travels in the dorsal root of the nerve to the posterior horn of the spinal cord where it divides into numerous branches. It may terminate in the cord or it may ascend in the cord to the brain and terminate there. The other branch of the afferent neuron is the long peripheral fiber which comes from a receptor. It travels in a nerve trunk to the vicinity of the appropriate dorsal root ganglion where it unites with the cell body via the short stemlike process mentioned above (Fig. 3–1, *B*).

Authorities differ in their choice of nomenclature for the parts of a sensory neuron. Some apply the term "axon" to the short stemlike process; others apply this term to the central fiber, i.e., the branch that enters the spinal cord. This text adopts the latter use of the term as it is in keeping with a commonly accepted definition, namely that an axon is the fiber over which impulses are conducted *away from* the cell body, as opposed to dendrites which convey impulses *toward* the cell body. When referring to a sensory neuron, the term dendrite is applied not to the long fiber which conveys impulses from peripheral regions to the cell body, but rather to its branches. The long sensory fiber itself is known simply as the peripheral fiber. Some authorities, however, do not designate any part of the sensory neuron as a dendrite, but say merely that the peripheral fiber and its branches *function like dendrites*.

It was noted above that the dendrites of efferent (motor) neurons make contact within the spinal cord either with the terminal branches of afferent (sensory) neurons or with connector neurons. Connector neurons, also known as internuncial neurons, are a third type of nerve cell. They exist completely within the central nervous system and serve as connecting links. They may vary from a single small neuron, connecting a sensory neuron with a motor neuron, to an intricate system of neurons whereby a sensory impulse may be relayed to many motor cell bodies. We know from common experience that a complex motor act may result from a single sensory impulse. For instance, a sudden loud noise may cause us to jump, turn around and tense nearly every muscle in our body. The connector neurons are responsible for this widespread response to the single sensory impulse. Thus there may be only one connector neuron participating in a movement, or there may be an intricate network making possible an almost limitless number of connections with other neurons.

Nerves. Just as an electric cable is an insulated bundle of wires for the transmission of electric currents, so a nerve is a bundle of fibers, enclosed within a connective tissue sheath, for the transmission of impulses from one part of the body to another. A nerve, or nerve trunk as it is frequently called, may consist entirely of outgoing fibers from the central nervous system to the muscles and other tissues; or it may consist only of incoming fibers from the sensory organs to the central nervous system. The typical spinal nerve, how-

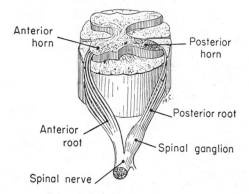

Figure 3–2 Section of the spinal cord showing the anterior and posterior roots of a spinal nerve.

ever, is mixed, that is, it contains both outgoing and incoming fibers. Each spinal nerve is attached to the spinal cord by a ventral (motor) root and a dorsal (sensory) root (Fig. 3–2). The dorsal root bears a ganglion and it is just beyond the ganglion that the two roots unite to form the spinal nerve. Once outside the vertebral canal, each spinal nerve divides into an anterior and a posterior branch, each of which contains both motor and sensory fibers. The anterior branches supply the trunk and limbs, the posterior branches the back.

THE MOTOR UNIT

To recapitulate, the structural units of the nervous and motor systems are, respectively, the neuron and the muscle fiber. Functionally, the two systems combine to form the neuromuscular system. The functional unit of the neuro-muscular system is the *motor unit,* and it consists of a single motor neuron (Fig. 3–1, *A*) together with all of the muscle fibers that its axon supplies.

Motor units vary widely in the number of muscle fibers supplied by one motor neuron. In some motor units there may be as many as 1000 or more muscle fibers; in others there may be fewer than 100. The number of motor units in a muscle depends in part upon the total number of fibers in the muscle and in part upon the number of fibers in a single motor unit.[6] A muscle which has a large number of motor units in relation to the total number of fibers, that is, a small ratio of muscle fibers to motor neurons, is capable of more precise movements than is the muscle with a small number of motor units for the same number of muscle fibers. Hence the ratio of muscle fibers to motor neurons has a direct bearing on the precision of the movements executed by the muscle. For example, the small muscles of the thumb and index finger are capable of effecting movements of great precision because their motor units have such a low ratio of muscle fibers to motor neurons, or to state it differently, such a large number of motor neurons per muscle. By way of contrast, the gluteus maximus has a relatively small number of motor neurons for its size, hence a large number of muscle fibers per neuron. It does not need to be pointed out that the movements for which the gluteus maximus is responsible can scarcely be described as precise.

RECEPTORS

The receptors are the sensory nerve terminals which respond to various stimuli. There are two major classifications, exteroceptors and interoceptors. The former receive and transmit stimuli that come from outside of the body and include the receptors of the familiar five senses: sight, hearing, smell, taste and touch; the latter include other cutaneous sensations, such as heat, cold, pain and pressure (Fig. 3–3). The interoceptors may be subdivided into the receptors that receive impulses from the viscera and those that receive impulses from the tissues directly concerned with musculoskeletal movements and positions. The former are known as visceroceptors and the latter as proprioceptors.

Proprioceptors

It is the proprioceptors with which students of activity and posture are especially interested for these are the receptors that receive impulses from muscles, tendons and joints, that is, the surrounding and protective tissues such as capsules, ligaments and other fibrous membranes. The proprioceptors are responsible for transmitting a constant flow of information from these structures to the spinal cord. This information has to do with the appropriate-

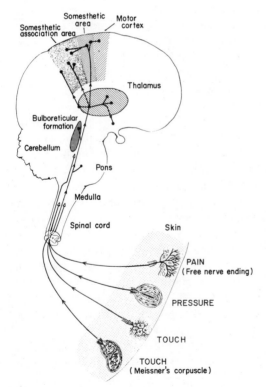

Figure 3–3 Transmission of exteroceptive sensation to the brain, showing the sensory receptors and the nerve pathways into the brain. (From Guyton, A. C.: Function of the Human Body, 4th Ed. Philadelphia: W. B. Saunders Company, 1974.)

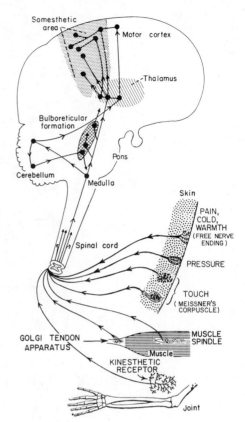

Figure 3-4 Transmission of proprioceptive sensations to the brain, showing the sensory receptors and the nerve pathways for transmitting these sensations into the brain. (From Guyton, A. C.: Function of the Human Body, 4th Ed. Philadelphia: W. B. Saunders Company, 1974.)

ness of the response, i.e., appropriateness regarding the degree, the direction and the rate of change in muscle tension. The proprioceptors include the following: muscle spindles, Golgi tendon organs, pacinian corpuscles, Ruffini end-organs, labyrinthine receptors and neck receptors (Figs. 3–4 and 3–5).

Muscle Spindles and Golgi Tendon Organs. These are found within the muscle itself. The *muscle spindles* are scattered throughout the fleshy part of the muscle, lying between the muscle fibers and parallel with them. A single spindle is a tiny capsule (about 1 mm long) which is filled with fluid and contains some specialized muscle fibers known as intrafusal fibers to distinguish them from the extrafusal or "regular" muscle fibers. There are two kinds of these fibers, nuclear bag fibers and nuclear chain fibers (Fig. 3–6). They are similar in that they both have central noncontractile areas where the nuclei are situated, and both have polar ends which are contractile. They differ in size and in the arrangement of the nuclei. The nuclear bag fiber is the larger of the two, and the nuclei appear crowded into the bag-like central area which gives the fiber its name. The small nuclear chain fiber is named for the single-line, chain-like arrangement of the nuclei in its slim, noncontractile central portion. There are differences also in the intricate system of innervation.

Each spindle is supplied with one afferent neuron which has a characteristic ending known as the primary or annulospiral ending. This ending is

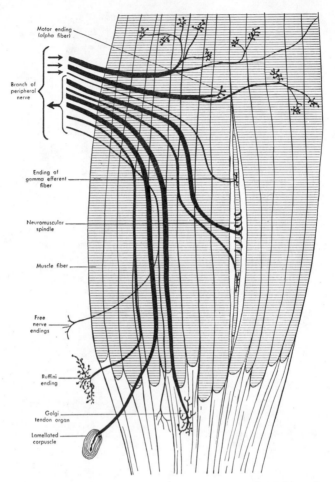

Motor ending
(alpha fiber)

Branch of
peripheral
nerve

Ending of
gamma efferent
fiber

Neuromuscular
spindle

Muscle fiber

Free
nerve
endings

Ruffini
ending

Golgi
tendon organ

Lamellated
corpuscle

Figure 3–5 Schematic representation of a muscle and its nerve supply. (From Gardner, E.: Fundamentals of Neurology, 6th Ed. Philadelphia: W. B. Saunders Company, 1975.)

divided into as many branches as there are intrafusal fibers, and each branch is coiled around the noncontractile midsection of the intrafusal fiber. The annulospiral (AS) ending is sensitive to changes in fiber length and by virtue of this sensitivity is credited with being responsible for the stretch reflex. In addition to the AS ending, most of the muscle spindles also have from one to five sensory endings which, because of their appearance, are given the picturesque name of flower-spray (FS) endings. Each FS ending has its own sensory fiber. The flower-spray endings (also called secondary endings) are found at either end of the noncontractile midsection of the intrafusal fibers. They are believed to register static muscular length, but their precise function is yet to be determined. One theory is that they inhibit further contraction of a muscle if the spindle is being overstretched.

Muscle spindles are also supplied with their own small efferent fibers. To differentiate these fibers from the motor neurons of the "regular" muscle fibers they are termed *gamma fibers* in contrast to the "regular" motor neurons whose axons are termed *alpha fibers* (Fig. 3–5). As a group, the gamma fibers form a *gamma fiber system.* Impulses conveyed by gamma fibers (also called gamma efferents) cause the intrafusal muscle fibers to contract. This shortening of the spindle muscle fibers stretches their central noncontractile region where the AS endings are situated, and this stimulates them, causing their rate of firing to increase. Hence the effect of the gamma system is to increase the sensitivity of the spindle afferents. The AS endings can be caused to fire, not only by passive stretch of the muscle as a whole, but also in the absence of such stretch by the function of the gamma system.

In brief, the spindles have the responsibility for controlling the coordination of our muscular behavior. The feedback which they keep supplying continuously assures a constant adjustment of muscular contraction. An exaggerated but familiar example of a single adjustment of this nature is seen when one starts to pick up an object that he has been led to believe is heavy. When the opposite proves to be the case his correction in muscular effort is almost instantaneous. Less spectacular examples of this kind of coordination take place in all movements all the time.

The *Golgi tendon organ* is another special receptor for impulses from muscles (Fig. 3–5). It consists of a mass of nerve endings which are enclosed within a connective tissue capsule and embedded in a muscle tendon. It is situated close to the junction of the tendon with the fleshy part of the muscle in such a way that it has an end-to-end relationship with the muscle fibers. These organs are stimulated by stretch, and much more by the stretch produced by the contraction of the muscle in which they are situated than by passive stretch. They appear to facilitate flexors and to inhibit extensors, and they have a protective, inhibitory effect on their own muscle when its tension increases to the danger point.

Pacinian corpuscles, Ruffini endings (flower spray or FS organs) and other joint proprioceptors are found in tissues related to joints, such as capsules and ligaments. Pacinian corpuscles exist in muscle fascia as well as in joint tissues. They are all activated by pressure and by changes in joint position.

Although *cutaneous receptors* are fundamentally exteroceptors, the ones that receive stimuli from touch, pressure and pain serve as proprioceptors when they show sensitivity to texture, hardness-softness and shape, and also when they participate in the pain or flexion withdrawal reflex and in the extensor thrust reflex.

Labyrinths. The labyrinths of the inner ear consist of the cochlea, the three semicircular canals, and the utricle and saccule. The cochlea is concerned with hearing, but the rest of the labyrinth is concerned with the sense of balance or equilibrium. Each of the canals contains a membranous tube, and the bony spaces for the maccule and saccule contain membranous sacs correspondingly named. The entire membranous labyrinth is filled with fluid. Certain parts are specialized in that the membrane consists of hair cells which are sensitive to the movement of the fluid as the head moves and which are intimately related to branches of the eighth cranial nerve. Thus, movement of the head is translated into nerve impulses reaching the brain. The hair cells in the maccule and saccule have, in addition, an overlying gelatinous substance in which otoliths

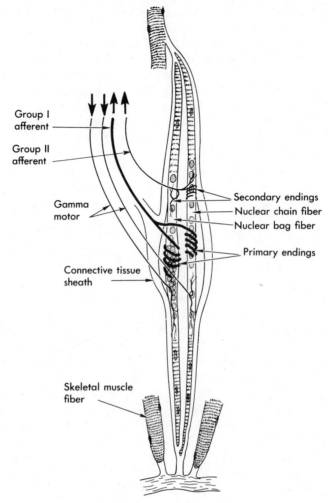

Group I afferent

Group II afferent

Gamma motor

Secondary endings

Nuclear chain fiber

Nuclear bag fiber

Primary endings

Connective tissue sheath

Skeletal muscle fiber

Figure 3–6   Schematic representation of a neuromuscular spindle. (From Gardner, E.: Fundamentals of Neurology, 6th Ed. Philadelphia: W. B. Saunders Company, 1975.)

(small carbonate of lime crystals) are embedded. The otoliths accentuate the effects of gravity on the hair cells. The maccule and saccule are thus sensitive to position as well as to movement of the head. The anatomic arrangement of the entire labyrinth is such that some part of it is especially sensitive to any position or direction of movement of the head.*

THE SYNAPSE

As was mentioned in the discussion of neurons, the connection between neurons in the central nervous system is known as a synapse. A synapse, and

---

*The authors are indebted to Dr. Ernest Gardner for this discussion of the labyrinths.

there may be thousands between any two neurons, is a contiguity of the membrane of an axon and the membrane of a dendrite or a cell body. There is no physical union between them. Conduction of impulses takes place in one direction only, namely from the axon of one neuron to the dendrites or cell body of another. The transmission of an impulse across a synapse depends upon the release of a transmitter substance by the axon. This substance diffuses through the membranes and stimulates or inhibits the next cell.*

REFLEX MOVEMENT

A reflex movement is one which occurs without volition and without the need of direction from the cerebrum. The anatomic basis for a reflex act is the reflex arc (Fig. 3–7). This consists of an afferent neuron which comes from a receptor organ, enters the spinal cord, and there makes a synaptic connection either directly with the dendrites and the cell body of an efferent neuron, or indirectly through one or more connector neurons. The axon of the efferent neuron extends from the·cord to the muscle where its distal branches terminate in muscle fibers. (It will be recalled that the axon of the efferent neuron together with all of the muscle fibers that it serves constitutes a motor unit.) The point of contact between an axon and a muscle fiber is known as a myoneural junction, also as a motor end-plate. The number of reflex arcs and the number of motor units involved depend both upon the nature of the reflex and upon the extent of muscular activity needed.

As could be inferred from the discussion of receptors, there are two main classes of reflexes related to skeletal movements, namely exteroceptive and proprioceptive. Many of the exteroceptor reflexes exhibited by animals and man are familiar to us. A horse will twitch its skin when flies alight on it; a dog will scratch when its skin is irritated by a flea, or perhaps tickled by a man. A human being jumps when he hears a sudden loud noise. He also blinks when a foreign body strikes his eyeball, or even threatens to strike it. Three exteroceptive reflexes which may be of special interest are the extensor thrust, the flexor and the crossed extensor reflexes.

Extensor Thrust Reflex.   Pressure against the sole of the foot stimulates the pacinian corpuscles in the subcutaneous tissue and elicits the reflex contraction of the extensor muscles of the lower extremity. When the weight is supported by the feet the pressure of the floor is sufficient to bring about this reaction. Some authorities classify this reflex as a proprioceptor, rather than an exteroceptor reflex.[7] (See page 58.)

Flexor Reflex.   The flexor reflex operates in response to pain and is a device for self-protection. Because of the flexor reflex we quickly withdraw a part of the body the instant it is hurt. If a finger is pricked by a pin or if it inadvertently touches a hot pan, we do not have to decide to remove our hand from the source of pain; we jerk it back even before we realize what has happened to it. Furthermore, all of the necessary muscles for withdrawing it are innervated promptly, not just those in the immediate vicinity of the injury.

---

*The authors are indebted to Dr. Ernest Gardner for his help in this definition of a synapse.

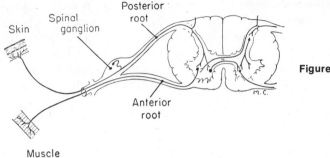

Figure 3-7 Reflex arc mechanism.

Although we are all too aware of the pain, this awareness plays no part in the reflex action of withdrawal. The value of the awareness is rather in teaching us to avoid repetition of the act that caused the pain.

Crossed Extensor Reflex.   This reflex functions cooperatively with the flexor reflex in response to pain in a weight-bearing limb. For instance, when an animal injures its paw, the flexor reflex causes it to withdraw the paw. Simultaneously, owing to the crossed extensor reflex, the extensor muscles of the opposite limb contract to support the additional weight thrust upon it. Similarly, if a man who is barefoot happens to step on a tack with his right foot he quickly shifts his weight to his left foot and withdraws his right foot from the floor. As the flexors of his right limb contract to enable him to lift his foot, the extensors of his left limb contract more strongly to support the weight of his entire body.

Guyton also cites the example of a non-weight bearing limb in man responding in like manner.[8] For example, if a pain stimulus is applied to one hand, at the same moment that the hand is withdrawn the opposite arm will extend as though to push the body away. The majority of authorities, however, appear to look upon the crossed extensor reflex as a mechanism for providing support for the body when one foot has been lifted.

Proprioceptive Reflexes.   Earlier in this chapter receptors were classified as exteroceptors and interoceptors, the latter being subdivided into visceral receptors and proprioceptors. Proprioceptive reflexes are generally described as those reflexes which occur in response to stimulation of receptors which are located in the skeletal muscles, the tendons and the joints. According to this interpretation the only proprioceptive reflexes are those related to the effect of stretch on muscles and tendons and the effect of movement on the connective tissues associated with joints.

Many texts use the term *myotatic reflex* synonymously with *stretch reflex* and this would appear to be logical as the word comes from the Greek words for muscle (mys) and stretching (tasis).[6] Other authorities classify stretch reflexes as a special type of myotatic reflex.[5] This should not disturb the student, however, for it is obvious that classifications are man-made devices for facilitating study and research. It is not surprising that there should be discrepancies in such classifications and even in the interpretations of the same classification.

Stretch Reflexes.   This type of reflex is of particular interest to the physical educator. In its simplest form the stretch reflex is a local response to stretch. For example, a muscle is subjected to stretch. The muscle spindles pick up the stretch stimulus and transmit it by way of the afferent neuron to the spinal cord. There the central terminal branches of the sensory neuron synapse direct-ly with the dendrites of the motor neuron which innervates the same muscle fibers that were stretched. These fibers then contract. This is the simplest type of reflex arc and is commonly known as a monosynaptic arc. Gardner prefers the term "two-neuron reflex arc" and describes it as involving one "area of synaptic junction." This is more accurate as an arc consisting of a single sensory neuron and a single motor neuron is not restricted to a single synapse. The important characteristic of this type of reflex arc is that it does not make use of connector neurons in the spinal cord. (Many authorities state that *all* stretch reflexes have this characteristic, but some state more cautiously that *most* of them do.[5,6])

Gardner classifies stretch reflexes as phasic and static types. The phasic type is the kind described above and includes familiar clinical tests like the knee jerk. Reflexes of this type are extremely rapid and the contraction is of brief duration. The word "jerk" gives an accurate picture. While it is true that the cause of the stimulus in this instance is exteroceptive in nature (it being a rubber-headed hammer or the edge of the hand) it is nevertheless classed as a proprioceptive reflex. Another example of a phasic type of stretch reflex is probably present in the violent movement of the arms in certain gymnastic exercises and sport skills. If the stretch is sudden and sufficiently severe the stretched muscle contracts, apparently in an attempt to protect itself from injury.

In the static type of stretch reflex the muscle is stretched slowly. This causes several spindles to be stimulated, not simultaneously but in succession and re-sults in a more sustained muscular contraction. When such a reflex is elicited by the stretch that is caused by the tendency of weight-bearing joints to flex, the response of the extensor muscles is commonly referred to as the *antigravity reflex.* This term is also used by some to include the response of lower extremity and trunk muscles to the involuntary forward-backward swaying that usually occurs when a person stands in one position for a long time.

Ralston and Libet, who have made extensive electromyographic studies of muscular action, apparently do not accept this concept of an antigravity reflex.[15] In 1953 they stated that investigators did not find electrical activity accompany-ing stretch unless the stretch was of such speed that it invoked the jerk type of reflex. They also stated that the short bursts of activity that accompanied sway-ing were apparently not simple stretch reflexes in spite of the fact that they were probably initiated by local stretch receptor impulses. As evidence of the latter conclusion they stated that the contraction of the tibialis anterior and the soleus which had been observed in a "standing at ease" position was initiated by a degree of angular motion at the ankle joint that they claimed was far less than that which is required to elicit a stretch reflex. They concluded that the hypothesis that stretch reflex discharge occurs automatically to help maintain a given postural attitude in normal man was not supported by the available evidence. In 1957 Ralston reaffirmed this conclusion.[16] Clearly this matter needs further investigation.

Posture and Locomotor Mechanisms.   Whether due to reflex action or to some other mechanism, it seems apparent that there are certain provisions in

the human body for remaining more or less erect and for engaging in locomotion, and that these follow the general pattern of reflex behavior. The coordinated efforts of the body to resist the downward pull of gravity include the
extensor thrust reflex, the static type of stretch reflex in response to gravitational pull, the muscular action evoked by forward-backward swaying and the
various mechanisms for preserving equilibrium, including visual orientation
and labyrinthine reflexes.

In regard to locomotion, the action of the legs of a four footed animal has
been attributed to reflex action. Some classify this reflex as a division of the
crossed extensor reflex;[17] others refer to it simply as a walking reflex.[8] Because
the research in this area has been done primarily on dogs and cats it has been
suggested that this reflex exists only in quadrupeds. Nevertheless, it is logical
to assume that it exists also in man inasmuch as his early forms of locomotion —
creeping and crawling — resemble the locomotion of quadrupeds. Even after he
assumes the erect position the swing of his arms in opposition to his lower
extremities reflects his earlier four-footed gait.

MUSCLE TONUS

Concepts of muscle tonus are so varied and seem to be so subject to revision
that this text is not attempting to define the term. It is recommended that the
reader refer to modern texts on general physiology, or physiology of muscular
activity, in order to learn the current thinking on this subject.

VOLITIONAL MOVEMENT

This topic involves such an extensive and complex body of knowledge that
only the bare essentials and a few of the newer concepts can be touched upon
here. The chief anatomic structures concerned with volitional movement, in
addition to those mentioned earlier (skeletal muscle, basic nerve structures,
motor units and sensory receptors) are the cerebral cortex, the cerebellum, the
brain stem, the corticospinal tracts and the numerous motor pathways, both
pyramidal and extrapyramidal.

The portion of the cerebral cortex in which impulses for the majority of
volitional acts are thought to arise is the fold situated just in front of the transverse central fissure. Because of its location, this is known as the precentral
gyrus; and because it was originally thought to consist entirely of motor cells,
it is referred to as the motor area of the cortex (Fig. 3–8). In front of this area
is another area having to do with movement. It is called the premotor area and
is thought to be responsible for the more complex movement patterns.[7,8]

Regarding the topography of the motor area, it used to be thought that
this area was divided into distinct sub-areas, each of which was solely responsible
for the contraction of particular muscles or groups of muscles. Recent studies,
however, have revealed that there is considerable overlapping of motor unit
territories.[7,9] This appears to be a provision for the performance of complex
movement patterns as well as for a variety of movement combinations.

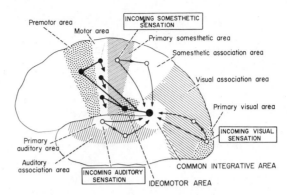

Figure 3–8 Integration of sensory signals from several different sources into a common thought by the common integrative area of the brain, showing also the primary and association areas for vision, for auditory sensations, and for somesthetic sensations. (From Guyton, A. C.: Function of the Human Body, 4th Ed. Philadelphia: W. B. Saunders Company, 1974.)

The axons of the motor cells, called Betz's cells, descend through the brain stem and the spinal cord. Together, these axons form the corticospinal tracts. They pass through the anterior portions of the medulla which constitute the pyramids, and it is here that most of the fibers cross to the opposite side. Because of their route through the pyramids the fibers are known collectively as the pyramidal system and their cell bodies as pyramidal cells. The fibers from the premotor area and from other parts of the cortex do not pass through the medulla pyramids; hence they are referred to as the extrapyramidal system.

It was originally thought that the pyramidal system consisted exclusively of Betz cell axons. More recently, however, it has been discovered that the majority of pyramidal fibers actually come from cortical cells outside of the traditional motor area, and that the extrapyramidal system also includes many fibers from the motor area.[7] Furthermore, the precentral gyrus is no longer thought to be exclusively a motor area, but rather a sensorimotor area because it is now known to receive some afferent impulses. There is experimental evidence to show that proprioceptive impulses have been received by the motor area after the sensory area in the postcentral gyrus had been removed.[7]

One of the most important of the newer concepts concerning volitional movement is that continued sensory stimulation is essential to motor unit function. There has been ample clinical evidence to show that when sensory innervation is impaired there is a noticeable impairment of volitional movement. It is realized now that for the successful and appropriate execution of volitional acts, sensory stimuli are as indispensable as motor stimuli. This is true throughout all stages of the movement.[7,9] It is obvious from this that the stimulus-response concept, as formerly interpreted, is no longer adequate for explaining volitional acts.[9]

It has been discovered that the position of a limb is a factor in the intensity of response when a given muscle is made to contract by means of cortical stimulation. For instance, in an electromyographic study of the triceps muscle it was found that the response of the muscle to stimulation of the appropriate cortical area differed according to the size of the angle at the elbow joint. When the joint angle was acute, the response of the triceps to cortical stimulation was stronger than when the joint angle was obtuse. The significance of this experiment is the evidence it presents of the part played by the proprioceptors in relaying information about the position of the joint.[7,9]

A concept that has received wide attention is known as the reafferent or servo-mechanism concept of overt behavior.[4, 9] This mechanism is responsible for feeding back inhibitory impulses to motor neurons and thereby keeping the discharge frequency of the latter under control and safeguarding them against possible convulsive activity.[9, 12]

Many of the structures and mechanisms which influence volitional movement belong to the extrapyramidal system. Among these is the cerebellum which has the important task of controlling the timing and governing the intensity with which the muscles contract (Fig. 3–9). There is also the reticular formation in the brain stem, a mechanism for exerting facilitatory and inhibitory influence on spinal centers, especially the centers for the antigravity muscles,[12] and thus providing for finer coordinations. The thalamus in the brain stem is responsible for receiving sensory impulses and integrating them in coordinated patterns of movement; and the hypothalamus, which responds to emotional stimuli, is responsible for eliciting increased muscle power.[7] These are but a few of the ways in which the pyramidal and the extrapyramidal systems are seen to work together in volitional movement.

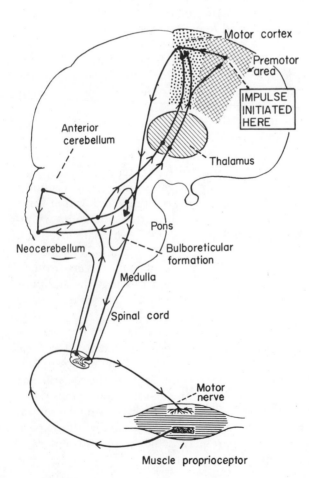

Figure 3–9 Feedback circuits of the cerebellum for damping motor movements. (From Guyton, A. C.: Function of the Human Body, 4th Ed. Philadelphia: W. B. Saunders Company, 1974.)

GRADATIONS IN THE STRENGTH OF
MUSCULAR CONTRACTIONS

Common experience indicates that the same muscles contract with various gradations of strength according to the requirements of the task. The elbow flexors, for example, are able to contract just enough to enable the hand to lift a piece of paper from the desk; they can also contract forcefully enough to lift a fifteen pound briefcase. How do they adjust to such extremes?

There are two major factors in the gradation of contraction. These are (1) the number of motor units which participate in the act, and (2) the frequency of stimulation. If the stimulus is of threshold value, all of the muscle fibers in the motor unit will contract maximally. If the stimulus is subliminal, in other words, below threshold value, none of the muscle fibers in the unit will contract at all. This characteristic is known as the *all-or-none principle of muscular contraction.* It must be emphasized that the principle applies only to individual motor units, not to entire muscles. To reiterate, if the stimulus is of threshold value, each muscle fiber in the participating unit will contract. Hence it follows that, other things being equal, the more motor units that contract, the greater will be the total strength developed.

If stimuli are discharged at low frequency, the muscle fibers will partially relax between impulses, but if the stimuli are discharged at high frequency the fibers will have insufficient time to relax and the result is summation or maximal contraction. If these two factors are combined, that is, if the maximum number of fibers are stimulated with the impulses being discharged at high frequency, the resulting contraction is of maximal strength.

RECIPROCAL INNERVATION AND INHIBITION

One of the mechanisms that provides for economical and coordinated movement is the one known as reciprocal innervation and inhibition, first described by Sherrington. According to this concept, when motor neurons are transmitting impulses to muscles, causing them to contract, the motor neurons that supply their antagonists are simultaneously and reciprocally inhibited. The antagonistic muscles, therefore, remain relaxed and the movers, or agonists, contract without opposition. Reciprocal inhibition operates automatically in movements elicited by the stretch reflex, also in familiar volitional movements. In more complicated and in less familiar coordinations its operation depends upon the degree of skill developed by the performer.

Not all investigators are in agreement with respect to the operation of reciprocal innervation and inhibition in volitional movement. Some believe that muscles that are antagonistic to each other do contract concurrently under certain conditions and they refer to this as cocontraction (see page 49). Others are of the opinion that simultaneous contraction of antagonistic muscles, when it does occur, is indicative of unskillful performance, and that skillful performance is characterized by the absence of antagonistic action.[1, 13]

REFERENCES

1. Basmajian, J. V.: Muscles Alive. 3rd Ed. Baltimore: The Williams & Wilkins Company, 1974.
2. de Vries, H. A.: Muscle tonus in postural muscles. Am. J. Phys. Med., 44:275–291, 1965.
3. Eldred, E.: The dual sensory role of muscle spindles. J. Am. Phys. Ther. Assn., 45:290–313, 1965.
4. Fischer, E.: Physiological basis of volitional movements. Phys. Ther. Rev., 38:405–412, 1958.
5. Fischer, E.: Neurophysiology a physical therapist should know. Phys. Ther. Rev., 38:741–748, 1958.
6. Gardner, E.: Fundamentals of Neurology, 6th ed. Philadelphia: W. B. Saunders Company, 1975.
7. Gellhorn, E.: The physiology of the supraspinal mechanism. In Johnson, W. R., and Buskirk, E. (Eds.) Science and Medicine of Exercise and Sports. 2nd Ed. New York: Harper & Row, 1973.
8. Guyton, A. C.: Function of the Human Body, 4th Ed. Philadelphia: W. B. Saunders Company, 1974.
9. Harrison, V. F.: Review of the neuromuscular bases for motor learning. Res. Quart. Am. Assn. Health, Phys. Ed. & Recrn., 33:59–69, 1962.
10. Huxley, H. E.: The contraction of muscle. Sci. Am., Nov. 1958 (offprint).
11. Karpovich, P. V., and Sinning, W. E.: Physiology of Muscular Activity, 7th Ed. Philadelphia: W. B. Saunders Company, 1971.
12. Loofburrow, G. N.: Neuromuscular integration. In Johnson, W. R., and Buskirk, E. (Eds.): Science and Medicine of Exercise and Sports, 2nd Ed. New York, Harper & Row, 1973.
13. O'Connell, A. L., and Gardner, E. B.: Understanding the Scientific Bases of Human Movement. Baltimore: The Williams & Wilkins Co., 1972.
14. Ralston, H. J.: Mechanics of voluntary muscle. Am. J. Phys. Med., 32:166–184, 1953.
15. Ralston, H. J., and Libet, B.: The question of tonus in skeletal muscle. Am. J. Phys. Med., 32:85–92, 1953.
16. Ralston, H. J.: Recent advances in neuromuscular physiology. Am. J. Phys. Med., 36:94–120, 1957.
17. Ruch, T. C., and Patton, H. D.: Medical Physiology and Biophysics, 19th Ed. Philadelphia: W. B. Saunders Company, 1965.

RECOMMENDED READING

Gardner, E. B.: Proprioceptive reflexes and their participation in motor skills. Quest, Monograph XII, Spring Issue: 1–25 (May), 1969.

Chapter Four

THE UPPER EXTREMITY: THE SHOULDER REGION

Anatomic cooperation is beautifully illustrated in the movements of the arms on the trunk. The arm travels through a wide range of movements, and in each of these the scapula cooperates by placing the glenoid fossa in the most favorable position for the head of the humerus. When the arm is elevated sideward, for instance, the scapula rotates upward; when it is elevated forward, the scapula not only rotates upward but it tends to slide partially around the rib cage. Occasionally this movement is deliberately repressed, as in the arm placings and flingings of the old Swedish type of calisthenics and in some posture exercises, but in all natural movements, the scapula shares with the humerus in the movements of the arm on the trunk.

The upper extremity is suspended from the axial skeleton (head and trunk) by means of the shoulder girdle. The latter consists of the sternum and two clavicles in front, and two scapulae in back with their connecting joints, the sternoclavicular between the sternum and each clavicle and the acromioclavicular between the acromion process of each scapula and the corresponding clavicle. Since there is no union between the two scapulae in back, this is an incomplete girdle. The upper extremity's connection with the shoulder girdle is made through the glenohumeral joint, the joint between the head of the humerus and the glenoid fossa of the scapula, better known as the shoulder joint.

The sternoclavicular joint is an exceedingly small one, about the size of the joint between the great toe and the first metatarsal bone, yet it is the sole skeletal connection between the upper extremity and the trunk. This anatomic arrangement accounts for the extensive freedom of motion enjoyed by the upper extremity and is a vital factor in the superb cooperation that exists between the shoulder joint and the shoulder girdle. The upper arm has a remarkably wide range of motion owing largely to its ball and shallow socket construction. Its movements are further amplified by the cooperative actions of the shoulder girdle which were described in the preceding paragraph.

In order to understand and appreciate the great variety of movements of the arm on the trunk it is essential that one be thoroughly familiar with the structure and function of each joint that is involved and be able to distinguish between the contributions of each in any given movement.

71

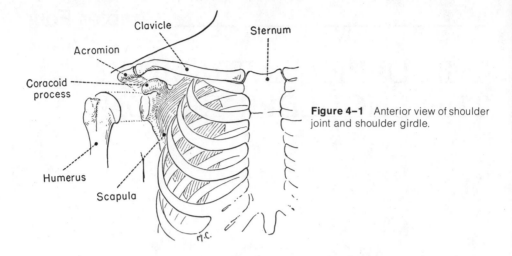

Figure 4-1 Anterior view of shoulder joint and shoulder girdle.

THE SHOULDER JOINT (GLENOHUMERAL ARTICULATION)

Structure. The shoulder joint is formed by the articulation of the spherical head of the humerus with the small, shallow, somewhat pear-shaped glenoid fossa of the scapula (Fig. 4–1). It is a ball-and-socket joint. The structure of the joint and the looseness of the capsule (permitting between one and two inches of separation between the two bones) account for the remarkable mobility of the shoulder joint. Both the humeral head and the glenoid fossa are covered with hyaline cartilage. The cartilage on the head is thicker at the center, while that which lines the cavity is thicker around the circumference. The glenoid fossa is further protected by a flat rim of white fibrocartilage, also thicker around the circumference. Called the glenoid labrum, this cartilage serves both to deepen the fossa and to cushion it against the impact of the humeral head in forceful movements (Fig. 4–2).

The joint is completely enveloped in a loose sleevelike articular capsule which is attached proximally to the circumference of the glenoid cavity and distally to the anatomic neck of the humerus. The capsule is lined with synovial membrane which folds back over the glenoid labrum, covers all but the upper portion of the anatomic neck of the humerus and extends through the intertubercular groove in the form of a sheath for the tendon of the long head of the biceps. There are several bursae in the region of the shoulder joint. Among the larger are the one between the deltoid muscle and the capsule and the one on top of the acromion process.

Ligamentous and Muscular Reinforcements. The shoulder joint is protected and stabilized by both ligaments and muscles. Inspection of the illustrations on these pages supplemented by study of the Table of Muscular Attachments in Appendix C will help the reader to gain an understanding of the relationships of the ligaments and muscles to the joints they reinforce.

The coracohumeral ligament, the three bands of the glenohumeral ligament and the bridge-like coracoacromial ligament constitute the *ligamentous*

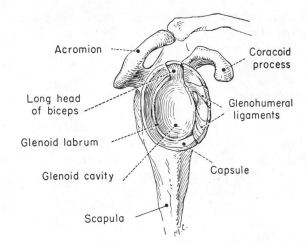

Acromion

Coracoid
process

Long head
of biceps

Glenohumeral
ligaments

Glenoid labrum

Glenoid cavity

Capsule

Scapula

Figure 4-2 Lateral view of right scapula showing glenoid cavity.

reinforcements of the shoulder joint. *Muscular reinforcement* is provided above by the supraspinatus muscle and the long head of the biceps brachii, below by the long head of the triceps brachii, in front by the subscapularis muscle and the fibrous prolongations of both the pectoralis major and teres major muscles and behind by the infraspinatus and teres minor muscles. (See Figs. 4-4 through 4-8.)

Apparently these reinforcements do not prevent downward dislocation, however. Two electromyographic investigations have thrown light on the role of certain structures in stabilizing the shoulder joint and, in particular, preventing downward dislocation. In their extensive study of the shoulder region in 1944, Inman, Saunders and Abbott noted the stabilizing function of the four muscles that constitute the "rotator cuff"—the supraspinatus, infraspinatus, teres minor and subscapularis.[9] In 1959 Basmajian and Bazant investigated the muscles whose fibers cross the shoulder joint vertically, as compared with those

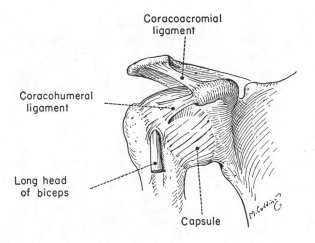

Coracoacromial
ligament

Coracohumeral
ligament

Long head
of biceps

Capsule

Figure 4-3 Anterior view of shoulder joint showing ligaments.

whose fibers cross it horizontally. To their surprise they discovered that it was the horizontal fibers and not the vertical that were active in preventing downward dislocation of the humerus. After doing a dissection of the shoulder joint, they agreed that the slope of the glenoid fossa was an important factor. Because of this slope, the head of the humerus was forced laterally as it was pulled downward, and it took the horizontally directed muscle fibers to check this lateral movement which, in turn, stopped the downward movement. They concluded that downward dislocation of the humerus was prevented primarily by three factors, namely, (1) the slope of the glenoid fossa, (2) the tightening of the upper part of the capsule and of the coracohumeral ligament and (3) the activity of the supraspinatus muscle and, to a lesser extent, of the posterior fibers of the deltoid.[1]

MOVEMENTS.   The movements of the humerus, all of which take place at the glenohumeral articulation, are as follows.

Flexion and Hyperflexion.   A forward upward movement in a plane at right angles to the plane of the scapula. If the movement exceeds 180 degrees, it is hyperflexion.

Extension.   Return movement from flexion.

Hyperextension.   A backward movement in a plane at right angles to the plane of the scapula.

Abduction.   A sideward upward movement in a plane parallel with the plane of the scapula.*

Adduction.   Return movement from abduction.

Outward Rotation.   A rotation of the humerus around its mechanical axis so that when the arm is in its normal resting position, the anterior aspect turns laterally.

Inward Rotation.   A rotation of the humerus around its mechanical axis so that when the arm is in its normal resting position, the anterior aspect turns medially.

Horizontal Flexion.   A forward movement of the abducted humerus in a horizontal plane (i.e., from a plane parallel to the plane of the scapula to a plane at right angles to it).

Horizontal Extension.   A backward movement of the flexed humerus in a horizontal plane (i.e., from a plane at right angles to the plane of the scapula to a plane parallel to it).

Circumduction.   A combination of flexion, abduction, extension, hyperextension and adduction performed sequentially in either direction so that the extended arm describes a cone and the fingertips a circle.

MUSCLES.**   The muscles of the shoulder joint are listed below according to their position in relation to the joint. This position is not always apparent, as a look at the illustrations will show.

---

*Some authorities interpret abduction as the sideward movement of the arm away from the body, thus including the action of the shoulder girdle with that of the shoulder joint. When reading the literature, one should note which interpretation is intended.

**Attention is called to the electromyographic investigations reported in the Supplementary Material at the end of this chapter.

Anterior	Posterior
Pectoralis major	Posterior deltoid
Coracobrachialis	Infraspinatus
Anterior deltoid	Teres minor
Subscapularis	
Biceps brachii	

Superior	Inferior
Middle deltoid	Latissimus dorsi
Supraspinatus	Teres major
	Triceps brachii, long head

CHARACTERISTICS AND FUNCTIONS OF SHOULDER JOINT MUSCLES*

Coracobrachialis (Fig. 4–4.)   The muscle's line of pull passes in front of the shoulder joint which suggests that it participates in *forward movements of the humerus*. It undoubtedly does this, especially if the arm starts in a position of hyperextension, or hyperhorizontal extension, but its angle of pull is so small that the muscle's chief function would appear to be *stabilization of the shoulder joint* rather than movement of the humerus. It may be palpated on the front of the upper arm between the anterior deltoid and the pectoralis major, but it is a difficult muscle to identify. The method suggested by Brunnstrom is recommended.[4]

Deltoid (Figs. 4–5 and 4–7.)   The complex structure of the deltoid, with the multipenniform arrangement of the bundles making up the middle portion, gives it a potential for great strength without undue bulk. The muscle is a *powerful abductor of the humerus*, its greatest activity occurring when the humerus is raised between 90 and 120 degrees, and it is capable of supporting the weight of the upper extremity for long periods while the hand is working at a height. The multipenniform arrangement of fibers compensates for the middle deltoid's rather poor angle of pull. The latter, however, serves the useful purpose of providing the muscle with a strong stabilizing component of force. This is fortunate because in this position the shoulder joint depends more upon its muscles than upon its ligaments for holding the head of the humerus on the glenoid fossa.

The anterior portion of the deltoid aids in *all forward movements* of the arm and in *inward rotation* of the humerus. There is disagreement in the literature concerning the movements effected by the posterior deltoid but there seems to be sufficient evidence to conclude that, in addition to the movements already mentioned, the lowest fibers, being situated below the axis of motion, assist in forceful adduction of the humerus from an overhead position. On the other hand, some of the upper fibers (those closest to the middle deltoid) probably act

---

*Listed in alphabetical order.

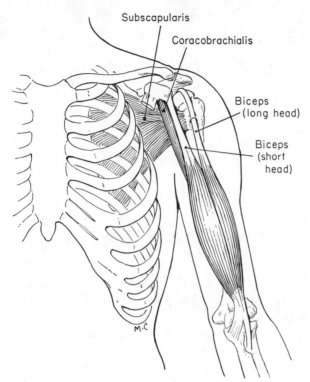

Subscapularis

Coracobrachialis

Biceps
(long head)

Biceps
(short
head)

Figure 4–4 Anterior view of muscles of shoulder joint, deep layer.

with the latter in contributing to abduction. In fact, Shevlin, Lehmann and Lucci stated that in their experiments the posterior deltoid elevated the humerus in the frontal plane (i.e., abduction) at all the levels tested (45, 90 and 110 degrees of elevation). Unfortunately they did not test above the 110 degree level; furthermore they used only one electrode for the posterior deltoid, placed "in the middle of its bulk."[15]

Infraspinatus and Teres Minor (Figs. 4–5, 4–6, *B* and 4–8.) These two muscles, which seem to act as one, have two notable functions. In addition to their *outward rotatory* action, they aid materially in holding the head of the humerus in the glenoid fossa. Together with the supraspinatus and subscapularis these muscles are known as the *rotator cuff muscles*. Their important function in this capacity is to prevent dislocation of the shoulder joint, especially when the humerus is in the abducted position. They may be palpated on the posterior surface of the scapula, medial to and below the posterior deltoid muscle.

Latissimus Dorsi (Fig. 4–5.) This is a broad sheet of muscle which covers the lower and middle portions of the back. Coming mainly from the lower half of the thoracic spine and the entire lumbar spine, the fibers gradually converge as they pass upward and laterally toward the axilla. Here the fibers twist on themselves in such a way that the lowest fibers become the uppermost. They end in the narrow flat tendon of the distal attachment. The muscle has a favorable angle of pull for *depression* of the arm, particularly when the latter is raised between 30 and 90 degrees. Scheving and Pauly found it to be more important than the pectoralis major as an *inward rotator* of the humerus.[1] The muscle may be palpated on the posterior border of the axilla just below the teres major.

Pectoralis Major (Fig. 4-7.) This large fan-shaped muscle of the chest converges to a flat tendon which, like that of the latissimus dorsi, twists on itself so that the lowest fibers become the uppermost at its point of attachment. The muscle is divided functionally into two parts, the clavicular and the sternal (or sternocostal). The clavicular portion lies close to the anterior deltoid muscle and acts with it in *flexion, horizontal flexion* and *inward rotation* of the humerus, participation in the latter movement, according to Scheving and Pauly, occurring only against resistance.[1]

Ordinarily the line of pull of the clavicular portion of the pectoralis major lies below the axis of the shoulder joint. Steindler claims, however, that when the arm is raised sideward well above the horizontal, the line of pull of the upper clavicular fibers shifts above the center of the shoulder joint, and these

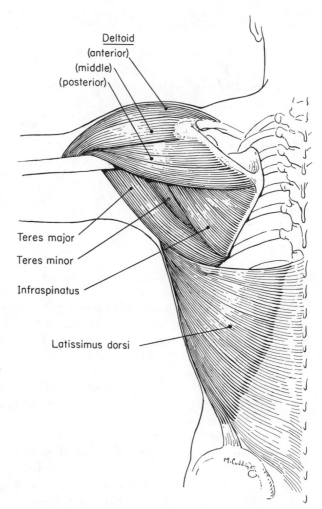

Deltoid
(anterior)
(middle)
(posterior)

Teres major

Teres minor

Infraspinatus

Latissimus dorsi

M.Coddings

Figure 4-5 Posterior view of muscles of shoulder joint, superficial layer.

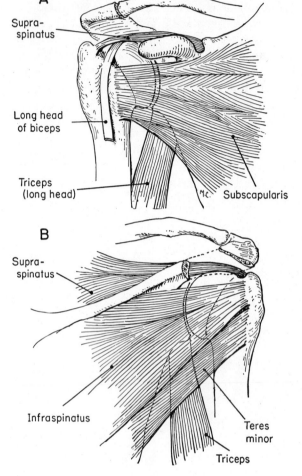

Figure 4–6 Muscular reinforcements of shoulder joint. *A*, Anterior view; *B*, posterior view.

fibers then cease to adduct and become abductors of the humerus.[16] (See Fig. 2–3.) The sternocostal portion acts only in downward and forward movements of the arm. The pectoralis major as a whole is particularly important in all pushing, throwing and punching activities. The clavicular portion may be palpated just below the medial two-thirds of the clavicle, the sternal portion just lateral to the sternum and below the clavicular part, and the muscle as a whole at the anterior border of the axilla.

Subscapularis (Figs. 4–4 and 4–6, *A*.)   Its chief action is *inward rotation* which it performs most effectively when the arm is at the side or is elevated posteriorly. It also contributes significantly to *stabilization* of the glenohumeral joint. It cannot be palpated.

Supraspinatus (Figs. 4–6 and 4–8.)   Like the deltoid, this muscle's greatest abductory activity occurs between 90 and 180 degrees of elevation. It plays a major part in *preventing downward dislocation* of the shoulder joint,[1] and by this same holding action it enables the deltoid to abduct the humerus in spite of the latter muscle's poor angle of pull.[16] Its own angle of pull is particularly favorable for initiating *abduction*. It may be palpated above the spine of the scapula, provided the scapula is supported, e.g., when the armpit rests over the back of a chair.

Teres Major (Figs. 4–5 and 4–8.)   Structurally, this muscle appears to be in a favorable position to work with the latissimus dorsi in *downward* and *backward movements* of the humerus and also in *inward rotation,* but Inman, Saunders and Abbott could detect no sign of activity in this muscle during these movements. They observed that it contracted only in maintaining static positions and that it attained its maximum activity when the humerus was at approximately a 90 degree angle of elevation.[9]

Biceps Brachii and Long Head of Triceps Brachii. (Figs. 4–4, 4–6 and 4–8.) Although essentially muscles of the elbow joint these two muscles cross the shoulder joint and assist in some of the movements of the humerus, the biceps in flexion (especially against resistance), horizontal flexion and adduction, and the long head of the triceps in adduction, extension and hyperextension. Both help to stabilize the shoulder joint.

THE SHOULDER GIRDLE (ACROMIOCLAVICULAR AND STERNOCLAVICULAR ARTICULATIONS)

Structure of Acromioclavicular Articulation. (Fig. 4–9.)   The articulation between the acromion process of the scapula and the outer end of the clavicle

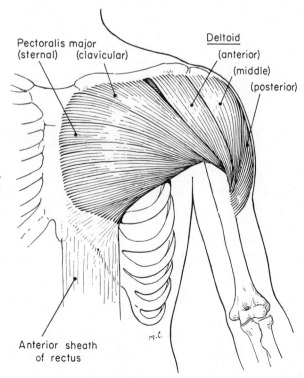

Figure 4–7 Anterior view of muscles of shoulder joint, superficial layer.

Pectoralis major
(sternal)   (clavicular)

Deltoid
(anterior)
(middle)
(posterior)

Anterior sheath
of rectus

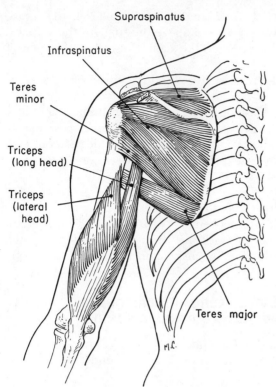

Supraspinatus

Infraspinatus

Teres
minor

Triceps
(long head)

Triceps
(lateral
head)

Teres major

Figure 4–8 Posterior view of muscles of shoulder joint, deep layer.

belongs to the diarthrodial classification. Within this group it is further classified as an irregular (arthrodial) joint. A small wedge-shaped disk may be found between the upper part of the joint surfaces, but this is frequently absent. The articular capsule is strengthened above by the acromioclavicular ligament, which passes from the upper part of the outer end of the clavicle to the upper surface of the acromion process, and behind by the aponeurosis of the trapezius and deltoid muscles. The clavicle is further stabilized by means of the coracoclavicular ligament (actually two ligaments, the conoid and the trapezoid) which, as the name suggests, binds the clavicle to the coracoid process.

The conoid ligament passes from the base of the coracoid process to the conoid tubercle on the underside of the clavicle. The trapezoid ligament extends from the top of the coracoid process to the trapezoid ridge on the underside of the clavicle.

Structure of Sternoclavicular Articulation. (Fig. 4–10.) The sternal end of the clavicle articulates with both the sternum and the cartilage of the first rib. It is classified as a double arthrodial joint because there are two joint cavities, one on either side of the articular disk. This round flat disk of white fibrocartilage is attached above to the upper and posterior border of the articular surface of the clavicle and below to the cartilage of the first rib near its junction with the sternum. The articular capsule is thin above and below but is thickened in front and behind by bands of fibers called the anterior and posterior sternoclavicular ligaments. The often overlooked importance of this capsule

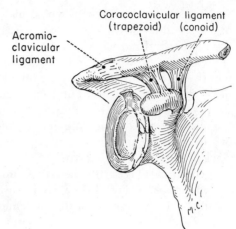

Figure 4-9 Anterior view of acromioclavicular articulation.

was demonstrated by Bearn in a series of experiments involving the loading of the lateral end of the clavicle both before and after cutting various structures. He presented convincing evidence that it is the capsule rather than the trapezius muscle that provides the chief support for the clavicle.[2]

The movements of the clavicle at this joint are as follows: elevation and depression which occur approximately in the frontal plane about a sagittal-horizontal axis; horizontal forward-backward movements which occur in the horizontal plane about a vertical axis; and a limited degree of forward and backward rotation which occurs approximately in the sagittal plane about the bone's own longitudinal axis. (In forward rotation the top of the clavicle revolves forward-downward.)

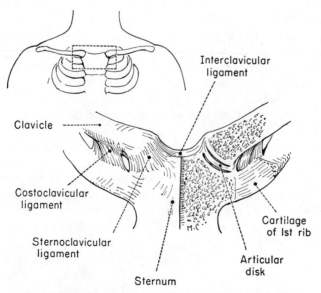

Figure 4-10 Anterior view of sternoclavicular articulation.

The sternoclavicular articulation is of great importance in the movements of the shoulder girdle and of the arm as a whole. It permits limited motion of the clavicle in all three planes, and because of the bone's attachment to the scapula at its distal end, this articulation is partially responsible for the latter's movements. It is reinforced by four ligaments: the anterior sternoclavicular, a band of fibers blending with the anterior fibers of the articular capsule; the posterior sternoclavicular, which blends with the posterior fibers of the articular capsule; the interclavicular, consisting of a flat band which passes across the upper margin of the sternum and attaches to the sternal end of each clavicle; and the costoclavicular, a short strong band of fibers which connects the upper border of the first costal cartilage with the costal tuberosity on the underside of the clavicle.

Movements. (Fig. 4–11.)   It is customary to define the movements of the shoulder girdle in terms of the movements of the scapulae. In doing this, there is some danger that the reader will visualize the movement as taking place solely in the joint between the scapula and the clavicle. It is well to emphasize the fact that every movement of the scapula involves motion in both joints, the acromioclavicular and the sternoclavicular.

The movements of the shoulder girdle expressed in terms of the composite movements of the scapula are as follows:

ELEVATION. (Fig. 4–11, *A.*)   An upward movement of the scapula with the vertebral border remaining approximately parallel to the spinal column. The elevation of the scapula is the direct result of elevation of the outer end of the clavicle, a movement which takes place at the sternoclavicular joint. This movement occurs to a slight extent during elevation of the humerus and to a greater extent in lifting the shoulders in a hunching gesture. The farther the clavicles depart from the horizontal position, the closer the scapulae move toward each other. The latter movement might well be called passive adduction as it is caused by the movement of the clavicles rather than by the adductor muscles of the scapulae.

DEPRESSION.   The return from the position of elevation. There is no depression below the normal resting position.

ABDUCTION OR PROTRACTION. (Fig. 4–11, *B.*)   A lateral movement of the scapula away from the spinal column with the vertebral border remaining approximately parallel to it. Pure abduction of the scapula is a hypothetical movement. Actually, because of two factors, (1) the rounded contour of the thorax and (2) the forward movement of the clavicle about a vertical axis at the sternoclavicular joint, a pure lateral movement of the scapula in the frontal plane is impossible. As the scapula abducts it turns slightly about its vertical axis in a movement known as a lateral tilt. This turning is characterized by a slight backward movement of the vertebral border and a corresponding forward movement of the axillary border. This movement causes the glenoid fossa to face slightly forward and the arms, if relaxed, to hang in a more forward position and in slight inward (medial) rotation.

ADDUCTION OR RETRACTION.   A medial movement of the scapula toward the spinal column combined with a reduction of lateral tilt.

UPWARD TILT. (Fig. 4–11, *D.*)   A turning of the scapula on its frontal-horizontal axis so that the posterior surface faces slightly upward and the inferior angle protrudes from the back. This is accompanied by a rotation of the clavicle about its mechanical axis so that the superior border turns slightly forward-downward and the inferior border backward-upward. It occurs only in conjunction with hyperextension of the humerus.

REDUCTION OF UPWARD TILT. The return movement from upward tilt.

UPWARD ROTATION. (Fig. 4–11, C.) A rotation of the scapula in the frontal plane so that the glenoid fossa faces somewhat upward. The movement occurs largely at the acromioclavicular joint but is accompanied by elevation of the outer end of the clavicle. Upward rotation is always associated with elevation

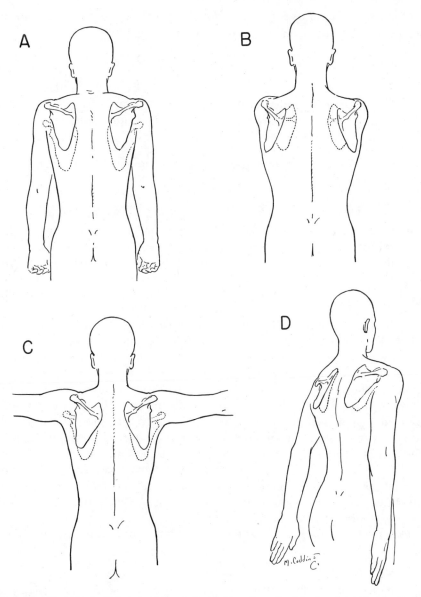

Figure 4–11 Movements of the shoulder girdle. *A*, Elevation; *B*, abduction (combined with lateral tilt and upward rotation); *C*, upward rotation; *D*, upward tilt.

of the humerus, either sideward or forward. It serves at least three useful purposes: (1) it puts the glenoid fossa in a favorable position for the upper extremity movement;[11] (2) by positioning the small glenoid fossa beneath the larger head of the humerus it contributes significantly to the stability of the shoulder joint;[8] and (3) by moving the origin of the deltoid medially at the same time that the latter muscle is elevating the humerus, the deltoid is prevented from shortening too much, thereby losing force too rapidly.[13]

DOWNWARD ROTATION.   The return from the position of upward rotation. There may be slight downward rotation beyond the normal resting position so that the glenoid fossa faces slightly downward.

Muscles.*   The muscles of the shoulder girdle are classified as anterior or posterior muscles according to their location on the trunk.

Anterior	*Posterior*
Subclavius	Levator scapulae
Pectoralis minor	Trapezius
Serratus anterior	Rhomboids

CHARACTERISTICS AND FUNCTIONS OF SHOULDER GIRDLE MUSCLES**

Levator Scapulae. (Fig. 4–13.) (Also listed with muscles of the neck.) Although one would expect the levator scapulae to elevate and adduct the scapula, Bowen pointed out that it actually causes *elevation* and *downward rotation* when the trunk is in the erect position.[3] His explanation of this action is that the weight of the arm at the acromial end of the scapula pulls that end down at the same time that the levator is lifting the medial angle. Thus these two forces act as a force couple to rotate the scapula.

In more recent years Basmajian[1] and Rasch and Burke,[14] who succeeded Bowen as authors of the textbook he originally wrote, appear to agree with Bowen in attributing the levator scapulae's movement of downward rotation to the weight of the arm and to the scapula's consequent need of postural support. Another author sees this weightsupporting function as a cooperative action of the levator scapulae and the rhomboids lifting the medial border of the scapula, and of the upper trapezius lifting its lateral angle.[7] Still another claims that the levator together with the rhomboid minor tends to rotate the scapula downward in the early phase of contraction, preliminary to elevating it.[4]

If the levator scapulae rotates the scapula downward only when the weight of the arm prevents it from adducting the scapula, it would be assumed that the trunk must be in the erect position for gravity to have this effect. In other positions, as when a person is swimming, one would expect the levator to adduct as well as to elevate the scapula. It might be enlightening if an electromyographic

---

*Attention is called to the EMG investigations reported in the Supplementary Material at the end of this chapter.
**Listed in alphabetical order.

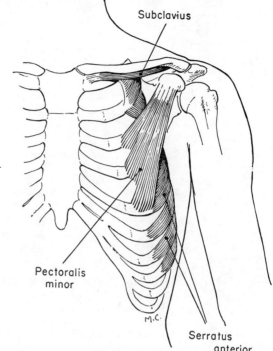

Figure 4-12 Anterior muscles of shoulder girdle.

study were to be made for the purpose of comparing the actions of the levator muscle when abduction of the humerus (and possibly other movements) is performed from two different starting positions: erect standing or sitting and prone lying.

The muscle is a difficult one to palpate successfully. The reader is referred to Brunnstrom for one method of doing this.[4]

Pectoralis Minor. (Fig. 4-12.) This muscle participates in several movements of the scapula, namely, *downward rotation, upward tilt, depression* and the combined movements of *abduction* and *lateral tilt.* Besides its action on the scapula, an important function of the pectoralis minor is its lifting effect on the ribs, both in forced inspiration and in maintaining good chest posture. When the scapulae are stabilized by the adductors, contraction of the pectoralis minor *elevates* the third, fourth and fifth ribs. Even without contracting, it exerts a slight upward and outward pull on these ribs if the muscle is well-developed. Thus the pectoralis minor can contribute either to good posture or to poor, depending upon whether its more effective pull is on the ribs or on the scapula. The key to its function as a muscle of good posture is stabilization of the scapulae by the adductors, i.e., the rhomboids and the middle trapezius.

It may be palpated midway between the clavicle and the nipple when the arm is elevated backward against resistance, provided the pectoralis major is relaxed, and also when the subject sits with the forearm resting on a table at his side and pushes both downward and laterally simultaneously.

Rhomboids, Major and Minor. (Fig. 4-13.) Functionally, the rhomboids may be regarded as one muscle. They cause *downward rotation, adduction* and

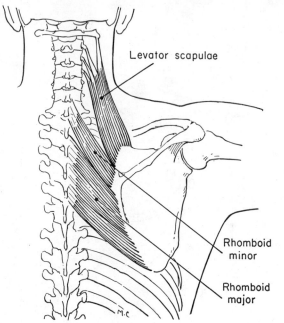

Levator scapulae

Rhomboid
minor

Rhomboid
major

Figure 4-13 Posterior muscles of shoulder girdle, deep layer.

elevation of the scapula. Their cooperative action with trapezius III, which has been discussed above, is an important factor in the maintenance of good shoulder posture. When the tonus of these two muscles is deficient, the unbalanced pull of the pectoralis minor and the serratus anterior results in habitually abducted and tilted scapulae. This in turn results in the failure of the pectoralis minor and serratus anterior to hold the chest in good posture. Thus one weak link in the chain of postural relationships leads to another.

These muscles are difficult to palpate as they are completely covered by the trapezius. The technique suggested by Brunnstrom is recommended.[4]

Serratus Anterior. (Figs. 4-12 and 4-15.) The upper portion causes *abduction* and *lateral tilt* of the scapula, the lower portion, *upward rotation*. Together they combine these movements and, in addition, pull the vertebral border of the scapula close to the ribs. See the report on the classic electromyographic study of the muscles of the shoulder region by Inman, et al in the Supplementary Material at the end of this chapter. The muscle may be palpated on the anterior-lateral surface of the upper thorax, especially on a thin, muscular subject.

Subclavius (Fig. 4-12.) The pull of this muscle, which is slightly *downward* and strongly *medialward*, suggests that its chief function is to protect and stabilize the sternoclavicular articulation. It also *depresses* the clavicle.

Trapezius (Fig. 4-14.) The trapezius is a fascinating muscle to study. As its location directly under the skin makes it easy to palpate, the student should investigate its action for himself. While some anatomists treat the muscle in three parts, it is more accurate to consider separately the four parts shown in

Figure 4–14. Parts I and II compose the upper trapezius, part III the middle, and part IV the lower. Its actions are as follows:

Part I.   Elevation.

Part II.   Elevation; upward rotation; assists in adduction.

Part III.   Adduction.

Part IV.   Upward rotation; depression; assists in adduction.

The relation of the trapezius to the rhomboids and serratus is interesting. The rhomboids and part III of the trapezius both adduct the scapulae. In this action they are partners. Parts II and IV, however, rotate the scapulae upward; the rhomboids rotate them downward. In this respect, then, they are antagonists.

Trapezius II and IV are partners with the lower serratus with respect to upward rotation, but trapezius III and the upper serratus are antagonistic, the former adducting and the latter abducting the scapulae. Parts II and IV of the trapezius act on the scapula as a force couple to rotate the scapula upward, part II pulling up on the acromial end of the scapular spine and part IV pulling down on the medial end or root. (See discussion of a force couple on p. 302, and Figs. 12–12 and 12–13 on pp. 302 and 303.)

Trapezius I and II have one important function which may be overlooked

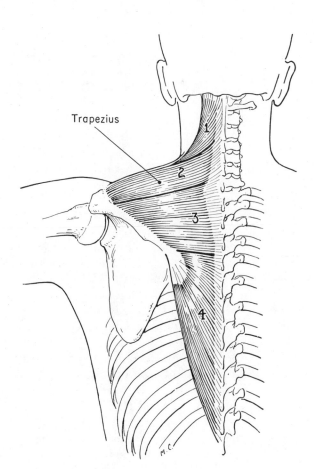

Trapezius

Figure 4–14   Trapezius.

because there is little, if any, actual movement involved. This is support for the distal end of the clavicle and the acromion process of the scapula when a heavy weight is held by the hand with the arm down at the side. Anyone who has carried a heavy suitcase for a long distance has doubtless experienced tension and subsequent soreness in these parts of the muscle. When no weight is carried, however, the capsule of the sternoclavicular articulation provides all the support necessary for the fully depressed clavicle.[2]

These various combinations of function are an excellent illustration of the cooperative action of the muscles and of the astonishing versatility of the musculoskeletal mechanism.

In their 1952 EMG study of the trapezius muscle, Wiedenbauer and Mortensen found that the trapezius showed definite activity during both elevation and retraction (adduction) of the scapula. In elevation, the upper portion showed the greatest activity and in retraction, the middle and lower portions. During abduction of the humerus and the accompanying upward rotation of the scapula, the lower two-thirds of the trapezius was most active, and during flexion of the humerus, the lower third was most active. The greatest activity of the muscle as a whole was seen in the upward rotation of the scapula accompanying abduction of the humerus. (See Basmajian.[1]) The muscle may be readily palpated in the kite-shaped area of the upper back and neck.

JOINT AND MUSCULAR ANALYSIS OF THE FUNDAMENTAL MOVEMENTS OF THE ARM ON THE TRUNK

As was stated earlier, the movements of the arm on the trunk involve the cooperative action of the shoulder joint and the shoulder girdle, the latter including both the acromioclavicular and the sternoclavicular joints. In order to analyze correctly the great variety of movements of the upper extremity it is essential that one understand this cooperative action of the three joints and their muscles.

The fundamental movements of the arm on the trunk, together with the anatomic analysis of each, are presented below.

Sideward Elevation.   Any distance up to the vertical (Fig. 4–15).

SHOULDER JOINT.   Abduction of the humerus by the middle deltoid and supraspinatus. True humeral abduction is the sideward elevation of the humerus in a plane parallel with the scapula. Hence, if the scapulae were slightly abducted and laterally tilted from poor posture, for instance, the abducted humeri would not be strictly in the frontal plane of the body but would be moving in an oblique plane, slightly anterior to the frontal plane.

Outward or lateral rotation by the infraspinatus and teres minor when palms are turned either out or up.

SHOULDER GIRDLE.   Upward rotation of the scapula by the serratus anterior and trapezius II and IV.

COMMENTS.   If the humerus is in a horizontally extended position when it is abducted (as is likely to be the case if both arms are raised simultaneously),

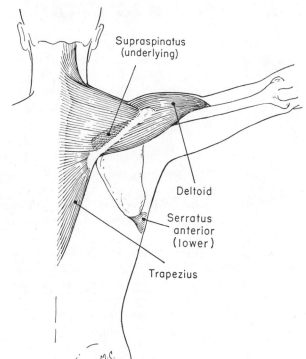

Supraspinatus
(underlying)

Deltoid

Serratus
anterior
(lower)

Trapezius

M.C.

Figure 4-15 Muscles which contract to produce sideward elevation of the arm.

the posterior deltoid, infraspinatus and teres minor would probably be active, and possibly the latissimus dorsi and teres major too, depending upon the forcefulness of the movement. This motion would doubtless be accompanied by slight adduction of the scapulae, produced chiefly by the rhomboids and middle trapezius.

Sideward Depression. From any degree of sideward elevation, either against resistance or in any position that rules out the help of gravitational force.

SHOULDER JOINT. Adduction of the humerus by the latissimus dorsi, the teres major, sternal portion of the pectoralis major and probably the lowest fibers of the posterior deltoid. Reduction of outward rotation mainly by the subscapularis and the teres major.

SHOULDER GIRDLE. Reduction of upward rotation by the rhomboids and pectoralis minor, with possible help from the levator scapulae.

Forward Elevation. Up to the horizontal.

SHOULDER JOINT. Flexion of the humerus by the anterior deltoid and clavicular portion of the pectoralis major, with probably some participation of the coracobrachialis and biceps brachii.

Slight outward rotation by the infraspinatus and teres minor.

SHOULDER GIRDLE. Slight upward rotation of the scapula by the serratus anterior and trapezius II and IV.

Abduction and lateral tilt of the scapula by the serratus anterior and pectoralis minor, unless intentionally inhibited.

Forward-Upward Elevation. From the horizontal to the vertical and beyond.

SHOULDER JOINT. Flexion of the humerus by the same muscles as above; hyperflexion if the humerus moves beyond the vertical.

Continued outward rotation by the infraspinatus and teres minor if the palms turn to face each other when the arms reach the vertical.

SHOULDER GIRDLE. Upward rotation of the scapula by the serratus anterior and trapezius II and IV.

Slight to moderate elevation of the scapula by the levator scapulae, trapezius I and II and rhomboids, unless effort is made to inhibit elevation.

Reduction of abduction and lateral tilt mainly by virtue of the overhead position.

Forward-Downward Depression. From the overhead vertical to the starting position, either against resistance or in a position that rules out the help of gravitational force.

SHOULDER JOINT. Extension of the humerus by the sternal portion of the pectoralis major (diminishing as the movement progresses), teres major, latissimus dorsi (especially during the lower 60 degrees of motion), the posterior deltoid and possibly the long head of the triceps brachii.

Reduction of outward rotation, probably by relaxation of outward rotator muscles but possibly aided by subscapularis, teres major, latissimus dorsi and pectoralis major.

SHOULDER GIRDLE. Reduction of elevation and upward rotation by relaxation of muscles. If the movement is performed against resistance the pectoralis minor, trapezius IV, subclavius and rhomboids would doubtless be active.

Backward Elevation (Fig. 4–16.)

SHOULDER JOINT. Hyperextension of the humerus by the posterior deltoid, latissimus dorsi and teres major.

SHOULDER GIRDLE. Upward tilt of the scapula by the pectoralis minor.

Elevation if movement is carried to the extreme. Possibly the hyperextension of the humerus pushes the scapula into a position of slight elevation. If any scapular muscles are acting, they would probably be the levator scapulae, trapezius I and II and rhomboids, with possibly the clavicular portion of the sternocleidomastoid (a neck muscle) helping.

Outward Rotation (Fig. 4–17.)

SHOULDER JOINT. Outward rotation of the humerus by the infraspinatus and teres minor with the posterior deltoid acting only if the humerus is also being adducted and extended, as in a calisthenic or postural exercise.

SHOULDER GIRDLE. Adduction of the scapulae and reduction of any lateral tilt which may have been present by the rhomboids and trapezius III, with some involvement of trapezius II and IV.

Inward Rotation

SHOULDER JOINT. Inward rotation of the humerus by the subscapularis, teres major, latissimus dorsi, anterior deltoid and pectoralis major. If the upper extremity is in a position of outward rotation to start with, the coracobrachialis and short head of the biceps would be active in the first part of the movement.

SHOULDER GIRDLE. Abduction and lateral tilt by the serratus anterior

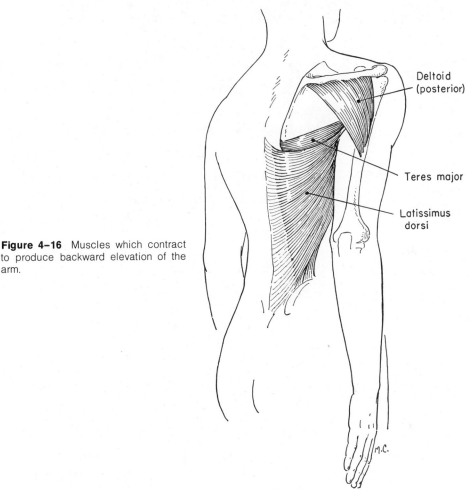

Deltoid
(posterior)

Teres major

Latissimus
dorsi

Figure 4-16 Muscles which contract to produce backward elevation of the arm.

and pectoralis minor, with a tendency toward elevation by the levator scapulae, trapezius I and II and rhomboids.

Horizontal Forward Swing from Side Horizontal Position

SHOULDER JOINT. Horizontal flexion of humerus by the subscapularis, pectoralis major, anterior deltoid and coracobrachialis with the biceps helping if the forearm is extended.

SHOULDER GIRDLE. Abduction and lateral tilt of scapula, unless deliberately inhibited. The movement is produced by the serratus anterior and pectoralis minor.

Horizontal Sideward Backward Swing from Forward Horizontal Position

SHOULDER JOINT. Horizontal extension of the humerus by the posterior deltoid, posterior portion of middle deltoid, infraspinatus and teres minor, with possible help from the latissimus dorsi and teres major.

SHOULDER GIRDLE. Adduction and reduction of lateral tilt of scapula by the rhomboids and trapezius III in particular, with II and IV also participating.

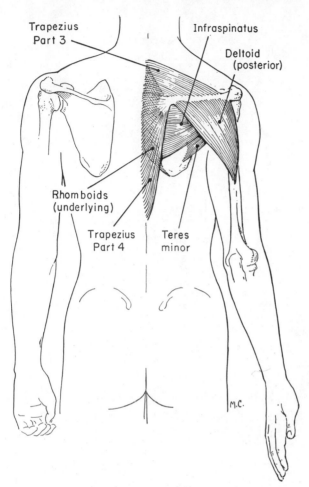

Figure 4–17 Muscles which contract to produce outward rotation of the arm and accompanying adduction of the scapula.

Shoulder Girdle Movements Not Involving the Arm.   In addition to these coordinated movements of the arm on the trunk there are three movements of the shoulder girdle in which movements of the arm are passive because they are produced by the changes in position of the shoulder girdle from which they are suspended. These are (1) a lifting or hunching of the shoulders, (2) protraction of the shoulders and (3) retraction of the shoulders.

Shoulder Lifting or Hunching

SHOULDER GIRDLE.   Elevation by the levator scapulae, trapezius I and II and rhomboids, with assistance by the sternocleidomastoid if the movement is performed against resistance. Reduction of the elevation is achieved by relaxing the muscles and letting the force of gravity have its way.

Shoulder Protraction

SHOULDER GIRDLE.   Forceful abduction and lateral tilt of scapula by the serratus anterior and pectoralis minor.

SHOULDER JOINT.   Slight passive inward rotation.

Reduction of the movement is achieved by relaxation of the muscles but may be followed by slight retraction.

Shoulder Retraction

SHOULDER GIRDLE.   Adduction and reduction of lateral tilt by the rhomboids, trapezius III and possibly II and IV.

APPLICATIONS TO COMMON MOVEMENTS

Unless performing calisthenic exercises one seldom uses pure fundamental movements of the arm on the trunk. Most of the sport and everyday movements are "in-between" or combination movements. In order to analyze these in terms of their muscular action, it is necessary to estimate the approximate proportions of the fundamental joint motions. For instance, a *tennis serve* might involve pure forward-downward depression of the arm (see shoulder joint and shoulder girdle analysis), or it might consist of forward-downward depression combined with a slight amount of "horizontal" forward swing and some inward rotation. (See Fig. 4–18.) In other words, this could be described as a diagonal forward-downward and slightly inward movement of the arm, consisting mainly of extension of the humerus combined with a slight degree of adduction. An appropriate term that is beginning to come into use is "diagonal adduction."

Figure 4–18   Tennis serve. (Courtesy of H. E. Edgerton.)

A true *forehand drive* might well consist of a pure horizontal forward swing from a side horizontal position (horizontal flexion of the humerus and abduction of the scapula), but the arm is more likely to start slightly above or below the horizontal and to move in a diagonal path.

An *underarm volleyball serve,* which is likely to have an upward as well as a forward component, would consist of a horizontal-forward swing from the side-horizontal position of the arm combined with a slight amount of forward-upward elevation. This would involve slight shoulder joint flexion accompanied by a combination of abduction, lateral tilt and upward rotation of the shoulder girdle.

COMMON ATHLETIC INJURIES OF THE SHOULDER REGION

Acromioclavicular Sprain.   This occurs if the acromioclavicular joint is forced beyond its normal range of motion, such as from a downward blow against the outer end of the shoulder, causing the acromion to be driven downward away from the clavicle. It is also caused by a fall in which the person catches himself on his outstretched hand or flexed elbow when the arm is in a vertical position and at an angle of 45 to 90 degrees flexion or abduction from the trunk. The damage consists of the tearing or severe stretching of the acromioclavicular ligaments.

Fracture of the Clavicle.   A fracture of the clavicle in its middle third may result from the same type of injury that causes acromioclavicular sprains, namely, either a direct downward blow to the acromion process or more commonly, landing on the hand from a fall with the arm rigidly outstretched. Such a fracture may be recognized or at least suspected if the injured person tends to support the arm with his good arm and carries his head tilted toward the injured side with his face turned to the opposite side. Teenagers and pre-teenagers are more likely to have a greenstick fracture from such injuries.[10]

Dislocation of the Shoulder.   There are three types of these dislocations: anterior-inferior or subcoracoid, inferior or subglenoid, and posterior. The most common type among young athletes is the anterior-inferior (subcoracoid) type. In this the head of the humerus, having slipped forward out of the glenoid fossa, comes to rest beneath the coracoid process. (See Fig. 4–19, *A.*) The injured arm is usually held out from the side in a position of slight abduction and lateral rotation.

Chronic Dislocation of the Shoulder.   This is usually an anterior dislocation and results either from a congenital abnormality of the shoulder joint or from repeated acute dislocations in an otherwise normal joint. With proper care following the acute dislocation there should be no recurrences. It is important to know which condition is the cause since congenital abnormalities are likely to require surgery.[12]

SUPPLEMENTARY MATERIAL

Electromyographic Studies of the Muscles of the Shoulder Joint and Shoulder Girdle.   In their extensive studies of the shoulder region, completed in 1944,

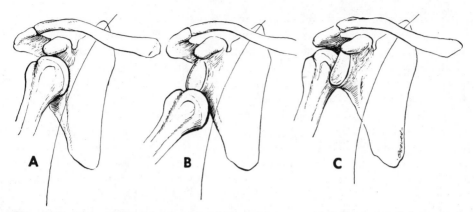

Figure 4-19   Dislocations of the shoulder. *A,* Typical subcoracoid dislocation. *B,* Subglenoid dislocation. *C,* Posterior dislocation. From O'Donoghue, D. H.: Treatment of Injuries to Athletes, 3rd Ed. Philadelphia: W. B. Saunders Company, 1976.

Inman, Saunders and Abbott reported the actions of the muscles in sideward and forward elevation of the upper extremity. The highlights of their findings are briefly summarized below.[9]

ABDUCTORS AND FLEXORS OF THE HUMERUS

Deltoid: Greatest activity is between 90 and 180 degrees of elevation.

Supraspinatus: Acts with the deltoid throughout the entire range of motion.

Pectoralis major: No activity was noted in sideward elevation. In forward elevation, the clavicular portion appeared to work synchronously with the anterior deltoid.

DEPRESSORS OF THE HUMERUS

Teres major: No activity in movements of the upper extremity but only in the maintenance of static positions.

Subscapularis, infraspinatus and teres minor: Continuous activity throughout both abduction and flexion.

SCAPULAR ROTATORS

Upper trapezius, levator scapulae and upper serratus anterior (acting as a unit): Passive support of the shoulder; active elevation of the shoulder girdle; constitute the upper component of a force couple in upward rotation of the scapula.

Lower trapezius and lower four digitations of serratus anterior: Constitute the lower component of a force couple in upward rotation of the scapula.

Middle trapezius and rhomboid muscles: Act in abduction of the humerus to stabilize the scapula. Are only slightly active in flexion of the humerus; permit the scapula to rotate around the thorax. (This is the combination movement described in this text as abduction and lateral tilt. See page 82 and Fig. 4-11,*B.*)

Shevlin, Lehmann and Lucci made an electromyographic study in 1969 of the functions of the ten major muscles that cross the glenohumeral joint. Twelve persons, including both male and female, their ages ranging from 17 to 55 years, served as subjects. For the testing, the arm was raised in three different planes: forward (sagittal plane), sideward (lateral plane) and halfway between. These were designated respectively as 0, 90 and 45 degree planes. As the muscular contractions were isometric, no actual movements took place during the testing. In each of the three planes the arm was positioned at three levels of elevation, these being at 45, 90 and 110 degrees from the body.

In each of these nine positions four movements were attempted: elevation, depression, forward horizontal adduction and backward horizontal abduction. The resistance given to these was of sufficient magnitude to prevent movement. This fact should be kept in mind when the results of the study are being considered.

The investigators made a statistical comparison between the amount of activity occurring during an attempted motion in one direction and an attempted motion in the opposite direction with the arm in the same position. They also compared the activity of a muscle contracting in the same direction with the arm in different positions. Their summary of these findings, which they believed offered new information, is as follows:

The anterior deltoid was found to be significantly active in elevation of the humerus rather than in depression in all positions tested.

The posterior deltoid was significantly active in elevation rather than depression in the frontal plane at all levels but only at the elevation of 110 degrees when the humerus was positioned at 45 degrees of horizontal abduction.

The clavicular fibers of the pectoralis major in the frontal plane at the level of 110 degrees were significantly active in elevation.

The supraspinatus and the middle deltoid functioned with statistically significant electrical activity in horizontal abduction rather than horizontal adduction.

The subscapularis showed significantly more electrical activity in elevation than in depression of the humerus and in horizontal abduction than in horizontal adduction.[15]

In interpreting the results of this study it would be well for the reader to keep the following points in mind:

1. The illustrations in the article show that elevation of the arm in all three planes was performed with the palms down. This means that, in the 0 (sagittal) and 45 degree planes at least, the humerus was rotated inward and the forearm was pronated.

2. Since the contractions were isometric, no movement took place during the testing.

3. The highest elevation of the arm at which tests were made was 110 degrees. The average individual can raise the arm considerably higher than this, especially if he is permitted to rotate the arm outward. At the higher elevations some muscle fibers shift to the other side of the center of motion and, hence, reverse their action.

4. When a muscle is said to "participate" in a movement, this does not necessarily mean that it is acting as a mover for that movement. It may be stabilizing the joint or maintaining a position, e.g., rotation, when the part is being moved in the sagittal or in the frontal plane. This is especially likely to be the case when it seems to be implied that a muscle is taking part in antagonistic

movements, such as when it is stated that a certain muscle is "more active in flexion than in extension."

5. If these findings are to be compared with those of similar studies it is important to note the placement of the electrodes.

Scapular Movements Accompanying Elevation of the Arm.   In 1945 Wells investigated the movements of the scapula accompanying forward and sideward elevation of the arm, using a series of x-rays of one subject. Each x-ray was traced, and measurements were then made on the tracings. Abduction of the scapula was measured in terms of the horizontal distance between the midpoint of the vertebral border of the scapula and the near margin of the spinal column. (A line connecting the spinous processes would have been the logical reference line, but it could not be used, since many of the spinous processes did not show in the x-ray.) Rotation was measured, by means of a protractor, in terms of the angle formed between a continuation of the vertebral border and the margin of the spinal column (Fig. 4–20). The results were as follows:

Position of Arm	Scapular Abduction	Scapular Rotation
At rest	5.5 cm.	−3° (downward rot.)
Sideward elev. about 45°	4.6 cm.	0 (parallel)
Sideward elev. about 90°	5.6 cm.	11° (upward rot.)
Sideward elev. about 135°	6.5 cm.	36° (upward rot.)
Sideward elev. about 180°	7.3 cm.	36° (upward rot.)
At rest	5.5 cm.	−3° (downward rot.)
Forward elev. about 45°	7.2 cm.	3.5° (upward rot.)
Forward elev. about 90°	10.1 cm.	8° (upward rot.)
Forward elev. about 135°	9.3 cm.	21° (upward rot.)
Forward elev. about 180°	8.2 cm.	31.5° (upward rot.)

The reader should not make any generalizations from a study such as this which uses only one subject. In order to make a study from which generalizations can safely be made it would be necessary to standardize the methods of measurement and to use a large number of subjects selected at random. Even then, use of this type of measurement technique is a precarious practice because of the distortion present in x-rays.

In their more sophisticated investigation of the functions of the shoulder joint, Inman et al. noted that after 30 degrees of side elevation and after 60 degrees of forward elevation of the arm, there appeared to be a constant two-to-one relationship between the movement of the humerus and that of the scapula. They observed that between 30 and 170 degrees of elevation, for every 15 degrees of total motion, abduction of the humerus (or flexion, in the case of forward elevation) was responsible for 10 degrees and upward rotation of the scapula for 5 degrees. They stated that, in the early phase of elevation, the scapula seemed to be establishing a precise position of stability with reference to the humerus. The exact movement that occurs during this phase is apparently determined by the individual's habitual shoulder posture.[9]

In 1966 Freedman and Munro, using 61 male subjects with an age range of 17 to 24 years, made a roentgenographic study of sideward elevation of the

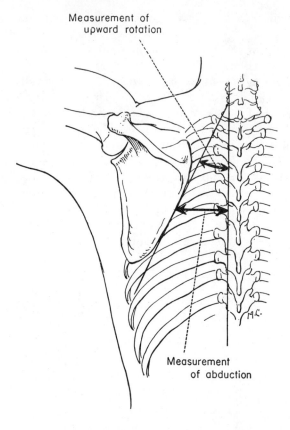

Measurement of
upward rotation

Measurement
of abduction

Figure 4–20 Measurements of the scapular movements accompanying sideward elevation of the arm. (The sketch is based on an x-ray.)

arm. They investigated the relative amounts of scapular and glenohumeral movements with the arm at five stages of abduction, namely, 0, 45, 90 and 135 degrees and maximum abduction. They used the scapular plane as their point of reference in preference to the coronal (frontal) plane as Inman, Saunders and Abbott had done in their 1944 study. Their chief findings were as follows:

In the resting position the glenoid fossa faced slightly downward in over 80% of the subjects, the downward inclination amounting to slightly more than 5 degrees.

The total rotation of the scapula averaged 65 degrees and the total glenohumeral movement, 103 degrees.

For every two degrees of scapular rotation accompanying abduction of the humerus in the scapular plane, there was an average of three degrees of movement in the glenohumeral joint. During the final stage of abduction a relative increase of glenohumeral motion occurred.

Statistics indicated that there was a considerable amount of individual variation in the movements.[6]

In 1970 Doody, Freedman and Waterland completed an investigation of the relative contributions of scapular and glenohumeral movements to abduction of the upper extremity in the scapular plane. Prior to the study they had developed a scapulohumeral goniometer which proved to be more reliable than the radiographic technique that Freedman and Munro had used in their earlier investigation. Their subjects consisted of 25 young women aged 17 to 21 years. On the basis of their findings the investigators concluded that:

The movements of the scapula and humerus were continuous throughout the abduction, irrespective of the application of resistance, and without added stress, the scapular movement accounted for 58.62 degrees of the total movement, and the humerus for 112.52 degrees.

What they called the "scapulohumeral rhythm" was found to vary among individuals, with some subjects experiencing a reverse rotation for the first 30 to 60 degrees of abduction.

Although there was a relationship between the glenohumeral angle and the position of the arm, it could not be adequately described by a linear function.

There was a continuous increase in the "mean relative amount of scapular movement" up to the position of maximum stress, which appeared to be between 90 and 140 degrees after which it fell off slightly.

The scapulohumeral rhythm was affected by an increase in stress, it being noted that the scapula's major participation began earlier when stress was added and that its total contribution showed a slight decrease.[5]

LABORATORY EXPERIENCES

Joint Structure and Function

1. Facing your partner's back, hold your thumb against the inferior angle of one scapula and your index or middle finger against the root of the spine at the scapula. Try to follow the movements of his scapula as he performs all of the fundamental movements of the arm on the body.

2. Using a form like that in Appendix A, record the essential information regarding the glenohumeral, acromioclavicular and sternoclavicular articulations. Study the movements of these joints both on the skeleton and on the living body.

3. In five different subjects measure the amount of abduction that occurs in the shoulder girdle (i.e., the separation of the scapulae) when the arms are raised to the forward-horizontal position. How much can this vary in one individual? In measuring the distance between the scapulae, measure the horizontal distance between the mid-points of the vertebral borders.

4. Using a protractor-goniometer, measure the amount of upward rotation of the scapula which occurs when the arm is raised sideward-upward to the overhead position. To make this measurement, center the instrument over the medial angle of the scapula, and adjust one of its arms in line with the normal resting position of the inferior angle and the other in line with the inferior angle after maximum upward rotation of the scapula has taken place.

Muscular Action

Directions. Work in groups of three, one person serving as the subject, the second as an assistant helping to support or steady the stationary part of the body and giving resistance to the moving part, and the third palpating the muscles and recording the results on the check list found in Appendix D.

5. SIDEWARD ELEVATION OF THE ARM. Shoulder joint: abduction and possibly outward rotation; shoulder girdle: upward rotation.

    Subject: In erect position, raise arm sideward to shoulder level, keeping elbow straight.

    Assistant: Resist movement by exerting pressure downward on subject's elbow. See to it that subject does not elevate shoulder.

    Observer: Palpate the three portions of the deltoid and tell which portions contract. Palpate the four parts of the trapezius. Which parts contract? Does the pectoralis major contract during any part of the movement?

6. SIDEWARD DEPRESSION OF THE ARM. (Fig. 4–21.) Shoulder joint: adduction and possibly reduction of outward rotation; shoulder girdle: downward rotation.

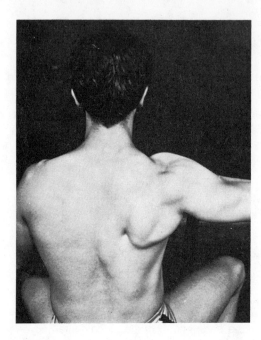

Figure 4-21 Sideward depression of the arm against resistance. The latissimus dorsi, teres major and rhomboids are in strong contraction.

Subject: In erect position with arm raised sideward to shoulder level, lower arm until 45 degrees from side.

Assistant: Place hand under subject's elbow and resist movement (If no resistance is given, the muscle action will be the same as in elevation, except that the contraction will be eccentric instead of concentric.)

Observer: Palpate the latissimus dorsi, teres major, pectoralis major and posterior deltoid. Do they each contract, and, if so, during which part of the movement?

7. FORWARD ELEVATION OF THE ARM. (Fig. 4–22.) Shoulder joint: flexion; shoulder girdle: upward rotation and probably abduction.

Subject: In erect position, raise arm forward to shoulder level, keeping elbow straight.

Assistant: Resist movement by exerting pressure downward on the subject's elbow. See that subject does not elevate shoulder.

Observer: Palpate the anterior deltoid and the pectoralis major. Do both the sternal and clavicular portions of the latter muscle contract?

8. FORWARD DEPRESSION OF THE ARM. (Fig. 4–23.) Shoulder joint: extension; shoulder girdle: downward rotation and probably adduction.

Subject: In erect position with arm raised forward to shoulder level, lower it until 45 degrees from side.

Assistant: Resist movement at underside of elbow.

Observer: Palpate the latissimus dorsi and the pectoralis major. Do they contract with equal force throughout the movement?

9. BACKWARD ELEVATION OF THE ARM. Shoulder joint: hyperextension; shoulder girdle; upward tilt.

Subject: Either in erect position or lying face down, raise arm backward, keeping elbow straight.

Assistant: Place hand over subject's elbow and resist movement.

Observer: Palpate the posterior deltoid, latissimus dorsi and teres major.

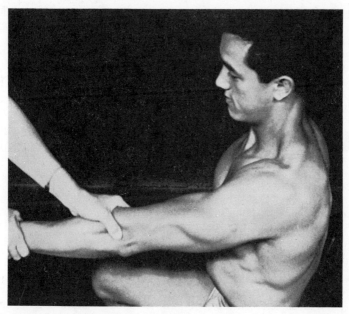

Figure 4–22   Forward elevation of the arm against resistance. The anterior and middle deltoid, upper trapezius and serratus anterior are in strong contraction.

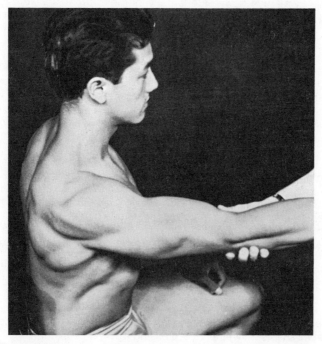

Figure 4–23   Forward depression of the arm against resistance. The latissimus dorsi and teres major are in strong contraction.

10. HORIZONTAL SIDEWARD-BACKWARD SWING OF THE ARM (from forward-horizontal position). Shoulder joint: horizontal extension and slight outward rotation; shoulder girdle: adduction and reduction of lateral tilt.

    a. *Subject:* In erect position with arms raised forward to shoulder level, palms down, swing arms sideward in horizontal plane as far as possible.

    Assistant: Stand facing subject between his arms and resist movement by grasping his elbows.

    Observer: Palpate the posterior deltoid and latissimus dorsi. What other muscles can be palpated?

    b. *Subject:* Lying face down on narrow plinth or on table close to edge with arm hanging straight down, raise arm sideward as far above the horizontal as possible.

    Assistant: Resistance may be given at elbow, but is not necessary, since gravity furnishes sufficient resistance.

    Observer: Same as in a.

11. HORIZONTAL SIDEWARD-FORWARD SWING OF THE ARM (from side-horizontal position). Shoulder joint: horizontal flexion and slight inward rotation; shoulder girdle: abduction and lateral tilt.

    a. *Subject:* In erect position with arm raised sideward to shoulder level, palm down, swing arm forward in horizontal plane.

    Assistant: Stand behind subject's arm and resist movement by holding elbow.

    Observer: Palpate pectoralis major and anterior deltoid.

    b. *Subject:* Lie on back on table with arm extended sideward, palm up. Raise arm to vertical position, keeping elbow straight.

    Assistant: Resistance may be given at elbow, but is not necessary, since gravity furnishes sufficient resistance.

    Observer: Same as in a.

12. OUTWARD ROTATION OF ARM. Shoulder joint: outward rotation; shoulder girdle: possibly adduction and reduction of lateral tilt.

    a. *Subject:* Lying face down on a table with upper arm at shoulder level, resting on table and forearm hanging down off edge of table. Keeping forearm at right angles to upper arm, raise hand and forearm forward-upward to limit of motion, without allowing upper arm to leave table.

    Assistant: Steady upper arm and resist movement of forearm by holding wrist.

    Observer: Palpate infraspinatus and teres minor.

    b. *Subject:* Sitting erect with upper arm at side-horizontal position and elbow bent at right angles with forearm at forward-horizontal position. Without moving upper arm raise forearm to vertical position (see Fig. 4–24).

    Assistant: Support upper arm at elbow and give resistance to forearm at wrist.

    Observer: Same as in a.

13. INWARD ROTATION OF ARM. Shoulder joint: inward rotation; shoulder girdle: abduction and lateral tilt, and tendency toward elevation.

    a. *Subject:* Same position as in 12,a. Raise forearm backward-upward.

    Assistant: Steady upper arm and resist movement of forearm by holding wrist.

    Observer: Palpate teres major and latissimus dorsi.

    b. *Subject:* Lie on back on table with upper arm at shoulder level resting on table and forearm raised to vertical position. Lower forearm forward-downward to the limit of motion.

    Assistant: Steady upper arm and resist forearm motion by holding wrist.

    Observer: Palpate anterior deltoid and clavicular portion of pectoralis major.

14. ELEVATION OF SHOULDER

    Subject: In erect position, lift shoulder toward ear, keeping arm muscles relaxed.

    Assistant: Resist movement by pressing down on shoulder.

    Observer: Palpate trapezius I and II.

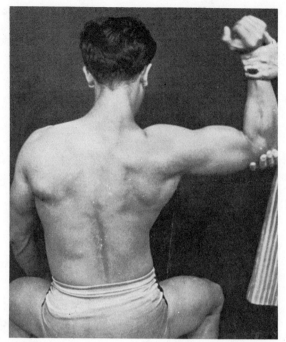

Figure 4-24 Outward rotation of the arm against resistance. The posterior deltoid, infraspinatus and teres minor are in strong contraction. (The hyperextension and lateral flexion of the trunk are caused by the extreme effort. The latissimus is contracting because he is pushing his elbow down.)

15. DEPRESSION OF SHOULDER
    a. *Subject:* In erect position with shoulder raised and elbow flexed, push down with elbow, lowering shoulder to normal position.
        Assistant: Resist movement by holding hand under elbow.
        Observer: Palpate trapezius IV.
    b. *Subject:* Take cross rest position between two chairs or parallel bars.
        Observer: Palpate trapezius IV.

16. ADDUCTION OF SHOULDER GIRDLE (retraction)
    Subject: In erect position with arms raised sideward, elbows flexed and fingers resting on shoulders, push elbows backward, keeping them at shoulder level.
    Assistant: Stand facing subject and resist movement by pulling elbows forward.
    Observer: Palpate middle and lower trapezius (parts III and IV). (This movement is somewhat similar to the one in 10, but here the emphasis is on the shoulder girdle rather than on the arm.)

17. ABDUCTION OF SHOULDER GIRDLE (protraction)
    Subject: In erect position with arms raised sideward, elbows flexed and fingers resting on shoulders, pull elbows forward, attempting to touch them in front of chest.
    Assistant: Stand behind subject and resist movement by pulling elbows back.
    Observer: Palpate serratus anterior.

Action of the Muscles Other Than the Movers
18. STABILIZATION OF THE SCAPULA DURING FORCEFUL FORWARD DEPRESSION OF THE ARM

Subject: In erect position with arm raised forward above shoulder level, lower arm against strong resistance.

Assistant: Resist the arm movement by placing hand under the arm just above the subject's elbow.

Observer: Palpate trapezius IV. Explain.

19. STABILIZATION OF SCAPULA DURING OUTWARD ROTATION OF HUMERUS
    Subject: Rotate the arm outward as it hangs at the side.
    Observer: Palpate the scapular adductors. Explain.

20. ROTATION OF ARM IN POSITION OF SIDE ELEVATION
    Subject: With one arm raised sideward to shoulder level, rotate it first outward, then inward.
    Observer: Palpate middle deltoid. Explain its action.

21. VIGOROUS ARM-FLINGING SIDEWARD TO THE HORIZONTAL
    Subject: Fling arm vigorously to the side horizontal position.
    Observer: Palpate the adductors of the shoulder joint. Do they contract momentarily at the very end of the movement? Explain.

22. VIGOROUS ARM-FLINGING DOWNWARD
    Subject: From an overhead position, fling arm vigorously forward-downward, stopping it at the body.
    Observer: Palpate the flexors of the shoulder joint. Do they contract momentarily at the end of the movement? Explain.

Applications

23. Work in groups of three with the members designated respectively as A, B and C. Equipment for each group: a volleyball and an empty twelve-ounce frozen juice can or other can of approximately same size.

    "A" stands at one end of playing area with left side toward the opposite end.

    "B" stands facing "A" about two arm-lengths away and holds can vertically in right hand with arm extended forward and with volleyball balanced on open end of can.

    "A" adjusts distance and swings extended right arm horizontally backward with thumb side up and palm flat. "A" then swings arm vigorously forward and strikes ball forcefully with palm, attempting to project ball as far as possible.

    "C" observes "A's" action and writes answers to following questions without saying them aloud.

    (a) What is the movement of "A's" humerus at the shoulder joint in the preparatory movement?

    (b) Same for the striking movement?

    (c) What is the position of "A's" humerus at the moment of impact?

    Repeat until each person has taken his turn at being A, B and C. Report answers to the rest of group and discuss if not in agreement.

24. Work in partners with one observing while the other performs.
    Starting position: Hang from horizontal bar with palms facing body and with feet hanging clear or, if necessary, with toes just touching floor or bench.
    Movement: Chin self with steady pull and hold end position.
    Observer: Write joint analysis of (a) starting position of humerus at shoulder joint, and of scapulae; and (b) movement of each. Discuss with partner.

REFERENCES

1. Basmajian, J. V.: Muscles Alive, 3rd Ed. Baltimore: The Williams & Wilkins Company, 1974. Chapter 10.
2. Bearn, J. G.: Direct observations on the function of the capsule of the sternoclavicular joint in clavicular support. J. Anat., 101:159–170, 1967.
3. Bowen, W. P., and Stone, H. A.: Applied Anatomy and Kinesiology, 7th Ed. Philadelphia: Lea & Febiger, 1953.
4. Brunnstrom, S.: Clinical Kinesiology, 3rd Ed. Philadelphia: F. A. Davis Company, 1972.
5. Doody, S. G., Freedman, L., and Waterland, J. C.: Shoulder movements during abduction in the scapular plane. Arch. Phys. Med. & Rehab., 51:595–604, 1970.
6. Freedman, L., and Munro, R. R.: Abduction of the arm in the scapular plane; scapular and glenohumeral movements. J. Bone & Joint Surg., 48A:1503–1510, 1966.
7. Hollinshead, W. H.: Functional Anatomy of the Limbs and Back, 3rd Ed. Philadelphia: W. B. Saunders Company, 1969.
8. Inman, V. T.: The shoulder as a functional unit. J. Bone & Joint Surg., 44A:977–978, 1962.
9. Inman, V. T., Saunders, J. B. deC. M., and Abbott, L. C.: Observations on the function of the shoulder joint. J. Bone & Joint Surg., 26:1–30, 1944.
10. Klats, C. E., and Arnheim, D. D.: Modern Principles of Athletic Training. St. Louis: C. V. Mosby Co., 1973.
11. Mollier, S.: On the Statics and Mechanics of the Human Shoulder Girdle under Normal and Pathological Conditions, trans. by F. E. Hastings and W. Skarstrom. Unpublished.
12. O'Donoghue, D. H.: Treatment of Injuries to Athletes. 3rd Ed. Philadelphia: W. B. Saunders Company, 1976.
13. Ralston, H. J.: Mechanics of voluntary muscle. Am. J. Phys. Med., 32:166–184, 1953.
14. Rasch, P. J., and Burke, R. K.: Kinesiology and Applied Anatomy, 5th Ed. Philadelphia: Lea & Febiger, 1974.
15. Shevlin, M. G., Lehmann, J. F., and Lucci, J. A.: Electromyographic study of the function of some muscles crossing the glenohumeral joint. Arch. Phys. Med. & Rehab., 50:264–270, 1969.
16. Steindler, A.: Kinesiology of the Human Body. Springfield, Ill.: Charles C Thomas, Publisher, 1970.
17. Wright, W. G.: Muscle Function. New York: Hafner Publishing Company, 1962.

RECOMMENDED READINGS

Conway, A. M.: Movements at the sternoclavicular and acromioclavicular joints. Phys. Ther. Rev., 41:421–432, 1961.
Dempster, W. T.: Mechanisms of shoulder movement. Arch. Phys. Med. & Rehab., 46:49–70, 1965.
Inman, V. T.: The shoulder as a functional unit. Arch. Phys. Med. & Rehab., 44:67, 1963. (Abstr.)
Singleton, M. C.: Functional anatomy of the shoulder. J. Am. Phys. Ther. Assn., 46:1043–1051, 1966.

Chapter Five

THE UPPER EXTREMITY: THE ELBOW, FOREARM, WRIST AND HAND

In much the same way that the shoulder girdle's cooperation with the shoulder joint contributes to the wide range of motion available to the hand, the cooperative movements of the elbow, radioulnar and wrist joints contribute to the versatility and precision of its movements. Although the hand is intrinsically skillful, its usefulness would be greatly impaired if anything interfered with the motions of the forearm or wrist. Injury to any one of the joints involved makes this painfully obvious to the sufferer.

THE ELBOW JOINT

Structure. The elbow is far more complex than the simple hinge joint that it appears to be. The two bones of the forearm attach to the humerus in totally different ways. The humeroulnar joint is indeed a true hinge joint, but the humeroradial joint is far from it. It has been classified as an arthrodial or gliding type of joint, but it would be more accurately described as a restricted or atypical ball-and-socket joint. Inspection of the articulating surfaces as depicted in Fig. 5–1 or of the skeleton itself will help to make this clear. The distal end of the humerus presents a spool-like process (trochlea) on the medial side and a spherical knob (capitulum) on the lateral side. The ulna articulates with the humerus by means of a semicircular structure which is cupped around the back and underside of the trochlea. The inner surface of this is known as the semilunar notch. It terminates below and in front in the small coronoid process, and above and in back in the broad olecranon process.

The radius articulates with the humerus by means of a slightly concave, saucer-like disk which is directly beneath the capitulum when the arm is hanging straight down. In spite of the joint's ball-and-socket structure the radius is unable to ab- or adduct because of the annular ligament which encircles the radial head and binds it to the radial notch of the ulna. Furthermore, because of this and other ligamentous connections with the ulna, the radius is unable to rotate independently (Figs. 5–2 and 5–3). Hence, the only movements it is free to engage in at the elbow joint are flexion and extension. For this reason one is justified in classifying the elbow joint as a whole as a hinge joint.

106

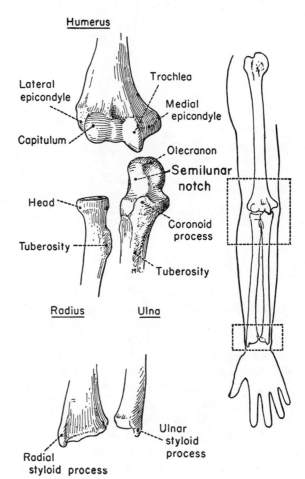

Figure 5-1 The bony structures of the elbow and radioulnar joints. (Anterior view.)

The two articulations of the elbow joint, as well as the proximal radioulnar articulation, are completely enveloped in an extensive capsule. This is lined by synovial membrane which extends into the proximal radioulnar articulation, covers the olecranon, coronoid and radial fossae, and lines the annular ligament. The capsule is strengthened by four ligaments, the *anterior, posterior, radial collateral* and *ulnar collateral.* The last named is the strongest. It is a thick triangular band, attached above by its apex to the medial epicondyle of the humerus and below by its base to the medial margins of the coronoid and olecranon processes of the ulna and the intervening ridge.

Movements

FLEXION.   From the anatomic position (Fig. 1–10, *B*) this is a forward-upward movement of the forearm in the sagittal plane.

EXTENSION.   Return movement from flexion. A few individuals are able to hyperextend the elbow joint. This is probably because of a short olecranon process, rather than loose ligaments.

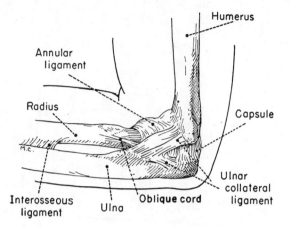

Figure 5–2 Medial aspect of elbow joint showing ligaments.

THE RADIOULNAR JOINTS

Structure of Proximal Radioulnar Joint. (Figs. 5–1, 5–2 and 5–3.) The disk-shaped head of the radius fits against the radial notch of the ulna and is encircled by the annular ligament. The notch and the annular ligament between them form a complete ring within which the radial head rotates. Inasmuch as the superior surface of the radial head articulates with the capitulum of the humerus, rotation must occur here too although, strictly speaking, this is not part of the radioulnar joint. The three joints in this region, the humeroulnar, humeroradial and proximal radioulnar all share a common capsule.

Structure of Distal Radioulnar Joint. (Fig. 5–1.) At the distal end of the forearm the radius articulates with the head of the ulna by means of a small notch. A triangular fibrocartilaginous disk lies between the head of the ulna and the proximal row of wrist bones (Fig. 5–10) and serves to reinforce the joint as well as to separate it from the wrist. The joint is also strengthened by the *volar radioulnar* and *dorsal radioulnar* ligaments. Both the proximal and the distal radioulnar joints are classified as pivot joints.

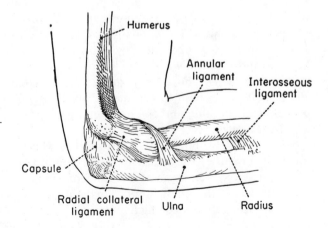

Figure 5–3 Lateral aspect of elbow joint showing ligaments.

Movements

PRONATION.   This is a rotation of the forearm around its longitudinal axis in such a way that the palm turns medially. It corresponds to medial or inward rotation of the humerus.

SUPINATION.   This is a rotation of the forearm around its longitudinal axis in such a way that the palm turns laterally. It corresponds to lateral or outward rotation of the humerus.

Note: When the elbow is in an extended position, pronation of the forearm tends to accompany inward rotation of the upper arm, and supination tends to accompany outward rotation. In the anatomic position of the arm (see page 21) the humerus is rotated outward and the forearm is supinated. The full range of pronation and supination is best seen when the elbow is maintained at a ninety degree angle. When the upper arms are at the sides of the body and the forearms are extended forward in the horizontal position, the mid or neutral position relative to pronation and supination is with the thumbs up and the palms facing each other. An excellent way to study what happens to the two forearm bones in these movements is suggested in Exercise 4 of the Laboratory Experiences on page 135.

Muscles.   The muscles of the elbow and radioulnar joints are listed below according to their position relative to the joints involved.

Anterior (elbow region)   *Posterior*
    Biceps brachii   Anconeus
    Brachialis   Supinator
    Brachioradialis   Triceps brachii
    Pronator teres

Anterior (wrist region)
    Pronator quadratus

CHARACTERISTICS AND FUNCTIONS OF INDIVIDUAL MUSCLES*

Anconeus. (Fig. 5–4.)   This *extends* the forearm. In an EMG study of elbow joint muscles made in 1967, Pauly et al. found that this muscle initiates extension of the elbow, helps to maintain the extended postion and appears to stabilize the joint during other movements of the upper extremity. It was also noted that the muscle was particularly active during pronation of the forearm.[11] The muscle may be palpated on the back of the elbow at the lateral margin of the olecranon process.

Biceps Brachii. (Fig. 5–5.)   This is primarily a muscle of the elbow and radioulnar joints, but as was shown in the last chapter, it also acts at the shoulder joint. Unless prevented from doing so (by action of neutralizers or by fixation of the hand when the subject is hanging from a bar), it simultaneously *flexes* and *supinates* the forearm. It may be palpated on the anterior surface of the upper arm when the forearm is flexed, especially in the supinated position (Fig. 5–27, *A* on p. 133).

---

*Listed in alphabetical order.

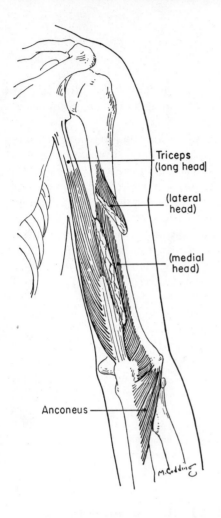

Triceps
(long head)

(lateral
head)

(medial
head)

Anconeus

Figure 5–4   Triceps and anconeus.

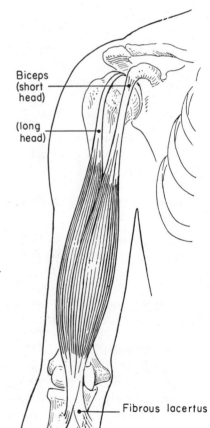

Biceps
(short
head)

(long
head)

Fibrous lacertus

Figure 5–5   Biceps muscle of the arm.

Brachialis. (Fig. 5–6.)   This muscle's sole function is *flexion* of the elbow joint and it is said to be the unexcelled flexor under all conditions.[1] It is partially covered by the biceps but can be palpated just lateral to this muscle if the contraction is sufficiently strong, and especially if the forearm is maintained in the pronated position as it is being flexed (Fig. 5–27, *B* on p. 133). It is a spurt muscle.

Brachioradialis. (Fig. 5–7.)   Although essentially an elbow *flexor,* it has been suggested that this muscle may tend to "de-rotate" the forearm as it flexes it, but this has not been confirmed by electromyographic research. Both Basmajian and Latif and DeSousa et al. found, however, that the brachioradialis neither supinates nor pronates the fully extended forearm unless the movement is strongly resisted.[1, 3] It has also been noted that this muscle is most active in quick movements and is, therefore, a shunt muscle.[1] It may be palpated on the anteroradial aspect of the upper half of the forearm.

Pronator Teres. (Fig. 5–7.)   This is primarily a *pronator* of the forearm, but it assists in flexing against resistance.[1] It is difficult to palpate.

Pronator Quadratus. (Fig. 5–8.)   This muscle's sole action is *pronation* of

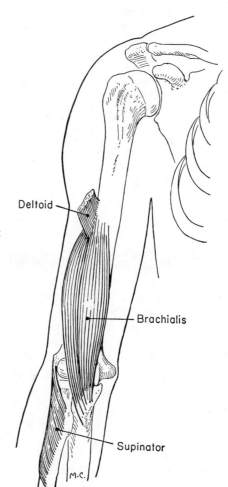

Figure 5–6 Deep muscles on front of right arm.

Deltoid

Brachialis

Supinator

M.C.

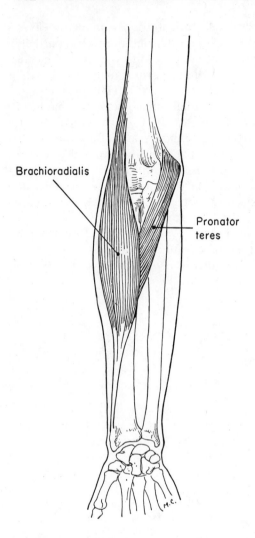

Brachioradialis

Pronator teres

Figure 5–7 Superficial muscles on front of right forearm.

the forearm. EMG experiments showed that the electrical activity of the pronator quadratus was definitely greater than that of the pronator teres, irrespective of the speed of the movement or the degree of the elbow flexion. It is too deep to palpate successfully.

Supinator. (Figs. 5–6 and 5–9.) Its only function is *supination*. Palpation with any degree of success is extremely difficult.

Triceps Brachii. (Figs. 5–4 and 5–9.) Virtually three muscles in one, the triceps covers the entire posterior surface of the upper arm. Its long head is the only one of the three to cross the shoulder joint. It is a powerful *extensor of the elbow joint,* having two factors in its favor, a large physiologic cross section (p. 293) and a favorable angle of pull (p. 294 ff.). Furthermore, it is a spurt muscle. In a comparison of the three heads it was noted that the medial head appeared to be the principal extensor of the elbow joint and that it was usually accompanied by the lateral head. All three heads participate when there is resistance.[1] The muscle is an easy one to see as well as to palpate.

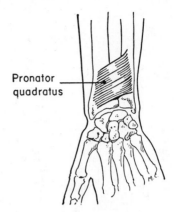

Pronator quadratus

Figure 5–8 Anterior view of distal end of forearm showing pronator quadratus.

MUSCULAR ANALYSIS OF THE FUNDAMENTAL MOVEMENTS OF THE FOREARM

FLEXION.   There are three important flexors of the forearm: the brachialis, brachioradialis and biceps—the three B's. The brachioradialis may help to reduce pronation or supination during flexion, and the biceps, being a supinator as well as a flexor, will tend to produce both movements unless supination is prevented by the action of a neutralizer, in this case probably the pronator teres, or by fixation of the hand, as when hanging from a bar.

As a flexor, the pronator teres functions chiefly as an assistant to give added strength when needed and as a neutralizer of the biceps' tendency to supinate.

EXTENSION.   When not produced by the force of gravity, extension of the elbow joint is effected by the triceps and anconeus.

PRONATION.   Movement of the forearm at the two radioulnar joints. Produced by the combined action of the pronator teres and pronator quadratus.

SUPINATION.   Movement of the forearm at the two radioulnar joints. Produced by the supinator and biceps brachii.

THE WRIST AND HAND

The hand and wrist owe their mobility to their generous supply of joints (Fig. 5–10). The most proximal of these is the radiocarpal or wrist joint. Just beyond this are the two rows of carpal bones, each row consisting of four bones. The carpal joints include the articulations within each of these rows, as well as the articulations between the two rows. The carpometacarpal joints are located at the base of the hand. Closely associated with them are the intermetacarpal joints, those points of contact between the bases of the metacarpal bones of the four fingers. The fingers unite with the hand at the metacarpophalangeal joints. Within the fingers themselves there are two sets of interphalangeal joints, the first between the proximal and middle rows of phalanges and the second between the middle and distal rows. The thumb differs from the four fingers in having a more freely movable metacarpal bone and in having only

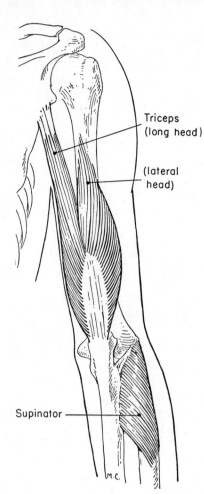

Triceps
(long head)

(lateral
head)

Supinator

M.C.

Figure 5–9   Triceps and supinator.

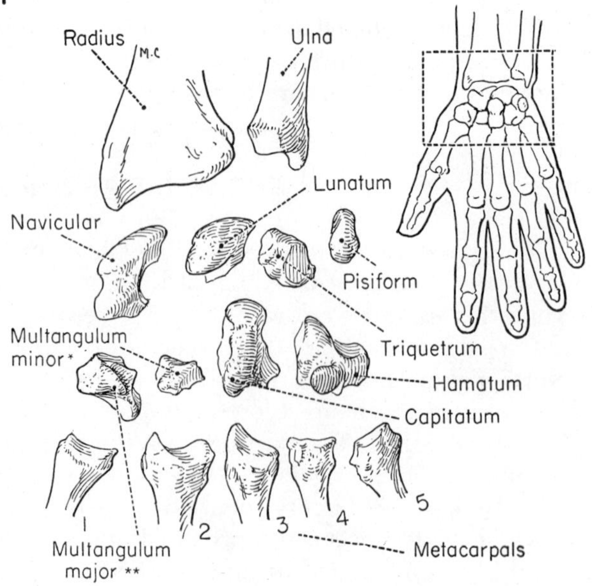

Radius   M.C   Ulna

Lunatum

Navicular   Pisiform

Figure 5–10   Bones of the wrist.
(Anterior view.)

Multangulum   Triquetrum
minor*
                                 Hamatum
                                 Capitatum

1   2   3   4   5

Multangulum   Metacarpals
major **

*Also called Trapezoid.
**Also called Trapezium.

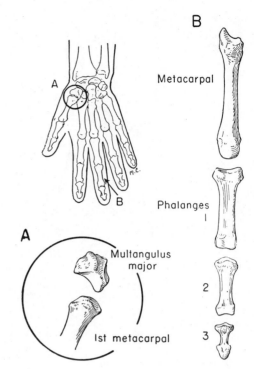

Figure 5–11 Bones of the hand showing selected joint surfaces. *A*, Carpometacarpal joint of thumb (a saddle joint). *B*, Metacarpal bone and phalanges of middle finger. (Anterior view.)

two phalanges instead of three. The metacarpal bone of the thumb is so similar to a phalanx that it might well be described as a cross between a phalanx and a metacarpal.

Structure of the Wrist (Radiocarpal) Joint. The wrist joint is an ovoid (condyloid) joint formed by the union of the slightly concave, oval-shaped surface of the proximal row of carpal bones (i.e., the navicular, lunate and triquetral bones, but not the pisiform). The distal radioulnar joint is in close proximity to the wrist joint and shares with it the articular disk which lies between the head of the ulna and the triquetral bone of the wrist. Yet it is not a part of the wrist joint, for each joint has its own capsule. The capsule of the wrist consists of four ligaments which merge to form a continuous cover for the joint. These are the volar radiocarpal, dorsal radiocarpal, ulnar collateral and radial collateral (Figs. 5–12 and 5–13).

Movements of the Hand at the Wrist Joint

FLEXION.   From the anatomic position (Fig. 1–10, *B*) this is a forward-upward movement in the sagittal plane, whereby the palmar surface of the hand approaches the anterior surface of the forearm.

EXTENSION.   Return movement from flexion.

HYPEREXTENSION.   A movement in which the dorsal surface of the hand approaches the posterior surface of the forearm—the exact opposite of flexion.

RADIAL FLEXION (ABDUCTION).   From the anatomic position this is a side-ward movement in the frontal plane, whereby the hand moves away from the body with the thumb side leading. The movement corresponds to abduction of the humerus.

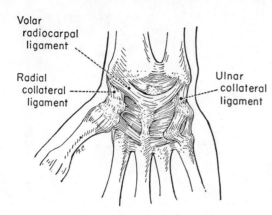

Volar
radiocarpal
ligament

Radial
collateral
ligament

Ulnar
collateral
ligament

Figure 5-12 Anterior view of right wrist joint showing ligaments.

ULNAR FLEXION (ADDUCTION).   From the anatomic position this is a sideward movement in the frontal plane, whereby the hand moves toward the body with the little finger side leading. The movement corresponds to adduction of the humerus.

CIRCUMDUCTION.   A movement of the hand at the wrist whereby the finger tips describe a circle, and the hand as a whole describes a cone. It consists of flexion, radial flexion, hyperextension and ulnar flexion occurring in sequence in either this or the reverse order. If there appears to be rotation when one performs this movement it is taking place in the radioulnar joints, not the wrist joint.

Structure and Movements of the Midcarpal and Intercarpal Joints.   These are the joints within the wrist itself. The articulation between the four carpal bones in the proximal row with the four in the distal row is known as the midcarpal articulation.* The joints between the adjacent bones within either row are known as the intercarpal joints of the proximal and distal rows, respectively.* These joints are all diarthrodial in structure. Within this classification they belong to the non-axial group and thus permit only a slight gliding motion between

---

*Anatomists differ in regard to these definitions. See both Gray's and Morris' Anatomy textbooks.[5, 13]

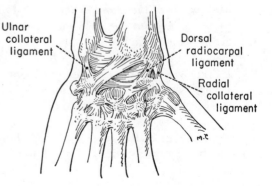

Ulnar
collateral
ligament

Dorsal
radiocarpal
ligament

Radial
collateral
ligament

Figure 5-13 Posterior view of right wrist joint showing ligaments.

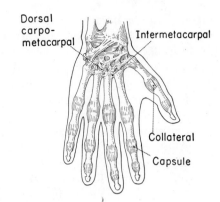

Figure 5–14 Posterior view of ligaments of right hand.

the bones. These slight movements, however, add up to a modified hinge type of movement for the midcarpal joint as a whole.

A further characteristic of the carpal region is that the bones are shaped and arranged in such a way that the anterior surface is slightly concave from side to side. This provides a protected passageway for the tendons, nerves and blood vessels supplying the hand. Among the many carpal ligaments, the radiate is the strongest. Its fibers radiate from the capitate to the navicular, lunate and triquetral bones on the anterior surface of the wrist.

Structure of the Carpometacarpal and Intermetacarpal Joints. (Figs. 5–10, 5–14, and 5–15.)   Although it has been customary to credit the carpometacarpal joint of the thumb with being the only saddle joint, this text agrees with Fick who is quoted by Morris as describing the carpometacarpal joints of all the fingers as modified saddle joints, the joint of the little finger more nearly approaching a true saddle joint than any other except that of the thumb.[13] The latter is a prime example of a saddle joint (Fig. 5–11, *A*). It is enclosed in an articular capsule which is stronger in back than in front. The capsule is thick but loose and serves to restrict motion rather than to prevent it. There are no additional ligaments.

The carpometacarpal joints of the four fingers are not only encased in capsules but are also protected by the dorsal, volar and interosseous carpo-

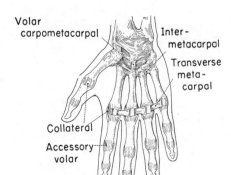

Figure 5–15 Anterior view of ligaments of right hand.

metacarpal ligaments (Figs. 5–14 and 5–15). Closely associated with these joints are the intermetacarpal articulations, the joints between the bases of the metacarpal bones of the four fingers. These are irregular joints. They share the capsules of the carpometacarpal joints and are further reinforced by the dorsal, volar and interosseous basal ligaments and also by the transverse metacarpal ligament, a narrow fibrous band which connects the heads of the four outer metacarpal bones.

Movements of the Carpometacarpal Joint of the Thumb

ABDUCTION. (Fig. 5–16, *A*.)   A forward movement of the thumb at right angles to the palm.

ADDUCTION.   Return movement from abduction.

HYPERADDUCTION. (Fig. 5–16, *B*.)   A backward movement of the thumb at right angles to the hand.

EXTENSION. (Fig. 5–16, *C*.)   A lateral movement of the thumb away from the index finger.

FLEXION. (Fig. 5–16, *D*.)   Return movement from extension.

HYPERFLEXION. (Fig. 5–16, *E*.)   A medialward movement of the thumb from a position of slight abduction. The thumb slides across the front of the palm.

CIRCUMDUCTION.   A movement in which the thumb as a whole describes a cone and the tip of the thumb describes a circle. It consists of all the movements described above, performed in sequence in either direction.

OPPOSITION. (Fig. 5–16, *F*.)   This movement, which makes it possible to touch the tip of the thumb to the tip of any of the four fingers, is essentially a combination of abduction and hyperflexion and, according to some investigators, slight inward rotation. Others claim that what appears to be inward rotation of the metacarpal is actually a slight medial movement of the greater multangular bone with which the metacarpal articulates. The movements of the metacarpal are accompanied by flexion of the two phalanges, especially the distal. The apparent rotatory movement is explained in part by the oblique axis of motion about which abduction and adduction of the thumb take place, and in part by the movement of the greater multangular bone which accompanies flexion of the thumb. The total movement of the thumb in opposition might well be described as a movement of partial circumduction.

Movements of the Carpometacarpal and Intermetacarpal Joints of the Fingers. Largely because of the short ligaments in this region, especially in the case of the second, third and fourth digits, the motion in both the carpometacarpal and intermetacarpal joints is almost non-existent, being limited to slight gliding. The fifth carpometacarpal joint is slightly more mobile and permits a limited motion of the fifth metacarpal bone, resembling in small degree the motion of the thumb.

Structure of the Metacarpophalangeal Joints. (Figs. 5–11, 5–14, and 5–15.) The joint at the base of each of the four fingers, uniting the proximal phalanx with the corresponding metacarpal bone, is an ovoid (condyloid) joint. The oval, convex head of the metacarpal fits into the shallow oval fossa at the base of the phalanx. The fossa is deepened slightly by the fibrocartilaginous volar accessory ligament. The joint is encased in a capsule and is protected on each side by strong collateral ligaments.

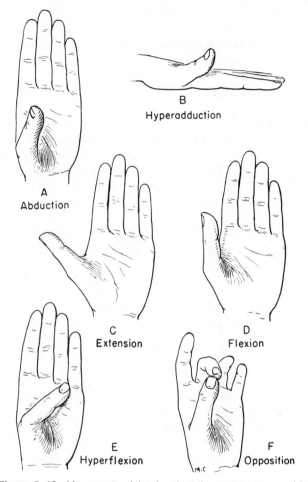

Figure 5–16   Movements of the thumb at the carpometacarpal joint.

The metacarpophalangeal joint of the thumb has flatter joint surfaces than do the corresponding joints of the four fingers and has more of the characteristics of a hinge joint. In addition to the articular capsule, it is protected by a collateral ligament on each side and by a dorsal ligament.

Movements of the Metacarpophalangeal Joints of the Four Fingers

FLEXION.   The anterior surface of the finger approaches the palmar surface of the hand.

EXTENSION.   Return movement from flexion. Most individuals are able to achieve slight hyperextension in these joints.

ABDUCTION.   For the fourth, fifth and index fingers this is a lateral movement away from the middle finger. This movement is limited and cannot be performed when the fingers are fully flexed.

ADDUCTION.   Return movement from abduction.

Note: In place of abduction and adduction, the lateral movements of the middle finger are termed radial and ulnar flexion. These are comparable to radial and ulnar flexion at the wrist.

CIRCUMDUCTION. The combination of flexion, abduction, extension and adduction performed in sequence in either direction.

Movements of the Metacarpophalangeal Joints of the Thumb

FLEXION. The volar surface of the thumb approaches that of the thenar eminence (base of thumb).

EXTENSION. Return movement from flexion. Individuals vary greatly in their ability to hyperextend the thumb at this joint.

The Interphalangeal Joints. These are the joints between the adjacent phalanges of any of the five digits. They are all hinge joints; hence, their only movements are flexion and extension. These correspond to flexion and extension of the first phalanx at the metacarpophalangeal joints. Hyperextension is slight, if present at all. Each joint is enclosed within an articular capsule which is strengthened in front by an accessory volar ligament and on each side by a strong collateral ligament.

Muscles. The muscles of the wrist, fingers and thumb are classified according to their location on the forearm or the hand and within each group are listed alphabetically.

Muscles of the Wrist

Anterior	*Posterior*
Flexor carpi radialis	Extensor carpi radialis brevis
Flexor carpi ulnaris	Extensor carpi radialis longus
Palmaris longus	Extensor carpi ulnaris

Muscles of the Fingers and Thumb

On the Forearm	*In the Hand (Intrinsic muscles)*
Fingers*	Fingers
Extensor digiti minimi	Abductor digiti minimi
Extensor digitorum	Flexor digiti minimi brevis
Extensor indicis	Interossei dorsales manus
Flexor digitorum profundus	Interossei palmaris
Flexor digitorum superficialis	Lumbricales manus
	Opponens digiti minimi
Thumb	Thumb
Abductor pollicis longus	Abductor pollicis brevis
Extensor policis brevis	Adductor pollicis
Extensor pollicis longus	Flexor pollicis brevis
Flexor pollicis longus	Opponens pollicis

---

*It is important to have an exact knowledge of the distal attachments of these muscles in order to understand their actions.

CHARACTERISTICS AND FUNCTIONS OF MUSCLE GROUPS

Wrist Muscles. (Figs. 5–17, 5–18 and 5–19, *A*.)   As one would expect from their location, the *flexor carpi radialis, flexor carpi ulnaris* and *palmaris longus* are *prime flexors* of the wrist joint. The tendons of these muscles may be readily palpated on the anterior surface of the wrist (Fig. 5–17), and the palmaris longus tendon is clearly visible if the hand is flexed against a slight resistance. The ulnaris tendon is best identified by its relation to the pisiform bone. It should not be confused with the tendon lying close on the ulnar side of the palmaris tendon. This is a tendon of the flexor digitorum superficialis, probably the one for the fourth finger (Fig. 5–20, *A*).

The *three wrist extensor muscles* may be palpated on the dorsal surface of the forearm when the forearm and hand are resting palm down on a table, the *carpi radialis longus* on the radial side at elbow level and slightly below, the *brevis* slightly

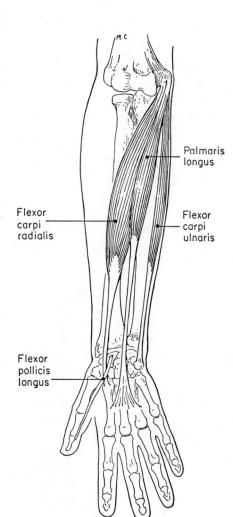

Palmaris
longus

Flexor
carpi
radialis

Flexor
carpi
ulnaris

Flexor
pollicis
longus

Figure 5–17 Superficial muscles on front of right forearm.

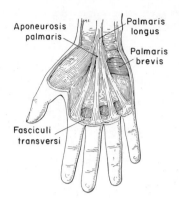

Aponeurosis palmaris

Palmaris longus

Palmaris brevis

Fasciculi transversi

Figure 5–18 Palmar aponeurosis and palmaris muscles of right palm.

below the longus and the *carpi ulnaris* on the ulnar margin of the dorsal surface about midway between the elbow and wrist. The tendon of the carpi radialis longus may be palpated on the dorsal surface of the wrist in line with the index finger.

The *flexor carpi radialis* and *extensor carpi radialis longus,* together with the *abductor pollicis longus* of the thumb, team up to produce *radial flexion (abduction)* of the wrist, and the *extensor* and *flexor carpi ulnaris* muscles team up similarly to produce *ulnar flexion (adduction).*

Muscles of the Fingers and Thumb. (Figs. 5–18 through 5–25.) These will not be discussed in detail. The names of the muscles indicate their chief functions. The role of the *abductor pollicis longus* (a thumb muscle) as a *radial flexor of the wrist* should, however, be emphasized since this is one of its important functions.

MUSCULAR ANALYSIS OF THE FUNDAMENTAL MOVEMENTS OF THE WRIST, FINGERS AND THUMB

The Wrist

These are movements of the hand as a unit. They occur chiefly at the radiocarpal joint but involve the midcarpal and intercarpal joints when flexion or hyperextension is carried to the limit of motion.

FLEXION. Performed by the palmaris longus and the flexors carpi radialis, carpi ulnaris and pollicis longus, with possible help from the flexors digitorum superficialis and profundus and the abductor pollicis longus.

EXTENSION AND HYPEREXTENSION. Performed by the extensors carpi radialis longus, carpi radialis brevis and carpi ulnaris, with possible help from the pollicis longus and extensors digitorum indices and digiti minimi.

RADIAL FLEXION (ABDUCTION). Performed by the extensors carpi radialis longus and brevis and the abductor pollicis longus, with possible help from the flexor carpi radialis and the extensors pollicis longus and brevis.

ULNAR FLEXION (ADDUCTION). Performed by the extensor carpi ulnaris and the flexor carpi ulnaris.

The Fingers

The muscular action of the fingers is given in terms of the movement of each phalanx. Movement of the proximal phalanx takes place at the meta-carpophalangeal joint, of the middle phalanx at the proximal interphalangeal joint, and of the distal phalanx at the distal interphalangeal joint. For convenience in referring to individual fingers, numbers are assigned as follows: 2 for the index finger, 3 for the middle finger, 4 for the ring finger and 5 for the little finger.

FLEXION

Proximal phalanx.   Flexed by the lumbricales manus (all fingers), interossei palmaris (palmar interossei) (2,4,5), and interossei dorsales manus (2,3,4),

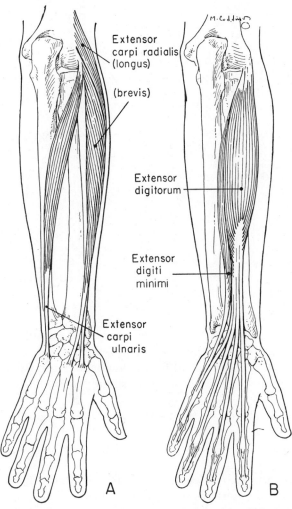

Figure 5-19   Muscles on back of right forearm. *A,* Extensor carpi radialis longus and brevis and extensor carpi ulnaris. *B,* Extensor digitorum and extensor digiti minimi.

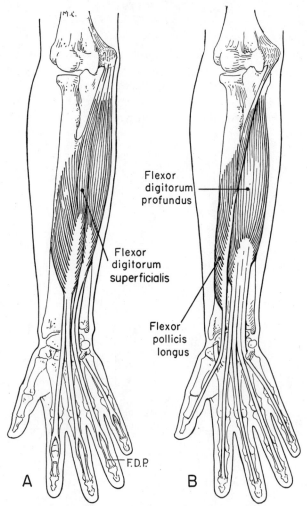

Figure 5–20   Deep muscles on front of right forearm. *A,* Flexor digitorum superficialis; *B,* flexor digitorum profundus and flexor pollicis longus.

flexor digiti minimi brevis (5) and opponens digiti minimi (5), with possible help from the flexors digitorum superficialis and profundus.

Middle phalanx.   Flexed by the flexor digitorum superficialis which acts on all four fingers and at the same time contributes to flexion of the metacarpal bones.

Distal phalanx.   Flexed by the flexor digitorum profundus which also acts on all four fingers and at the same time contributes to flexion of the proximal and middle phalanges.

Extension

Proximal phalanx.   Extended by the extensor digitorum (all fingers), extensor indicis (2) and extensor digiti minimi (5). All of these muscles contribute to the extension of the wrist. The extensor digitorum is also able to help extend the middle and distal phalanges.

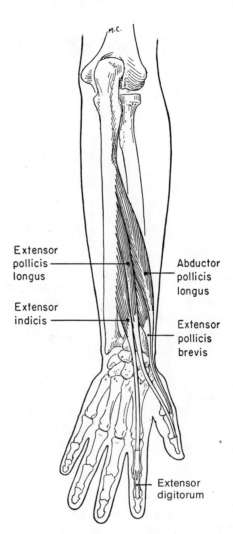

Figure 5-21 Posterior muscles of the thumb and index finger.

Extensor pollicis longus

Abductor pollicis longus

Extensor indicis

Extensor pollicis brevis

Extensor digitorum

Middle and distal phalanges. Extended by the lumbricales manus (all fingers) and interossei dorsales manus (dorsal interossei) (2,3,4). The abductor digiti minimi (5) and the extensor digitorum (all fingers) are also able to help extend the middle and distal phalanges at the same time that they are extending the proximal phalanx.

ABDUCTION AND ADDUCTION.   It must be remembered that in ab- and adduction of the fingers a different point of reference is used than in ab- and adduction of the hand as a whole. The center line of the hand, that is, the line passing through the middle finger when the latter is in its normal, extended position, is the reference line for the second, fourth and fifth digits. Comparable movements of the middle finger are called radial and ulnar flexion.

These lateral finger movements are actually movements of the proximal phalanx with the action occurring at the metacarpophalangeal joint, but the

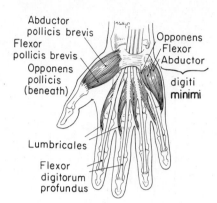

Figure 5–22 Muscles of right hand, anterior view.

entire finger moves as a unit, there being no lateral action possible at the interphalangeal joints.

Abduction is brought about by the interossei dorsales manus (2,4) and abductor digiti minimi (5), and adduction by the interossei palmaris (2,4,5).

Radial and ulnar flexion of the middle finger is performed by the interossei dorsales manus (3).

OPPOSITION. The fifth digit, or little finger, being at the outer margin of the hand, has greater freedom of movement than do the other fingers. Through the action of the opponens digiti minimi the metacarpal bone of this finger can engage in a slight degree of opposition at the carpi metacarpal joint. Together with the thumb, it participates in this movement when the hand is "cupped," as when scooping up water, and also when the tip of the little finger is brought forcibly against the tip of the thumb.

The Thumb

The muscular action of the thumb is given in terms of the movements of the metacarpal bone and the two phalanges, proximal and distal.

The Thumb Metacarpal

FLEXION. The metacarpal is flexed and hyperflexed after being slightly abducted by the flexor pollicis brevis and the adductor pollicis.

Figure 5–23 Deep muscles of thumb and fifth metacarpal.

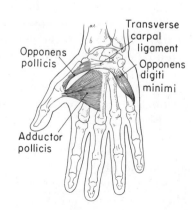

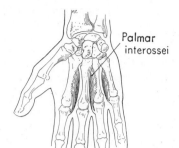

Figure 5-24   Palmar interossei, right hand.

EXTENSION.   Performed chiefly by the abductor pollicis longus with help from the extensors pollicis longus and brevis.

ABDUCTION.   Four muscles are responsible for this movement, two from the forearm: the abductor pollicis longus and the extensor pollicis brevis, and two from the thenar eminence: the abductor pollicis brevis and the opponens pollicis. Under some conditions these may be helped by the flexor pollicis brevis.

ADDUCTION.   This is performed mainly by the adductor pollicis, with some help from the flexor pollicis brevis and, in certain positions, from the extensor pollicis longus.

OPPOSITION.   This is performed mainly by the opponens, but with appreciable help from the flexor pollicis brevis. As opposition is not a single, well-defined movement but varies according to the finger that is being opposed and to the exact position of that finger, the muscles controlling the thumb must adapt to the demands of the situation. This includes the action of the phalanges as well as that of the metacarpal.

The Thumb Phalanges

FLEXION.   The flexor pollicis longus flexes both of the phalanges. Additional flexors of the proximal phalanx include the flexor pollicis brevis and the adductor pollicis, with help from the abductor pollicis brevis when necessary.

EXTENSION.   The extensor pollicis longus extends both of the phalanges. This is joined by the brevis in the extension of the proximal phalanx.

The plane in which flexion and extension of the thumb phalanges takes place is determined by the position of the metacarpal bone of the thumb.

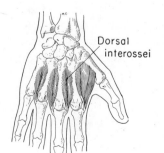

Figure 5-25   Dorsal interossei, right hand.

COOPERATIVE ACTIONS OF WRIST AND DIGITS

For a better understanding of all of the actions of the finger and thumb muscles, one should study them both on the skeleton (using an elastic band to represent muscles) and on another person. Particular attention should be paid to the relation of each muscle to every joint it crosses, to the muscle's line of pull and to the leverage involved. The relationship between the wrist movements and the finger movements in a variety of common skills and the advantage of the specific wrist movement or position to the activity of the hands should be noted.

As an aid to recognizing the secondary actions of the muscles, a record of the joints crossed by all of the finger and thumb muscles is summarized below.

Forearm Muscles of the Fingers. (See p. 120.) All five of these muscles cross four sets of joints: wrist, carpometacarpal, metacarpophalangeal and proximal interphalangeal. The extensor digitorum and extensor digiti minimi also cross both the elbow and the distal interphalangeal joint, making a total of six joints crossed. The flexor digitorum superficialis crosses the elbow, but not the distal interphalangeal, and both the extensor indicis and flexor digitorum profundus cross the distal interphalangeal joint, but not the elbow.

Intrinsic Muscles of the Fingers. Of these six muscles, only the abductor digiti minimi and the flexor digiti minimi brevis cross both the carpometacarpal and the metacarpophalangeal joints. The two interossei muscles, dorsales and palmares, and the lumbricales cross only the metacarpophalangeal joint, and the opponens digiti minimi, like the opponens pollicis, crosses only the carpometacarpal joint. The two work together in the cupping action of the palm as well as independently in other opposition movements.

Forearm Muscles of the Thumb. All four of these muscles cross both the wrist and the carpometacarpal joints, and all but the abductor pollicis longus also cross the metacarpophalangeal joint. The extensor and flexor pollicis longus muscles cross the interphalangeal joint as well. The thumb, of course, has no second interphalangeal joint.

Intrinsic Muscles of the Thumb. All four of these muscles cross the carpometacarpal joint and all but the opponens pollicis also cross the metacarpophalangeal joint.

Length of Long Finger Muscles Relative to Range of Motion in Wrist and Fingers. An interesting characteristic of the long finger muscles is that they do not have sufficient length to permit the full range of motion in the joints of the fingers and wrist at the same time. For instance, one cannot achieve complete flexion of the fingers and the wrist simultaneously because the extensor digitorum will not elongate enough to permit it. If maximum *finger* flexion is maintained, the wrist is able to flex only slightly. And similarly, if maximum *wrist* flexion is maintained, it will be impossible to achieve a real grip with the fingers. They flex incompletely and without appreciable force. Or if one first makes a tight fist and then determines to flex the wrist completely, no matter what he does, he will soon discover that the fingers loosen their grip and tend to open up in spite of his efforts to prevent it. This is not caused by contraction of the finger extensors, but by their inability to elongate sufficiently.

The same type of reaction occurs if one attempts to achieve maximum extension of the fingers when the wrist is fully hyperextended. This involuntary movement due to the tension of opposing muscles is known as the tendon or pulley action of multijoint muscles (see p. 47ff.). Because of this arrangement of the muscles, the strongest finger flexion can be obtained when the wrist is held rigid in either a straight or slightly hyperextended position and the strongest finger extension when the wrist is rigid in either a straight or slightly flexed position. The most powerful wrist action—either flexion or hyperextension— can take place only when the fingers are relaxed. In other words, strong finger action requires a rigid wrist; strong wrist action requires relaxed fingers. This aspect of wrist and finger action has been discussed exceptionally well by Wright.[16]

Examples of Using the Hands for Grasping.   In sports and gymnastics there is probably less concern with the fine, precision movements of the fingers and thumb than with the grosser movements such as the grasping of balls, striking implements and suspension apparatus. In general, grasping activities involve flexion of the fingers (usually all three joints), opposition of the thumb metacarpal and flexion of the phalanges. The degrees of these movements, together with the degree of abduction that may be present in the fingers, depend upon the shape and size of the object being grasped, as well as on the purpose of the movement. (See Figure 5–26.)

Whether pitching, throwing for distance or tossing a ball straight upward, the movements of the forearm and hand are of prime importance. The greater the force desired for moving the ball, the greater the contribution of the upper arm, but as this discussion applies only to the forearm and hand the upper arm is not considered here. Ignoring the finer movements, the essential action of the forearm in both overhand pitching and in throwing for distance is extension; of the wrist, "flexion" from the hyperextended to the extended position (with an abrupt check of the motion when the wrist is straight); and of the fingers, extension.

In a vertical toss, starting with the forearm forward at a slight downward slant, i.e., with the elbow at a slightly obtuse angle, the movements are elbow flexion followed by finger extension with the wrist held firm in an extended position. The active muscles are mainly the elbow flexors, the wrist flexors in static contraction and the finger extensors. For a stronger throw the wrist may start in a slightly hyperextended position and then flex to a straight line. The reader may find it of interest to experiment with other kinds of throws.

COMMON ATHLETIC INJURIES OF THE FOREARM, ELBOW, WRIST AND FINGERS

Fractures of the Forearm.   These are common among children and teenagers and are usually caused either by a direct blow or by falling on a rigidly outstretched arm. It is more usual for both the radius and ulna to break than for either one to break alone, and in the younger age group the fracture of either or both bones is likely to be of the greenstick type.

It is important to immobilize the elbow joint in the treatment of a fractured

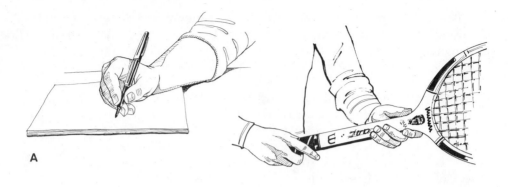

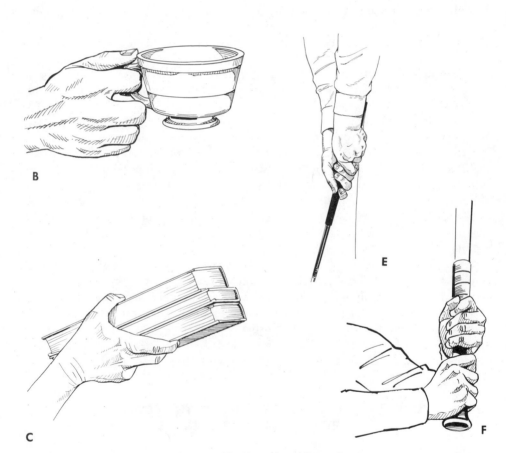

Figure 5-26 Examples of Grasps*

A. Pen
B. Cup handle
C. A handful of books
D. Tennis racket
E. Golf club
F. Baseball bat

G. Field hockey stick
H. Badminton racket
I. Basketball
J. Baseball
K. Flying rings

*Drawn from photographs.

(Illustration continued on opposite page.)

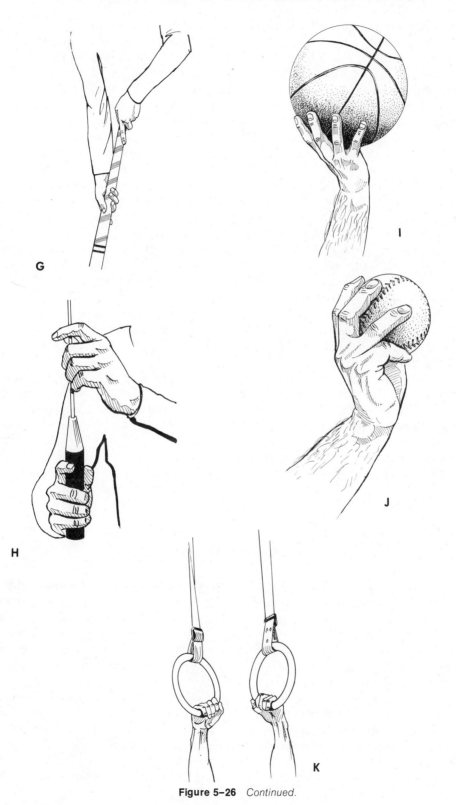

G

I

H

J

K

Figure 5–26 *Continued.*

radius, even though the fracture is close to the wrist. This is because in pronation and supination, as the radial head rotates against both the capitulum of the humerus and the radial notch of the ulna, the broad distal end swings half way around the ulna.[9] The need for immobilizing the elbow joint in the event of a radial fracture should be apparent to anyone who is conversant with kinesiology.

Elbow Dislocation.   The majority of these dislocations consist of the backward displacement of the ulna and radius in relation to the humerus. The most common cause is catching oneself from a fall by taking the weight on the outstretched hand with the elbow in rigid extension or hyperextension. This can be a very serious injury as it is likely to involve blood vessels and nerves.

Elbow Fracture-Dislocation.   Elbow dislocations are frequently accompanied by fractures, the most common being a fracture of the medial epicondyle, especially in the middle-to-late adolescent age group in those whose epicondylar epiphyses have not yet closed.

Sprained or Strained Wrist.   This type of wrist injury is very common and, like so many of the other upper extremity injuries, is caused by catching oneself from a fall by thrusting the arm downward and taking the weight on the palm with the hand hyperextended at the wrist and the elbow rigidly extended. Although the injury is usually called a sprain, it is more likely to be a strain as the site of the trouble tends to be at the tendon attachments rather than at the attachments of the anterior ligaments.[6,10] It may also involve the fracture of a carpal bone.

Baseball Finger and Less Severe Injuries Caused by a Blow from a Ball Against the Tip of a Finger.   These are the result of extending the fingers toward the oncoming ball when preparing to catch it. In a true baseball finger the ball forces the distal phalanx into flexion so sharply that the extensor digitorum tendon pulls off the bit of bone from the base of the phalanx to which it is attached.[10] This type of injury is known as an avulsion fracture. Less severe injuries from the same cause may result in damage to an interphalangeal cartilage.

SUPPLEMENTARY MATERIAL

Relation of Forearm Position to the Strength of Elbow Flexion.   Since Wells' early study[15] of this problem in which she adapted a grip dynamometer in a pull type holder to measure the strength of the elbow flexors of ten young women, there have been several reports of studies on larger numbers of subjects and using more appropriate equipment. With possibly one exception, these reverse her findings with respect to supination and the midposition of the forearm.

In 1952 Downer measured 30 female subjects, using a Beasley myodynemeter (an electronic instrument) in both a breaking point test and an isometric test. She found that the strongest contraction of the elbow flexors was obtained when the forearm was in the midposition and the least strong when the forearm was pronated.[4]

In 1955 Provins and Salter[11] measured eight male and four female subjects, and in 1956 Rasch[12] measured 24 male subjects. A strain gauge dynamometer was used in both investigations. In each study, as in Downer's, it was found that the greatest degree of elbow flexion strength was recorded when the forearm was in the midposition and the least when it was pronated.

A more recent study of the relation of forearm position to the strength of elbow flexion was made in 1969 by Larson.[7] He stated two objectives: the first, "to determine if electromyograms obtained from surface electrodes overlying the areas of the biceps brachii, the brachialis, the brachioradialis, and the

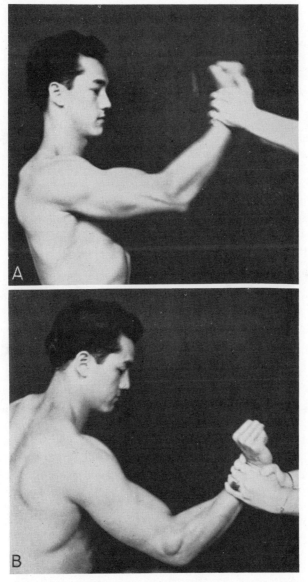

Figure 5–27   Flexion of the forearm. *A,* In a position of supination; *B,* in a position of pronation.

pronator teres muscles are affected by different forearm positions when performing several trials of maximal isometric elbow-flexor contractions," and the second, "to determine the effects of supination, pronation, and midposition on the force exerted by the elbow flexors during maximal isometric contractions." For subjects, he used thirty males with an age range of 17 to 31 years.

The subjects assumed the hook-lying position, the elbow was flexed to 65 degrees, the upper arm and elbow were fully supported on the table and the elbow was braced manually by an assistant. Instructions were given not to arch the back nor to raise the head or shoulders during maximal exertion. Maximal isometric elbow-flexor contractions were then performed three times in each of three forearm positions—supination, midposition and pronation. Cable-tensiometer scores were recorded and, at the same time, electromyographic recordings were obtained from the biceps-brachialis area, the brachioradialis area, and the pronator teres area. Larson assumed that the brachialis muscle was equally active in all three positions as it inserts into the ulna and would therefore not be affected by changes in the forearm position.

The results of this study led Larson to conclude that, within the scope of the study, (1) the biceps is most active electrically when the forearm is supinated and least active when it is pronated (see Fig. 5–27), (2) the brachioradialis is most active electrically when the forearm is either in the midposition or in supination and least active when the forearm is pronated, (3) the pronator teres, as a flexor, does not seem to be significantly affected by the position of the forearm and (4) the isometric force exerted by the elbow flexors during maximal voluntary contractions is greatest when the forearm is supinated or in midposition and least when the forearm is pronated.[7]

In their 1957 study of the biceps, brachialis and brachioradialis, Basmajian and Latif noted: (1) that the biceps flexed the supinated forearm and assisted in flexing the semiprone forearm when the movement was resisted; (2) that the brachialis flexed the forearm under all conditions, it being the "workhorse" of the elbow joint; and (3) that the brachioradialis was a rapid flexor of the forearm but that it also aided in slow flexion when the movement was resisted. They concluded that the three muscles act together with maximum electrical activity when the forearm is in the "semiprone" position; i.e., midposition, flexing against resistance.[1]

Relation of Different Forearm Positions to the Strength Exerted by the Elbow and Shoulder Muscles in Chinning.   In 1963 McCraw, using 51 young men as subjects, investigated the effect of forearm positions (pronation, supination, mid-position, one forearm pronated and the other supinated) on the muscular strength used in chinning. An aircraft cable tensiometer was used to measure strength. He found that the variation in strength from position to position was no greater than that from trial to trial in the same position. He concluded from this that there appeared to be little justification for requiring a particular position of the forearms for pull-ups.[8]

His study is significant for at least two reasons: first, his appreciation of the fact that the muscles used in extending the upper arms are as important in the performance of pull-ups as are the muscles that flex the elbows, and second, his recognition of the variations in day-to-day performance and his comparison of these with the variations due to the forearm position.

LABORATORY EXPERIENCES

Elbow and Forearm: Joint Structure and Function

1. Using a form like the one in Appendix A, record the essential information regarding the two articulations of the elbow joint and, likewise, the two radioulnar articulations. Study the movements of these joints both on the skeleton and on the living body.

2. Using a protractor-goniometer, measure the range of motion on five subjects for the following movements: flexion, pronation and supination of the forearm.

3. Repeat Exercise 24 from Chapter 4 (p. 104), this time writing the joint analysis of (a) the starting position of the forearm at the elbow and radioulnar joints, and (b) the movement from the starting position to the final pull-up position. Discuss with partner.

4. Assume a handshaking grasp with a skeleton with the elbow flexed and the forearm approximately horizontal. Slowly pronate your forearm and note the movement of the skeleton's forearm. Observe carefully each end of the radius and of the ulna and describe what happens. Now supinate your forearm as far as possible and carefully observe the radioulnar movements of the skeleton. Note the way the edge of the radial head rotates against the notch of the ulna and the way the superior surface of the radial head revolves against the capitulum of the humerus. At the distal end note the way the broad articular process of the radius swings around the head of the ulna and the radial shaft crosses over that of the ulna. Note that the ulna itself does not rotate although it may appear to do so when the elbow is fixed in extension and pronation of the forearm occurs in conjunction with inward rotation of the humerus.

Elbow and Forearm: Muscular Action.   Record the results on a chart similar to the one in Appendix D.

5. FLEXION
    Subject: Sit with entire arm resting on table. Flex forearm (a) with palm up (forearm supinated), (b) with thumb up (forearm in neutral position), and (c) with palm down (forearm pronated).
    Assistant: Resist movement by holding wrist. Steady upper arm if necessary.
    Observer: Palpate as many of the forearm flexors as possible. Do you notice any difference in the muscular action in a, b and c?

6. EXTENSION
    a. *Subject:* Lie face down on table with arm raised to shoulder level, with upper arm resting on table, forearm hanging down. Extend forearm without moving upper arm.
    Assistant: Steady upper arm and resist forearm at wrist.
    Observer: Palpate the triceps and anconeus.
    b. *Subject:* On hands and knees, bend and extend the elbows in a push-up exercise.
    Observer: Palpate the triceps and anconeus.

7. SUPINATION
    Subject: Assume hand-shaking position with assistant and turn forearm outward.
    Assistant: Assume same position with subject and resist his movement.
    Observer: Palpate and identify the muscles which contract.

8. PRONATION
    Subject: Assume hand-shaking position with assistant and turn forearm inward.
    Assistant: Assume same position with subject and resist movement.
    Observer: Palpate and identify the muscles which contract. What is their function? Can you palpate the principal movers?

Action of Muscles Other Than Movers

9. SUPINATION WITHOUT FLEXION
    Subject: Sit with arm supported, elbow in slightly flexed position and relaxed. Supinate forearm without increasing or decreasing flexion at elbow.
    Observer: Palpate the triceps. Explain.

10. Vigorous Flexion of Forearm

Subject: Flex forearm vigorously, then check movement suddenly before completing full range of motion.

Observer: Palpate the triceps. Does it contract during any part of the movement? Explain.

11. Perform a movement in which the supinator acts as a neutralizer.

Elbow and Forearm: Applications

12. Working with a partner execute a knee push-up, i.e., a push-up from the front lying position, hands under shoulders, onto the knees instead of the toes, until the elbows are fully extended. Keep body straight from knees to top of head. Return to starting position slowly and in good form.

(a) Analyze joint and muscular action of elbows in the push-up.

(b) Do the same for the return movement.

(c) What force is responsible for the movement in (a)? In (b)?

(d) What is the chief difference in the type of muscular action used in the push-up and in the let-down (return movement)? (See last paragraph on page 320.)

13. In reading the section on Common Injuries it may have been noted that several injuries to the forearm, elbow and wrist are caused by taking the weight on the outstretched hand with the elbow rigidly extended when catching oneself from a fall. The following exercise is designed to accustom one to the practice of giving at the elbow and other upper extremity joints at the moment the hand strikes the ground. If practiced frequently this technique should become a habit.

Kneel on a gymnasium mat with knees slightly separated, hips in extension and body erect. Shift your weight to the side until you lose your balance and fall to a side-sitting position with your arm outstretched and your hand reaching to catch your weight. At the moment of contact let your elbow give (i.e., flex) and, if the force is sufficient, roll onto your shoulder and back with knees drawn up. Practice this many times, both to right and left. Experiment with variations.

Wrist and Hand: Joint Structure and Function

14. Using a form like the one in Appendix B, record the essential information regarding the radiocarpal, the carpometacarpal, the metacarpophalangeal and the interphalangeal articulations. Study the movements both on the skeleton and on the living body. Pay particular attention to the carpometacarpal joint of the thumb.

15. With a protractor-goniometer measure the amount of hyperextension possible at the wrist, (a) with the fingers flexed; (b) with the fingers extended. Likewise measure the amount of flexion possible at the wrist, (a) with the fingers flexed; (b) with the fingers extended. Explain.

Wrist and Hand: Muscular Action. (See check lists in Appendix D.) If possible, get someone who plays the piano to serve as subject.

16. Flexion at Wrist

Subject: Sit with forearm resting on a table with palm up. Flex hand at wrist.

Assistant: Resist movement by holding palm.

Observer: Palpate, identify and explain the action of as many muscles as possible.

17. Extension and Hyperextension at Wrist

Subject: Sit with forearm resting on a table, palm down, hand hanging over edge of table. Extend hand at wrist.

Assistant: Resist movement by pressing on back of hand.

Observer: Palpate, identify and explain the action of as many muscles as possible.

18. Radial Flexion at Wrist

Subject: Sit with forearm resting on a table, ulnar side (little finger side of hand) down. Keeping thumb against hand, raise hand from table without moving forearm.

Assistant: May give slight resistance to hand.
Observer: Palpate and identify the muscles responsible for radial flexion.

19. ULNAR FLEXION AT WRIST
    Subject: Lie face down or bend forward in such a way that radial side of hand (thumb side) is on supporting surface, with forearm supported and wrist neither flexed nor hyperextended. Keeping little finger against hand, raise hand without moving forearm.
    Assistant: May give slight resistance to hand.
    Observer: Palpate and identify the muscles responsible for ulnar flexion.

20. FINGER FLEXION
    Subject: Sit with forearm resting on a table with palm up. Flex fingers without flexing wrist.
    Assistant: Resist movement by hooking own fingers over those of subject.
    Observer: Palpate, identify and explain the action of as many muscles as possible.

21. FINGER EXTENSION
    Subject: Sit with forearm resting on a table with palm down, fingers curled over edge of table. Extend fingers.
    Assistant: Resist movement by holding hand over subject's fingers.
    Observer: Palpate, identify and explain the action of as many muscles as possible.

22. ABDUCTION OF THUMB
    Subject: Place the hand on a table with the palm up and the thumb slightly separated from the index finger. Abduct the thumb at the carpometacarpal joint by raising it vertically upward.
    Assistant: Give slight resistance to the thumb at the proximal phalanx.
    Observer: Palpate the abductor pollicis brevis in the thenar eminence.

23. HYPERFLEXION OF THUMB IN POSITION OF SLIGHT ABDUCTION
    Subject: Place the hand on a table with the palm up and the thumb slightly raised from the table. Hyperflex the thumb at the carpometacarpal joint.
    Assistant: Give slight resistance to the proximal phalanx of the thumb.
    Observer: Palpate the flexor pollicis brevis in the thenar eminence.

24. EXTENSION OF THUMB
    Subject: Rest the fully extended hand on its ulnar border with the thumb uppermost. Extend the thumb as far as possible.
    Observer: Identify the tendons of the abductor pollicis longus, the extensor pollicis longus and the extensor pollicis brevis.

25. OPPOSITION OF THUMB
    Subject: Press the thumb hard against the tip of the middle finger.
    Observer: Palpate and identify the opponens pollicis and adductor pollicis.

Action of Muscles Other Than Movers
26. Perform a movement in which the extensor carpi ulnaris and extensor carpi radialis longus and brevis act as neutralizers to prevent flexion at the wrist.

27. Perform a movement in which the extensor carpi ulnaris and flexor carpi ulnaris act as mutual neutralizers.

Hands: Application
28. In Figure 5–26 on pages 130 and 131 inspect the various styles of grasping sport objects and analyze a few of these. First, identify the joint position of the wrist, fingers and thumb, and then determine the chief muscular involvement.

REFERENCES

1. Basmajian, J. V.: Muscles Alive, 3rd Ed. Baltimore: The Williams & Wilkins Company, 1974.
2. Beevor, C.: The Croonian Lectures on Muscular Movements. Reprint. New York: The Macmillan Company, 1951.
3. DeSousa, O. M., DeMoraes, J. L., and Viera, F. L. de M.: Electromyographic study of the brachio-radialis muscle. Anat. Rec., *139*:125–131, 1961.
4. Downer, A. H.: Strength of the elbow flexor muscles. Phys. Ther. Rev., *33*:68–70, 1953.
5. Goss, C. M. (Ed.): Gray's Anatomy of the Human Body, 29th Ed. Philadelphia: Lea & Febiger, 1973.
6. Klafs, C. E., and Arnheim, D. D.: Modern Principles of Athletic Training. St. Louis: C. V. Mosby Co., 1973.
7. Larson, R. F.: Forearm positioning on maximal elbow-flexor force. J. Am. Phys. Ther. Assn., *49*:748–756, 1969.
8. McCraw, L. W.: Effects of variations of forearm position in elbow flexion. Res. Quart. Am. Assn. Health, Phys. Ed. & Recrn., *35*:504–510, 1964.
9. O'Donoghue, D. H.: Treatment of Injuries to Athletes. 3rd Ed. Philadelphia: W. B. Saunders Company, 1976.
10. Pauly, J. E., Rushing, J. L., and Scheving, L. E.: An electromyographic study of some muscles crossing the elbow joint. Anat. Rec., *159*:47–53, 1967.
11. Provins, K. A., and Salter, N.: Maximum torque exerted above the elbow joint. J. Appl. Physiol., *7*:393–398, 1955.
12. Rasch, P. J.: Effect of position of forearm on strength of elbow flexion. Res. Quart. Am. Assn. Health, Phys. Ed. & Recrn., *27*:333–337, 1956.
13. Schaffer, J. P. (Ed.): Morris' Human Anatomy, 11th Ed. New York: Hafner Publishing Co., 1967.
14. Steindler, A.: Kinesiology of the Human Body. Springfield, Ill.: Charles C Thomas, Publisher, 1970.
15. Wells, K. F.: Kinesiology, 3rd Ed. Philadelphia: W. B. Saunders Company, 1960, p. 165.
16. Wright, W. G.: Muscle Function. New York: Hafner Publishing Company, 1962.

Chapter Six

THE LOWER EXTREMITY: THE HIP JOINT

THE RELATIONSHIP BETWEEN THE HIP JOINT AND THE PELVIC GIRDLE

The relationship between the hip joint and the pelvic girdle is somewhat similar to that between the shoulder joint and shoulder girdle. Just as the scapula tilts or rotates to put the glenoid fossa in a favorable position for the movements of the humerus, so the pelvic girdle tilts and rotates to put the acetabulum in a favorable position for the movements of the femur. There are these differences, however. Whereas the left and right sides of the shoulder girdle can move independently, the pelvic girdle can move only as a unit. Furthermore, whereas the movements of the shoulder girdle take place in its own joints (sternoclavicular and acromioclavicular), the pelvic girdle is dependent for its movements upon the lumbosacral and other lumbar joints, and the hip joints. Hence, an analysis of the movements of the pelvic girdle must always be stated in terms of spinal and hip action.

Structure. (Figs. 6–1, 6–2, 6–3, 6–4 and 6–5.) The hip joint, a typical ball-and-socket joint, is formed by the articulation of the spherical head of the femur with the deep cup-shaped acetabulum. The latter, being formed by the junction of the three pelvic bones (ilium, ischium and pubis) is also described as horsehoe-shaped as there is a gap (the acetabular notch) at the lower part of the "cup." The entire acetabulum is lined with hyaline cartilage. This is thicker above than below, and the center is filled in with a mass of fatty tissue covered by synovial membrane. A flat rim of fibrocartilage, known as the *glenoid labrum,* is attached by its circumference to the margin of the acetabulum (Fig. 6–2). It covers the hyaline cartilage and, since it is considerably thicker at the circumference than at the center, it adds to the depth of the acetabulum. Furthermore, being thicker above and behind, it serves to cushion the top and back of the acetabulum against the impact of the femoral head in forceful movements. The head also is completely covered with hyaline cartilage, except for a small pit near the center called the fovea capitis. The cartilage is thicker above and tapers to a thin edge at the perimeter.

Ligamentous Reinforcements. The *transverse acetabular* ligament is a strong,

139

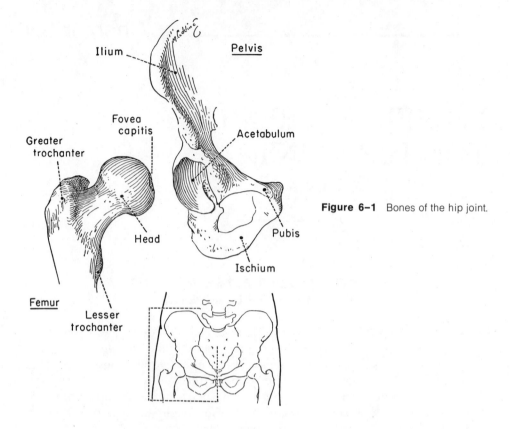

Figure 6–1   Bones of the hip joint.

flat band of fibers continuous with the glenoid, which bridges the acetabular notch and thus completes the acetabular ring.

The *teres femoris* is a flat, narrow triangular band which is attached by its apex to the fovea capitis near the center of the femoral head, and by its base

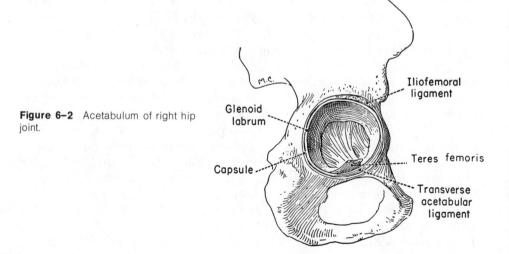

Figure 6–2   Acetabulum of right hip joint.

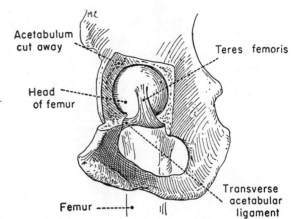

Figure 6-3   Right hip joint from within, looking toward head of femur.

to the margins of the acetabular ligament (Fig. 6–3). Its function is to "tie" the head of the femur to the lower part of the acetabulum and thus provide the joint with reinforcement from within.

Outer reinforcement is provided by the three ligaments of the femoral neck, one for each of the pelvic bones that unite to form the acetabulum (Figs. 6–4 and 6–5). The *iliofemoral* ligament, called the Y ligament because of its supposed resemblance to an inverted Y, is an extraordinarily strong band of fibers situated at the front of the capsule and intimately blended with it. Because of its position it serves to check extension and both outward (lateral) and inward (medial) rotation. The *pubofemoral* ligament consists of a narrow band of fibers at the medial anterior and lower portion of the capsule. It prevents excessive abduction and helps to check extension and outward rotation. The *ischiofemoral* ligament is a strong triangular ligament at the back of the capsule. It limits inward rotation and adduction in the flexed position.

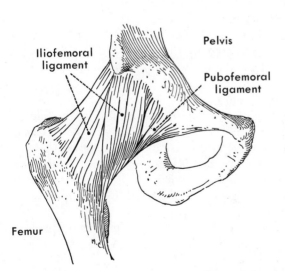

Figure 6-4   Anterior view of right hip joint.

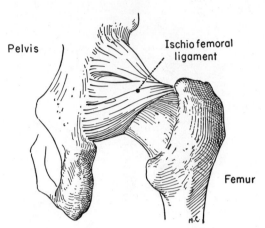

Pelvis

Ischiofemoral
ligament

Femur

Figure 6-5 Posterior view of right hip joint.

Position and Shape of Femur.   The movements of the femur are similar to those of the humerus, but are not quite so free as the latter because of the deeper socket. In studying the movements of the femur the student should first be aware of the position of the femur in the fundamental standing position. If viewed from the front, it is seen that the shaft of the femur is not vertical but that it slants somewhat medialward. This serves to place the center of the knee joint more nearly under the center of motion of the hip joint. Hence, the mechanical axis of the femur—a line connecting the center of the femoral head with the center of the knee joint—is almost vertical (Fig. 1-1). The degree of slant of the femoral shaft is related both to the size of the angle between the neck and shaft and to the width of the pelvis.

As seen from the side, the shaft of the femur bows forward. These characteristics of the femur—the obtuse neck-shaft angle and the forward bowing of the shaft—are, as Steindler has explained, provisions for resisting the strains and stresses sustained in walking, running and jumping, and for assuring the proper transmission of weight through the femur to the knee joint.[11]

Movements of the Femur at the Hip Joint

FLEXION.   A forward movement of the femur in the sagittal plane. If the knee is straight, the movement is restricted by the tension of the hamstring muscles. In extreme flexion the pelvis tilts backward to supplement the movement at the hip joint.

EXTENSION.   Return movement from flexion.

HYPEREXTENSION.   A backward movement of the femur in the sagittal plane. This movement is extremely limited. Except in dancers and acrobats, it is possible only when the femur is rotated outward and is probably completely absent in many individuals. The restricting factor is the iliofemoral ligament at the front of the joint. The advantage of this restriction of movement is that it provides a stable joint for weight-bearing without the need for strong muscular contraction.

ABDUCTION.   A sideward movement of the femur in the frontal plane so that the thigh moves away from the midline of the body. A greater range of movement is possible when the femur is rotated outward.

ADDUCTION.   Return movement from abduction. Hyperadduction is possible only when the other leg is moved out of the way. In extreme hyperadduction the teres femoris becomes taut.

OUTWARD ROTATION.   A rotation of the femur around its longitudinal axis so that the knee is turned outward.

INWARD ROTATION.   A rotation of the femur around its longitudinal axis so that the knee is turned inward.

HORIZONTAL FLEXION.   A forward movement of the abducted thigh in a horizontal plane, probably accompanied by reduction of outward rotation.

HORIZONTAL ABDUCTION.   A sideward movement of the flexed thigh in a horizontal plane, probably accompanied by outward rotation.

CIRCUMDUCTION.   A combination of flexion, abduction, extension and adduction performed sequentially in either direction.

Muscles.   The muscles acting at the hip joint are listed below according to their position in relation to the joint. They include several muscles which act with equal or greater effectiveness at the knee joint. These are known as the two-joint muscles of the lower extremity. Only their action at the hip joint is considered in this section.

Anterior

Iliopsoas (Fig. 6–13)
Pectineus (Fig. 6–13)
Rectus femoris (Fig. 6–14)
Sartorius (Fig. 6–14)
Tensor fasciae latae
   (Figs. 6–7 and 6–14)

Lateral

Gluteus medius (Fig. 6–10)
Gluteus minimus (Fig. 6–10)

Posterior

Biceps femoris ⎫ "Hamstrings"
Semimembranosus ⎬ (Figs. 6–11
Semitendinosus ⎭   and 6–12)
Gluteus maximus (Figs. 6–7, 6–8
   and 6–9)
Six deep outward rotators (Fig. 6–12)

Medial

Adductor brevis (Fig. 6–6)
Adductor longus (Fig. 6–6)
Adductor magnus (Fig. 6–6)
Gracilis (Figs. 6–6, 7–8 and 7–9)

CHARACTERISTICS AND FUNCTIONS OF INDIVIDUAL MUSCLES*

Adductor Brevis. (Fig. 6–6.)   This lies just above the adductor longus and consists of fibers that are almost horizontal when the thigh is in its normal resting or standing position. From this position it both *adducts* and *aids in flexing the femur*, but if the hip is flexed to a marked degree it combines extension with adduction.

Adductor Longus. (Fig. 6–6.)   This *adducts* and *assists in flexion of the femur*. Steindler has pointed out that while it ordinarily helps to flex the thigh, when the flexion exceeds about 70 degrees it becomes an extensor as a result of a shift in the relationship between the muscle's line of pull and the joint's center of motion.[11] In an EMG study made in 1966, de Sousa and Vitti found that this muscle

---

*Listed in alphabetical order.

was always active during free adduction and inward rotation.[2] The muscle may be palpated just below its proximal attachment at the medial aspect of the groin.

Adductor Magnus. (Fig. 6–6.)   This *extends the thigh as well as adducting it*, and the condyloid or *lowest portion also assists in inward rotation.* de Sousa and Vitti noted that this muscle was not active during free adduction unless the movement was performed against resistance.[2] Magnus may be palpated on the medial aspect of the middle half of the thigh. The uppermost portion of the muscle, i.e., the portion that comes from the pubis, is sometimes treated as a separate muscle called *adductor minimus.*

Gluteus Maximus. (Figs. 6–7, 6–8 and 6–9.)   This is the largest and most superficial of the three buttock muscles. It is a potentially *powerful hip extensor.* It also *rotates the femur outward* when the latter is extended. The *lower portion assists in adduction* from an abducted position, if the movement is resisted. The

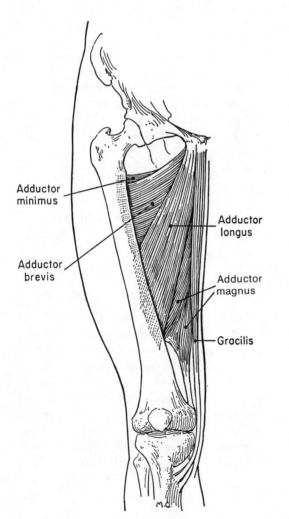

Adductor minimus

Adductor longus

Adductor brevis

Adductor magnus

Gracilis

Figure 6–6   Adductor muscles of right thigh.

upper portion abducts against strong resistance.[8] One can understand these seemingly contradictory functions more readily after studying the relation of the muscle to the hip joint's center of motion as seen from behind. Figure 6–9 shows that roughly one third of the muscle lies above the center of motion, and two thirds lie below it. This puts the uppermost fibers in position for abducting the thigh and the lower fibers in position for adducting it, whereas the fibers lying directly behind the femoral head are not in position for doing either. The entire muscle may easily be palpated on the posterior surface of the buttock.

In the light of findings from electromyographic investigations, earlier statements made in this text must now be modified. These findings are not in complete agreement, however. Basmajian agreed with Duchenne that ordinary walking is not affected by complete paralysis of this muscle.[2] Yet, the EMG study conducted by the Prosthetic Devices Research Project in Berkeley indi-

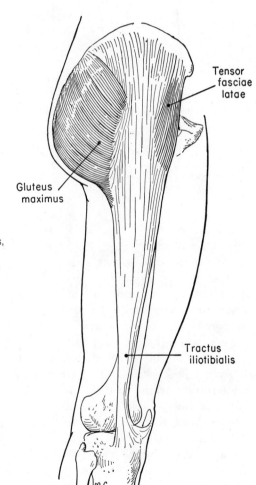

Tensor
fasciae
latae

Gluteus
maximus

Tractus
iliotibialis

Figure 6–7   Lateral view of gluteus maximus, tensor fasciae latae and iliotibial tract.

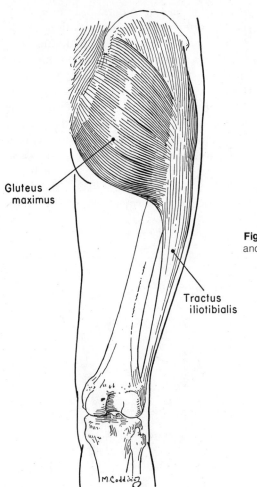

Gluteus
maximus

Tractus
iliotibialis

Figure 6-8 Posterior view of gluteus maximus and iliotibial tract.

cated that the muscle was active in the early part of the stance phase in both normal and fast walking on level ground.[1]

The latter study and one by Merrifield agree on its activity in stair climbing. It has also been found to be active in walking up an inclined plane, in extending the femur against resistance, in abducting the femur, especially against resistance and when rotated outward, and in adducting the femur against resistance when in an abducted position.[9] Surprisingly, Houtz and Fischer, the only investigators who have reported on its role in bicycling, stated that it was unimportant in this activity.[2] In a later, more extensive study of gluteus maximus function, the same investigators had some additional surprising results. After testing their subjects in the performance of several exercises commonly prescribed for strengthening the gluteus maximus, they found that the movements which elicited the greatest electrical activity were as follows: hyperextension movements of the thigh performed against resistance from the erect standing position, muscle setting and vigorous hyperextension of the

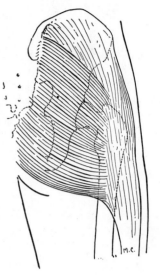

Figure 6–9 Diagram showing relation of gluteus maximus to hip joint.

trunk from an erect position. Furthermore, they found that lifting a 25 lb. weight from both a squat position and from a straight leg, trunk bend position elicited relatively minor electrical activity.[5]

If a person stands erect with feet parallel, voluntary contraction of the gluteus maximus, achieved by "pinching the buttocks together," produces two interesting postural effects. The pull on the femur causes a slight outward rotation at the hip joint, but since friction between the soles of the feet and the floor prevents the feet from turning laterally, the rotatory force is transmitted from the femur to the talus, thence to the other tarsal bones, and results in supination of the foot and a lifting of the medial aspect of the longitudinal arch. At the same time the pull at the muscle's proximal attachment decreases the lumbar lordosis. This setting or tensing of the gluteus maximus is frequently advocated as a corrective postural exercise.

Gluteus Medius. (Fig. 6–10, *A*.)   This is essentially an *abductor of the femur*. The *anterior fibers also rotate the thigh inward*. The muscle may be palpated about 2 or 3 inches above the greater trochanter.

The muscle is an important one in walking and in standing in good posture. When the weight is shifted onto one foot, tension of the gluteus medius and other abductors is an important factor in the stabilization of the hip. Lack of such stabilization results in an exaggerated sideward thrust of the supporting hip and drop of the pelvis on the opposite side. Paralysis of this muscle causes a typical limping gait known as the "gluteus medius gait." When the weight is borne on the affected side, the trunk tilts strongly to that side, and the opposite hip is thrust into prominence.

Gluteus Minimus. (Fig. 6–10, *B*.)   This *rotates inward and abducts*. It is a smaller muscle than the gluteus medius and is situated beneath it. Whereas the medius is primarily an abductor and secondarily an inward rotator, the minimus is primarily an inward rotator and secondarily an abductor. The muscles appear to work cooperatively, each one assisting in the other's primary function.

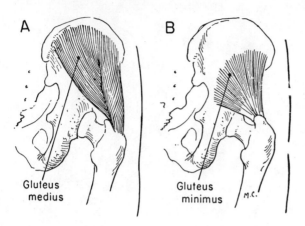

Figure 6-10 Gluteus medius and minimus.

Gracilis. (Figs. 6-6, 7-8 and 7-9.) (Also listed with the knee muscles.) This *adducts the femur and helps to flex it.* As the name indicates, it is a slender muscle. Being an adductor, it is sometimes called the adductor gracilis, and like the hamstrings, the sartorius and the rectus femoris, it is a muscle of the knee as well as of the hip joint. EMG studies have shown that it participates in hip flexion only when the knee is extended and that it is most active during the first part of flexion; it also helps to rotate the femur medially (inward).[12]

The Hamstrings. (Figs. 6-11 and 6-12.) (Also listed with the knee muscles.) The three hamstring muscles, *biceps femoris, semimembranosus* and *semitendinosus,* are situated on the back of the thigh, extending from the tuberosity of the ischium down just below the knee joint, the biceps femoris on the lateral aspect of the posterior surface and the two "semi" muscles on the medial aspect. They all *extend the femur,* or if the thighs are bearing weight as in either the standing or the long sitting position, they will extend the forward flexed trunk as a unit, i.e., from the hips. (Spinal action must not be confused with hip action or vice versa.) Their effectiveness as extensors of the hip is in inverse proportion to the degree of flexion at the knee joint. If the knee is sharply flexed, the muscles have insufficient tension to act effectively at the hip joint. The tendon or pulley action of the two-joint muscles is discussed on page 47.

Basmajian reports that some investigators found that all three hamstrings, in addition to extending the hip, help to stabilize it, except in erect standing; also they adduct the femur from the abducted position when the movement is resisted and help to rotate the extended femur, the long head of the biceps femoris rotating it laterally and the inner hamstrings rotating it medially.[2]

Biceps Femoris, Long Head. (Fig. 6-11.) The biceps femoris is the lateral hamstring muscle. Only its long head crosses the hip joint; the short head, therefore, has no part in hip joint movements. The tendon may be palpated on the lateral aspect of the posterior surface of the knee.

Semimembranosus and Semitendinosus. (Figs. 6-11 and 6-12.) Together, these constitute the medial component of the hamstring group. The *semimembranosus* lies anterior to the *semitendinosus* and has a shorter, deeper tendon which is extremely difficult to palpate. The *semitendinosus* tendon may easily be palpated on the medial aspect of the posterior surface of the knee when the leg is flexed against resistance from the prone lying position. It should not be confused with the gracilis tendon which lies slightly anterior to it.

Iliopsoas. (Fig. 6–13.) (Also listed with the spinal muscles.)   As the *psoas major* and the *iliacus* muscles share a common distal attachment and act as one muscle at the hip joint, the usual practice of treating them as one muscle is followed here. The muscle is a *strong hip flexor.* Depending upon the circumstances it will either *flex the thigh on the trunk* or will *flex the trunk as a unit on the thighs* from a supine lying position, or in any position when the movement is performed against resistance. It is also thought to help stabilize the hip joint in the standing position.

There has been considerable disagreement concerning additional functions. There has been some evidence of both outward and inward rotation, but it would be well to follow Basmajian's advice concerning this and abandon the controversy as there is insufficient evidence to support either side.[2]

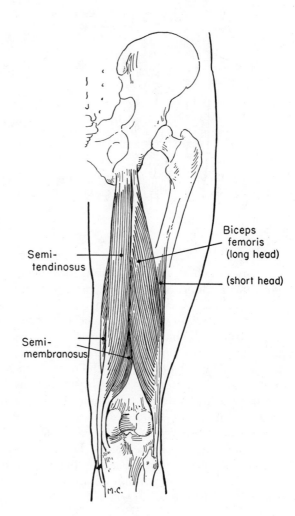

Figure 6–11   Hamstring muscles.

Semi-
tendinosus

Semi-
membranosus

Biceps
femoris
(long head)

(short head)

M.C.

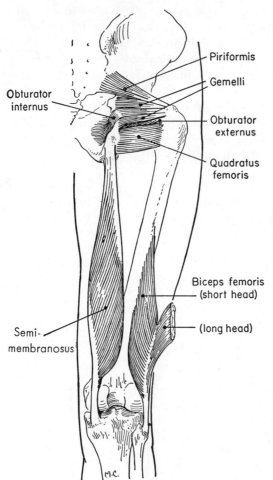

Obturator internus

Piriformis

Gemelli

Obturator externus

Quadratus femoris

Figure 6–12 Deep posterior muscles of right thigh.

Biceps femoris (short head)

(long head)

Semi-membranosus

In regard to abduction and adduction, Steindler assumed that from its position the iliopsoas would *adduct* the femur but that such movement would be negligible.[11] Close found in his EMG investigation that the iliopsoas was definitely active in *abduction,* especially as the limit of the range of motion was approached.[2] It may be of interest to the reader to look at Figure 1–1 which depicts the mechanical axis of the femur and to visualize the lines of pull of the iliopsoas. It will be noted that the only fibers that appear to be in a position to abduct are the outermost fibers of the iliacus which originate from the vicinity of the anterior superior iliac spine. It is the opinion of the authors of this text that conclusions regarding abduction or adduction should be postponed until additional investigations have been made.

The muscle is extremely difficult to palpate. It is impossible to palpate the iliacus but the *psoas major* may possibly be palpated on slender subjects who are able to keep the abdominal muscles relaxed during the testing. Two techniques are suggested.

1. The subject lies on his side, rolled toward the face, and flexes the thigh against slight resistance without contracting the abdominal muscles. The psoas may be palpated in the groin.

2. The subject lies on his back with the lower back arched as much as possible. From this position he flexes one thigh without contracting the abdominal muscles. An assistant should support the underside of the pelvis and try to keep it from moving. The psoas may be palpated through the abdomen.

Pectineus. (Fig. 6–13.)   This is a short, thick, quadrilateral muscle situated lateral and superior to the adductor longus and more or less parallel to it. It *flexes the thigh* and *assists in adduction* when the hip is in a flexed state. Whether it also contributes to outward rotation is debatable. As a flexor it has a good angle of pull which, together with its internal structure, accounts for its ability to overcome considerable resistance. It may be palpated at the front of the pubis, just lateral to the adductor longus, but it is difficult to distinguish from the latter muscle.

Rectus Femoris. (Fig. 6–14.) (Also listed with the knee muscles.)   This *flexes the thigh*. It is a large bipenniform muscle, located superficially on the front of the thigh. It acts on the knee joint as well as the hip and is therefore a two-joint muscle. For the pulley or tendon action of such muscles see page 47. Accord-

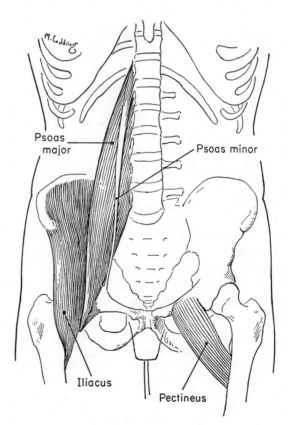

Figure 6–13 Anterior view of pelvic region showing psoas major and minor, iliacus and pectineus.

Psoas major

Psoas minor

Iliacus

Pectineus

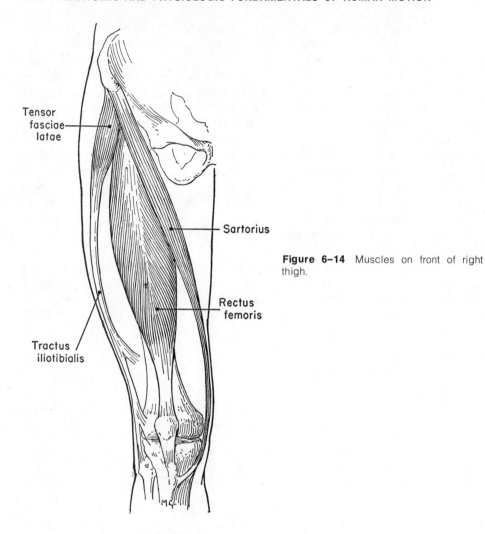

Tensor
fasciae
latae

Sartorius

Figure 6–14 Muscles on front of right thigh.

Rectus
femoris

Tractus
iliotibialis

ing to Wright, it serves as an anterior ligament of the hip in addition to being a flexor.[13] It may be palpated as well as seen on the anterior surface of the thigh.

Sartorius. (Fig. 6–14.) (Also listed with the knee muscles.) This also is a two-joint muscle. Its action on the thigh is *flexion.* It is a long, slender, ribbon-like muscle and is directed obliquely downward and medialward across the front of the thigh. It is the most superficial of the anterior thigh muscles and may be readily seen and palpated on slender subjects. On others, it may be palpated at the anterior superior iliac spine. Its name is derived from its alleged function of enabling one to sit with the legs in "tailor-fashion."

The Six Deep Outward Rotators. (Obturator externus and internus, gemellus superior and inferior, quadratus femoris, and piriformis.) (Fig. 6–12.) These six muscles form a compact group behind the hip joint. Their fibers run horizontally for the most part. The piriformis, the most superior of the group, is slightly above the joint, and the quadratus femoris, the most inferior, is slightly below it. Some of the muscles have a secondary function such as ab- or adduction, but neither of these functions compares in importance with that of *outward rotation*. They are favorably situated for helping to hold the femoral head in the acetabulum.

   Tensor Fasciae Latae. (Figs. 6–7 and 6–14.)   This muscle *flexes* and *abducts the femur* and *tenses the fascia lata.* Whether it also rotates the femur inward is debatable. It is a small muscle located close in front of and slightly lateral to the hip joint and may be palpated about two inches anterior to the greater trochanter. Because its pull on the fascia lata is transmitted by means of the iliotibial tract down to the lateral condyle of the tibia, it helps to extend the leg at the knee. Together with the gluteus maximus, which also unites with the fascia lata, it helps to stabilize the knee joint in weight-bearing positions. When the lower extremities are fixed, both of these muscles help to steady the pelvis and trunk on the thighs.

   Not all kinesiologists agree that it contributes to inward rotation, but Wheatley and Jahnke claimed that their EMG experiments showed it to be a medial (inward) rotator in all of the positions tested.[12]

COOPERATIVE MOVEMENTS OF THE PELVIS

   Since the pelvis appears to be as closely associated with the spine as with the lower extremities, its structure and movements will be discussed in greater detail in the chapter on the spinal column. Nevertheless, an elementary understanding of its structure and movements is necessary in order to appreciate its relation to the hip joint and thigh. In brief, it is a rigid bony basin which serves as a massive connecting link between the trunk and the lower extremities. It is firmly united to the sacrum by a pair of joints which do not permit voluntary motion. These are the right and left sacroiliac articulations. Changes in the position of the pelvis are brought about by virtue of the motions of the lumbar spine and the hip joints. Movements in these joints permit the pelvis to tilt forward, backward and sideward, and to rotate horizontally.

   As was stated earlier the pelvis can move only as a unit. It can, however, supplement three types of lower extremity movements: movements of both limbs acting in unison, as when swinging them forward or backward from a position of suspension; movements of both limbs acting in opposition, as when walking, running or doing a flutter kick in swimming; and movements of one limb, as when kicking or when raising one leg to the side. In double leg swinging the pelvis tilts backward or forward, decreasing or increasing its inclination; in opposition movements it rotates in the horizontal plane; and in single limb movements it tilts backward for a kick (Fig. 6–15) and laterally for a sideward leg lift. In each of these examples the pelvis positions itself so as to favor the movement of the thigh or thighs.

Figure 6-15 A punt, illustrating hip flexion combined with backward tilt of the pelvis. (Courtesy of Springfield College.)

MUSCULAR ANALYSIS OF THE FUNDAMENTAL MOVEMENTS OF THE THIGH

FLEXION. This is performed chiefly by the tensor fasciae latae, pectineus (both of these especially during the first half of range), iliopsoas, rectus femoris and sartorius. The gracilis and adductors longus and brevis assist in flexion.

EXTENSION. The three hamstring muscles are the chief hip extensors. The gluteus maximus extends only against resistance. The adductor magnus also extends, especially against resistance and when the thigh is flexed beyond a 45 degree angle.

ABDUCTION. The chief abductors are the gluteus medius and minimus, the former being the more effective of the two. The uppermost fibers of the gluteus maximus abduct during the early part of the movement, and the tensor fasciae latae abducts the thigh when it is extended.

ADDUCTION. The adductors magnus, longus and brevis and the gracilis are the important adductors. The pectineus adducts the flexed thigh and the lower third of the gluteus maximus assists in the movement when it is performed against resistance. (See Fig. 6-9.)

OUTWARD ROTATION. This is performed by the six deep outward rotators and the gluteus maximus.

INWARD ROTATION. The chief inward rotators are the gluteus medius and minimus, the latter being the more effective of the two. The lower fibers of the adductor magnus rotate the thigh inward when it is extended. Some say that the tensor fasciae latae also helps, but this is debatable.

HORIZONTAL FLEXION.   Probably performed by the adductors longus and brevis, gracilis, iliopsoas, pectineus, rectus femoris, sartorius and tensor fasciae latae, and accompanied by the relaxation of the outward rotators.*

HORIZONTAL ABDUCTION.   Probably performed by the gluteus medius, minimus and upper maximus, and the six deep outward rotators.*

TABLE 6–1   Common Examples of Movements of the Thigh in Sports, Calisthenics and Daily Life Activities

FLEXION
   The swing or recovery phase of walking.
   Stepping up onto a high step.
   Downward stroke in the flutter kick.
   A punt in football (Fig. 6–15).

EXTENSION
   The support and push-off phases of walking.
   Downward stroke in bicycling.
   Upward stroke in the flutter kick.
   Rising from a squat position with the knees pointing forward.

ABDUCTION
   Jumping to a side-stride position.
   Lying on the back with the legs closed, move the legs apart.
   Lying on one side with legs straight, raise the top leg.
   Recovery phase of the kick in the standard breast stroke.

ADDUCTION
   Lying on the back with the legs wide apart, bring the legs together.
   Using the right foot, pass a soccer ball to the left.
   Force phase of the kick in the standard breast stroke.

OUTWARD ROTATION
   From the standing position turn the feet out in a first ballet position.

INWARD ROTATION
   From a standing position turn the feet in to a pigeon-toed position.

HORIZONTAL FLEXION
   Ballet dancing.
   Figure skating.
   Hurdling.
   Gymnastics: straddle vault; movements on parallel bars.

HORIZONTAL ABDUCTION
   Ballet dancing.
   Figure skating.
   Gymnastics: movements on parallel bars.

COMMON ATHLETIC INJURIES OF THE THIGH AND HIP JOINT

Contusion of the Thigh Muscles.   The muscles of the thigh are in a particularly vulnerable position in contact sports, especially in football. It is fortu-

*So far as the authors know these movements have not yet been analyzed electromyographically.

nate for the femur that it is so well protected in front by the heavy quadriceps muscles. It is likewise fortunate for the rectus femoris that the vasti muscles lie between it and the bone and thus cushion the former against the blows it frequently receives. In spite of such cushioning, however, and in spite of the external protection usually worn by the player, the quadriceps muscles do suffer contusions, the vasti lateralis and intermedius in particular, but the rectus femoris also on occasion. The symptoms of thigh contusions tend to be delayed and more diffused than those of contusions occurring in less fleshy areas. Nevertheless, they can be severe, causing disability, especially when the injured muscle is put on a stretch such as when the knee is flexed beyond 90 degrees.[10]

Myositis Ossificans. This is a condition in which calcification develops following repeated traumas of the muscle. It is likely to occur when the symptoms of muscle injury are so mild that the player insists on continuing to play. The front of the thigh and the brachialis muscle of the upper arm appear to be the most vulnerable area so affected. O'Donoghue suggests that the frequency of this condition is caused in large part by poor treatment such as over-vigorous massage, manipulation under anesthesia, over-strenuous exercise and too early return to participation in the sport in which a severe muscle injury has occurred. In other words, myositis ossificans can often be prevented if muscle contusions are given proper treatment.[10]

Strains of the Hamstring Muscle Group. There is high incidence of hamstring strains among athletes. These tend to occur in running more than in any other activity, especially when a muscular imbalance occurs through fatigue or other condition. A disturbance of the player's coordination often results. A frequent site of the strain is the distal attachment of the biceps femoris on the fibular head. This is close to the attachment of the collateral fibular ligament and it is often difficult to differentiate between strain of the bicipital tendon and sprain of the fibular ligament. At a slightly higher, i.e., more proximal site, at the junction of the tendon with the fleshy part of the muscle, it may be difficult to differentiate between a muscle strain and a contusion or hematoma.[10] A correct diagnosis is essential in order that the appropriate treatment may be selected. It is therefore important that the diagnosis be made by a physician.

Although this section is headed "Common Athletic Injuries of the Thigh and Hip Joint," no hip conditions are discussed here. This is because of the relatively low incidence of hip joint injuries in athletics. The structure of the joint accounts for the rarity of dislocations, and fractures of the hip joint region are fortunately not a serious threat to athletes. The dangerous age when hip fractures are a real threat is old age when the bones have lost their toughness and have become brittle.

SUPPLEMENTARY MATERIAL

Variations in Femoral and Tibial Torsion; Relation to Gait. Elftman investigated the torsion of both the femur and the tibia in 35 male cadavers. It was his opinion that extremes at either end of the scale might well account for peculiarities of gait. The possibility of femoral or tibial torsion should be taken into consideration when judging exaggerated toeing-in or toeing-out gaits. The results of Elftman's findings are recorded in Table 6-2.

TABLE 6-2   Measurements of Femoral and Tibial Torsion (Elftman) (N = 35)

	RANGE	MEAN	S.D.
Femoral torsion	0°–26°	11.86°	6.21 ± 0.74
Tibial torsion	12°–44°	27.40°	7.40 ± 0.89

An interesting study on the relation of femoral torsion to in-toeing and out-toeing was reported by Crane in 1959.[3] He noted that the out-toeing group was capable of 60 to 80 degrees of lateral rotation but less than 20 degrees of medial rotation. The in-toeing group, on the other hand, was capable of only 10 to 20 degrees of lateral rotation and 60 to 80 degrees of medial rotation. X-rays showed abnormal femoral torsion in both of these groups. Although the cause could not be determined, Crane suggested that it might be traced either to fetal positions or, as was thought by Fitzhugh, to sleeping positions during infancy.

In comparing a group of "normal" children, aged 6 months to 9 years, with data on "normal" adults, he found that femoral torsion was three or four times greater during the first year of life than it was in adulthood and that the decrease in torsion occurred gradually.

A striking contrast was seen in a comparison of two young boys who had opposite patterns of sitting. Boy A, aged 7, habitually assumed a kneel-sitting position with the knees close and the feet widely separated and everted like a letter W. Boy B, aged 5, habitually assumed the familiar position known as "tailor sitting" or "Indian sitting." Their rotation and torsion measurements were as follows:

	Lat. Rot.	*Med. Rot.*	*Femoral torsion (anteversion)*
Boy A	5–10°	75°	R 50; L 53°
Boy B	80°	10°	Less than 10°

EMG Investigation of Iliopsoas Function.   Because of divergent opinions expressed by earlier investigators, LaBan, Raptou and Johnson undertook a study of the function of the iliopsoas muscle in 1965. They considered that their use of a flexible wire electrode had an advantage over the rigid ones used by previous investigators.

Using five subjects whose ages ranged from 20 to 29 years they tested the action of the iliopsoas in quiet standing, in walking at normal speed and in performing a number of movements from the long-lying and hook-lying supine positions. They detected no electrical activity of the iliopsoas during quiet standing. In the forward swing phase of walking they found considerable activity.

Their most interest findings were from the comparison of sit-ups executed from the long-lying supine position with those done from the hook-lying (flexed knee and hip) supine position. They noted that the iliopsoas muscle showed considerable electrical activity throughout the entire range of movement when the sit-ups were performed from the hook-lying position, but in the straight leg lying position it showed little or no activity for the first 30 degrees of movement. After that it produced considerable activity. They assumed that the implication from this was that the abdominal muscles are responsible for the first 30 degrees of a sit-up performed from the long-lying position, with the rectus femoris being responsible for stabilizing the pelvis.[7]

LABORATORY EXPERIENCES

Joint Structure and Function

1. Using a form like the one in Appendix A, record the essential information regarding the hip joint. Study the movements both on the skeleton and on the living body.

2. Using a protractor type of goniometer, measure the range of motion in the following joint movements on five different subjects:
   a. Hip flexion, with straight knee.
   b. Hip flexion, with flexed knee.
   c. Total abduction of both thighs.

3. From an erect standing position with the feet together take a fairly long step forward with the right foot, stopping with weight mostly over the right foot and with the left foot still in place but with the heel raised and the ball of the foot bearing just enough weight to maintain balance. Analyze the joint action that has taken place at each hip joint.

4. Analyze the joint action of each hip joint in each phase of riding a bicycle.

   Muscular Action.   (See Appendix D for muscle check list.) Identify as many muscles as possible in the following experiments.

5. HIP FLEXION
   a. *Subject:* Sit on table with legs hanging over edge. Raise thigh.
      Assistant: Resist movement slightly by pressing down on knee.
      Observer: Palpate pectineus, tensor fasciae latae, sartorius, rectus femoris and adductor longus. Does the gracilis contract?
   b. *Subject:* Lie on one side, rolled toward face. Flex thigh of top leg, allowing knee to flex passively.
      Assistant: Resist movement by pushing against knee.
      Observer: Palpate iliopsoas.

6. HIP EXTENSION
   a. *Subject:* Stand facing table with trunk bent forward until it rests on table. Grasp sides of table. Raise one leg, keeping the knee straight.
      Assistant: Resist movement by pushing down on thigh close to knee. Second time, give resistance at heel.
      Observer: Palpate gluteus maximus, adductor magnus and hamstrings.
   b. *Subject:* Lie face down on table and raise one leg with knee straight.
      Assistant: Resist movement by pushing down on knee.
      Observer: Palpate same muscles as in a.

7. HIP ABDUCTION
      Subject: Lie on one side and raise top leg.
      Assistant: Resist movement by pushing down on knee.
      Observer: Palpate gluteus maximus, gluteus medius and tensor fasciae latae.

8. HIP ADDUCTION
      Subject: Lie on one side with top leg raised; then lower it.
      Assistant: Resist movement by pressing up against knee.
      Note: Unless resistance is applied, the action will be performed by means of the eccentric contraction of the abductors.
      Observer: Palpate three adductors and name them.

9. Outward Rotation of Thigh

Subject: Stand on one foot with the other knee bent at right angles so that the lower leg extends horizontally backward. Rotate the free thigh outward by swinging the foot medially.

Assistant: Steady subject's knee and resist movement of leg at ankle.

Observer: Palpate gluteus maximus.

10. Inward Rotation of Thigh

Subject: Stand on one foot with other knee bent at right angles so that the lower leg extends horizontally backward. Rotate the free thigh inward by swinging the foot laterally.

Assistant: Steady subject's knee and resist movement of leg at ankle.

Observer: Palpate gluteus medius, tensor fasciae latae and lower adductor magnus.

REFERENCES

1. Advisory Committee on Artificial Limbs, National Research Council: The Pattern of Muscular Activity in the Lower Extremity During Walking. Berkeley, Cal., Prosthetic Devices Research Project, Institute of Engineering Research, University of California. Series II, 1953.
2. Basmajian, J. V.: Muscles Alive, 3rd Ed. Baltimore: The Williams & Wilkins Company, 1974.
3. Crane, L.: Femoral torsion and its relation to toeing-in and toeing-out. J. Bone & Joint Surg., 41A:421–428, 1959.
4. Elftman, H.: Torsion of the lower extremity. Am. J. Phys. Anthrop., 3 (new series): 255–265, 1945.
5. Fischer, F. J., and Houtz, S. J.: Evaluation of the function of the gluteus maximus muscle. Am. J. Phys. Med., 47:182–191, 1968.
6. Klafs, C. E., and Arnheim, D. D.: Modern Principles of Athletic Training. St. Louis: C. V. Mosby Co., 1973.
7. LaBan, M. M., Raptou, A. D., and Johnson, E. W.: Electromyographic study of function of iliopsoas muscle. Arch. Phys. Med. & Rehab., 46:676–679, 1965.
8. MacConaill, M. A., and Basmajian, J. V.: Muscles and Movements. Baltimore: The Williams & Wilkins Co., 1969.
9. Merrifield, H. H.: An electromyographic study of the gluteus maximus, the vastus lateralis and the tensor fasciae latae. Diss. Abstr., 21:1833, 1961.
10. O'Donoghue, D. H.: Treatment of Injuries to Athletes, 3rd Ed. Philadelphia: W. B. Saunders Company, 1976.
11. Steindler, A.: Kinesiology of the Human Body. Springfield, Ill.: Charles C Thomas, Publisher, 1970.
12. Wheatley, M. D., and Jahnke, W. D.: Electromyographic study of the superficial thigh and hip muscles in normal individuals. Arch. Phys. Ther., 31:508–522, 1951.
13. Wright, W. G.: Muscle Function. New York: Hafner Publishing Company, 1962.

RECOMMENDED READINGS

Inman, V. T.: Functional aspects of the abductor muscles of the hip. J. Bone & Joint Surg., 29A:607–619, 1947.
Mendler, H. M.: Relationship of hip abductor muscles to posture. J. Am. Phys. Ther. Assn., 44:98–102, 1964.

Chapter Seven

THE LOWER EXTREMITY: THE KNEE, ANKLE AND FOOT

THE KNEE JOINT

The knee joint is a masterpiece of anatomic engineering. Placed midway in each supporting column of the body, it is subject to severe stresses and strains in its combined functions of weight-bearing and locomotion. As Steindler has pointed out, it meets the requirements made of it with remarkable efficiency.[11] To take care of the weight-bearing stresses it has massive condyles; to facilitate locomotion it has a wide range of motion; to resist the lateral stresses due to the tremendous lever effect of the long femur and tibia, it is reinforced at the sides by strong ligaments; to combat the downward pull of gravity and to meet the demands of such violent locomotor activities as running and jumping, it is provided with powerful musculature. It would be difficult indeed, to find a mechanism better adapted for meeting the combined requirements of stability and mobility than the knee joint.

In this connection, however, mention should be made of two forms of malalignment at the knee joint, one of which is common. These are the conditions popularly known as "knock-knees" and "bowlegs." In "knock-knees" (genu valgum) the knees are closer to the midline of the body than is normal. In the standing position the knees are closer together than the feet, so that when the feet are placed side by side, the knees are either pressed together or are slightly overlapping with one behind the other. Mechanically, the condition means that the weight-bearing line of the lower extremity passes lateral to the center of the knee joint. This puts the medial ligament (tibial collateral) under increased tension and subjects the lateral meniscus to increased pressure and friction. Such a joint is an unstable one. Not only is it more prone to injury than a well-aligned joint, but in all weight-bearing positions postural strains are constantly present. The condition of "bowlegs" (genu varum) is just the reverse of "knock-knees," with the additional complication of the long bones themselves being curved laterally.

Structure. Although the knee is classified as a hinge joint, its bony structure resembles two ovoid or condyloid joints lying side by side, yet not quite parallel. (See Fig. 7–1.) The lateral flexion which is permitted in a single ovoid joint is not possible in the knee joint because of the presence of the second

160

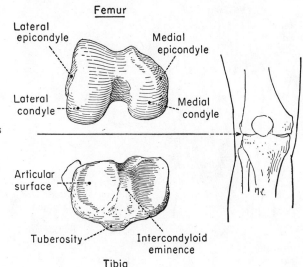

Figure 7-1 Articulating surfaces of knee joint.

condyle. The two rocker-like condyles of the femur rest on the two slightly concave areas on the top of the tibia's broad head. These articular surfaces of the tibia are separated by a roughened area, called the intercondyloid eminence, which terminates both anteriorly and posteriorly in a slight hollow, but rises at the center to form two small tubercles not unlike miniature twin mountain peaks (Fig. 7–2). The medial articular surface is oval; the lateral is smaller and more nearly round. Each is overlaid by a somewhat crescent-shaped fibro-cartilage, known as a semilunar cartilage or meniscus.

The lower end of the femur terminates in the two rocker-like condyles already mentioned. The lateral condyle is broader and more prominent than the medial. The medial condyle projects downward farther than the lateral.

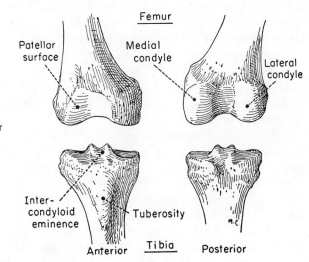

Figure 7-2 Anterior and posterior views of bones of knee joint.

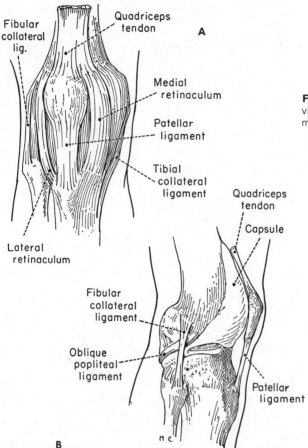

Figure 7-3 Anterior and lateral views of knee joint showing ligaments.

This, however, is evident only when a disarticulated femur is held vertically. In its normal position in the body the femur slants inward from above downward. This slant is known as the obliquity of the femoral shaft. Observation of the mounted skeleton will show that the downward projection of the medial condyle compensates for the obliquity of the femoral shaft.

Another interesting feature of the condyles is that they are not quite parallel. While the lateral condyle lies in the sagittal plane, the medial condyle slants slightly medially from front to back. This is an important factor in the movements of the knee.

Anteriorly, the two condyles are continuous with the smooth, slightly concave surface of the patellar facet for the articulation of the patella. The patella, or knee cap, is a large sesamoid bone located slightly above and in front of the knee joint. It is held in place by the quadriceps tendon above, by the patellar ligament below and by the intervening fibers which form a pocket for the patella (Fig. 7-3).

The articular cavity is enclosed within a loose membranous capsule which lies under the patella and folds around each condyle but which excludes the

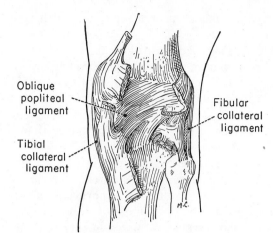

Figure 7-4 Posterior view of knee joint showing popliteal and collateral ligaments.

intercondyloid tubercles and the cruciate ligaments. It is supplemented by expansions from the fascia lata, iliotibial tract and various tendons. The oblique popliteal ligament covers the posterior surface of the joint completely, shielding the cruciate ligaments and other structures not enclosed within the capsule (Fig. 7-4).

The synovial membrane of the knee joint is the most extensive of any in the body. It folds in and around the joint in a manner far too complicated to attempt to describe here. There are numerous bursae in the vicinity of the knee joint, among the largest and most important being the prepatellar, infrapatellar and suprapatellar bursae.

The Semilunar Cartilages. (Fig. 7-5.) These cartilages, or menisci as they are called, are somewhat circular rims of fibrocartilage, situated on the articular surfaces of the head of the tibia. They are relatively thick at their peripheral borders, but taper to a thin edge at their inner circumferences. Thus they deepen the articular facets of the tibia and, at the same time, serve in a shock absorbing capacity. The inner edges are free, but the peripheral borders are attached loosely to the rim of the head of the tibia by fibers from the inner surface of the capsule.

The lateral semilunar cartilage forms an incomplete circle, conforming closely to the nearly round articular facet. Its anterior and posterior horns,

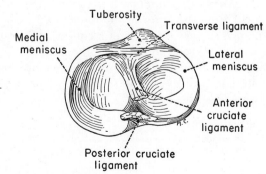

Figure 7-5 The menisci (semilunar cartilages) of the knee joint.

which almost meet at the center of the joint, are attached to the intercondyloid eminence.

The medial cartilage is shaped like a large letter C, broader toward the rear than in front. Its anterior horn tapers off to a thin strand which is attached to the anterior intercondyloid fossa. It is not so freely movable as the lateral cartilage because of its secure anchorage to the tibial collateral ligament at the medial side of the knee. Largely because of this point of attachment, the medial cartilage is more frequently injured than the lateral.

Ligaments of the Knee*

PATELLAR LIGAMENT. (Fig. 7–3.) This is a strong flat ligament connecting the lower margin of the patella with the tuberosity of the tibia. Passing over the front of the patella, the superficial fibers are continuations of the central fibers of the quadriceps femoris tendon.

COLLATERAL TIBIAL LIGAMENT. (Figs. 7–3, *A*, 7–4 and 7–6.) This is a broad, flat, membranous band on the medial side of the joint. It is attached above to the medial epicondyle of the femur below the adductor tubercle, and below to the medial condyle of the tibia. It is firmly attached to the medial meniscus. This fact should be noted because of its significance in knee injuries. It serves to check extension and to prevent motion laterally.

COLLATERAL FIBULAR LIGAMENT. (Figs. 7–3, 7–4 and 7–6.) This is a strong, rounded cord, attached above to the back of the lateral epicondyle of the femur and below to the lateral surface of the head of the fibula. It serves to check extension and to prevent motion medially.

OBLIQUE POPLITEAL LIGAMENT. (Figs. 7–3, *B*, and 7–4.) This is a broad, flat ligament, covering the back of the knee joint. It is attached above to the upper margin of the intercondyloid fossa and posterior surface of the femur and below to the posterior margin of the head of the tibia. Medially, it blends with the tendon of the semimembranosus muscle and laterally with the lateral head of the gastrocnemius.

THE CRUCIATE LIGAMENTS. (Fig. 7–6.) These are two strong, cordlike ligaments situated within the knee joint, although not enclosed within the joint capsule. They are called cruciate from the fact that they cross each other and are further designated anterior and posterior, according to their attachments to the tibia. They serve to check certain movements at the knee joint. They limit extension and prevent rotation in the extended position. They also check the forward and backward sliding of the femur on the tibia, thus safeguarding the anteroposterior stability of the knee.

ANTERIOR CRUCIATE LIGAMENT. (Fig. 7–6.) This passes upward and backward from the anterior intercondyloid fossa of the tibia to the back part of the medial surface of the lateral condyle of the femur.

POSTERIOR CRUCIATE LIGAMENT. (Fig. 7–6.) This is a shorter and stronger ligament than the anterior. It passes upward and forward from the posterior intercondyloid fossa of the tibia to the lateral and front part of the medial condyle of the femur.

---

*Detailed descriptions of individual ligaments are included here because of their importance to a good understanding of the complex injuries experienced by this joint.

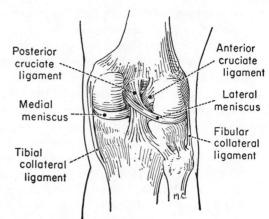

Figure 7-6 Posterior view of knee joint showing cruciate ligaments.

TRANSVERSE LIGAMENT. (Fig. 7-5.)   This is a short, slender cordlike ligament, connecting the anterior convex margin of the lateral meniscus to the anterior end of the medial meniscus.

THE ILIOTIBIAL TRACT. (Figs. 6-7 and 6-8.)   The iliotibial tract is said to act like a tense ligament which connects the iliac crest with the lateral femoral condyle and the lateral tubercle of the tibia. At the knee joint the tract serves as a stabilizing ligament between the lateral condyle of the femur and the tibia. The attachment to the femoral condyle is then a fixed point and the distal end moves forward in knee extension and backward in knee flexion.[4]

Movements.   The movements which occur at the knee joint are primarily flexion and extension. A slight amount of rotation can take place when the knee is in the flexed position and the foot is not supporting the weight.

FLEXION AND EXTENSION.   The movements of flexion and extension at the knee are not so simple as are those of a true hinge joint. This can be demonstrated in the classroom by holding a disarticulated femur and tibia together in a position of extension, then, holding the tibia stationary, flexing the femur on the tibia as though the individual were assuming a squat or sitting position. If no other adjustment is made, the femoral condyles will roll back completely off the top of the tibia. What prevents this in real life is the fact that as the condyles roll backward they simultaneously glide forward and thus remain in contact with the menisci throughout each phase of the movement. Conversely, when the femur extends on the tibia, the forward roll of the femoral condyles is accompanied by a backward glide.

Because the femoral condyles are not quite parallel and differ in size, a slight degree of rotation occurs during the initial phase of flexion and the final phase of extension. This can be readily seen on the living subject if he stands with the knees slightly flexed and then extends them completely. The patellae are seen to turn slightly medialward, indicating slight inward rotation of the thighs. Because of the inequality of the two condyles, the medial condyle continues to roll forward after the lateral condyle has ceased its movement. The inward rotation of the femur which accompanies the completion of extension is commonly known as "locking" the knees. In persons who tend to hyper-extend their knees habitually the rotation is more pronounced.

When the leg is flexed or extended in a non-weight-bearing position, the tibia rotates on the femur, instead of vice versa. The final phase of extension is accompanied by slight outward rotation of the tibia. At the beginning of flexion the tibia rotates inward until the mid-position is attained.[9]

The rotation which occurs in the final stage of extension and the initial phase of flexion is an inherent part of these movements and should not be confused with the voluntary rotation that can be performed when the leg is not bearing weight and the knee is in a flexed position.

INWARD AND OUTWARD ROTATION IN THE FLEXED POSITION.   When the leg has been flexed at the knee to a right angle and beyond, it is possible to rotate the leg on the thigh through a total range of about 50 degrees. This can occur, however, only when the leg is not bearing the body weight. It is impossible, for instance, to rotate either the leg or the thigh in this manner when the body is in a stooping position. A good way to demonstrate rotation of the tibia is to sit on a chair with the heel resting lightly on the floor. In this position, with the knee and thigh held motionless, the foot should be turned first in and then out. The action will be that of inward and outward rotation of the tibia. The movement taking place within the foot itself should be discounted.

Muscles.   The muscles acting on the knee joint are classified as anterior or posterior according to the relation of their distal tendons to the transverse axis of the joint.

Anterior	*Posterior*
Quadriceps femoris group	Hamstring group
Rectus femoris	Biceps femoris
Vastus intermedius	Semimembranosus
Vastus lateralis	Semitendinosus
Vastus medialis	Sartorius
	Gracilis
	Popliteus
	Gastrocnemius

CHARACTERISTICS AND FUNCTIONS OF INDIVIDUAL MUSCLES*

Biceps Femoris. (Figs. 6–11 and 7–7.) (Also listed with the hip muscles.) This is the lateral hamstring muscle. It consists of two heads, the long head which comes from the tuberosity of the ischium and the short head which originates from the linea aspera on the posterior surface of the thigh. The two join at the distal tendon close to the lateral condyle of the femur, not far above the tendon's attachment to the head of the fibula. It is an important *flexor of the knee.*

---

*Listed in alphabetical order.

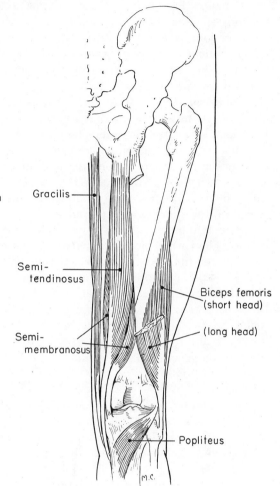

Figure 7-7 Posterior muscles of thigh and knee.

Gracilis

Semi-tendinosus

Biceps femoris (short head)

(long head)

Semi-membranosus

Popliteus

M.C.

When the knee is flexed and not bearing weight, *the biceps can rotate the lower leg outward.* Its tendon may be palpated behind the knee on its lateral aspect.

Gastrocnemius. (Fig. 7-20.) (Also listed with the ankle muscles.)   This large calf muscle, although primarily a muscle of the ankle joint, has an important function at the knee joint. It is in a position to help *flex the knee* and does so when the leg is not bearing weight. However, according to Wright, its most important function at the knee is serving as a *posterior ligament* to protect the joint in movements involving violent extension, as in running and jumping.[13]

Hollingshead makes the interesting observation that when the foot is fixed in weight-bearing, *the gastrocnemius can help to maintain knee extension.*[3] It does this when the hip and knee are in strong extension and when plantar flexion of the ankle is inhibited. Under these circumstances the *gastrocnemius* is able to pull back and down on the femoral condyles, thus contributing to knee extension. The muscle is easy to palpate, including both the muscle belly in the calf and the tendon behind the ankle.

Gracilis. (Figs. 6–6, 7–7 and 7–9.) (Also listed with the hip muscles.)   This is a long slender muscle situated on the medial aspect of the thigh. Its action at the knee joint is *flexion.* It also aids in *inward rotation of the tibia when the knee is in a flexed position and the foot is not bearing weight.* It may be palpated on the medial aspect of the posterior surface of the knee, anterior to the semitendinosus tendon, but close to it.

Hamstring Group. (Figs. 6–11 and 6–12.) (Also listed with the hip muscles.) The hamstrings, so named from their large, cordlike tendons behind the knee joint, consist of the biceps femoris, semimembranosus and semitendinosus muscles. Although the biceps femoris constitutes the lateral hamstring, its long head lies approximately along the midline of the posterior aspect of the thigh, as far down as the popliteal space. At about this level the two heads unite to form their common tendon of attachment. The long head is fusiform in construction; the short head is penniform.

The semimembranosus and semitendinosus constitute the medial hamstrings. The former lies deeper than the latter and attaches higher on the tibia. The semitendinosus is attached to the medial surface of the tibia below the head, just below the attachment of the gracilis and behind that of the sartorius.

Although the hamstrings act at both the knees and the hips, their primary function is *knee flexion.* Wright called attention to the usefulness of the hamstrings in preventing hyperextension at the knee, and in unlocking the knee (i.e., reducing hyperextension) when one is returning from a position in which the line of gravity falls in front of the knee joints (e.g., inclining the trunk forward without bending the knees.)[13] Nearly everyone is familiar with the limiting effect of the hamstrings. The difficulty experienced by many people in touching the toes with the fingers without bending the knees and in sitting erect on the floor with the legs extended straight forward is due to the fact that the hamstrings are frequently not long enough to permit such extreme stretching at the hips and knees simultaneously.

Popliteus. (Fig. 7–7.)   This *rotates the tibia inward* and *helps to flex the knee.* In structure and function it resembles the pronator teres muscle of the elbow. In a subject who is standing, it "unlocks" the knee joint preliminary to flexion. It also helps to protect and stabilize the knee joint when a squatting position is assumed and maintained.[1]

Quadriceps Femoris Group. (Figs. 7–3, 7–8 and 7–9.)   This consists of the rectus femoris and the vasti: vastus intermedius, vastus lateralis and vastus medialis. Of these, only the rectus femoris, the most superficial of the four, crosses the hip joint. The vastus intermedius lies posterior to the rectus and is completely covered by it. The distal portions of the four muscles unite to form a single broad, flat tendon which attaches to the base of the patella, the base being the upper border. In some texts this is given as the distal attachment of the quadriceps group with no further explanation. If this ended the matter, one would wonder how muscles which did not cross the knee joint could extend it. Obviously, the patellar ligament which connects the patella with the tuberosity of the tibia is a vital part of the quadriceps femoris. Actually, the patella is a sesamoid bone which is encased within the quadriceps tendon, the patellar ligament being but a continuation of this and the tibial tuberosity being the true distal point of attachment. All four muscles extend the leg at the knee joint.

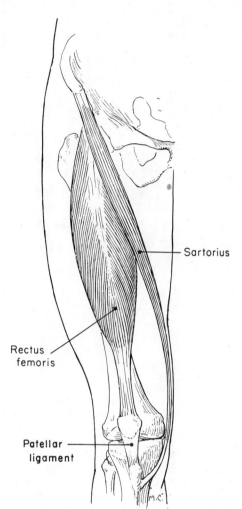

Figure 7-8   Front of thigh showing rectus femoris and sartorius muscles.

Sartorius

Rectus femoris

Patellar ligament

The vastus lateralis and vastus medialis, with their fibers converging toward the patella, together with the vastus intermedius and rectus femoris, with their longitudinal approach, serve to steady the knee joint in all weight-bearing positions and to maintain a balanced tension on the patella. As the three vasti are one-joint muscles, they are *powerful knee extensors,* regardless of the position of the hip joint. They are responsible for completing the last part of knee extension. When the knee is fully extended, static contraction of the quadriceps serves to pull up or "set" the patella, a mild exercise used in physical therapy. These muscles are not active in ordinary standing.[1]

Pocock concluded from his EMG investigation of the quadriceps muscles that they function as a unit and do not have any particular timing pattern as had been previously suggested.[1]

Rectus Femoris. (Fig. 7-8.) (Also listed with the hip muscles.)   This is of bipenniform structure with all except the lowest fibers slanting obliquely downward and sideward from the central tendon and the lowest fibers being

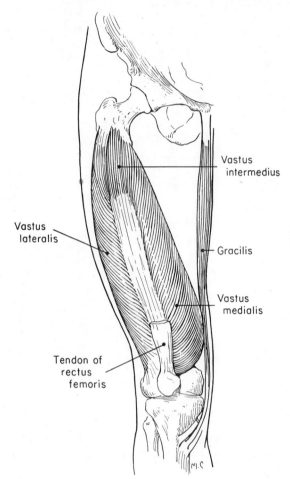

Vastus
intermedius

Vastus
lateralis

Gracilis

Vastus
medialis

Tendon of
rectus
femoris

Figure 7–9   Front of thigh showing the
three vasti muscles and the gracilis.

approximately vertical. The upper three-quarters of the muscle consist of muscle
fibers, the last quarter, down to the base of the patella, being the muscle's distal
tendon. The muscle may be palpated on the central-anterior surface of the thigh.

Vastus Lateralis. (Fig. 7–9.)   The majority of the fibers slant downward
and medialward to the tendon. The muscle may be palpated on the anterolateral
aspect of the thigh, lateral to the rectus femoris.

Vastus Medialis. (Fig. 7–9.)   The majority of fibers slant downward and
lateralward to the tendon, the lowest ones being almost horizontal in direction.
If the lateralis and medialis were looked upon as one muscle, it would be considered of bipenniform construction, with the fibers slanting in direct opposition to those of the rectus femoris. The fleshy part of both the medialis and
lateralis extends down almost to the level of the base of the patella. The vastus
medialis may be palpated on the anteromedial aspect of the lower third of the
thigh, medial to the rectus femoris.

Sartorius. (Fig. 7–8.) (Also listed with the hip muscles.)   This is a long,
slender, ribbon-like muscle, superficially located and directed obliquely down-

ward and medialward across the front of the thigh. On its way to its distal attachment it curves around behind the bulge of the medial condyles in such a way that its line of pull is posterior to the axis of the knee joint. Thus, in spite of the fact that at least two-thirds of the muscle, including both its proximal and distal attachments, lie on the anterior aspect of the lower extremity, its action at the knee joint is not extension, but *flexion*. It also assists in *inward rotation of the tibia when the knee is flexed*. Its line of pull is determined by the direction of its distal tendon between the latter's point of contact with the medial condyle of the tibia and its attachment to the upper anteromedial surface of the tibial shaft, almost as far forward as the anterior crest. It may be palpated at the anterior superior iliac spine, as well as along its entire length where it is clearly visible on a thin, well-muscled subject.

Semimembranosus and Semitendinosus. (Fig. 7–7.) (Also listed with the hip muscles.)   These are the two medial hamstring muscles and, like the biceps femoris, they *flex the knee joint*. When the leg is flexed without bearing weight, these muscles can *rotate it inward*. The semitendinosus may be palpated on the medial aspect of the posterior surface of the knee. The tendon of the semimembranosus is almost impossible to palpate successfully as it is shorter than its partner and is partially covered by the latter as well as by the gracilis tendon.

MUSCULAR ANALYSIS OF THE FUNDAMENTAL MOVEMENTS OF THE LEG AT THE KNEE JOINT

FLEXION.   The knee joint has five important flexors, namely, the three hamstring muscles (biceps femoris, semimembranosus and semitendinosus), the sartorius and the gracilis; the latter is especially important during the early part of flexion, provided that the knee is not flexing simultaneously. Two additional muscles that help with flexion are the popliteus and the gastrocnemius.

It should be remembered that when the weight is borne by the feet and the knees are allowed to flex as in stooping, the knee flexors are not responsible for the movement. The flexion is produced by the force of gravity and is controlled by the extensor muscles which are contracting eccentrically, that is, in lengthening contraction.

EXTENSION.   This is performed by the four muscles that make up the quadriceps femoris group: the rectus femoris, vastus intermedius, vastus lateralis and vastus medialis.

Muscles sometimes act in surprising ways. A good example of this is the action of the gastrocnemius at the knee when the weight is on the feet. When the weight is not on the foot, the gastrocnemius is an assistant flexor of the knee. Its primary function is extension (plantar flexion) of the ankle joint. When the foot is bearing weight, flexion of the knee cannot take place unless the ankle is dorsiflexing at the same time. If this dorsiflexion is prevented, the weight-bearing knee is unable to flex. Under these circumstances the gastrocnemius contracts in what might be called the reverse direction, that is, it acts on its proximal attachments and pulls backward and downward on the femoral condyles, and with the foot fixed, this contributes to knee extension. It is because of such reversals as this that it is not desirable for a student to memorize muscular actions. The circumstances under which the movement is performed are of vital importance.

Outward Rotation of the Tibia. This is performed by the biceps femoris. It can only occur when the knee is flexed in a non-weight-bearing situation.

Inward Rotation of the Tibia. This is performed chiefly by the semi-membranosus, semitendinosus and popliteus, with possible help from the gracilis and sartorius. As with outward rotation, it can occur only when the knee is flexed and the foot is not bearing weight.

THE ANKLE AND THE FOOT

The foot has two functions of great importance — support and propulsion. In studying the structure of the foot, these functions should be kept constantly in mind, for only by seeing the foot in terms of the combined static and dynamic demands made upon it can one fully appreciate its intricate mechanism.

The foot is united with the leg at the ankle joint. Within the foot itself are the seven tarsal bones. Two of the joints in this region are of sufficient importance to the kinesiologist to merit special attention. These are the subtalar and midtarsal joints, the latter including the talonavicular and calcaneocuboid articulations. The movements within the foot occur mainly at these two joints.

The structure of the ankle, the tarsal joints and the toes will be described separately, but the muscles of these three regions will be discussed together as many of them act on more than one joint.

Structure of the Ankle. (Figs. 7–10, 7–11 and 7–12.) The ankle is a hinge joint. It is formed by the articulation of the talus (astragalus) with the malleoli of the tibia and the fibula. The latter bones, bound together by the transverse tibiofibular ligament, the anterior and posterior ligaments of the lateral malle-

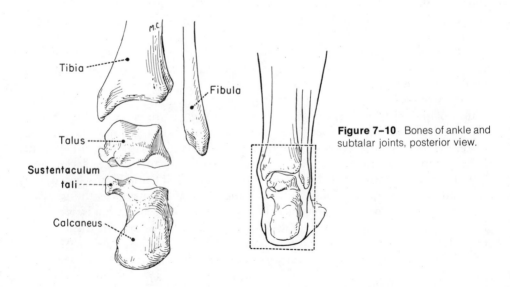

Tibia

Fibula

Talus

Sustentaculum tali

Calcaneus

Figure 7–10 Bones of ankle and subtalar joints, posterior view.

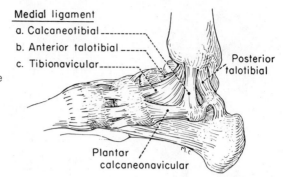

Medial ligament
a. Calcaneotibial
b. Anterior talotibial
c. Tibionavicular
Posterior talotibial
Plantar calcaneonavicular

Figure 7–11   Medial ligaments of ankle joint.

olus and the interossei, constitute a mortise into which the upper, rounded portion of the talus fits. The joint is surrounded by a thin, membranous capsule which is thicker on the medial side of the joint. In the back it is a thin mesh of membranous tissue and is not continuous as are most capsules. It is reinforced by several strong ligaments.

Ligamentous Reinforcement. (Figs. 7–11, 7–12 and 7–15.)   The medial side of the ankle joint is protected by five strong ligamentous bands, four of them connecting the medial malleolus of the tibia with posterior, tarsal bones: calcaneus, talus and navicular. The fifth band provides a horizontal connection between the navicular bone and the sustentaculum tali projection on the medial aspect of the calcaneus.

The lateral side of the ankle is reinforced by three ligaments which connect, respectively, the lateral malleolus with the upper lateral aspect of the calcaneus and with anterior and posterior portions of the talus. Inspection of the two Figures, 7–11 and 7–12, gives one the impression that the lateral side of the ankle is less protected than the medial. If this is true, it might be a factor in the high incidence of ankle sprains.

Structure of the Foot. (Figs. 7–13 and 7–14.)   The foot as a whole is usually described as an elastic arched structure, the keystone of the arch being the talus. This bone has several marks of distinction. Aside from being the connecting

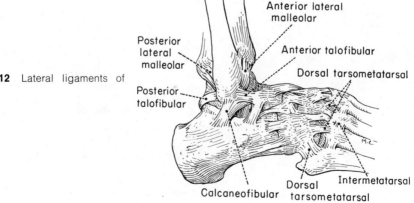

Anterior lateral malleolar
Posterior lateral malleolar
Anterior talofibular
Dorsal tarsometatarsal
Posterior talofibular
Intermetatarsal
Calcaneofibular
Dorsal tarsometatarsal

Figure 7–12   Lateral ligaments of ankle joint.

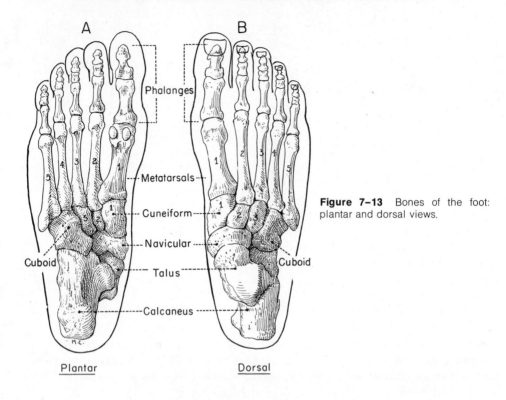

Figure 7-13 Bones of the foot: plantar and dorsal views.

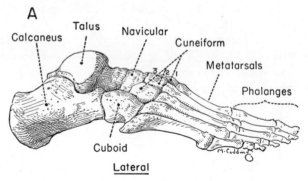

Figure 7-14 Bones of the foot: lateral and medial views.

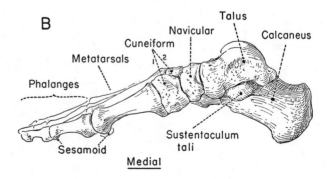

link between the foot and the leg, it is distinguished by having no muscles attached to it and by receiving and transmitting the weight of the entire body (with the exception of the foot itself), a function which requires great strength and firm support.

The foot has two arches, a longitudinal and a transverse. The longitudinal arch extends from the heel to the heads of the five metatarsals. It is sometimes described as made up of an inner and an outer component. The outer component includes the calcaneus, cuboid and fourth and fifth metatarsals (Fig. 7–14, *A*.). The inner component consists of the calcaneus, talus, navicular, three cuneiforms and the three medial metatarsals (Fig. 7–14, *B*.). The outer component has a nearly flat contour and lacks mobility; hence, it is better adapted to the function of support, whereas the inner component with its greater flexibility and its curving arch is adapted to the function of shock absorption, so important in all forms of locomotion. Contrary to popular opinion, the height of the longitudinal arch is not indicative of the strength of the arch. Thus a low arch is not necessarily a weak one, *provided it is not associated with a pronated (i.e., abducted and everted) foot.*

The transverse arch is the side-to-side concavity on the underside of the foot formed by the anterior tarsal bones and the metatarsals. The anterior boundary of this arch under the metatarsal heads is known as the metatarsal arch. There is some disagreement as to whether this should be called an arch, since it flattens completely when bearing weight. The metatarsal arch exists, therefore, only in non-weight-bearing situations.

The toes, especially the large and powerful "big toes," are largely responsible for propulsion. They provide the push-off at the end of the step. Their use in locomotion is directly proportional to the vigor and speed of the walk or run.

The strength and elasticity of the foot are due in large measure to the ligaments which bind the bones together and to the muscles which work to preserve the balance of the foot. Thus both ligaments and muscles share the responsibility for maintaining the integrity of the arches.

SUBTALAR JOINT. (Fig. 7–15.)   This is the joint between the underside of the talus and the upper and anterior aspects of the calcaneus or heel bone. It is reinforced by four small talocalcaneal ligaments. A fifth ligament, the *plantar calcaneonavicular,* is probably the most important of all. It is a broad, thick ligament which connects the sustentaculum tali projection of the calcaneus with the underside of the navicular bone. It passes under the talus and aids in supporting it. It is actually part of the subtalar joint, as it contains a fibrocartilaginous facet which is lined with synovial membrane. This is commonly called the *spring ligament* because of the yellow elastic fibers which give it its elasticity. The importance of this ligament can be readily seen when one remembers that the talus receives the weight of the entire body. The shock absorbing function of this elastic support is obvious. It is probably equally obvious that excessive prolonged pressure on this ligament through improper use of the feet will cause it to stretch permanently and thus result in a lowered arch.

Unfortunately Figure 7–15, *B* gives a somewhat misleading picture of this ligament. Though it looks like a cord-shaped ligament on the medial aspect of the ankle, the part that shows in the picture is actually just the medial border of a broad ligament which extends beneath the head of the talus like a taut hammock.

A

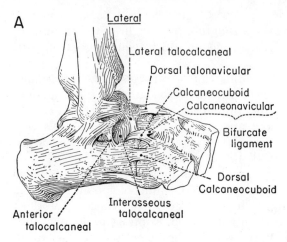

Lateral

Lateral talocalcaneal

Dorsal talonavicular

Calcaneocuboid

Calcaneonavicular

Bifurcate ligament

Dorsal Calcaneocuboid

Interosseous talocalcaneal

Anterior talocalcaneal

Figure 7-15   Ligaments of tarsal joints.

B

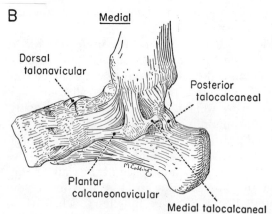

Medial

Dorsal talonavicular

Posterior talocalcaneal

Plantar calcaneonavicular

Medial talocalcaneal

MIDTARSAL JOINT (TRANSVERSE TARSAL; CHOPART'S).   This consists of two articulations, the lateral one being the calcaneocuboid joint and the medial one, the talonavicular. On looking down on these from above, the continuous line of articulation—the talonavicular and calcaneocuboid—is seen to form a somewhat shallow letter S (Figs. 7–13, B and 7–16). The talonavicular joint is a modified ball-and-socket joint and permits somewhat restricted movements about three axes. The calcaneocuboid joint is non-axial and permits only slight gliding motions. These seem to be supplementary or secondary to the freer motions of the talonavicular joint. There are several ligaments that reinforce these joints but the ones that give the most support are the *long and short plantar (calcaneocuboid) ligaments.* These are both wide, thick ligaments of great strength.

TARSOMETATARSAL JOINTS. (Fig. 7–17.)   These are non-axial joints, with the possible exception of the great toe joint which looks slightly like a saddle joint. The movements are of a gliding nature which resembles a restricted form of flexion, extension, abduction and adduction.

INTERMETATARSAL JOINTS. (Figs. 7–12 and 7–17.)   These include two sets of side-by-side articulations, those between the bases and those between the

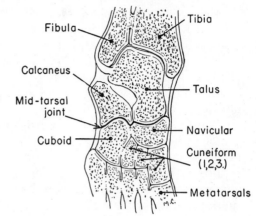

Figure 7–16 Oblique section of tarsal bones showing midtarsal joint.

heads of the metatarsal bones. They are all non-axial joints. The articulations between the heads of the metatarsal bones are an important part of the meta-tarsal arch. The total result of the movements occurring there is a spreading or flattening of the arch when the weight is on it and a return to its plantar con-cavity when the weight is taken off it.

METARTARSOPHALANGEAL JOINTS. (Fig. 7–17.)   These may best be described as a modified form of ovoid joint. The joint of the great toe differs from the others in that it is larger and has two sesamoid bones beneath it.

INTERPHALANGEAL JOINTS.   As is true of the fingers, these are all hinge joints.

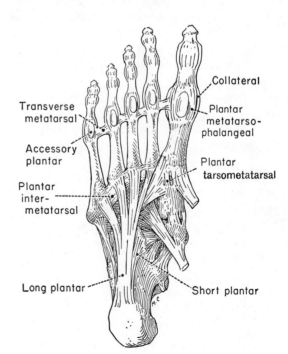

Figure 7–17 Plantar ligaments of foot.

Movements of the Foot at the Ankle, Tarsal and Toe Joints

ANKLE JOINT. The movements of the ankle joint occur about an axis which is usually described as frontal-horizontal, but which is actually slightly oblique, as evidenced by the slightly posterior position of the lateral malleolus relative to the medial. This is of minor significance but explains the tendency of the foot to turn out when it is fully elevated in dorsiflexion and to turn in when fully depressed in plantar flexion.

Dorsiflexion (flexion). A forward-upward movement of the foot in the sagittal plane, so that the dorsal surface of the foot approaches the anterior surface of the leg.

Plantar flexion (extension). A forward-downward movement of the foot in the sagittal plane, so that the dorsal surface of the foot moves away from the anterior surface of the leg.

TARSAL JOINTS. The movements that take place at the *midtarsal, subtalar* and other *tarsal* joints occur together and are usually closely related to the ankle joint movements. Except for the talonavicular joint which belongs to the ball-and-socket category, they are all non-axial joints and therefore permit only slight gliding movements.

Dorsiflexion. Slight decrease in convexity of dorsal surface and in concavity of plantar surface of tarsal region. Accompanies dorsiflexion of ankle.

Plantar flexion. Increase in convexity of dorsal surface and in concavity of plantar surface of tarsal region. Accompanies plantar flexion of ankle.

Inversion and adduction (supination). A lifting of the medial border of the arch combined with a medial bending of the front of the foot.

Eversion and abduction (pronation). A slight raising of the lateral border of the foot combined with a slight lateral bending of the front of the foot.

TARSOMETATARSAL AND INTERMETATARSAL JOINTS. Slight gliding motion. The first metatarsal bone has a slightly greater degree of motion at these joints than do the other metatarsals because of the absence of any ligament between its base and the base of the second metatarsal.

METATARSOPHALANGEAL JOINTS. Flexion, extension and limited abduction and adduction.

INTERPHALANGEAL JOINTS. Flexion and extension; also hyperextension, especially of the great toe.

Muscles. The muscles of the ankle and foot are classified below according to their location.

Anterior Aspect of Leg

Tibialis anterior
Extensor digitorum longus
Extensor hallucis longus
Peroneus tertius

Posterior Aspect of Leg

Gastrocnemius
Soleus
Tibialis posterior
Flexor digitorum longus
Flexor hallucis longus

Lateral Aspect of Leg

Peroneus longus
Peroneus brevis

(See page 184 for a brief discussion of the intrinsic muscles of the foot.)

CHARACTERISTICS AND FUNCTIONS OF
INDIVIDUAL MUSCLES*

Extensor Digitorum Longus. (Figs. 7–18, *B* and 7–22.)   This *extends the four lesser toes.* It also *dorsiflexes both the ankle and the tarsal joints* and *helps to evert and abduct the latter.* It is a penniform muscle and is situated lateral to the tibialis anterior muscle in the upper part of the leg and lateral to the extensor hallucis longus in the lower part. Just in front of the ankle joint the tendon divides into four tendons, one for each of the lesser toes. The muscle may be palpated on the anterior surface of the ankle and the dorsal surface of the foot, lateral to the tendon of the extensor hallucis longus.

Extensor Hallucis Longus. (Fig. 7–18, *A.*)   This *extends and hyperextends the great toe.* It also *dorsiflexes the tarsal joints and helps to dorsiflex the ankle.* Like the

*Listed in alphabetical order.

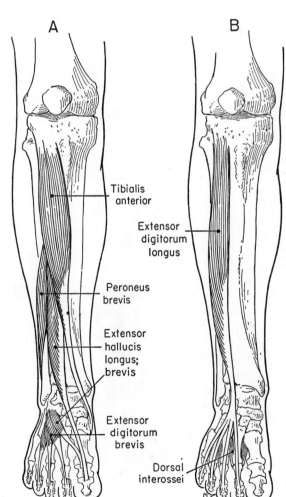

Figure 7–18   Anterior muscles of the leg.

A

B

Tibialis anterior

Extensor digitorum longus

Peroneus brevis

Extensor hallucis longus; brevis

Extensor digitorum brevis

Dorsal interossei

preceding muscle, this is penniform in structure. Its upper portion lies beneath the tibialis anterior and extensor digitorum longus, but about halfway down the leg the tendon emerges between these two muscles, thus becoming superficial. After it reaches the ankle the tendon slants medially across the dorsal surface of the foot to the top of the great toe. It may be palpated on the dorsal surface of the foot and great toe.

Flexor Digitorum Longus. (Fig. 7–19.)   This *flexes the four lesser toes, plantar flexes and helps to invert and adduct the tarsal joints* and *helps to plantar flex the ankle.* The muscle is situated on the medial side of the back of the leg behind the tibia. It is penniform in structure. Its distal tendon passes behind the medial malleolus between the tendons of tibialis posterior and flexor hallucis longus. Beneath the tarsal bones it divides into four tendons which go to the distal phalanx of each of the four lesser toes.

Flexor Hallucis Longus. (Fig. 7–19.)   This *flexes the great toe, plantar flexes and helps to invert and adduct the tarsal joints* and *helps to plantar flex the ankle.* It is situated on the lateral side of the back of the leg behind the fibula and the

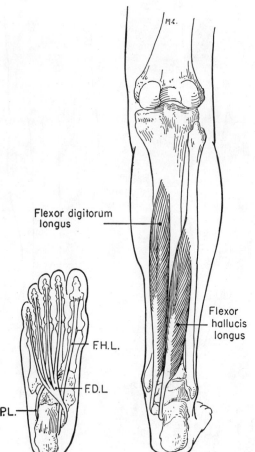

Flexor digitorum longus

Flexor hallucis longus

F.H.L.

F.D.L

P.L.

M.c.

Figure 7–19   Flexor digitorum longus and flexor hallucis longus. (*F.H.L.* = Flex. hal. long.; *F.D.L.* = flex. dig. long.; *P.L.* = per. long.)

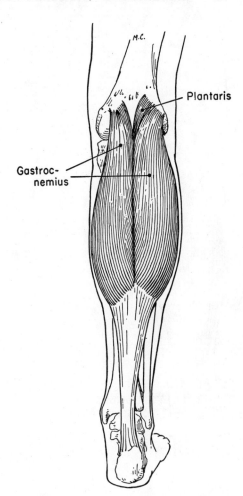

Figure 7–20   Gastrocnemius.

lateral portion of the tibia. The fibers unite with the distal tendon in a penni-form manner. The tendon crosses behind the ankle to the medial side, passes behind and beneath the sustentaculum tali, the projection on the medial side of the calcaneus, and runs forward under the medial margin of the foot to the distal phalanx of the great toe. It is the most posterior of the three tendons that pass behind the medial malleolus. One of its important functions is to provide the push-off in walking, running and jumping. It may be palpated on the medial border of the calcaneal tendon close to the calcaneus.

Gastrocnemius. (Fig. 7–20.) (Also listed with the knee muscles.)   This is a powerful muscle for *plantar flexing the foot at the ankle joint*. It is the most super-ficial muscle on the back of the leg and can be seen as two bulges in the upper part of the calf when it is well developed. Its two heads, together with the soleus, constitute the triceps surae. The lateral and medial portions of the muscle remain distinct from each other as far down as the middle of the back of the leg. Then they fuse to form the broad tendon of Achilles.

The most familiar function of this muscle is to *enable one to rise on the toes.*

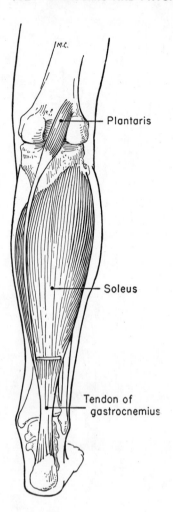

- Plantaris

- Soleus

Tendon of
gastrocnemius

Figure 7–21 Posterior muscles of the leg, middle layer.

Many anatomists have thought that it acted only when the movement was resisted, but an EMG investigation by Sheffield, Gersten and Mastellone revealed that it was active in unresisted *plantar flexion* in subjects lying in the supine position.[1] It has a large angle of pull, approximately 90 degrees when the foot is in its fundamental position. Its internal structure and its leverage combine to make it an exceedingly powerful muscle. In a 1967 EMG study Herman and Bragin concluded that its most important role was plantar flexing in large contractions and in the rapid development of tension.[1] It may be palpated in the calf of the leg and on the back of the ankle.

Peroneus Brevis. (Figs. 7–18, *A* and 7–22.) This *plantar flexes and everts and abducts the tarsal joints* and *helps to plantar flex the ankle*. It is a penniform muscle, lying beneath the peroneus longus on the lower half of the lateral aspect of the leg. Its tendon passes behind the lateral malleolus immediately anterior to the tendon of longus and continues forward just above the longus tendon to its attachment on the tuberosity of the fifth metatarsal, below the attachment of peroneus tertius. It may be palpated on the lateral margin of the foot, just posterior to the base of the fifth metatarsal.

Peroneus Longus. (Fig. 7–22.) This *plantar flexes, everts and abducts the tarsal joints,* and *plantar flexes the ankle.* It is situated superficially on the lateral aspect of the leg. Its distal tendon passes behind the lateral malleolus and proceeds forward and downward to the margin of the foot where it passes behind the tuberosity of the fifth metatarsal. At this point it turns under the foot, passes through the peroneal groove of the cuboid and slants forward across the plantar surface of the foot to its attachment at the base of the first metatarsal and first cuneiform, not far from the attachment of the tibialis anterior. The muscle belly may be palpated on the lateral surface of the upper half of the leg and the tendon on the lateral surface of the lower half of the leg and just above and behind the lateral malleolus.

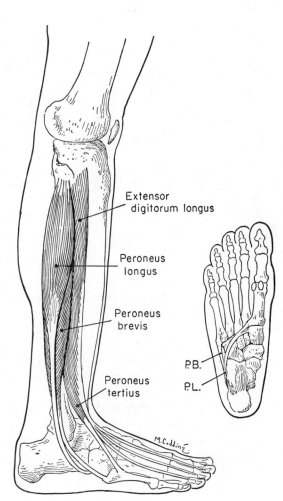

Figure 7–22 Lateral muscles of the leg. (*P.B.* = Peroneus brevis; *P.L.* = peroneus longus.)

Extensor
digitorum longus

Peroneus
longus

Peroneus
brevis

Peroneus
tertius

P.B.

P.L.

Peroneus Tertius. (Fig. 7–17.) This *dorsiflexes and pronates (everts and abducts) the tarsal joints* and *dorsiflexes the ankle.* It is a small muscle that lies lateral to the extensor digitorum longus and is sometimes described as the fifth tendon of the latter muscle. It may be palpated on the dorsal surface of the foot close to the base of the fifth metatarsal.

Soleus. (Fig. 7–21.) Like the gastrocnemius, this *plantar flexes the foot at the ankle joint.* It lies beneath the gastrocnemius, except along the lateral aspect of the lower half of the calf where a portion of it lies lateral to the upper part of the calcaneal tendon. Its fibers are inserted into the calcaneal tendon in a bipenniform manner. In an EMG study of the leg muscles when the subjects balanced on one foot, it was found that the soleus was consistently more active than the gastrocnemius.[1] In another study it was found that the soleus was most active in minimal contractions and when the foot was in a dorsiflexed position. This seems to imply that it was especially active in the reduction of dorsiflexion.[1] The muscle may be palpated slightly lateral to and below the lateral bulge of the gastrocnemius.

Tibialis Anterior. (Fig. 7–18, *A.*) This lies along the full length of the anterior surface of the tibia from the lateral condyle down to the medial aspect of the tarsometatarsal region. Approximately one-half to two-thirds of the way down the leg it becomes tendinous. The tendon passes in front of the medial malleolus on its way to the first cuneiform. The muscle *dorsiflexes the ankle* and *dorsiflexes and supinates (inverts and adducts) the tarsal joints.* In an EMG study of the action of the leg muscles in movements of the free foot (the subject standing on the other foot), O'Connell found that the tibialis anterior initiates dorsiflexion.[1] The muscle may be palpated on the anterior surface of the leg just lateral to the tibia.

Tibialis Posterior. (Fig. 7–23.) This *supinates (inverts and adducts) and plantar flexes the tarsal joints* and *helps to plantar flex the ankle.* It is the deepest of the muscles on the back of the leg. The main part of the muscle covers the intermuscular septum between the tibia and the fibula. In the lower front of the leg its tendon slants across the medial side of the ankle, passes behind the medial malleolus and above the sustentaculum tali, then turns under the foot around the medial margin of the navicular bone to insert into its underside. The muscle is penniform in structure. Because of its direction of pull and its numerous attachments on the plantar surface of the tarsal bones, an important function of this muscle appears to be maintenance of the longitudinal arch.

Intrinsic Muscles of the Foot. (Figs. 7–24, 7–25 and 7–26.) There are eleven of these small muscles or muscle groups. All but one, the extensor digitorum brevis, are on the plantar surface and are usually described as being arranged in four layers. The dorsal interossei muscles, although included in the deepest layer, are situated between the metatarsal bones, rather than on either surface (Fig. 7–18, *B*). The extensor digitorum brevis, which includes the hallucis, although the latter is sometimes described as a separate muscle, is situated on the dorsal surface of the foot (Fig. 7–18, *A*). With the exception of the *lumbricales* and the *quadratus plantae,* which help to flex the lesser toes, the names of these muscles indicate their functions. As one might expect, these intrinsic

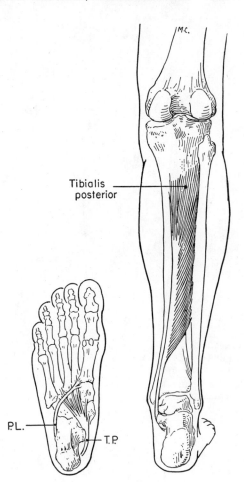

Tibialis
posterior

Figure 7–23 Tibialis posterior. (*P.L.* = Peroneus longus; *T.P.* = tibialis posterior.)

P.L.

T.P.

muscles are much more highly developed in primitive people than in people
who habitually wear shoes.

Various research investigations have shown that the intrinsic muscles act
as a functional unit, have a significant role in stabilization of the foot during
propulsion, tend to show more activity in feet which are habitually pronated,
do not show activity during relaxed standing in either normal or pronated feet,
are not active in the normal *static* support of the longitudinal arches, but do
show definite activity in voluntary attempts to increase the height of the arches.
They are also definitely active in the movement of rising on the toes.

Plantar Fascia. (Fig. 7–27.)   On the plantar surface of the foot the muscles
are covered by fascia. This is divided into medial, central and lateral portions.
The central portion, known as the plantar aponeurosis, is particularly strong
and fibrous. It extends under the whole length of the foot, connecting the
tuberosity of the calcaneus with the bases of the proximal phalanges of the five
toes. This is an exceedingly strong band which serves as an effective binding
rod for the longitudinal arch.

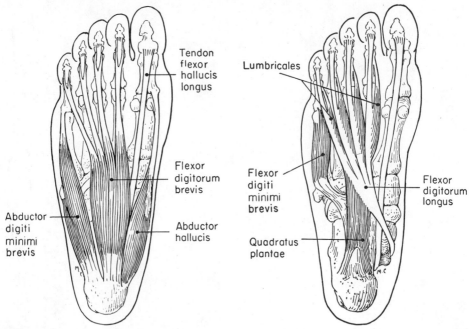

Figure 7–24   Plantar muscles of the foot, superficial layer.

Figure 7–25   Plantar muscles of the foot, middle layer.

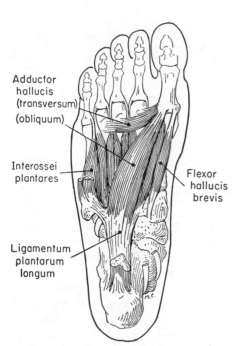

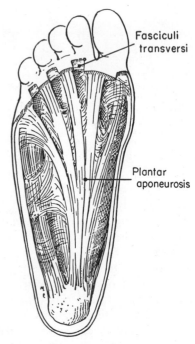

Figure 7–26   Plantar muscles of the foot, deep layer.

Figure 7–27   Plantar fascia of the foot.

MUSCULAR ANALYSIS OF THE FUNDAMENTAL MOVEMENTS OF THE ANKLE AND FOOT (TARSAL JOINTS AND TOES)

The Ankle

DORSIFLEXION.   Performed by the tibialis anterior, peroneus tertius and extensor digitorum longus, with possible help from the external hallucis longus.

PLANTAR FLEXION.   Performed by the gastrocnemius, soleus and peroneus longus, with possible help from the tibialis posterior, peroneus brevis, flexor digitorum longus and flexor hallucis longus.

The Tarsal Joints

DORSIFLEXION.   The same as for dorsiflexion of the ankle.

PLANTAR FLEXION.   Performed by the tibialis posterior, flexor digitorum longus, flexor hallucis longus and peroneus longus and brevis.

SUPINATION (INVERSION AND ADDUCTION). (Fig. 7–28, *B*.)   Performed by the tibialis anterior and tibialis posterior, with possible help from the flexor digitorum longus and flexor hallucis longus.

PRONATION (EVERSION AND ABDUCTION). (Fig. 7–28, *A*.)   Performed by the peroneus longus, brevis and tertius, with possible help from the extensor digitorum longus.

The Toes (Exclusive of the intrinsic muscles)

FLEXION.   Performed by the flexor digitorum longus and flexor hallucis longus.

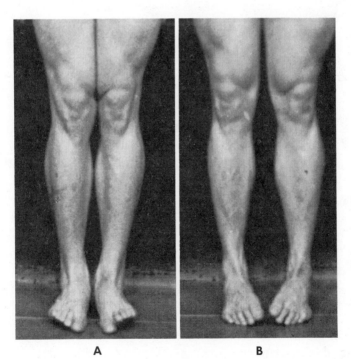

A   **B**

Figure 7–28   The feet and legs in weight-bearing position. *A*, In eversion and abduction; *B*, in inversion and adduction.

EXTENSION.   Performed by the extensor digitorum longus and extensor hallucis longus.

APPLICATIONS TO COMMON MOVEMENTS

The most common movements of the lower extremity are undoubtedly walking and running, but as these are discussed in Part Three they will not be taken up here. Squatting, or deep knee bending, is a movement that is used in many ways, both in daily life activities and in sports and other physical education activities. It is used by the baseball catcher as his ready-to-catch position. It is also used as a starting position for running races, for executing various stunts, as an exercise for physical fitness or training and for landing after jumping down from a height. In the home, on the street and almost anywhere it is used for picking up objects from the floor or ground. Whether performed slowly or quickly, the basic muscular pattern is the same. In downward movement, the hip and knee joints are flexing and the ankle joints are dorsiflexing. The joint movements are *caused* by the force of gravity; they are *controlled* by the muscles that normally cause the opposite movements but which, for this purpose, are engaged in *eccentric contraction*. In the return movement, that is, the return to the erect standing position, the same muscles are working but this time in *concentric contraction*.

If one were interested in making a joint and muscular analysis of the movement it would be important to define it exactly. The following would be some of the major factors to consider.

I. Stance
   A. Distance between feet
      1. Feet close
      2. Feet separated
         a. Laterally
         b. Forward-backward
         c. Obliquely
   B. Direction of feet
      1. Parallel, pointing straight forward
      2. Angle between feet; toes turned out

Question: What effect does the foot position have on the thighs and the hip joints?

II. Trunk position
   A. As erect as possible during movement and in full squat position
   B. Inclined slightly forward in a comfortable position.

Question: How is balance affected?

III. Arms
   A. Extended horizontally sideward or forward and used for balance
   B. Extended vertically downward, fingers touching floor when full squat is reached, at the sides of the body if knees are close; between the feet if knees are separated

IV. Speed of movement
   A. Slowly for balance
   B. Quick bend and quick return
   C. Jumping to and from squat

It is suggested that students of kinesiology carefully think through each of these factors in preparation for the time when, as physical education instructors or as trainers, they consider assigning exercises involving repeated full squats or long-held squat positions, or stunts like the duck walk or the familiar Russian dance step. Attention is called to related discussions in the sections on Athletic Injuries and Supplementary Material.

COMMON ATHLETIC INJURIES OF THE LEG, KNEE AND ANKLE

The Leg

Shin Bruises (Contusions).   These are very common in sports because of the exposed position of the tibia and its lack of protection. A direct blow may cause an injury that varies in severity all the way from a simple bruise to a severe traumatic tibial periostitis, a condition in which the periosteum may be seriously damaged. Unlike the femur, the tibia has no anterior muscles to cushion it against sharp blows. It is important, therefore, to make every effort to protect the bone by the use of shin guards or other form of padding.

Shin Splints.   In view of the broad and inexact use of this term it is impossible to be definitive in regard to the causes, symptoms and preventive measures. The following general measures are considered essential for a good recovery: a moderately long period of rest, supportive strapping and local heat provided it does not increase the feeling of tension. More precise treatment depends upon the diagnosis. As there is considerable likelihood of a recurrence of the condition, it is important to supervise the player carefully when he resumes activity.[10]

Leg Fracture.   The most common leg fracture experienced in athletics is that of the fibula, a fracture that tends to occur in the lower two thirds of the leg.[5, 10] A fibular fracture is not usually of serious consequence, provided it is not accompanied by damage to the ankle joint, the condition of greatest concern being rupture of the tibiofibular ligament. A complicating condition which is likely to accompany this is displacement of the bones owing to the forceful pull of antagonistic muscles. If this results in instability of the ankle joint, the consequences can be extremely serious, causing a permanent disability.[5, 10]

The Knee

There can be no question as to the vulnerability of the knee. It is probably the most susceptible to injury of any of the joints in the body. Two factors appear to be responsible for this: its complicated structure and its position mid-way between the hip and the sole of the foot. Superficially, it looks like a hinge joint, but its action combines the movements of a hinge with the gliding of an irregular joint. (See page 12.) Furthermore, when it is flexed it is capable of a slight degree of medial and lateral rotation. Only a few of the many common knee injuries are discussed here.

Contusion. This occurs frequently among athletes and can be caused either by a fall or by a blow against the front or side of the knee. The problem presented by a contusion of the knee is that it often masks a more serious injury, the most likely being a tear of the medial collateral ligament at either its femoral or its tibial attachment, or severe damage to the lower part of the quadriceps tendon or to the patellar ligament and the attachment of the latter to the tuberosity of the tibia. O'Donoghue warns about the need for particular care in diagnosing the condition and recommends treating it, when in doubt, as though it were the more serious injury.[10]

Collateral Ligament Sprain and "The Unhappy Triad." This is doubtless one of the most, if not *the most* frequently reported knee injury in the world of sports.[5] To understand the reason for this, a thorough knowledge of the structure of the joint is essential. Although classified as a hinge joint, it is by no means a typical one like the interphalangeal finger joints, for instance. In flexion and in the return from flexion, a certain amount of gliding occurs. When the knee is flexed it is capable of a slight amount of voluntary rotation. When it receives a blow from the side or when it is subjected to severe wrenching in the weight bearing position, it can easily be forced beyond its normal range of rotatory motion. Furthermore, although abduction and adduction are not normal knee motions, that is, one cannot voluntarily perform them, the leg can be passively ab- or adducted by an outside force. A slight degree of this probably does no harm, but a severe lateral blow or violent wrenching is likely to tear the ligament on the opposite side.

The majority of knee sprains are caused by a blow from the lateral side toward the medial side or by a severe medialward twist.[5] This means that the leg has been violently adducted and medially rotated at the knee joint. O'Donoghue describes the classic athletic knee injury as follows: ". . . the foot is fixed to the ground, the thigh rotates inward and the leg outward, the knee is forced inward toward the opposite leg and the stress is primarily received on the ligaments on the inner side of the knee." If the force is great enough to be transmitted to the deep layer of this ligament, it is likely to affect the medial meniscus which is attached to the ligament. In the severe triple injury known as "The Unhappy Triad," the two layers of the medial collateral ligament are torn near their attachment to the tibia, and both the medial meniscus and the anterior cruciate ligament are ruptured (Fig. 7–29). The same type of injury can occur to the lateral side, but this is much less common.[10]

The Ankle

Of all the injuries to which athletes are prone, those affecting the ankle joint have the highest incidence. One reason for this is thought to be the arrangement of the muscles. The long tendons cross the ankle in a way that makes for lack of bulkiness and for good leverage but contributes little to stabilization.[5] Consequently, this joint is unusually susceptible to strains, sprains, dislocations and fractures.

Strains. A strain, it will be remembered, is a muscle injury. This includes the muscle tendon and the connective tissue by means of which the muscle is

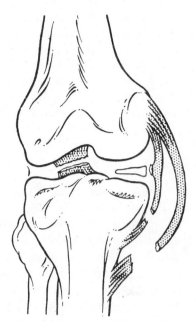

Figure 7–29 Triple injury to the knee involving sprain, or in more severe cases, rupture of medial collateral ligament and anterior cruciate ligament, and damage to medial meniscus. (From O'Donoghue, D. H.: Treatment of Injuries to Athletes, 2nd Ed. Philadelphia: W. B. Saunders Company, 1970.)

attached to the bone. Landing from jumping exposes the tendons of the ankle and foot muscles to the danger of strain. O'Donoghue points out the particular danger of broad jumping. As the jumper lands, his feet may be in severe dorsiflexion; and the impact of landing then forces them beyond their normal range of motion. This gives the Achilles tendon a sudden wrench which may cause tearing either at the point of the tendon's attachment to the bone or at the junction between the tendon and the muscle belly.[10]

The distal tendons of both the anterior and posterior tibial muscles are also subject to strain. The aftereffects of each of these can be quite troublesome as they are both inverters (supinators) of the foot, in addition to which the posterior tibial has the important function of helping to support the longitudinal arch.

Tenosynovitis.   This is the term used for inflammation of the synovial membrane that surrounds a tendon, a condition which tends to follow strains. It occurs frequently at the ankle, but instead of resulting from a specific injury, it is caused most often by overuse of a tendon.[10]

Sprains.   A sprained ankle is all too familiar. It results from a sudden wrench or twist and is usually associated with forced inversion of the foot with the lateral ligaments being stretched or torn and sometimes ruptured or pulled off of the bone. The affected ligaments are any of those on the lateral aspect of the ankle, i.e., the calcaneofibular, the anterior talofibular and the posterior talofibular. The interosseous talocalcaneal ligament, while not strictly an ankle ligament, may also be affected.

Fractures.   Ankle fractures are usually caused by a sudden wrenching or twisting, the same factors that cause sprains but, whereas sprains are the result of excessive inversion of the foot, fractures result from excessive eversion. The majority of ankle fractures occur to the malleoli, especially the lateral malleolus. In the more serious fractures, there is also likely to be some dislocation as the result of a separation between the tibia and fibula with a consequent widening of the socket or mortise. Prompt and adequate treatment is all important if permanent damage is to be avoided. Emphasis is placed upon the importance of restoring the integrity of the mortise and maintaining the weight-bearing bones in proper relationship to one another.[10]

SUPPLEMENTARY MATERIAL

Vulnerability of the Knee Joint.   Several writers have called attention to the strains and stresses to which the knee is subject and have emphasized the need for physical therapists and physical educators to be aware of the relation of these forces to knee functions. Williams and Lissner have pointed out the demands made on the quadriceps muscles when the knee is flexed in the weight-bearing position, as when climbing stairs, seating oneself and rising from a chair, and deep knee bending. They have described methods for analyzing both tension and compression forces acting on the structures of the knee and have suggested the application of these to exercise procedures.[12]

Some denounce the use of deep squat exercises as taught in weight training and football conditioning programs and suggest that they be eliminated. Such exercises, they believe, tend to weaken the ligaments and increase the instability of the joint.[8]

The Pennsylvania State University Studies.[2, 8]   New light has been thrown on this problem by two investigations made during the early seventies. Both were directed by C. A. Morehouse and were undertaken because of the concern he and his co-workers felt regarding the high incidence of knee injuries in athletics and because they were also disturbed by the lack of objective evidence to support the assumption of some authorities that ligaments are the first line of defense against knee injury and that a stretched ligament is inevitably a weaker one. They undertook to devise equipment for providing objective and reliable measurements of knee stability as judged by the amount of abduction and adduction of which the knee was capable. Using this apparatus they investigated the effect of vigorous exercises including squat jumps on the lateral stability of knees, the possible relationship between knee stability and the occurrence of injuries to knee ligaments in college football, and the effectiveness of adhesive strapping in providing support to the knee joint prior to and following vigorous exercise.

To summarize their results briefly:

1. They developed an instrument which had acceptable reliability but which they hoped to improve before using it for future studies.

2. The effects of football practice and scrimmage on knee stability yielded results that were inconclusive but tended to indicate a *decrease* in ab- and adduction.

3. Squat jumping was found *not* to increase ab- and adduction of the knee joint.

4. Adhesive strapping was found to provide support for a brief time but no support was apparent after five minutes of vigorous exercise.

When a number of cases of knee ligament injuries which occurred in football were analyzed, it was learned that this group had had less abduction rather than more. This suggested that the person with more taut ligaments is more prone to injury.[8]

In a follow up study conducted by Goldfuss, Morehouse, and LeVeau a few years later for the purpose of investigating the effect of muscular tension on ab- and adduction of the leg at the knee joint, it was found that:

1. Unconscious muscular activity in the quadriceps and hamstring muscles had no effect on knee ab- and adduction measures.

2. Conscious contraction of the quadriceps and hamstring muscles was found to stabilize the knee joint against excessive ab- and adduction. The investigators felt that this finding had important implications for the rehabilitation of injured knees and that it indicated the need for maintaining the strength of these muscles during the recovery period of the injured joint.[2]

Action of the Muscles in the Support of the Arches. In 1963 Basmajian and Stecko reviewed the question of the mechanics of arch support and investigated three theories regarding the maintenance of the arches. These are that they are maintained by muscular contraction alone, by bones and ligaments alone or by the combination of muscular contraction and passive structures.

Using 20 young men as subjects, they investigated six muscles electromyographically. These were the tibialis anterior, tibialis posterior, peroneus longus, flexor hallucis longus, abductor hallucis and flexor digitorum brevis. They found that the men could support loads of 100–200 lbs. standing on one foot without any evidence of muscular action, and that with loads of 400 lbs. some muscles became active, but many still remained inactive. They concluded from these findings that the arches' first line of defense is ligamentous and that the muscles constitute a dynamic reserve which is called into action reflexively when the load is excessive.[1]

Flexibility and Stability of Feet. In a study of the flexibility and stability and other characteristics of the feet of 100 young women, Lawrence noted that there was no significant relationship between flexibility and stability, and that the size and weight of the body had very little effect upon the measurements of foot size, flexibility, stability or degree of out-toeing. Lawrence also observed that long, narrow feet tended to be more flexible, but less stable, than feet of other proportions.[7]

Action of the Muscles in Movements of the Free Foot. Basmajian and O'Connell, in independent studies, reached similar conclusions regarding the action of muscles in movements of the non-weight-bearing foot. Briefly, these are as follows:

1. Dorsiflexion is initiated by tibialis anterior and assisted by extensor digitorum longus and extensor hallucis longus.

2. Plantar flexion is initiated either by peroneus longus or soleus.

3. Tibialis anterior is definitely active in inversion of the foot only when the latter movement is accompanied by dorsiflexion.[1]

Action of the Foot and Ankle Muscles in Standing. Although their studies were not entirely comparable, some investigators found that the gastrocnemius was active in relaxed standing and others found that the soleus was active, but the gastrocnemius was not unless the body swayed forward. Several investigators agreed that the tibialis anterior and peroneus longus were not active in relaxed standing but noted that the tibialis anterior became active when the body swayed backward.[1]

For additional findings the reader is referred to *Muscles Alive* by Basmajian or to the original reports listed in the back of that book.

LABORATORY EXPERIENCES

Knee Joint: Joint Structure and Function

1. Using a form like that in Appendix A, record the essential information regarding the knee joint. Study the movements both on the skeleton and on the living body.

Muscular Action (See Appendix D for muscle check list.)

2. FLEXION AT KNEE
    Subject: Lie face down and flex leg at knee by raising foot.
    Assistant: Steady subject's thigh and resist movement by pushing down on ankle.
    Observer: Palpate biceps femoris, semitendinosus, gracilis, sartorius and gastrocnemius.

3. EXTENSION AT KNEE
    a. *Subject:* Rise from a squat position.
       Observer: Palpate quadriceps femoris.
    b. *Subject:* Sit on table with legs hanging over edge. Extend leg.
       Assistant: Steady subject's thigh and resist movement by holding ankle down.
       Observer: Palpate quadriceps femoris.

4. OUTWARD ROTATION OF LEG WITH KNEE IN FLEXED POSITION
    Subject: Sit on table with legs hanging over edge. Turn foot laterally as far as possible without moving thigh.
    Assistant: Steady subject's thigh and give slight resistance by holding foot.
    Observer: Palpate biceps femoris.

5. INWARD ROTATION OF LEG WITH KNEE IN FLEXED POSITION
    Subject: Sit on table with legs hanging over edge. Turn foot medially as far as possible without moving thigh.
    Assistant: Steady subject's thigh and give slight resistance by holding foot.
    Observer: Palpate semitendinosus, gracilis and sartorius.

Ankle and Foot: Joint Structure and Function

6. Using forms like the one in Appendix A, record the essential information regarding the ankle joint, the subtalar joint and the midtarsal joints. Study the movements of these joints both on the skeleton and on the living body.

7. Using a protractor-goniometer, compare the total range of plantar and dorsal flexion of the ankle in a group of five or more subjects, (a) with the knee straight; (b) with the knee flexed.

8. Make a similar comparison between two groups, one consisting of three to five varsity level swimmers and the other of the same number of recreational swimmers, or make a similar comparison between ballet and non-ballet dancers.

Ankle and Foot: Muscular Action (See Appendix D for muscle check list.)

9. PLANTAR FLEXION
    Subject: (a) Stand and rise on the toes. (b) Hold one foot off the floor and extend it vigorously.
    Observer: Compare the muscular action of the leg in (a) and (b).

10. DORSIFLEXION
    Subject: Sit on a table with the legs straight and with the feet over the edge. Dorsiflex one foot as far as possible
    Assistant: Resist the movement by holding the foot.
    Observer: Identify the tibialis anterior, peroneus tertius, extensor digitorum longus and extensor hallucis longus.

11. PRONATION (EVERSION AND ABDUCTION)
    Subject: In same position as above, turn one foot laterally without extending it.
    Assistant: Steady the leg at the ankle and resist the movement by holding one foot.
    Observer: Identify the muscles that contract.

12. SUPINATION (INVERSION AND ADDUCTION)
    Subject: In same position as above, turn one foot medially as far as possible.
    Assistant: Steady the leg at the ankle and resist the movement by holding the foot.
    Observer: Identify the muscles that contract.

13. It is suggested that those who are interested in strengthening their ankles try rising high on their toes 20 times a day, holding weights in each hand. Start with a 5 lb. dumbbell in each hand and gradually increase the weights to 25 lbs. or more, using whatever weights are available, such as weighted suitcases or books strapped together.

REFERENCES

1. Basmajian, J. V.: Muscles Alive, 3rd Ed. Baltimore: The Williams & Wilkins Company, 1974.
2. Goldfuss, A. J., Morehouse, C. A., and LeVeau, B. F.: Effect of muscular tension on knee stability. Medicine and Science in Sports, 5:267–271, 1973.
3. Hollinshead, W. H.: Functional Anatomy of the Limbs and Back, 3rd Ed. Philadelphia: W. B. Saunders Company, 1969.
4. Kaplan, E. B.: The iliotibial tract. J. Bone & Joint Surg., 40A:817–832, 1958.
5. Klafs, C. E., and Arnheim, D. D.: Modern Principles of Athletic Training. St. Louis: C. V. Mosby Co., 1973.
6. Klein, K. K.: The knee and the ligaments. J. Bone & Joint Surg., 44A:1191–1192, 1962.
7. Lawrence, S.: A Study of the Flexibility and the Stability of the Feet of College Women. Unpublished master's thesis, Smith College, 1955.
8. Morehouse, C. A.: Evaluation of knee abduction and adduction. The effects of selected exercise programs on knee stability and its relationship to knee injuries in college football. Final Project Report, Grant No. RD-2815M, Division of Research and Demonstration Grants, Social and Rehabilitation Service, Dept. of Health, Education and Welfare, Washington, D.C., 1970. (Mimeographed copies available upon request.)
9. Schaeffer, J. P. (Ed.): Morris' Human Anatomy, 11th Ed. New York: McGraw Hill, Inc., 1953.
10. O'Donoghue, D. H.: Treatment of Injuries to Athletes. 3rd Ed. Philadelphia: W. B. Saunders Company, 1976.
11. Steindler, A.: Kinesiology of the Human Body. Springfield, Ill.: Charles C Thomas, Publisher, 1970.
12. Williams, M., and Lissner, H. R.: Biomechanical analysis of knee function. J. Am. Phys. Ther. Assn., 43:93–99, 1963.
13. Wright, W. G.: Muscle Function. New York: Hafner Publishing Company, 1962.

Chapter Eight

THE SPINAL COLUMN AND PELVIC GIRDLE

THE SPINAL COLUMN

If one were faced with the problem of devising a single mechanism that would simultaneously (1) give stability to a collapsible cylinder, (2) permit movement in all directions and yet always return to the fundamental starting position, (3) support three structures of considerable weight (a globe, a yoke and a cage), (4) provide attachment for numerous flexible bands and elastic cords, (5) transmit a gradually increasing weight to a rigid basin-like foundation, (6) act as a shock absorber for cushioning jolts and jars and (7) encase and protect a cord of extreme delicacy, he would be staggered by the immensity of the task. Yet the spinal column fulfills all these requirements with amazing efficiency. It is at the same time an organ of stability and mobility, of support and protection and of resistance and adaptation. It is an instrument of great precision, yet of robust structure. Its architecture and the manner in which it performs its many functions are worthy of careful study. From the kinesiologic point of view, we are interested in the spine chiefly as a mechanism for maintaining erect posture and for permitting movement of the head, neck and trunk.

In order to understand these functions of the spine, it is necessary to have a clear picture, first of the spinal column as a whole and second of the distinguishing characteristics of the different regions. The spinal column, consisting of seven cervical, twelve thoracic and five lumbar vertebrae, the sacrum and the coccyx, presents four curves as seen from the side. The cervical and lumbar curves are convex forward, the thoracic and sacrococcygeal curves convex to the rear (Fig. 8–1). The thoracic and sacrococcygeal curves are called primary curves because they exist before birth. The cervical and lumbar curves develop during infancy and early childhood and hence are called secondary curves. From the first cervical to the fifth lumbar vertebra, the vertebral bodies become increasingly larger, an important factor in the weight-bearing function of the spine.

There are two sets of interspinal articulations, those between the vertebral *bodies* and those between the vertebral *arches*. The latter are in pairs, there being one on either side of each vertebra. The articulations of the first two vertebrae are atypical and will be described separately.

There is such a close relationship between the structure of the spinal column and the movements that take place in its different regions that the

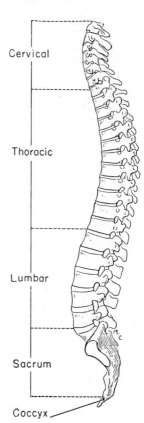

Cervical

Thoracic

Lumbar

Sacrum

Coccyx

Figure 8–1 Lateral view of the spinal column showing antero-posterior curves.

student will find it well worth the effort to acquire a thorough grasp of the structure, particularly of the joints, before proceeding to the movements. If possible, he should refer frequently both to a skeleton and to a strung set of vertebrae while studying spinal structure.

Articulations of the Vertebral Bodies. (Fig. 8–2.)   These joints are classified as synchondroses or cartilaginous joints. The bodies of the vertebrae are united by means of fibrocartilages, otherwise known as intervertebral disks. These correspond to the surfaces of the adjacent vertebral bodies, except in the cervical region where they are smaller from side to side. They adhere to the hyaline cartilage both above and below, there being no articular cavity in this type of joint. In thickness they are fairly uniform in the thoracic region, but in the cervical and lumbar regions they are thicker in front than in back. Altogether, they constitute one fourth of the length of the spinal column. Each disk consists of two parts, an outer fibrous rim and an inner pulpy nucleus known as the nucleus pulposus. This is a ball of firmly compressed elastic material, a little like the center of a golf ball. It constitutes a pivot of motion and permits compression in any direction, as well as torsion. The intervertebral disks are also important as shock absorbers.

Ligamentous Reinforcement. (Figs. 8–3 and 8–4.)   The joints of the spinal column are reinforced by several ligaments. The vertebral bodies are held

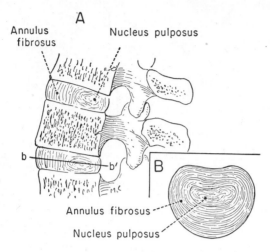

Figure 8–2 *A,* Sagittal section of lumbar vertebrae and intervertebral fibrocartilages. *B,* Transverse section of intervertebral fibrocartilage.

together by two long ligaments, one in front and one in back. The *anterior longitudinal* ligament starts as a narrow band and widens as it descends from the occipital bone to the sacrum. The *posterior longitudinal* ligament, descending from the occipital bone to the coccyx, is relatively narrow throughout but has lateral expansions opposite each intervertebral fibrocartilage. Both ligaments are stronger in the thoracic region than in either the cervical or the lumbar region.

Articulations of the Vertebral Arches. (Fig. 8–5.)   The articulations between the facets of the vertebral arches are non-axial diarthrodial joints. Each of these joints has an articular cavity and is enclosed within a capsule. A slight amount of gliding motion is permitted. The resultant movement of each vertebra is determined largely by the direction in which the articular facets face. The cervical spine appears to be somewhat of an exception, however. The facets in this region slant at about a 45 degree angle, lying halfway between the horizontal

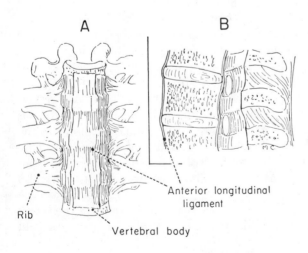

Figure 8–3 Anterior longitudinal ligament of the spine. *A,* Anterior view; *B,* sagittal section of vertebrae showing lateral view of ligament.

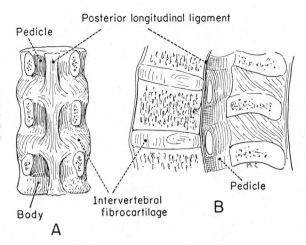

Figure 8-4 Posterior longitudinal ligament of spine. *A*, Frontal section of vertebrae showing posterior view of ligament. *B*, Sagittal section of vertebrae showing lateral view of ligament.

and the frontal planes (Fig. 8-6, *A*). Such a slant would seem to favor rotation and lateral flexion and to be unfavorable to flexion and hyperextension. Yet these latter movements occur as freely as does lateral flexion, whereas rotation from the second cervical vertebra down can be rated only as moderate. In the thoracic region they lie slightly more in the frontal and less in the horizontal plane than do the cervical articulations, and they have a slight inward and outward slant (Fig. 8-6, *B*). The upper facets face backward, slightly upward and lateralward; the lower facets face forward, slightly downward and medialward. They are adapted equally well to rotation and to lateral bending. In the lumbar region, except at the lumbosacral articulation, the articular facets lie more nearly in the sagittal plane (Fig. 8-6, *C*). The upper facets face inward and slightly backward; the lower facets face outward and slightly forward. Furthermore, the upper facets present slightly concave surfaces and the lower facets, convex. By this arrangement of the facets, the lumbar vertebrae are virtually locked against rotation. The slight amount of rotation that does occur is made possible by the looseness of the capsules. At the lumbosacral articula-

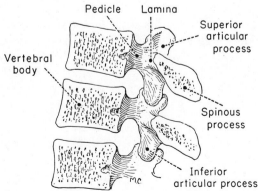

Figure 8-5 Sagittal section of vertebrae showing articulations of the vertebral arches.

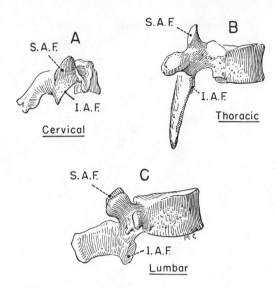

Figure 8–6 Articular facets of vertebrae. *A,* Cervical; *B,* thoracic; *C,* lumbar. *S.A.F.* = Superior articular facet. *I.A.F.* = Inferior articular facet.

tion the facets lie somewhat more in the frontal plane than is true of the other lumbar joints.

The ligaments reinforcing these joints may be identified in Figures 8–7 and 8–8. The *ligamenta flava* and the *interspinous* and *supraspinous* ligaments are all thickest and strongest in the lumbar region. There remain two rather thin ligaments, the *intertransverse,* connecting the transverse processes of adjacent vertebrae, and the *ligamentum nuchae,* which is the continuation of the supraspinous ligament in the cervical region.

Atlanto-occipital Articulation. (Fig. 8–9.) This is the articulation between the head and the neck. It consists of a pair of joints, one on each side. Each condyle of the occipital bone of the skull articulates with the corresponding superior articular fossa of the first vertebra, known as atlas. Each articulation by itself belongs to the ovoid (condyloid) classification, but the movement which occurs in the two joints together is more like that of a hinge joint. The rigid relationship between the two joints results in a restriction of the lateral motion that would normally occur in an ovoid joint. The movements which take place at the atlanto-occipital articulation are chiefly flexion and extension, with a slight amount of lateral flexion. There is no rotation.

Atlantoaxial Articulation. (Fig. 8–10.) This is a perfect example of a pivot joint—a joint whose sole function is rotation. The toothlike peg (odontoid process) that projects upward from the second cervical vertebra, otherwise known as axis or epistropheus, fits into the ring formed by the inner surface of the anterior arch of atlas and the transverse ligament which bridges across the tips of the arch. Since no rotation occurs at the atlanto-occipital joint, rotation of atlas on axis will carry the head with it; thus the movement occurring at the atlantoaxial joint contributes to the movement of the head on the trunk.

Movements of the Spine as a Whole

The movements of the spinal column, which resemble those of a ball-and-socket joint, are described as follows.

FLEXION. (Fig. 8–11, *A*.)   This is a forward-downward bending in the sagittal plane about a frontal-horizontal axis. It involves a compression of the anterior parts of the intervertebral disks and a gliding motion of the articular processes. It occurs more freely in the cervical, upper thoracic and lumbar regions. The cervical curve may be reduced to a straight line and the lumbar curve, in flexible individuals, may be reversed.

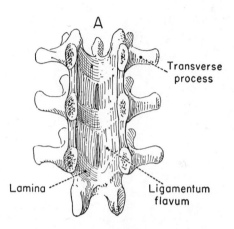

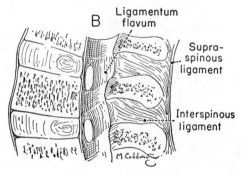

Figure 8–7 *A*, Frontal section of three lumbar vertebrae showing anterior view of vertebral arches and ligamenta flava. *B*, Sagittal view of lumbar vertebrae showing ligaments of vertebral arches.

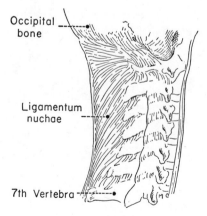

Figure 8–8 Side view of cervical spine showing ligamentum nuchae.

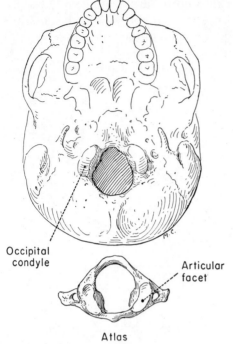

Figure 8-9 Bones forming atlanto-occipital articulation.

Occipital
condyle

Articular
facet

Atlas

EXTENSION AND HYPEREXTENSION. (Fig. 8–11, *B*.) Extension is the return movement from flexion. Hyperextension is a backward-downward movement in the sagittal plane. It occurs most freely in the cervical and lumbar regions and particularly at the lumbosacral junction. In the thoracic region hyperextension is limited by the overlapping of the spinous processes.

LATERAL FLEXION. (Fig. 8–11, *C*.) This is a sideward bending in the frontal plane about a sagittal-horizontal axis. It is freest in the cervical region and quite free in the lumbar region and at the thoracolumbar junction. But it is limited in the thoracic region by the presence of the ribs. Each rib (except the first, tenth, eleventh and twelfth) articulates with two adjacent vertebrae and the intervening disk, and each rib (except the eleventh and twelfth) articulates with the transverse process of the lower of the two vertebrae (Fig. 8–12). Thus it is seen that the ribs serve as splints, restricting lateral flexion of the thoracic spine

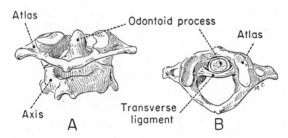

Atlas

Odontoid process

Atlas

Axis   A

Transverse
ligament   B

Figure 8-10 Atlantoaxial articulation. *A*, Posterior view; *B*, superior view.

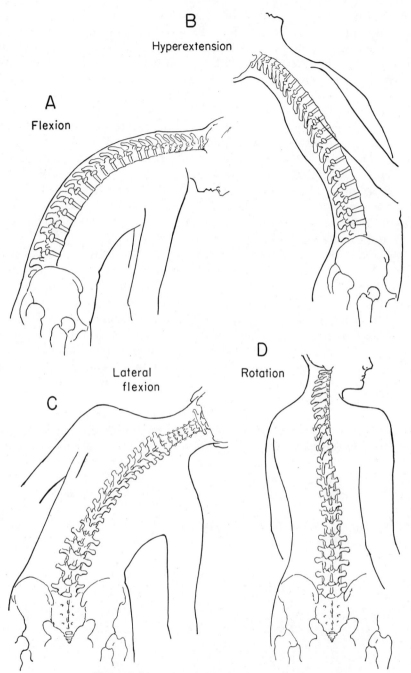

Figure 8–11 Movements of the spinal column.

to a marked degree. It is amazing that any motion can take place there at all. For several reasons—the slant of the articular processes, the presence of the anteroposterior curves of the spine, and muscular and ligamentous tensions— lateral flexion is always accompanied by a certain amount of torsion.

ROTATION. (Fig. 8–11, *D*.)   This is a rotatory movement of the spine in the horizontal plane about a vertical axis. Spinal rotation is named by the way the front of the upper spine turns with reference to the lower part. Thus a turning of the head and shoulders to the right constitutes rotation to the right. A turning of the legs and pelvis to the left, without turning the upper part of the body, also constitutes rotation of the spine to the right since the anatomic relationships are the same as in the former example. The movement of rotation is most free in the cervical region, 90% of the movement being attributed to the atlantoaxial joint. It is next most free in the thoracic region and at the thoracolumbar junction.[9] Owing to the interlocking of the articular processes, it is extremely limited in the lumbar region, there being only about 5 degrees of rotation to each side. In the cervical region there is no rotation between atlas and the skull, but free rotation at the pivot joint between atlas and axis. Whenever rotation occurs in the spine, it is accompanied by a slight amount of unavoidable lateral flexion to the same side.

INFLUENCE OF THE STARTING POSITION ON LATERAL FLEXION AND THE TORSION ACCOMPANYING IT.   When lateral flexion is performed from the erect position, the maximum movement occurs in the lumbar region and at the thoracolumbar junction, with only slight involvement of the lower thoracic spine. (The cervical spine is excluded from this discussion.) The torsion occurs in the same part of the spine and consists in a turning of the vertebral bodies toward the side of the lateral flexion. Thus, if the spine bends to the right (forming a curve concave to the right), the vertebral bodies of the lumbar and lower thoracic vertebrae turn slightly to the right, the spinous processes, therefore, turning to the left.

If the lateral flexion is performed from a position of hyperextension, and the hyperextension is maintained throughout the movement, the lateral flexion moves lower in the spine, occurring almost entirely below the eleventh thoracic vertebra. The torsion occurs in this same region and in the same manner that it does when the lateral flexion is performed from the erect position. The position of hyperextension seems to lock the thoracic spine against lateral movements.

If the lateral flexion is performed from a position of forward flexion, the movement occurs higher in the spine than ordinarily, the greatest deviation

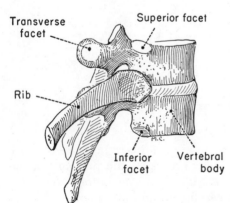

Transverse facet

Superior facet

Rib

Inferior facet

Vertebral body

Figure 8–12   Articulation of a rib with two adjacent vertebrae.

being at the level of the eighth thoracic vertebra. The torsion in this case reverses itself. Thus, in a side bend to the right the vertebral bodies turn to the *left* and the spinous processes to the right. This reversal is not inconsistent. It is directly related to the anteroposterior curves of the spine. In the first two examples, that is, when the lateral flexion is performed either from the erect or from the hyperextended position, most of the movement takes place in the lower part of the spine, the part that is concave to the rear. The rotation that accompanies the side bend in these two cases is called concave-side rotation because the bodies turn in the direction of the concave or inner side of the laterally curved spine. When the side bend is performed from the flexed position, most of the movement takes place in the thoracic spine, the region that is convex to the rear. The rotation that accompanies the lateral flexion in this case is called convex-side rotation because the vertebral bodies turn in the direction of the convex or outer side of the laterally curved spine.

INFLUENCE OF THE STARTING POSITION ON ROTATION AND THE LATERAL FLEXION ACCOMPANYING IT. When performed from the erect position, rotation of the spine (below the seventh cervical vertebra) occurs almost entirely in the thoracic region. When performed from the position of hyperextension, the movement shifts lower in the spine, occurring in the vicinity of the thoracolumbar junction. When performed from the flexed position, the rotation is higher than usual, occurring in the upper thoracic spine. Regardless of the position in which the rotation is performed—whether erect, flexed or hyperextended—the slight lateral flexion which accompanies it is always to the same side as the rotation. Thus if the spine rotates to the left, it flexes slightly to the left. This movement is very slight, however, and can scarcely be detected.[15]

CIRCUMDUCTION. This is a circular movement of the upper trunk on the lower, being a combination of flexion, lateral flexion and hyperextension, but not including rotation.

Summary of Spinal Movements
    Flexion; extension; hyperextension
        Free in all three regions
        Cervical and thoracic curves may be reduced to straight lines
        Lumbar curve may be reversed in flexible subjects
    Lateral flexion
        Free in cervical and lumbar regions
        Limited in thoracic region by rib attachments
        Accompanied by torsion
    Rotation
        Freest at top, least free at bottom of spine
        Accompanied by slight lateral flexion
    Circumduction
        Sequential combination of flexion, lateral flexion and hyperextension

Regional Classification of Spinal Movements
    Occipitoatlantal joint
        Flexion and extension
        Hyperextension
        Slight lateral flexion

Atlantoaxial joint
> Rotation

Remaining cervical joints
> Free flexion and extension
> Free hyperextension
> Free lateral flexion
> Free rotation

Thoracic region
> Moderate flexion
> Slight hyperextension
> Moderate lateral flexion
> Free rotation

Lumbar region
> Moderate to free flexion and extension
> Free hyperextension
> Free lateral flexion
> Slight rotation

Summary of Factors Which Influence the Stability and Mobility of the Spinal Column. Before considering the muscular analysis of the spinal movements it would be advisable to review some of the special characteristics which contribute to the spine's stability and which modify its mobility in one way or another.

1. Pressure and Tension Stresses. The tendency of the compressed intervertebral disks to push the vertebrae apart, combined with the tendency of the ligaments to press them together, is an important factor in the stability of the spinal column.

2. Anteroposterior Curves. The alternating anteroposterior curves of the spinal column influence the nature and the degree of movements that occur in the different regions. Individual variations from the so-called normal curves cause variations in the movement patterns (see pages 229 to 231). The anteroposterior curves are said to serve as a safeguard against the development of abnormal lateral curves (curvature of the spine; scoliosis).

3. Relative Thickness and Shape of the Intervertebral Disks. There is a direct relationship between the thickness of the disks and the degree of movement permitted, there being greater freedom of motion where the disks are thick.

4. Thickness and Strength of the Ligaments. These differ in the different regions and have a corresponding influence on the motions permitted in each region.

5. Direction and Obliquity of the Articular Facets. These are characteristic for each region and play an important part in determining the type of motion permitted in each.

6. Size and Obliquity of the Spinous Processes. These overlap like shingles in the thoracic region, hence limiting hyperextension. In the lumbar region they are horizontal, and, although they are wide, they do not restrict motion.

7. Articulations of the Ribs with the Vertebrae. These limit lateral flexion in the thoracic region.

Muscles. The muscles responsible for the movements of the spine, with the exception of two groups, have at least one attachment on the spinal column or the skull. The exceptions are the abdominal and the hyoid muscles. Both of these groups are superficially located on the front of the body. Nevertheless both groups, the abdominal muscles in particular, are effective movers of the spine. The muscles are listed below according to aspect and region.

 Anterior Aspect
  Cervical Region
   Prevertebral muscles (longus capitis and colli, rectus capitis anterior and lateralis)
   Hyoid muscles (suprahyoids and infrahyoids)
  Thoracic and Lumbar Regions
   Abdominal muscles
    Obliquus externus abdominis
    Obliquus internus abdominis
    Rectus abdominis
 Posterior Aspect
  Cervical Region only
   Splenius capitis and cervicis
   Suboccipitals (rectus capitis posterior major and minor; obliquus capitis superior and inferior)
  Cervical, Thoracic and Lumbar Regions
   Erector spinae (iliocostalis, longissimus and spinalis)
   Deep posterior spinal muscles (multifidi, rotatores, interspinales, intertransversarii and levatores costarum)
   Semispinalis thoracis, cervicis and capitis
 Lateral Aspect
  Cervical Region
   Scalenus anterior, posterior and medius (commonly called the Three Scalenes)
   Sternocleidomastoid
   Levator scapulae
  Lumbar Region
   Quadratus lumborum
   Psoas major

CHARACTERISTICS AND FUNCTIONS OF INDIVIDUAL MUSCLES AND SMALL MUSCLE GROUPS*

Anterior Aspect

Prevertebral Muscles. (Fig. 8–13.) As the illustration shows, the longus colli and capitis extend vertically up the front of the vertebrae, the colli from the upper three thoracic to the first cervical (atlas) and the capitis from the lower

---

*Listed in same order as in previous list.

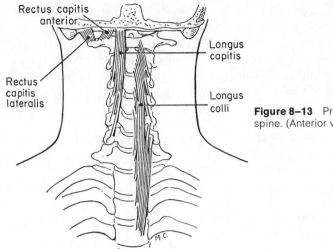

Figure 8–13 Prevertebral muscles of cervical spine. (Anterior view.)

cervical to the occipital bone. The rectus capitis muscles pass obliquely upward from atlas to the skull, the anterior slanting medially and the lateralis laterally. When the left and right muscles act together they *flex the head and neck.* Acting separately, they *flex the head and neck laterally* or *rotate it to the opposite side.*

Hyoid Muscles. (Fig. 8–14.) Also called the strap muscles, these are small anterior muscles in the cervical region. There are four suprahyoids and four infrahyoids. Together they *flex the head and neck.* They are primarily muscles of some phase of swallowing, but they contract in cervical flexion whenever the movement is performed against resistance. By neutralizing one another's pull

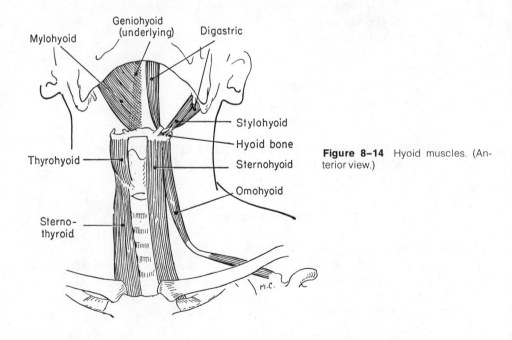

Figure 8–14 Hyoid muscles. (Anterior view.)

on the hyoid bone their action is transferred to the head and thence to the cervical spine. They may be palpated just below the jaw bone.

Obliquus Externus Abdominis. (Fig. 8–15.) (Also listed with muscles of respiration.) The fibers of this muscle run diagonally upward and outward from the lower part of the abdomen, the two muscles together forming an incomplete letter V, as seen from the front. When both sides contract they *flex the thoracic and lumbar spine* against gravity or other resistance. When only one side contracts in combination with other anterior, lateral and posterior muscles on the same side, it *flexes the spine laterally.* When it combines with other spinal rotators, it *rotates the spine to the opposite side,* i.e., the right muscle rotates the spine to the left.

Investigators have found that the external obliques show the greatest activity in movements performed from the supine position, e.g., forward and lateral flexion of the spine, decrease of the pelvic tilt, forward flexion combined with rotation and double knee circling.[18, 20] The external and internal obliques working together were found to show marked activity in two types of movement, namely straining and bearing down when the breath is held[1, 4] and forced exhalation.[1, 4, 8] The external oblique may be palpated at the side of the abdomen.

Obliquus Internus Abdominis (Fig. 8–16.) (Also listed with the muscles of respiration.) This muscle lies beneath (i.e., deeper than) the external oblique.

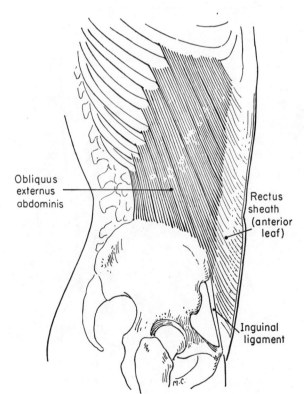

Figure 8–15 External oblique abdominal muscle (obliquus externus abdominis).

Obliquus externus abdominis

Rectus sheath (anterior leaf)

Inguinal ligament

Its fibers fan out from the crest of the ilium, most of them passing diagonally forward and upward toward the rib cartilages and sternum, some horizontally forward toward the linea alba and some diagonally forward and downward toward the crest of the pubis. Of the three abdominal muscles acting on the spine, this one is most active in rotation. EMG experiments have also shown it to have marked activity in the following movements: leaning backward, decreasing the pelvic tilt, from the supine position, lifting the knees to the chest and lowering them from side to side and lifting the knees over the head until the buttocks are raised from the supporting surface.[18] In summary, the internal oblique *flexes the lumbar and thoracic spine, flexes the spine laterally,* and *rotates the spine to the same side.* It may be palpated at the side of the abdomen, below the external oblique. It may also be palpated through the external oblique when the latter is relaxed, as in rotation.

Rectus Abdominis (Fig. 8–17.) (Also listed with the muscles of respiration.) This is the most superficial of the abdominal muscles. It is situated on the anterior surface of the abdomen on either side of the linea alba. It is a long flat band of muscle fibers extending longitudinally between the pubis and the lower part of the chest. At three different levels transverse fibrous bands known as tendinous inscriptions cross the muscle fibers. The muscle is enclosed within a sheath formed by the aponeuroses of the other muscles making up the abdominal wall. EMG studies have shown the rectus to be strongly active in head raising from the supine position[4, 8] and inclining the trunk backward from the erect position.[18, 20] The upper rectus was found to be more active in exercises

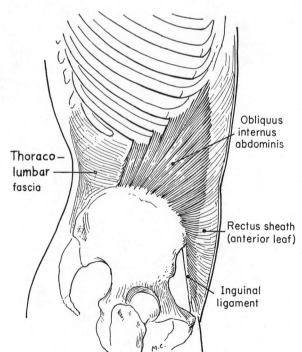

Thoraco—
lumbar
fascia

Obliquus
internus
abdominis

Rectus sheath
(anterior leaf)

Inguinal
ligament

Figure 8–16 Internal oblique abdominal muscle (obliquus internus abdominis).

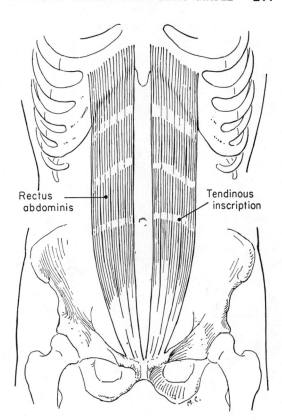

Rectus abdominis

Tendinous inscription

Figure 8–17   Rectus abdominis.

involving the upper part of the body, such as spine flexion from the supine position.[20] In the latter movement it was also found to start contracting a moment before the lower rectus.[6] The lower rectus was found to be more active in movements involving a decrease of pelvic tilt, e.g., in the supine position bending the knees and lifting them toward the face until the fifth lumbar vertebra is raised approximately five inches above the supporting surface.[20] In brief, the rectus abdominis *flexes the lumbar and thoracic spine,* and *one side working alone helps to flex the spine laterally.* The muscle may be palpated on the front of the abdomen about two or three inches from the mid-line, from the pubis to the sternum.

The Abdominal Muscles as a Group

As Spinal Flexors.   The rectus abdominis and the external and internal obliques work together to flex the lumbar and thoracic spine. They play a small part, however, in flexing the spine from an erect position. They initiate the movement but relax almost immediately as the extensors take over in lengthening contraction to control the movement which is now produced by the force of gravity. The only circumstance that would necessitate continued contraction of the abdominal muscles would be if the spine were being flexed against resistance such as would occur if a person were lifting a weight by pulling down on a pulley rope and were supplementing his arm strength by flexing his spine instead of by the more efficient method of bending the knees and using the body weight.

The abdominal muscles are markedly active when the spine is being flexed from a supine position, especially at the beginning of this movement before the hips start to flex. Their activity is increased if a weight is held against the chest or on top of the head. (Obviously, the head and neck flexors are also working hard.) Once the hips start to flex, the abdominal muscles play a double role, namely, as movers in flexing the spine and as stabilizers of the pelvis against the pull of the hip flexors.

When a straight-spine sit-up is performed, the abdominal muscles *do not act as movers* at all. In this exercise, the trunk as a whole is flexing at the hip joints on the lower extremities. As the hip flexors are attached to the movable pelvis, the latter needs to be stabilized against their pull, and this is done by means of the *static contraction* of the abdominal muscles. If the latter are not strong enough to prevent the tilting of the pelvis, the abdominal action then becomes involuntary eccentric or lengthening contraction. If the student is thoroughly familiar with the attachments of the abdominal muscles, he will know that they cannot be movers in this exercise as they do not cross the hip joints.

The Abdominal Wall.   The abdominal wall consists of the three abdominal muscles just discussed and the transversus abdominis (Fig. 9–11). The latter muscle is a broad sheet of horizontal fibers whose function is to compress the abdomen. It is primarily a muscle of respiration and other physiologic functions. Together, these four muscles form a strong anterior support for the abdominal viscera. They are subject to considerable stress from the pressure of the latter against their inner surface. The more stretched they become, as in the case of a protruding abdomen, the more heavily the organs rest upon the abdominal wall, subjecting it to direct gravitational stress. Thus a vicious circle is set in motion. The pressure against the lower abdominal wall stretches it still more, causing its protrusion to increase and subjecting it to ever increasing gravitational stress. As is so often the case, correction of this postural fault is much more difficult than its prevention. A strong abdominal wall is greatly to be desired.

Posterior Aspect

Splenius Capitis and Cervicis. (Fig. 8–18.)   These two muscles consist of bands of parallel fibers, slanting outward as they ascend from their centrally located lower attachments to their more laterally located upper attachments. The capitis is much broader than the cervicis. The illustration clearly shows the left cervicis and the right capitis muscles. The viewer should try to visualize both muscles on both sides. When the left and right sides contract together, they serve to *extend and hyperextend the head and neck.* They also help to *support the head* in erect posture. One side contracting alone can *flex the head and neck laterally,* also *rotate them to the opposite side.* The muscles may be palpated on the

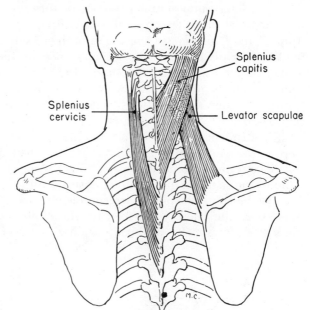

Splenius
capitis

Splenius
cervicis

Levator scapulae

Figure 8–18   Posterior and lateral
muscles of cervical spine.

back of the neck just lateral to the trapezius and posterior to the sternocleidomastoid above the levator scapulae, especially if the head is extended against
resistance in the prone position and the shoulders are kept relaxed. It is difficult
to identify them, however.

Suboccipital Group. (Fig. 8–19.)   This is a group of four short muscles
situated at the back of the lower skull (occipital bone) and upper two vertebrae
(atlas and axis). It includes the obliquus capitis superior and inferior, and the
rectus capitis posterior major and minor. Acting together on both sides, this
group *extends and hyperextends the head.* When one side acts alone it *flexes the head
laterally* or *rotates it to the same side.*

Erector Spinae. (Fig. 8–20.)   The muscle commences as a large mass in
the lumbosacral region but soon divides into three branches.

The iliocostalis branch consists of lumbar, thoracic and cervical portions
which are named lumborum, thoracis and cervicis, respectively. It receives an
additional tendon of origin from each rib throughout the thoracic region and
gives off small slips to insert into the ribs in the thoracic region and into the
transverse processes of the vertebrae in the cervical region.

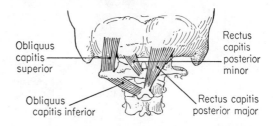

Obliquus
capitis
superior

Rectus
capitis
posterior
minor

Figure 8–19   Suboccipital muscles. (Posterior view.)

Obliquus
capitis inferior

Rectus capitis
posterior major

The longissimus branch consists of three distinct portions which, in fact, appear to be three separate muscles (see Fig. 8–20). Longissimus thoracis is a broad band lying against the angles of the ribs; longissimus cervicis is narrower and lies slightly closer to the spine, connecting the transverse processes of the upper thoracic vertebrae with those of the lower cervical vertebrae; and longissimus capitis is a thin strand which lies against the vertebrae for its lower two thirds and then slants outward and upward to the mastoid process of the temporal bone.

The spinalis branch lies against the vertebrae and is attached by separate slips to the spinous processes. It is of significance in the thoracic region only.

Electromyographic studies have shown that the erector spinae contributes little to the maintenance of erect posture unless a deliberate effort is made to extend the thoracic spine more completely or unless the weight is carried forward over the balls of the feet, in which case some static contraction of the muscle is required. In ordinary standing, however, the muscle is relaxed.[1]

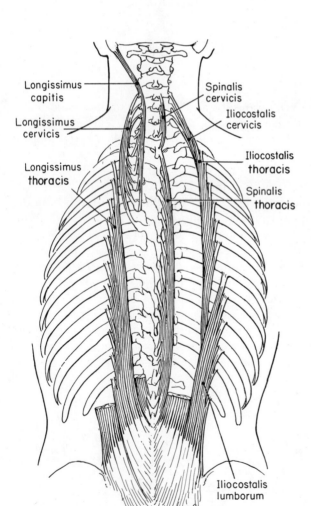

Figure 8–20   The erector spinae.

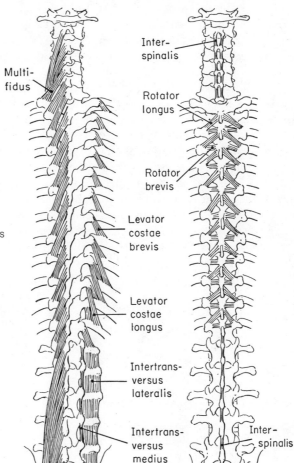

Multi-
fidus

Inter-
spinalis

Rotator
longus

Rotator
brevis

Levator
costae
brevis

Figure 8–21   Deep posterior muscles of the spine.

Levator
costae
longus

Intertrans-
versus
lateralis

Intertrans-
versus
medius

Inter-
spinalis

In forward flexion from the standing position, the erector spinae undergoes eccentric contraction until the weight of the trunk is supported by the ligaments. When the trunk returns from this position the muscle contracts concentrically until the body is again erect and balanced.[1]

The muscle engages most forcefully in its functions of extension, hyperextension and lateral flexion when these movements are performed against gravity or other resistance. Hyperextension from the prone lying position is considered the best exercise for strengthening the erector spinae.[19]

In brief, when the two sides of the muscle contract with equal force, the erector spinae *extends the head and spine* (assuming that all of its branches are contracting). When one side contracts alone, especially in conjunction with lateral and anterior muscles of the same side, it causes *lateral flexion*. And when one side alone contracts in a certain precise combination with lateral and anterior muscles—some on the same side, some on the opposite—it *rotates the head and spine to its own side.* The lumbar and lower thoracic portions of the muscle may be palpated in the two broad ridges on either side of the spine.

Deep Posterior Spinal Muscles. (Fig. 8–21.)   This group includes the multifidi, the rotatores, the interspinales, the intertransversarii and the levatores costarum. The latter is primarily a muscle of the thorax but is included here as a possible assistant in extension and lateral flexion. These muscles consist of small slips, in most cases inserting into the vertebrae immediately above their lower attachments. Some of the fibers run vertically, and some slant medially as they ascend. The former are best developed in the cervical and lumbar regions where their action is that of extension. The latter are best developed in the thoracic region where they either extend or rotate. It has been suggested that the muscles in this group are responsible for localized movements. It seems likely that they also help to stabilize the spine. In brief, acting symmetrically they *extend and hyperextend the spine,* and acting asymmetrically they *rotate the spine to the opposite side* and *assist in lateral flexion.*

Semispinalis Thoracis, Cervicis and Capitis. (Fig. 8–22.)   These muscles lie close to the vertebrae beneath the erector spinae. The thoracis and cervicis portions consist of small bundles of fibers that slant medially as they ascend to

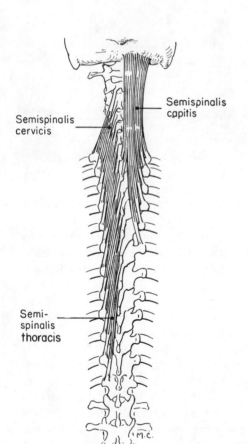

Semispinalis
capitis

Semispinalis
cervicis

Semi-
spinalis
thoracis

Figure 8–22   Semispinalis. (Posterior view.)

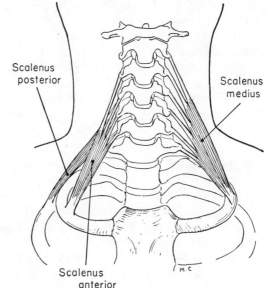

Scalenus
posterior

Scalenus
medius

Figure 8-23   The three scaleni muscles.
(Anterior view.)

Scalenus
anterior

the spinous processes several vertebrae above. The lower portion of the semi-spinalis capitis, that is, the portion starting from the upper thoracic vertebrae, have a slight medial slant, but the bundles in the cervical region attaching to the occipital bone are vertical. Like the muscles in the preceding group they *extend and hyperextend the thoracic and cervical spine* when both sides contract together, and when only one side contracts they cause *lateral flexion and rotation to the opposite side.*

Transversospinalis.   This is not a different muscle from those already listed but represents a different organization of the deep muscles of the back. Some texts use this term for the three spinal muscles whose fibers slant medially as they ascend, namely the *semispinalis,* the *multifidi* and the *rotatores* (Fig. 8-21 and 8-22).

Thoracolumbar Fascia.   (Fig. 8-16.)   Although not a muscle, the thoracolumbar fascia is described here because of its importance to the deep muscles of the spine and to the erector spinae. It binds these muscles together, holding them close to the skeletal structure and separating them from the more superficial muscles of the back. In the lumbar region it curves around the lateral margin of the erector spinae and folds in front of it to attach to the tips of the transverse processes of the vertebrae and to the intertransverse ligaments. Its lateral portion provides attachment for the transverse abdominis (Fig. 9-11), and its posterior portion blends with the aponeurosis of the latissimus dorsi (Fig. 4-6).

Lateral Aspect

Scalenus Anterior, Posterior and Medius.   (Fig. 8-23.)   The three scalenes run diagonally upward from the sides of the two upper ribs to the transverse processes of the cervical vertebrae. Acting together, they *flex the cervical spine,* and acting on one side at a time, they *flex the neck laterally.* They may be palpated on the side of the neck between the sternocleidomastoid and the upper trapezius but are difficult to identify.

Sternocleidomastoid. (Fig. 8–24.) This muscle arises from two heads, one from the top of the sternum and the other from the top of the clavicle about two inches away from the first. They unite to attach to bones of the skull close below and behind the ear. Acting together, they *flex the head and neck.* Acting on one side at a time, they *flex the head and neck laterally;* they also *rotate them to the opposite side* (Fig. 8–26, *A*). They may be easily palpated, as well as seen, on the side of the neck from just under the ear to the front of the neck on either side of the sternoclavicular joint.

Campbell observed that both the sternocleidomastoid and the three scalenes show marked activity as soon as a person begins to raise the head from a supine position, and Vitti et al. in a 1973 EMG study confirmed the movements stated in the preceding paragraph.[1]

Levator Scapulae. (Fig. 8–18.) (Also listed with the muscles of the shoulder girdle.) When one scapula is fixed, the muscle on that side will help to *flex the cervical spine laterally.* If both muscles contract at the same time when both scapulae are fixed, they neutralize each other without effecting any movement. This action may possibly help to stabilize the neck, especially when the body is in the prone position, supported on "all fours."

Quadratus Lumborum. (Fig. 8–25.) This is a flat muscle, situated behind the abdominal cavity at the side of the lumbar spine. It extends from the crest of the ilium to the lowest rib and has slips branching medially to attach to the tips of the transverse processes of the upper four lumbar vertebrae. Acting bilaterally, it is credited with *stabilizing the pelvis and lumbar spine.* Acting unilaterally, it *flexes the lumbar spine to the same side.* In a 1972 EMG study, Waters

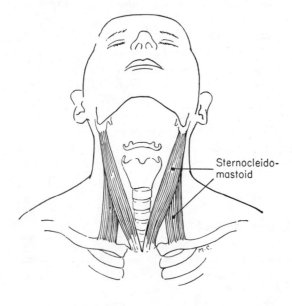

Sternocleido-
mastoid

Figure 8–24 Sternocleidomastoid muscle.

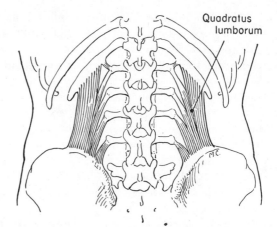

Quadratus lumborum

Figure 8-25   Quadratus lumborum. (Posterior view.)

and Morris found that together with other posterior spinal muscles as well as with the abdominal muscles it contracted regularly in each cycle of walking. According to the electromyogram reproduced in *Muscles Alive*,[1] its action appears to coincide with the moment of heel contact. The muscle may be palpated on a thin, muscular subject just lateral to the erector spinae in the lumbar region.

Psoas. (Fig. 6–13.) (Also listed with the muscles of the hip.)   Like the quadratus lumborum, the psoas is situated at the back of the abdominal cavity. Together, these two form the posterior abdominal wall. Although the psoas is primarily a muscle of the hip joint, its action on the lower spine and pelvis is of interest. (See the section on the Psoas Major and the Lumbar Spine in the Supplementary Material.) When the distal attachment is fixed, as when lying in the supine position, contraction of the psoas muscle, in addition to flexing the entire trunk on the thighs, may contribute either to flexion or to hyperextension of the lumbar spine, depending upon various factors. Its more important role, however, would seem to be *stabilization or balancing of the spine* in response to other forces acting on the latter. Unilateral contraction contributes to *lateral flexion of the lumbar spine.*

MUSCULAR ANALYSIS OF THE FUNDAMENTAL MOVEMENTS OF THE HEAD AND SPINE

In general, the muscles situated anterior to the spine flex it; those posterior to it extend it; and those lateral to it, when acting on one side only, either flex it laterally or rotate it, depending upon the requirements of the intended movement. Because of the effect of gravity, however, the anterior muscles fulfill their function as flexors most successfully when the body is supine, the posterior muscles as extensors when the body is prone and the lateral muscles as lateral flexors when the body is resting on the side. These facts should be kept in mind when one is analyzing the muscular actions of the fundamental movements.

Cervical Spine and Atlanto-occipital Joint

FLEXION.   This is performed chiefly by the sternocleidomastoid, the three scalenes and the prevertebral muscles. The supra- and infrahyoid muscles, whose chief function is to move the hyoid bone up or down in movements related to swallowing and vocalizing, give added force to cervical flexion when they contract together and movements of the mouth are prevented.

EXTENSION AND HYPEREXTENSION.   Many muscles contribute to these movements: the splenius capitis and cervicis, the capitis and cervicis portions of the erector spinae, semispinalis, deep posterior spinal muscles and the suboccipitalis. When the left and right sides of trapezius I contract together, they also help to extend the head and neck.

LATERAL FLEXION.   This is performed by the simultaneous contraction of the extensors and flexors of the same side. Specifically, the chief lateral flexors include the capitis and cervicis portions of the splenius, erector spinae, semispinalis, three scalenes and the sternocleidomastoid. The suboccipitals, cervical portions of the deep posterior spinal muscles and the levator scapulae are in a position to aid in lateral flexion when they are needed.

ROTATION. (Fig. 8–26.)   The sternocleidomastoid and deep posterior spinal muscles rotate the head and neck to the opposite side, and the splenius, erector spinae and occipitals rotate them to the same side.

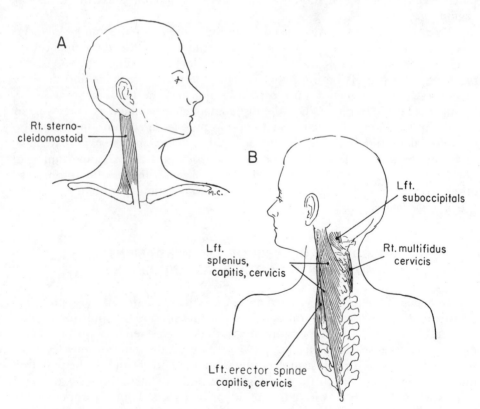

Figure 8–26   Muscles which contract to rotate the head and neck to the left.

Thoracic and Lumbar Spine

FLEXION. This is performed by the three abdominal muscles: rectus abdominis, and the external and internal obliques. As an aid to their effective action, the pelvis must often be stabilized by the hip flexors, especially when the movement is performed from the supine position.

EXTENSION AND HYPEREXTENSION. The thoracic and lumbar portions of the erector spinae and the semispinalis thoracis are the chief extensors, but the deep posterior spinal muscles also have a significant role. When hyperextension is performed from the prone lying position, the erector spinae is particularly active.

LATERAL FLEXION. Many muscles are active in this movement, the erector spinae, internal and external oblique abdominals, and quadratus lumborum in particular, with the semispinalis thoracis, rectus abdominis, deep posterior spinal muscles, psoas and latissimus dorsi supplying additional force if needed. When the trunk is flexed to the right from a side lying position on the left, the working muscles are those on the right side of the trunk.

ROTATION. (Fig. 8–27.) Rotation to the left is effected by the left internal oblique abdominal muscle and the thoracic and lumbar portions of the left

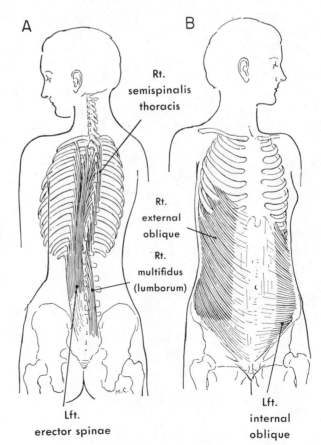

Figure 8-27 Muscles which contract to rotate the trunk to the left.

erector spinae, especially the iliocostalis thoracis branch, the right external oblique abdominal muscle, semispinalis thoracis, multifidus and other deep posterior spinal muscles.

THE PELVIC GIRDLE

Structure. (Fig. 8–28.)   Each hip bone (os innominatum) is made up of three bones—the ilium, ischium and pubis. These bones become fused into a single bone by about the time of puberty. The two hip bones together form the pelvic girdle. This bony girdle or basin is firmly attached to the sacrum at the sacroiliac articulation, an articulation that is difficult to classify. It presents some of the characteristics of a diarthrodial joint, an articular cavity being present for part of the articulation. It is unlike other diarthrodial joints in one important respect, however. No movement can be voluntarily effected at the sacroiliac joint. Any movement which does occur is involuntary. Just how much motion can take place at the sacroiliac joint is debatable. Some anatomists say that a slight "giving" may occur there as a shock absorption device; others claim that no motion occurs at the joint normally, except in women during pregnancy and parturition, when the ligaments relax in order to permit a slight spreading of the bones. (See report of study by Clayson et al., page 228.)

The sacrum is firmly bound to the two iliac bones by means of the anterior, posterior and interosseus sacroiliac ligaments (Figs. 8–29 and 8–30). It is further reinforced by the iliolumbar, sacrotuberous and sacrospinous ligaments and by the lower portion of the erector spinae muscle. Because of this firm attachment, the sacrum might well be considered a part of the pelvic girdle. From the point of view of function it is more truly a part of the pelvis than of the spine.

The joints at which the movements of the pelvic girdle occur are the two hip joints and the joints of the lumbar spine, particularly the lumbosacral articulation.

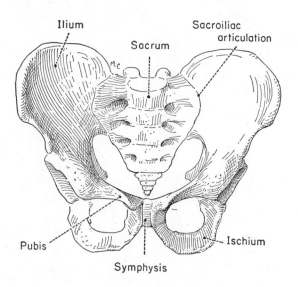

Figure 8–28   Anterior view of pelvis.

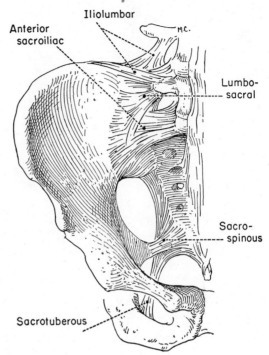

Figure 8-29 Anterior view of sacroiliac articulation showing ligaments.

Movements. The pelvic movements may be defined as follows:

1. Increased inclination (forward tilt) (Fig. 8–31, *C*). A rotation of the pelvis in the sagittal plane about a frontal-horizontal axis in such a manner that the symphysis pubis turns downward and the posterior surface of the sacrum turns upward.

2. Decreased inclination (backward tilt) (Fig. 8–31, *B*). A rotation of the pelvis in the sagittal plane about a frontal-horizontal axis in such a manner that the symphysis pubis moves forward-upward and the posterior surface of the sacrum turns somewhat downward.

3. Lateral tilt. A rotation of the pelvis in the frontal plane about a sagittal-horizontal axis in such a manner that one iliac crest is lowered and the other is raised. The tilt is named in terms of the side which moves downward. Thus in a lateral tilt of the pelvis to the left, the left iliac crest is lowered and the right is raised.

4. Rotation (lateral twist). A rotation of the pelvis in the horizontal plane about a vertical axis. The movement is named in terms of the direction toward which the front of the pelvis turns.

The Relationship of the Pelvis to the Trunk and Lower Extremities. Architecturally, the pelvis is strategically located. Linking the trunk with the lower extremities, it must cooperate with the motion of each, yet at the same time contribute to the stability of the total structure. When the body is in the erect standing position, the pelvis receives the weight of the head, trunk and upper extremities, divides it equally and transmits it to the two lower extremities. Whenever an individual stands on only one foot, the pelvis automatically adapts itself to this position and transmits the entire weight of the upper part of the

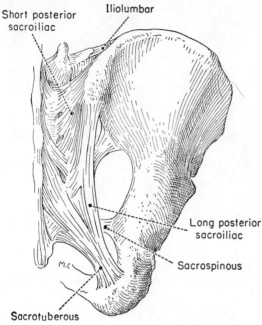

Short posterior
sacroiliac

Iliolumbar

Figure 8–30 Posterior view of sacroiliac articulation showing ligaments.

Long posterior
sacroiliac

Sacrospinous

Sacrotuberous

body to one of the lower extremities. It requires a fine adjustment to do this in such a way that the balance of the total structure is preserved.

Since the pelvis depends upon the joints of the lower spine and those of the hips for its movements, it is not surprising that its motion is sometimes associated with the motion of the trunk or spine, and sometimes with that of the thighs. In such cases the movement of the pelvis may be said to be secondary to that of the spine, or of the thighs, as the case may be. In fact, most of its motion belongs in one or the other category. Occasionally, however, the move-

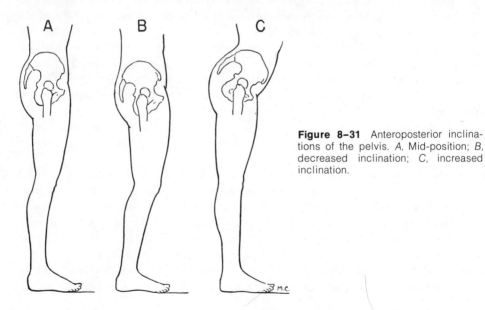

A B C

Figure 8–31 Anteroposterior inclinations of the pelvis. *A,* Mid-position; *B,* decreased inclination; *C,* increased inclination.

ment seems to be initiated in the pelvis itself, with the spine and thighs cooperating with it. In such an event, the movement of the pelvis might be considered primary, and that of the spine and hips, secondary. One sees this type of movement when the individual "tucks his hips under" as he would have to do to change from *C* to *B*, or even *C* to *A*, in Figure 8–31.

It is not always easy to judge the habitual tilt of the pelvis from the contours of the body. Prominent buttocks, heavy layers of fat or an unusually convex sacrum can easily mislead the observer. Figure 8–32 shows a sketch based on an x-ray which illustrates a type of build in which the contour of the lower back and pelvic region does not correspond to the bony structure. In this illustration the tilt, as judged by the position of the sacrum, is greater than it appears to be from the contour of the lower back. This observation is of importance to those who tend to place emphasis on the position of the pelvis in giving posture instruction.

The joint analyses of the primary and secondary movements of the pelvis are given below.

JOINT ANALYSIS OF THE PRIMARY MOVEMENTS OF THE PELVIS AS PERFORMED FROM THE FUNDAMENTAL STANDING POSITION.

Pelvis	*Spinal Joints*	*Hip Joints*
Increased tilt	Hyperextension	Slight flexion
Decreased tilt	Slight flexion	Complete extension
Lateral tilt to left	Slight lateral flexion to right	R: Slight adduction L: Slight abduction

Rotation to left
  (without turning the head
  or moving the feet)
	Rotation right	R: Slight outward rotation
		L: Slight inward rotation

JOINT ANALYSIS OF MOVEMENTS OF THE PELVIS SECONDARY TO THOSE OF THE SPINE

Spine	*Pelvis*
Flexion	Decreased tilt
Hyperextension	Increased tilt
Lateral flexion to left	Lateral tilt to left
Rotation to left	Rotation to left

There are also movements of the pelvis which may be considered as secondary to the movements of the lower extremity. A good example of this is seen in the high kick or a punt. (See Fig. 6–15.) In activities such as this the pelvis seems to move with the lower extremity for the purpose of supplementing the latter's range of motion. Hence, when the thigh is flexed at the hip joint, the pelvic inclination is decreased; when the lower extremity is raised backward

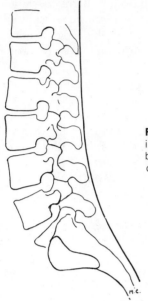

Figure 8–32 Lumbar and lumbosacral regions of the spine showing discrepancy in the lower lumbar curve as seen in the vertebral bodies and as seen in the contour of the back. (The sketch is based on an x-ray.)

in apparent hyperextension, the pelvic inclination is increased; when one thigh is widely abducted, the pelvis tilts laterally; and when one leg is placed forward and the other backward as though taking a long stride, the pelvis rotates in the horizontal plane about a vertical axis.

All the muscles which attach to the pelvic bones or to the sacrum serve either to initiate or to control pelvic movements. As one would expect, these are all muscles either of the hip joint or of the lumbar spine, including the lumbosacral junction. The precise combination of movements at these joints depends upon whether the pelvic movement is primary or whether it is secondary, supplementing either the spinal movements or those of the hip joint.

COMMON ATHLETIC INJURIES OF THE
NECK, BACK AND PELVIS

The Neck and Back

Neck Injuries. While these fortunately are not common among athletes, they are of prime concern. If there is the slightest suspicion of serious injury it is literally of vital importance that the individual not be moved *at all* until the physician has examined him, and then only under the physician's close supervision. *The danger of death or paralysis from the neck down cannot be over-emphasized.*

Contusion of the Spine. These are undoubtedly much more common among athletes than among non-athletes. The muscles involved are usually those on either side of the spinous processes. Ordinarily the contusion is not serious but it may cause a hematoma. Another possible complication is painful stiffness which may last for several days. Muscle spasm often occurs in the more severe contusions of the lower back.

Back Strains and Sprains.   Strains (injuries to muscles) and sprains (injuries to ligaments) are both common in athletics largely because there are so many muscles and ligaments in the region of the spine. In the early stages of these injuries it is often difficult to distinguish between them. The strain is usually the result of either a violent contraction or a movement which causes the muscles to overstretch.[17] A sprain may be caused by the same kind of movements that cause a strain, but in the latter case the damage is a tearing of the ligaments.

An acute back *strain* which is not given proper treatment is likely to develop into a chronic strain and become a perpetual problem. This is usually more common in the lower back than in the upper. Prevention of back strain and sprain is of major concern in the planning of conditioning programs.

Fractures of Transverse Process of Lumbar Vertebra.   These occur quite frequently in sports, either from a severe blow or from a violent muscular contraction. In either case, the damage to the muscle which attaches to the bone is of greater significance than the damage to the bone itself.[17] This is understandable when one reviews the attachments of the back muscles, especially those of the semispinalis muscle and the deep posterior muscles of the spine.

Herniated Disk.   O'Donoghue believes that the conditions which cause this, namely, the compression of two adjacent vertebrae with such magnitude that the annulus fibrosus is ruptured, is rarely brought about by participation in sports.[17] Repeated heavy lifting with the body in poor alignment is a more likely cause. If this has happened to an athlete, however, participation in athletics is unwise until the rupture can be repaired. Otherwise the nucleus pulposus is likely to protrude through the break in the disk and press on the spinal cord or a spinal nerve. The area most likely to be affected is the lumbar spine, especially between the fourth and fifth lumbar vertebrae. This condition can be very painful.

The Pelvis

Contusion of Buttocks Area.   This is common and not usually of serious consequence. If, however, the tuberosity of the ischium receives a direct blow, the contusion may be accompanied by a fracture.

Contusion and Strain of Iliac Crest.   (Hip pointer.)   This is likely to occur from a blow in football or other contact sport, especially if the crest is not adequately protected. The injury may consist of a simple contusion, or it may involve a strain of the muscles that attach to the crest or even a muscular avulsion, a condition in which the muscle pulls away from the crest taking some bone with it. If the latter occurs and the injury is not properly diagnosed and therefore not adequately treated, there is likely to be a recurrence.[13, 17]

Contusion of Sacrum and Coccyx.   Contusion of the sacrum is a common injury in contact sports and can be very painful but is not usually serious, provided it is only a contusion and the bone is not cracked or fractured. It can be prevented or minimized by the wearing of adequate protection. Contusion of the coccyx may also result from a direct blow or from a fall in which the subject lands heavily in a sitting position.

Muscle Strain. A common strain in the pelvic area is one that occurs where the semitendinosus and the long head of the biceps femoris attach to the lower and medial impression on the tuberosity of the ischium. This is usually caused by a forceful movement of the lower extremity involving flexion of the thigh with the knees held in extension. In severe strains there may also be an avulsion fracture, especially if the ossification of the epiphysis is not yet complete.

SUPPLEMENTARY MATERIAL

Movements of the Lower Spine and Pelvis. In 1962 Clayson and his co-workers reported their investigation of the mobility of the hip joints and lumbar vertebrae. Their subjects were 26 normal young women who had no history of disabilities of the back or hips. The movements studied were flexion and extension of the hip joint combined with flexion and extension of the lumbar spine. For their complete findings the reader is referred to their published report.[5]

A few of their measurements and observations were as follows:

Average maximum flexion and maximum extension of the hip joint, as measured by the pelvifemoral angle, were 60 ± 6.7 degrees and 186 ± 6 degrees, respectively.

The average pelvifemoral angle in the relaxed standing position was 175 ± 3.4 degrees.

The greatest anteroposterior motion in the lumbar spine took place between the fifth lumbar vertebra and the sacrum.

In flexion, the lumbar curve became reversed in all but four subjects.

Anteroposterior motion at the sacroiliac joint ranged from 1 degree to 21 degrees, the average being 8 ± 4.9 degrees.

The combined anteroposterior motion taking place in the lumbar spine and hip joints together averaged 181 degrees from maximum flexion to the relaxed standing position and 41 degrees from the latter to maximum extension, making a total average movement of 222 degrees.

The Psoas Major and the Lumbar Spine. Because the psoas major muscle at its proximal end attaches to the sides of the bodies and to the front and lower borders of the transverse processes of all the lumbar vertebrae, it has been thought to be a mover of the lumbar portion of the spinal column. A review of textbooks of kinesiology and of corrective exercises shows that there are conflicting statements concerning such movements. Some say that when its distal attachment is fixed, it flexes the lumbar spine; some say that it hyperextends it; others say that sometimes it flexes and sometimes it hyperextends, according to the current relation of its line of pull to the lumbar joints. This relationship is thought to be affected by the position of the body, by the anteroposterior postural curve of the lumbar spine and by its current status, whether in a position of flexion or hyperextension.

In the hope of having some light thrown on this subject, the writings of four experimental clinicians (physicians or physical therapists of known repute for their wide experience in observing the muscular action of patients)[3, 6, 12, 23] and the statement of four researchers (or teams of researchers) based on their electromyographic experimentation,[7, 11, 14, 16] were carefully examined. Unfortunately, this perusal served only to bring to light more conflicting statements.

What is the reader to conclude from this? Does it actually imply opposing points of view? It seems to this reviewer that there may be a number of logical explanations for the seeming disagreements. For instance, the writer may not have been explicit regarding techniques used or specific conditions at the time of examining or experimenting; he may use terminology that is subject to misinterpretation; variations in muscular action may have been caused by variations in anatomic structure or in habitual posture; and finally, for one reason or another, the reader may have simply misunderstood the writer's meaning.

When there appear to be diverse opinions regarding muscular actions, it seems likely that the differences are not of great importance. Frequently, when there is lack of agreement regarding movement, one may safely assume that the true function of the muscular contraction, with reference to the joints in question, is more likely to be stabilization or balance than purposeful movement. This, in fact, has been suggested as a function of the psoas muscle by two investigators, Keagy et al, and Nachemson. The latter's study of the stabilizing action of the psoas appeared in a Scandinavian journal and has been brought to our attention both by Basmajian and by Jonsson.[10] Brunnstrom has described this type of action with unusual clarity. She likens the muscles that are situated close to the spinal column (erector spinae, psoas major, etc.) to guy ropes that support an upright pole. When the pole starts to tip, the tension of the ropes on the opposite side increases. In like manner, if a person starts to lean backward, possibly to favor weak posterior muscles, the muscles on the front of the spine spring into action. She told of a patient with paralysis of the psoas muscles who, when he sat on a stool, always inclined his trunk forward. When she gently pushed his trunk to the erect position he had to grasp the sides of the stool to keep from falling over backward. The other hip flexors, largely because of their poor leverage, were not equal to the task of holding the trunk erect. While this does not necessarily exemplify spinal action, it emphasizes an important function of the psoas muscle which is often overlooked.[3]

Atypical Spinal Contours. Wells investigated the spinal contours of 100 college women as recorded in routine anteroposterior posture photographs in which the MacEwan pointers were used to show the location of the tip of the spinous processes. These 100 photographs were selected from 1200, fifty of them on the basis of a predominantly convex spine, that is, a spine in which the thoracic convexity involves a portion, possibly all, of the lumbar region; and fifty on the basis of a predominantly concave spine, that is, a spine in which the lumbar concavity extends well up into the thoracic region. Because the convex spine is characteristic of the anthropoid apes, this group was called the "anthropoid spine" group; and because a lumbar curve is charactertistic of the human spine, the second group was called the "humanoid spine" group (Fig. 8–33). Measurements made on the photographs revealed that significant measurable differences existed between the two types of spine. The mean values of these measurements are presented in Table 8–1.[21]

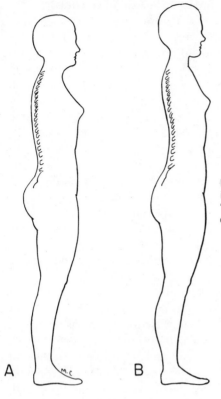

Figure 8-33 Lateral views of two female figures illustrating variations in spinal type. *A*, Convex or "anthropoid" type of spine. *B*, Concave or "humanoid" type of spine.

TABLE 8-1   Comparison of "Anthropoid" and "Humanoid" Types of Spines with Reference to the Depth and Length of the Anteroposterior Curves of the Thoracic and Lumbar Portions of the Spine (Wells)

(Mean values of measurements taken from the posture photographs of 100 college women, 50 representing the "anthropoid" type and 50 the "humanoid" type.)

ASPECT OF SPINE MEASURED	"ANTHROPOID" SPINE	"HUMANOID" SPINE
Total length of thoracic and lumbar portion of spine	3.54 cm.	3.54 cm.
Length of posterior convexity	2.79 cm. (79%)	1.48 cm. (42%)
Length of posterior concavity	0.75 cm. (21%)	2.06 cm. (58%)
Depth of posterior convexity	0.22 cm.	0.08 cm.
Depth of posterior concavity	0.06 cm.	0.16 cm.

Patterns of Anteroposterior Spinal Flexibility.   An interesting study of the flexibility of the spinal column of four individuals was made by Wiles. Two of the subjects were normally active women; two were acrobatic dancers, one of them a child and the other a man. While too small in scope to be of any real significance, this study is interesting because it suggests the wide variation in flexibility found in the human spine. In the light of Wells' study, it is interesting to note that the photograph of Miss P. showed a spine of "normal" contours;

TABLE 8–2 Anteroposterior Spinal Flexibility of Four Selected Cases (Wiles)

SUBJECT	FLEXION	HYPEREXTENSION	TOTAL
Miss P	64°	35°	99°
Miss R	62°	19°	81°
Child	76°	39°	115°
Man	50°	71°	121°

that of Miss R. showed a long convexity or "anthropoid type" of spine; that of the child showed a marked lordosis; and that of the man showed a shallow but long concavity or "humanoid type" of spine. The range of motion in each spine, as measured on x-rays, is recorded in Table 8–2. The relationship between the type of spine and the degree and pattern of flexibility should be noted. The Wiles study, although it involves only four individuals, two of whom were highly atypical from the point of view of agility, nevertheless suggests a relationship between structure and function.[22] It is interesting to note that Miss R., whose spine seemed to be of the "anthropoid type," showed a marked limitation in hyperextension, whereas the adult male acrobat, who seemed to represent the extreme "humanoid type," showed extreme hyperextension, but limited flexion.[22] A study of the flexibility of a large sampling of these two spinal types might prove to be of value to the physical educator and the athletic coach.

The significance of studies such as the two preceding ones lies in their implication for posture education and for recommendations regarding activity. Such studies are valuable to the degree that they give (1) a broad concept of the "normal," (2) an appreciation of the relatedness between structural type and physical skills and (3) an awareness of the limitations characteristic of each type. Physical educators and therapists should realize that identical goals of posture, flexibility and function cannot be laid down for all types of body build. Just what the specific abilities and limitations of each type are, and just what the goals for each type should be, are problems that are still open for investigation.

Comparison of Surface Measurements of Lumbosacral Portion of Spine with Similar Measurements Made on X-ray. In 1934 Boynton made a study of the pelvis and lumbar spine, using for her subjects fifty college women.[2] Her data consisted both of anthropometric measurements and of measurements taken from lateral x-rays. She found considerable variation in the contour and position of the sacrum, and she observed a close relationship between these and the slope of the lower lumbar vertebrae. In her opinion the slope of the lower lumbar vertebrae is determined by the slope of the top of the sacrum and the position of the sacrum in the pelvis. She also observed that the angle of pelvic obliquity varies with these factors. Furthermore—and this is probably Boynton's most

TABLE 8–3 Coefficients of Correlation Between Measurements Made on Surface of Body and Measurements Made on X-ray

Position of sacrum	.0222
Slope of sacrum	.2430
Slope of lower lumbar vertebrae	.0465

important contribution—she found that the correlation between the measurements on the surface of the body and those on the x-rays was so low that it was impossible to judge accurately the slope of the lower lumbar vertebrae and the angle of pelvic obliquity from the external measurements (Fig. 8–32). The coefficients of correlation which she computed give further emphasis to this revealing observation (See Table 8–3.)

LABORATORY EXPERIENCES

Joint Structure

1. Study the bones of the spinal column, then fill out an outline like the one in Appendix A for each of the following joints, including the articulations of both the bodies and the arches.
   a. Atlanto-occipital
   b. Atlantoaxial
   c. A middle cervical joint
   d. The joint between the seventh cervical and the first thoracic vertebra
   e. A middle thoracic joint
   f. The joint between the twelfth thoracic and the first lumbar vertebra
   g. A middle lumbar joint
   h. The lumbosacral joint

Joint Action

2. Have a subject sit tailor-fashion on a table and flex his spine as completely as possible. Observe the shape of the spine as seen from the side. Compare the three regions of the spine as to forward flexibility. Make a line drawing of the side view of the spine.

3. Have a subject sit astride a chair, facing its back, and hyperextend the spine as completely as possible. Observe and record the shape of the spine as in 2.

4. Have a subject sit astride a bench and bend sideward as far as possible, first to one side and then to the other. Observe from the rear and draw a line representing the spine in maximum lateral flexion, both left and right.

5. Have a subject sit astride a bench with the hands at the neck, then rotate the trunk as far as possible, first to one side, then to the other. Observe and compare the regions of the spine as to rotating ability.

6. Observe flexion, hyperextension, lateral flexion and rotation of the spine in several subjects, preferably subjects representing different body builds, and note individual differences.

7. Have a subject lie face down on a table with the legs and pelvis supported on the table, the trunk extending forward beyond the table, and the hands clasped behind the neck.
   a. Have the subject bend laterally. Compare the thoracic and lumbar regions. Note the torsion accompanying the lateral flexion.
   b. Have the subject flex the spine and then flex it laterally. Observe as in a.
   c. Have the subject hyperextend the spine (with someone helping to support the elbows) and then flex laterally. Observe as in a.
   d. Have the subject rotate the trunk to one side as far as possible. Compare the thoracic and lumbar regions. Is any lateral bending apparent in the spine?
   e. Have the subject flex the spine and then rotate it. Observe as in d.
   f. Have the subject hyperextend the spine and then rotate it. Observe as in d.

Muscular Action

The purpose of these exercises is not to test the strength of the muscles, but to enable the observer to study the action of the muscles in simple movements of the body. The procedure, therefore, is quite different from that followed by the physical therapist in testing muscle strength. It is suggested that students work in groups of three: one acting as the subject, one as an assistant helping to support or steady the stationary part of the body and giving resistance to the moving part, and one palpating the muscles and recording the results. The check lists in Appendix D may be used for this purpose. They may also be used for the analysis of other movements.

8. FLEXION OF THE NECK
   a. *Subject:* Lie on the back and lift the head, bringing the chin toward the chest.
      Observer: Palpate and identify as many of the contracting muscles as possible.
   b. *Subject:* Lie on the back and lift the head, leading with the chin.
      Observer: Compare the action of the sternocleidomastoid in *b* with its action in *a*.

9. EXTENSION AND HYPEREXTENSION OF THE NECK
   a. *Subject:* Lie face down on a table with the head over the edge. Raise the head as far as possible, hyperextending both the head and the neck.
      Assistant: May resist the movement if stronger muscular action is desired.
      Observer: Palpate and identify as many of the contracting muscles as possible.
   b. *Subject:* Lie face down on a table with the head over the edge. Raise the head as far as possible with the chin tucked in.
      Assistant: Resist the retraction of the chin.
      Observer: Compare the muscular action in (*b*) with that in (*a*).

10. LATERAL FLEXION OF THE HEAD AND NECK
    Subject: Lie on one side and raise the head toward the shoulder without turning the head or tensing the shoulder.
    Assistant: Give slight resistance at the temple.
    Observer: Palpate and identify as many muscles as possible.

11. ROTATION OF THE HEAD AND NECK
    Subject: Sit erect and turn the head to the left as far as possible.
    Assistant: Give fairly strong resistance to the side of the jaw.
    Observer: Palpate the sternocleidomastoids. Which one contracts?

12. FLEXION OF THE THORACIC AND LUMBAR SPINE
    Subject: Lie on the back with the arms folded across the chest. Raise the head, shoulders and upper back from the table, keeping the chin in. There is no need to come to a sitting position, since this is intended as a movement of spinal, not hip, flexion.
    Assistant: Hold the thighs down.
    Observer: Palpate the rectus abdominis and the external oblique abdominal muscle.

13. EXTENSION AND HYPEREXTENSION OF THE THORACIC AND LUMBAR SPINE
    Subject: Lie face down with the hands on the hips. Raise the head and trunk as far as possible.
    Assistant: Hold the feet down.
    Observer: Palpate the erector spinae and the gluteus maximus (the large hip extensor muscle located in the buttocks). What is the function of the latter muscle in this movement?

14. LATERAL FLEXION OF THE THORACIC AND LUMBAR SPINE
    Subject: Lie on one side with the under arm placed across the chest and the hand resting on the opposite shoulder, and with the hand of the top arm resting on the hip. Raise the trunk sideways.
    Assistant: Hold the legs down. If necessary, help the subject by pulling at the elbow.

Observer: Palpate the rectus abdominis, external oblique abdominal muscle, erector spinae and latissimus dorsi (the large superficial muscle of the lower back whose tendon of insertion forms the posterior margin of the armpit).

15. ROTATION OF THE THORACIC AND LUMBAR SPINE
    Subject: Sit astride a bench with the hands placed behind the neck. Twist to one side as far as possible without leaving the bench.
    Assistant: Resist the movement by grasping the subject's arms close to his shoulders and pushing (or pulling) in the opposite direction.
    Observer: Palpate as many of the spinal and abdominal muscles as possible. Disregard the muscles of the scapula and arm.

16. DECREASE OF PELVIC INCLINATION
    Subject: Lie on back with knees drawn up and feet resting on floor. Tilt pelvis in such a manner that lumbar spine becomes flatter.
    Assistant: Kneeling at subject's head and facing his feet, place thumbs on his anterior superior iliac spines and fingers under his lower back. Resist movement by pushing iliac spines toward subject's feet.
    Observer: Palpate rectus abdominis and gluteus maximus. Palpate the hamstrings. Do they contract?

17. INCREASE OF PELVIC INCLINATION
    Subject: In erect standing position, stiffen the knees and push the buttocks as far back as possible.
    Observer: Palpate tensor fascia latae, sartorius, pectineus and iliocostalis. Does the adductor longus or gracilis contract?

18. LATERAL TILT OF PELVIS
    Subject: Stand on one foot on stool with other leg hanging free. Pull free hip up as far as possible.
    Assistant: Give slight resistance by holding ankle down.
    Observer: Palpate oblique abdominals, iliocostalis, adductor magnus, adductor longus and gracilis on side of free leg.

Action of the Muscles Other Than the Movers
19. THE SIT-UP
    Subject: Lie on the back and come to a sitting position, keeping the spine as rigid as possible.
    Assistant: Hold the feet down.
    Observer: Palpate the abdominal muscles, the erector spinae and the sternocleidomastoid. Explain the function of each.

20. DOUBLE LEG LOWERING
    Subject: Lie on the back. Raise both legs, then slowly lower them half way.
    Observer: Palpate the abdominal muscles and the erector spinae. Explain the function of each.

21. TRUNK BENDING FORWARD
    Subject: Stand with the feet slightly separated. Bend forward from the hips, keeping the back flat.
    Observer: Palpate the erector spinae. Explain its function.

22. PUSH-UP
    Subject: Assume a front-leaning-rest position on the hands and toes with the body straight. Let the elbows bend until the chest almost touches the floor, then push up again, keeping the body straight the entire time. Do not let it sag or hump.
    Observer: Palpate the abdominal muscles. Explain their function.

REFERENCES

1. Basmajian, J. V.: Muscles Alive, 3rd Ed. Baltimore: The Williams & Wilkins Company, 1974.
2. Boynton, B.: Individual differences in the structure of pelvis and lumbar spine as a factor in body mechanics. Thesis, State University of Iowa, 1934.
3. Brunnstrom, S.: Clinical Kinesiology, 2nd Ed. Philadelphia: F. A. Davis Company, 1966.
4. Campbell, E. J. M.: An electromyographic study of the role of the abdominal muscles in breathing. J. Physiol., *117*:222–233, 1952.
5. Clayson, S. J., Newman, I. M., Debevec, D. F., et al: Evaluation of mobility of hip and lumbar vertebrae of normal young women. Arch. Phys. Med. & Rehab., *43*:1–8, 1962.
6. Crowe, P., O'Connell, A. L., and Gardner, E. B.: An electromyographic study of the abdominal muscles and certain hip flexors during selected sit-ups. Report presented at National Convention of the American Association for Health, Physical Education, and Recreation, 1963.
7. Flint, M. M.: An electromyographic comparison of the function of the iliacus and the rectus abdominis muscles. J. Am. Phys. Ther. Assn., *45*:248–252, 1965.
8. Floyd, W. F., and Silver, P. H. S.: Electromyographic study of patterns of activity of the anterior abdominal wall muscles in man. J. Anat., *84*:132–145, 1950.
9. Hollinshead, W. H.: Anatomy of the spine. J. Bone & Joint Surg., *47A*:209–215, 1965.
10. Jonsson, B.: Morphology, innervation, and electromyographic study of the erector spinae. Arch. Phys. Med. & Rehab., *50*:638–641, 1969.
11. Keagy, R. D., Brumlik, J. B., and Bergan, J. J.: Direct electromyography of the psoas major muscle in man. J. Bone & Joint Surg., *48A*:1377–1382, 1966.
12. Kendall, H. O., and Kendall, F. P.: The role of abdominal exercises in a program of physical fitness. J. Health & Phys. Ed., *14*:480, 481, 504–506, 1943.
13. Klafs, C. E., and Arnheim, D. D.: Modern Principles of Athletic Training. St. Louis: C. V. Mosby Company, 1973.
14. LaBan, M. M., Raptou, A. D., and Johnson, E. W.: Electromyographic study of function of iliopsoas muscle. Arch. Phys. Med. & Rehab., *46*:676–679, 1965.
15. Lovett, R. W.: Lateral Curvature of the Spine and Round Shoulders, 5th Ed. Philadelphia: P. Blakiston's Son and Co., Inc., 1931, Chapter 3.
16. Nachemson, A. *Quoted in* Jonsson, B.: Morphology, innervation, and electromyographic study of the erector spinae. Arch. Phys. Med. & Rehab., *50*:638–641, 1969.
17. O'Donoghue, D. H.: Treatment of Injuries to Athletes. 3rd Ed. Philadelphia: W. B. Saunders Company, 1976.
18. Partridge, M. J., and Walters, C. E.: Participation of the abdominal muscles in various movements of the trunk in man. Phys. Ther. Rev., *39*:791–800, 1959.
19. Pauly, J. E.: An electromyographic analysis of certain movements and exercises. I. Some deep muscles of the back. Anat. Rec., *155*:223–234, 1966.
20. Walters, C. E., and Partridge, M. J.: Electromyographic study of the differential action of the abdominal muscles during exercise. Am. J. Phys. Med., *36*:259–268, 1957.
21. Wells, K. F.: An investigation of certain evolutionary tendencies in the female human structure. Res. Quart. Am. Assn. Health, Phys. Ed. & Recrn., *18*:260–270, 1947.
22. Wiles, P.: Movements of the lumbar vertebrae during flexion and extension. Proc. Roy. Soc. Med., *28*:647–651, 1935.
23. Wright, W. G.: Muscle Function. New York: Hafner Publishing Company, 1962.

RECOMMENDED READINGS

Jonsson, B.: Morphology, innervation and electromyographic study of the erector spinae. Arch. Phys. Med. & Rehab., *50*:638–641, 1969.
Morris, J. M., Lucas, D. B., and Bresler, B.: Role of the trunk in stability of the spine. J. Bone & Joint Surg., *43A*:327–351, 1961.

Chapter Nine

THE MOVEMENTS OF THE THORAX IN RESPIRATION

STRUCTURE

The thorax is a bony-cartilaginous cage with an inverted V-shaped opening in front beneath the sternum (Fig. 9–1). It is formed mainly by the ribs and their cartilages but also includes the sternum which constitutes the anterior base of attachment for the ribs, and the thoracic portion of the spine, which provides the posterior base of attachment. The upper seven ribs whose cartilages articulate directly with the sternum are called true ribs and the remaining five, false ribs. This is a misleading term, the only difference being that the latter do not articulate with the sternum. In each case the cartilages of the eighth, ninth and tenth ribs unite with the cartilage above; the eleventh and twelfth ribs, known as the "floating ribs," have no anterior attachment but end anteriorly in cartilagenous tips.

The angle formed by the margins of the lower rib cartilages at the front of the chest is known as the subcostal angle. This is characteristically wider in individuals of stocky build than in those of slender build. The thorax is wider from side to side than it is from front to back and is slightly flattened in front. An infant or young child has a more "barrel-shaped" chest than does an adult, that is, a thorax whose anteroposterior diameter more nearly approaches its transverse diameter than is the case in an adult.

Before studying the articulations and the movements of the thorax, the student should review the ribs by observing them on a skeleton, noting especially their shape and the way in which they twist. If no skeleton is available, he should look carefully at pictures of the ribs such as those shown in Figure 9–2.

ARTICULATIONS

All but the lowest two ribs articulate anteriorly with the sternum, either directly or indirectly, and all articulate posteriorly with the vertebrae. More specifically, with the exception of the first, tenth, eleventh and twelfth ribs, the head of each rib articulates with two adjacent vertebrae, thus spanning the disk between. Each of the other ribs articulates with a single vertebra. Except in

236

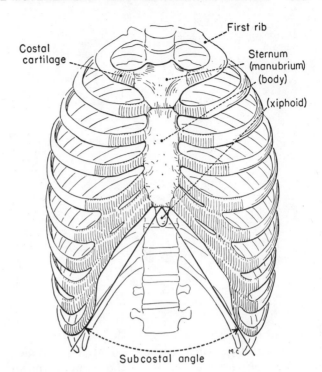

First rib

Costal
cartilage

Sternum
(manubrium)
(body)

(xiphoid)

Subcostal angle

Figure 9-1 Anterior view of
thorax.

the case of the last two ribs, each rib has an additional vertebral articulation
between the tubercle of the rib and the adjacent transverse process of the
vertebra. All of these articulations are non-axial, diarthrodial joints and permit
only a slight gliding action.

There are four groups of sternocostal articulations: (1) the *sternocostal
joints* between the costal cartilages and the sternum; (2) the joints between each

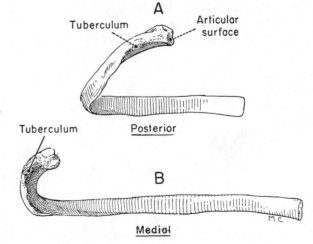

A

Tuberculum

Articular
surface

Posterior

Tuberculum

B

Medial

Figure 9-2 Rib. *A*, Posterior
view; *B*, medial view.

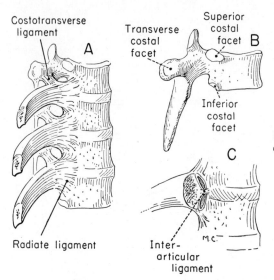

Figure 9–3 Anterior and lateral views of costovertebral articulations.

rib and its cartilage, known as the *costochondral joints;* (3) the joints between one costal cartilage and another, called the *interchondral joints;* and (4) the two *intersternal joints,* one between the manubrium and body of the sternum, the other between the body and the xiphoid process.

MOVEMENTS

Because most of the ribs are attached both posteriorly and anteriorly, their movement is extremely limited. In the thoracic expansion associated with inhalation the anterior ends of the ribs are elevated in a flexion type of movement. This is accompanied by a slight eversion in which the lower margin of the central portion of the rib turns upward and lateralward, the inner surface being made to face somewhat downward. As the anterior ends of the upper ribs move upward, they also push forward, carrying the sternum forward and upward with them. In the case of the lower ribs, the anterior ends move laterally, thus "opening" the chest and widening the subcostal angle.

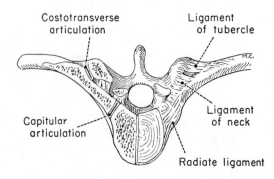

Figure 9–4 Superior view of costovertebral articulations.

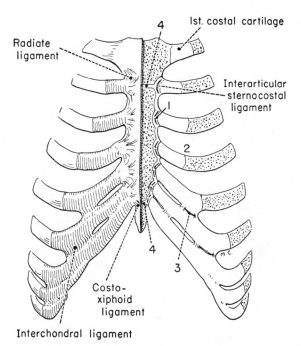

Figure 9–5 Sternocostal articulations. Key: *1*, Sternocostal; *2*, costochondral; *3*, interchondral; *4*, intersternal.

Although expansion of the thorax is ordinarily associated with inhalation for the purpose of providing the body with oxygen, there is another purpose. Whenever one exerts maximal muscular effort of short duration, he first takes a deep breath and then holds it while exerting the effort. This serves the purpose of stabilizing the ribs and sternum and thus provides firm anchorage for the upper extremity and trunk muscles which are used in forceful lifting, pushing and pulling.[3]

In inhalation the thorax is enlarged in three diameters: transverse, anteroposterior and vertical.

Increase in the Transverse Diameter. (Fig. 9–6.) This results from the elevation and eversion of the lateral portion of the ribs. The shape and twist of the ribs together with their anterior and posterior attachments are responsible for what has so aptly been called their "bucket handle inspiratory movement." The elevation of the lower ribs is accompanied by a lateral movement of their anterior ends. This widening of the lower thorax increases the power of the diaphragm by putting it on a stretch.

Increase in the Anteroposterior Diameter. (Fig. 9–6.) This is produced by the elevation of the anterior ends of the obliquely placed ribs and of the body of the sternum, the latter being caused by the rib movement. The elevation of the anterior ends of the ribs causes the ribs to assume a more horizontal position

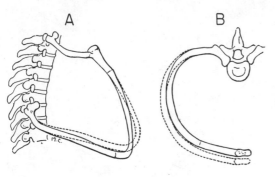

Figure 9-6 Expansion of thorax during inhalation. *A*, Lateral view; *B*, superior view.

and results in a straightening of the costal cartilages. The movements of the thorax in the anteroposterior and transverse diameters are inseparable. The expansion in both directions when the ribs are elevated is the inevitable result of their shape and of the oblique direction of their axes in motion.

Increase in the Vertical Diameter. This is brought about primarily by the depression of the central tendon of the diaphragm, but elevation of the upper two ribs makes a slight contribution. In forced inspiration the thoracic spine may extend to its limit, and this also contributes to a further increase in the vertical diameter.

Analysis of Respiration

Phases of Respiration. Basing his conclusions on his own findings as well as on those of several other investigators, Basmajian recognizes four phases of respiration. In brief, these are as follows.

PRE-INSPIRATION. This is a brief static phase which precedes the intake of air.

INSPIRATION. This is characterized by expansion of the thorax and the taking in of air.

PRE-EXPIRATION. This is a brief static phase which follows inspiration and precedes expiration.

EXPIRATION. This is characterized by an outflow of air accompanying a decrease in thoracic volume.[1]

Muscular Action. Undoubtedly, the muscular analysis of respiration is of less interest to the average physical education major student, whose chief concern is with performance in sports and other activities, than it is to research-minded graduate students. It is discussed briefly in this text for those who may be interested.

On the whole, *EMG* studies have tended to reinforce the muscular analysis of respiration as presented in older kinesiology texts, but there have been a few unexpected revelations. The student who is interested in pursuing this subject is advised to read Basmajian's excellent summaries of EMG investigations before examining the original reports of individual studies.[1]

CHARACTERISTICS AND FUNCTIONS
OF INDIVIDUAL MUSCLES*

Diaphragm. (Fig. 9–7.)   This is a dome-shaped sheet of muscle which separates the thoracic and abdominal cavities from each other. Its contraction causes depression of its central tendon, and this increases the vertical dimension of the thorax. It also has a tendency to lift the lower ribs but this appears to be resisted by the quadratus lumborum and iliocostalis lumborum. As the diaphragm moves downward it presses against the abdominal organs which, in turn, push forward against the relaxed abdominal wall. By increasing the intra-abdominal pressure it helps in defecation, vomiting and other forms of expulsion. Although primarily a muscle of inspiration, a number of EMG studies have revealed the presence of electric activity in the diaphragm during both the pre-expiratory and expiratory phases.[1] It was suggested that this continuation of activity in the expiratory phase might be a braking action which serves the purpose of resisting or slowing down the elastic recoil of the lungs. This appears to imply that the contraction is eccentric or lengthening in nature, much like the action of the knee and hip extensors in resisting gravitational force in a slow deep knee bend. The finding that the diaphragm did not show any activity in forced expiration would seem to bear this out. Two other findings were brought to light by EMG studies, one, that all portions of the diaphragm contract simultaneously, a positive indication that the muscle functions as a unit, and the other, that the diaphragm is unquestionably the chief muscle of inspiration.[1]

---

*Listed in alphabetical order.

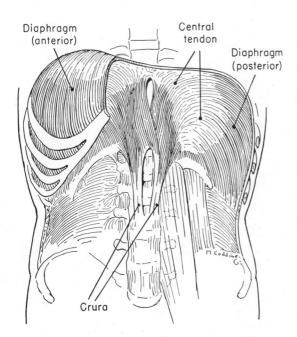

Diaphragm
(anterior)

Central
tendon

Diaphragm
(posterior)

Crura

Figure 9–7   The diaphragm.

Erector Spinae. (See Chapter 8 for discussion and illustrations.) This extensive muscle of the back serves to stabilize the spine and pelvis against the pull of the abdominal muscles. By resisting the tendency of the latter to flex the spine, it forces them to concentrate their activity on abdominal compression.

Extensors of Cervical and Thoracic Spine. (See Chapter 8 for discussion and illustrations.) These stabilize the head and neck against the pull of the scalenes and the sternocleidomastoid.

Intercostales, Externi and Interni. (Fig. 9–8.) These are two layers of similar sets of muscles, each set consisting of short, parallel fibers which connect adjacent ribs. The fibers of the outer set slant downward and forward from one rib to the rib below, and those of the inner set slant in the reverse direction, that is, downward and backward. An interesting point is that the slant of each set is similar to the slant of the corresponding oblique abdominal muscle. Both sets extend posteriorly as far as the angles of the ribs. In front, the external layer extends only as far forward as the costal cartilages, whereas the internal extends to the sternum. Hence the anterior portion of the internal intercostals is not covered by the external layer.

These muscles have long been regarded as important respiratory muscles, second only to the diaphragm, but for many years there has been a lack of agreement concerning their specific functions. Some investigators have claimed that both sets elevate the ribs, some that one set elevates and the other depresses, and some that both the external intercostals and the anterior (uncovered) portion of the internal layer elevate, and the remainder of the internal depresses. Even electromyographic research has not settled the question of functions. One reason may be that, as refinements are made in techniques, investigators do not want to repeat the old methods, thus making comparisons

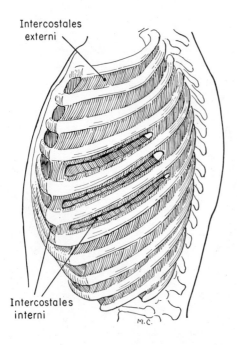

Intercostales externi

Intercostales interni

M.C.

Figure 9–8 The intercostal muscles.

invalid. If several research teams could agree on using the same techniques under similar conditions, the findings of one or more studies might confirm those of others.

In the past, it has been assumed that if a muscle is active during a certain phase of breathing it is making a direct contribution to the movement characteristic of that phase. For instance, if a muscle that attaches to the ribs, as do the intercostals, were to contract during the inspiratory phase, it would be assumed that it was helping to expand the thorax. Jones et al, however, have suggested a theory concerning the intercostals that deserves serious consideration. In a 1958 study their group noted that both sets of intercostals were constantly active during quiet breathing, but that they showed no rhythmic fluctuation as one would expect if they were causing the rhythmic movements of the thorax. They explained this observation by suggesting that the function of the intercostals was to supply the tension needed to keep the ribs at a constant distance from each other and to increase the intrathoracic pressure.

At the risk of putting too much emphasis on the findings from a single study, the results of Taylor's EMG investigation of the intercostal muscles, in which he used very fine needle electrodes, are briefly reported below.

External intercostals:

    a. No action at all in quiet breathing.

    b. Where two layers of muscles are present (i.e., both external and internal), the external acts in inspiration only. (In the light of the first notation it is assumed that this means in deep or forced inspiration.)

Internal intercostals:

    a. Where two layers of muscles are present, the internal acts during expiration only. This was noted in the lower lateral part of the thorax during quiet expiration.

    b. In the cartilaginous region in front where the internal is not covered by the external, electrical activity was noted during inspiration.[1]

Levatores Costarum (Fig. 9-9.)   These little muscles, slanting down and slightly outward from the tip of the transverse process of each vertebra to the rib below, with additional bands in the case of the 7th, 8th, 9th and 10th vertebrae passing to the second rib below, are in a position to exert a lifting effect on the ribs, but they have poor leverage for this as their attachments to the ribs are quite close to the costovertebral joints. In spite of this, it is assumed that they help to elevate the ribs during inspiration.

Pectoralis Major and Minor. (See Chapter Four for discussion and illustrations.)   A few investigators have reported activity of the pectoralis major in deep inspiration but have not made it clear what function the muscle is performing. Wells suggests that when a person holds his arms vertically upward or is suspended by the hands, it seems reasonable to assume that the pectoralis major would help to elevate the sternum and upper six ribs. The pectoralis minor is likewise in a position to lift the third, fourth and fifth ribs when the thoracic spine is extended and the scapulae are stabilized.

Quadratus Lumborum. (See Chapter Eight for discussion and illustration.) An EMG study conducted in 1965 by Boyd et al confirms the assumption that

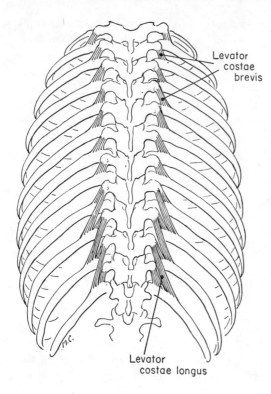

Figure 9-9 Levatores costarum (levator costae).

this muscle anchors the last rib against the pull of the diaphragm which would otherwise tend to lift it and in so doing would lose some of its force for depressing its central tendon.[1]

Scalenes, Anterior, Posterior and Medius. (See Chapter Eight for discussion and illustration.) These three muscles (in former editions of this text called the "three scaleni") are assuming greater importance as respiratory muscles as the result of EMG research. They connect the transverse processes of the cervical vertebrae with the first two ribs and were formerly thought to be primarily lateral flexors of the neck and secondarily accessory or stabilizing muscles of respiration, their function being to anchor the first two ribs for the intercostals. Two investigations over ten years apart give strong evidence of *the scalenes' role as true respiratory muscles in quiet inspiration as well as in forced.*[1] These muscles may be palpated on the side of the neck between the sternocleidomastoid and upper trapezius muscles.

Serratus Posterior Inferior. (Fig. 9–10.) Like four chevrons, these broad bands connect the lower borders of the lowest four ribs with the spinous processes and ligaments of lower vertebrae (lower two thoracic and upper two or three lumbar). They are assumed to depress the four ribs and to stabilize them against the pull of the diaphragm. They are too deep to palpate or to test electromyographically by present techniques.

Serratus Posterior Superior. (Fig. 9–10.) Like four steeply slanted, inverted chevrons, these bands connect the upper borders of the 2nd, 3rd, 4th and 5th ribs with the spinous processes and ligaments of the lower two or three cervical and the upper two thoracic vertebrae. They are assumed to help elevate the four ribs and in so doing to expand the upper thorax. Like the inferior, this muscle is too deep to palpate or to check by present EMG means.

Sternocleidomastoideus. (See Chapter Eight for discussion and illustration.) As an accessory muscle of respiration, this muscle showed marked electrical activity in forced inspiration. It helps to elevate the sternum and clavicle. In vigorous inspiration the head is usually held firmly erect, and instead of flexing the head and neck, the sternocleidomastoid has a slight lifting effect on the sternum and sternal end of each clavicle. It may be palpated on the side of the neck just below the ear and on the front of the neck at the junction of the clavicle and sternum.

Transversus Abdominis. (Fig. 9–11.)   This is one of the four muscles form-ing the abdominal wall. (See Chapter Eight for discussion of this.) Its fibers run horizontally from the thoracolumbar fascia and cartilages of the lower ribs

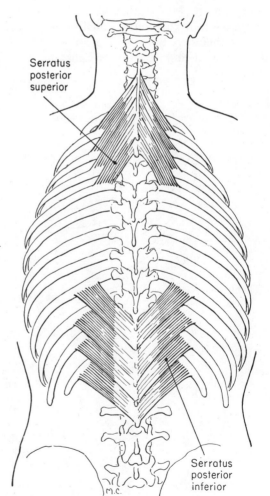

Serratus
posterior
superior

Figure 9–10 Serratus posterior superior and inferior.

Serratus
posterior
inferior

forward to the linea alba. Its pull is inward against the abdominal viscera; hence it is a strong muscle of exhalation and expulsion. It also helps to stabilize the trunk when acts requiring great effort are performed. Together with the other muscles of the abdominal wall, it is credited with compressing the abdominal contents into a semi-rigid cylinder.

The *transversus abdominis* and the *two obliques* were found by Campbell to be the most important muscles of *forced expiration*. He also noted that they do not initiate expiration but help to complete it. Although the rectus also contracts in expiration, he found it to be of little importance compared with the other abdominals.[1]

Transversus Thoracis. (Fig. 9–12.)   This connects the lower half of the inner surface of the sternum and adjoining costal cartilages with the lower borders and inner surfaces of the costal cartilages of the 2nd, 3rd, 4th, 5th and 6th ribs. It consists of flat bands which radiate upward and outward from the inner surface of the sternum to the ribs, the lowest fibers being continuous with those of the transversus abdominis.

Trapezius I & II. (See Chapter Four for discussion and illustration.)   In reviewing EMG studies of the trapezius, Basmajian was unable to find confirmation of Duchenne's inclusion of this muscle as an accessory in respiration. It is included here as a possible stabilizer of the shoulder girdle against the downward pull of the pectoralis minor. As yet, there is no confirmation of this theory.

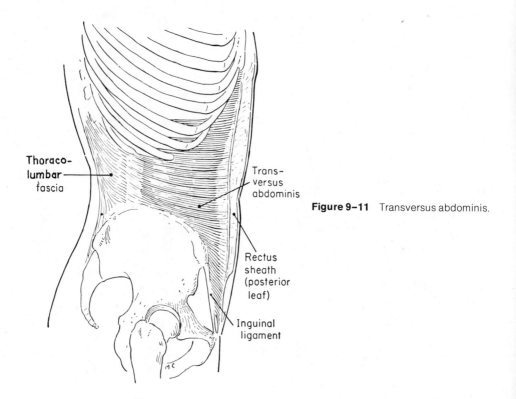

Thoraco-
lumbar
fascia

Trans-
versus
abdominis

Rectus
sheath
(posterior
leaf)

Inguinal
ligament

Figure 9–11   Transversus abdominis.

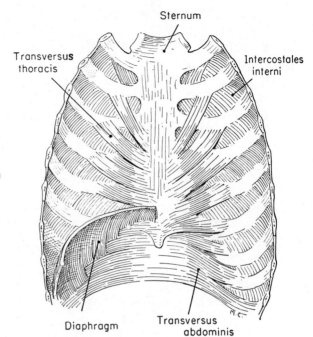

Figure 9–12   Posterior (inner) view of anterior wall of thorax.

COMMON ATHLETIC INJURIES OF THE THORAX

Rib Fractures.   These are fairly common in contact sports like football and wrestling. The usual causes are either direct blows or forceful compressions. Sudden, violent, muscular contraction may also be a cause. In most fracture injuries two or more ribs are likely to be involved. A fracture should be suspected if breathing is accompanied by severe pain. A possible serious complication of rib fractures is damage to the soft tissues when the broken ends of the bone are pushed inward.[2,4]

LABORATORY EXPERIENCES

1. MOVEMENT OF THE THORAX IN RESPIRATION
      Subject: Breathe naturally for a while, then as deeply as possible.
      Observer: (*a*) Place the hands on the sides of the thorax and note the movement in the lateral diameter. (*b*) Place one hand on the ribs at the subcostal angle (just below the sternum) and the other hand against the back at the same level. Note the movement in the anteroposterior diameter. (*c*) Place the fingers on the sternum. Can you detect any movement in normal respiration? In deep respiration?

2. MUSCULAR ACTION IN FORCED INHALATION
      a. Subject: Inhale through a small rubber tube, pinching it slightly in order to furnish resistance
      Observer: Note the action of the sternocleidomastoid, cervical and thoracic extensors, and upper trapezius. Can any other muscular action be detected? If so, explain.

b. Subject: Run in place or around the room until short of breath. Hang from a horizontal bar.

Observer: Can you detect any action of the pectoralis major accompanying inhalation? (By stabilizing the arms, the hanging position causes the pectoralis major to act on the ribs.)

3. Muscular Action in Vigorous Exhalation

Subject: Blow through a small rubber tube, pinching it slightly or holding a finger loosely over the end. (Or blow into a spirometer, flarimeter or toy balloon.)

Observer: Note the action of the abdominal muscles and of the erector spinae.

REFERENCES

1. Basmajian, J. V.: Muscles Alive, 3rd Ed. Baltimore: Williams & Wilkins Company, 1974.
2. Klafs, C. E., and Arnheim, D. D.: Modern Principles of Athletic Training. St. Louis: C. V. Mosby Company, 1973.
3. Morris, J. M., Lucas, D. B., and Bresler, B.: Role of the trunk in stability of the spine. J. Bone & Joint Surg., *43A*:327–351, 1961.
4. O'Donoghue, D. H.: Treatment of Injuries to Athletes, 3rd Ed. Philadelphia: W. B. Saunders Company, 1976.

FUNDAMENTALS OF BIOMECHANICS

INTRODUCTION
TO PART TWO

As seen by the kinesiologist the human body is a highly complex machine constructed of living tissue. As such it is subject to the laws and principles of mechanics as well as those of biology. The principles of mechanics are directly applicable both to the movements of the human body and to the sports implements it handles. Principles of balance and equilibrium, motion and the application of forces apply equally to man in motion as they do to rockets and wheels, gears and missiles. A study of the fundamental principles of mechanics as they apply to movement skills will aid the teacher and coach in the analysis of skills for the purposes of correction of error and the intelligent evaluation of new techniques as they come along. Applications in research can lead to the development of techniques yet unheard of.

Interest in mechanical analysis and study as a part of physical education was due in large measure to the influence of C. H. McCloy, University of Iowa, who toured the country in the late thirties and forties giving lectures with demonstrations showing specific ways in which performance could be improved by the application of appropriate mechanical principles. He was the first to develop a course in the Mechanical Analysis of Motor Skills. Pioneer efforts in cinematographic analysis by Ruth Glassow at the University of Wisconsin also contributed to interest among physical educators in the United States. Currently there is a lively interest in the mechanical analysis of man in motion, and a new area of study in physical education called the biomechanics of sport has emerged. The branch of science called biomechanics is broad, and the biomechanics of sport is only one of the areas in which applications of the same common core of knowledge and fundamental research based in physics, mathematics, anatomy and physiology are made. Other fields of applied biomechanics include industrial engineering and ergonomics, physical rehabilitation, medicine and biomedical physics, and aerospace science.

Of the fields of applied biomechanics the biomechanics of sport and physical education is the least advanced, but increased availability and use of advanced technology in the form of computers and electronic recording devices currently is making possible research and study which previously was practically prohibitive because of the agonizing amount of time it consumed. Additional impetus has also been supplied through the founding of an international society of biomechanics whose focus is multidisciplinary. The influence of this society in stimulating study and disseminating knowledge through international meetings is doing much to advance knowledge in this fascinating field of applied biomechanics, the biomechanics of sport and physical education.

Part II introduces the student to some of the elementary concepts necessary for beginning to understand the biomechanics of sport and physical education. Chapter 10 presents mechanical concepts and terminology which are basic to the study of mechanics as an aspect of kinesiology. The need for the understanding of basic mathematical concepts for the purpose of being able to use appropriate formulas and to understand basic principles is identified. The level of mathematics understanding needed for this and subsequent chapters is relatively elementary, and with the aid of the examples given and the mathematics review in Appendix E, the average kinesiology student should have no difficulty. Under no circumstances, however, should the student become so involved with juggling numbers in this part that the sight of the forest is lost for the trees.

Part II continues with a chapter on the fundamentals of motion description with particular emphasis placed upon an understanding of projectiles and "free flight." Specific applications are made to sport and physical education activities. A similar approach is followed in subsequent chapters on force, force and motion, and force and equilibrium. Each chapter concludes with a variety of problems and exercises designed to help the student understand the direct application of principles of mechanics to the execution of skills in sport and physical education.

REFERENCES

1. Nelson, R. C.: Biomechanics of sport: An overview. *In* Cooper, J. M., (Ed.): Selected Topics in Biomechanics. Chicago: The Athletic Institute, 1971.
2. Wartenweiler, J.: The manifold implications of biomechanics. *In* Nelson, R. C., and Morehouse, C. A., (Eds.): Biomechanics IV. Baltimore: University Park Press, 1974.

Chapter Ten

MECHANICS
OF HUMAN MOTION

As it is presently constituted, kinesiology is an area of study concerned with the musculoskeletal analysis of human motion and with the study of mechanical principles and laws as they relate to the study of human motion. Students of human motion capable of accurately analyzing the musculoskeletal actions occurring in the execution of a movement are well on their way toward knowing what is happening during that movement. Those who have taken the further step of acquiring a working knowledge of how human motion is governed by physical laws and principles have added an additional dimension of understanding how and why the motion occurs as it does. Together, these knowledges provide a scientific foundation upon which to make appropriate decisions concerning the most effective execution of any movement pattern. It is only through such study that definitive answers may be found concerning the "best" way for an individual to perform a skill and the reasons *why* the method selected is indeed the "best." The record breaking "form" of one person may or may not be appropriate for another of differing body build and size. In fact, although they break records, top performers' techniques may include actions which if eliminated would result in even greater performance. Unless subjected to scientific scrutiny, discrimination between the success factors and deterrent factors may be confused or not even identified.

Mechanics.   Where *forces* and *motion* are concerned, the scientific study which provides accurate answers to what is happening, why it is happening and to what extent it is happening is called *mechanics*. It is that branch of physics concerned with the effect that forces have on bodies and the motion produced by those forces. The study of mechanics is engaged in by those people whose occupations or professions require an understanding of force, matter, space and time. Engineering, to a large extent, is the application of mechanics. Navigation, astronomy, space and communications experts all study mechanics. The same is true of individuals concerned with the study of human motion and the forces causing it. The laws and principles used to explain the motion of planets or the strength of buildings and bridges apply equally to man in motion. All motion, including motions of the human body and its parts, is the result of the application of forces and is subject to the laws and principles which govern force and motion.

Biomechanics.   When the study of mechanics is limited to living structures, especially the human body, it is called biomechanics. For our purposes biomechanics may be considered to be that aspect of the science of movement (kinesiology) which has to do with the effect forces have upon the state of motion or rest of living bodies. Anatomists, orthopedists, space engineers, industrial engineers, specialists in physical medicine, physical educators and coaches all have an interest in biomechanics. The study of biomechanics is divided into two areas, *statics* and *dynamics*. Statics covers situations in which all forces acting on a body are balanced and the body is in equilibrium. With a knowledge of the principles of statics one may have a better understanding of levers and a greater ability to solve problems such as locating the body's center of gravity or the center of buoyancy. That branch of biomechanics which deals with bodies subject to unbalanced forces is called dynamics. Principles of dynamics explain circumstances where an excess of force in one direction or a turning force cause an object to change speed or direction. Principles of work, energy and accelerated motion are covered in the study of dynamics.

The terms *kinematics* and *kinetics* are also part of the vocabulary of the study of mechanics. Kinematics has been referred to as the geometry of motion. It describes the motion of bodies in terms of time, displacement, velocity and acceleration. The motion occurring may be in a straight line (linear kinematics) or about a fixed point (angular kinematics). Kinematics is not concerned with the forces which cause the object to move. That is covered in the kinetics of motion. Kinetics is that branch of mechanics which considers the *forces* that produce or change motion. Admittedly the most complex of biomechanics studies, it is the area least developed in physical education and sport, and of most challenge to research today.

Measurement and Mathematics in Biomechanics. In the study of human motion as in the study of any science, careful measurement and the use of mathematics are essential for the classification of facts and the systematizing of knowledge. Mathematics is the language of science. It enables us to express relationships quantitatively, rather than merely descriptively. It provides objective evidence of the superiority of one technique over another and thus forms the basis for developing effective measures for improving performance. Furthermore, it makes possible continuing advancement of knowledge through research. Had it not been for the use of mathematics, the contributions of great scientists like Archimedes, Galileo and Newton would not have been possible.

In the biomechanical aspects of kinesiology, as in all mechanics, the depth of understanding of the principles and laws that apply to it is greatly increased through experimental and mathematical evidence. Hence, it is to the kinesiologist's advantage to become conversant with appropriate mathematical concepts and techniques. The mathematics needed for the quantitative treatment of the simple mechanics discussed in this text is not difficult. It consists of elementary algebra and right triangle trigonometry. A review of these essential mathematical concepts is presented in Appendix E.

Units of Measurement. The units of measurement employed in the study of biomechanics are expressed in terms of length, time, and mass. Presently there are two systems of measurement having units for these quantities. They are the English system and the metric system. Since both systems are currently used in research and literature, a comparison of equivalent values is helpful. Table 10–1 presents the common units used in biomechanics study and their English-metric equivalents.

UNITS OF LENGTH.   In the metric or decimal system, all units differ in size by a multiple of ten. In ascending order, linear units are millimeters, centimeters, meters and kilometers. In the English system the basic unit of length is the foot. Other possible units are inches, yards and miles.

UNITS OF AREA OR VOLUME.   In the metric system, square centimeters or square meters are used for area, and cubic centimeters or cubic meters are used for volume. A cubic meter equals one liter. In the English system area units are square inches or feet, and cubic inches, cubic feet, quarts or gallons denote volume.

UNITS OF MASS AND FORCE (WEIGHT).   *Mass* is the quantity of matter a body contains. The *weight* of a body depends upon its quantity of matter and the strength of the gravitational attraction acting on it. The measure of gravitational *force* is called weight. The mass of an object will not change even if taken to the moon, but its weight will. The kilogram, equal to the mass of a liter of water, is the unit of mass in the metric system. The unit of force (weight) is the newton (nt), and for most of the United States a mass of one kilogram weighs approximately 9.80 newtons. In the English system the pound is the basic unit of force (weight). The mass unit is the slug (from the English word for sluggish). A mass of one slug weighs approximately 32 pounds for the gravitational pull present at the latitude and longitude of most of the United States.

UNITS OF TIME.   The basic unit of time for both systems of measurement is the second.

Scalar and Vector Quantities.   The units of measure described in the previous section are quantities which possess size or amount. Units of length, volume, area, mass, and time are examples of such quantities. They are called *scalar* quantities or scalars. When one knows that a person has run five miles, one has an indication of the *amount* of distance run. Distance is a measure of magnitude; it is a scalar. Similarly, the rate of running (speed) of five miles per hour, a temperature of 70 degrees, an area of two square miles and a mass of 10 kilograms are all magnitude or amount measures. Quantities which are not completely described by a magnitude measure alone also exist. For a full de-

TABLE 10-1   Comparison of English and Metric Systems of Measurement

UNIT	METRIC SYSTEM	ENGLISH SYSTEM	EQUIVALENTS
Length	Centimeter (cm.) meter (100 cm.)	inch (in.) foot (ft.)	2.54 cm. = 1 in. 0.305 m. = 1 ft.; 1 m. = 39.37 in.
Area	square meter (100 cm.^{2})	square foot (144 in.^{2})	6.45 cm.^{2} = 1 in.^{2}
Volume	cubic meter (1000 cm.^{3}) liter (1000 cm.^{3})	cubic foot (1728 in.^{3}) quart (57.75 in.^{3})	16.39 cm.^{3} = 1 in.^{3} 0.946 l. = 1 qt.
Mass	Kilogram (kg.)	slug (32 lb.)	14.53 kg. = 1 slug
Force (weight)	newton (.102 kg.)	pound	0.454 kg. = 1 lb.; 1 kg. = 2.2 lb.
Time	second	second	————————

scription of these quantities, a knowledge of magnitude and direction is needed. These quantities are called *vector* quantities. If two people, each on opposite sides of a door push with equal amounts of force, the door will not move. If on the other hand, they both push on the same side of the door thus changing the *direction* of one of the forces, the result will be very different. The movement of the door depends upon both the *amount* and the *direction* of the force. Force, therefore, is a vector quantity. If the individual who ran five miles runs five more miles, he will have run a total distance of ten miles. If, however, he runs five miles in one direction, reverses himself and runs back to the starting point, his change in position or *displacement* is zero. He is zero miles from his starting point. Displacement is also a vector quantity as it possesses both magnitude and direction. Numerous quantities in biomechanics are vector quantities. In addition to force, displacement and velocity already mentioned, some other examples are momentum, acceleration, friction, work and power. Vector quantities exist whenever direction and amount are inherent characteristics of the quantities.

Vector Representation.   A vector is represented by an arrow whose length is proportional to the magnitude of the vector. The direction in which the arrow points indicates the direction of the vector quantity. Figure 10–1 shows examples of arrows indicating vector quantities of force, displacement and velocity.

Two vectors are the same if both magnitude and direction are the same. Although all the vectors below are of the same length (magnitude) only two are equal vector quantities. They are the two which also have the same direction (d and f).

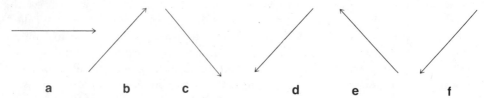

| a | b | c | d | e | f |

Combination of Vectors.   Vectors may be combined by addition, subtraction or multiplication. Vectors are added by joining the head of one with the tail of the next while accounting for magnitude and direction. The combination of the vectors results in a new vector called the *resultant.* The resultant vector is represented by the distance between the last head and the first tail. Figure 10–2 shows examples of vectors which have been combined by addition. Note that the head of the resultant meets the *head* of the last component vector. These drawings also show that very different component vectors may produce the same resultant. The subtraction of vectors is done by changing the sign of one vector (multiply by −1) and then adding as before (Fig. 10–3, *A*). The multiplication of a vector by a number changes its magnitude only (Fig. 10–3, *B*).

Resolution of Vectors.   As we have seen, the combination of two or more vectors results in a new vector. Conversely any vector may be broken down or resolved into two component vectors acting at right angles to each other. The vector in Figure 10–1, *C* represents the velocity with which the shot was put. Should one wish to know how much of that velocity was in a horizontal direction and how much in a vertical direction the vector must be resolved into hori-

B. Displacement

Figure 10–1 Examples of vector amounts represented by arrows.

A. Force

C. Velocity

zontal and vertical components. In Figure 10–4, A and B are the vertical and horizontal *components* of resultant R. The vector addition of these components once again would result in the resultant vector R. The arrows over A, B, and R, indicate that they are vector quantities.

Location of Vectors in Space. In describing motion it is helpful to have a frame of reference within which one can locate a position in space or change in position. It is possible to locate an object in three dimensions, but to simplify understanding, the description which follows is limited to motion in two dimensions, i.e., one plane. By constructing an x and y axis interacting at point 0, any point in the plane may be located with respect to 0. Rectangular coordinates (x, y) are used to locate a point, P, with respect to the x and y axes. (Fig. 10–5). R is a vector with magnitude and direction describing point P with

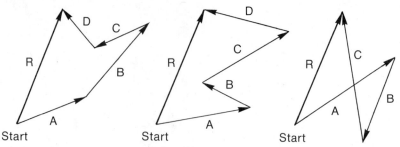

Figure 10-2 Vectors are added by joining the head of one with the tail of the next. The same resultant vector **R** may be obtained from the combination of dissimilar components.

respect to 0. $P = (13,5)$. Point P may also be described using *polar* coordinates (r, θ). Point P is r distance from 0 and θ degrees from the x axis. $P = (r, \theta)$. If r is 14 units in magnitude and $\theta = 25$, then P in polar coordinates is $(14,25°)$. $P = (14,25°)$.

In this coordinate system degrees are customarily measured in a counter-clockwise direction. Also, by convention, x values to the right of the y axis are positive $(+)$ and those to the left are negative $(-)$. Y values above the x axis are positive and those below are negative (Fig. 10–6). Point A in Figure 10–6 has (x, y) coordinates of $(4.3,2.5)$ and (r, θ) coordinates of $(5,30°)$. The (x, y) coordinates for Point B are $(-1.5, -3)$ and the polar coordinates are $(3.4,240°)$.

Graphic Resolution and Combination of Vectors. Within this frame of reference quantities encountered in the study of biomechanics may be portrayed and handled graphically. Consider a broad jumper who takes off with a velocity of 31.6 ft./sec. at an angle of 18 degrees (Fig. 10–7). By selecting a linear unit of measurement to represent a unit of velocity such as 0.25 inch to represent 2 feet per second of velocity and by constructing a line of the appropriate length at an angle of 18 degrees to the x axis, one can determine the horizontal and vertical components of velocity for that jump. This is done by constructing a right triangle in which the hypotenuse is the vector representing the total velocity of the jump, the vertical side is the vertical velocity and the horizontal

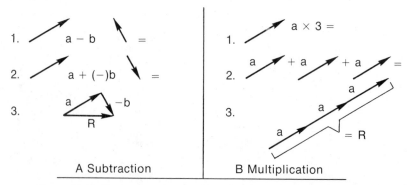

A Subtraction | B Multiplication

Figure 10-3 Vectors may be combined by subtraction or multiplication.

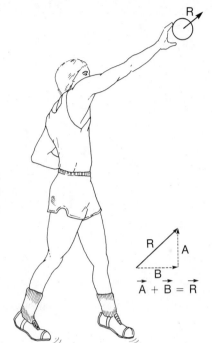

Figure 10–4 A resultant vector may be resolved or broken down into two component vectors acting at right angles to each other. The velocity vector **R** has a horizontal component **B** and a vertical component **A**.

side is the horizontal velocity. The horizontal and vertical velocity components are determined by carefully measuring the lengths of the respective sides of the triangle and converting those amounts to velocity values. This is done by using the conversion factor (0.25 in. = 4 ft./sec.) The values obtained are 30 ft./sec., horizontal velocity component, and 10 ft./sec. of vertical velocity.

The illustration just given shows how a vector quantity can be resolved into its components using the graphic method. The combination of vectors to determine the resultant vector may also be determined graphically by the construc-

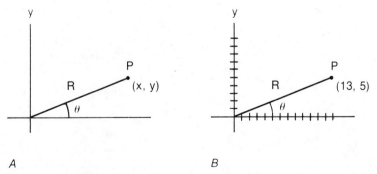

Figure 10–5 A point in space may be located in two dimensions using an X and Y axis as a frame of reference. In A, point P is x units from the Y axis and y units from the X axis. In B, point P is 13x units from the Y axis and 5y units above the X axis.

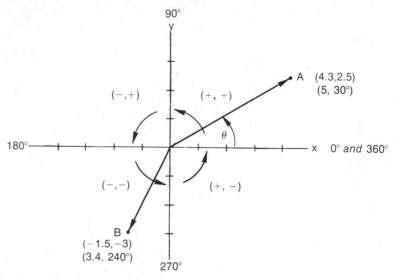

Figure 10-6   Coordinate Quadrants. Values of x and y are positive in upper right hand quadrant and negative in lower left. X is negative in upper left and y is negative in lower right.

tion of a parallelogram, the sides of which are linear representations of the two vectors. The first step is to mark a point on a piece of paper. This represents the point at which the two vectors are applied. From this point two lines are drawn to scale, with the correct angle between them, that is, the same angle which actually exists between the two vectors. By using these two lines as two sides of a parallelogram, the other two sides are constructed by a simple geometric method (Fig. 10–8). The diagonal is then drawn from the point of application to the opposite corner. This diagonal represents both in magnitude and in direction the composite effect of the two separate vectors. It is the resultant vector. When one wishes to determine the resultant of *three* or more vectors acting at one point a similar procedure is followed. The resultant of two of the vectors is found. A second parallelogram is then constructed using the third vector as

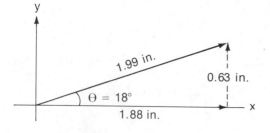

Velocity of jump = 31.6 ft./sec.
Angle of takeoff = 18°

Let 0.25 inches = 4 ft./sec.

Then: velocity of jump = 1.99 inches
Horizontal velocity x = 1.88 inches =
30 ft./sec. and vertical velocity y =
0.63 inches = 10 ft./sec.

Figure 10-7   Graphic method of vector resolution. The horizontal and vertical velocity components of broad jump with initial velocity of 31.6 ft./sec. at a direction of 18 degrees are determined by drawing vector components to scale.

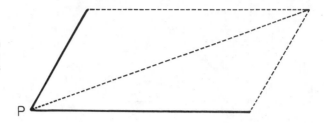

Figure 10-8 A "parallelogram of forces" used for determining the composite effect of two forces applied to the same point.

one side and the resultant of the first two vectors as the second side. The resultant vector of this second parallelogram is the resultant of all three vectors (Fig. 10-9).

Another graphic method combines the vectors by adding them head to tail. Suppose muscle *J* has a force of 200 pounds and is pulling on bone *E-F* at an angle of 10 degrees, and muscle *K* has a force of 175 pounds and is pulling at an angle of 40 degrees (Fig. 10-10). The composite effect of these two muscles may be described in terms of the amount of force and the direction or angle of pull of that composite force. Again a linear unit of measure is selected to represent a unit of force, and the vectors are placed in reference to the *x, y* axes so that the force vector for muscle *K* is added to the force vector for muscle *J* (Fig. 10-10). The resultant vector is drawn connecting the tail of A with the head of B. Its length times the selected force conversion factor (0.1 in. = 20 lb.) represents the resultant force of the two muscles. The angle between the X axis and the resultant (measured with a protractor) indicates the direction of the resultant force. Careful use of a protractor and ruler produces an *r* of 335 pounds pulling in a direction of 24 degrees. Again, this method is not limited to the combination of two vectors. Any number of vectors may be combined in this fashion.

Trigonometric Resolution and Combination of Vectors. Although the graphic method has value for portraying the situation, it does have serious drawbacks. Accuracy is difficult to control in the drawing and measuring process and the procedure is slow and unwieldy. A more accurate and efficient

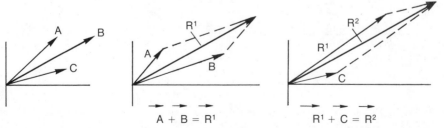

$A + B = R^1$ $R^1 + C = R^2$

Figure 10-9 Parallelogram method used for determining the composite effect of three or more forces applied to the same point. R_1 is resultant of combined forces *A* and *B*. R_2 is resultant of combined forces R_1 and *C*. $\vec{A} + \vec{B} + \vec{C} = \vec{R_2}$.

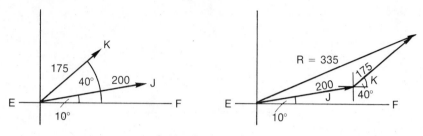

Scale: 0.1 in. = 20 lb.

Figure 10–10 Combination of vectors using graphic method. Vector *J* is added to Vector *K* taking into account magnitude and direction. Resultant *R* is drawn by connecting tail of *J* to head of *K*.

approach makes use of trigonometric relationships in combining and resolving vectors. Any vector may be resolved into horizontal and vertical components if the trigonometric relationships of a right triangle are employed. Let us use the previous example of the broad jumper whose velocity at take-off was 31.6 ft./sec. in the direction of 18 degrees with the horizontal (Fig. 10–7). To find his horizontal velocity (V_x) and vertical velocity (V_y) at take-off a right triangle is constructed. With the take-off velocity (*R*) as the hypotenuse of the triangle, the vertical and horizontal components of velocity become the vertical and horizontal sides of the triangle (Fig. 10–11). To obtain the values of V_x and V_y the sine and cosine functions are used.* V_y has a value of 10 ft./sec. and V_x a value of 30 ft./sec.

The combination of vectors also makes use of trigonometric relationships. Although other trigonometric solutions are possible the method shown here requires a knowledge of right triangle trigonometry only.

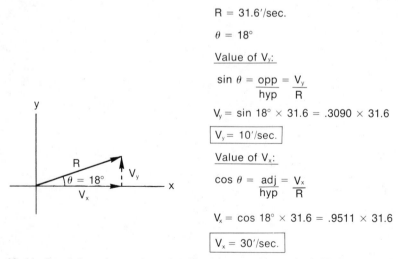

R = 31.6'/sec.

$\theta = 18°$

Value of V_y:

$$\sin \theta = \frac{opp}{hyp} = \frac{V_y}{R}$$

$V_y = \sin 18° \times 31.6 = .3090 \times 31.6$

$V_y = 10'/sec.$

Value of V_x:

$$\cos \theta = \frac{adj}{hyp} = \frac{V_x}{R}$$

$V_x = \cos 18° \times 31.6 = .9511 \times 31.6$

$V_x = 30'/sec.$

Figure 10–11 Resolution of a vector using the trigonometric method. Horizontal and vertical components are determined using cosine and sine functions.

*Refer to trigonometric table in Appendix F for values of trigonometric functions.

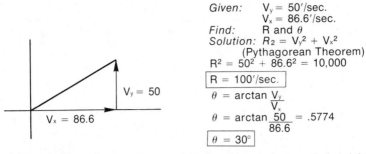

Given: $V_y = 50'/\text{sec.}$
$\quad\quad\quad\quad V_x = 86.6'/\text{sec.}$
Find: R and θ
Solution: $R^2 = V_y^2 + V_x^2$
$\quad\quad\quad\quad$ (Pythagorean Theorem)
$\quad\quad R^2 = 50^2 + 86.6^2 = 10,000$

$\boxed{R = 100'/\text{sec.}}$

$\theta = \arctan \dfrac{V_y}{V_x}$

$\theta = \arctan \dfrac{50}{86.6} = .5774$

$\boxed{\theta = 30°}$

Figure 10–12 Trigonometric solution to combination of two vectors applied at right angles.

If two vectors are applied at right angles to each other the solution should appear reasonably obvious since it is the reverse of the example just explained. If a baseball is thrown with a vertical velocity of 50 ft./sec. and a horizontal velocity of 86.6 ft./sec., the velocity of the throw and the angle of release may be determined as shown in Figure 10–12.

If more than two vectors are involved or if they are not at right angles to each other as shown in previous examples, the resultant may be obtained by determining the *x* and *y* components for each individual vector and then summing these individual components to obtain the *x* and *y* components of the resultant. Once the *x* and *y* components are known, the magnitude and direction of *R* may be obtained. Let us consider the problem treated graphically on p. 261 where muscles *J* and *K* were pulling on bone *E-F*, and we were interested in determining the composite force of these two muscles and the resultant direction or angle of pull (Fig. 10–10). To solve this problem trigonometrically, the horizontal and vertical components for each muscle must be determined first (Fig. 10–13).

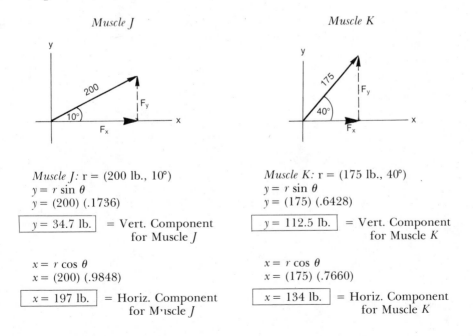

Muscle J

Muscle K

Muscle J: $r = (200 \text{ lb.}, 10°)$
$y = r \sin \theta$
$y = (200) (.1736)$

$\boxed{y = 34.7 \text{ lb.}}$ = Vert. Component
$\quad\quad\quad\quad\quad\quad\quad$ for Muscle *J*

$x = r \cos \theta$
$x = (200) (.9848)$

$\boxed{x = 197 \text{ lb.}}$ = Horiz. Component
$\quad\quad\quad\quad\quad\quad\quad$ for Muscle *J*

Muscle K: $r = (175 \text{ lb.}, 40°)$
$y = r \sin \theta$
$y = (175) (.6428)$

$\boxed{y = 112.5 \text{ lb.}}$ = Vert. Component
$\quad\quad\quad\quad\quad\quad\quad\quad$ for Muscle *K*

$x = r \cos \theta$
$x = (175) (.7660)$

$\boxed{x = 134 \text{ lb.}}$ = Horiz. Component
$\quad\quad\quad\quad\quad\quad\quad$ for Muscle *K*

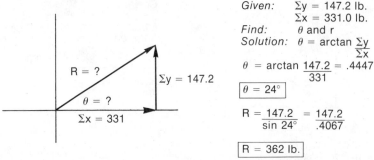

Given: $\Sigma y = 147.2$ lb.
$\Sigma x = 331.0$ lb.

Find: θ and r

Solution: $\theta = \arctan \dfrac{\Sigma y}{\Sigma x}$

$\theta = \arctan \dfrac{147.2}{331} = .4447$

$\boxed{\theta = 24°}$

$R = \dfrac{147.2}{\sin 24°} = \dfrac{147.2}{.4067}$

$\boxed{R = 362 \text{ lb.}}$

Figure 10–13 Trigonometric combination of summed vectors. The sum of all x components become the horizontal vector component and the sum of all y components become the vertical vector component. R and θ are determined by combining Σx and Σy.

To obtain the y component of the resultant effect of the *two* muscles, the y values for muscles J and K are summed: ($\Sigma y = 34.7 + 112.5$; $\Sigma y = 147.2$ lb.). The x component for R is the sum of the x values for J and K: ($\Sigma x = 197 + 134$; $\Sigma x = 331$ lb.).

As we have seen before, a knowledge of the horizontal (x) and vertical (y) components makes it possible to determine the resultant vector. A triangle is formed and the unknown parts are found (Fig. 10–13), showing the composite muscle pull to be 362 pounds, pulling at an angle of 24 degrees.

In the explanation of coordinate systems it was shown that values of x and y may be negative and that values of θ may exceed 90 degrees (Fig. 10–6). An example of a problem with these additional factors is that of the hiker who plots the stated course and then must determine her resultant displacement at the completion of the course.

A hiker walks the following course: 2000 yards at 30 degrees, 1000 yards at 100 degrees, and 500 yards at 225 degrees. What is her resultant displacement? The solution is presented in Figure 10–14.

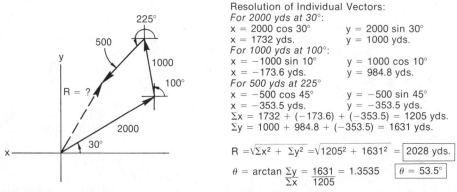

Resolution of Individual Vectors:
For 2000 yds at 30°:
$x = 2000 \cos 30°$ $\qquad$ $y = 2000 \sin 30°$
$x = 1732$ yds. $\qquad$ $y = 1000$ yds.
For 1000 yds at 100°:
$x = -1000 \sin 10°$ $\qquad$ $y = 1000 \cos 10°$
$x = -173.6$ yds. $\qquad$ $y = 984.8$ yds.
For 500 yds at 225°
$x = -500 \cos 45°$ $\qquad$ $y = -500 \sin 45°$
$x = -353.5$ yds. $\qquad$ $y = -353.5$ yds.
$\Sigma x = 1732 + (-173.6) + (-353.5) = 1205$ yds.
$\Sigma y = 1000 + 984.8 + (-353.5) = 1631$ yds.

$R = \sqrt{\Sigma x^2 + \Sigma y^2} = \sqrt{1205^2 + 1631^2} = \boxed{2028 \text{ yds.}}$

$\theta = \arctan \dfrac{\Sigma y}{\Sigma x} = \dfrac{1631}{1205} = 1.3535$ $\qquad \boxed{\theta = 53.5°}$

Figure 10–14 Combination of vectors involving negative values of x and y and values of θ larger than 90 degrees.

The ability to handle variables of motion and force as vector or scalar quantities should improve one's understanding of motion and the forces causing it. The effect that a muscle's angle of pull has on the force available for moving a limb is better understood when it is subjected to vector analysis. Similar study of the direction and force of projectiles improves one's understanding of the effect of gravity, the angle of release and the force of release upon the flight of a projectile. The effect of several muscles exerting their combined forces on a single bone is clarified when treated quantitatively as the combination of vector quantities to obtain a *resultant*. Indeed, the effect which a change in any variable may produce becomes much more apparent. Without the use of a vector relationship, it would be difficult if not impossible to describe motion and forces in meaningful, quantitative terms.

LABORATORY EXPERIENCES

1. Express the following units in metric terms:
   a. a force of 25 pounds
   b. a mass of 5 slugs
   c. a distance of 11 inches
   d. a velocity of 20 feet per second
   e. a volume of 3 quarts

2. A basketball official runs 60 ft. along the sideline in one direction, reverses himself and runs 25 ft. How far has he run? What is his displacement? Draw a vector diagram.

3. The muscular force of a muscle is 160 pounds and the muscle is pulling on the bone at an angle of 15 degrees. What are the vertical and horizontal components of this force?

4. At the moment of release, a baseball has a horizontal velocity of 80 feet per second and a vertical velocity component of 45 feet per second. At what angle was it released, and what was its initial velocity in the direction of the throw?

5. A child is being pulled in a sled by a person holding a rope that has an angle of 20 degrees with the horizontal. The force being used to move the sled at a constant forward speed is 25 pounds. How much of the force is horizontal? Vertical?

6. An orienteer runs the following course:

   1000 meters at 45°
   1500 meters at 120°
    500 meters at 190°

   a. Accurately draw the course to scale.
   b. Determine the resultant displacement graphically.
   c. Determine the resultant displacement trigonometrically.
   d. Explain any differences you have between your graphic and trigonometric results.
   e. Express the orienteer's position at the end of the course in terms of rectangular coordinates; polar coordinates.

7. A football lineman charges an opponent with a force of 175 pounds in the direction of 310 degrees. The opponent charges back with a force of 185 pounds in the direction of 90 degrees. What is the resultant force and in what direction will it act?

8. Referring to Figures 1–1 and 6–6 make a tracing of the femur and adductor longus muscle. Draw a straight line to represent the mechanical axis of the femur and another to represent the muscle's line of pull.
   a. Using a protractor, determine the angle of pull of the muscle (angle formed by muscle's line of pull and mechanical axis of bone).
   b. Assuming a total muscle force of 250 pounds, calculate the force components.

9. Muscle A has a force of 100 pounds and is pulling on a bone at an angle of 15 degrees. Muscle B has a force of 150 pounds and is pulling on the same bone at the same spot but at an angle of 30 degrees. Muscle C has a force of 75 pounds and is pulling at the same spot with an angle of pull of 10 degrees. What is the composite effect of these muscles in terms of amount of force and direction?

10. Name as many vector and scalar quantities as you can think of which are a part of the games of football, tennis or golf.

REFERENCES

1. Basford, L.: The Science of Movement. London: Sampson Low, Marston, & Co., 1966.
2. Dull, C. E., Metcalfe, H. C., and Williams, J. E.: Modern Physics. New York: Holt, Rinehart and Winston, 1963.
3. Evans, F. G.: Biomechanical implications of anatomy. In Cooper, J. M. (Ed.): Selected Topics on Biomechanics. Chicago: Athletic Institute, 1971.
4. Hay, J. G.: The Biomechanics of Sports Techniques. Englewood Cliffs, N.J.: Prentice-Hall Inc., 1973.
5. Kelley, D. L.: Kinesiology—Fundamentals of Motion Description. Englewood Cliffs, N.J.: Prentice-Hall Inc., 1971.
6. Nelson, R. C.: Biomechanics of sport: An overview. In Cooper, J. M. (Ed.): Selected Topics on Biomechanics. Chicago: Athletic Institute, 1971.
7. Widule, C. J.: Analysis of Human Motion—Experiences, Experiments and Problems. Lafayette, Indiana: Balt Publishers, 1974.

Chapter Eleven

MOTION

If we are to understand the movements of the human musculoskeletal system and the implements put into motion by this system, we need first to turn our thoughts to the concepts of motion itself. What determines the kind of motion that will result when an object or a part of the human body is made to move? How is motion described in mechanical terms? And finally, how do these generalities about motion apply to movements of the musculoskeletal system?

What is Motion?   How does one know that motion is occurring? When one walks down the street or rides a bicycle or serves a tennis ball, it is obvious that movement is involved. We can either see it or feel it. Less obvious is the movement of the earth through space or that of a sleeping passenger in a smoothly flying airplane traveling at a constant velocity. In order to tell if motion has occurred a reference point is needed. Whenever an object is in the process of changing place or position with respect to some point it is in motion. The flying passenger is in motion with respect to some reference point on the earth. He is not in motion with respect to any point within the plane — at least not until sleep is replaced with moving about. *Motion, then, is the act or process of changing place or position with respect to some reference point.*

Cause of Motion.   It is difficult to think of motion without visualizing a specific object in the act of moving. If we did not actually see how it changed from a stationary condition to a moving one, we might wonder what caused it to be set in motion. Did someone pull on it, or push against it, or perhaps blow on it or even attract it with a magnet? What are these assumed causes of motion? Without exception, they are a form of force. *Force* is the instigator of movement. If we see an object in motion, we know that it is moving because a force has acted upon it. We know, too, that the force must have been sufficiently great to overcome the object's inertia, for unless a force is greater than the resistance offered by the object, it cannot produce motion. We can push against a stone wall all day without moving it so much as one millimeter, but a bulldozer can knock the wall down at the first impact. The magnitude of the force *relative to the magnitude of the resistance* is the determining factor in causing an object to move.

Kinds of Motion.   What are the ways in which an object may move? A hockey puck slides across the ice without turning. On the other hand, it may revolve as it slides. A figure skater spins in place. Arrows, balls and jumpers move through the air in a pathway known as a parabola. The hand moves in an arc when the forearm turns at the elbow joint and the neighboring joints are held motionless. As we note the different ways in which objects move, we are impressed with the almost limitless variety in the patterns of movement. Objects

267

move in straight paths and in curved paths; they roll, slide and fall; they bounce; they swing back and forth like a pendulum; they rotate about a center, either partially or completely; and they frequently rotate at the same time that they move as a whole from one place to another. Although the variety of ways in which objects move appears to be almost limitless, careful consideration of these ways reveals the fact that there are, in actuality, only *two* major classifications of movement patterns. These are *translatory* and *rotatory*. Either an object turns about a center of motion, or it moves in its entirety from one place to another. Sometimes it does both simultaneously. The former kind of movement is termed translatory because the object is translated as a whole from one location to another. Translatory movement may be further classified as rectilinear and curvilinear motion. Rectilinear motion, commonly called simply linear motion, is defined as the linear progression of an object as a whole, with all its parts moving the same distance in the same direction at a uniform rate of speed (Fig. 11–1). Curvilinear motion refers to all translatory, nonrectilinear movement. The object moves in a curved but not necessarily circular pathway. The paths of a ball or any projectile in flight, the wrist during the force phase in bowling, or the gondola on a moving Ferris wheel are curvilinear (Fig. 11–2). A form of translatory motion which on the surface does not appear to be translatory is that called *circular* motion. Circular motion occurs when an object moves along a curved path of constant radius. As the arm moves around in windmill fashion, the hand or any other point on the arm is moving in a circular path and is engaged in circular motion. This type of motion is a special case of curvilinear motion. It occurs when an unbalanced force acts on a moving body to keep it in a circle. If that unbalanced force stops acting on the object and the object is free to move, it will move in a linear path tangent to the direction it is moving at the moment of release. This is what may happen to external objects which are projected into space as the result of movements of body segments. A ball held in the hand moves in the same circular path as the hand until it is released. Then it flies off at a tangent moving in a linear path until gravity alters its flight.

Rotatory or *angular* motion is the kind of motion that is typical of levers and of wheels and axles. Rotatory or angular motion occurs when any object acting as a rigid bar moves in an arc about a fixed point. The arc may be small or it may be a complete circle. Most of the joint motions in the body are angular movements in which the body part moves in an arc about a fixed point. The arm engages in rotatory motion when it moves in windmill fashion about a fixed point or axis in the shoulder. The head's motion in the act of indicating "no," the lower leg in kicking a ball or the hand and forearm in turning a door knob are all examples of rotatory or angular motion. In each instance the moving body segment may be likened to the radius of a circle. The arm moving in windmill fashion and the lower leg and foot in kicking are the radii. In the "no" action of the head and in the door knob being turned by the forearm and hand, the radius is perpendicular to the long axis running vertically through the middle of the head and lengthwise through the middle of the forearm and hand, respectively (Fig. 11–3). These movements are not to be confused with circular motion. Circular motion describes the motion of any *point* on the radius whereas angular motion is descriptive of the motion of the whole radius.

Figure 11-1 An example of rectilinear motion.

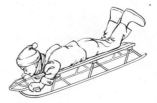

Reciprocating motion denotes repetitive movement. The use of the term is ordinarily limited to repetitive translatory movements, as illustrated by a bouncing ball or the repeated blows of a hammer, but technically it includes all kinds. The term *oscillation* refers specifically to repetitive angular movements, that is, movements in an arc. Familiar examples of this type of movement are seen in the pendulum, the metronome and the tuning fork. Not infrequently an object displays a combination of rotatory and translatory movement. This is sometimes referred to as *general motion.* The bicycle, the automobile, and the train move linearly as the result of the rotatory movements of their wheels, provided there is enough friction between the wheels and the supporting surface to keep the former from spinning in place. Likewise, man, as he walks or runs down the street, experiences translatory motion because of the angular movement of his body segments. The angular motions of several segments of the body are frequently coordinated in such a way that a related segment will move linearly. This is true in throwing darts, in putting the shot and in a lunge in fencing. Because of the angular motions of the forearm and upper arm, the hand is enabled to travel linearly and thus is able to impart linear force to the dart and to the shot prior to their release, and to the foil (Fig. 11–4).

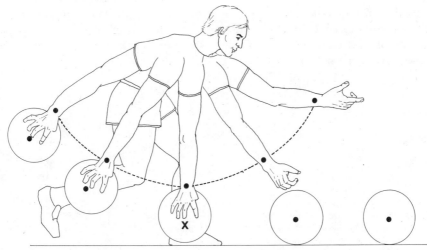

Figure 11-2 The wrist follows a curvilinear path during the delivery of a bowling ball. (Drawn from motion picture film tracing.)

Figure 11–3 Example of angular motion. The lower leg rotates about an axis in the knee joint. Similarly, the thigh engages in rotatory motion moving about an axis in the hip joint. (Drawn from motion picture film tracing.)

Kinds of Motion Experienced by the Body. The human body experiences all kinds of motion. As most of the joints are axial, the body segments must undergo primarily angular motion (Fig. 11–5). A slight amount of translatory motion is seen in the gliding movements of the plane or irregular joints. These movements are negligible in themselves. They occur chiefly in the carpal and tarsal joints and in the joints of the vertebral arches in conjunction with angular movements in neighboring axial joints. The body as a whole experiences rectilinear movement when it is acted upon by the force of gravity, as in coasting (Fig. 11–1), or in a free fall (Fig. 11–7), and likewise when acted upon by an external force, as in water skiing (Fig. 11–6). It experiences general motion in forward and backward rolls on the ground and in somersaults in the air, and rotatory motion in twirling on ice skates. It experiences curvilinear translatory motion in diving, broad jumping, high jumping and hurdling, and it experiences reciprocating motion on the trampoline and when swinging back and forth on the rings, trapeze or horizontal bar.

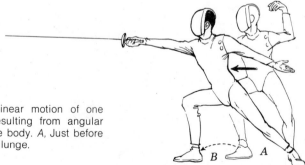

Figure 11–4 General motion: linear motion of one part of the body (the hand) resulting from angular motion of several segments of the body. *A,* Just before lunge (thrust). *B,* At completion of lunge.

Figure 11–5 An example of movement of the body caused by the body's own muscular activity. Movements of individual body segments are primarily angular. (Drawn from motion picture film tracing.)

Factors Which Determine the Kind of Motion.   Thus far we have considered the cause of motion and the various kinds of motion based on movement patterns or paths. Now we must turn to the question: What determines the kind of motion that will result when an object is made to move? The best way for the student to discover the answer is to produce each kind of motion and then to analyze what he did to obtain the kind of motion he wanted.

In order to make an object move linearly, we discover that either we must apply force uniformly against one entire side of the object, or we must apply it directly in line with the object's center of gravity. The object will move in a straight line provided it does not meet an obstacle or resistance of some sort. If its edge hits against another object or encounters a rough spot, the moving

Figure 11–6 An example of movement of the body caused by an external force.

Figure 11-7 An example of movement of the body caused by the force of gravity. (Drawn from motion picture film tracing.)

object will turn about its point of contact with the interfering factor. If we attempt to push a tall cabinet across a supporting surface which provides excessive friction such as a cement floor, for instance, the cabinet will tip, even though we place our hands exactly in line with the cabinet's center of gravity and push in a horizontal direction. In order to move it linearly it will be necessary to apply the push lower than the cabinet's center of gravity to compensate for the friction.

If rotatory motion of a freely movable object is desired, it is necessary to apply force to it "off center" or to provide an "off center" resistance which will interfere with the motion of part of the object. A lever undergoes rotatory motion because, by definition, one portion of it remains in place. If it is desired to move an object in the manner of a lever, it is necessary to provide a fulcrum and to apply force to it at some point other than its point of contact with the fulcrum.

Reciprocating motion is caused by a uniform repetition of opposing force applications, and the oscillation of a pendulum is produced by repeated applications of gravitational force to a suspended object which is free to move back and forth and which is in any position other than its resting position.

In summary, it may be said that the kind of motion that will be displayed by a moving object depends first of all upon the kind of motion permitted that particular kind of object. If it is a lever, it is permitted only angular motion; if it is a pendulum, oscillatory motion, and so on. If it is a freely movable object, it is permitted either translatory or rotatory motion, depending upon the circumstances. These circumstances include the point at which force is applied with reference to the object's center of gravity, the environmental pathways of movement available to the object and the presence or absence of additional external factors which modify the motion.

Factors Modifying Motion. Motion is usually modified by a number of external factors, such as friction, air resistance, water resistance and the like. Whether these factors are a help or a hindrance depends upon the circumstances and the nature of the motion. The same factor may facilitate one form of motion, yet hinder another. For instance, friction is a great help to the runner because it enables him to exert maximum effort without danger of slipping, yet on the other hand, friction hinders the rolling of a ball, as in field hockey, golf and crocquet. Again, wind or air resistance is indispensable to the sailboat's motion, but unless it is a "tail wind" it impedes the runner. Likewise, water resistance is essential for propulsion of the body by means of swimming strokes and of boats through the use of oars and paddles, yet at the same time it hinders the progress of both the swimmer and the boat, especially if these present a broad surface to the water. It is for this reason that swimmers keep the body level and that boats are streamlined. One of the major problems in sports is to learn how to take advantage of these factors when they contribute to the movement in question, and on the other hand, how to minimize them when they are detrimental to the movement. A more detailed discussion of forces influencing motion is presented in the chapter on force and motion.

There are also anatomic factors which modify the motion of the segments of the body. These include friction in the joints (minimized by synovial fluid), tension of antagonistic muscles, tension of ligaments and fasciae, anomalies of bone and joint structure, atmospheric pressure within the joint capsule and the presence of interfering soft tissues. Except for the limitations due to fleshiness, these modifying factors come under the heading of "internal resistance."

KINEMATIC DESCRIPTION OF MOTION

Motion has been defined as the act or process of changing place or position with respect to some reference point. Thus, in order to talk about motion a starting point must be located and the resultant motion described in terms of that point. The description of that motion, regardless of whether it is translatory or angular, may deal with how far the object has moved or how fast it has moved. The description of motion in such terms is called *kinematics.* The kinematics of motion describes motion with respect to displacement, velocity and acceleration. The forces causing or modifying the motion are not considered in the study of kinematics.

Linear Kinematics

Displacement. The distance an object is removed from a reference point is called its *displacement*. Displacement does not indicate how far the object travels in going from point *A* to point *C*. It only indicates the final change of position. A person who walks north for three miles to point *B* and then east for four miles to point *C* has walked a distance of seven miles, but the *displacement* with respect to the starting point is only five miles (Fig. 11–8).

To describe the displacement adequately the direction as well as the amount of position change must be indicated. This makes displacement a vector quantity since it has both magnitude and direction. Distance on the other hand is a scalar quantity possessing only amount.

Speed and Velocity. Speed and velocity are two words that are frequently used to describe how fast an object is moving. These terms are often used interchangeably, but in fact there is a significant difference. Speed tells how fast an object is moving, i.e., the distance an object will travel in a given time, but it tells nothing about the direction of movement.

$$\text{Average Speed} = \frac{\text{distance traveled}}{\text{time}}.$$

Velocity, on the other hand, involves direction as well as speed. Speed is a scalar quantity while velocity is a vector quantity. In most sports activities this difference is of no concern, but in others it is of extreme importance. The speed of a football player carrying the ball may be impressive but, if not directed toward his opponent's goal, it is not providing yardage for a first down. Although the speed may be great, the velocity in the desired direction may indeed be zero.

Velocity is the amount of *displacement* per given unit of time. This is the same as saying that velocity is the *rate* of displacement. Velocity may be constant or it may change. When velocity is constant the amount of displacement per unit time does not change. In the graphs in Figure 11–9, displacement values (s) are plotted along the y axis and the time values (t) along the x axis. The line formed by connecting different values of displacements for different points in time represents velocity (v).

In *A*, *B*, and *C* the rate of displacement is constant and the velocity is shown as a straight line. The steeper the slope, the greater the change in displacement

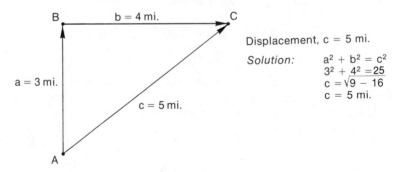

Displacement, c = 5 mi.

Solution:
$a^2 + b^2 = c^2$
$3^2 + 4^2 = 25$
$c = \sqrt{9 - 16}$
$c = 5$ mi.

Figure 11–8 Displacement is the resultant distance an object is removed from its starting point.

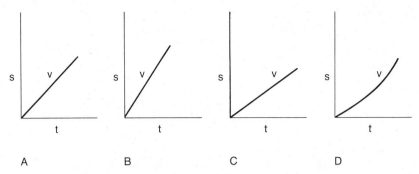

Figure 11–9 Examples of displacement–time graphs.

per unit of time. Graph B, shows the fastest velocity and C, the slowest. In D, the rate of displacement changes. This means that the velocity is not constant. It starts at a slow rate and then starts to increase. If A, B, C and D represent runners on a straight track, A, B and C would each be running at a constant but different velocity with B's velocity the fastest and C's the slowest. Runner D starts out at a slow velocity but increases the rate of displacement until his velocity is the fastest of all four. Where velocity is constant as in A, B and C, the motion is said to be uniform. When the amount of displacement per unit of time varies, nonuniform motion occurs. Uniform motion is not a common characteristic of human motion. Most human movements are apt to have many variations in the rate of displacement, and where the velocity of human motion is given, it is usually an average velocity which tells only the total displacement occurring in a stated period of time. In equation form, average velocity is $\bar{v} = \dfrac{s}{t}$ where $\bar{v}$ is average velocity, s is the displacement and t represents time. Although a long distance runner who runs the Boston Marathon, a distance of 26 miles, 385 yards, in two and one half hours, has an average velocity of 10.4 mph, it is doubtful that his velocity was 10.4 mph for any appreciable time throughout the run.

The average velocity of an object in motion may also be determined if the initial and final velocities are known. In the equation $\bar{v} = \dfrac{u + v}{2}$, u represents initial velocity, and v is final velocity. A cyclist whose initial velocity was 8 ft./sec. and whose velocity 10 seconds later was 23 ft./sec. had an average velocity of 15.5 ft./sec. during that time period. $\left(\dfrac{8 + 23}{2} = 15.5\right)$

Acceleration.   When velocity changes, its rate of change is called acceleration. A sprint runner has an initial velocity of zero ft./sec. When the gun signals the beginning of a race, the sprinter's velocity begins to change by increasing. The rate of change in velocity is *acceleration.* Acceleration may be positive or negative. An increase is considered positive and a decrease such as slowing down at the end of the race is considered negative. Negative acceleration is also called deceleration. When velocity is plotted against time as shown in Figure 11–10, the line formed by connecting the values of the velocity for a unit of time represents acceleration. In A the velocity does not change. It remains constant and

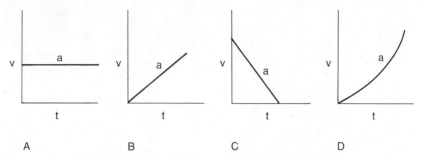

A   B   C   D

Figure 11-10 Examples of velocity — time graphs.

therefore there is no acceleration. In *B* the acceleration is positive and uniform. As *t* increases, *v* increases at a constant rate. In *C* acceleration is negative and uniform. As *t* increases, *v* decreases a constant amount per unit of time. In *D* acceleration is positive but it is nonuniform. Its rate of change is not constant. Again, taking the case of the runners on a straight track, the runner in *B* starts at 0 velocity and increases the velocity at a constant rate; the runner in *C* steadily decreases the velocity at a constant rate until it is zero; the runner in *D* has an acceleration (rate of velocity change) which is initially slow but then proceeds to speed up.

In equation form acceleration is expressed as $\bar{a} = \dfrac{v - u}{t}$ where $\bar{a}$ represents average acceleration, *v*, final velocity, *u*, initial velocity and *t*, time. A runner whose velocity changes from 2 ft./sec. at the end of the first second to 4 ft./sec. at the end of the second second, to 6 ft./sec. at the end of the third second has accelerated motion. The rate of change of velocity $\left(\bar{a} = \dfrac{6 - 0}{3}\right)$ is 2 feet per second for each second he runs, or two feet per second per second. *Acceleration is the time rate of change of a time rate of change.* Therefore, time appears twice in acceleration units. The acceleration in this example can also be written as 2 ft./sec./sec. or 2 ft./sec.^{2}

Uniformly Accelerated Motion.   In the example just given the acceleration rate was constant, i.e., during each second of the run the amount of velocity change remained the same. When this is the situation, motion is said to be *uniformly* accelerated, and the relationships among displacement, velocity, acceleration and time may be expressed in equations of motion:

$$v = u + at \qquad (1)$$
$$s = ut + \tfrac{1}{2} at^2 \qquad (2)$$
$$v^2 = u^2 + 2 as \qquad (3)$$

These equations apply to any type of linear motion where acceleration is uniform. Perhaps the most common situation in which we encounter a uniform acceleration has to do with objects in flight. Neglecting air resistance, objects allowed to fall freely will speed up or accelerate at a uniform rate due to the acceleration of gravity. Conversely objects projected upward will be retarded at a uniform rate due to the acceleration of gravity. The value for the acceleration of gravity changes with different locations on the earth's surface, but for most of the United States this value can be considered to be 32 ft./sec.² Regardless of its size or density, a falling object will be acted on by gravity so that its velocity will increase 32 ft./sec. each second it is in the air. A dropped ball starting out with a velocity of 0 ft./sec. will have a velocity of 32 ft./sec. at the end of one second, 64 ft./sec. at the end of 2 seconds, 96 ft./sec. at the end of 3 seconds, and so on. A second ball weighing twice as much will fall with exactly the same acceleration. It too will have a velocity of 96 ft./sec. at the end of 3 seconds.

Because the acceleration of gravity is constant, the distance traveled by a freely falling body, as well as its downward velocity, can be determined for any point in time by making use of the motion equations (Table 11–1).

Projectiles

Vertical Projections.   When a ball is allowed to fall freely its behavior is determined by gravity. When it is thrown straight up, its upward flight is governed by the upward force of the throw and the downward force of gravity. Objects projected upward are decelerated by the downward force of gravity at the same rate that those projected downward are accelerated. Consequently an upward thrown ball will have the same speed when it falls again into the hand as it did at the moment of leaving the hand. Its upward force is a vector quantity as is its downward force (Fig. 11–11).

Downward directed vectors have plus values and upward directed vectors have minus values. The speed (magnitude) of the ball starting up will be equal to the speed of the ball landing. The only difference is one of direction. The initial velocity ($-u$) equals the final velocity ($+v$). Proof that release velocity and landing velocity are equal in amount but opposite in direction ($-u = v$), can be shown by substitution of values in the motion equations.

Example: Assuming that a ball is thrown to a height of eight feet, what is its initial velocity as it leaves the hand? What is its final velocity as it lands in the hand?

Upward Throw Velocity   *Downward Landing Velocity*

$u = ?$ $v = 0$ $v = ?$ $u = 0$
     $a = 32$ $a = 32$
     $s = 8$ $s = 8$

Using Equation (3): $v^2 = u^2 + 2as$

$v^2 = u^2 + 2as$ $v^2 = u^2 + 2as$
$0 = u^2 + (2 \times 32 \times 8)$ $v^2 = 0 + (2 \times 32 \times 8)$
$u^2 = -(2 \times 32 \times 8)$
$u^2 = -512$ $v^2 = 512$
$u = -\sqrt{512}$ ft./sec. $v = \sqrt{512}$ ft./sec.
$u = -22.6$ ft./sec. $v = 22.6$ ft./sec.

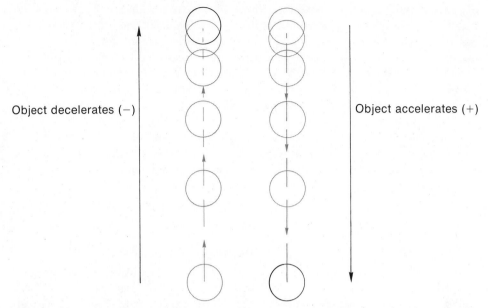

Object decelerates (−)   Object accelerates (+)

Figure 11–11 Objects projected upward are decelerated by the downward force of gravity at the same rate as those allowed to fall downward are accelerated. Both objects will cover the same distance in the same time. (Drawn from motion picture film tracing.)

When any object is thrown upward, it continues to slow down until it reaches a point at which the force of the velocity upward is neutralized by the downward force of gravity. The greater the force of the upward projection, the longer it takes for the upward velocity to be reduced to zero by gravity and the higher the ball will go. Referring to Table 11–1 it can be seen that a ball thrown upward with an initial velocity of 32 ft./sec. will rise 16 feet and take one second to reach its high point while a ball thrown upward with an initial velocity of 64 ft./sec. will continue upward for 64 feet reaching its peak in two seconds. The greater the force of the upward projection, the longer it takes for the upward velocity to be reduced to zero by gravity and the higher the ball will go. The greater the initial upward velocity of a projected object, the longer it will remain in the air before returning to its starting point. Consequently upward velocity should be emphasized in activities when it is desirable to allow as much time as possible in the air. Gymnasts and divers who desire to perform intricate stunt patterns in the air need time and therefore would benefit from the increased height which comes as a result of increased vertical velocity.

The statement that objects fall at the same rate of 32 ft./sec.² regardless of

TABLE 11–1   Effect of Gravity on a Freely Falling Object

TIME	DISTANCE TRAVELED $S = ut + \frac{1}{2}at^2$	FINAL VELOCITY $v = u + at$	AVERAGE VELOCITY $\bar{v} = \dfrac{u+v}{2}$
1 sec.	16 ft.	32 ft./sec.	16 ft./sec.
2 sec.	64 ft.	64 ft./sec.	32 ft./sec.
3 sec.	144 ft.	96 ft./sec.	48 ft./sec.
4 sec.	256 ft.	128 ft./sec.	64 ft./sec.
5 sec.	400 ft.	160 ft./sec.	80 ft./sec.

weight holds true of course only when air resistance is not a factor. A shuttle-cock dropped from the same height as a golf ball is affected more by air resistance and descends at a slower rate than the golf ball. The equations of motion can only be applied with reasonable accuracy where objects of considerable density, such as baseballs, are affected little by air resistance. Even heavy objects such as skydivers falling from great distances eventually reach a downward speed large enough to create an opposing air resistance equal to the accelerating force of gravity. When this happens, the diver no longer speeds up but continues to fall at a steady speed. This speed is called *terminal* velocity and amounts to approximately 120 mph (176 ft./sec.) for a falling skydiver. With his parachute open, the diver's velocity reduces to 12 mph steady velocity.

Horizontal Projection.   The flight path of a ball thrown horizontally is also determined by the force of the throw (in this case horizontal) and the downward acceleration of gravity. A horizontally projected object starts out horizontally but immediately begins to follow a downward-curved path because of the additional effect of gravity's force acting on it. The resultant displacement of the ball is the resultant of the horizontal displacement vector due to the force of the throw plus the vertical displacement vector resulting from the force of gravity (Figure 11–12). Balls thrown horizontally with different forces will have differing horizontal velocities and will travel different horizontal distances in a given time $\left(s = \dfrac{v}{t}\right)$, but they all will travel the same vertical distance downward since the acceleration due to gravity does not change (a = 32 ft./sec./sec.), and the vertical drop depends entirely on the time gravity has to act on the object (s = ut + ½ at²). (See Figure 11–13). Note: s = ut + ½ at² becomes s = ½ at² because u = 0. From this it can be seen that the horizontal force or velocity of a projected object is independent of the vertical force or velocity of the object and that the horizontal force of the object only has influence over the horizontal distance that the object will cover while it remains in the air and none over the amount of time that the object remains in the air. An object projected horizontally from the same height and at the same time as one allowed to drop downward will land at the same level as the dropped object in the same amount of time. As with the vertically projected object, the time that a horizontally projected object remains in the air depends upon the amount of vertical distance between the landing point and the high point (s = ½ at²).

The horizontal distance the projectile travels is governed by both the horizontal velocity of the object and the amount of time the object is able to

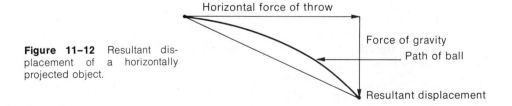

Figure 11–12 Resultant displacement of a horizontally projected object.

Horizontal force of throw

Force of gravity
Path of ball

Resultant displacement

Figure 11-13 Flight path of balls with different horizontal velocities. Each ball is released at the same height as the other balls, and therefore each remains in the air for the same amount of time as the other balls before hitting the ground.

remain in the air before it hits the ground. A ball thrown horizontally from a height of 8 feet above the ground with a horizontal velocity of 50 ft./sec. will go 35 feet before hitting the ground. A ball thrown with the same velocity but from a height of 4 feet will hit the ground just 25 horizontal feet from its release point. These values may be determined as follows:

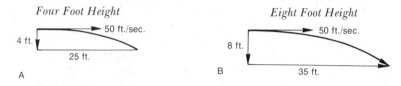

Time object will be in air before it drops to ground: Use Equation (2),
$S = ut + \frac{1}{2} at^2$ and solve for t.

$$s = 4 \qquad\qquad\qquad\qquad\qquad\qquad s = 8$$
$$u = 0 \qquad\qquad\qquad\qquad\qquad\qquad u = 0$$
$$a = 32 \qquad\qquad\qquad\qquad\qquad\qquad a = 32$$
$$4 = 0\,t + (\tfrac{1}{2}\,32t^2) \qquad\qquad\qquad 8 = 0\,t + (\tfrac{1}{2}\,32t^2)$$
$$t^2 = \frac{4}{16} = \frac{1}{4} = .25 \qquad\qquad\qquad t^2 = \frac{8}{16} = \frac{1}{2} = .50$$

$$\boxed{t = .5 \text{ sec.}} \qquad\qquad\qquad\qquad \boxed{t = .7 \text{ sec.}}$$

Horizontal distance the object will travel before it hits the ground:
Using velocity equation, $\bar{v} = \frac{s}{t}$, solve for s.

$$\bar{v} = 50 \text{ ft./sec.} \qquad\qquad\qquad\qquad \bar{v} = 50 \text{ ft./sec.}$$
$$t = .5 \qquad\qquad\qquad\qquad\qquad\qquad t = .7$$
$$50 = \frac{s}{.5} \qquad\qquad\qquad\qquad\qquad\qquad 50 = \frac{s}{.7}$$
$$s = 50 \times .5 \qquad\qquad\qquad\qquad\qquad s = 50 \times .7$$

$$\boxed{s = 25 \text{ ft.}} \qquad\qquad\qquad\qquad\qquad \boxed{s = 35 \text{ ft.}}$$

Diagonal Projections. More often than not, objects put in flight will be sent in directions other than exactly vertical or horizontal. They will be projected at some angle with respect to the horizontal or vertical. If no other force acts on such an object except that which propels it into space, the object's inertia will cause it to continue to move at the same speed and in the same direction it had at the moment of release. It would be at point *A* in Figure 11–14. But the projectile does not do this. As with the horizontally projected object, this object begins dropping the instant it is projected into space. It moves downward with an increasing velocity according to the constant acceleration of gravity following a flight path the shape of a parabola. At the end of one half second the object will have dropped 4 feet ($s = \frac{1}{2}at^2$ or $s = 16 \times .5^2 = 4$) and be at point *B*. At the end of one second it will have dropped a total of 16 feet (Table 11–1) and be at point *C*.

Since this type of projectile flight has both horizontal and vertical velocity imparted to it initially, its flight will be determined by the nature of each of these components. The vertical flight of the object is the resultant of the imparted upward vertical velocity and the downward acceleration due to gravity (32 ft./sec.²). This resultant velocity is a vector quantity which diminishes in amount until it reaches zero at the high point. It then continues to increase in the opposite direction until it is equal in size but opposite in direction to its release value when it lands at the same level as the release (Fig. 11–15). The horizontal flight is governed only by the horizontal velocity of the projection. This velocity is shown as a vector of constant length throughout the flight. Unlike the vertical velocity, the horizontal velocity remains constant because no other horizontal force is introduced (air resistance excluded). As long as the object is in the air, the horizontal distance covered is the product of the horizontal velocity and the time in flight.

Optimum Angle of Flight. It has been shown that the horizontal distance that an object will travel in space depends upon both its horizontal velocity and the length of time that the object is in flight. The length of time the object is in flight depends upon the height of its high point and that in turn is governed by the vertical velocity imparted to the object at release. Thus the horizontal distance an object will travel depends upon both the horizontal and vertical components of velocity which the projectile has at the initiation of flight. The size of the vertical and horizontal velocity components depends upon the flight angle (Fig. 11–16). Flight *A* has a projection angle of 30 degrees and Flight *B* has a projection angle of 60 degrees. The initial projection velocity of each projectile is the same.

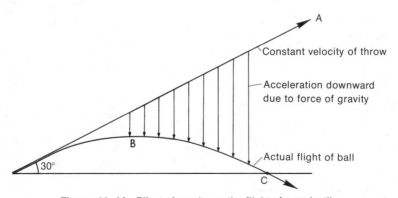

Figure 11–14 Effect of gravity on the flight of a projectile.

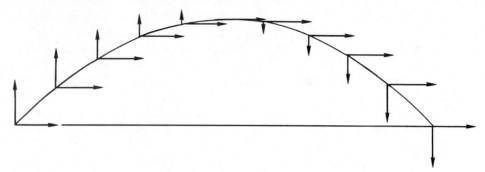

Figure 11-15 Magnitude of horizontal and vertical velocities during projectile flight.

From the diagram it can be seen that the horizontal velocity component for flight *A* is greater than its vertical component and that it is also greater than the horizontal velocity component for *B*. In contrast, the vertical velocity of *B* is greater than its horizontal velocity as well as that of *A*'s. This can be shown mathematically using right triangle relationships:

	Flight A	*Flight B*
Initial Velocity	80 ft./sec.	80 ft./sec.
Angle of Release	30°	60°
Horizontal Velocity	80 × cos 30° = 80 × .866 = ⟦69.3 ft./sec.⟧	80 × cos 60° = 80 × 0.50 = ⟦40 ft./sec.⟧
Vertical Velocity	80 × sin 30° 80 × 0.50 = ⟦40 ft./sec.⟧	80 × sin 60° = 80 × 0.866 = ⟦69.3 ft./sec.⟧

A simple experiment with a garden hose demonstrates that a stream of water projected vertically or at 90 degrees will go higher than a stream projected at any other angle and drops from that stream will remain in the air longer. This stream has no horizontal velocity and therefore no horizontal distance is covered. A stream projected at 0 degrees at ground level has no vertical velocity component but consists entirely of horizontal velocity. The stream will not travel any vertical distance, but neither will it travel any horizontal distance in space in spite of its horizontal velocity. Vertical distance is needed for time in flight and this stream has none. Various other angles imparted to the water stream result in differing heights and horizontal distances reached by the water drops. These heights and distances show a pattern related to the angle at which the hose nozzle is held (Fig. 11–17).

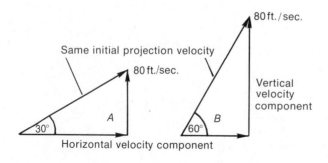

Figure 11-16 Effect of projection angle upon the magnitude of horizontal and vertical velocity components. As the angle decreases, the horizontal component increases and the vertical component decreases.

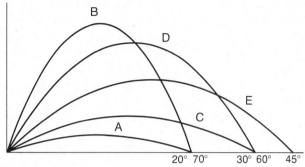

Figure 11–17 The angle of projection influences the horizontal and vertical distance covered by a projectile. Complementary angles of projection produce the same horizontal displacement.

Flight paths *A* and *B* result in the least amount of horizontal displacement and although the amount of horizontal displacement for both is the same, the vertical displacements are quite different. The angle of elevation for *A* is the complement ($90° - B$) of the angle for *B*. This is also true for *C* and *D*. The angle for *C* is 60 degrees and for *D* it is 30 degrees. Either elevation angle will result in the same landing spot, but flight *D* will go *higher* and take *longer* to land. Tennis lobs and high football punts are examples of flights *B* or *D* and are used when extra time is desired. On the other hand, the longer an object is in the air, the greater the time for air and wind resistance to alter the flight. Where this is a detriment, flight patterns like *A* or *C* should be selected. Moreover there are many occasions when the speed with which the object gets from *A* to *B* is

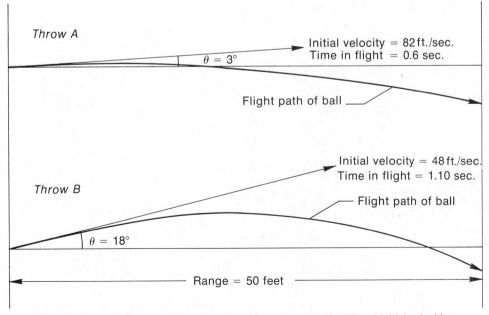

Figure 11–18 Comparison of flight paths of balls thrown with different initial velocities.

extremely important. Base throwing in baseball is an example. The flatter the trajectory the faster the ball will reach its destination, providing of course, its horizontal velocity is sufficiently great to get it to its destination before gravity causes it to drop too much. Figure 11–18 shows the trajectories of two balls thrown at a spot on a wall fifty feet away. Each ball was thrown as "hard and as fast" as the thrower was capable of throwing. Throw *A* reached the wall in .61 second while throw *B* took 1.10 seconds. The release angle for *A* was 3 degrees; for *B* it was 18 degrees. The velocity of the throw for *A* was 82 ft./sec. and for *B* it was 48 ft./sec.

Path E in Figure 11–17 shows the flight when the initial angle is 45 degrees. At this angle the vertical and horizontal velocity components are equal. An angle of 45 degrees is the optimum angle for greatest horizontal distance, but only when air resistance is not a factor and when the release and landing occur at the same level. If the landing is lower than the release, an angle less than 45 degrees is called for. How much less depends on how great the difference is between release and landing level, as well as on the initial velocity. The greater the difference between release and landing, the more the optimum angle decreases. Also, the greater the initial velocity, the less the angle will differ from 45 degrees. Table 11–2 shows the effect of speed, height and angle upon the horizontal range in putting the shot.

The characteristics of a projectile flight also affect the way one must aim for accuracy. A baseball pitcher must account for gravity by aiming at a point above the batter's head in order to compensate for gravity. In target archery there is only one distance away from the target where a given archer with his particular equipment, uses "point blank" aim. At all other distances the arrow tip is aimed either above or below the target (Fig. 11–19).

This discussion of projectiles should point out that how far one can throw a ball depends both upon the velocity one is capable of imparting to the ball

**TABLE 11–2 Variation of Optimum
Angle With Height and Speed of Release***

HEIGHT OF RELEASE	SPEED OF RELEASE					
	28 ft./sec.	32 ft./sec.	36 ft./sec.	40 ft./sec.	44 ft./sec.	48 ft./sec.
8 ft. 0 in.	38° (31.34 ft.)	39° (38.99 ft.)	40° (47.58 ft.)	41° (57.13 ft.)	42° (67.65 ft.)	42° (79.15 ft.)
7 ft. 6 in.	38° (30.95 ft.)	39° (38.58 ft.)	40° (47.15 ft.)	41° (56.69 ft.)	42° (67.21 ft.)	42° (78.69 ft.)
7 ft. 0 in.	39° (30.55 ft.)	40° (38.16 ft.)	41° (46.73 ft.)	41° (56.25 ft.)	42° (66.76 ft.)	42° (78.23 ft.)
6 ft. 6 in.	39° (30.16 ft.)	40° (37.75 ft.)	41° (46.29 ft.)	42° (55.81 ft.)	42° (66.31 ft.)	43° (77.78 ft.)

*The distance obtained by the indicated combinations of speed of release, height of release and optimum angle are shown in parentheses. These distances do not include the extra distance (approximately one foot) that the shot is in advance of the inside edge of the stop board at the instant of release. (From Hay, J. G.: The Biomechanics of Sports Techniques. Englewood Cliffs, N.J.: Prentice-Hall, Inc. 1973.)

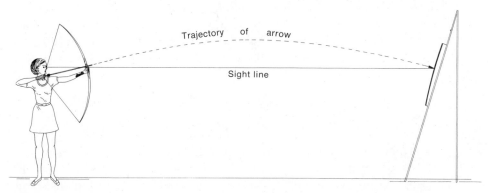

Figure 11–19 The force of gravity affects the flight of an arrow. An archer must account for this effect when aiming.

and the angle of release. A person may execute a short throw because of a poor angle choice or because of inability to impart speed to the ball. Since alterations in angle are readily changed, it would seem that a measure of speed of the throw would be a better measure of skill than distance thrown. Improvements in throwing ability then would be noted by increases of speed of release. Cooper and Glassow present a method for determining the speed of a throw when the time of flight, range, release height and landing height are known.[3]

Angular Kinematics

Angular Displacement.   The human skeleton is made up of a system of levers which by definition are rigid bars that rotate about fixed points when force is applied. When any object acting as a rigid bar moves in an arc about an axis, the movement is called rotatory or angular movement. An attempt to describe angular motion in linear units presents real problems. As an object moves in an arc, the linear displacement of particles spaced along that lever vary. Particles nearer to the axis have a displacement in inches, meters, feet or centimeters which is less than those farther away. In the underarm throw pattern the hand moves through a greater distance than the wrist and the wrist a greater distance than the elbow. Rotatory motion needs rotatory units to describe it. As might be expected, these units relate to the units of a circle and the fact that the circumference of a circle, C, is equal to $2\pi r$, where r is the radius and π is a constant value of 3.1416. There are three rotatory or angular units of displacement. Degrees, revolutions or radians are interchangeable units used to describe angular motion. One full revolution of displacement is the same as 360 degrees or 2π radians of displacement. The word revolution is not stated, but it is understood when we say that a diver executed a 1½ somersault tuck. The dive could also be described as a tuck somersault of 540 (360 + 180) degrees or 3 π radians. Degrees are used most frequently in the measurement of angles, and radians, the term favored by engineers and physicists, are the units often needed in equations of angular motion. The symbol for angular displacement is the Greek letter θ (theta).

Angular Velocity. The rate of rotatory displacement is called angular velocity, symbolized as ω (omega). Angular velocity is equal to the angle through which the radius turns divided by the time it takes for the displacement,

$$\overline{\omega} = \frac{\theta}{t},$$

and is expressed as degrees/second, radians/second or revolutions/second. A softball pitcher who moves his arm through an arc of 140 degrees in 0.1 second has an average angular velocity of 1400 degrees per second. This could also be expressed as 3.88 revolutions per second or 24.43 radians/second. This velocity is called average velocity because film studies of pitchers show that the angular displacement during the execution of the skill is not uniform and a velocity such as this represents the average velocity over the time span through which the displacement is measured. Most human movements are more likely to be variable and not uniform. The longer the time span through which the displacement is measured the more variability is averaged. Thus, if one is interested in the velocity at a specific instant in a skill the displacement must be measured over an extremely small time span. Figure 11–20 shows variations in displacement during the execution of the golf drive.

Angular Acceleration. In the discussion of linear velocity, a change in velocity was called acceleration. The same is true for changes in angular velocity. Angular acceleration α (alpha) is the rate of change of angular velocity and is expressed in equation form as:

$$\alpha = \frac{\omega_v - \omega_u}{t}$$

where ω_v is final velocity, ω_u is initial velocity and t is time. If, in Figure 11–20, the angular velocity is 25 rad./sec. at point A and 50 rad./sec. at point B, and the time lapse between A and B is 0.11 seconds, the angular acceleration between points A and B is 241 rad./sec./sec. This value for α indicating that the velocity increased 241 radians per second each second would be true, of course, only if the velocity increased at a uniform rate. Otherwise this value has to be considered an average of accelerations which may have been higher or lower during the time period studied.

Radius Length. The description of angular motion in terms of displacement, velocity and acceleration can tell us a great deal about human movements, but nothing in such a description accounts for or shows the effect of the length of the radius on the outcomes of such movements. We know that a baseball hit in the middle of a bat will not go as far as one hit at the end, or that a ball hit by a tennis racquet as an extension of the arm will travel farther than a ball hit with the hand and that in golf a driver will cause a struck ball to travel farther than a nine iron. In each instance greater force is imparted to the struck object when the radius (distance between axis and point of contact) is longer causing

Figure 11-20 Variations in angular displacement of golf club over equal time intervals during the execution of a golf drive. (Drawn from motion picture film tracing.)

greater linear velocity to be generated at its end. As can be seen in Figure 11–21, lever *A* is shorter than *B*, and *B* is shorter than *C*. If all three levers are moved through the same angular distance in the same amount of time, it is apparent that the end of lever *A* would move with less speed than would the ends of either *B* or *C*. All three levers have the same angular velocity, but linear velocity of the circular motion at the end of each lever is proportional to the length of the lever. An object moved at the end of a long radius will have a greater linear velocity than one moved at the end of a short radius, providing the angular velocity remains constant. Thus, it is to the advantage of a performer to use as long a lever as possible to impart linear velocity to an object, providing the lever length does not cause too great a sacrifice in angular velocity. The optimum length of the lever for a person depends upon the individual's ability to maintain angular velocity. A child who cannot handle the weight of a long radius is better off with a shortened implement which he can control and swing rapidly, whereas a strong adult profits by using a longer radius.

    In the same way that the radius affects the linear velocity in circular motion when the angular velocity is held constant, the radius length determines the angular velocity of the radius when the linear velocity at the end of the radius is held constant. Once an object is engaged in rotatory motion, the linear velocity at the end of the radius stays the same due to the conservation of momentum. The

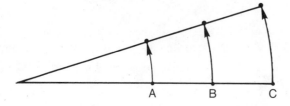

Figure 11–21 Lever A < B < C. Although the angular displacement for all three levers is the same, the linear displacement at the end of the longer levers is greater than that at the end of the shorter levers.

radius of rotation for a pike somersault dive is longer than that for a tuck somersault, and the radius for a layout somersault is longer than that for a pike somersault. If one starts a dive in an open position and then tucks tightly, the radius of rotation decreases, but because the linear velocity does not change, the angular velocity increases. The same situation occurs when a figure skater rotating slowly about a vertical axis with arms and one leg out to the side brings the arms and leg close to the axis. The radius decreases and the angular velocity increases. To slow down, the skater again reaches out with arms and leg. Figure 11–22 shows the effect of shortening the radius while maintaining a constant linear velocity at the end of the radius. *Shortening the radius will increase the angular velocity and lengthening it will decrease the angular velocity.* Points *a* and *b* on radii *A* and *B* have moved through the same linear distance, but the angular displacement for *A* is greater than that for *B*. If the displacements of *a* and *b* each take place in the same amount of time, the linear velocities will be equal, but the angular velocity for *A* must be the greater.

The relationship which exists between the angular velocity of an object moving in a rotary fashion and the linear velocity at the end of its radius is expressed with the equation:

$$\bar{v} = \omega r$$

To use the equation in this form, ω must be expressed in radians. If the angular velocity is expressed in degrees/second, the equation becomes:

$$\bar{v} = \frac{\omega r}{57.3}$$

Either form of the equation shows the direct proportionality which exists between linear velocity and the radius. For any given angular velocity, the linear velocity is proportional to the radius. If the radius doubles, the linear velocity does likewise. And for any given linear velocity, the angular velocity is inversely proportional to the radius. If the radius doubles, the angular velocity decreases one half.

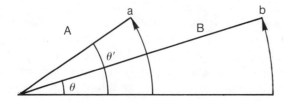

Figure 11–22 Increasing the length of the radius decreases the angular velocity when the linear velocity remains constant.

LABORATORY EXPERIENCES

1. With the help of several classmates prepare a displacement/time graph and a velocity/time graph for your performance on the 50 or 100 yard dash. Class members should be spaced at five yard intervals along your running path, each with a stopwatch. On the signal for you to go, each timer will start his watch and stop it when you pass that timer's position. Prepare a table with the following data for each run:
   a. Distance intervals
   b. Times recorded at each interval
   c. Times over each 5 yard interval (subtract adjacent times)
   d. Average velocity over each 5 yard interval $\left(\overline{v} = \frac{s}{t} = \frac{15}{t_2 - t_1} \right)$

   For each set of data prepare a displacement/time graph and a velocity/time graph for the whole run. Describe your run in terms of displacement, velocity and acceleration. Compare your graphs with other members of the group, and note any differences.

2. Throw a ball so that it is projected vertically upward, Catch it at the same height it was released. Have a partner measure the time the ball is in the air, i.e., from the time of release to the time the ball lands in your hand. Determine the velocity of the ball at the moment of release and the distance the ball traveled before it started its descent. Graph the flight of the ball on a piece of graph paper.

3. Have someone drop a ball, letting go of it at the same time and height that you project another ball horizontally. Two other people should measure the time in flight for each ball from the time of release to the time of landing. Compare the times and explain the results.

4. While walking along at a constant speed, project a ball vertically into the air. If you continue to walk without changing your speed or direction, where will the ball land? Explain. Draw a diagram of the ball's flight indicating the forces acting on it.

5. Assume that you are able to throw a ball with a velocity of 80 ft./sec. and at an angle of 45 degrees with the horizontal. If it is caught at the same height from the ground at which it was released, neglecting air resistance, how far will it go? How long will it be in flight? Repeat with a 30 degree angle of release. How would these values change if the landing height were lowered?

6. Using Figure 11–3 determine the angular velocity of the lower leg at the knee joint at the beginning of the force phase and at the moment of foot contact with the ball. The time between each stick figure tracing is .0156 second. What is the linear velocity at the ankle at the moment of contact if the lower leg is 16 inches (knee joint to ankle joint).

REFERENCES

1. Atwater, A. E.: The overarm softball throw. In Sisley, B. (Ed.): D.G.W.S. Softball Guide. Washington: A.A.H.P.E.R., 1968.
2. Basford, L.: The Science of Movement. London: Sampson Low, Marston & Co., 1966.
3. Cooper, J. M., and Glassow, R. B.: Kinesiology, 3rd Ed. St. Louis: C. V. Mosby Co., 1972.
4. Dull, C. E., Metcalfe, H. C., and Williams, J. E.: Modern Physics. New York: Holt, Rinehart, and Winston, 1963.
5. Dyson, G.: The Mechanics of Athletics, 5th Ed. London: University of London Press, 1970.
6. Hay, J. G.: The Biomechanics of Sports Techniques. Englewood Cliffs, N.J.: Prentice-Hall Inc., 1973.

7. Jensen, C. R., and Schultz, G. W.: Applied Kinesiology. New York: McGraw-Hill Book Company, 1970.
8. Kelley, D. L.: Kinesiology–Fundamentals of Motion Description. Englewood Cliffs, N.J.: Prentice-Hall Inc., 1971.
9. McCloy, C. H.: The mechanical analysis of motor skills. *In* Johnson, W. R. (Ed.): Science and Medicine of Exercise and Sports. New York: Harper & Row Publishers, Inc., 1960.
10. Miller, D. L., and Nelson, R. C.: Biomechanics of Sport. Philadelphia: Lea & Febiger, 1973.
11. Mortimer, E. M.: Basketball shooting. Res. Quart. Am. Assn. Health, Phys. Ed. & Recrn., *22*:234–243, 1951.
12. Ruchlis, H.: Orbit: A Picture Story of Force and Motion. New York: Harper & Row Publishers, Inc., 1958.
13. Williams, M., and Lissner, H. R.: Biomechanics of Human Motion. Philadelphia: W. B. Saunders Company, 1962.

Chapter Twelve

FORCE

Nature of Force. Force produces motion, stops motion and prevents motion. It may increase speed, decrease speed or cause objects to change direction. Forces may push or pull to cause motion, or balance each other so that bodies remain stationary. *Force is the effect that one body has on another.* How a force affects a body is determined by the size or *magnitude* of the force, the *direction* in which the force is acting and the exact point at which the force is *applied* to the object. In order to describe force fully, all three of these characteristics must be identified and taken into account. A change in any one of them

Figure 12–1 Graphic representation of a force vector. The magnitude of the force is the vector line, *A*; the point of application is the beginning of the vector, *B*; and the direction of the vector is represented by the arrowhead and the angle, *θ*. (Drawn from motion picture film tracing.)

alters the nature of the motion. Two fifty pound forces applied in the same direction and in line with the center of an object will result in linear motion. The same forces also applied in the same direction but off center will cause rotatory motion. Finally, no motion will occur if these forces are applied at the same point but in opposite directions.

Since force has the qualities of both magnitude and direction, it is a vector quantity. Force vectors are represented and treated in the same fashion as kinematic vectors. Graphically, the magnitude of the force is represented by the length of the vector line. The point of application of the force is the point where the force vector starts, and the force is always represented as a pull away from the point of application. The vector line represents the line of force, and the arrowhead indicates the direction of the force application (Fig. 12–1). Force vectors may also be resolved and combined using trigonometric relationships in the same fashion as was demonstrated with kinematic quantities.

The action of a force may be internal or external. Internal forces are defined as forces exerted by bodies on other bodies within a defined system, whereas external forces are forces exerted by bodies within a specified system on bodies outside of the specified system. In kinesiology, internal forces are usually classified as muscle forces which act on the various structures of the body, and external forces are those outside the body. The best known external force is gravity. Wind or water resistance forces, friction or forces due to other objects acting on the body also are external forces.

ASPECTS OF FORCE

Magnitude. The force of gravity is the external force with which the human body must contend in all movement experience. It is the force which gives bodies weight, and it is measured in terms of the body's weight. When one holds a ball in the hand, the pull of gravity is felt as the weight of the ball. The ball stays in the hand as long as an equal and opposite force acting between the hand and the ball balances the downward gravitational force. In this example the equal and opposite force is muscular. When the opposing force is removed, the ball drops and gravity's pull is apparent in the downward motion of the ball. The weight of the ball is the *magnitude* of the force of gravity acting on the ball.

The magnitude of force that a body can exert varies with its location. The farther away an object is from the earth's center, the less gravitational pull it has and therefore less weight. The equation for weight is $W = mg$ where m is the mass or quantity of matter of the object and g is the accelerative rate of gravity which we can accept as 32 ft./sec./sec. The basic unit of force (weight) in the English system is the pound and in the metric system it is the newton. (See Table 10–1.) The pound is defined as the weight of a standard pound at sea level and at 45 degrees latitude. A newton is the force needed to lift a mass of 0.102 kilogram under the same conditions.

The magnitude of muscular force is in direct proportion to the number and size of the fibers in the muscle which is contracting. If muscles contracted individually, it would be a relatively easy matter to measure the force exerted by each one in a given movement. Since they normally act in groups, however, their force or strength is measured collectively. It is customary to measure maximum muscular strength by performing a simple movement against the resistance of a dynamometer, spring balance or similar instrument. The instrument thus serves as the resistance to an anatomical lever whose force is provided by a group of muscles which act as a functional team to produce the movement of the lever. Among the muscle groups which are frequently measured by this method are the finger flexors (grip strength), elbow flexors and knee extensors.

Although there is no way of determining the amount of force exerted by a single muscle in the living body, its potential strength can be calculated from its measurements, its internal structure and the approximate number of pounds (or kilograms) which the average human muscle is known to exert per square inch (or centimeter). The muscle's external measurements and its internal structure form the basis for determining its physiologic cross section, a term which refers to the perpendicular section of all of the muscle's fibers. A study of the internal structure of various muscles reveals a variety of arrangements. In some muscles the fibers are arranged longitudinally; in some, in spindle-like fashion; in some, fanlike; and in some, feather-like (see page 38). Obviously a simple cross section of a penniform or a bipenniform muscle will miss a large number of the fibers; hence a true cross section of the muscle's fibers is one which cuts across every fiber in the muscle. Figure 12–2 illustrates the method of measuring the physiologic cross section of several types of muscles. The cross section does not reveal the actual number of fibers, to be sure, but it corresponds closely enough for us to use this measurement in estimating the muscle's potential force. The physiologic cross section is found by adding the lengths of the lines that cut perpendicularly across the fibers and multiplying their sum by the average thickness of the muscle. Such measurements can, of course, only be made on dissected muscles, but in the living body they can be roughly estimated from the approximate circumference and length of the muscle belly and from a knowledge of the muscle's internal structure. Suppose a penniform muscle is 7 inches long, exclusive of its tendons, and its average thickness is $3/4$ of an inch. Suppose further that it takes three lines, measuring respectively 4, 5 and 3 inches, to cut perpendicularly across the fibers. The physiologic cross section of such a muscle is $3/4$ $(4 + 5 + 3) = 3/4 \times 12 = 9$ square inches.

  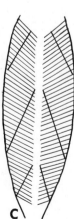

Figure 12–2 Method of measuring the physiologic cross section of three types of muscles. *A*, A fusiform or spindle muscle; *B*, a penniform muscle; *C*, a bipenniform muscle.

The amount of force which the average human muscle can exert has been determined by several experimenters. Fick, one of the early investigators, found that human muscles exerted a force of 6 to 10 kilograms per square centimeter of their physiologic cross section.[5,6] This is approximately 85 to 141 pounds per square inch. Recklinghausen, according to Steindler,[10] concluded from his experimentation that human muscles exerted only 3.6 kilograms per square centimeter (approximately 51 pounds per square inch) of cross section. It is assumed that these two investigators used male subjects. A more recent investigator, Morris,[9] found that the muscles of male subjects exerted 9.2 kilograms per square centimeter (130 pounds per square inch), and of female subjects, 7.1 kilograms per square centimeter (101 pounds per square inch). Because of the wide range of figures presented to date, further investigation of this matter would seem desirable. A study of the effect of training on muscular force per unit of cross section would also be of interest. If 95 pounds per square inch is arbitrarily selected as the force which an average human muscle can exert, the hypothetical muscle described above, having a physiologic cross section of 9 square inches, would have a potential force of 9×95, or 855 pounds.

Point of Application. The point of application of a force is that point at which the force is applied to an object. Where gravity is concerned this point is always through the center of gravity of an object. For practical purposes it may be assumed that the point of application of muscular force is the center of the muscle's attachment to the bony lever. This usually corresponds to the muscle's insertion or distal attachment. Technically, however, it is the point of intersection between the line of force and the *mechanical axis* of the bone or segment serving as the anatomic lever. This axis does not necessarily pass lengthwise through the shaft of the bony lever. If the bone bends or if the articulating process projects at an angle from the shaft, the greater part of the axis may lie completely outside the shaft, as in the case of the femur. *The mechanical axis of a bone or segment is a straight line which connects the midpoint of the joint at one end with the midpoint of the joint at the other end, or in the case of a terminal segment, with its distal end.*

Direction. The direction of a force is along its action line. Because the force of gravity pulls all objects toward the earth's center, the direction of gravitational forces is vertically downward. The force of gravity acting on an object would be represented as a downward directed vector starting at the center of gravity of the object.

The direction of muscular force is represented by the direction of the muscle's line of pull. This direction is identified by the muscle's angle of pull which is bounded by the muscle's line of pull and the portion of the mechanical axis that lies between the point of application and the fulcrum. Figure 12–3, *A* shows a muscle (the biceps) applying its force to a lever (the radius) at an angle of 30 degrees, while Figures 12–3, *B* and *C* illustrate other angles of pull.

Components of Force. As with any vector, a force may be resolved into a vertical and a horizontal component, and the relative size of these components depends upon the angle at which the force is applied. Where muscles are involved, the size of a muscle's angle of pull changes with every degree of joint motion and consequently, so do the sizes of the horizontal and vertical components. These changes have a direct bearing on the effectiveness of the mus-

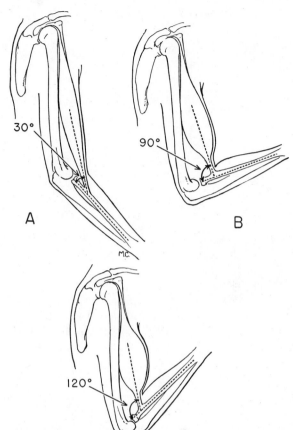

Figure 12-3 Angles of muscle pull. *A*, An angle less than 45 degrees; *B*, an angle of 90 degrees; *C*, an angle greater than 90 degrees.

cle's pulling force in moving the bony lever. The larger the angle between 0 degrees and 90 degrees the greater the vertical component and the less the horizontal component. The vertical component of muscle pull is always perpendicular to the lever and is called the rotatory component. It is that part of the force which moves the lever. The horizontal component is parallel to the lever and is the nonrotatory component. It does not contribute to the lever's movement. The angle of pull of most muscles in the resting position is less than a right angle and it usually remains so throughout the movement (Fig. 12-3, *A*). This means that the nonrotatory component of force is directed toward the fulcrum which gives it a stabilizing effect. By pulling the bone lengthwise toward the joint it helps to maintain the integrity of the joint. Under most circumstances, therefore, muscular force has two simultaneous functions, namely, movement and stabilization. In the latter capacity it supplements the ligaments, an excellent example of the body's efficiency, as muscles perform this stabilizing function only during the period when the segment is moving, at which time the integrity of the joint may be threatened.

Occasionally the angle of pull becomes greater than a right angle which means that the nonrotatory component of force is directed away from the fulcrum and is therefore a dislocating component. This does not happen in many instances, however, and when it does, the muscle is close to the limit of its

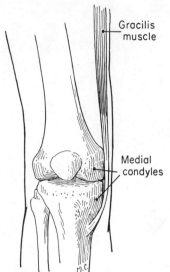

Gracilis
muscle

Medial
condyles

Figure 12–4 The medial condyles at the knee joint serving as a pulley to increase the angle of pull of the gracilis tendon.

shortening range and is therefore not exerting much force. (See Fig. 12–3, C.)

When the angle of pull is 90 degrees, the force is completely rotatory. When it is 45 degrees the rotatory and stabilizing components are equal. Since the angle of pull usually remains less than 45 degrees, more of the muscle's force serves to stabilize the joint than to move the lever. In fact, there are some muscles whose angles of pull are always so small that their contribution to motion would seem to be negligible. This appears to be true of the coracobrachialis and the subclavius muscles. It is interesting to note that the upper extremity is frequently called upon to perform violent, powerful movements, as well as to support the body weight in suspension. The joints which bear the brunt of this violence and strain are the shoulder and sternoclavicular joints. They might well become dislocated more easily than they do were it not for the coracobrachialis and the subclavius muscles which pull the bones lengthwise toward their proximal joints and thus serve to stabilize these joints.

The small angle of pull that most muscles have when in their normal resting

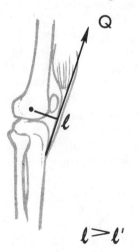

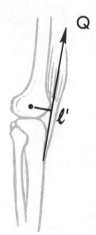

Q   Q

ℓ ℓ'

$\ell > \ell'$

Figure 12–5 By increasing the angle of pull the patella increases the rotatory force component of the quadriceps femoris. (From Williams, M., and Lissner, H. R.: Biomechanics of Human Motion. Philadelphia, W. B. Saunders Company, 1962.)

position has already been noted. Were it not for anatomic devices that serve as fixed single pulleys for increasing such angles, some muscles would probably be unable to effect any movement whatsoever. For instance, the condyles both above and below the knee joint serve this purpose for the gracilis muscle (Fig. 12–4); the patella for the quadriceps (Fig. 12–5); and the external malleolus for the peroneus longus (Fig. 12–32).

The effect the angle of pull has upon the rotatory force of a muscle for a given angle is demonstrated in the following problem. The solution clearly shows an increase in rotatory force with each increase in angle size.

Muscle *M* exerts a force of 100 pounds at insertion and is pulling at an angle of 30 degrees. How much of its force is rotatory? stabilizing? How do these values change when the angle of pull is 10 degrees? 75 degrees? (See Fig. 12–6.)

Solution: Angle of Pull of 30°: Construct a right triangle where $\sin 30° = \dfrac{A}{100}$.

Rotatory component equals $100 \times \sin 30° = 50$ *lb.*
Stabilizing component equals $100 \times \cos 30° = 86.6$ *lb.*
Angle of Pull of 10°:
Rotatory component A equals $100 \times \sin 10° = 17.36$ *lb.*
Stabilizing component B equals $100 \times \cos 10° = 98.48$ *lb.*
Angle of Pull of 75°:
Rotatory component equals $100 \times \sin 75° = 96.59$ *lb.*
Stabilizing component equals $100 \times \cos 75° = 25.88$ *lb.*

The resolution of a single external force into component forces acting at right angles to each other is accomplished in the same manner as that explained for muscular forces and would be used when the force is applied at an oblique angle. If, instead of giving a piece of furniture a horizontal push, one pushes it by standing close to it with the arms held at a forward-downward slant, only part of the force will push the table forward (Fig. 12–7). The force is applied to the table at an oblique angle and thus will have a vertical and horizontal component. Whether or not the table moves forward depends upon the amount of the total force which is applied in the horizontal direction. If sufficient, only the horizontal component of force will overcome the table's resistance to move. The downward

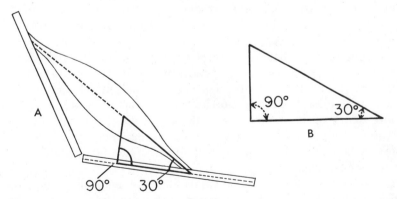

Figure 12–6 Method of constructing a right triangle for the purpose of determining the components of muscular force by the trigonometric method. Note that the hypotenuse coincides with a portion of the muscle's line of pull, and the side adjacent with the mechanical axis of the bone into which the muscle is inserted.

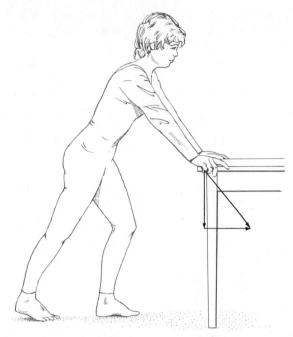

Figure 12–7   The diagonal pushing force consists of a horizontal and a vertical component. Only the horizontal component serves to overcome the table's resistance to being moved. (Drawn from photograph.)

component merely pushes the table against the floor and increases the friction between the floor and the table. The closer one can come to applying all of the available force in the desired direction of movement the more efficient will be the action. Another example of this principle is demonstrated in pulling actions. If a child's sled or cart is drawn by too short a rope, there will be a relatively large lifting component and a small forward-pulling component. Since the purpose is to pull the cart horizontally, it is more efficient to use a long rope because this gives a relatively greater horizontal or pulling component.

Composite Effects of Two or More Forces.   Frequently two or more forces are applied to the same object. A canoe may be acted upon by both the wind and the paddler, one force tending to send the canoe north and the other east. While in flight a punted ball's path is the result of the force imparted to it by the kicker, the downward force of gravity and the force of the wind, if any. In the body it is rarely, if ever, the case that an individual muscle acts by itself. For example, there are at least four muscles that may act in flexion of the forearm, and more than five that contribute to flexion of the leg at the knee joint. The effect which composite forces have on the human body to cause or modify motion may be classified according to their direction and application as linear, concurrent or parallel.

LINEAR FORCES.   Forces applied in the same direction along the same action line are called *linear* forces. If a horizontal push is applied to a piece of furniture and the push is applied in line with the object's center of gravity, the object will move forward in a horizontal direction, providing of course that there is no additional conflicting force or resistance. If another force is applied to the furniture in line with and in the same direction as the first force, the resultant of the two forces has a value equal to the sum of the two forces (a + b = c).

$$\xrightarrow{\hspace{2cm} a \hspace{2cm}} + \xrightarrow{\hspace{2cm} b \hspace{2cm}} = \xrightarrow{\hspace{3cm} c \hspace{3cm}}$$

Similarly, if the forces act in opposite directions, the resultant still equals the algebraic sum of the two forces. (a + (−b) = c). This might be the case in a tug of war.

$$\xrightarrow{\hspace{2cm} a \hspace{2cm}} + \xleftarrow{\hspace{2cm} b \hspace{2cm}} = \xrightarrow[\hspace{2cm} a \hspace{2cm}]{\xleftarrow{\hspace{1.5cm} b \hspace{1.5cm}}} = \xrightarrow{\hspace{1cm} c \hspace{1cm}}$$

Examples of more than one force applied at the same point and acting in identical directions in the body are rare. Possibly there are two such examples, the gastrocnemius and the soleus acting at the ankle joint, and the psoas and the iliacus acting at the hip joint. In each of these examples, it will be noted that the two muscles have a common tendon for their distal attachments.

CONCURRENT FORCES.   Forces acting at one point but at different angles are called *concurrent* forces. Several football players opposing each other in a blocking situation furnish opposing forces acting at one point (Fig. 12–8). The resultant outcome of the blocking is found using the method known as the combination of forces described in Chapter Ten, page 261. This method assumes a common point of application. While this situation is common externally, it is not true of the majority of muscles which act on the same bone. Very few muscles have a common point of attachment. Nevertheless, the principle of finding

Figure 12–8 Opposing forces acting at one point but at different angles are called concurrent forces.

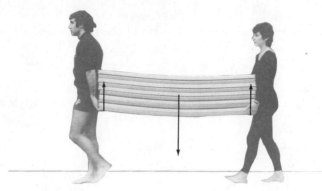

Figure 12–9 Examples of parallel forces. The mats exert a downward force while the carriers each exert parallel forces upward.

the composite effect of two or more forces, both as to magnitude and direction, is as true for forces acting on body segments as for forces acting on external objects. The important thing to remember is that the resultant magnitude of two or more concurrent forces is not their arithmetic sum, and the resultant direction of two concurrent forces is not halfway between them unless the two forces are of equal magnitude. The resultant of two or more concurrent forces depends upon both the magnitude of each force and the angle of application, i.e., the direction of each force.

PARALLEL FORCES. In addition to linear forces in which all forces occur along the same action line and concurrent forces in which forces acting at different angles are applied at the same point, another situation exists in which forces not in the same action line but *parallel* to each other act at different points on a body. The two students in Figure 12–9 are carrying a weight between them. Each one exerts an upward force on each end while the weight exerts a downward force between them. There are three parallel forces here, two in one direc-

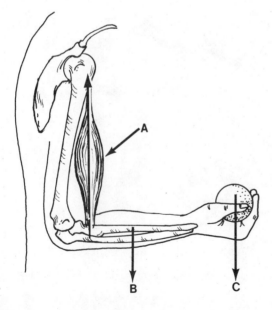

Figure 12–10 Example of parallel forces in equilibrium. The force of the biceps (A) balances the opposite force of gravity acting on the forearm at its center of gravity and on the weight held in the hand.

tion and the third in an opposite direction. All three forces are acting on the same object but at different points. Another example of this situation would be that of holding a 10-pound weight in the hand when the forearm is flexed so that the angle of pull of the biceps is 90 degrees. The force of gravity may be represented as acting at two different points to push the forearm and the weight down while the force of the biceps acting in the opposite direction at another point pulls the forearm up. All three of these forces are parallel to each other but acting at different points (Fig. 12–10).

The effect parallel forces have on the object they act upon depends on the magnitude, the direction and the application point of each force. Parallel forces may act in the same or opposite directions. They may be balanced and cause no motion or they may cause linear or rotatory motion. When parallel forces act on an object, their relationship to the object's fixed axis or to its center of gravity if it can move freely determines the resultant action. In the case of the weight (mats) held at opposite ends by two students, the mats will remain balanced and motionless if all the forces about the center of gravity are balanced. The mats will move upward in a linear fashion if the students exert equal parallel forces upward which are greater than the downward force of the weight, and they will move in a curvilinear fashion about their center of gravity if one student exerts a force greater than the other. If the students exert equal and opposite parallel forces, rotatory motion about the center of gravity of the weight will occur. The effect of equal parallel forces acting in opposite directions is called *a couple* or *force couple*. An example of this type of movement is seen in steering a car or a boat when both hands are used on opposite sides of the wheel (Fig. 12–11). There are a number of examples in the human body in which two muscles rotate a bone by acting cooperatively as a force couple; for instance, trapezius II and the lower portion of serratus anterior are a force couple, rotating the scapula upward. Trapezius II and IV, acting on the two extremities of the spine of the scapula, similarly serve as a force couple to help rotate the scapula upward (Fig. 12–12). Other examples of parallel forces are shown in Figure 12–13.

Torque. The effect the location of the point of force application has on a parallel force system is evident in the previously cited example of the 10-pound

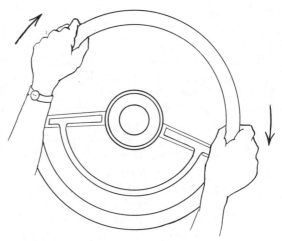

Figure 12–11 When one steers with two hands, the hands act as a force couple.

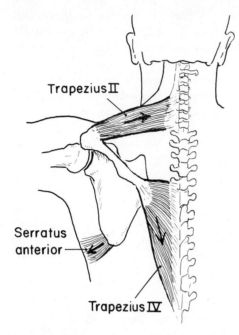

Trapezius II

Serratus anterior

Trapezius IV

Figure 12-12 Two force couples acting on the scapula to rotate it upward. (Trapezius II and lower Serratus Anterior are an excellent example. Trapezius II and the lower fibers of IV also tend to act as a force couple although their pulls are not in opposite directions.

weight held in the hand of the flexed forearm. If the weight is moved closer to the elbow joint, the force of the elbow flexors needed to maintain the forearm and weight in a horizontal position is less. It also takes less effort to move the forearm upward in a rotatory fashion about the elbow joint with the weight in this position. The weight has not changed its mass and neither has the arm. The only thing which has changed is the distance between the weight and the elbow. It appears then that the effectiveness of the arm and weight in causing rotation is dependent upon the weight held in the hand, the weight of the arm, and the distance of these weights from the axis of rotation. The farther from the axis a force is applied, the greater is its turning effect and the greater the effort needed to resist the turning.

The turning effect of a force is called the torque or moment of force. *The torque about any point equals the product of the force magnitude and its perpendicular distance from the direction of force to the point or axis of rotation.* The perpendicular distance is called the moment arm or torque arm. Neglecting the weight of the arm for now, the torque or turning effect caused by a five pound weight held in the hand is the product of the weight times its perpendicular distance or moment arm length from the elbow joint. If this distance is one foot, the amount of torque or downward turning force is five foot-pounds. To keep the arm motionless in this position the elbow flexors must exert an equal and opposite torque or upward directed turning force of five foot-pounds.

Since a force moment is the product of force and moment arm length, it may be increased or decreased by increasing or decreasing either the force or the moment arm length. A small force some distance away from the turning point can have the same torque or moment as a large force near the axis. We have already seen one way of altering the torque when we moved the weight from the hand to the middle of the forearm. Another way is demonstrated when the forearm's position is shifted from the horizontal to one of 45 degrees of flexion with the horizontal. Now the force line of the weight is not at right angles to the forearm (Fig. 12–14). This means that the length of the moment arm is no longer the length of the forearm, because by definition it is the perpendicular distance from the direction or line of force and the axis or center of motion. The moment arm now is considerably shorter. Using trigonometric relations we find that the moment arm length is .707 feet. Consequently, the torque decreases from 5 foot-pounds to 3.5 foot-pounds, and the amount of muscular effort needed to counteract this downward force decreases proportionately.

In the human body the mass or weight of a segment cannot be altered.

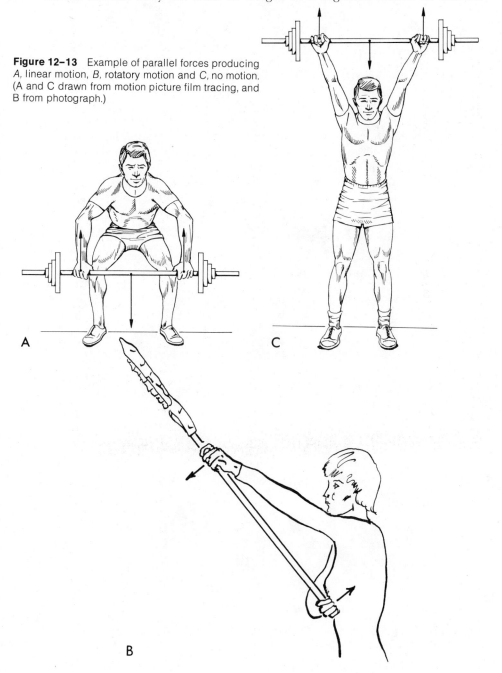

Figure 12–13 Example of parallel forces producing A, linear motion, B, rotatory motion and C, no motion. (A and C drawn from motion picture film tracing, and B from photograph.)

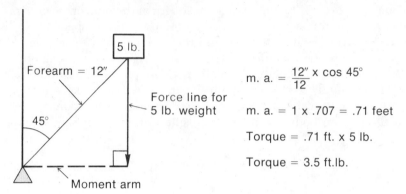

$$m.\ a. = \frac{12'' \times \cos 45°}{12}$$

m. a. = 1 x .707 = .71 feet

Torque = .71 ft. x 5 lb.

Torque = 3.5 ft.lb.

Figure 12–14 The torque of the 5-pound weight about the elbow joint is the product of the weight and the perpendicular distance between the force line of the weight and the axis of rotation (elbow joint).

Therefore the torque of a segment due to gravitational force can only be changed by changing the length of the moment arm in relation to the axis. As is shown in Figure 12–14 this is done by moving the force line of the weight closer to or farther from the axis. The effect of doing this is quite apparent in stages of the sit up. Compare the gravitational torque on the trunk when the trunk is just

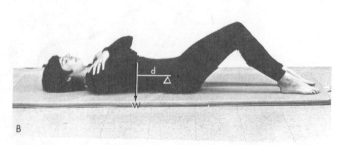

Figure 12–15 Gravitational torque (d) decreases as the force line moves closer to the axis. The torque is zero at 90°.

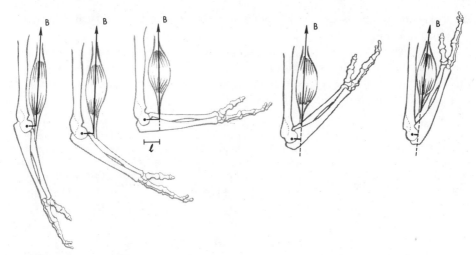

Figure 12–16 The biceps (B) at various points of elbow flexion, showing variations in the moment arm. (From Williams, M., and Lissner, H. B.: Biomechanics of Human Motion. Philadelphia, W. B. Saunders Company, 1962.)

leaving the floor with the torque when the trunk is at a 30 degree angle from the floor (Fig. 12–15).

Muscle forces also exert torque on rotating segments. The amount of torque depends upon both the magnitude of the muscle force and the moment arm length. Unlike gravitational torque, each of these factors can be altered. The moment arm length depends upon the point of insertion of the muscle and the position of the body segment at any point in a given motion. Figure 12–16 shows how the moment arm of the biceps changes for every change of arm position during elbow flexion. The magnitude of the force of the muscle contributing to the torque changes also as its length, tension and angle of pull change.

Summation of Moments.   In the case of parallel forces, more than one moment acts on a body at any given time. The resultant effect of these moments is expressed in the principle of the summation of moments which states that the *resultant moment of a force system must be equal to the sum of the moments of the individual forces of the system about the same point.* Because moments are vector quantities the summation must consider both magnitude and direction. The direction of rotation is expressed either as clockwise or counterclockwise direction. Clockwise moments are usually labeled as negative and counter-

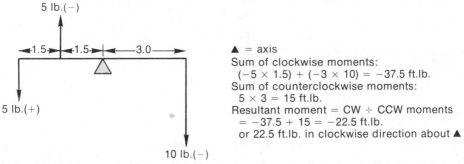

▲ = axis
Sum of clockwise moments:
   $(-5 \times 1.5) + (-3 \times 10) = -37.5$ ft.lb.
Sum of counterclockwise moments:
   $5 \times 3 = 15$ ft.lb.
Resultant moment = CW + CCW moments
   $= -37.5 + 15 = -22.5$ ft.lb.
   or 22.5 ft.lb. in clockwise direction about ▲

Figure 12–17 Summation of moments. The resultant moment about a point is equal to the sum of the moments of the individual forces about the same point. Clockwise moments are negative, and counterclockwise moments are positive.

clockwise moments as positive. Their signs must be accounted for when they are summed (Fig. 12–17).

In Figure 12–17 all of the forces are perpendicular to the lever. When forces are applied at an angle as in Figure 12–13, the moment arms perpendicular to the force lines must be resolved using trigonometric functions. An example of this procedure is shown in the following problem.

What muscular force F pulling at an angle of 25 degrees would be required to keep the abducted arm in a position of 20 degrees with the horizontal? The muscle inserts 4 inches from the shoulder joint. The arm weighs 13 pounds and its center of gravity is located 12 inches from the shoulder. A 10-pound weight is held in the hand 23 inches from the shoulder joint. For the arm to be held stationary the sum of the counterclockwise moments must equal the clockwise moments. (ΣCCW = ΣCW) (See Figure 12–18 for solution.)

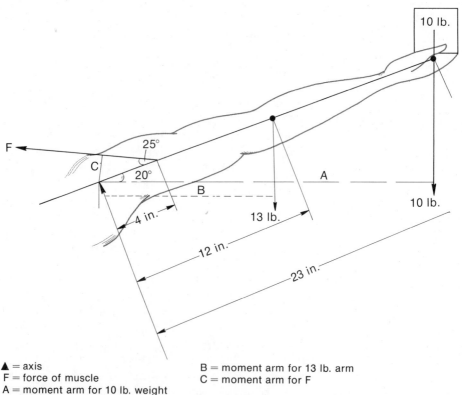

▲ = axis
F = force of muscle
A = moment arm for 10 lb. weight

B = moment arm for 13 lb. arm
C = moment arm for F

To balance, clockwise moments must equal counterclockwise moments.

1. *Clockwise moments*
   a. 10 lb. × A = 10 × 23 cos 20°
   b. 13 lb. × B = 13 × 12 cos 20°
2. *Counterclockwise moments*
   a. F × C = F × 4 sin 25°
3. CW = CCW
   F × C = (10 × A) + (13 × B)

4. 230 cos 20° + 156 cos 20° = 4 sin 25° × F
5. $F = \dfrac{230 \cos 20° + 156 \cos 20°}{4 \sin 25°}$
6. $F = \dfrac{(230 \times .940) + (156 \times .940)}{4 \times .422}$

   $F = \dfrac{362}{1.69} = 215$ lb.

Figure 12–18 Summation of force moments using trigonometric functions. The amount of muscle force needed to counteract the force of gravity in this example is 215 pounds.

When the sum of counterclockwise moments equals the sum of clockwise moments no turning will occur. This idea may also be expressed by stating that rotation will be absent when the sum of the moments of all forces about any point or axis equals zero (Fig. 12–19). When the sum of clockwise moments

Figure 12–19 Rotation is absent when the sum of the moments of all forces about any point or axis equals zero.

does not equal the sum of the counterclockwise moments, the resultant torque will be the difference between the two opposing forces and in the direction of the larger.

SIMPLE MACHINES AND THEIR ANATOMIC COUNTERPARTS

The Lever

A simple machine which operates according to the principle of moments is the *lever*. A lever is a rigid bar which can rotate about a fixed point when a force is applied to overcome a resistance. When they move, levers serve two important functions. They are used either to overcome a larger resistance than the effort applied or to increase the distance a resistance can be moved through use of an effort greater than the resistance. When there is no motion, the effort turning effect (moment or torque) equals the resistance turning effect, and the lever system is said to be balanced.

We use levers every day of our lives. In the kitchen the old-fashioned hand can opener, the nut pick, the punch can opener and the bottle opener or lid pry are all examples of simple levers. In the workshop or about the house and grounds, the tack lifter, the crowbar, the pinch bar and the wheelbarrow are likewise levers. What do these implements have in common? Even though their shapes vary and their structures differ in complexity, each of these is a rigid bar. When a force is applied to one of them, it turns about a fixed point known as a fulcrum, and it overcomes a resistance which may, in some cases, be no more than its own weight. All the levers mentioned are for the purpose of using a relatively small force to overcome a relatively large resistance. In levers such as these the range of movement is relatively slight. The tack lifter, for instance, lifts the tack only a fraction of an inch. In other words, the power to overcome a considerable resistance is gained at the expense of range of motion.

The striking implements used in sports are levers that do the opposite of this. The golf club, for instance, is used for gaining range of motion at the expense of force. The length of the shaft enables the club head to travel through a large arc of motion, but it is used to overcome the relatively slight resistance of the weight of the club itself. Tennis and squash rackets, baseball bats, hockey sticks and fencing foils are other examples of levers used for the purpose of gaining distance at the expense of force. These levers do not save the strength of the user, as do the household levers mentioned, but they increase his range and speed of movement. By striking a ball with a racket, for instance, he can impart more speed to it and send it a greater distance than he could by striking it with his hand. This is because the head of the racket travels a greater distance, and therefore at a greater speed, than the hand alone is able to do.

A still different kind of lever is seen in the seesaw on the playground, the scales in the laboratory and the yoke used for carrying balanced loads across the shoulders. These levers gain neither force nor distance, but provide for a balancing of weights. If the loads are equal, they will balance each other when they are equidistant from the fulcrum. If they are unequal, they will balance only if the heavier load is placed closer to the fulcrum. There is an exact relationship between the magnitude of the weights and their respective distances from the fulcrum.

This kind of lever may also be used to balance a force and a load. The skier carrying skis over one shoulder, balanced by a hand holding the other end, is using this kind of lever. The amount of effort exerted by the hand depends upon what portion of the ski is in contact with the shoulder. If the weight of the skis is evenly distributed on each side of the shoulder, the hand needs to exert little or no effort.

The Body Segments as Levers.   But where in the human body do we have anything even faintly resembling a punch can opener, a hockey stick or a seesaw? When we recognize each of these levers as a rigid bar which turns about a fulcrum when force is applied to it, it is then apparent that nearly every bone in the skeleton can be looked upon as a lever. The bone itself serves as the rigid bar, the joint as the fulcrum and the contracting muscles as the force. A large segment of the body, such as the trunk, the upper extremity or the lower extremity, can likewise act as a single lever if it is used as a rigid unit. When the entire arm is raised sideward, for instance, it is acting as a simple lever. The center of motion in the shoulder joint serves as the fulcrum. The effort is supplied mainly by the deltoid muscle and the resistance in this instance is the weight of the arm itself. The point at which the effort is applied to the lever is approximately the point at which the deltoid inserts into the humerus and the point at which the resistance is applied is the center of gravity of the extended arm. If a weight is held in the hand, the resistance point is then the center of gravity of the arm plus its load and is located closer to the hand than before.

If a relatively heavy weight is lifted, for practical purposes the weight of the arm may be disregarded and the resistance point may be assumed to be the center of the object's point of contact with the hand.

Anatomic levers do not necessarily resemble bars. The skull, the shoulder blade and the vertebrae are notable exceptions to the definition. The resistance point, also, may be difficult to identify, especially in the seesaw type of lever. It is not always easy to tell whether the resistance is the weight of the lever itself or is the resistance afforded by antagonistic muscles and fasciae which are put on a steadily increasing stretch as the movement progresses. For instance, when the head is turned easily to the left, the resistance point may be regarded as the center of gravity of the head. We can only guess at the approximate location of this. If the turning of the head is resisted by the pressure of some-one's hand against the left side of the chin, the resistance point is the midpoint of the contact area. If the head is turned without external resistance, but is forced to the limit of motion, resistance to the movement is afforded by the antagonistic rotators, and possibly by the ligaments and fasciae. The resistance *point* in such a case is the midpoint of the area over which these resisting forces act on the head. As in the first example, the location of this point can only be estimated.

Classification of Levers. In the examples cited, three points on the lever have been identified: the point about which it turns, the point at which effort is applied to it and the point at which the resistance to its movement is applied or concentrated. Since there are three points, there are three possible arrange-ments of these points. Any one of the three may be situated between the other two. The arrangement of these three points provides the basis for the classifica-tion of levers.

1. In a first class lever the fulcrum lies between the effort and resistance points (Fig. 12–20, *1*).

2. In a second class lever the resistance point lies between the fulcrum and the effort point (Fig. 12–20, *2*).

3. In a third class lever the effort lies between the fulcrum and the re-sistance point (Fig. 12–20, *3*).

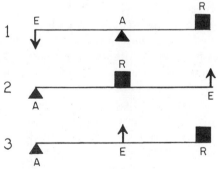

Figure 12–20 Levers. *1.* A lever of the first class; *2*, a lever of the second class; *3*, a lever of the third class.

E = Effort
A = Axis or fulcrum
R = Resistance or weight

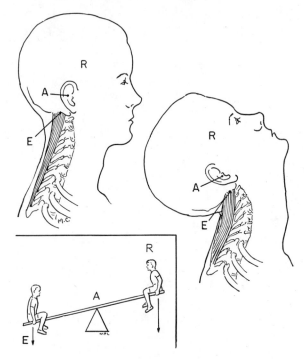

Figure 12–21 The head acting as a first class lever like the seesaw. $A =$ The approximate position of the axis or fulcrum; $E =$ the point where the force is applied; $R =$ the approximate point where the resistance is concentrated.

Examples of external levers are as follows:

First Class: seesaw, balance scales, crowbar, scissors, automobile jack.
Second Class: wheelbarrow, door (effort applied at knob), nut cracker.
Third Class: screen door with spring closing.

Examples of Anatomic Levers. The head, tipping forward and backward, is a good example of a first class lever in the body (Fig. 12–21). To be sure, it is a sphere rather than a bar, and the axis of motion would seem to be an imaginary one located in the frontal plane approximately between the ears. The effort is supplied by the extensors of the head, notably the splenius and upper portions of the semispinalis, and is applied to the head at the base of the skull. The resistance to the movement is furnished by the weight of the head itself, together with the tension of the antagonistic muscles and fasciae, as the limit of motion is approached. The center of concentration of the resistance is difficult to determine. If the head is acting like a seesaw, the resistance would seem to be centered in the front half of the head for hyperextension, and in the rear half for flexion. Additional resistance is provided by the tension of opposing muscles and ligaments, the resistance point being the point at which the various resistant forces are concentrated.

Another first class lever is seen in the foot when it is not being used for weight-bearing, as when the knees are crossed in the sitting position. As the soleus pulls upward on the heel, the foot plantarflexes at the ankle joint where the fulcrum is situated. The resistance seems to be provided by the tonus of the dorsiflexor muscles. The weight of the foot apparently is not a factor here, since the foot has already relaxed into a position of partial plantar flexion. The picture would be changed, however, if the person were lying face down with the leg bent at the knee and the lower leg extended vertically upward. If the

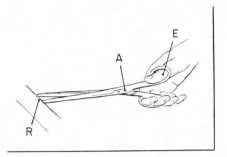

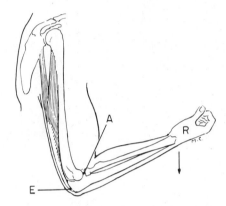

Figure 12–22   The forearm acting as a first class lever similar to a pair of paper shears.

foot were then plantar-flexed, the weight of the foot would be a factor in the resistance.

The forearm is another example of a first class lever when it is being extended by the triceps muscle (Fig. 12–22). The fulcrum is situated at the elbow joint, the effort is applied at the olecranon process and the resistance point is located at the forearm's center of gravity when no external resistance is present, and at the hand when the latter is pushing against an external resistance. Internal resistance does not appear to be a factor in this movement.

Whether or not there are any second class levers in the body seems to be a controversial matter among anatomists and kinesiologists. Some claim that when the foot is being plantar-flexed in a weight-bearing position, as when rising on the toes, it is a second class lever. The fulcrum is said to be at the point of contact with the ground, the effort point at the heel where the tendon of Achilles attaches and the resistance at the ankle joint where the weight of the body is transferred to the foot. Another second class lever might be the forearm if it were being flexed by the brachioradialis alone, but this could occur only if the other flexors were paralyzed.

The forearm is a good example of a third class lever when it is being flexed by the biceps and the brachialis (Fig. 12–23). Another third class lever is seen in the example cited earlier, namely the arm as it is raised sideward-upward by the deltoid muscle (Fig. 12–24).

Lever Arms.   Lever arms are commonly defined as the portion of the lever between the fulcrum and the force points. The effort arm is the distance between the fulcrum and the effort point, and the resistance arm is the distance

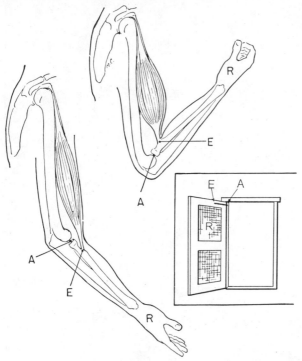

Figure 12–23 The forearm acting as a third class lever similar to a screen door.

between the fulcrum and the resistance point. These definitions are valid, however, only when the effort and resistance are applied at right angles to the lever. When the effort and resistance are applied at some angle other than 90 degrees to the lever, these definitions are inaccurate. A better definition of a lever arm which applies regardless of the angle of force application is one which is synonymous to that of a moment arm. Indeed, a lever arm is a moment arm. In a lever the perpendicular distance between the fulcrum and the line of force of

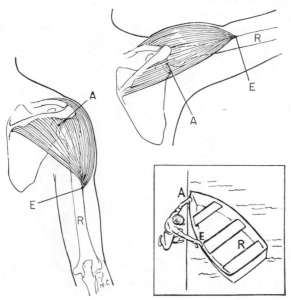

Figure 12–24 The humerus acting as a third class lever somewhat like a boat being pulled alongside the dock.

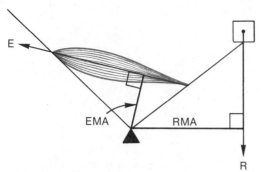

RMA is perpendicular distance from line of resistance to fulcrum.
EMA is perpendicular distance from effort line to fulcrum.

Figure 12-25 Lever arms, like moment arms, are the perpendicular distance between the fulcrum and the force line.

the effort is the *effort moment arm* or *effort arm*. Similarly, the perpendicular distance between the fulcrum and the line of resistance force is the *resistance moment arm* or *resistance arm*. In Figure 12–25, EMA is the effort arm and RMA, the resistance arm.

The Principle of Levers. A lever of any class will balance when the product of the effort and the effort arm equals the product of the resistance and the resistance arm. This is known as the *principle of levers*. It enables us to calculate the amount of effort needed to balance a known resistance by means of a known lever or to calculate the point at which to place the fulcrum in order to balance a known resistance with a given effort. If any three of the four values are known, the remaining one can be calculated by using the following equation:

$$E \times EMA = R \times RMA$$

(effort times effort arm equals resistance times resistance arm)

The equation restates a principle already studied: When the force moments in one direction equal the force moments in the opposite direction, equilibrium exists. $E \times EMA$ is a force moment as is $R \times RMA$. If RMA in Figure 12–25 is 10 inches, R is 5 pounds and EMA is 3 inches, the effort needed to balance the weight in the hand would be $E \times 3 = 5 \times 10$ or E would be 16.7 pounds. The equation also shows the importance of the lever arm lengths in determining the amount of effort needed to balance a given resistance. If EMA is lengthened while $R \times RMA$ remains constant, the amount of effort needed to balance the lever decreases, but if on the other hand RMA is increased, the amount of effort must increase. Generally speaking, for this reason second class levers require less effort to balance or move heavier resistances, while third class levers require more effort than the resistance they seek to balance or move (Figs. 12–23 and 12–24). The first class lever may have either a longer EMA or RMA depending upon the placement of the fulcrum (Figs. 12–21 and 12–22).

A lever whose effort arm is the longer of the two, whether it be a first or second class lever, is said to favor *force*. Less effort is required to overcome a resistance with this kind of lever than it would take to overcome the same resistance without the aid of the lever. It gains this advantage at the expense of speed and range of movement. The heavier resistance will always move through a smaller distance than the effort (Fig. 12–26). Conversely, a lever whose resistance arm is the longer, whether it be a first or a third class lever, is said to favor speed and distance. However, more effort is required to move it

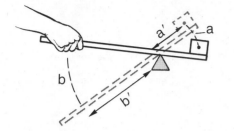

$a < b$

$a' < b'$

$\dfrac{b}{a} = \dfrac{b'}{a'}$

Figure 12–26 The range of motion increases as the lever arm length increases.

than would be the case if the relative lengths of the effort and resistance arms were reversed. Furthermore, an object of negligible weight can be moved a greater distance and more rapidly by this kind of lever than it could be without the aid of the lever.

Relation of Speed to Range in Movements of Levers. The reader will have noticed that in the foregoing discussion of levers the terms "speed and range" were usually linked together. There is a reason for this. In angular movements speed and range are interdependent. For instance, if two third class levers of different lengths each move through a 40-degree angle at the same angular velocity, the tip of the longer lever will be traveling a greater distance or range than the tip of the shorter lever. Since it covers this distance in the same time that it takes the tip of the shorter lever to travel the shorter distance, the former must be moving faster than the latter. This is easily seen if the shorter lever is superimposed on the longer, as in Figure 12–27. Here the shorter lever, *AB*, has been superimposed on the longer lever, *AC*. The levers are moving from the horizontal position to the diagonal one. Since the point *C* travels to its new position, *C'*, in the same time that it takes *B* to travel to *B'*, point *C* must obviously be moving faster than point *B*.

Characteristics of Anatomic Levers. With few exceptions, the effort arm in skeletal levers is shorter than the resistance arm. Thus, anatomic levers tend to favor speed and range of movement at the expense of effort. Examples of this preference are seen in the throwing of a baseball or the kicking of a soccer ball. The hand in the one case and the foot in the other travel through a relatively long distance at considerable speed. Both these movements require strong muscular action, in spite of the fact that the balls are relatively light in weight. This type of leverage is the reverse of the kind usually seen in mechanical implements such as the crowbar and the automobile jack, both of which are used to move heavy weights a relatively short distance. Sports implements which may serve as levers in themselves or as artificial extensions of the human

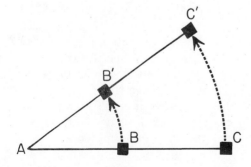

Figure 12–27 Comparison of a long and a short lever turning the same number of degrees. It takes *B* the same amount of time to reach *B'* that it takes *C* to reach *C'*.

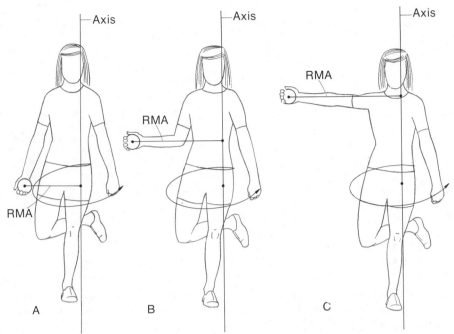

Figure 12–28 The length of the RMA determines the linear velocity at the end of the lever. In the positions pictured, when the pelvis rotates to the left, the linear velocity of the ball is least in *A* and most in *C*. The movement occurs at the left hip and results in the lower extremity being medially rotated, relative to the pelvis.

arm also favor speed and range of movement. Frequently the sport implement, the arm and a large part of the rest of the body act together as a system of levers. In batting a baseball, for instance, the trunk forms one lever, the upper arms another, the forearms another and the hands and bat still another. This use of multiple leverage is for the purpose of building up speed at the tip of the bat, for the greater this speed, the greater the force that can be imparted to the ball.

Selection of Levers.   Skill in motor performance depends upon the effective selection and use of levers, both internal and external. Long golf clubs are selected for distance and shorter clubs for accuracy at close range. Heavy baseball bats are chosen by those with the strength to swing them, whereas children are often taught tennis with short handled racquets. In most instances external levers are designed for a specific purpose and are selected accordingly. The levers of the human body on the other hand are not designed for one action or purpose. Body parts or segments may be held in numerous positions for any given joint action and thus provide a great variety of lever arrangements. When muscles supply the effort, skill depends upon the right choice of joint axis, joint action and moment arm length. Short levers increase angular velocity while the positioning of body parts to form the longest possible resistance moment arms will favor linear speed and range of motion if the performer has sufficient strength to move the long third class lever as quickly as desired. In all three instances in Figure 12–28, the ball in the hand is carried forward by virtue of the counterclockwise (as seen from above) rotation of the pelvis which takes place at the left hip joint. The pelvis carries the trunk with it but no movement occurs in any joint other than the left hip. In all three positions the resistance movement arm for the action is the perpendicular distance between the hip axis and the line of action of the resistance (the ball). However, the resistance moment

Figure 12–29 A straight arm perpendicular to the desired line of flight provides the greatest linear velocity to the ball when the joint action is shoulder flexion.

arm is a different length in each situation. It is smallest in *A* and largest in *C*. Consequently the linear velocity of the ball is largest in *C* and smallest in *A* when the angular velocity is the same in each stance. (See Fig. 12–27.)

Similarly if flexion of the shoulder is the joint action, the position of the arm which will provide the greatest linear velocity to the object in the hand at the moment of release is one in which the elbow is extended and the arm is perpendicular to the desired direction of flight (Fig. 12–29).

Identification and Analysis of Levers. Figures 12–21 to 12–24 depict certain anatomic levers and their mechanical counterparts. These should enable the student to understand the principle of leverage as it applies in the human body and to see how the anatomic levers compare with the levers of everyday life. For each of these levers and for every lever that the student observes, he should answer these questions: (1) What is the location of the fulcrum, of the effort point and of the resistance point? (2) At what angle is the effort applied to the lever? (3) At what angle is the resistance applied to the lever? (4) What is the effort arm of the lever? (5) What is the resistance arm of the lever? (6) What are the relative lengths of the effort and resistance arms? (7) What kind of movement does this lever favor? (8) What class of lever is this?

The Wheel and Axle

The wheel and axle device consists of a wheel attached to a central axle about which it revolves. Force may be applied to the wheel either at the rim, as in the case of the steering wheel of the automobile, or to the axle, as in the case of the automobile's rear wheels. The steering wheel is an example of a wheel and axle which magnifies force at the expense of speed and distance. The larger the diameter of the wheel, the greater the magnification of force. Quantitatively, the turning effect of the wheel is the product of the force and the radius. The radius thus corresponds to the effort arm of a lever. The doorknob, the water wheel and the helm of the ship are common examples of this kind of wheel and

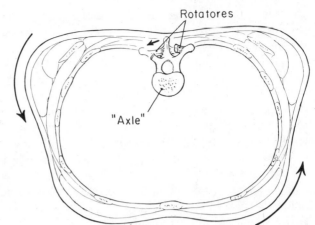

Rotatores

"Axle"

Figure 12–30 A cross section of the trunk representing a "wheel and axle" in which the force of the rotatores muscles is applied to the "axle."

axle. In the helm of the ship the rim of the wheel is absent, but the spokes constitute a wheel nevertheless. In many respects the wheel and axle device is similar to the lever, particularly when the "wheel" consists of a single spoke, as in the case of the meat grinder, the pencil sharpener and the hand-operated clothes wringer. These correspond to a second class lever, in which the fulcrum (actually the center of the axle) is at one end, the effort is applied to the other end and the resistance is applied close to the fulcrum.

The type of wheel and axle which is used to gain speed and distance at the expense of effort is seen less commonly, perhaps, yet it is present in many of our vehicles. In the automobile the rear wheels are turned by means of effort applied to their axles. The same is true of the bicycle, the velocipede and the old-fashioned bicycle, in which the pedals are attached directly to the axle. The Ferris wheel and the merry-go-round are additional examples of this kind of wheel and axle. In each of these the effort is applied to the axle and the resistance to the outer circumference of the wheel. More careful inspection of these examples reveals that they are actually combinations of both kinds of wheels and axles. In the velocipede, for instance, the pedal represents the first type of wheel and axle. The effort is applied to the outer end of the pedal. This serves to revolve the common axle of the pedal and the front wheel of the velocipede. The front wheel represents the second type of wheel and axle.

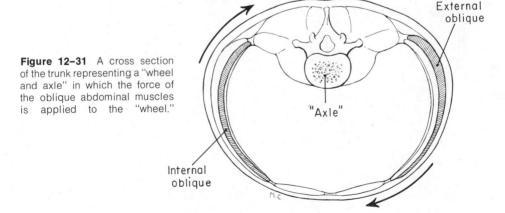

External oblique

"Axle"

Internal oblique

Figure 12–31 A cross section of the trunk representing a "wheel and axle" in which the force of the oblique abdominal muscles is applied to the "wheel."

Effort is applied to it at the axle (as the result of the action of the pedal) and resistance, in the form of friction and pressure, is applied to the rim at its point of contact with the ground.

Further consideration of wheels and axles, as seen in common household and industrial devices, shows that they frequently are combined in such a way that a wheel and axle of the first type alternates with one of the second type. There may be several such combinations within one relatively simple mechanism. The common rotary egg beater, for instance, is found to combine four wheel and axle devices, the two types alternating with each other.

Most of the examples of the wheel and axle in the body, like anatomic levers, are arranged for gaining distance and speed at the expense of effort. Both kinds are represented, however. A cross section of the upper trunk is a good example. The multifidus, rotatores and semispinalis act on the "axle," that is, the spinal column, and the oblique abdominal muscles and the iliocostalis exert their force on the perimeter of the "wheel"—the ribs in this case (Figs. 12–30 and 12–31). The head and neck also illustrate a wheel and axle mechanism, the effort being applied to the perimeter of the "wheel" by the sternocleidomastoid and splenius muscles and to the "axle" by the deep spinal muscles.

A cross section of the arm or the thigh likewise presents the characteristics of a wheel and axle. Here the shaft of the long bone serves as the axle and the peripheral tissues as the wheel. Rotation of the limb about its mechanical long axis constitutes the movement of the wheel and axle, with the effort being furnished by the muscles producing the rotation and the resistance by the antagonistic muscles, or by an external resistance, as the case may be. Unlike the usual mechanical wheel and axle, the resistance in an anatomic wheel and axle is frequently applied at the same distance from the center of motion as the effort. This is the case when antagonistic muscles provide the only resistance to the movement.

The Pulley

A pulley is usually a spool or wheel with a rope running over it. Although we do not have wheels and ropes in the body, we do have pulleys. In the field

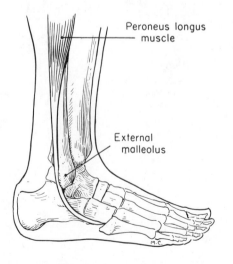

Peroneus longus muscle

External malleolus

Figure 12–32   The external malleolus serving as a pulley for the peroneus longus tendon.

of mechanics there are simple pulleys and there are complicated arrangements of block and tackle. Only the fixed single pulley is represented in the musculoskeletal system. It serves the same purpose as the mechanical fixed single pulley, namely, that of changing the direction of a force. This may take the form of giving a muscle a greater angle of pull than it would otherwise have or of enabling it to produce a totally different movement than it could otherwise produce. For instance, the angle of pull of the gracilis muscle is increased by means of the bulging medial condyles of the knee over which the tendon passes just before it attaches to the tibia (Fig. 12–4). A pulley changing the nature of a movement is illustrated by the peroneus longus muscle, which, by passing behind the lateral malleolus before it turns under the foot to attach to the first cuneiform and base of the first metatarsal bone, plantar-flexes the foot at the ankle (Fig. 12–32). If it passed in front of the malleolus, its pull would be shifted in front of the ankle joint and this would cause it to dorsiflex the foot. In the first example the medial condyles of the femur and tibia are the "fixed single pulley," and in the second example the lateral malleolus serves in this capacity.

Mechanical Advantage

Machines are judged good if they are efficient, poor if they are inefficient. How is the efficiency of a machine measured? Since the machines used in industry and in the workshop are usually for the purpose of magnifying force, it is customary to measure their efficiency in terms of their *mechanical advantage,* in other words, their ability to magnify force. Another way of expressing this ability is to state the "output" of the machine relative to its "input." In levers this is the ratio between the effort applied to the lever and the resistance overcome by the lever. It may be expressed in terms of the equation:

Mechanical Advantage = the ratio of the resistance overcome to the effort applied, or simply, $M.A. = \dfrac{R}{E}$

Since the balanced lever equation (p. 313) may also be expressed

$$\frac{R}{E} = \frac{EA}{RA}$$

it is seen that the mechanical advantage may be expressed in terms of the ratio of the effort arm to the resistance arm. Hence, if

$$M.A. = \frac{R}{E}$$

it also holds that

$$M.A. = \frac{EA}{RA}$$

When a muscle is said to have poor leverage it means that it has poor mechanical advantage. In other words, the effort arm of the lever upon which it is acting is short compared with the resistance arm.

The mechanical advantage of a wheel and axle is measured in a similar manner, in terms of the ratio of the radius of the wheel (R) to the radius of the axle (r), or

$$M.A. = \frac{R}{r}$$

We need not concern ourselves with the mechanical advantage of pulleys as the fixed single pulley affects only the direction of a force, not its magnitude.

WORK, POWER AND ENERGY

Work.   Simple machines such as the lever or wheel and axle are devices designed to do work. In each instance the machine aids in the use of a force to overcome a resistance. When the resistance is overcome for a given distance, *work* is done. Mechanically speaking, *work is the product of the amount of force expended and the distance through which the force succeeds in overcoming a resistance it acts upon.* This may be expressed as

$$W = Fd$$

where W stands for work, F for force and d as the distance along which the force is applied. Units for expressing work are numerous because any force unit may be combined with any distance unit to form a work unit. In the English system the foot-pound is the most common work unit while the joule is the most frequently used unit in the metric system. A joule is equivalent to $10^7 \times$ one gram of force exerted through one centimeter.

In computing work, the distance d must always be measured in the direction the force acts even though the object whose resistance is overcome may not be moving in the same direction. If one lifts a 20-pound suitcase from the floor to place it on a shelf five feet above the floor, the work accomplished is 100 foot-pounds. If, on the other hand, that same weight is lifted an equal distance upward but along a ten foot inclined plane, the amount of work done is still 100 foot pounds (Fig. 12–33). The work done along the incline is the same as the work done to lift the weight to the height of the incline. The horizontal distance the suitcase moves is not included.

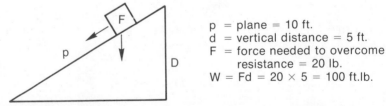

p = plane = 10 ft.
d = vertical distance = 5 ft.
F = force needed to overcome
     resistance = 20 lb.
W = Fd = 20 × 5 = 100 ft.lb.

Figure 12–33   Work is the product of force needed to overcome a resistance and the direction over which the force is applied. The force lifting the 20 pound weight 5 vertical feet does 100 foot-pounds of work even though the 20 pounds are moved 10 feet along the plane.

Work done in the same direction that the body moves is called *positive* work, whereas work done in the opposite direction is called *negative* work. When an individual does a deep knee bend, the extensor muscles of the leg contract eccentrically to resist the effect of gravity on the body. The body moves in a direction opposite to the upward force of the muscles, and thus negative or resistive work is performed by the muscles. In the return to standing from the knee bend position, the body moves in the same direction as the concentrically contracting extensors, and the work of the muscles is positive. The net work accomplished during the down and up movement of the knee bend is the vector sum of the positive and negative work. Negative forces resisting gravity perform less work over a given distance than positive forces overcoming gravity. For example, one performs more work walking up a mountain than walking back down.

When the exertion of effort produces no motion, such as might happen during a tug of war, mechanically speaking, no work is accomplished. Static contraction of muscles may be evident and considerable effort may be expended, but, in the strict mechanical sense, no work is being done. The physiologic measure of such efforts may be determined by obtaining the energy costs. This is usually measured by computing the amount of oxygen consumed during the effort and converting it to calories per minute.

Theoretically, the mechanical work performed by an individual muscle can also be determined using the equation W = Fd. Suppose, for instance, that there is a rectangular muscle, 4 inches long and 1½ inches wide, that exerts 66 pounds of force as it turns a bony lever. Since the average muscle fiber shortens to one-half of its resting length and the fibers of a small rectangular muscle run the full length of the muscle, the force of the muscle in question is exerted over a distance of two inches (the amount of shortening, equal to one-half the resting length). Therefore, since F = 66 pounds and d = 2 inches ($^2/_{12}$ or $^1/_6$ of a foot), the muscle is performing 132 inch pounds, or 11 foot pounds, of work. In brief: W = F(66 lb.) × d($^1/_6$ ft.).

If the force of the muscle is not known it is computed from the muscle's cross section (see page 293). It must also be remembered that "d" in the work force per square inch of cross section to be 90 pounds, the following steps are taken.

1. Find the muscle's cross section.
   Cross section = width × thickness.
   1½ in. × ½ in. = ¾ sq. in. (cross section)
2. Find the amount of force exerted by the muscle.
   Average force = 90 lb. per sq. in.
   Cross section = ¾ sq. in.
   F = 90 × ¾ = $^{270}/_4$ = 67½ lb.
3. Find the amount of work performed by this muscle, first in inch pounds, then in foot pounds.
   W = Fd
   W = 67½ lb. × 2 in. = $^{135}/_2$ × 2 = 135 in. lb.
   $^{135}/_{12}$ = 11¼ ft. lb.

For purposes of simplification the internal structure of the hypothetical muscle used in these examples was rectangular. This means that a simple geometric cross sectional measure could be used. For penniform and bipenniform muscles, however, it would be essential to determine the physiologic cross section (see page 293). It must also be remembered that "d" in the work equation represents one-half the length of the average fiber in the muscle and that this may or may not coincide with the total length of the fleshy part of the muscle, depending upon its internal structure.

The number of pounds of force per square inch exerted by the average human muscle must be selected arbitrarily, depending upon whose research the student accepts as his source.

A single equation for computing the work performed by a muscle whose average fiber length is known and whose physiologic cross section (PCS) has been determined, would be as follows:

$$W = 90 \times PCS(\text{in sq. in.}) \times \tfrac{1}{2} \text{ the length of the fibers(in inches)}$$

This will give work in terms of inch pounds. Since it is customary to measure work in terms of foot pounds, the result should be divided by 12. The following equation includes this step:

$$W = \frac{90 \ (\text{PCS in sq. in.})(\tfrac{1}{2} \text{ the fiber length in inches})}{12}$$

Power. Any measure of work does not account for the time involved in performing the work. When one lifts 200 pounds a distance of three feet, 600 foot-pounds of work are done regardless of the time it takes to do it. The rate at which work is done is called power, and may be expressed as

$$P = \frac{Fd}{t} \quad \text{or} \quad P = \frac{W}{t}$$

where *P* stands for power, *W* for work and *t* for time. Either form of the equation clearly points out that the machine or person who can perform more work in a given unit of time or who takes less time to do a specified amount of work is more powerful.

In the English system, power is expressed as ft.-lb./sec. or as horsepower (550 ft.-lb./sec. = 1 horsepower). The metric system unit is the watt, equivalent to one joule/second.

Energy. Energy is defined as the capacity to do work. A body is said to possess energy when it can perform work and the energy that the body possesses is measured as the work accomplished. Energy may take numerous forms, and it is common for it to be converted from one form to another, although according to the Law of Conservation of Energy it can neither be created nor destroyed. Some forms which energy may take are heat, sound, light, electric, chemical, atomic and mechanical. When a ball is hit with a bat, some of the mechanical energy is converted to sound and heat energy, but none of the energy is lost. The total amount of energy possessed by a body or an isolated system remains constant.

Potential energy and *kinetic energy* are two classifications of energy which have important implications in biomechanics. Potential energy is the capacity for doing work that a body has because of its position or configuration. A raised weight such as a diver standing on a platform, a bent bow or a compressed spring all have potential energy. Measured in work units potential energy is the product of the force an object has and the distance over which it can act. The potential energy of a 150-pound diver whose center of gravity is 20 feet above the water surface is 3000 foot pounds. In this instance the appropriate form for the potential energy equation is

$$P.E = mgh$$

where m is the mass of the body, g is the force of gravity and h is the height between the diver's center of gravity and the water surface. The product of m and g (mg) is the same as the diver's weight. The distance represented by h is established by choosing an arbitrary zero level. The potential energy of someone standing on a table three feet from the floor can be changed by boring a large hole in the floor directly in front of the table. The individual's potential for dropping farther is now increased.

The kinetic energy of a body is the energy due to its motion. The faster a body moves, the more kinetic energy it possesses. When a body stops moving the kinetic energy is lost. This is readily seen in the equation for kinetic energy:

$$K.E = \frac{1}{2} \, mv^2$$

where m is the mass of the object and v is its velocity. According to the principle of the conservation of energy the work done is equal to the kinetic energy acquired, and therefore

$$Fd = \frac{1}{2} \, mv^2$$

This relationship is extremely helpful in explaining the value of "giving" when receiving the impetus of any moving object. In attempting to catch a fast moving ball, one's chances of success are improved by increasing the distance used for stopping the ball's motion. As d increases in $Fd = \frac{1}{2} \, mv^2$, the force of the impact F, must decrease. The work of the kinetic energy against the hands depends on the kinetic energy the ball possesses when it hits the hand. Whether that work consists of a large F and a small d or a small F and a large d depends on the technique used by the catcher. The skillful performer knows he will decrease the possibility of injury and increase the chances of holding onto the ball if the latter choice of a small F and a large d is made. Achieving a gradual loss of kinetic energy is likewise advantageous when landing from a jump or a fall (Fig. 12–34).

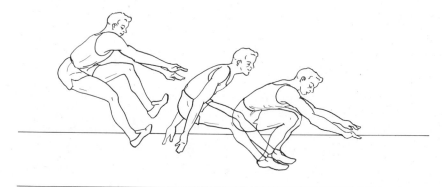

Figure 12–34 Effecting a gradual loss of kinetic energy by bending the knees upon landing from a jump.

Energy is frequently transformed from kinetic into potential energy or conversely from potential to kinetic energy. The diver who jumps from a platform above the water immediately begins to lose potential energy in proportion to his gain in kinetic energy. At platform height all of the diver's energy is potential. At zero elevation all of the potential energy has been converted into an equivalent amount of kinetic energy. Barring no conversion of energy to other forms (heat, sound, etc.) the potential energy at the top equals exactly the kinetic energy at the bottom.

The transformation from one energy state to another is interesting to note in a gymnast swinging on the flying rings. Like a pendulum, the swinger's energy is transformed from kinetic to potential on every swing. As the suspended body moves upward, the kinetic energy is continuously changed to potential energy, and the higher the swinger goes the greater the potential becomes for doing work on the downswing. At the top of the swing the conversion to potential energy is complete. As the gymnast begins to fall kinetic energy again develops, becoming the greatest at the bottom of the swing when the speed is greatest and potential energy is zero. Theoretically the swinging should continue uninterrupted, but because of friction some energy is converted to heat and eventually the "pendulum" will come to rest.

LABORATORY EXPERIENCES

Note: Assume that the muscles can exert a force of 100 pounds per square inch of cross section.
1. How much force can each of the following muscles exert?
   Muscle A, having a cross section of 2 square inches.
   Muscle B, having a cross section of 4 square inches.
   Muscle C, having a cross section of 13 square inches.

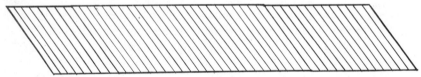

Figure 12–35 What is the approximate force that this muscle can exert? (Scale ½ inch = 1 inch).

2. Find the approximate force of which the muscle shown in Figure 12–35 is capable. Assume that the diagram is drawn to scale, ½ inch being the equivalent of 1 inch. The muscle is 1 inch thick.

3. Estimate the cross section of your own biceps muscle. Approximately how much force should it be able to exert?

4. Approximately how much force should your triceps be able to exert?

5. In the diagram of the biceps muscle in Figure 12–36, find the size of the angle of pull.

6. Using the scale, ⅛ inch = 1 inch, determine the effort moment arm of the forearm lever in Figure 12–36.

7. For each of the following anatomic levers estimate the approximate length of the effort moment arm, i.e., the perpendicular distance. Refer to anatomic illustrations or to a muscle manikin to help you estimate the angle of pull of the muscles. Unless otherwise stated, assume that the segments are in their normal resting position. (*Hint:* Use the mechanical axis of the segment for the lever.)
   a. The forearm lever with the biceps providing the effort.
   b. The upper arm lever with the middle deltoid providing the effort.
   c. The upper arm lever in the side-horizontal position with the entire pectoralis major

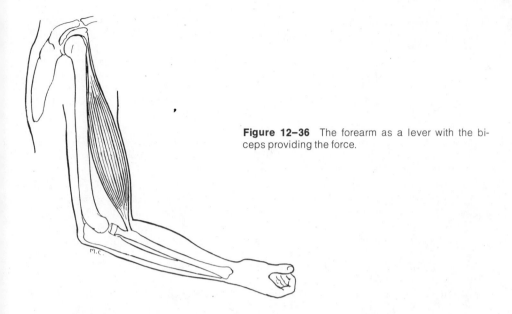

Figure 12–36 The forearm as a lever with the biceps providing the force.

providing the effort. (*Hint:* Which view would show you the angle of pull for this movement, facing the subject or looking down from above?)

  d. Same lever as in *c,* with the anterior deltoid providing the effort.

8. Referring to the diagrams in Figure 12–3, assume that a weight is suspended from the wrist. Find the resistance moment arm of the forearm lever in positions *A, B* and *C.* Consider that the scale for these diagrams is 9 inches to the inch.

9. Assume that a muscle having a force of 300 pounds is pulling at an angle of 75 degrees. Find the components of force (*a*) by the trigonometric method; (*b*) by the graphic method.

10. Assuming that the weight used in question 8 is 8 pounds, determine the rotatory and nonrotatory components of the weight (*a*) by the trigonometric method; (*b*) by the graphic method.

11. Determine the amount of work (in foot pounds) performed by each of the following hypothetical muscles:
   Muscle A, capable of a total force of 240 pounds and having fibers with an average length of 6 inches.
   Muscle B, capable of a total force of 150 pounds and having fibers with an average length of 24 inches.
   Muscle C, having a cross section of 4 square inches and fibers with an average length of 12 inches.

12. Referring to Figure 6–6, make a tracing of the femur and the adductor longus muscle. Draw a straight line to represent the mechanical axis of the femur and another to represent the muscle's line of pull (connecting the midpoints of the proximal and distal attachments).
   a. Using a protractor, measure the angle of pull, i.e., the angle facing the hip joint, formed by the intersection of the muscle's line of pull with the bone's mechanical axis.
   b. Measure the effort moment arm of the lever, i.e., the perpendicular distance from the fulcrum (center of hip joint) to the muscle's line of pull. To convert this to a realistic figure use the scale $^3/_{16}$ in. = 1 in.
   c. Assuming the muscle's total force to be 250 pounds, calculate the moment of force (i.e., the torque) of the lever.
   d. Calculate the rotatory and the nonrotatory components of force.

13. Place a pole across the back of a chair, hang a pail or basket containing a 5-pound weight on one end and hold the other end of the pole. Now adjust the pole so that it becomes increasingly difficult to balance the weight of the pail with one hand. Stop when you reach the point where you are barely able to lift the pail by pushing down on the opposite end of the pole. Have an assistant measure the effort arm and the resistance arm of the lever. Without shifting the position of your hand, draw the pole toward you until you can easily lift the pail by pushing down on the opposite end of the pole with one finger. Again, have an assistant measure the effort and resistance arms of the lever. What do you conclude concerning the relative length of two arms? In which case does the pail move through the greater distance? What do you conclude about the relationship between the effort required to move an object by leverage and the distance that the object is moved?

14. Balance a pole across the back of a chair, hanging a 5-pound weight at each end. Let one of these represent the effort and the other the resistance. The effort arm and the resistance arm should be exactly equal if the pole is symmetrical. Now add 5 more pounds at another point on the resistance end and adjust the pole until it balances. Measure the effort and resistance moment arms. What do you conclude about:
    a. The relationship between the resistance and the resistance arms, between the effort and the effort arm?
    b. The relationship between the resistance and the resistance arm, given a changing resistance and a constant effort?
    Explain the following equation: $E \times EMA = R \times RMA$

15. Compute the amount of effort necessary to lift a resistance of 20 pounds with a 6-foot, first class lever whose fulcrum is located 2 feet from the point at which the weight is attached, and 4 feet from the point at which the effort is applied. Assume that both the effort and the resistance are applied at right angles to the lever.

16. Where would the fulcrum have to be located in the above-mentioned 6-foot first class lever if there were only 5 pounds of effort available to balance the 20-pound weight? Determine this by experiment. Check your answer by the algebraic method.

17. For each of the anatomic levers listed below identify the class of lever represented; identify the fulcrum, the effort point and the resistance point; and name the kind of movement favored by this type of lever.
    a. Leg being flexed at knee by hamstrings.
    b. Leg being extended at knee by quadriceps femoris.
    c. Pelvis being tilted to right by left quadratus lumborum.
    d. Clavicle being elevated by trapezius I.
    e. Lower extremity being abducted by gluteus medius.
    f. From supine lying position, lower extremities being raised by hip flexors.
    g. From supine lying position, trunk being raised by hip flexors.

18. Perform the following paired movements, noting the difference in the effort needed. Diagram and explain the reasons for the difference.
    a. A push-up from the toes and a push-up from the knees.
    b. A sit-up with hands on the thighs and a sit-up with a five pound weight held behind the head.
    c. A five pound weight held in the hand with the arm outstretched horizontally sideward and a five pound weight suspended from the elbow crotch when the arm is outstretched sideward.

19. Explain the difference in effort needed to hold the body levers in 18 a, b, c, at a 10-degree angle with the horizontal compared with holding them at a 30-degree angle; a 45-degree angle.

20. What muscular effort E pulling at an angle of 80 degrees would be required to keep the lower leg in a position of 10 degrees with the horizontal? The muscle inserts 3 inches from the knee joint. The lower leg and foot weighs 8 pounds and its center of

gravity is located 7 inches from the knee joint. A 10-pound weight is hung from the ankle 13 inches from the knee joint.

REFERENCES

1. Basford, L.: The Science of Movement. London: Sampsom Low, Marston & Co., 1966.
2. Bunn, J. W.: Scientific Principles of Coaching, 2nd Ed. Englewood Cliffs, N.J.: Prentice-Hall, 1972.
3. Dull, C. E., Metcalfe, H. C., and Williams, J. E.: Modern Physics. New York: Holt, Rinehart, and Winston, 1963.
4. Dyson, G.: The Mechanics of Athletics, 5th Ed. London: University of London Press, 1970.
5. Fick, R.: Handbuch der Anatomie und Mechanik der Gelenke. Jena: G. Fischer, 1910.
6. Fick, R.: Review of literature on mechanics of joints and muscles. Z. Orthop. Chir., *51*:320–337, 1929.
7. Hay, J. G.: The Biomechanics of Sports Techniques. Englewood Cliffs, N.J.: Prentice-Hall, 1973.
8. Miller, D. I., and Nelson, R. C.: Biomechanics of Sport. Philadelphia: Lea & Febiger, 1973.
9. Morris, C. B.: The measurement of the strength of muscle relative to the cross section. Res. Quart. Am. Assn. Health, Phys. Ed. & Recrn., *19*:295–303, 1948.
10. Steindler, A.: Kinesiology of the Human Body. Springfield, Ill.: Charles C Thomas, Publisher, 1970.
11. Tricker, R. A. R., and Tricker, B. J. K.: The Science of Movement. New York: American Elsevier, 1967.
12. Williams, M., and Lissner, H. R.: Biomechanics of Human Motion. Philadelphia: W. B. Saunders Company, 1962.

Chapter Thirteen

MOTION AND FORCE

NEWTON'S LAWS OF MOTION

Up to this point both the characteristics of motion and the principles governing the ways in which objects move, as well as the nature of force, have been described, but little has been said about the exact nature of how forces cause or prevent motion. That motion is related to force in a precise manner was observed by Sir Isaac Newton in the seventeenth century. He formulated three laws of motion which explain why objects move as they do. Although all of these laws cannot be proved on earth even in ideal experimental situations, they are accepted as universal truths to explain the effects of force.

Law of Inertia. Newton's first law of motion states that *a body continues in its state of rest or of uniform motion unless an unbalanced force acts on it.* This means that an object at rest remains at rest, and one in motion will continue at a constant speed in a straight line unless acted on by a force. The fact that objects at rest need a force to move them seems obvious, but the need for force to slow or stop an object in motion is not always as apparent. We have all seen moving objects come to rest of their own accord, or what seems to be their own accord. Actually, another force in the form of friction or air resistance causes the change in velocity. The tendency for a body to stay in motion for long periods of time is possible to observe more clearly in laboratory conditions where the effects of friction and air resistance can be minimized, but nevertheless, numerous examples of Newton's first law can still be observed in sport and every day experiences. Baserunners in baseball know it takes force to change velocity suddenly in order to avoid overrunning a base. Skiers continue into space if they traverse a hill or mogul at high speed (Fig. 13–1). And everyone at sometime or other has experienced the sometimes frightening situation of continuing forward when the vehicle in which the person is riding stops suddenly.

That property of an object which causes it to remain in its state of either rest or motion is called its *inertia.* Because of inertia force is needed to change the velocity of an object. The amount of force needed to alter the object's velocity is directly related to the amount of inertia it has. The measure of inertia in a body is its mass, i.e., the quantity of matter it possesses. The greater the mass of an object, the greater its inertia. A medicine ball obviously has greater inertia than does a volleyball. A tennis racquet has greater inertia than a badminton racquet and a baseball more than a whiffle ball.

Law of Acceleration. The second law of motion concerns acceleration and momentum, and it tells how the quantities of force, mass and acceleration are

328

Figure 13–1   An example of Newton's first law of motion.

related. The law states that *the acceleration of an object is directly proportional to the force causing it, is in the same direction as the force, and is inversely proportional to the mass of the object.* It is quite easy to show that change in velocity (acceleration) of an object is proportional to the force and in the direction of the force. The velocity of a pitched ball reflects the force with which it is thrown, and it moves in the direction of the line of force at the moment of release. Similarly it takes less "braking force" to stop a baseball moving at 10 feet per second than it does to stop a pitch of 100 feet per second. In both instances the change in velocity is directly proportional to the amount of force and in the direction of the force. The mass of the ball is a measure of its inertia, and the greater the inertia the more force it takes to change the object's velocity. Thus, acceleration is inversely proportional to mass. A bowling ball requires more force to put it in motion than a playground ball and the same is true for stopping it.

These relationships among force, acceleration and mass when combined and stated symbolically become:

$$a \propto \frac{F}{m} \quad or \quad F \propto ma$$

By defining terms, physicists have assigned values to units of force, mass and acceleration so that an equals sign may be substituted for the proportion sign, and Newton's second law may be expressed in equation form as

$$F = ma$$

For this to be possible the force unit is the pound when acceleration is in feet/second/second and mass is in slugs. When acceleration is in meters/second/second and mass is in kilograms, force will be in newtons. (See Table 10–1.)

With this equation it is now possible to determine the force needed to produce a given linear acceleration of a body if the weight of the body is known. Since we know that w = mg, F = Ma can be written $F = \dfrac{w}{g} \times a$. For example, the force needed to accelerate a 160 pound object, 2 ft./sec./sec. is $\dfrac{160}{32} \times 2$ or 10 pounds.

Impulse and Momentum. Acceleration has been defined as the rate of change of velocity, or $a = \dfrac{v-u}{t}$. Substitution of this value for *a* in the equation, F = ma, changes it to $F = m\dfrac{(V-u)}{t}$ or Ft = m(V−u). *Ft*, the product of a force and the time over which it acts is called *impulse.* As the change in velocity of an object of given mass increases, so must the impulse increase proportionately. Conversely, if either force or time is increased the change in velocity must also increase. Doubling either the force or time over which a force is applied will double the velocity change. The importance of creating as large an impulse as possible is evident in the skillful execution of many sports' techniques. A baseball pitcher uses a form which allows the longest time over which to apply the force to the ball before releasing it. This same long "wind up" is seen in the technique used by hammer throwers, discus throwers and shot putters. In each instance the performer accelerates the object to be thrown as much as possible by generating as much force as strength permits and by using body segment adjustments which increase the time over which the force can be applied (Fig. 13–2).

The impulse relationship also shows that force cannot be generated to cause a change in velocity unless time is available over which the force is ap-

Figure 13–2 Example of impulse generation. (Drawn from motion picture film tracing.)

plied. This helps to explain the value of the follow-through in throwing and striking objects. Although the follow-through does not affect the flight of the object once the object has left the throwing or striking implement, it does help to assure that the missile will stay in contact with the implement which is imparting force to it for as long as possible. The ball is actually carried along by the foot, the golf club or the tennis racquet, and the longer the time that the force of the implement can be applied to the ball the greater will be the change in velocity in the ball.

The impulse equation is usually written as:

$$Ft = mv - mu$$

The product of mass and velocity (*mv* or *mu*) is *momentum*. Momentum is a quantity of motion which when mass is constant may be increased or decreased by increasing or decreasing velocity. The shot putter who is able to push his shot with a greater speed than his opponent will cause his shot to have greater momentum at the moment of release. And even though his mass is less, a smaller tackler may "take out" a larger opponent in football if his faster speed is sufficient to afford him a larger momentum than the person he tackles. Momentum may also be increased or decreased by altering the mass. Heavier bowling balls released with the same speed as lighter balls have greater momentum. Similarly, a heavier tennis racquet will strike a tennis ball with greater momentum and cause a greater change in momentum in the tennis ball than will a lighter racquet.

An increase in momentum occurs when the force causing the increase is applied in the direction of the motion. Force applied in the opposite direction produces a slowing down or decrease in momentum. This is what happens when one catches a fast ball or lands from a jump. In both instances relatively large momentums must be reduced to zero, (the momentum of the ball is large because or its large velocity and the momentum of the jumper is great because of his large mass). Large impulses occur as the result of these changes in momentum. Looking again at the impulse equation, $Ft = mv - mu$, it can be seen that a short stopping time will require a large stopping force and that an increase in stopping time will reduce the amount of stopping force needed to change the momentum of the object to zero. This is why it is necessary to increase the stopping time by "giving" when catching the ball or when landing from a jump or fall. Without the "give" the momentum will not decrease to zero and the ball will not be caught, or the momentum will reach zero but the force will be so great that injury in the form of damaged bones and joints may result. A five pound force falling for five seconds has the same impulse as a twenty-five pound force falling for one second.

Law of Reaction. The third law of motion considers the way forces act against each other. A book lying on a table (Fig. 13–3) exerts a downward force on the table, and because the book is stationary, another equal and opposite force must be acting on the book. Newton's first law states that unbalanced forces produce motion. Since we have no motion here, we must have a balanced force system. The downward force of the book on the table is balanced by an upward force of the table on the book. The same is true when a person walks

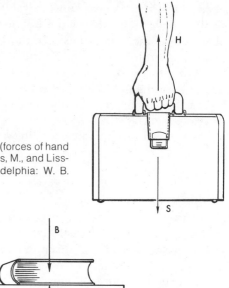

Figure 13–3 Equal and opposite reactions. H = S (forces of hand and bag) and B = T (book and table). (From Williams, M., and Lissner, H. R.: Biomechanics of Human Motion. Philadelphia: W. B. Saunders Company, 1962.)

across a floor. The feet push back against the floor with the same magnitude as the floor pushes forward against the feet. Without the forward push of the floor against the feet, forward progress would not be possible. Starting blocks are used by runners to push against at the beginning of a race so that a strong forward reaction push can be received from the blocks. In each of these instances, forces of equal magnitude are exerted in opposite directions. One force is called the action force and the other is the reaction force. Newton's third law of motion states that *for every action there is an equal and opposite reaction*. Whenever one body exerts a force upon a second body, the second exerts an equal and opposite force upon the first. This is the reason one makes less progress in walking on wet ice or in walking on soft sand, than on firm nonslippery surfaces. Because of a lack of friction between the feet and the supporting surface, the foot's force pushing back against the ice or sand is diminished, and therefore the ice or sand pushes the body forward with less force. To overcome the lack of friction, players engaged in activities involving quick starts, stops and direction changes wear shoes with special cleats. The cleats allow the player to dig in and push without slippage or loss of force. The maximum equal and opposite reaction then pushes the player in the desired direction. Consider the problem of trying to walk on ice with ball bearings attached to the shoe soles.

Action and reaction show up in countless ways when objects are in motion. When a boat is rowed, the oars exert a force against the water, and the water pushes against the oars with an equal and opposite reaction causing the boat to be pushed forward as the force is transferred from the oar to the boat through the oarlock. The force of a volleyball can be felt pushing back against the hand as it is served with a forward force. A similar force is observed when a gun is shot or an arrow is released from a bow. The recoil of the gun or bow is due to the reaction force of the bullet or arrow to the action force of the gun or bow.

Conservation of Momentum.   When an object is set in motion by a force, the momentum (*mv*) of the object is changed. Since the force which causes this change in momentum must have an equal and opposite force, another equal and opposite momentum change must occur in the object producing the reactive force. The time the objects are in contact with each other would also be equal, and therefore the impulses (*Ft*) would be equal. This means that $m_1 v_1 - m_1 u_1 = m_2 v_2 - m_2 u_2$. This principle is summarized in the law of conservation of momentum which states that *in any system where forces act on each other the momentum is constant.* Thus, if an impact or action between objects occurs, the momentums before impact must equal the momentums after the impact, providing, of course, that no momentum is lost through friction or other forces. The momentum of a golf ball changes from zero to a larger quantity after it is struck by a club. Neglecting air resistance and friction, the momentum of the club will also change so that the momentum of ball and club before impact will equal the momentum of ball and club after impact. This is proved by using the impulse equation,

$$m_b v_b - m_b u_b = m_c v_c - m_c u_c$$

where the subscript *b* refers to the ball and *c* to the club. Rearranged, this equation becomes

$$m_b u_b - m_c u_c = m_b v_b - m_c v_c$$

Figure 13–4 Momentum of club and ball before impact equals momentum of club and ball after impact. (Drawn from motion picture film tracing.)

That is, the combined momentums before impact equal the combined momentums after impact. Momentum is conserved; none is lost.

The conservation of momentum may be easily apparent in some instances whereas in others it is harder to visualize. When one steps out of a canoe onto a dock, the canoe is pushed back by the passenger as the passenger is pushed forward by the canoe. The change in momentum of the canoe backward ($m_1v_1 - m_1u_1$) will equal the change in momentum of the passenger forward ($m_2v_2 - m_2u_2$) Here the action-reaction relationship is evident. But if the same person steps off an ocean liner, the change in momentum of the ship is imperceptible. Yet, it will still equal the change in momentum of the passenger. Because the mass of the ship is so great, its velocity is not apparent. In *both* instances, the change in the mass-velocity product of the passenger equals the change in the mass-velocity product of the boat (canoe or ship), and momentum is conserved. Incidently, if the passenger disembarking from the canoe does not account for the backward acceleration of the canoe, the step toward the dock may be a wet one.

NEWTON'S LAWS AND ROTATIONAL EQUIVALENTS

Moment of Inertia.   In the preceding discussion of Newton's laws of motion, the quality of a body to resist change in its state of motion was identified as inertia. The inertia of a body with respect to linear motion was shown to be directly proportional to the mass of the object. The heavier an object the more force it takes to start it moving and the more force to stop it. This is also true in rotatory motion. Once they are set in motion, spinning bodies tend to keep spinning. As with linear motion, the amount of force needed to start or stop a spinning object is related to its mass. However, there is an additional factor to be considered. The hammer thrower knows that it takes more effort to start the weight moving in a circular fashion at the end of the wire than it does to start it moving in a linear fashion. It is also true that once the hammer is moving in a circular fashion it is more difficult to slow it down than if it were moving in a straight line. Therefore it seems that the hammer's inertia is greater when moving in an angular pattern than when moving in a linear path. Since the mass of the hammer does not change, this increase in inertia must be due to some other element. In the same way that the torque causing rotatory motion is dependent upon the magnitude of force and the perpendicular distance from the line of action of the force to the axis, the inertia of a rotatory body is affected by the distance between the mass and the axis of rotation. A ball rotating on the end of a long string is harder to stop and start than one on a short string. As the distance between the axis and the mass increases, the inertia increases. This angular inertia is called the moment of inertia (I). It is the moment about the axis due to inertia and is directly related to the distribution of the mass around the axis. If the mass of an object is concentrated close to the axis of rotation, the object is easier to turn than if the mass is concentrated farther away from the axis. The exact nature of this relationship is shown in the equation for the moment of inertia, $I = \Sigma mr^2$, where m is the mass of a particle in the rotating body and r, the perpendicular distance between the mass particle and the axis of rotation. Therefore,

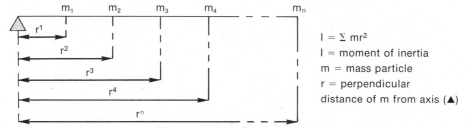

$$I = \Sigma \, mr^2$$

I = moment of inertia
m = mass particle
r = perpendicular
distance of m from axis (▲)

Figure 13–5 The moment of inertia about an axis is the sum of the mass particles multiplied by the square of the distance of each particle from the axis.

the moment of inertia of an object is the sum of each of the particles multiplied by the square of the distance to the axis (Fig. 13–5).

In the human body the mass distribution may be altered by changing the body position, and thus the moment of inertia will change. A runner is able to move his recovery leg forward more rapidly when it is in a flexed position than when it is extended. The mass of the leg is the same in both instances, but it is closer to the axis when the leg is flexed and the moment of inertia is less. Using data for average mass proportions of body segments and the location of the center of gravity of each segment, Dyson estimated that a person standing on a frictionless turntable with arms outstretched to the side has a moment of inertia three times greater than when the arms are at the side (Fig. 13–6).[8] When the

A   B

Figure 13–6 The moment of inertia about an axis decreases when the mass is concentrated close to the axis of rotation. The moment of inertia in *A* is greater than that in *B*.

person lies horizontally on the table, the arms at sides and the vertical axis passing through the center of gravity, I becomes 14 times greater. The moment of inertia of the body is least about a vertical axis passing through the center of gravity when the arms are raised and held close to the head, and greatest when the body is in a fully extended position rotating about the hands as in the giant swing on the high bar.

Using a method similar to finding the center of gravity of the body by the segmental method (see Chapter Fourteen, p. 370), Hay reported the moment of inertia of the human body in some common rotating positions.[9] In the tuck position, I about the body's center of gravity was 2.58 slug-ft.^{2}, in the pike position it was 4.89 slug-ft.^{2} and in the layout, 11.15 slug-ft.^{2} The moment of inertia about the hands of the giant swing position was 60.90 slug-ft.^{2} These figures verify that inertia to rotation increases as the mass is distributed farther away from the axis. When one is interested in the moment of inertia of a specific body segment, it is usually taken about the center of the joint serving as the axis, although other axes may be chosen. If another axis is selected such as the center of gravity of the segment, I will change accordingly because values of r will be different in $I = \Sigma mr^2$.

Angular Momentum. Momentum is a measure of the force needed to start or stop motion. Objects undergoing angular motion have momentum in the same fashion as objects engaged in linear motion. Linear momentum is the product of mass and velocity. Angular momentum is the product of the angular equivalents of mass and velocity, that is, the moment of inertia, I, and angular velocity, ω.

$$\text{angular momentum} = I\ \omega$$
$$\text{linear momentum} = m\ v$$

The momentum of a skater skating in a straight line is mv. The momentum of the skater spinning is $I\omega$.

The law of conservation of momentum applies to rotatory motion as well

Figure 13–7 The speed of rotation is controlled by the radius of rotation. (Drawn from motion picture film tracing.)

as to linear motion. Like linear momentum, angular momentum is conserved. Once a spinning body is in motion its angular momentum will not alter, providing, of course, no outside forces are introduced. Divers, trampolinists, dancers and any other rotating performers all make use of the conservation of angular momentum to control the speed of bodily spin. A skater starts to spin with the arms outstretched. After she is spinning slowly in this position, she brings her arms in close to her body and immediately begins to spin rapidly. The increase in angular velocity occurs with no effort on the skater's part. By bringing her arms in closer to her axis of rotation she has decreased her moment of inertia about that axis, and since her angular momentum must remain constant, a decrease in I produces an increase in ω. Increasing I by stretching the arms and perhaps a leg out to the side will again slow down the skater. A diver performing a tuck somersault can control the speed of rotation by changing the tightness of his tuck, thus changing his moment of inertia. If he thinks his entry into the water will be spoiled because he is rotating too rapidly, he will increase I and therefore slow down by "opening up" or loosening his tuck.

Action and Reaction.   The force for angular motion is torque. When a torque is applied by one body to another the second body will exert an equal and opposite torque on the first. This is an example of Newton's third law of motion applied to angular movement. A force which causes a change in angular momentum must have an equal and opposite force creating an equal and opposite momentum change; that is, angular momentum is conserved: $I_1 (\omega_{v_1} - \omega_{u_1}) = I_2 (\omega_{v_2} - \omega_{u_2})$. When one jumps straight up from a trampoline bed with arms stretched upward and then swings the legs forward and up, the body will jack-knife at the hips. The torque acting on the legs results in an equal and opposite torque acting on the rest of the body. A change in angular velocity is observed in both body segments, although that in the trunk segment is less because I is greater. Another jump upward followed by a sharp flexion of the wrists only will also produce an equal and opposite torque upon the rest of the body. However, in this case the change in angular velocity of the arms and trunk resulting in forward upward motion will be barely visible. I for the arms and trunk is so large compared to I for the hands that the opposite rotation will be very slight. The angular velocity of the two moving parts is inversely proportional to their moments of inertia about the axis of motion (the wrist joint in the example just given). Axes for such actions may be in any plane but the reactions must be in the same or parallel planes. The arms swinging horizontally across in front of the trunk will produce an opposite action of the rest of the body in the transverse plane (Fig. 13–8). Movement of one arm downward in the frontal plane produces an equal and opposite action of the rest of the body in the frontal plane. This is the movement which may be used to regain balance on a beam or tightrope. If one falls to the left, a downward movement of the left arm produces a reaction of the rest of the body to the right and hopefully prevents a fall.

Sometimes action and reaction of specific body parts is not desired and should be controlled. This can be done by substitution or absorption of the undesired action. In running, the rotation of the pelvis and legs about a vertical axis produces an undesired reaction of the upper trunk in the opposite direction if it is not compensated in some fashion. To prevent this, the arms move in opposition to the legs to "absorb" the reaction by producing a counter twist

Figure 13–8 Angular action and reaction. As the arms swing across the body in one direction, an equal and opposite reaction occurs in the rest of the body.

which cancels out the reaction of the body to the leg action. The faster one moves or the more massive the legs, the more vigorous must be the arm action. The arms are used in the same fashion to prevent undesired trunk reaction to leg action in hurdling, diving and jumping.

Transfer of Momentum.   Because of the law of conservation of momentum, angular momentum may be transferred from one body or body part to another as the total angular momentum remains unaltered. In the suspended balls shown in Figure 13–9, the sudden checking of motion in ball *A* produces a comparable action in ball *E*. Similarly, the checking of simultaneous motion in *A* and *B* produces equal momentum in *D* and *E*. Examples of transfer of angular momentum in movement patterns are numerous. As a back diver leaves the board, the arms are swung upward until the motion is checked by the limitation of range of motion in the shoulder joint. The checked momentum transfers to the body and increases its angular momentum, thus helping to turn the body in the air. In the racing dive, the angular momentum of the diver's arms is also transferred to the body as the diver stops the upward movement of the arms in the forward reach, and in a jump twist the dancer transfers twisting momentum from the upper arms and trunk to the legs as the feet leave the ground. In each of these instances the body is in contact with the ground while the momentum is developing. Otherwise, an equal and opposite reaction, rather than a transfer, would occur.

Centripetal and Centrifugal Force.   According to Newton's first law, a moving body left alone travels uniformly in a straight line. To make that body leave the straight path requires force. When one swings a weight around on the

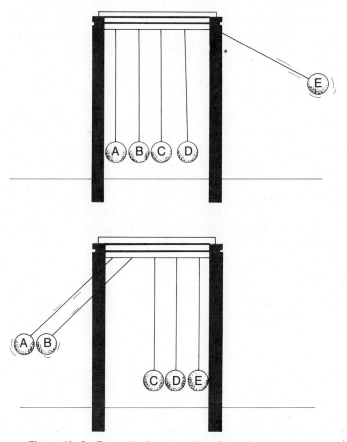

Figure 13–9 Example of conservation of angular momentum.

end of a piece of string, the force causing the weight to change direction constantly is called *centripetal* force (center seeking force). It is a constant force acting to move the object at right angles to the direction it is moving at any instant and therefore causing it to move in a circular path. Even though the velocity of the whirling object is constant, its direction changes continually. This means that acceleration is occurring, since by definition acceleration is a rate of change in velocity. The acceleration occurring as an object moves around a circle at a constant speed is of the magnitude $\frac{v^2}{r}$, where v is the linear velocity of the object and r is the radius or distance from the axis of motion to the object. From Newton's second law we know that F = ma. Therefore, the centripetal force needed to keep a body moving in a circle at constant speed is

$$F_c = \frac{mv^2}{r}$$

The centripetal force has to be applied to the object moving in a circle by another object. Newton's third law states that the second object which applies the force must be acted on by an equal and opposite force. In the case of the weight on a string, the finger applies the force to the weight through the string. The finger, in turn, has a force pulling on it. This outward pulling force is called *centrifugal* force (center fleeing) and is felt in the tension exerted on the finger by the string attached to the circling object. Centrifugal force is equal in magnitude to centripetal force. Like the latter, it may be written as $F_c = \dfrac{mv^2}{r}$. If centripetal force ceases, there is no longer an inward pull on the object and the latter then flies off at a tangent to the direction in which it was moving at the instant the force stopped. Without centripetal force, there will be no centrifugal reaction, and the object will once more travel uniformly in a straight line.

From the equation for centripetal force it can be seen that the amount of centripetal force necessary to keep an object moving in a circular path is directly proportional to its mass. Doubling the mass doubles the centripetal force. If the radius is shortened but the speed is not changed, the amount of centripetal force needed will also increase. Dividing the radius in half doubles the force required. The effect of increasing the speed of the movement is more dramatic.

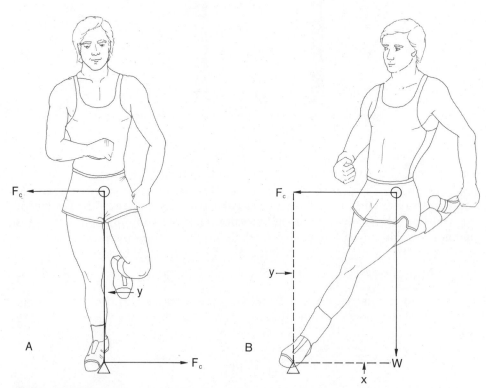

Figure 13–10 A runner must lean in when going around a corner to balance an outward pulling torque ($F_c y$).

Doubling the velocity along the curve increases fourfold the force essential for keeping the object moving in a circle.

When runners or bicyclists negotiate corners with any speed they lean into the curve. If they did not, they would tend to topple outward. Centripetal force is exerted on the body by the ground through the feet or the bicycle wheel. While it pulls horizontally inward at that point, it tends to cause the rest of the body to topple outward because it creates a torque (F_cy) by exerting a force not in line with the center of gravity of the body (Fig. 13–10, A). When one leans in (Fig. 13–10, B), the outward rotating force moment about the feet is balanced by an opposite reacting force moment, Wx, (due to the individual's weight) which is also about the feet. The individual leans in until $F_cy = Wx$. This relationship demonstrates that as F_c increases the amount of lean will also have to increase. When this occurs, x increases, y decreases and W, of course, remains the same. Where speeds are too great or radii too small for participants to negotiate curves successfully, the track may be banked. The amount of banking is determined for the particular radius and the average expected velocity so that the performer may remain perpendicular to the surface as he rounds the curve.

Centripetal–centrifugal forces are also evident in many instances where the body imparts force to an external object. Overarm, side-arm or underarm

Figure 13–11 Centripetal-centrifugal forces operating in weight event. (Boris Djerassi, A.A.U. and N.C.A.A. Hammer throw Champion, 1975. Photograph courtesy of Northeastern University.)

throwing patterns all involve the application of force to the object to be thrown in order to keep it moving in a circular path for all or part of the time before it is released. As soon as the object is released its inertia causes it to move in a straight line. In the hammer throw, the thrower transmits force to the head of the hammer along the flexible wire. This is a centripetal force directed inward toward the axis of rotation. As the performer increases the speed of his rotation the velocity of the hammer increases, and the increased centripetal force the thrower must exert is proportional to the square of the velocity. The outward pulling centrifugal force increases accordingly on the thrower, and he must adjust by leaning back or be pulled off balance. Considerable strength is needed by the thrower to resist the centrifugal force (Fig. 13–11). This is also true with discus throwers who generate considerable centripetal force during the turn prior to delivery, or baseball pitchers whose elbows are subject to great forces because of the tremendous speed with which the forearm is whipped forward in the pitch. Another instance where centripetal force is an important factor is in all swinging activities in gymnastics. Cureton[6] found that although the centrifugal force acting on a 160 pound gymnast was only 121.2 pounds at the top of a giant swing, it was 789.2 pounds at the bottom of the swing.

FORCES MODIFYING MOTION

Friction. Friction is a force which opposes efforts to slide or roll one body over another. Without friction it would be impossible to walk or run or do much of any kind of moving, but on the other hand it increases the difficulty of moving objects about with its deterrent effect. There are numerous examples where we attempt to *increase* friction for more effective performance. The use of rubber soled shoes on hardwood floors or wet decks, spikes on golf shoes and cleats on football shoes improve friction with the supporting surface. Chalk on the gymnast's hands, golf gloves and rubber grips on field hockey sticks are all used to decrease slipping. Even the surfaces of balls are designed to increase friction through irregularities such as the fuzz on the tennis ball or the dimples on a golf ball. Attempts to *decrease* friction are also evident in sports. The sole of one of a bowler's shoes is made to have little friction so that it can slide more easily in the approach. Sharp ice skates apply pressure on the ice and cause slight melting, thus making it easier for the skates to move across the ice, and ice covered with a slight film of water is more slippery than colder, drier ice. Skis are waxed, bicycles are greased and roller skates have ballbearings, each for the purpose of minimizing the retardant effect of friction.

The amount of friction between one surface and another depends upon the nature of the surfaces and the forces pressing them together. Generally speaking, smooth surfaces have less friction than rough surfaces. The area of surfaces in contact with each other does not affect friction. A footlocker pulled along on one end would take as much force to pull as one on its side. But an empty footlocker would take less force than one full of books. *Friction is proportional to the force pressing two surfaces together.*

The force of friction acts parallel to the surfaces which are sliding over each other and opposite to the direction of motion. In Figure 13–12 the book is

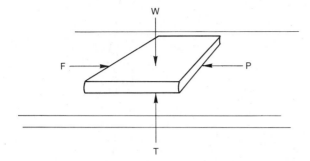

pressing down on the table with a force W equal to its weight. The reactive force of the table, T, pushes up against the book. The force needed to put the book in motion is P. The force resisting the motion, F, is the force due to friction. F equals in magnitude the force P attempting to move the book. The ratio of the force needed to overcome the friction, P, to the force holding the surface together, W, is called the coefficient of friction, μ (mu).

$$\mu = \frac{P}{W}$$

This coefficient indicates the starting friction ratio for these two surfaces. The larger the coefficient the more the surfaces cling together. The smaller the coefficient the easier it is for the two surfaces to begin sliding over each other. A coefficient of 0.0 would indicate completely frictionless surfaces. The equation also shows that the coefficient of friction is totally dependent upon the force holding the surfaces together *(W)* and the force needed to slide one surface over the other *(P)*. The coefficient will decrease as P decreases. Friction is overcome by changing either the surface or the force. If one attempts to push an object forward with a force directed diagonally downward, the force holding the surfaces together is increased and so is the friction. Part of the moving effort is lost. On the other hand, a force directed diagonally forward-upward would decrease the force holding the surfaces together, diminish the friction and make the moving task somewhat easier.

Starting friction, the friction which resists the start of motion, is greater than sliding friction, the friction which resists continued motion. It takes less force to keep something sliding than it does to start it sliding. At low speeds friction usually decreases as speed increases, but at extremely rapid speeds friction increases proportionately until the heat it generates causes the sliding surfaces to disintegrate. While sliding friction is less than starting friction, rolling friction is much less than sliding friction. The movement of heavier objects is much easier when they are put up on wheels. As with sliding friction, rolling friction varies with the nature of the surfaces and the magnitude of the force pushing the two surfaces together. Smooth hard surfaces roll or are rolled upon easier than soft, irregular surfaces. Field hockey players and the golfers know this and must adjust their games to varying surfaces. Obviously, the rolling friction over thick high, wet grass will be greater than that over a hard, dry, closely cropped surface.

The coefficient of friction between two objects may also be found by placing

Figure 13-13   An inclined plane may be used to determine the coefficient of friction, μ, between two surfaces.

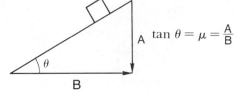

one object on the second and tilting the second until the first starts to slide. The tangent of the angle of the second object with the horizontal is the coefficient of friction (Fig. 13–13). Bunn cites an interesting application of the use of μ with respect to the gripping power of basketball shoes.[4] The amount of lean a player may safely take is equal to the angle θ which the player makes with the vertical, whose tangent $= \dfrac{P}{W}$ (Fig. 13–14). P is the amount of horizontal force needed to cause the feet to start sliding horizontally and W is the weight of the player. Shoes allowing a greater lean would certainly afford their wearers an advantage in the game. For this information to be of use to shoe manufacturers a standard type floor surface and a standard weight or prototype ball player would have to be determined and used in the ratio.

Fluid Forces.   The external forces of air and water have considerable effect upon the movements of the human body and of external implements. The influence of these forces is noticeable in many circumstances. A discus sails, a baseball curves, a volleyball "wobbles" and a shuttlecock drops because of contact with air currents. Skyjumpers and hang gliders control their flight paths by interacting with the air currents, while downhill racers, swimmers and divers streamline their bodies to minimize the effect of fluid resistance.

Water and air are both fluids and are subject to many of the same laws and principles. If one were to place a hand in a moving stream of water or in the air stream of a circulating fan, so that the hand is perpendicular to the path of the flow, considerable pressure would be felt on the hand as the fluid pushed against it. Turning the hand so that it is now horizontal to the fluid flow diminishes the pressure against the hand considerably. In fact very little if any pressure is felt and it is quite easy to hold the hand in this position. A position halfway between these two, i.e., at 45 degrees to the flow direction, results in the feeling of some uplift pressure as well as backward pressure (Fig. 13–15). The flat hand allows the layers of air or water to flow over it with little distortion, and only some small resistance or *drag* is evident at the leading edge of the hand. In

Figure 13-14   The amount of lean a basketball player can safely assume depends upon the friction between the floor and his shoes.

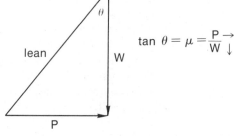

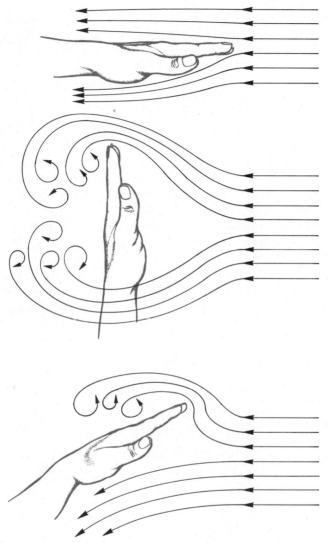

Figure 13-15 Patterns of air flow around an object vary with the shape of the frontal surface.

contrast, the vertical hand has considerable pressure or drag on the front edge, and in addition, more resistance due to suction behind the hand as the displaced air goes around the hand and tries to fill in the vacuum behind. Numerous examples exist of technique forms which attempt to minimize this frontal drag through streamlining. In all instances as little frontal surface as possible is presented. Skaters, skiers, bicyclists and divers all assume positions which diminish as much as possible the frontal surface area. In addition they wear tightly fitted clothing to assist with the streamlining.

The tilted hand experiences both lift and drag. The lift is due to a build-up of air pressure on the underside compared to the topside, and the drag comes from frictional or surface forces acting on the tilted hand as well as the drag due to its form. The ratio between lift and drag becomes extremely important in sports like discus throwing or ski jumping. Any changes in the angle of tilt or the air speed with respect to the object or body will produce a variation in lift and drag, and resultant differences in distance traveled by the object.

The air pattern which surrounds a moving object may be smooth or turbulent. Air passing around a smooth surface at slow speeds is usually smooth or laminar air while high speeds and rough surfaces may cause laminar air to break up and become turbulent. Rotating balls act differently with respect to laminar flow than straight balls. A straight ball may cause laminar air to break up and become turbulent. This is likely to happen if the ball has an uneven or irregular surface or a large surface area. The result is a wobbling or wavering such as is observed when a volleyball is served or thrown with no spin. A ball traveling at high speeds with no initial spin may also curve as a result of the laminar air becoming turbulent. This is often seen in baseball.

An extremely important principle which applies to laminar air was discovered by Bernoulli. Simply stated, he determined that *the pressure in a moving fluid decreases as its speed increases.* A sheet of paper held by two corners will rise at its loose end if one blows over the surface of the paper. The air moving over the top of the paper is moving at a faster speed than the air

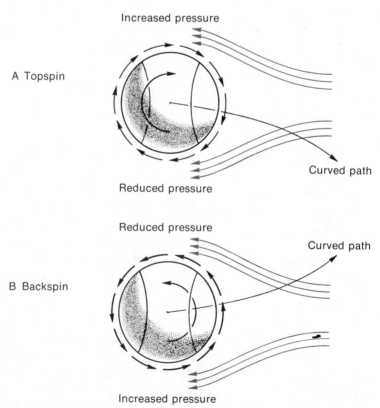

Figure 13–16 A spinning ball follows a curved path moving in the direction of least pressure. (The curve is exaggerated for clarity.)

under the paper. The pressure on top therefore is less and the paper rises. Similarly if one hangs two tennis balls on strings and then blows a stream of air between them, the balls will move closer to each other in the direction of the lowered pressure. Bernouilli's principle applies for moving objects passing through a stationary fluid as well as for fluids passing stationary objects. A ball moving through the air will also move in the direction of least air pressure. If the ball is spinning it will follow a curved path. As shown in Figure 13–16, A, the ball spinning in a clockwise direction drags around a boundary layer of air. At the bottom of the ball this air current is moving in the same direction as the on-coming air. At the top, the boundary air is moving in the opposite direction. The air at the bottom is moving faster, and therefore the pressure is reduced. The air at the top moves more slowly and the pressure is increased. Thus the ball will move in a downward curve in the direction of least pressure. Viewed from the side this would be the behavior of a ball with top spin imparted to it. Balls with top spin drop sooner than balls with no spin. A ball with a counterclockwise or back spin will move in an upward curve and thus stay aloft longer than a ball with no spin (Fig. 13–16, B). Balls spinning about a vertical axis have side spin. Right spin causes the ball to curve to the right and occurs when the forward edge of the ball moves to the right. Left spin is the opposite.

The amount of air a ball drags around with it when spinning depends upon the surface of the ball and the speed of the spin. Rough or large surfaces, small mass and a fast spin speed will all produce a more noticeable spin and curve deflection. The small mass of a table tennis ball, the fuzz on a tennis ball and the seams on a baseball all enhance spin, an important element in each game's strategy. The deflection will also be more pronounced if the forward velocity is slow. This may occur because of little force imparted to the ball or a strong head wind. Spin on a ball may also smooth its flight by acting as a stabilizer. Like a gyroscope, a football or discus spinning around one axis resists spinning about another axis and therefore is less likely to tumble through the air.

Rebounding Forces. Objects which rebound from each other do so in a fairly predictable manner. The nature of a rebound is governed by the elasticity, mass and velocity of the rebounding surfaces, the friction between the surfaces and the angle with which one object contacts the second.

ELASTICITY. Any time two or more objects come into contact with each other some distortion or deformation occurs. Whether or not the distortion is permanent depends upon the elasticity of the interacting objects. Elasticity is the ability of an object to resist distorting influences and to return to its original size and shape when the distorting forces are removed. The force which acts on an object to distort it is called *stress.* The distortion which occurs is called *strain,* and is proportional to the stress causing it. Stress may take the form of tension, as in the stretching of a spring, compression, as in the squeezing of a tennis ball, flexion, such as the bending of a fencing foil or torsion, as in the twisting of the spring (Fig. 13–17). In all cases the object tends to resume its original shape when the stress is removed. If the stress is too large the elastic limit of the object is exceeded and permanent distortion occurs.

Substances vary in their resistance to distorting forces and in their ability to regain their original shape after being deformed. One usually thinks of a material such as rubber as being highly elastic since it yields easily to a dis-

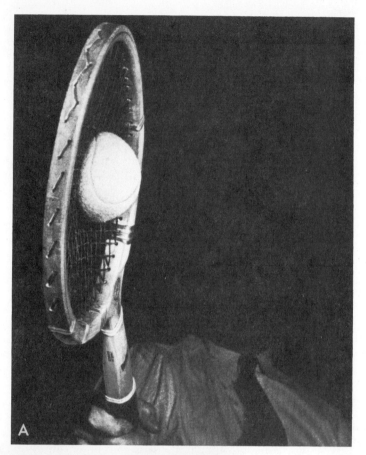

Figure 13–17 Compression of tennis ball (*A*) and golf ball (*B*) at moment of impact. (Courtesy of H. E. Edgerton.)

torting force and returns to its original shape. Actually, substances which are hard to distort and return perfectly to their original shape are more elastic. Gasses, liquids, highly tempered steel and brass are examples. In comparing the elasticity of different substances, coefficients of elasticity are used. A *coefficient of elasticity* or restitution is defined as the stress divided by the strain. The coefficient of elasticity most commonly determined in sports activities is that caused in the compression of balls. If one drops a ball onto a hard surface like a floor, the coefficient of restitution may be determined by comparing the drop height with the bounce height:

$$e = \sqrt{\frac{\text{bounce height}}{\text{drop height}}}\,.$$

(e = coefficient of restitution or elasticity)

The closer the coefficient approaches 1.0 the more perfect the elasticity. Rules require that a basketball should be inflated to rebound to a height of 49 to 54 inches at its top when its bottom is dropped from a height of 72 inches. For the maximum bounce height this is a coefficient of .781. In comparison, a volleyball dropped from the same height and inflated to 6 psi (pounds per square inch) rebounds to 51 inches and has a coefficient of .84. A tennis ball has a coefficient of .73 and a leather covered softball one of .46. The coefficient of restitution may also be found in another way. Because the law of conservation of momenum states that the total momentum in any impact between the objects must remain the same, the momentum of one object may be reduced, but the momentum of the other will increase proportionately. Since the mass of neither object changes,

$$e = \frac{V_2 - V_1}{U_1 - U_2}$$

where V_2 and V_1 are the velocities after impact and U_1 and U_2 are the velocities before impact.

ANGLE OF REBOUND.   An elastic object dropped vertically onto a rebounding surface will compress uniformly on its underside and rebound vertically upward. An elastic object which strikes a rebounding surface obliquely will compress unevenly on the bottom and rebound at an oblique angle. The size of the angle compared to the striking angle depends upon the elasticity of the striking object and the friction between the two surfaces. The rebound of a perfectly elastic object is similar to the reflection of light: *the angle of incidence is equal to the angle of reflection* (Fig. 13–18). Variations from this ideal are to be expected as the coefficient of restitution varies. Low coefficients will generally produce angles of reflection greater than angles of incidence. For example, an underinflated volleyball or basketball will rebound at an angle closer to the surface than it struck it. Friction also affects the angle. Whereas the coefficient of elasticity affects the vertical component of the rebound, friction will affect the horizontal component and decrease it. It is possible that a decreased horizontal component related to the coefficient of elasticity could occur in proportion to the decreased vertical velocity so that although the resultant velocity of the rebound

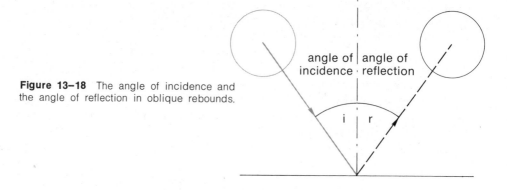

Figure 13–18 The angle of incidence and the angle of reflection in oblique rebounds.

would be less than the initial velocity, the angle of reflection would equal the angle of incidence.

Spin also influences rebounding angles. Balls thrown with topspin will rebound from horizontal surfaces lower and with more horizontal velocity than that with which they struck. They will tend to roll farther also, an action often desirable on long golf drives. Balls hitting a horizontal surface with backspin rebound at a higher bounce and are slower. Balls with back spin also roll for shorter distances than those with top or no spin. Because of the compression of the ball and the friction between it and the surface, a ball with no spin hitting the surface at an angle will develop some top spin on the rebound, and a ball hitting with top spin will develop greater top spin upon rebounding. With back spin however, the spin may be completely stopped or reversed. A ball with side spin will rebound in the direction of the spin. A ball spinning or curving to the right will "kick" to the right upon rebounding and a left spinning ball will do the reverse.

When spinning balls hit vertical surfaces such as a basketball backboard or a squash court wall, they will respond in relation to the surface in the same manner as with horizontal surfaces. When the vertical surface is struck from below, a ball with no spin or top spin will have added spin on rebound, and the angle of reflection will be greater than the angle of incidence. With back spin the spin will stop or reverse and the angle of reflection will be less than the incidence angle. For this to be true, a back spinning ball approaching a vertical wall from above must be regarded as moving with top spin in relation to the rebounding surface. Similarly a top spinning ball hitting the vertical surface from above is in actuality spinning backwards with respect to the rebounding surface.

When a spinning ball meets a forward moving object as in tennis or table tennis, the ball will rebound in a direction that will be the resultant of the forces acting on it at impact. For example, a ball with top spin striking a stationary vertical surface head on will rebound upward. That same ball (with top spin) striking a moving vertical surface, like a tennis racquet, will also rebound upward but not as much because the resultant rebound has a horizontal force component from the forward moving tennis racquet. Nevertheless, the upward direction may be sufficient to send the ball out of bounds. To counteract the upward direction the racquet face can be turned obliquely downward, thus adding a downward compensating force component, as well as changing the spin of the ball. The resultant force path of a rebounding ball is controlled by several factors. When one attempts to predict the direction of the rebound, the momentums of both the ball and the striking implement must be considered, as well as the elasticity of the two objects, the spin of the ball and the angle of impact. Awareness of these factors and the ways in which they affect play have numerous and valuable applications in sports such as handball, squash racquets, racquetball, table tennis, paddleball and tennis.

LABORATORY EXPERIENCES

1. Place a book on a table and stand a small bottle on top of it. Pull the book toward you with a quick jerk. Note the action of the bottle. Stand the bottle on the book again and pull the book across the table with a steady pull. How does the bottle move? Now pull the book and stop it suddenly. Explain the action of the bottle in all three instances.

2. Stand on a frictionless turntable or sit on a swivel stool. Hold a 5-pound weight in each hand and hold the arms out to the side. Have a partner spin you around. Alternately bring your hands into your shoulders and move them out to the side. Explain the changes in your angular velocity.

3. Stand on a frictionless turntable or sit on a swivel stool. Determine how you can rotate yourself moving just your arms. Explain why your arm motions make the rotation possible.

4. Hit a softball with a bat from a tee, from a self toss and from a pitch. Which hit goes the farthest? Explain.

5. Determine the coefficient of restitution for each of the following objects dropped from a height of 72 inches onto a wooden floor:
   a. hockey ball
   b. lacrosse ball
   c. golf ball
   d. soccer ball
   e. baseball
   Repeat the calculations for the above objects rebounding from concrete, from asphalt tile, from artificial turf and from a tumbling mat.

6. Lie on your back in the water with your arms over your head. Raise your legs by flexing your hips. What happens to your arms and trunk? Explain. Devise another experiment which demonstrates the same principle.

7. Perform a vertical jump with and without the use of your arms. Have someone compare the height of the two jumps by noting the level of the top of your head. A chart with numbered horizontal lines on the wall behind you will help in scoring. The observer's eyes should be at the level of the top of your head at the peak of the jump. Repeat several times and compare your results with those of others doing the same experiment. Explain the results.

8. Using a tennis racquet or a paddle, impart top spin, back spin, no spin and side spin to a ball. Note the effect on the velocity and angle of reflection when the ball rebounds from a horizontal surface; from a vertical surface when struck from above; and from a vertical surface when struck from below.

9. While both of you have on ice skates or roller skates, stand facing someone whose weight is the same as yours. Push against each other. Observe and compare the distance and velocity each of you move. Repeat the procedure with someone who weighs considerably more or less than you do. Explain the difference between the two performances.

REFERENCES

1. Basford, L.: The Restlessness of Matter. London: Sampson Low, Marston & Co., 1966.
2. Basford, L.: The Science of Movement. London: Sampson Low, Marston & Co., 1966.
3. Broer, M.: Efficiency of Human Movement, 3rd Ed. Philadelphia: W. B. Saunders Company, 1973.
4. Bunn, J. W.: Scientific Principles of Coaching, 2nd Ed. Englewood Cliffs, N.J.: Prentice-Hall, Inc., 1972.
5. Cooper, J. M., and Glassow, R. B.: Kinesiology, 3rd Ed. St. Louis: C. V. Mosby, 1972.
6. Cureton, T. K.: Elementary principles and techniques of cinematographic analysis. Res. Quart. Am. Assn. Health, Phys. Ed. & Recrn., 10:3–24 (May), 1939.
7. Dull, C. E., Metcalfe, H. C., and Williams, J. E.: Modern Physics. New York: Holt, Rinehart and Winston, 1963.
8. Dyson, G.: The Mechanics of Athletics, 5th Ed. London: University of London Press, 1970.
9. Hay, J. G.: The Biomechanics of Sports Techniques. Englewood Cliffs, N.J.: Prentice-Hall, Inc., 1973.
10. Ruchlis, H.: Orbit: A Picture Story of Force and Motion: New York: Harper & Row Publishers, Inc., 1958.
11. Tricker, R. A. R., and Tricker, B. J. K.: The Science of Movement. New York: American Elsevier, 1967.
12. Williams, M., and Lissner, H. R.: Biomechanics of Human Motion. Philadelphia: W. B. Saunders Company, 1962.

Chapter Fourteen

FORCE
AND EQUILIBRIUM

One's body is constantly subject to forces even when no motion is evident. When this condition exists, the sum of all the forces acting on the body are balanced and the forces are said to be in *equilibrium*. The sum of all of the horizontal forces equals zero, the sum of all the vertical forces equals zero and the sum of all the moments which would cause rotation is also zero. The person in Figure 14–1 is balanced because the sum of all the forces acting on her equals zero. The forces are in equilibrium.

CENTER OF GRAVITY

The location of the center of gravity in the human body is extremely important in determining the state of equilibrium at any moment. The performer's body in Figure 14–1 is made up of numerous particles with each particle having weight and exerting a downward force. All of these forces are parallel, and if they are summed, the total is the resultant vertical force acting on the performer. This resultant force equals the actual weight of the body. The point where it is applied to the whole body is called the *center of gravity* of the body. The center of gravity is the point where the sum of all the forces and force moments acting on the body is zero. It is the equilibrium point.

The center of gravity of a body is sometimes described as its balance or pivot point. A simple experiment to locate the pivot point consists of suspending an irregularly shaped object by a string and letting it hang until it ceases to move. A vertical line is then drawn on the object from its point of suspension as a continuation of the string. The object is then suspended from another point, and the vertical continuation line is drawn again (Fig. 14–2). This procedure is repeated once more. The point *G* where the three lines intersect is the center of gravity of the object. If the object is suspended from *G*, it will hang in whatever position it is placed as if the weight of the object were all concentrated at this point. It is for this reason that the center of gravity is sometimes defined as the point where all of the weight of the object is concentrated. More accurately, it is the point where the weight of the body may be said to act.

The location of the center of gravity of any object remains fixed as long as the body does not change shape. In rigid bodies of homogeneous mass, the center of gravity is at the geometric center. Where the density of a rigid body

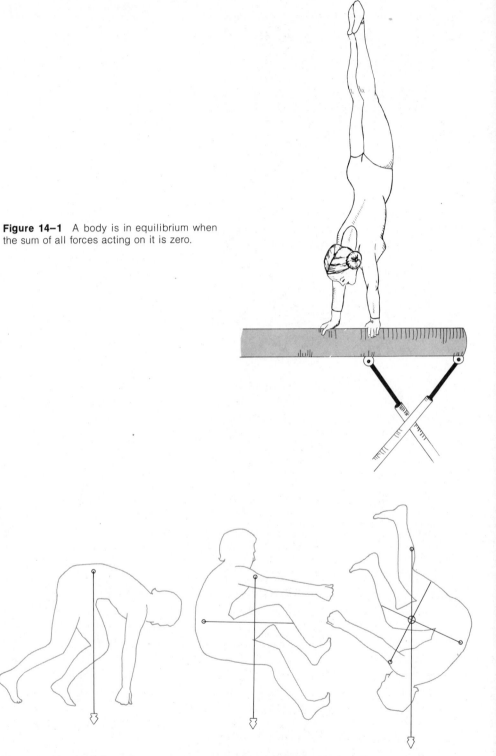

Figure 14–1 A body is in equilibrium when the sum of all forces acting on it is zero.

Figure 14–2 Location of center of gravity in irregularly shaped object.

varies, the center of gravity is not at the geometric center but is shifted toward the more weighted section. If an object's shape or position changes, the location of the center of gravity will also change. This happens in the human body (Fig. 14–3). It is a segmented structure, capable of numerous positions, and the location of its center of gravity changes accordingly. This is an important consideration in the execution of sports skills. The evolution of the technique for the high jump shows how the change of placement of the center of gravity in the body increased the height of the bar over which the jumper could project himself (Fig. 14–4). As one changes the relationship of the body segments to each other, the center of gravity may even be located completely outside of the body itself.

The location of the center of gravity of a human being in the normal standing position varies with body build, age and sex. A number of experiments relating to the center of gravity were made by Hellebrandt[8] at the University of Wisconsin. She found the height of the center of gravity in women to be 55 per cent of their standing height. In other studies, Croskey, Dawson, Luessen, Marohn and Wright found the center of gravity in men to be 56.18 per cent of their height and in women, 55.44 per cent.[2] They also found that the height of the center of gravity was considerably more variable in women than in men. They found no correlation between the height of the center of gravity and body weight or height.

In a series of studies on the relation of age to the height of the center of gravity, Palmer[12] found that the latter maintained a fairly constant ratio to the height of the individual at all ages, ranging from 55 to 59 per cent. From the age of 6 fetal months to 70 years the center of gravity was found to descend gradually from the level of the seventh thoracic vertebra to the level of the first sacral segment. Swearingen, et al[15] substantiated these results in their studies of the center of gravity of infants. In addition they found that the height of the center of gravity above the crotch remains more or less constant at six inches throughout life.

Hellebrandt also studied the way in which the body sways when a person attempts to stand still[9] and observed that although the center of gravity of the body as a whole shifts constantly during relaxed and effortless standing, the

Figure 14–3 A shift in segment configuration results in a relocation of the body's center of gravity. (Drawn from motion picture film tracing.)

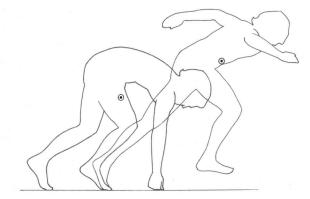

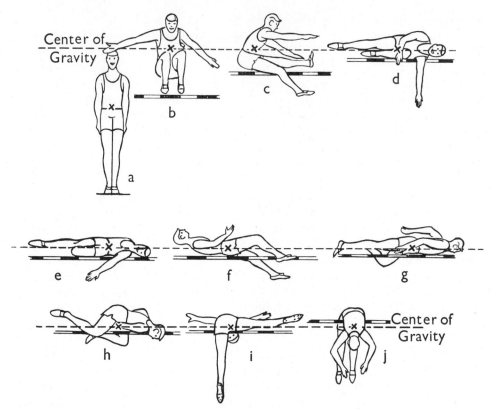

Figure 14–4 Effect of shift in center of gravity on high jump performance. (From Dyson, G. H. G.: The Mechanics of Athletics. London: University of London Press, 1970.)

patterns formed by a trajectory of the shifting center of weight and the mean position of the vertical projection of this theoretical point (i.e., the line of gravity) are relatively constant. She found that the average area of maximal sway for a group of men and women was only 4.09 square centimeters and that the differences between the men and the women were not statistically significant. It was noted that although the line of gravity intersected the base of support close to its center, in the majority of subjects it was slightly to the left and behind the exact center. In a study on the influence of shoes on the position of the center of gravity, Hellebrandt found that shoes of low and of moderate heels had a negligible effect upon postural stability and the position of the line of gravity, but that high heeled shoes tended to cause a forward shifting of the line of gravity and to increase the amount of swaying, apparently indicating a decrease in stability.

STABILITY AND EQUILIBRIUM

Objects in equilibrium are classified according to the stability of that equilibrium. If the position of an object is slightly altered and the object tends to return to its original position, the object is in *stable* equilibrium. Stable equilibrium occurs when an object is placed in such a fashion that an effort to disturb it would require its center of gravity to be raised. Thus it would tend to fall back in place (Fig. 14–5, *A*). The more its center of gravity has to be raised to up-end it, the more stable it is. A brick on its side is more stable than one on end because its center of gravity needs to be raised higher to up-end it. The wrestler and the defensive lineman both know the value of shifting body position to increase stability by lowering the center of gravity. In fact, if for any reason, the equilibrium is too precarious, assuming a crouching, kneeling or sitting position will lower the center of gravity and increase stability.

Unstable equilibrium exists when it takes only a slight push to destroy it. This is the situation when the center of gravity of the object drops to a lower point when the object is tilted (Fig. 14–5, *B*). A pencil on end or a tightrope walker displays unstable equilibrium because the center of gravity is bound to be lowered if either loses its balance. Swimmers standing on the starting block poised for the start of a race or sprint runners at the start of their race are in unstable equilibrium, as are toe dancers on point or balance beam performers. In each instance the center of gravity will be lowered if the individual is disturbed so that rotation occurs around the point of support.

The third classification of equilibrium is called *neutral* equilibrium, and exists when an object's center of gravity is neither raised nor lowered when it is disturbed (Fig. 14–5, *C*). A ball lying on a table is in neutral equilibrium. Objects in neutral equilibrium will come to rest in any position without a change in level of the center of gravity. Upon receiving a slight push such objects neither fall backward nor forward.

STABILITY AND THE HUMAN BODY

Because man ordinarily holds himself in an upright position and because the law of gravity is always in operation on this earth, the problems of stability are ever present. Probably the only time the human body is not adjusting itself in response to gravitational force is when it is in a position of complete repose. Either consciously or unconsciously, man spends most of his waking hours adjusting his position to the type of equilibrium best suited to the task.

The ability to maintain one's balance under unfavorable circumstances is recognized as one of the basic motor skills. Standing on tiptoes or on one foot without losing one's balance, or maintaining a headstand or a handstand for an

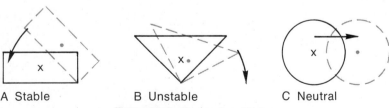

A Stable   B Unstable   C Neutral

Figure 14–5 Types of equilibrium.

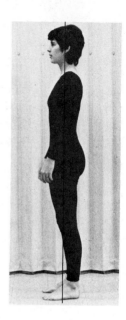

Figure 14–6 Position of the body in which the line of gravity falls approximately through the center of the base of support. This is a stable position.

appreciable length of time is such a skill. These particular feats are examples of static balance, and the mark of skill is to accomplish them with a minimum of motion.

Familiarity with the following factors of stability will enable the student to analyze his balance problems and may suggest to the teacher the means of helping his less skillful students. It should also enable the physical therapist to help amputees and paralytics regain their lost sense of equilibrium.

The Relation of the Line of Gravity to the Base of Support. An object retains its equilibrium only so long as its line of gravity falls within its base of support. When the force that the body is resisting is the downward force of gravity, the

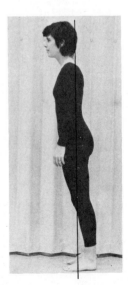

Figure 14–7 Position of the body in which the line of gravity falls near the anterior margin of the base of support. This position is less stable than the one shown in Fig. 14–6.

Figure 14–8 Compensating for a unilateral load by bending to opposite side.

nearer the line of gravity to the *center* of the base of support, the greater the stability (Fig. 14–6), and conversely, the nearer the line of gravity to the *margin* of the base of support, the more precarious the equilibrium (Fig. 14–7). Once it passes beyond the margin, stability is lost and a new base must be established. It is this factor which constitutes the major problem in some modern dance techniques, in balance stunts, in walking a tightrope and in building pyramids. For developing the neuromuscular control necessary for acquiring such skills as these, there is no substitute for repeated practice. There are, however, a few devices that help one to keep the center of gravity centered over the base of support. One of these we do almost unconsciously. If we carry a heavy weight

Figure 14–9 Compensation for a unilateral load by inclining the entire body to the opposite side.

at one side of the body (e.g., a suitcase or a pail of water), *this constitutes a unilateral* load which, if uncompensated, would shift the center of gravity to that side, bringing it dangerously close to the margin of the base of support. By raising the opposite arm sideways, by bending or leaning to the opposite side, or by a combination of these, we counterbalance the external load and keep the line of gravity close to the center of the base of support (Figs. 14–8 and 14–9). Another application of the principle of keeping the line of gravity over the center of the base of support is seen in the tightrope walker who carries a balancing pole or, to a lesser degree, in the gymnast walking on a balance beam with his arms extended sideward.

When the external force acting on a body is a lateral one, stability is increased if the line of gravity is placed so that it will continue to remain over the base even when forced to move by the external force. Leaning into the wind (Fig. 14–10) or pushing a heavy chest are examples where the line of gravity should be close to the edge of the base of support nearest the oncoming force. Pulling in a tug of war is an example of having the gravity line near the edge of the base of support farthest away from the external force. When one is not certain from which direction an external force may be applied, equilibrium is most stable when the line of gravity is in the center of the base of support.

There are also occasions in movement activities when a person may wish to place the line of gravity so that the equilibrium is unstable. Swimmers and runners waiting for the start of a race assume a position in which the line of gravity is as close to the front edge as possible, since they wish to lose balance rapidly.

 The Height of the Center of Gravity. Ordinarily, man's center of gravity is located approximately at the level of the upper third of the sacrum. This is true only for the normal standing position. If the arms are raised or if a weight is carried above waist level, the center of gravity shifts to a higher position and it becomes more difficult to maintain one's equilibrium. Activities and stunts such as walking on stilts, canoeing and balancing a weight on the head are difficult or dangerous because of the relatively high center of gravity. Lowering the center of gravity will increase the stability of the body because it allows

Figure 14–10 Leaning into the wind to balance the effect of its force on the body.

greater angular displacement of the center of gravity within the bounds of the base of support (Fig. 14–11).

The Size and Shape of the Base of Support.   It is obvious that a wide base of support adds to the stability of an object. In addition to the height of the center of gravity, much of the difficulty experienced in walking on a balance beam, a railroad track or a tightrope, or in ice skating and toe dancing is due to the narrow base of support. The problem is to keep the center of gravity over the base of support, a requisite for maintaining equilibrium. The wider the base, the easier this is.

In a man whose weight is supported entirely by his feet, the base of support includes not only his two feet but also the intervening area (Fig. 14–12). If the feet are separated, the base is widened and the equilibrium improved. An individual on crutches will be more stable if he places the crutches forward, making a triangular base instead of a linear one (Fig. 14–13, *A*). There is another factor, however, that must not be overlooked. If one takes a stance that is wider than the breadth of the pelvis, the legs will assume a slanting position. This introduces a horizontal component of force. If this is accompanied by insufficient friction between the feet and the supporting surface, as when standing on ice, obviously a widening of the base of support does not make for greater stability. In fact, the wider the stance, the less one can control the sliding of the feet. From this we see that we must observe *all* the principles which apply to a situation. Observance of only one may not bring the results expected.

In addition to the size of the base of support, the shape is also a factor in

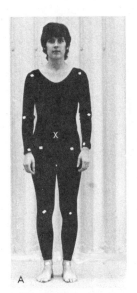

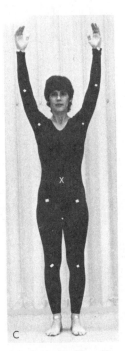

Figure 14–11 The height of the center of gravity changes with a change in body position. X = center of gravity.

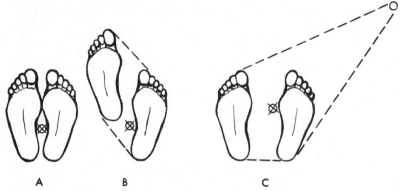

Figure 14–12 The position of the feet determines the size of the supporting area beneath the body. Use of a cane greatly extends the base of support in *C* and the area over which the body is stable. (From Williams, M., and Lissner, H. R.: Biomechanics of Human Motion. Philadelphia: W. B. Saunders Company, 1962.)

stability. To resist lateral external forces the base should be widened in the direction of the oncoming force. In Figure 14–13, *C* the position provides great stability for lateral forces from the side but very little from the front or back. Where the forces are known to be coming from a forward-backward direction, as when catching a swift ball or spotting a performer in gymnastics, a forward-

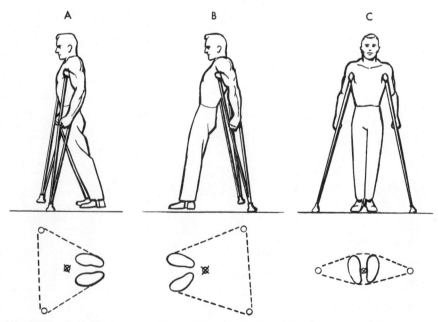

Figure 14–13 Bases of support with varying degrees of stability. Can you rank these from most stable to least stable? The subject in *A* and *B* is secure primarily in the anteroposterior direction; the position in *C* provides greater stability in the frontal plane than in the sagittal plane. (From Williams, M., and Lissner, H. R.: Biomechanics of Human Motion. Philadelphia: W. B. Saunders Company, 1962.)

backward stance is recommended. A similar adjustment is made when one stands in a bus or a subway train. The tendency to be thrown backward when the vehicle starts up is resisted either by standing sideways with the feet in a moderately wide stance, or by facing forward and leaning forward with one foot placed forward. These automatic reactions to external forces are for one purpose only, namely, to enable one to keep the center of gravity over the base of support in spite of the disturbing lateral forces. When the direction of on-coming force cannot be predicted, a square stance is probably best.

The Mass of the Body. The mass or weight of an object is a factor in equilibrium only when motion or an external force is involved. It is a matter of common observation that an empty cardboard carton is more likely to blow down the street than one filled with canned goods. Likewise, a 250-pound lineman is less likely to be brushed aside than is a 130-pound one. In all sports involving physical contact, the heavy, solid individual stands a better chance of keeping his footing than does the lightweight one. When all factors are considered, how-ever, mass is less of a factor in stability than are the location of the line of gravity and the height of the center of gravity.

Friction. Friction as a factor in stability has already been suggested in relation to the size of the base of support. It has even greater influence when the body is in motion or is being acted upon by an external force. Inadequate friction is what makes it difficult to keep one's equilibrium when walking on an icy pavement, particularly if a frisky dog tugs unexpectedly on its leash. When the supporting surface presents insufficient friction, the footgear can make up for it. The person who must walk on icy pavements can wear "creepers" on his shoes; the golfer and the field hockey player can wear cleats; and the gym-nast and basketball player can wear rubber-soled shoes.

Segmentation. If, instead of being in one solid piece, an object consists of a series of segments placed one above the other, the problem of retaining its equilibrium is a multiple one. Maximum stability of a segmented body is assured when the centers of gravity of all the weight-bearing segments lie in a vertical line which is centered over the base of support. In a column of blocks, this means that each block must be centered over the block beneath. In a jointed column, as in the human body, one segment cannot slide off another, but it is quite possible for the segments to be united in a zigzag alignment. Such is all too often the case in man's posture. In fact, the alignment of the body segments is a widely used criterion for judging standing posture. When the segments are aligned in a single vertical line, the posture is not only more pleasing in appear-ance to most of us, but there is less likelihood of strain to the joints and muscles. When one segment gets out of line, there is usually a compensatory disalign-ment of another segment in order to maintain a balanced position of the body as a whole. (In other words, for every "zig" there is a "zag.") At every point of angulation between segments there is uneven tension thrown on the ligaments and uneven tonus in opposing muscle groups. This causes fatigue, if not actual strain.

The addition of an external weight to the body, as when one carries books, babies or suitcases, may be thought of as the addition of a segment. The addi-tional segment will add mass to the body and change its stability somewhat. More important, though, is the effect on the height of the center of gravity and the location of the line of gravity. The center of gravity will be displaced in the direction of the added weight, and the line of gravity will shift accordingly. Its new location will be governed by the nature of compensation made to accommodate the additional weight (Figs. 14–8 and 14–9).

Visual and Psychologic Factors. Factors which belong in this category are less easily explained than the others but are familiar to everyone. The giddiness that many experience when walking close to an unprotected edge high above the ground or when crossing a swirling river on a foot bridge is a real detriment to one's equilibrium. Even if the supporting surface is entirely adequate, the sense of balance may be disturbed. A common means of preserving the balance, both in this type of situation and when walking on a narrow rail, is to fix the eyes on a stationary spot above or beyond the "danger area." This seems to facilitate neuromuscular control by reducing the disturbing stimuli.

Physiologic Factors. Besides the visual and psychologic factors there are also physiologic factors related to the physical mechanism for equilibrium, namely, the semicircular canals. In addition to actual lesions of this mechanism, any disturbance of the general physical condition is likely to affect the sense of balance. Feelings of dizziness accompanying nausea or any form of debility reduce one's ability to resist other factors which threaten the equilibrium. These physiologic factors are largely beyond our control. One principle which can be derived from them, however, is that it is better to avoid situations which are likely to threaten the equilibrium when there is a temporary physiologic disturbance.

PRINCIPLES OF STABILITY

The principles of stability are stated here as simply and concisely as possible, and brief applications are suggested in each case.

Principle I. Other things being equal, the lower the center of gravity, the greater will be the body's stability.

Applications

a. The easiest and safest pyramids for beginners are those in which the participants are on their hands and knees. This position provides for a lower center of gravity than the kneeling or standing position.

b. In canoeing the kneeling position represents a compromise position which combines the advantages of stability and ease of using the arms for paddling. Kneeling is preferable to sitting on the seat because the lowering of the center of gravity makes the position a more stable one. While it is less stable than sitting on the floor of the canoe, it is a more convenient position for paddling. A position frequently recommended is kneeling and sitting against a thwart or the edge of a seat.

c. A performer on a balance beam quickly squats when she feels herself losing her balance.

d. A wrestler tries to remain as stable as possible by lowering his center of gravity.

Principle II. Greater stability is obtained if the base of support is widened in the direction of the line of force.

Applications

a. This helps an individual to keep from being thrown off balance when he punches with force, pushes a heavy object or throws a fast ball. It also enables him to "put his weight behind his punch" because with a relatively wide forward-backward stance he can shift his weight from the rear foot to the forward foot as he delivers the impetus.

b. In pushing and pulling heavy furniture he can put his whole body into the act without loss of balance.

c. When catching a fast moving object like a baseball or a heavy one like a medicine ball, widening the base in line with the direction of the force enables the catcher to "give" as he catches, and in this way to provide a greater distance in which to reduce or stop the motion of the object. It also assures greater accuracy by reducing the likelihood of rebound.

d. The military "at ease" is more stable than the position of "attention."

e. Keeping one's balance when standing on a bus or train which is accelerating or decelerating is facilitated by widening the stance in the direction that the vehicle is moving, that is, in a forward-backward direction in relation to the vehicle.

Principle III.   For maximum stability the line of gravity should intersect the base of support at a point which will allow the greatest range of movement within the area of the base in the direction of forces causing motion.

Applications

a. A football player knowing he will be pushed from in front should lean forward so that he can "give" in a backward direction without losing his balance.

b. A person in a tug-of-war line leans backward in preparation for absorbing a strong forward pull from the opponent.

c. A tennis player anticipating her opponent's return will keep her line of gravity centered so that she can shift her center of gravity quickly in any direction without loss of balance.

d. Dragging a heavy box forward on a high shelf and then lifting it down is an activity in the home to which this principle applies. Assuming a forward-backward stance and leaning forward for this act gives the individual a wider distance for receiving the weight of this forward moving object. This decreases the likelihood of his being thrown off balance when the box suddenly comes free of the shelf. It also enables him to take a step backward which makes it easier for him to lower the box in front of him and to keep control of it. With a sideward stance he would be likely to be thrown off balance as the box comes free. There is also the danger of his exerting so much horizontal force that instead of lowering the box in front of him he swings it back overhead, hyperextending his spine and running the risk of straining his back.

e. Basketball and other team games involving running often require sudden reversals of direction. If the player tries to turn while his feet are close together his momentum is likely to throw him off balance. This can be prevented if he spreads his feet to check his forward motion and leans back so that his line of gravity will be toward the rear. He can then quickly pivot to reverse his direction.

Principle IV.   Other things being equal, the greater the mass of a body, the greater will be its stability.

Application.   In sports in which resistance to impact is a factor, heavy, solid individuals are more likely to maintain their equilibrium than lighter ones. This provides one basis for selecting linemen in football.

Principle V. Other things being equal, the most stable position of a vertical segmented body (such as a column of blocks or the erect human body) is one in which the center of gravity of each weight-bearing segment lies in a vertical line centered over the base of support or in which deviations in one direction are exactly balanced by deviations in the opposite direction.

Applications

a. This applies to postural adjustments for achieving a pleasing, well-balanced alignment of the body segments, both with and without external loads.

b. In pyramid building and other balance stunts in which one person (or group of persons) supports the weight of another person or persons, the chief problem is one of either aligning or balancing the several centers of gravity over the center of the base of support.

Principle VI. Other things being equal, the greater the friction between the supporting surface and the parts of the body in contact with it, the more stable the body will be.

Application. The wearing of cleats and rubber-soled shoes for sport activities not only aids in locomotion but also serves to increase one's stability in positions held momentarily between quick or forceful movements, as in basketball, fencing, football, field hockey, lacrosse and other sports.

Principle VII. Other things being equal, a person has better balance in locomotion under difficult circumstances when he focuses his vision on stationary objects rather than on disturbing stimuli.

Application. Beginners learning to walk on a balance beam or perform balance stunts and others who for any reason have difficulty in keeping their balance can minimize disturbing visual stimuli by fixing their eyes on a stationary spot in front of them, either at eye level or somewhat above eye level.

Principle VIII. There is a positive relationship between one's physical and emotional state and the ability to maintain balance under difficult circumstances.

Application. Persons should not be permitted to attempt dangerous balance stunts or activities requiring expert balance ability when their physical or emotional health is impaired.

Principle IX. Regaining equilibrium is based on the same principles as maintaining it.

Applications

a. After an unexpected loss of balance, such as when starting to fall or after receiving impetus when "off balance," equilibrium may be more quickly regained if a wide base of support is established and the center of gravity is lowered.

b. Upon landing from a downward jump, stability may be more readily regained if the weight is kept evenly distributed over both feet or over the hands and feet, and if a sufficiently wide base of support is provided.

c. Upon landing from a forward jump, the balance may be more readily regained if one lands with the weight forward and uses the hands if necessary in order to provide support in the direction of motion.

From this emphasis on stability it might seem that one should seek maximum stability in all situations. This is not true regarding certain stunts and gymnastic activities that are designed for the purpose of testing and developing body control under difficult circumstances. In many gymnastic vaults, for instance, "good form" stipulates that the performer shall land with the heels close, the knees separated, the arms extended sideward and the trunk as erect as possible, while he lets his knees bend to assure a light landing. In teaching beginners it would seem wiser to postpone emphasis on form from the point of view of appearance and to stress good mechanics and safety.

FINDING THE CENTER OF GRAVITY IN THE HUMAN BODY

The location of the center of gravity in man is of interest to scientists in many areas. Anatomists, kinesiologists, orthopedists, physical therapists, space engineers and equipment design engineers have all shown interest in means to determine the location of the human center of gravity. Earliest experiments located the center of gravity by balancing the body over a wedge. Various other methods have since been developed to estimate the location of the center of gravity either at rest or in motion. Two of these procedures, easily replicated with a minimum of equipment, are described here.

Reaction Board Method.   It is a fairly simple matter to find an estimate of the center of gravity of a motionless body using the *reaction board method.* Making use of the principle of moments, this procedure relies on the fact that the sum of the moments acting on a body in equilibrium is zero. Using this information the location of the gravitational line is found for each plane. The center of gravity of the body becomes the intersection of the values for each of these three planes. Directions for locating the center of gravity in three planes follow.

DIRECTIONS FOR DETERMINING THE POSITION OF THE CENTER OF GRAVITY
Apparatus (See Fig. 14–14)
1. Scales: preferably either the Toledo or the spring balance type.
2. A stool or block the same height as the platform of the scales.
3. A board about 40 cm. wide and 200 cm. long. A knife edge should be attached to the underside of each end in such a way that when the board is placed in a horizontal position it will rest on the knife edges. For simplifying the calculations the distance from knife edge to knife edge should measure exactly 200 cm. The front edge of the board should be marked in centimeters. The board should be tested with a level to make certain it is horizontal.

Directions (Refer to Fig. 14–14)
1. Find the subject's total weight.
2. Put one knife edge of board on scale platform and the other edge on box platform. Use a spirit level to make sure board is horizontal. Note the reading on the scales. This is the partial weight of the board, B.
3. Have the subject lie supine on the board with the heels against the foot rest at the end of the board away from the scales. The position the subject assumes should be as much like the standing position as possible. Record the reading on the scales. This is the partial weight of the subject and scales $(S + B)$.
4. For equilibrium to exist about the point P, the counterclockwise moments must equal the clockwise moments. If W is the total weight of the subject, B the

partial weight of the board, $S + B$ the partial weight of the subject and board, L the length of the board and d the perpendicular distance from P to W, then:

$$d \times W = [(S + B) - B] \, L$$

(clockwise moments = counterclockwise moments)

Rearranged,

$$d = \frac{[(S + B) - B] \, L}{W}$$

The distance between the subject's feet and center of gravity is "d." This is comparable to the distance between the ground and the center of gravity when the subject is standing, but must be viewed as an estimate due to shifts in body organs and tissues when lying down.

5. The percentage height of the center of gravity with respect to the subject's total height is found by dividing the value of "d" in the transverse plane (supine lying position) by the subject's total height and multiplying by 100.

$$\text{Per cent} = \frac{d \text{ in transverse plane}}{\text{subject's height}} \times 100$$

6. To locate the center of gravity in the frontal or sagittal planes the procedure must be repeated with the subject standing on the board (preferably near the middle). For the sagittal plane, the subject stands with the side to the scales and for the frontal plane location, the subject stands facing the scales (Fig. 14–15). Use the same formula.

$$d = \frac{[(S + B) - B] \, L}{W}$$

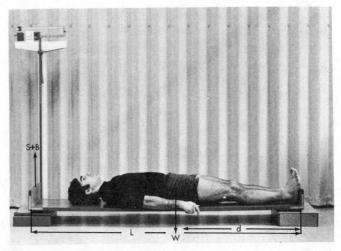

Figure 14–14 Reaction board method for locating the height of the center of gravity.

to solve for "d." The value of "d" represents the distance from the knife edge P to the plane in which the subject's center of gravity is located.

7. If it is desired to find the single point representing the spot where the line of gravity intersects the base of support, a piece of paper should be placed under the subject's feet for the side-view measurement. The outline of the feet is traced on the paper. When the first "d" is found, the distance is measured and marked on both the left and right sides of the paper. The paper should then be removed and the points connected by a straight line. When the subject faces forward for the second measurement, the paper should be placed on the board so that the subject's feet will fit in the foot prints. When the second "d" is found, the distance should be measured and marked on both edges of the paper, and the place where two lines intersect represents the approximate position of the point where the line of gravity strikes the base of support. This is a crude method of locating this point and is not strictly accurate since the subject may not be standing in exactly the same posture for both measurements. Furthermore, the element of swaying always introduces a source of error.

A modification of the reaction board method involves the use of a large triangular board supported by scales on two corners and a platform of equal height under the third corner.[17] Each corner makes contact with its support through a pointed bolt. Again it is important that the board be horizontal. If the triangle is equilateral, the moments are taken about lines forming two sides of

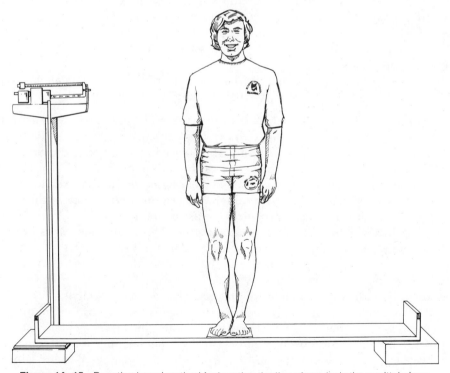

Figure 14–15 Reaction board method for locating the line of gravity in the sagittal plane.

the triangle, and the perpendicular distance from each line to the center of gravity is determined as follows:

$$d_1 = \frac{[(S + B)_y - B_y]\ L}{W}$$

$$d_2 = \frac{[(S + B)_x - B_x]\ L}{W}$$

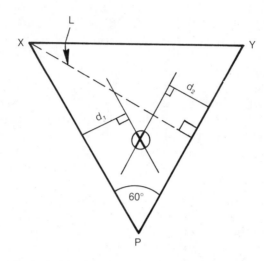

d_1 = distance between XP and center of gravity
d_2 = distance between YP and center of gravity
$(S + B)_x$ = partial weight of subject and board on scale X
$(S + B)_y$ = partial weight of subject and board on scale Y
B_x = partial weight of board recorded on scale X
B_y = partial weight of board recorded on scale Y
W = weight of subject
L = altitude of triangle (perpendicular distance from scale to line about which moment is being taken)

Segmental Method. Experiments using the reaction board are convincing in showing how the body automatically compensates for external loads and segmental adjustments. It is revealing also to see how the body adjusts for the sideward raising of an arm, for the forward bending of the trunk, for a brief-case carried in one hand or a load of books carried on the hip. Such analysis, however, is limited to the body in a stationary position. The location of the center of gravity of someone in action requires the use of another method. A highly useful procedure is one called the *segmental method*. This technique makes use of a photograph of the subject and involves finding the location of the center of gravity of each of the body segments, the position of these individual gravity points with respect to an arbitrarily placed *x, y* axis and knowledge of the ratio between the individual segment weights and the total body weight.

Considerable research has been done to determine values for the propor-tionate weights of body segments and the locations of the segmental centers of gravity. These data have been obtained through the weighing and suspension of cadaver segments, determination of the weight of segments of living subjects through the amount of water displaced by the immersed segment, and through

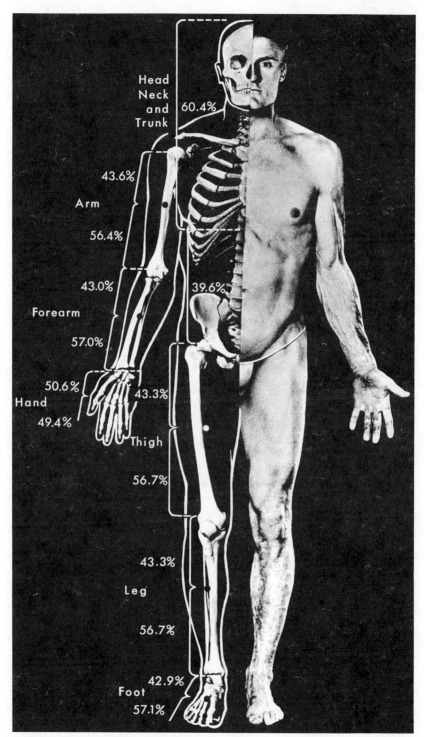

Figure 14–16 Joint centers and percentage distance of centers of gravity from joint centers. (From Williams, M., and Lissner, H. R.: Biomechanics of Human Motion. Philadelphia: W. B. Saunders Company, 1962.)

Figure 14–17   Immersion tanks for determination of segmental weights. Using segment landmarks as defined by Dempster, the segment is immersed in water. The displaced water is weighed and multiplied by the specific gravity of the segment to obtain the segmental weight. (From O'Connell, A. L., and Gardner, E. B.: Understanding the Scientific Bases of Human Movement. Baltimore: Williams & Wilkins Co., 1972.)

the formation of mathematical models. Probably the most commonly used data today are those of Dempster.[4] He weighed eight elderly male cadavers, dismembered them, weighed the segments and determined the proportion of total weight for each segment. In addition he located the center of gravity and specific gravity for each segment. The percentage distance of segment centers of gravity from joint centers is shown in Figure 14–16.

The locations of segmental centers of gravity have not been determined in living subjects, but the weights of individual body segments of men and women have been calculated through the determination of the amount of water displaced by an individual segment (Fig. 14–17).

Using specific gravity data from Dempster and the volumetric displacement method, Plagenhoef[13] reported body segment weights as percentages of total body weight for living college-age males, and quoted Kjeldsen as having obtained the same information for college-age females. These results are summarized in Table 14–1.

TABLE 14–1   Body Segment Percentages of Total Body Weight For Living Men and Women*

SEGMENTS	MEN	WOMEN
Hands	1.3	1.0
Forearms	3.8	3.1
Upper arms	6.6	6.0
Feet	2.9	2.4
Shanks	9.0	10.5
Thighs	21.0	23.0
Trunk (including head and neck)	55.4	54.0

*From data presented in Plagenhoef, S.: Patterns of Human Motion, pp. 25, 27.

Unfortunately, when applied to women and children, calculations using Dempster's data have to be considered as estimates since all of Dempster's work was done with male subjects. Use of the data with living adult males is considered accurate even though much of the basic research was done on cadavers.

With information on the proportionate mass of body segments and the location of the center of gravity of each segment, the center of gravity of the whole body may now be determined by making use of the principle of moments. The sum of the moments of the individual segments about arbitrarily placed *x* and *y* axes will produce the location of the center of gravity of the whole body with respect to the *x* and *y* axes. That is, the total body weight acting at the center of mass is the resultant of the combined segment weights acting at their mass centers. The resultant moment of the total body weight about the *x, y* axes is the sum of the individual segment moments about the same axes.

The segmental method for determining the center of gravity requires a considerable amount of measurement and calculation and therefore can be time consuming. The use of computer programs speeds up the process considerably as does the use of film analyzers with built in *x-y* coordinate systems. When these technical aids are not available, the process may be simplified with an inexpensive device called the Walton template (Fig. 14–18). The template makes use of the principle of similar triangles and eliminates the need to calculate the location of the mass center for each segment.

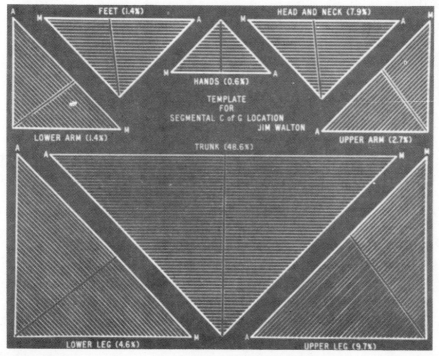

Figure 14–18   Walton template for use in segmental determination of center of gravity. (From J. S. Walton, A template for locating segmental centers of gravity. Research Quarterly of the American Association for Health, Physical Education, and Recreation *41*:615–618, 1970.)

Procedure for Determining Center of Gravity Using Segmental Method and Walton Template*

Apparatus

1. Walton template.
2. Line drawing on graph paper taken from photographic image of subject.
3. Worksheet with Dempster proportions listed. (See Figure 14–20.)

Method

1. The locations of the extremities of the individual segments must be marked according to the link boundaries shown in Figure 14–16. This will result in marks at the end of the second toe, ankle, knee, hip, knuckle III of the hand, wrist, shoulders, seventh cervical vertebra and top of the head. Where these points are obscured by other body parts, an estimate must be made. The upper trunk mark is the seventh cervical, located slightly above the midpoint of the transverse line joining the hips.

2. The extremity limits are joined to form a stick figure consisting of fourteen segments (Fig. 14–19, *A*).

3. The appropriate triangle on the Walton template is placed over one of the body segment lines so that the proximal end of one of the triangle lines

---

*Template dimensions can be found in Walton, J. S.: A template for locating segmental centers of gravity. Res. Quart. Amer. Assoc. Health, Phys. Ed. & Recrn., *41*:617, 1970. The template is available commercially through James S. Walton, Department of Applied Engineering, Stanford University.

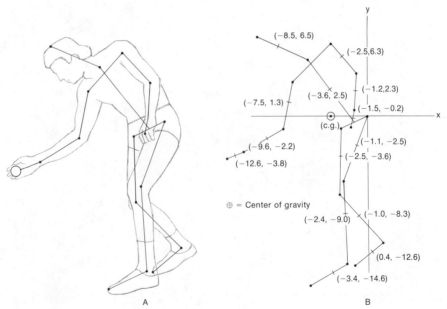

Figure 14–19 Segmental determination of the center of gravity. *A,* Location of body segments. *B,* The center of mass of each body segment is marked, and x, y coordinates are found using an arbitrarily placed x, y axis.

coincides with the proximal end of the body segment line, and the distal end of the same triangle line coincides with the distal end of the body segment.

4. The center of mass of the segment is marked on the tracing by drawing a short line through the slot in the triangle. (The location of the slot in the triangle is positioned according to proportions given by Dempster). This process is repeated for the remaining segments, selecting the appropriate triangle each time (Fig. 14–19, *B*). If the Walton template is not used, the mass center location for each segment length is found using the data given in Figure 14–16, where centers of gravity are located as a percentage of the distance between segment end points.

5. *x* and *y* axes are drawn on the paper in any convenient location.

6. The *x, y* coordinates for each of the 14 segment mass centers are determined and recorded on the diagram of the figure at the respective mass centers.

7. A worksheet such as that shown in Figure 14–20 is used to record the *x, y* coordinate values and the moments of those segments about the *x* and *y* axes. *Note* that the positive and negative values of the *x* and *y* coordinates must be retained. The individual moments are the products (Col. III) of the coordinate values (Col. II) and their related body segment proportions (Col. I).

8. The algebraic sum of the *x* products represents the *x* coordinate of the total body's mass center, and the algebraic sum of the *y* products is the *y* coordinate. These values are located and marked on the tracing (Fig. 14–19, *B*).

EQUILIBRIUM IN WATER

If a swimmer stands in shoulder deep water and abducts her arms as she lays her head back on the water's surface, most likely her feet will leave the bottom as her legs begin to rise. At some point between the vertical and horizontal, the swimmer will come to rest and she will be in a motionless backfloat. She will be in static equilibrium with the sum of all of the forces equal to zero. For this to occur an upward force must counterbalance the weight (force) of her body, acting vertically downward at the center of gravity. This upward force is called *buoyancy* and according to *Archimedes' principle* the magnitude of this force is equal to the weight of water displaced by the floating body. Specifically, Archimedes' principle states that *a solid body immersed in a liquid is buoyed up by a force equal to the weight of the liquid displaced.* This principle explains why some objects float and others do not, why some individuals float motionless like bobbing corks and why others struggle to keep their noses above water while attempting a back float. When a body is immersed in water, it will sink until the weight of the water it displaces equals the weight of the body. Sinking objects never do displace enough water to equal their body weight and eventually settle to the bottom. If such objects are weighed under water, they will be found to weigh less than when weighed in air. That difference in weight equals the weight of the water displaced and is the buoyant force acting on the immersed objects. Even a body which floats has some part of its volume beneath the surface, and thus displaces a volume of water. The weight of the water it displaces equals the *total* weight of the floating object. Any object stops sinking when the weight of the water it displaces equals its weight.

Body Segment	Propor-tion of Body Wt.	x + or – Value	Products	y + or – Value	Products
1. Trunk	.486	–3.6	–1.75	2.5	1.22
2. Head & Neck	.079	–8.5	–0.67	6.5	0.51
3. R. Thigh	.097	–2.5	–0.24	–3.6	–0.35
4. R. Lower Leg	.045	–1.0	–0.05	–8.3	–0.37
5. R. Foot	.014	0.4	0.01	–12.6	–0.18
6. L. Thigh	.097	–1.1	–0.11	–2.5	–0.24
7. L. Lower Leg	.045	–2.4	–0.11	–9.0	–0.41
8. L. Foot	.014	–3.4	–0.05	–14.6	–0.20
9. R. Upper Arm	.027	–7.5	–0.20	1.3	0.04
10. R. Lower Arm	.014	–9.6	–0.13	–2.2	–0.03
11. R. Hand	.006	–12.6	–0.08	–3.8	–0.03
12. L. Upper Arm	.027	–2.5	0.07	6.3	0.17
13. L. Lower Arm	.014	–1.2	0.02	2.3	0.03
14. L. Hand	.006	–1.5	0.01	–0.2	–0.00
Total-Plus Products			0.01		1.97
Total-Minus Products			3.49		1.81
x - y Resultants (Larger-Smaller) product total			–3.48		0.16

x Coordinate = ‾3.48

y Coordinate = +0.16

Figure 14–20 Worksheet for locating the center of gravity using the segmental method.

The ratio of body weight and the weight of an equal volume of water is called *specific gravity*. Objects which displace an amount of water equal in weight and volume to their weight and volume have a specific gravity of 1.0. Objects which displace a volume of water less than their volume have a specific gravity less than 1.0 and will float with some part above the surface. When the volume of water displaced weighs less than the weight of the object, the object will sink.

Human beings differ in specific gravity. Individuals with a greater proportion of fat will have a lower specific gravity than those with greater muscle mass
and large bones. Men and children usually have higher specific gravities than
women and consequently are poorer "floaters." The position in which one floats
is also determined by the distribution of muscle, bone and fat within the body,
since the specific gravity of the various body parts differs accordingly. Usually the
legs have a high specific gravity and consequently are the part of the body
which most often sinks during the back float. The thoracic region is the most
buoyant part, having the lowest weight for its volume. A person can increase
the buoyancy of this region by keeping the lungs inflated with air, thus increasing
the ease of floating. Some few individuals have overall specific gravities greater
than 1.0. It is impossible for these people to do a motionless float for they are
"sinkers." A practical way to determine whether a person is a floater or sinker is
to have him assume the tucked jellyfish float position with lungs inflated. If any
portion of the individual's back is on or above the surface, he can learn to
maintain a motionless floating position which, even though it may be more
nearly vertical than supine, is still called a back float.

As previously stated, a floater has to be concerned with two forces, the
downward force of his weight and the upward buoyancy of the water. When
these forces act on the body so that their resultant is zero, the forces will be in
equilibrium and the body will be in a motionless float. The downward force acts
at the center of gravity of the body, a point somewhere in the pelvis. The
buoyant force acts at the center of buoyancy of the body, a point which varies
with individuals but is usually closer to the head than is the center of gravity.
If the body were of uniform density, the center of gravity and the center
of buoyancy would coincide, but since the body has less mass toward the
head, the center of buoyancy is usually higher in the body than is the center of
gravity. The center of buoyancy is the point where the center of gravity of the
volume of displaced water would be if the water were placed in a vessel the shape
and size of the floater's body. Because the water is of uniform density, its center
of gravity will be in the direction of the greater volume, i.e., near the chest
region. If the center of gravity and center of buoyancy are not in the same force
line with each other, as shown in Figure 14–21, *A,* the body will rotate in the
direction of the forces until the forces are equal and opposite in line, direction

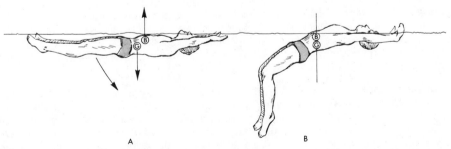

A   B

Figure 14–21   A balanced float occurs when the center of gravity and the center of buoyancy are
in the same force line. G = downward force of body weight. B = upward force (buoyancy) of water.

and magnitude. At this point the floater will be in a balanced float (Fig. 14–21, *B*). Individuals who float horizontally start out with the center of gravity and center of buoyancy in the same vertical line. These are usually individuals whose bodies contain a high percentage of fat. Those floaters whose legs tend to drop when attempting the back float will have a balanced position somewhere between the horizontal and vertical at that point where the center of gravity and center of buoyancy are in the same vertical line. The angle of the floating position with the horizontal may be decreased by making those body adjustments which move the center of gravity closer to the center of buoyancy. Raising the arms over the head, arching the back, bending the knees and flexing the wrists to bring the hands out of the water all contribute to moving the center of gravity closer to the head and thus closer to the center of buoyancy (Fig. 14–21, *B*).

LABORATORY EXPERIENCES

1. *a.* Working with a partner, determine the position of your line of gravity using the reaction board method. Locate the point where this line intersects your base of support by marking it on a tracing of your feet.
   b. Determine the position of your line of gravity leaning as far forward as possible with the body in a straight line from the top of the head to the ankles. Repeat leaning as far backward as possible.
   c. Locate the line of gravity in the sagittal plane while leaning as far as possible to one side.
   d. Determine the height of your center of gravity with your arms at your side and then with them stretched over your head. What per cent of your total height is your center of gravity? How does this compare with averages for your sex?
   e. Choose an original position with a small or unstable base of support. Locate the point where the line of gravity intersects the base of support.

2. Make a tracing on graph paper of a picture of a person engaged in a motor skill. Locate the center of gravity using the segmental method.

3. Walk on a low balance beam:
   a. Looking ahead at the wall.
   b. Looking at a person who is in front of the balance beam doing a vigorous exercise such as a jumping jack.
   c. With your eyes blindfolded.
   d. Walk along with a partner beside you. Without warning, the partner is to give you a slight, but sudden sideward push. What measures do you take to maintain your balance? If you fail, explain why.

4. Build two columns of blocks, one with the blocks carefully centered one over the other, the second column with the blocks staggered but balanced. Grasping the lowest block of each column, slide the columns back and forth, changing the speed frequently and suddenly until the blocks tumble. Which column is the first to topple? Why?

5. Assume a back lying position in the water with your arms at your side. Note and explain any shift in body position. Slide your arms from your sides to a side horizontal position, keeping them close to and parallel to the surface of the water. What effect does this have on body position? Continue moving your arms until they are overhead. Next flex the wrists so the hands are out of the water. Finally, flex the legs at the knees. Explain the effect of these last three moves upon your position in the water.

REFERENCES

1. Basford, L.: The Science of Movement. London: Sampson Low, Marston & Co., 1966.
2. Croskey, M. I., Dawson, P. M., Luessen, A. C., Marohn, I. E., and Wright, H. E.: The height of the center of gravity in man. Am. J. Physiol., 61:171–185, 1922.
3. Cureton, T. K., and Wickens, J. S.: The center of gravity of the human body in the antero-posterior plane and its relation to posture. Springfield College Suppl. to Res. Quart. Am. Assn. Health, Phys. Ed. & Recrn., 6:93–105, 1935.
4. Dempster, W. T.: Space Requirement of the Seated Operator. Ohio: Wright-Patterson Air Force Base (WADC TR 55-199), 1955a.
5. Dull, C. E., Metcalfe, H. C., and Williams, J. E.: Modern Physics. New York: Holt, Rinehart and Winston, 1963.
6. Hanavan, E. A.: A Mathematical Model of the Human Body. Ohio: Wright-Patterson Air Force Base (AMRL-TR-64-102), 1964.
7. Hay, J. G.: The center of gravity of the human body. In Kinesiology III. Washington, D.C.: Am. Assn. Health, Phys. Ed. & Recrn., 1973.
8. Hellebrandt, F. A., Riddle, K. S., Larsen, E. M., and Fries, E. C.: Gravitational influences on postural alignment. Physiother. Rev., 22:143–149, 1942.
9. Hellebrandt, F. A., and Franseen, E. B.: Physiological study of vertical stance of man. Physiological Rev., 23:220–225, 1943.
10. Miller, D. I., and Nelson, R. C.: Biomechanics of Sport. Philadelphia: Lea & Febiger, 1973.
11. O'Connell, A. L., and Gardner, E. B.: Understanding the Scientific Basis of Human Movement. Baltimore: Williams & Wilkins Co., 1972.
12. Palmer, C. E.: Studies of the center of gravity in the human body. Child Develop., 15:99–180, 1944.
13. Plagenhoef, S.: Patterns of Human Motion: A Cinematographic Analysis. Englewood Cliffs, N.J.: Prentice-Hall, Inc., 1971, pp. 25, 27.
14. Reynolds, E., and Lovett, R. W.: Method of determining the position of the center of gravity in its relation to certain bony landmarks in the erect position. Am. J. Physiol., 24:286–293, 1909.
15. Swearingen, J. J., Braden, G. E., Badgley, J. M., and Wallace, T. F.: Determination of centers of gravity in children. Federal Aviation Administration (report AM 69-22), (Nov.) 1969.
16. Walton, J. S.: A template for locating segmental centers of gravity. Res. Quart. Amer. Assoc. Health, Phys. Ed. & Recrn., 41:615–618, 1970.
17. Waterland, J. D., and Shambes, G. M.: Biplane center of gravity procedure. Percept. Motor Skills, 30:511–514, 1970.
18. Williams, M., and Lissner, H. R.: Biomechanics of Human Motion. Philadelphia: W. B. Saunders Company, 1962.

Part Three

MOTOR SKILLS: PRINCIPLES AND APPLICATIONS

INTRODUCTION
TO PART THREE

Part Three opens with a chapter on Approaches to the Kinesiologic Analysis of Motor Skills. It contains a comprehensive outline of motor skills organized in accordance with the major objectives of these skills. These are (1) the maintenance of erect posture, (2) the giving of impetus both to one's own body and to external objects and (3) the receiving of impetus both from one's own body and from external objects. The next six chapters, which follow this outline closely, include discussions of the different types of skills. They draw on both the anatomic and the mechanical information found in Parts One and Two and present the principles that provide the basis for the successful performance of each skill.

This group of chapters is followed by a single chapter on Exercises for Special Purposes. The exercises that are discussed fall into three general classifications, namely, exercises for increasing the range of joint motion, exercises for strengthening muscles and exercises for correcting posture faults. Inasmuch as the exercises incorporate several of the types of motor skills listed in the outline, this chapter does not fit into any one particular motor skill category, and for that reason it follows the chapters that are based on the outline.

The final chapter in Part Three is addressed particularly to physical education major students who will soon be joining the ranks of instructors in physical education. It discusses the implications of kinesiology for effective instruction in the activity program. It presents different views concerning the value of teaching biomechanical principles to students as an aid to learning motor skills. Some investigators have found this practice beneficial, although others have not. As to the value of a sound knowledge of mechanical principles to the instructor himself, there can be no question. The increased understanding which this gives him provides a scientific basis for selecting one particular technique in preference to another; it enables him to diagnose individual needs and difficulties; it reveals basic similarities between motor skills in the same category and thus enables him to present more clearly new sports that involve the same movement patterns as a sport with which the class is already familiar; it enables him to make pertinent suggestions with true insight. A thorough grasp of this subject adds immeasurably to the instructor's background. In short, the intelligent use of one's knowledge of kinesiology often makes all the difference between effective and ineffective teaching.

Chapter Fifteen

APPROACHES TO THE KINESIOLOGIC ANALYSIS OF MOTOR SKILLS

KINESIOLOGIC ANALYSIS

What Is a Kinesiologic Analysis? In the preceding chapters the anatomic components of human movement — the bones, the joints, the muscles and the related portions of the nervous system — were presented, and both the anatomic and the mechanical aspects of human motion were discussed. The basic movements of the body segments were described, and it was shown how observation of both anatomic and mechanical principles contributes to the efficient use of the body.

A kinesiologic analysis of a motor skill consists of breaking the skill down into its constituent elements, of determining the nature of each movement and of identifying the appropriate mechanical and anatomic principles. It attempts to give specific answers to the following questions:

1. What joints are involved, and what are their exact movements in the motor skill?

2. Are any of the joints used to the limit of their range of motion?

3. What muscles are responsible for the joint actions, and what is the nature of their contraction?

4. Do any of the muscle groups exert maximal or near maximal effort?

5. What anatomic and mechanical principles contribute to maximal efficiency and accuracy in the performance of the motor skill?

6. What principles are directly related to the avoidance of injury?

Why Make Kinesiologic Analyses of Motor Skills? The simplest answer is that such analyses are an aid to effective teaching of the skills. This does not necessarily mean, however, that the instructor should explain the analysis to an activity class unless the class shows an interest in knowing. What it does mean is that it provides the instructor with a sound background for presenting a motor skill to a class and for knowing what points to emphasize. It also provides the instructor with the knowledge that enables him to view each student's performance with an "x-ray eye" and to diagnose any difficulty. Furthermore, it makes the

385

instructor more aware of the types of injuries that are likely to occur in a particular skill and thus enables him to make the appropriate suggestions for preventing these. The instructors who can apply their knowledge effectively to individual needs are the ones best qualified for their task of teaching others and of helping them to develop proficiency in a variety of motor skills.

The undertaking of analysis assumes an organization of the factors and circumstances related to the area of investigation. Hence, in the field of motor skills it is appropriate first to identify major categories and then the subdivisions to which the skills belong. This approach makes it possible to categorize the nature of a given motor skill with a fair degree of precision.

Many systems of classification have appeared in the literature. Although a review of these is of interest because of the different points of view they represent, it is unprofitable to spend time comparing their relative merits since a classification should be judged solely on the basis of its meaningfulness to the persons using it. The classification presented below has been of use to the authors as a basis for discussing the kinesiologic aspects of human motion. It is based on three major divisions of motor skills according to their objectives, on the subcategories relating to the media in which they take place and on the nature of the body's support (or lack of it in some instances).

Classification of Motor Skills

I. Maintaining erect posture

II. Giving impetus

    A. To one's own body

        1. Supported by the ground or other resistant surface

           a. Movements on a stationary or limited base

           b. Locomotion on foot, on wheels and blades, on hands, on hands and knees (or feet); rotatory locomotion

        2. Supported in suspension

           a. Swinging activities on trapeze, flying rings or similar equipment

           b. Hand traveling on traveling rings or horizontal ladder

        3. Unsupported, i.e., projected into or falling through the air

           a. Diving

           b. Trampoline activities

           c. Acrobatics

        4. Supported by water

           a. Aquatic locomotion

               1. Swimming

               2. Boating

           b. Aquatic stunts

    B. To external objects

        1. Throwing with hand or implement

        2. Pushing, pulling, thrusting, lifting

        3. Striking, hitting, kicking

III. Receiving impetus
   A. Of one's own body in landing from a jump or fall
   B. Of external objects in catching, trapping, spotting or intercepting

It may have been noticed that the three major headings in this outline are Maintaining Erect Posture, Giving Impetus and Receiving Impetus. Some may question the reason for treating the maintenance of erect posture as a major catetory instead of including it under Giving Impetus to One's Own Body. The rationale for this decision is that the emphasis here is on *adjustment to the immediate environment,* rather than on "making a movement" in the sense that one usually interprets this concept. With one exception, the adjustments are made from a stationary position, the exception being a shift in stance necessitated by standing on a moving base. This does not involve moving from one place to another, but only widening the stance and facing in a different direction for the purpose of maintaining balance.

The initial step in the analysis is to determine in which major category the skill belongs, and then in which secondary, and possibly tertiary, category. A forehand drive in tennis, for instance, belongs in the primary category of "giving impetus to an external object" and in the secondary one of "striking." Turning a cartwheel is a form of "giving impetus to one's own body, when it is supported by the ground," and is classified further as "rotatory locomotion."

In addition to pinpointing the exact categories to which the skill belongs, there are a number of factors which should be considered. Many skills consist of a series of phases that cut across different categories, and these must be considered separately. A tennis serve, like the forehand drive, is a form of striking, but it also involves tossing the ball, a skill which should not be overlooked. Vaults over a gymnasium box or horse consist of the approach, the placement of the hands almost simultaneously with the jump or take-off, the momentary support by the hands and the push-off from the box, followed by the projection of the body together with the necessary adjustments of the bodily segments, and finally the landing which involves movements of the upper extremities and trunk as well as of the lower extremities. In pole vaulting and in hand-over-hand rope climbing using feet as well as hands (the only method that assures continuous movement and avoids the necessity for overcoming inertia at every step), there is a smooth transition from pulling to pushing. In hurdling there is repeated alternation between the run and the hurdle without any break in the rhythm. In many basketball throws for the basket, the throw is accompanied by a jump. All phases of the skill should be included in the analysis.

In many skills, especially those involving either the giving or the receiving of a force of appreciable magnitude, the ability to maintain balance is an important feature. To do so effectively means observing the principles of balance and posture adjustment as well as those relating to the specific form of giving or receiving impetus. Lifting a heavy weight from the floor is a good example of an impetus-giving activity that depends in large part for its effectiveness upon the maintenance of a posture that favors lifting.

The specific objective of the motor skill must also be considered. For instance, if the skill is a form of throwing or striking, which is the primary purpose, achieving maximum distance or accuracy of aim? If it is running or swimming, is it in a sprint or a long distance race?

Having classified the skill according to the categories in the outline and having considered the related factors, one is now ready to analyze the skill both anatomically and mechanically.

ANATOMIC ANALYSIS

Techniques and Equipment

JOINT ANALYSIS. The most commonly used laboratory method of studying joint action consists of measuring the range of motion either with a protractor type of goniometer or with a Leighton Flexometer. The newest instrument used for research at the present time is the Elgon, an electronic instrument for electrogoniometry. (These techniques were mentioned in Chapter One.)

MUSCULAR ANALYSIS. A technique low on the scale of sophistication and objectivity is theoretical analysis, sometimes referred to in a rather derogatory manner as "armchair analysis." This technique is based on the use of anatomy texts and implies judging the actions of a muscle from the muscle's attachments, together with its relation to the joint in question. Even this method cannot be called strictly theoretical because the information in the textbooks was originally derived by dissection. The theoretical method is of use when experimental methods are not readily available. It must be used with caution, however, as its validity is questionable. Assumed muscular actions should be verified whenever possible. Referring to a number of textbooks and research reports is helpful.

There is one experimental technique that is available to everyone. This is palpation and inspection of superficial muscles. In spite of the limitations of this method and its subjective nature, it is recommended for students, as it is a valuable learning experience. They should be cautious, however, about applying their findings to sport skills which, in most cases, are performed under circumstances that differ widely from those under which basic movements are executed.

The most reliable laboratory method of investigating muscular action in present use is electromyography. (See Chapter Two, also the sections on Supplementary Material which may be found in several chapters in Parts One and Three.)

The recording of isokinetic contraction is a relatively new technique for making precise evaluations of muscular and joint performance. It requires the use of an electromechanical device designed specifically for this purpose. This method is discussed in Chapter Twenty-Two. The student who has the opportunity of experiencing or even just observing this laboratory method is fortunate. Those who do not have such an opportunity can enrich their backgrounds by reading firsthand reports of research investigations using this technique.

Procedure

For each phase of a motor skill and for each joint participating in that phase, the precise joint action should be identified and, if it seems desirable, the degree of motion should be measured. This would necessitate measuring the angle at the beginning of the movement and again at the end. If the subject is one whose performance is poor, the joint action should be judged on the basis of its accuracy and on the adequacy of its range of motion. Insofar as is possible, the instructor should decide from this analysis whether the joint needs to have its range increased and whether it is being used in such a way that strain or injury is likely to result.

Likewise, the muscular action is identified for each joint movement in each phase of the motor skill. This implies identifying not only the muscles that are contracting but also their precise function in the movement, the kind of contraction they are undergoing (concentric, eccentric or static) and an estimate of the force of their contraction (strong, medium or mild).

A sample analysis is shown in Table 15–1. Similar forms are appropriate for recording analyses of the movements illustrated in Appendix G or any other motor skills. If it is desired to indicate the names of individual muscles, see the charts in Appendix F.

MECHANICAL ANALYSIS

The mechanical analysis of an activity involves the identification of laws and principles which help to explain the most appropriate form for the execution of the activity and to identify the mechanical reasons for success or failure. In order to assess the mechanical nature of a technique and to make use of this information in helping performers choose movements which will result in skillful motion, the analyzer should attempt to identify those principles and laws which verify the actions as desirable. Once the movement is classified according to an outline such as that on page 386, the analyzer should determine exactly how and when the movements of the performance do or do not satisfy the standards of good performance as explained by the laws and principles of mechanics. Each aspect of the motion should be explained by identifying the appropriate laws and principles of stability and equilibrium, motion, force, work, energy and power. Once this process is accomplished, a greater depth of understanding of the skill is achieved, and the basis for making change is founded upon sound knowledge and understanding of the reasons "why."

Procedures which help to analyze and quantify the mechanical nature of human movement performance are numerous and involve a variety of instrumentations. Perhaps the most used is some form of motion picture photography. When appropriate precautions are taken, accurate records of human perform-

TABLE 15-1 Chart for Anatomic Analysis of a Motor Skill*

Skill being analyzed: Standing broad jump. (See Fig. 11-5.)
Phase being analyzed: Force phase.

Name of Joint	Starting Position	Observed Joint Action	Force for Movement	Main Muscle Groups Active	Kind of Contraction	Force of Contraction
Metatarsal phalangeal	Extended	Hyperextension/flexion	Muscle	Extensors/flexors	Concentric	Strong
Ankle	Dorsiflexed	Plantar flexion	Muscle	Plantar flexors	Concentric	Strong
Knee	Flexed	Extension	Muscle	Extensors	Concentric	Strong
Hip	Flexed	Extension	Muscle	Extensors	Concentric	Strong
Pelvis	Decreased tilt	Increased tilt	Muscle	Spinal extensors	Concentric	Moderate
Lumbar spine	Flexion	Extension	Muscle	Spinal extensors	Concentric	Moderate
Thoracic spine	Slight flexion	Extension	Muscle	Spinal extensors	Concentric	Moderate
Cervical spine	Hyperextended	Flexion	Gravity	Spinal extensors	Eccentric	Mild
Shoulder girdle	Upward tilt	Upward rotation, abduction	Muscle	Upward rotators Abductors	Concentric Concentric	Moderate Moderate
Shoulder joint	Hyperextension, medial rotation	Flexion	Muscle	Flexors	Concentric	Strong
Elbow	Extended	—	—	—	Static	Mild
Radioulnar	Pronated	—	—	—	—	—
Wrist	Extended	—	—	Extensors	Static	Mild
Phalanges	Extended	—	—	Extensors	Static	Mild

*This form for recording an anatomic analysis may be reproduced for class use without specific permission.
(Patterned after format presented in Rasch, P. J., and Burke, R. K.: Kinesiology and Applied Anatomy, 5th ed. Philadelphia, Lea & Febiger, 1974, pp. 415–422.)

ance may be obtained on film. The quantitative analysis of the film then requires the use of some type of motion analyzer which permits measurements to be taken from single frames. This may be done by making tracings of the projected picture from which linear or angular measures may be obtained. This approach is simple but time consuming. More sophisticated models of analyzers allow the direct feeding of coordinate points from the film image into a computer. This more advanced procedure helps to eliminate a large amount of the tedium involved in such analyses. Segmental centers of gravity, as well as linear and angular measures of displacement, velocity and acceleration, may be obtained from film. With these data, force determinations are also possible. In addition, for a more complete understanding of a given motion, cinematography is often combined with other devices, such as electromyograms, elgons or external force measuring devices.

External force measures usually involve some form of electronic instrumentation. A great variety of measures of force and acceleration are possible with the variety of instruments available. One instrument worthy of recognition is the force platform. Force sensing instruments capable of recording forces in three planes as well as force movements about the three axes are attached to a platform. As some part of the performer's body lands on the platform, forces and torques which develop are identified. This procedure has been used to identify forces in a variety of activities, and increased use is already evident in research. The combination of the force platform with cinematography increases its value even more.

Probably the form of instrumentation that has most influenced analysis and research procedures in the mechanical analysis of motion is the high speed computer. Without it the volume of data which can be generated through the use of film and force measuring devices would never be analyzed. The availability of computers is undoubtedly responsible for the rapid advances in biomechanical research in recent years. Without this availability many of the necessary mathematical procedures would be impossible. In addition to the facilitation of data treatment, the computer also contributes to the analysis of motion in two other significant ways. A relatively new application is computer simulation. Complex mathematical equations are used to develop mathematical models which simulate human movement patterns. Once these models are validated against experimental conditions, they may be used to determine the effect of altering selected variables upon the total performance. The third use of computers applied to the analysis of motion is computer graphics, i.e., computer data are displayed graphically. Drawings of the human body have been made by the computer as have other illustrative charts, graphs and diagrams. The display of computer simulations is also often "drawn" through the use of computer graphics.

The future of research in the mechanics of human motion will probably be as varied as present and future technologies allow. The use of gamma ray scanners and laser beams are already under investigation as are procedures for automating much of the data gathering which now requires endless hours of attention.

LABORATORY EXPERIENCES

1. Select three motor skills from different sections of Appendix G and classify them according to the Outline of Motor Skills. Analyze them anatomically, using a chart similar to the one on page 390. List the mechanical principles that are particularly pertinent for efficient performance of the skill.

REFERENCES

1. Miller, D. I., and Nelson, R. C.: Biomechanics of Sport. Philadelphia: Lea & Febiger, 1973.
2. Plagenhoef, S.: Patterns of Human Motion—A Cinematographic Analysis. Englewood Cliffs, New Jersey: Prentice-Hall, Inc., 1971.
3. Rasch, P., and Burke, K.: Kinesiology and Applied Anatomy, 5th ed. Philadelphia: Lea & Febiger, 1974.

Chapter Sixteen

ERECT POSTURE: CONCEPTS, PRINCIPLES AND ADJUSTMENTS

There are innumerable concepts of human posture and innumerable interpretations of its significance. Posture may well claim to be "all things to all men." To the physical anthropologist posture may be a racial characteristic, or it may be an indication of phylogenetic development; to the orthopedic surgeon it may be an indication of the soundness of the skeletal framework and muscular system; to an artist it may be an expression of the personality and the emotions; to the actor it serves as a tool for expressing mood or character; to the physician, the biologist, the fashion model, the employer, the sculptor, the dancer, the psychologist—to each of these, posture has a different significance. Each sees posture within the framework of his own profession and interest. This is no less true of the kinesiologically oriented physical educator. To him, posture is a gauge of mechanical efficiency, of kinesthetic sense, of muscle balance and of neuromuscular coordination.

PERSONAL POSTURE

Most of the following discussion has to do with what might be called "personal posture," its analysis, evaluation, adjustment and the principles that apply to it.

No individual's posture can be adequately described. Posture means position, and a multisegmented organism such as the human body cannot be said to have a single posture. It assumes many postures and seldom holds any of them for an appreciable time. Although characteristic patterns become apparent as we observe an individual over an extended period, it is difficult, if not well nigh impossible, to measure, or even record, these patterns. It would take a series of candid camera motion pictures to do so.

Another difficulty is the varieties of human physique represented, such as those defined by Sheldon.[28] The importance of considering these individual differences of build when evaluating posture has been emphasized by Frost.[11] Hence we see that posture norms are appropriate only for the mythical average figure and apply only to the static standing position, which may or may not be representative of a person's habitual postural patterns.

In view of the fact that activity postures should be of greater concern to the physical educator than static postures, it may be well to say a word in defense of the practice of examining and photographing the posture of subjects in the erect standing position. It is admitted that the posture in such a position is of little importance in itself. It becomes significant, however, when it is taken as the point of departure for the many postural patterns assumed by the individual, both at rest and in motion. Since there is an almost endless variety of activity postures and since these are extremely difficult to judge, it is a convenient custom to accept the standing posture as the individual's basic posture from which all his other postures stem. Hence, as a reflection of the individual's characteristic postural patterns, the standing posture takes on an importance it would not otherwise have. It should be kept in mind, however, that its importance is in direct proportion *to the extent to which it represents the individual's habitual carriage.*

Factors Related to Stability

1. Hellebrandt demonstrated that even the erect standing posture is not literally static. "Standing," she concluded, "is, in reality, *movement upon a stationary base.*"[15] Her experiments revealed that the center of gravity did not remain motionless above the base of support no matter how still the subject attempted to stand, but moved forward, backward and sideward. This motion indicated that the subjects were constantly swaying. When the swaying was prevented by artificial means, there was a tendency to faint. Hence the involuntary swaying was seen to serve the purpose of a pump, aiding the venous return and assuring the brain of adequate circulation for retaining consciousness.

2. In the same experiments Hellebrandt found that the oscillations of each individual were balanced so exactly that the average position of the line of gravity, relative to the base of support, was remarkably constant. From this it would seem that we can assume the presence of a controlling factor in our tendency to sway. Apparently the stretch reflex, the kinesthetic sense and vision all operate here to confine the oscillations to a limited area, an area well within the boundaries of the base of support.

3. Some experimenters have investigated the possibility of a relationship between the position of the line of gravity, relative to the base of support, and the quality of posture. The findings of the different investigators do not agree, however. It seems obvious that however close the line of gravity is to the center of the base of support, this condition does not necessarily indicate good segmental alignment. One can assume an exaggerated zigzag alignment and still stand in such a way that the line of gravity intersects the center of the base of support, provided his "zags" balance his "zigs," yet his posture may leave much to be desired. The summaries of investigations by Cureton and Wickens, by Crowley, and by Johnston in the Supplementary Material at the end of this chapter present two conflicting conclusions from their line-of-gravity experiments. In this connection students may find number 3 of the Laboratory Experiences of particular interest.

4. In informal class experiments it was found that the relation of the line of gravity to the base of support was not affected significantly or consistently when the subject assumed different positions of the upper extremities or held

external objects such as books, a suitcase or a tray. This would seem to provide evidence of the body's tendency to compensate for deviations of some of its parts from the fundamental standing position. The principle would appear to be established that, under ordinary circumstances, the disalignment of one segment of the body, whether anteroposteriorly or laterally, is accompanied by a compensatory disalignment of another segment or segments. If the disalignment is not exactly balanced, excessive tension in certain muscle groups results. This is particularly apparent when external loads are not adequately compensated. Objective evidence is suggested but is as yet inconclusive.

Factors Related to the Alignment of Body Segments

1. In the literature on posture, statements are frequently seen to the effect that, in the ideal standing posture as viewed from the side, the line of gravity bears a definite relation to certain anatomic landmarks, such as the mastoid process, the acromion process, the junctions of the anteroposterior curves of the spine, the hip joint (greater trochanter of the femur), the knee joint and the

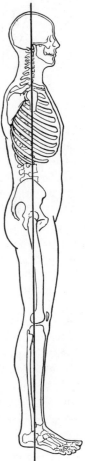

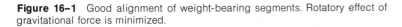

Figure 16–1 Good alignment of weight-bearing segments. Rotatory effect of gravitational force is minimized.

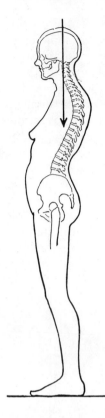

Figure 16–2 Zigzag alignment of weight-bearing segments increases rotatory effect of gravitational force.

lateral malleolus.* This seems to be too rigid a definition, as it ignores the factor of body sway. It might be more realistic to determine a "normal zone" within which the line of gravity might reasonably be expected to lie when the subject is standing in erect posture.

2. It has been stated that a standing posture in which each weight-bearing segment was balanced vertically upon the segment beneath it made less demand on the muscles than a posture in which the segments formed a zigzag alignment.[2, 22] Good posture, it was said, takes less muscular effort to maintain than poor. The explanation given was that when a segment is not in vertical alignment, the force of gravity is not parallel with its long axis, and hence exerts a rotatory component of force. Although this reasoning may seem logical, it overlooks two facts: first, that one of the most poorly aligned postures is actually a fatigue posture in which the muscles have let go and have left it to the ligaments to prevent complete collapse (see Fig. 16–2); and secondly, that even in the most ideal posture some rotatory force is present, owing to (1) the supporting column of the trunk (i.e., the spine) being situated closer to the posterior surface of the body than to the anterior, (2) the supporting base (the feet) being projected forward from the lower extremities instead of centered beneath them,

*According to Brunnstrom this belief is the result of an incorrect translation and interpretation of Braune and Fischer's discussion of "Normalstellung."[4]

(3) the spinal column being curved anteroposteriorly and (4) the chest forming an anterior load upon which gravity is constantly exerting a rotatory force (see Fig. 16–1). The weight of the breasts in women constitutes an additional anterior weight and thus causes an even greater rotatory component of gravitational force.

3. There appears to be a definite relationship between the alignment of the body segments and the integrity of the joint structures. It is generally accepted that prolonged postural strain is injurious to these structures. Ligaments that are repeatedly subjected to stretch become permanently stretched, and cartilages that are subjected to uneven pressures and to abnormal friction become damaged. There is adequate clinical evidence to support the contention that prolonged postural strain is a factor in the arthritic changes which take place in the weight-bearing joints. Objective evidence may be lacking, but it might not be difficult to secure if postural records and x-rays of the weight-bearing joints could be obtained for an adequate number of subjects over a ten- or twenty-year period. Such an investigation might prove or disprove the claim that the human machine functions more efficiently when the weight-bearing segments are in "proper" alignment with a minimum of stress and strain on them.

Factors Related to Energy Cost.   The question of the energy cost of standing posture has been investigated by both Hellebrandt[17] and McCormick.[23] Both concluded that when standing, the increase of metabolic rate over the basal rate was so small, compared with the metabolic cost of moving and exercising, as to be negligible. McCormick included both anteroposterior and lateral measurements of body alignment. From these she concluded that the type of posture which involved a minimum of metabolic increase appeared to be one in which the knees are hyperextended as completely as the joints permit, the hips are pushed forward to the limit of extension, the thoracic curve is increased, the head is projected forward and the upper trunk is inclined slightly backward in a posterior list (see Figs. 16–3, *B* and 16–4, *B*). As one might expect, this is a typical picture of fatigue posture. A common variation of it is a shift of the weight to one foot with accompanying asymmetric adjustments in the spine and lower extremities.

From these two studies and from the writings of other investigators, such as Basmajian, Evans, Joseph, Steindler and others, it is seen that there is a lack of agreement concerning the degree of muscular activity required for maintaining upright posture. Doubtless this is partly due to confusion in what is meant by "upright posture." To some, it may mean merely the ability to stay on one's feet and resist the downward pull of gravity. To others, it may mean "good" alignment as opposed to a "zigzag" alignment. The studies based on energy cost appear to indicate that, although it takes little more energy to stand erect than to sit, *minimum* energy expenditure cannot be accepted as a criterion of good posture. Metabolic economy is desirable to a point, as it implies the absence of hypertonicity, but from the physical educator's point of view well balanced segmental alignment should not be sacrificed for it.

It would seem that the energy requirement for maintaining erect posture in reasonably good alignment bears a direct relationship to the individual's habitual carriage. It is a matter of common observation that there is a wide

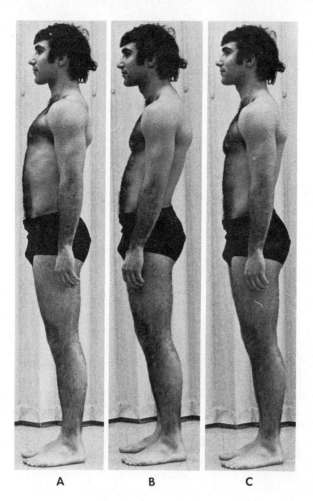

Figure 16–3 *A,* Individual in position of "attention." He is overtense and has exaggerated lumbar curve. *B,* Individual is overrelaxed and has zigzag alignment. *C,* Individual has slightly forward head, round shoulders and slight posterior list of trunk; otherwise there is fairly good alignment.

A   B   C

range of body alignments seen in "upright posture." Any physical educator who has had the task of evaluating the posture of large groups of students and of giving help to those with "poor posture" is impressed with the variation in effort it takes for a student to stand in "good posture." Whereas one individual apparently has no difficulty in assuming this posture because it is his natural one, another cannot assume it even momentarily without the instructor's help and without becoming overtense. It is obvious that the second student is using much more muscular energy than is the first. The physical education teacher who is concerned with posture instruction would like to see these individual variations explored more thoroughly. The combination of metabolic determination and electromyography should prove a good tool for such research. It would be of particular interest to the posture and corrective exercise instructor to learn whether such instruction over a specified period would reveal a relationship between posture improvement and a decrease in the amount of muscular energy required for assuming an "acceptable posture" and maintaining it while participating in selected activities for a specified period of time.

Factors Related to Evolutionary and Hereditary Influences

1. In tracing the evolution of the human structure and its posture, Morton[26] has shown the influence that the force of gravity has had on the morphologic development, first of the terrestrial quadrupeds, then of the arboreal primates and finally of man. The evolution from horizontal to vertical posture was achieved, he claimed, by the force of gravity pulling on the suspended body of the arboreal primates when they engaged in brachial locomotion. The changes which developed in man's structure, he stated, were the direct result of the shift from a vertically suspended position to a vertically supported one. This shift was responsible not only for the changes in the weight-bearing parts of the musculoskeletal structure, but also for changes in the upper extremities, which were now freed for the development of a great variety of manipulative skills. While no specific principle is derived from this explanation of the role played by the force of gravity in the evolution of man's structure, an awareness of it might be of help in the analysis of individual postures.

2. Attention has already been called to individual variations in posture. In

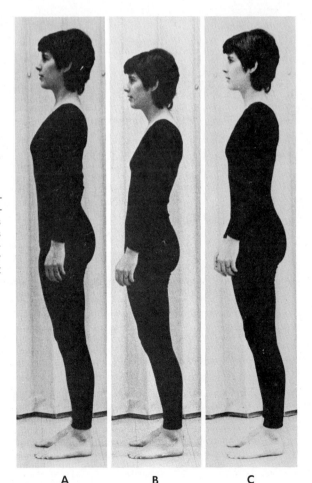

Figure 16–4 *A*, Individual in position of "attention." She has exaggerated lumbar curve but does not show strain. *B*, Individual is overrelaxed and has zigzag alignment. *C*, Individual has a nice easy posture and good alignment except for very slightly forward head.

A   B   C

attempting to correct a person's posture one must be realistic and accept the limits imposed by a possible hereditary factor. Improvement can doubtless be made, but one must not expect to effect a radical change in the basic shape of the spine.

3. Certain pathologic conditions, such as congenitally dislocated hips, tuberculosis of the spine, cerebral palsy and poliomyelitis with resultant paralysis of trunk muscles, may cause such changes in an individual's posture that the usual hereditary and environmental influences are obscured.

Factors Related to Organic Function.   One frequently mentioned criterion of good posture is the relationship of the alignment of the body to organic function.[12, 22] Postural patterns are not thought to be good unless they both permit and encourage normal function of the vital physiologic processes, particularly those of respiration, circulation, digestion and elimination. Considerable clinical evidence has been presented to substantiate this belief, but experimental evidence is scarce.[8, 16, 21]

In this regard, Hellebrandt commented that the concept of the harmful effect of poor posture on visceral function was "based on more or less tenuous evidence without regard for the wide margin of safety under which all organ systems function and the paucity of proof that the anatomical position of a viscus is a valid criterion of the adequacy of its physiologic behavior."[16] There is, however, some evidence of a relationship between menstrual function and posture. Hoffman studied the findings of the routine orthopedic examination for two groups of college women, one group known as the "dysmenorrhea group," the other as the "no-pain group." The two groups were found to differ significantly with respect to two postural traits, namely anteroposterior pelvic tilt and bilateral hip asymmetry.[19]

Fox also studied the relation of certain aspects of posture to dysmenorrhea.[10] She investigated the incidence of dysmenorrhea in three groups of young women, one a control group, one a group characterized by sway back (posterior list of the trunk), and one group characterized by faulty pelvic tilt (increased inclination). She found that dysmenorrhea occurred with greater severity among the sway back group than among the control group. Unlike Hoffman, however, she did not find a significant relationship between pelvic tilt and dysmenorrhea.

Factors Related to Strength and Flexibility.   That strength and flexibility are factors in posture would seem to be a universally accepted thesis, judging by the preponderance of strength and flexibility exercises included in the majority of corrective programs and also by the strength and flexibility measurements included in posture tests. Interest has been shown particularly in the strength of the abdominals, scapular adductors and thoracic spinal extensors, and in the flexibility of the pectorals and the hamstrings. There seems to have been little scientific investigation of the relation of these strengths and flexibilities to posture. It would seem that the widespread assumption of such a relationship may have been responsible for the attitude that there was no need for such investigation. Yet nowhere in the literature can the authors find a clear statement as to what constitutes optimal strength or optimal flexibility for the maintenance of good posture. Possibly one is justified in assuming it to be a matter of balance between opposing muscle groups, rather than of strength or flexibility *per se*, or of relative muscle length. These aspects would seem to bear investigation.

In comparing the abdominal strength of a control group with that of two faulty posture groups — one characterized by sway back and the other by faulty pelvic tilt — Fox did not find that abdominal strength was a differentiating factor. She recommended that further study be made of this problem, especially as her sway back group was much smaller than the others.[10]

Factors Related to Psychological Aspects of Posture. There are several psychological aspects of postural problems with which the instructor should be prepared to deal. For instance, not all posture problems can be explained in terms of physical causes, either musculoskeletal or environmental. Atypical postures may be symptoms of personality problems or emotional disturbances. The hanging head and drooping shoulders of some adolescent girls are often not physical in origin but are symptoms of shyness and lack of self-confidence. Postural exercises will do little to help such girls unless they are used in conjunction with psychological help. The same is true of the small man whose bantam-cock posture is merely an overcompensation for his feelings of inferiority. Proficiency in some sport in which physical size is not important (e.g., swimming or diving) might be much more effective for correcting his lordosis than hours of posture exercises in the corrective gym.

One pernicious psychological cause of undesirable posture among girls is the example set by dress models. This influence on certain girls is more difficult to combat than almost any other cause of poor posture.

Another type of psychological problem is demonstrated by the emotional reaction of an overly sensitive individual to a conspicuously abnormal posture or body build. As is true of other physical handicaps, it may interfere with the individual's personal and social development unless he learns to see it in its right perspective. The abnormal posture or build may be impossible to correct, in which case the problem is to achieve as much improvement as possible and then to discover ways of standing, sitting and walking that will minimize the conspicuousness of what cannot be corrected. As in the case of the undersized man, proficiency in some sport can be effective in providing a healthy type of compensation. The instructor's role here is to offer suggestions and to present opportunities. He should be matter-of-fact and should avoid over-persistence.

In the types of problems described above, the chief principles to follow are (1) to learn as much as possible about the psychology of behavior and adjustment and (2) when feasible, to work with or at least to seek the advice of a psychiatrist or psychologist who is treating the student in question.

An important role of psychology in posture education is that of motivation. No matter how well the teacher or the therapist has selected the exercises, and no matter how conscientiously the student or the patient practices them, they will have little effect in improving the individual's habitual postural patterns unless he is motivated to *want* to improve them.

And finally, psychology is used as a technique of treatment by those who like the method of using mental concepts to change neuromuscular pathways.[30, 31] For success in this method they depend completely upon the cooperation of the individual in mental participation, for it is by this means, they believe, that the changes in the neuromuscular pathways are effected.

POSTURAL PRINCIPLES

The following areas appear to be the only ones for which there is objective support:

1. Postural reflex action
2. Stability of the erect standing position as evidenced by the relationship of the line of gravity to the base of support
3. The influence of heredity and environment on posture
4. The relationship between certain postural faults and one type of faulty organic function, namely dysmenorrhea.

Since so much emphasis is placed on posture, it is indeed unfortunate that there is so little objective evidence that our efforts are being made in the right direction. The authors are inclined to be sympathetic toward Miller's conclusions:

. . . although orthopedists and physical educators have been working actively for the past fifty years with the problems involved in posture, there is still a seemingly unwarranted lack of agreement among practitioners of both fields. Three basic differences of opinion are implicated in this bewildering lack of unanimity: (1) whether any particular posture is more advantageous physiologically than any other posture; (2) whether prescribed physical activity can actually modify posture; and (3) whether it is possible to agree upon a definition of "good" posture and upon a method of accurately measuring such a concept. Eminent authorities in both physical education and medical circles can be found to support either side of any of these questions.[25]

In view of this lack of evidence and these differences of opinion, what stand shall the kinesiologist take in regard to posture education? Shall he ignore it, or shall he formulate tentative principles to guide him in posture education and correction, and shall he adhere to these until they are definitely disproved and indications for other principles have become apparent? The authors believe that, either consciously or unconsciously, the physical educator is bound to be guided by *some* principles of posture, whether they are founded on fact or conjecture. In recognition of the difficulty of devising an accurate measure of habitual posture, the formulation of some guiding principles based on the best knowledge available, incomplete though it may be, would seem to be justifiable, even imperative, if we are to continue to teach "good body mechanics" in our schools and clinics. In full recognition of their limitations and knowing that they may be superseded as new evidence is revealed by further research or by clinical evidence, the following postural principles are suggested:

1. The weight-bearing segments of the body are so aligned in good standing posture* that the line of gravity passes through these segments within certain "normal" limits yet to be defined. Such a definition should either be applicable to all physiques or else indicate to what types of physique it is, or is not, applicable.
2. Inasmuch as Hellebrandt found that in *every* individual she had observed, the average location of the center of gravity was close to the geometric

---

*The term "good standing posture" is used advisedly. Allowances should be made for atypical builds.

center of the supporting base, it would seem that the relation of the line of gravity to the base of support is not indicative of body alignment and therefore does not serve as a measure of posture.

3. Good standing posture is a position of extension of the weight-bearing joints. This should be an easy extension and should not be accompanied by strain or tension (Fig. 16–5).

4. From the point of view of energy expenditure, good posture would seem to be a position which requires a minimum expenditure of energy *for the maintenance of good alignment.* Excess energy expenditure indicates hypertonicity or poor neuromuscular coordination, or both. A posture requiring an absolute minimal energy expenditure does not fulfill the requirements of good posture because it is characterized by "hanging on the ligaments," that is, a dependence upon the ligaments of the weight-bearing joints, rather than upon muscle tonus, for resisting the downward pull of gravity.

5. Good posture, in repose and in activity, permits mechanically efficient function of the joints. In other words, friction in the joints is minimized, ten-

Figure 16–5 Except for a slightly forward head, the subject shows good alignment and extension without strain.

sions of opposing ligaments are balanced and pressures within the joints are equalized. Hence the skeletal structure is architecturally and mechanically sound and there is a minimum of wear and tear on the joints.

6. Good posture, both static and dynamic, requires normal muscle tonus. This implies adequate development of the antigravity muscles to resist the pull of gravity successfully and to maintain good alignment without excessive effort or tension. It also implies a balance between antagonistic muscle groups. There is no indication, however, that "the stronger the muscles the better the posture."

7. Good posture, both static and dynamic, requires sufficient flexibility in the structures of the weight-bearing joints to permit good alignment without interference or strain. Poor flexibility may be caused by tight ligaments or fasciae, by short muscles or by hypertrophied muscles. The flexibility should not be so great, however, that excessive muscular effort is needed to keep the weight-bearing joints in alignment.

8. Good posture requires good coordination. This implies good neuromuscular control and well-developed postural reflexes.

9. Adjustments in posture can be made more readily by individuals who have a good kinesthetic awareness of the postures they assume and of the degree of tension in their muscles.

10. Good posture, both static and dynamic, is favorable, or at least not detrimental, to organic function.

11. A relationship exists between habitual posture and personality, also between habitual posture and extreme emotional states.

12. In view of the great variety of human physiques and individual differences in structure, due either to heredity or to early environmental influence, there can be no single detailed description of good posture (Figs. 16–3, *C* and 16–4, *C*).

13. In the last analysis, both the static and the dynamic posture of any individual should be judged on the basis of how well it meets the demands made upon it throughout his lifetime.

THE MECHANISM FOR MAINTAINING AND ADJUSTING ERECT POSTURE

1. The proprioceptors are responsible for most of the reflex movements necessary for the maintenance of the erect standing position and for the adjustments that must be made to meet changing conditions. They include the receptors of the muscles, joints and labyrinths and are accompanied by two exteroceptors—one visual and the other cutaneous, the latter serving as a proprioceptor together with the pressure receptors, especially in connection with the extensor thrust reflex.

2. Volitional postural adjustments are made by the same mechanism that is responsible for all volitional movements (p. 66) and, of necessity, are governed by the structural limitations of the individual.

3. There are several schools of thought regarding the method of changing habitual postural patterns. Some believe that it can be accomplished by the

frequent repetition of carefully selected exercises performed with control and with constant attention to correct form.[12, 14, 22, 24, 27] Others believe that the rebuilding of the necessary neuromuscular pathways can be accomplished only by the indirect method, that is, by influencing the individual's neuromuscular response by means of his thought processes. Mental concepts are utilized for this purpose.[30, 31] Still others seek to establish new postural habits by practicing movements which are believed to develop the natural postural reflexes.[13] All groups recognize that the establishing of new postural patterns can take place only within the limits of the individual's structural heritage.

4. The kinesthetic sense is believed to be a vital factor in the mechanism for establishing and adjusting postural patterns, but this has not yet been demonstrated satisfactorily.

POSTURAL ADAPTATION TO EXTERNAL CONDITIONS AND SPECIAL PROBLEMS

There are a number of conditions which necessitate postural adjustment if one is to maintain a reasonably balanced standing position. These include standing on either an uphill or a downhill slope; standing on the level but wearing high heels; standing on a moving surface, such as bus, streetcar, subway or other train; holding a heavy bundle against the front of the body; pregnancy; and standing on one foot. In all of these the body can be relied upon to adjust automatically through the function of proprioceptors and the feedback mechanism. From the point of view of "good body mechanics," however, the nature of the adjustment may not always be desirable. For instance, one can *balance* when standing on an inclined plane by bending at the knees, hips or spine, but it would be mechanically preferable to maintain vertical segmental alignment, as well as balance. To achieve this position one would need to stand so that the center of gravity of each weight-bearing segment was centered above the base of support. This centering can be achieved only by making the adjustment at the ankles and feet.[3] The same is true for the person wearing high heels and for the pregnant woman, although some women lack the necessary abdominal strength for this action. It is highly desirable for them to strengthen these muscles in order to resist the tendency to lean back from the waist, an adjustment that is almost sure to cause trouble in the lower back. The person carrying a heavy bundle against the front of the body may find that adjustment at the ankles is not enough, especially if the load is excessively heavy. In this case some adjustment at the knees and hips will help, but every effort should be made not to lean back at the waist because of the danger of lower back strain.

When standing in a moving bus, streetcar or train, there are three adjustments one should be prepared to make: adjustment to acceleration, to deceleration and to side-to-side sway. The same principle applies to all three, namely, establishing a comfortably wide stance in the direction of motion (forward-backward for acceleration and deceleration, and sideward for a steady speed, especially if there is a pronounced sway). During sudden acceleration especially, the person tends to be thrown toward the back of the vehicle, in keeping with

Newton's first law of motion. The foot toward the rear, therefore, should be well braced and more weight should be borne by the forward foot in anticipation of the jerk. The reverse is true during deceleration and stopping. In both acceleration and deceleration the body will be less likely to be thrown off balance if the knees are slightly flexed as this shortens the lever upon which the vehicle's motion acts.

In a crowded vehicle that makes frequent stops it may not be possible to keep adapting the stance, and one may have to rely on a hand grasp to supplement the foot adjustment. A slightly oblique stance, favoring the forward-backward direction, serves as an acceptable compromise.

The adjustment to standing on one foot is a delicate one but is usually managed automatically by the muscle, joint and labyrinthian proprioceptors and the reflex response. The adjustment consists of a shift in the body weight to the single supporting limb and in the support of the pelvis on the side of the free limb. The latter adjustment requires additional effort by the quadratus lumborum and the abductors (gluteus medius and minimus, tensor fasciae latae and oblique abdominal muscles on the support side). The iliopsoas, which is continuously active during all standing, undoubtedly increases its activity in steadying the lumbar spine.[1] In addition, there is probably a continuous interplay of the deep muscles of the lumbar spine and possibly of many of the lower extremity muscles. The alternating action of the foot and ankle muscles, especially the tarsal pronators and supinators, is quite pronounced in their effort to keep the center of gravity over the narrow base of support. This problem can be helped somewhat by turning the toes slightly outward (i.e., rotating the thigh slightly outward) before the one-legged stance is assumed. For a more precise muscular analysis of the adjustments made in standing on one foot, an electromyographic investigation is needed.

SUPPLEMENTARY MATERIAL

A few investigators have been interested in the possibility of a relationship between the line of gravity and standing posture. In their historic survey of this subject Cureton and Wickens noted that no quantitative studies had been found which related the center of gravity to the area of the base as a diagnostic test for posture.[7] Using the reaction board technique for determining the position of the line of gravity and their own method of analyzing anteroposterior posture, they made a number of correlation studies. They concluded that there was a definite relationship between the position of the line of gravity and posture, strength, physical fitness and athletic ability. The coefficient of correlation between their measure of kyphosis and the line of gravity measurement was 0.256. The relationship between body lean and the line of gravity was indicated by a coefficient of 0.864. This denotes a high degree of positive relationship, but on the other hand, body lean *is* the position of the body which is associated with the anteroposterior shifting of the line of gravity. They are one and the same thing. In fact, one wonders why the relationship was only 0.864 instead of 1.000. In correlating body lean with kyphosis, Cureton and Wickens obtained a coefficient of 0.363.[7] They interpreted this as an indication of a trend for men who habitually stood with their weight more forward to have straighter upper backs. The authors apparently did not investigate the relationship between the anteroposterior position of the line of gravity and the alignment of body segments.

Crowley and Johnston in two separate studies could find no relationship between the anteroposterior position of the line of gravity and the total anteroposterior posture as measured by the Wellesley (MacEwan-Howe) objective method.[32] Likewise, Hellebrandt and her co-workers, using this method on a larger number of subjects, could find no relationship between the objective posture score and the anteroposterior shifting of the line of gravity. They suggested that this surprising failure to find a relationship between the two might indicate that the posture criterion in common use is based on an aesthetic concept of posture rather than on a physiologic one.[17]

Directions for Making Line-of-Gravity Photographs

For this purpose a camera, such as the kind employed for taking posture photographs, is set up facing the equipment used for the reaction board method of determining the location of a person's center of gravity as viewed from the side. Computations will be simpler if the distance from the camera to the board is adjusted so that the length of the board in the photograph is in round numbers such as 5 or 10 cm. It is possible to do this by taking the back off the camera and looking through a piece of ground glass held behind the camera. The dimensions of the image on the glass will be the same as those on the film. The anteroposterior position of the center of gravity is found as described on page 386, no. 6. The length measurements (i.e., total length of board and distance "d") are made on the photograph instead of on the board itself. A vertical line is then erected from the point at which the line of gravity intersects the board to a point beyond the level of the top of the subject's head. Some interesting experiments can be performed through the use of line-of-gravity photographs. This technique has the advantage of making it possible to take a series of photographs of one subject assuming a variety of positions and to make the computations and measurements at a later time. Another advantage is that several prints of the same photograph can be made and used by the entire class.

LABORATORY EXPERIENCES

1. To demonstrate the alignment of the body segments take from five to seven large wooden blocks, each having a vertical line painted in the center of one side. A layer of thick felt should be glued to the top and bottom of each block and a small hook screwed into each of two opposite sides.
   a. Arrange the blocks in a straight column with the painted lines in front. Connect the hooks on the sides with elastic bands. The elastic "ligaments" will be under equal tension and the felt "cartilages" under equal pressure when the column is in perfect alignment.
   b. Now insert wedges between the blocks in such a way that every other block tips to the left and the alternate blocks tip to the right. The elastic "ligaments" will now be under unequal tension and the felt "cartilages" under unequal pressure.

The zigzag alignment of the painted lines illustrates graphically the poor alignment of the segments.

2. To demonstrate good and poor alignment of a single weight-bearing joint, such as the knee, two blocks arranged like those described above may be used in a similar manner.

3. Take two anteroposterior line of gravity photographs of one or more subjects, one photograph representing the subject's "best posture," and the other an exaggerated zigzag posture, but with the weight centered over the feet. Compare the postures and the anteroposterior positions of the line of gravity in the two photos.

4. Take anteroposterior line of gravity photographs of several subjects representing various postures. After drawing the line of gravity on each photograph, observe them carefully and note the relation of the line to the head, shoulders, upper trunk, lower trunk, pelvis, knees and ankles.

5. Take ten anteroposterior line of gravity photographs of one subject within a period of one week. Compare these.

6. Take anteroposterior line of gravity photographs of several subjects representing different physique types. Can you make any generalizations about the relation of physique to posture?

7. Do an original posture study using a small number of subjects.

REFERENCES

1. Basmajian, J. V.: Muscles Alive, 3rd Ed. Baltimore: The Williams & Wilkins Company, 1974.
2. Bowen, W. P., and Stone, H. A.: Applied Anatomy and Kinesiology, 7th Ed. Philadelphia: Lea & Febiger, 1953.
3. Broer, M.: Efficiency of Human Movement, 3rd Ed. Philadelphia: W. B. Saunders Company, 1973.
4. Brunnstrom, S.: Clinical Kinesiology, 3rd Ed. Philadelphia: F. A. Davis Company, 1972.
5. Campbell, D. G.: Posture: A gesture toward life. Physiother. Rev., 15:43–47, 1935.
6. Cowell, C. C.: Bodily posture as a mental attitude. J. Health & Phys. Ed., 1:14–15, 56, 1930.
7. Cureton, T. K., and Wickens, J. S.: The center of gravity of the human body in the antero-posterior plane and its relation to posture. Res. Quart. Am. Assn. Health & Phys. Ed. (Suppl.), 6:93–105, 1935.
8. Deaver, G. G.: Posture and its relation to mental and physical health. Res. Quart. Am. Assn. Health & Phys. Ed., 4:221–228, 1933.
9. Evans, F. G. (Ed.): Biomechanical Studies of the Musculo-Skeletal System. Springfield, Ill.: Charles C Thomas, Publisher, 1961.
10. Fox, M. G.: The relationship of abdominal strength to selected posture faults. Res. Quart. Am. Assn. Health, Phys. Ed. & Recrn., 22:141–144, 1951.
11. Frost, L. H.: Individual structural differences in the orthopedic examination. J. Health & Phys. Ed., 9:90–93, 122, 1938.
12. Goldthwait, J. E., Brown, L. T., Swaim, L. T., and Kuhns, J. G.: Essentials of Body Mechanics in Health and Disease, 5th Ed. Philadelphia: J. B. Lippincott Company, 1952.
13. Haller, J. S., and Gurewitsch, A. D.: An approach to dynamic posture based on primitive motion patterns. Arch. Phys. Med., 31:632–640, 1950.
14. Hawley, G.: Kinesiology of Corrective Exercise, 2nd Ed. Philadelphia: Lea & Febiger, 1949.
15. Hellebrandt, F. A.: Physiology and the physical educator. Res. Quart. Am. Assn. Health, Phys. Ed. & Recrn., 11:12–29, 1940.
16. Hellebrandt, F. A.: Postural adjustments in convalescence and rehabilitation. Fed. Proc., 3:243–246, 1944.
17. Hellebrandt, F. A., and Franseen, E. B.: Physiological study of the vertical stance of man. Physiol. Rev., 23:220–255, 1943.
18. Hellebrandt, F. A., Riddle, K. S., and Fries, E. C.: Influence of postural sway on stance photography. Physiother. Rev., 22:88, 1942.
19. Hoffman, E.: Certain Physical and Physiological Characteristics as Related to the Incidence of Severe Dysmenorrhea. Unpublished M.S. thesis. Wellesley College, 1942.

20. Joseph, J.: Man's Posture; Electromyographic Studies. Springfield, Ill.: Charles C Thomas, Publisher, 1960.
21. Karpovich, P. V., and Sinning, W. E.: Physiology of Muscular Activity, 7th Ed. Philadelphia: W. B. Saunders Company, 1971.
22. Kelly, E. D.: Adapted and Corrective Physical Education, 4th Ed. New York: Ronald Press Company, 1965.
23. McCormick, H. G.: The Metabolic Cost of Maintaining a Standing Position, with Special Reference to Body Alignment. New York: King's Crown Press, 1942.
24. Mensendieck, B.: Mensendieck System of Functional Exercises. Portland, Me.: Southworth-Anthoensen Press, 1937.
25. Miller, K. D.: A physical educator looks at posture. J. Sch. Health, *21*:89–94, 1951.
26. Morton, D. J.: Human Locomotion and Body Form. Baltimore: The Williams & Wilkins Company, 1952.
27. Rathbone, J. L., and Hunt, V. V.: Corrective Physical Education, 7th Ed. Philadelphia: W. B. Saunders Company, 1965.
28. Sheldon, W. H., Stevens, S. S., and Tucker, W. B.: The Varieties of Human Physique. New York: Harper, 1940.
29. Steindler, A.: Kinesiology of the Human Body. Springfield, Ill.: Charles C Thomas, Publisher, 1973, Lecture XIV.
30. Sweigard, L. E.: Human Movement Potential; Its Ideokinetic Facilitation. New York: Dodd, Mead & Company, 1974.
31. Todd, M. E.: The Thinking Body. Boston: Charles T. Branford Company, 1949.
32. Wellesley College Studies in Hygiene and Physical Education: Factors in antero-posterior posture. Res. Quart., A.A.H.P.E. (Suppl.) 9:89–96, 1938.

RECOMMENDED READINGS

Kendall, H. O., and Kendall, F. P.: Developing and maintaining good posture. J. Am. Phys. Ther. Assn., *48*:319–336, 1968.
Metheny, E. R.: Body Dynamics. New York: McGraw-Hill Book Co., Inc., 1952, Chap. 7.
Wells, K. F.: What we don't know about posture. J. Health, Phys. Ed. & Recrn., *29*:31–32, 1958.

Chapter Seventeen

MOVING ONE'S BODY ON THE GROUND OR ON OTHER RESISTANT SURFACES

This category includes both nonmanipulative movements performed on a stationary or limited base and all forms of locomotion by self-propulsion performed on the ground.

MOVEMENTS OF THE BODY ON A STATIONARY OR LIMITED BASE

This group embraces the majority of calisthenic exercises, such as those for warming-up purposes and for improving muscle tonus, flexibility, agility and postural alignment. These are segmental movements rather than movements of the body as a whole. The only movement that involves the body as a whole and is performed on a stationary base on the ground is the rotation of the body about its own vertical axis, as when pirouetting on the toes or on ice skates. Rotation about successive points of contact with the ground, such as in a single cartwheel or a single forward roll, might be included, depending upon one's interpretation of "limited base." When performed in a series these activities constitute forms of locomotion.

The following are suggested as the major principles applying to nonmanipulative movements of the body when it is supported by the ground on a stationary or limited base. They are in addition to the principles relating to stability which were discussed in Chapter Fourteen.

Principle I. Law of Inertia: An object which is at rest will remain so unless acted upon by a force. When the "object" is the human body itself, or a segment of it, the force giving impetus to it is usually internal, i.e., muscular contraction. Another force which must not be overlooked is the force of gravity, which is always operative, except in outer space. In many instances a movement is initiated by muscular action and then carried on by gravitational force because of the position in which the segment has been placed. If this is the desired direction of the movement, the muscles which normally perform the opposite movement

410

contract eccentrically in order to control the speed of the segment. These same opposing muscles will check the movement if it is not desired. A common example of this controlling and checking action is seen in slow deep knee bending as the body assumes a squatting position. The movement is started by the momentary contraction of the hip, knee and ankle flexors and then is carried on by the lengthening contraction of the extensor muscles. If one wishes to stop the movement before a full squat is reached, the same muscles must contract statically with just the right amount of force to balance the gravitational force acting on the lower extremity levers.

Principle II.   Law of Action and Reaction: To every action there is an equal and opposite reaction. In all movements performed in the standing position, the counterpressure of the ground against the feet is essential to the accurate performance of a movement of one or more parts of the body. The performer is usually unaware of this in easy movements, but if he were to attempt vigorous movements standing on soft sand he would notice the difference. The principle holds true no matter what part of the body is in contact with the supporting surface.

Principle III.   A long lever has greater velocity at the end than does a short lever moving at the same angular velocity. Hence, in a vigorous arm-swing from the shoulder, the hand will have greater velocity if the elbow is kept fully extended. Likewise, in a vigorous movement of the lower extremity, such as a kick, the foot will have greater velocity if the knee is fully extended.

Principle IV.   Centrifugal force is developed in circular movements of bodily segments, as in vigorous arm circling. This should be recognized as a potential source of injury to the shoulder joint as the centrifugal force creates a dislocating tendency.

Principle V.   The momentum of any part of a supported body can be transferred to the rest of the body. For instance, if one sits on the end of a table with the legs hanging down, then lies down on the back and raises the legs overhead until the feet almost touch the table behind the head, and then vigorously swings both limbs forward-downward, then suddenly checks their motion when they touch the table, the trunk will rise to a vertical position. Or if one stands with one arm extended forward and then flings it horizontally sideward-backward as far as possible, the whole body will tend to follow the arm in horizontal rotation. It is through the application of this same principle that the ballet dancer and the figure skater are enabled to spin in place. In both cases friction is minimized by the footwear worn and by the smoothness of the supporting surface.

Principle VI.   Rotational movement of the body as a whole may be decelerated by lengthening the radius, and accelerated by shortening the radius while the spin is in progress. When spinning on the toes (or skates) the dancer and the skater lengthen the radius by extending the arms sideward at shoulder level, and shorten it by bending the arms in close to the body. The spectacular increase in the speed of the spin when the arms are bent gives the impression that an additional force has acted upon the body, whereas the acceleration is merely the result of decreasing the moment of inertia about the vertical axis. The extended arms cause the moment of inertia of the spinning body to increase. Because the angular momentum is conserved the angular velocity decreases and the spinning body slows down.

LOCOMOTION BY SELF-PROPULSION

Ordinarily the propulsion is provided by the lower extremities, but it is occasionally provided by all four extremities, as in creeping, or by the upper extremities alone, as in walking on the hands or in suspension. It may involve the use of wheels, blades, skis or other equipment attached to the feet, or it may involve a vehicle such as a bicycle or wheel chair, or a small craft such as a boat, canoe or surfboard propelled by means of the arms or legs, with or without the use of a propelling implement like oars, paddles or poles. Locomotion by self-propulsion may be on the ground or in the water, but, at the present writing, not in the air without support. Aside from locomotor activities which are used mostly for utilitarian purposes, there are many skills in which man indulges for sport and pleasure. For purposes of systematizing the study of locomotor skills the following classification is suggested.

Forms of Locomotion by Self-Propulsion

1. On Foot
Walking
Running
Climbing (inclined plane, stairs, ladder)
Descending (inclined plane, stairs, ladder)
Jumping, leaping, hurdling
Skipping, hopping, sliding, side-stepping
Progressive dance steps, e.g., polka, mazurka
Snow shoeing
Ski touring (cross country skiing)
Walking on stilts
2. On Wheels and Blades
Bicycling
Roller skating
Ice skating
Propelling self in wheel chair
3. On Hands
Walking on hands
Hand traveling suspended from boom, horizontal ladder, traveling ring
4. On Hands and Knees or Hands and Feet
Creeping
Crutch walking
Stunts, e.g., dog running, rabbit hopping
5. Rotatory Locomotion
Cartwheels
Handsprings
Forward, backward and sideward rolls

Walking

To the casual observer, the movements involved in walking appear to be relatively simple, yet kinesiologic analysis shows them to be exceedingly complex. The dovetailing of muscular action and the synchronization of joint movements beautifully illustrate the teamwork present in all bodily movements. Not even the most complex piece of machinery designed by the most skillful engineers exceeds the movements of the human machine in perfection of detail or in potential smoothness of function.

Research on the gait, such as that conducted at the University of California as part of the Prosthetic Devices Research Project and that of Dr. Patricia Murray, Dr. J. V. Basmajian, and many, many others, has served to emphasize the complexity of human locomotion. In the third edition of his book, *Muscles Alive,* Basmajian has written an excellent chapter on this subject and has reported on numerous electromyographic studies.[1, 11, 12, 13, 14, 15]

Neuromuscular Considerations. Walking is a reflex action; no conscious control is necessary. On the contrary, if attention is focused on any part of the gait, tension is likely to develop and the natural rhythm and coordination are disturbed. Reflexes control not only the movements of the limbs but also the extension of both the supporting limb and the trunk in resisting the downward pull of gravity. This extension serves to give stability to the body in the supporting phases of locomotion, a stability which provides for effective muscular action in producing the necessary movements. Thus, in walking, as in all the motions of the body, smooth, coordinated movement requires properly functioning reflexes, normal flexibility of the joints and optimum stability of the body as a whole in the weight-bearing phases of the act.

Mechanical Considerations. Walking is accomplished by the alternating action of the two lower extremities. (See Fig. 17-1.) It is an example of translatory motion of the body as a whole brought about by means of the angular motion of some of its parts. It is also an example of a periodic or pendulum-like movement in which the moving segment (in this case, the lower extremity) may be said to start at zero, pass through its arc of motion and fall to zero again at

Figure 17-1 An example of linear motion of the body as a whole resulting from the angular motion of some of its parts.

the end of each stroke. In walking, each lower extremity undergoes two phases, the swinging or recovery phase and the supporting phase. The supporting phase is further divided into a restraining phase (from the moment the foot touches the ground until it is directly under the center of the body) and the propulsion phase (from the moment when the foot is under the center of gravity until it leaves the ground). The beginning of the restraining phase of one leg overlaps the end of the propulsive phase of the other leg. Thus it constitutes a brief phase of double support when both feet are on the ground. This is characteristic of the walk and serves to differentiate it from the run. In the swinging phase of the walk, the action of the lower extremity may be likened to that of the pendulum of a clock and, in the supporting phase, to that of the inverted pendulum of a metronome. Gravity and momentum are the chief sources of motion for the swinging phase; hence, this phase represents a ballistic type of movement (p. 49), particularly when the individual is walking at his natural pace. The source of motion for the supporting phase is, for the first half, the momentum of the forward-moving trunk (provided by the propulsive action by the other leg) and, for the second half, the contraction of the extensor muscles of the supporting leg. Whether the supporting phase can also be classed as ballistic movement is open to question. Even the swinging phase varies in its ballistic quality according to the speed of the gait and the skill, flexibility and build of the walker. A tense individual will tend to substitute muscular action for the pendulum swing of the lower extremity, and an individual with tight hamstrings will have to exert additional muscular force to overcome the restraining action of the short hamstrings. An individual who has knock-knees or fat thighs will also have difficulty in achieving a natural, pendulum swing because of friction and interference between the two limbs. In order to avoid this interference he must increase the lateral distance between his limbs and thus introduce an undesirable lateral component of motion.

Walking and other similar forms of locomotion involve a balancing of forces. Only the most obvious of these are mentioned here.

1. The inertia of the stationary body is overcome by the horizontal component of force. Since periodic movement is characterized by an alternating increase and decrease of speed, inertia must be overcome at every step. As the center of gravity moves forward, it momentarily passes beyond the anterior margin of the base of support and a temporary loss of balance results. At this point the downward pull of gravity threatens a complete loss of equilibrium. A timely recovery of balance is brought about, however, as the foot is placed on the ground. Thus a new base of support is established and a new supporting phase is begun.

2. When forward motion has been imparted to the trunk by means of the backward thrust of the leg and foot, it tends to continue unless restrained by another force. Once the center of gravity passes beyond the base of support, it is essential to restrain the action of the trunk until a new base of support is established. Hence, as the foot is brought to the ground in front of the body at the close of its recovery phase, a restraining phase is constituted. This diminishes as the leg approaches a vertical position. During the period that the foot is in front of the center of gravity, there is a *forward* component of force in the

thrust of the foot against the ground. This results in a *backward* counterpressure of the ground against the foot which is transmitted to the leg and thence to the trunk.

3. In the same phase of the step as that discussed above in section 2, the trunk is acted upon by the downward pull of gravity as well as by momentum. This downward force is counteracted by the vertical component of force of the supporting leg. During the phase of double support each leg exerts some vertical force. If the vertical force exceeds that needed to balance the gravitational force, it results in an exaggerated lift to the body, causing a gait characterized by a bounce or unusual spring.

4. The forward-moving trunk meets with air resistance which tends to push it backward. By inclining the body forward, the pull of gravity is utilized to balance the force of the air resistance. When walking against a strong wind, it is necessary to incline the body farther forward in order to maintain balance. (See Fig. 14–10.) If the air resistance is not balanced by the force of gravity, it must be balanced by the contraction of the abdominal and other anterior muscles of the neck and trunk. If the body is inclined too far forward, however, the force of gravity acts too strongly on it and must be counteracted by tension of the posterior muscles. Thus the proper degree of forward inclination is a factor in muscular economy.

5. The degree to which the pressure of the foot actually imparts motion to the body in the propulsive phase and restrains it in the restraining phase is in direct proportion to the counterpressure of the supporting surface. If the surface lacks solidity, as in the case of mud, soft snow and sand, it offers too little resistance to give the needed counterpressure. The pressure of the foot results in slipping or sinking, and more pressure must be applied in order to achieve even a slow forward progress. Hence the efficiency of the gait depends upon the right balance between the pressure of the foot and the counterpressure of the supporting surface (Fig. 17–2).

6. Like counterpressure, friction is also an essential factor in the effective application of the forces needed in walking. Because of the diagonal thrust of the leg at the beginning and end of the supporting phase, friction between the foot and the ground is essential in order that the counterpressure of the ground may be transmitted to the body. For efficient walking, friction must be sufficient to balance the horizontal component of force. If it is insufficient, the thrust of

Figure 17–2 The ground reaction force R is equal in action line and magnitude to the downward thrust of the foot during walking, but is opposite in direction. The force is greater at heel-strike than at mid-stance because of the body's momentum, and greater at push-off due to the plantar flexion thrust of the calf muscles driving the body forward. (From Williams, M., and Lissner, H. R.: Biomechanics of Human Motion. Philadelphia: W. B. Saunders Company, 1962.)

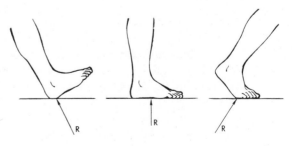

the foot results in a slipping of the foot itself, rather than in the desired propulsion of the body. The greater the horizontal component of force (as when walking with a long stride), the greater the dependence upon friction for efficient locomotion.

Mechanical Principles Applied to Walking

Principle I.   A body at rest will remain at rest unless acted upon by a force. Since walking is produced by a pendulum-like motion of the lower extremities, the inertia of the body must be overcome at every step.

Principle II.   A body in motion will continue in motion unless acted upon by a force. Since motion is imparted to the trunk by the backward thrust of the leg, the trunk has a tendency to continue moving forward, even beyond the base of support. A brief restraining action of the forward limb serves as a check on the momentum of the trunk.

Principle III.   Force applied diagonally consists of two components, horizontal and vertical. The vertical component in walking serves to counteract the downward pull of gravity. The horizontal component serves (1) in the restraining phase, to check forward motion, and (2) in the propulsive phase, to produce it. The horizontal component of force in the propulsive phase must exceed that in the restraining phase if the end result is to be progressive forward locomotion.

Principle IV.   Translatory movement of a lever is achieved by the repeated alternation of two rotatory movements, the lever turning first about one end and then the other end.[19] In walking, the lower extremity alternates between rotating about the foot's point of contact with the ground and the hip joint.

Principle V.   The speed of the gait is directly related to the magnitude of the pushing force and to the direction of its application. This force is provided by the extensor muscles of the hip, knee and ankle joints, and the direction of application is determined by the slant of the lower extremity when the force is being applied.

Principle VI.   The economy of the gait is related to its timing with reference to the length of the limbs. The most economical gait is one which is so timed as to permit pendular motion of the lower extremities.

Principle VII.   Walking has been described as an alternating loss and recovery of balance.[19] This being so, a new base of support must be established at every step.

Principle VIII.   As propulsion of the body is brought about by the diagonal push of the foot against the supporting surface, the efficiency of locomotion depends upon the counterpressure and friction provided by this surface.

Principle IX.   Stability of the body is directly related to the size of the base of support. In walking, the lateral distance between the feet is a factor in maintaining balance.

a. Too narrow a lateral distance between the feet, such as occurs when one foot is placed directly in front of the other, increases the difficulty of maintaining balance as it decreases the width of the base of support.

b. Too wide a lateral distance between the feet increases stability, but tends to cause a weaving gait and to make the body sway from side to side.

c. The optimum position of the feet appears to be one in which the inner borders fall approximately along a single straight line.

Anatomic Analysis of Walking

The action taking place in the joints of the lower extremity consists essentially of flexion and extension. But in much the same way that the shoulder girdle cooperates with the arm movements of the upper extremity, the pelvic girdle cooperates in movements of the lower extremities. The pelvis has the double task of transmitting the weight of the body alternately first over one limb, then over the other, and of putting each acetabulum in a favorable position for the action of the corresponding femur. The adaptations of the pelvic position are made in the joints of the thoracic and lumbar spine as well as in the hip joints. Thus, as first one foot and then the other is put forward, the flexion and extension movements of the thigh are accompanied by slight rotatory movements and ab- and adduction at the hips, and by slight lateral flexion and rotation of the spine. (Figures 17–3 and 17–4.)

The muscular analysis presented in the original edition of this text was based on Wells' own investigations (using palpation and inspection), supplemented by information from the literature available prior to 1950. It was later revised to incorporate the findings of two electromyographic investigations, the Prosthetic Devices Research Project at the University of California in Berkeley,[1] and a study by Sheffield, Gersten and Mastellone.[17] Since then a number of revisions have been made to incorporate findings from subsequent EMG investigations. The last word on locomotion has not yet been written, so it behooves all kinesiologists to keep abreast of the research being done in this area.

Swinging Phase.   The swinging phase begins with toe-off and ends with heel-strike.

Spine and Pelvis.   *Movements:* Rotation toward opposite side; prevention of dropping of pelvis over unsupported side.

Muscles.   Semispinalis, rotatores, multifidus and external oblique abdominal muscle on side toward which the pelvis rotates. Erector spinae and internal oblique abdominal muscle on opposite side. (Note: Rotation of the pelvis to the right constitutes rotation of the spine to the left. See p. 225.) The psoas and quadratus lumborum help to support the pelvis on the side of the swinging limb.

Hip.   *Movements:* Flexion; outward rotation (because of pelvic rotation); adduction at beginning and abduction at end of phase, especially if long stride is taken (also because of pelvic rotation, as well as stride length).

Muscles.   The sartorius, tensor fasciae latae, pectineus, iliopsoas, rectus femoris and the short head of the biceps femoris contract during the early part of the swing phase, each in its own particular pattern, the sartorius and short head of the biceps, for instance, chiefly at toe-off and the tensor at both toe-off and mid-swing.

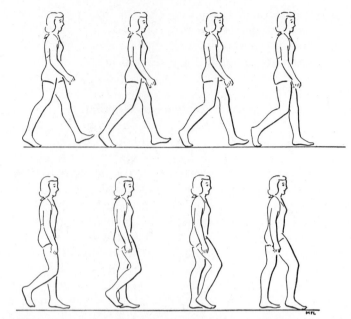

Figure 17-3   A normal gait at moderate speed. (Traced from a motion picture film.)

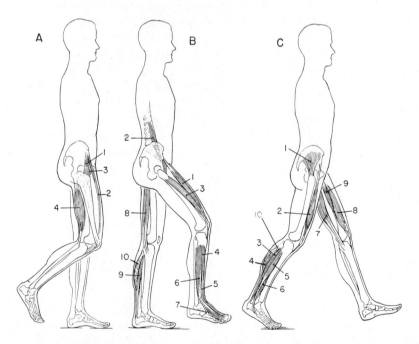

Figure 17-4   The muscles of the lower extremity used in walking. *Key: A:1,* Tensor fasciae latae; *2,* sartorius; *3,* pectineus; *4,* biceps femoris. *B: 1,* Rectus femoris; *2,* iliopsoas; *3,* vastus lateralis (medius and intermedius are not shown); *4,* tibialis anterior; *5,* extensor hallucis longus; *6,* extensor digitorum longus; *7,* peroneus tertius; *8,* semitendinosus and semimembranosus; *9,* soleus; *10,* gastrocnemius. *C: 1,* Gluteus medius; *2,* rectus femoris; *3,* soleus; *4,* tibialis posterior (underneath); *5,* peroneus longus; *6,* peroneus brevis; *7,* semimembranosus and semitendinosus; *8,* vastus medialis and intermedius (lateralis not shown); *9,* adductor longus; *10,* gastrocnemius.

In the latter part of the swing phase there is no appreciable action of the hip flexors in normal walking on level ground. This is consistent with the ballistic nature of the movement. The hamstrings, particularly the long head of the biceps femoris, contract with moderate intensity, and the gluteus maximus and medius contract slightly at the very end of the swing. The adductors longus and magnus, and presumably brevis, contract slightly after the swinging limb has passed the halfway mark. Just what the function of the adductor magnus is, is not clear. It may help to steady and guide the forward-swinging limb. In any event its action is extremely slight, even in rapid walking.

In rapid walking there is a noticeable increase in the activity of the sartorius and the rectus femoris and also a slight increase in that of the tensor fasciae latae.

KNEE.   *Movements:* Flexion during the first half; extension during the second half.

Muscles.   As was true in hip flexion (and for the same reason), so also in knee flexion is there remarkably little muscular action in the swing phase of normal walking. The quadriceps extensors contract slightly at the end of this phase. The action of the sartorius, a two-joint muscle, has already been mentioned in connection with the hip. The action of these muscles, as well as that of the medial hamstrings, increases in rapid walking. In an easy gait the movement appears to be initiated by gravitational force and continued by momentum. This force is sufficient to extend the leg at the knee, except perhaps at the very end of the movement. In more vigorous walking the quadriceps femoris provides the force for leg extension.

ANKLE AND FOOT.   *Movements:* Dorsal flexion; prevention of plantar flexion.

Muscles.   The tibialis anterior, extensor digitorum longus, extensor hallucis longus and probably the peroneus tertius contract with slight to moderate intensity at the beginning of the swinging phase and taper off during the middle portion of this phase. Basmajian and his co-workers found that the tibialis anterior was actually completely quiescent at midswing. They observed that the foot everted in the early phase and maintained this eversion during the middle part. This seemed to them to serve the important purpose of providing sufficient clearance between the foot and the ground.[3]

Toward the end of the swing phase this group of muscles contracts again with considerable force in preparation for heel-strike. The plantar flexors are completely relaxed throughout the entire swing phase.

Supporting Phase

The supporting phase begins with heel-strike and ends with toe-off. The portion between heel-strike of the forward foot and toe-off of the other, i.e., the rear foot, constitutes a period of double support which is characteristic of walking but does not occur in running.

SPINE AND PELVIS.   See comments under Swinging Phase.

HIP.   *Movements:* Extension; reduction of outward rotation, followed by slight inward rotation; prevention of adduction of thigh and dropping of pelvis to opposite side.

Muscles.   During the first part of the supporting phase all three gluteal muscles contract with moderate intensity; then the contractions of maximus and medius taper off during the middle part. There is disagreement in the literature as to whether the gluteus maximus participates at all in normal walking but, until the evidence is conclusive, this text is inclined to accept the views of the EMG researchers who found evidence of gluteus maximus activity in the early part of the supporting phase.[3] The gluteus minimus continues to contract moderately during the middle portion. The only muscles of the hip which contract appreciably during the last part of the supporting phase are the adductors magnus, longus and gracilis, and possibly brevis.

In rapid walking the gluteus maximus and minimus contract with appreciable intensity during the first part of the support phase, and the adductor longus during the last part. The hamstrings apparently have but a small part in the supporting phase of normal walking. Only the long head of the biceps contracts at all, and it contracts only slightly at the very beginning of this phase. In rapid walking both the long head of the biceps and the semitendinosus contract with moderate intensity during the first half of the support phase.

KNEE. *Movements:* Slight flexion at moment of contact, following immediately by extension.

Muscles. The quadriceps extensors contract moderately in the early part of the support phase, then gradually relax. They appear to control the slight flexion which occurs in the knee at the moment of heel-strike. The vastus intermedius continues to contract throughout the first half of this phase. As the leg reaches the vertical position, the knee apparently locks and makes contraction of the extensors unnecessary. The tension of the stretched hamstrings at the end of the swinging phase, especially when a long stride has been taken, may well be the factor which initiates the slight flexion at heel-strike. The hamstrings again show activity at the end of the supporting phase. In rapid walking all of these muscles contract more strongly and for a long duration. There is an abrupt increase in their action in the second half of the support phase which would seem to indicate that the extension of the leg at the knee is much more forceful in rapid walking than in normal walking.

ANKLE AND FOOT. *Movements:* Slight plantar flexion, followed by slight dorsal flexion; prevention of further dorsal flexion which the body weight tends to cause. Plantar flexion of ankle and hyperextension of metatarsophalangeal joints at end of propulsive phase, especially in vigorous walking.

Muscles. EMG studies reviewed by Basmajian show that there is considerable action of the tibialis anterior in the early part of the supporting phase, especially at heel-strike. It seems likely that this is related to the controlled lowering of the foot by eccentric contraction in order to prevent the foot from slapping down too hard. Contrary to earlier opinions, it does not continue to show activity during the major weight-bearing period, but it becomes active again at toe-off.[3] The extensor digitorum longus and hallucis longus follow a similar pattern. They reach their peak of contraction almost at the moment of transition between the swinging and the supporting phases; they relax early in the supporting phase, commencing to contract slightly at the end of this phase.

Carlin emphasized the importance of recognizing the influence of the weight-bearing position on the action of the dorsiflexors of the ankle joint. In the stance or support phase of walking the leverage of the leg is reversed because the foot is fixed on the ground. Instead of acting on the foot, the dorsiflexors act on the tibia to pull the upper end forward over the foot.[6] This is an important point and it is good to have it brought to our attention. It is also suggested here, however, that the relative force which these muscles have to exert is probably strongly influenced by individual variations in walking patterns. The tibialis anterior, extensor digitorum longus and extensor hallucis longus doubtless have to exert more force in a person who habitually walks with a backward list than in a person who tends to keep his weight over his forward foot. It would also seem that the length of stride might be a factor, as it is related to the slant of the forward leg at the moment of contact with the ground, that is, at heel-strike.

The tibialis posterior is most active during the middle part of the support phase, one of its functions, according to Basmajian, being to prevent eversion (pronation) of the foot. He points out that the peroneus longus and tibialis posterior apparently cooperate in stabilizing the leg and foot in weight-bearing.[3] The gastrocnemius and soleus likewise appear to act merely as stabilizers, for even in the push-off their activity is notably less than in the movement of rising on tip-toes.[3] In *rapid* walking, however, their activity is much more pronounced. The peroneus longus follows a similar pattern but does not seem to contract quite so strongly as the others, except in rapid walking. The peroneus brevis does not start to contract until about the middle of the supporting phase, but it contracts more strongly than the longus. In rapid walking it starts earlier and contracts with intensity soon after the halfway point has been reached.

The flexor digitorum longus contracts slightly during the middle portion of the supporting phase and increases abruptly to moderate contraction in the last portion. In rapid walking the contraction becomes strong. The flexor hallucis longus follows the same pattern, except that it does not start to contract until the middle of the phase.

The toe muscles, flexor hallucis longus, flexor digitorum longus and the short, intrinsic flexors of the toes, contract in response to the pressure of the ground against the toes. In the propulsive phase, especially in vigorous walking, this contraction is intensified. In all parts of the supporting phase the contraction of the toe flexors is greater in barefoot walking than when shoes are worn. This is especially noticeable when walking on turf or sand.

Action of Upper Extremities in Walking.   Unless restrained, the arms tend to swing in opposition to the legs, the left arm swinging forward as the right leg swings forward and vice versa. This is usually accomplished without obvious muscular action and serves to balance the rotation of the pelvis. It is a reflex action. When the arm swing is prevented, the upper trunk tends to rotate in the same direction as the pelvis, causing a tense, awkward gait.

Murray and her co-workers, using the technique of interrupted light photography, investigated the action of the upper extremities in walking. They noted "patterns of sagittal rotation of the shoulder and elbow," or flexion and extension of both joints. They found that, although the amplitudes of the arm swing pattern varied considerably from one subject to another, each individual had a similar pattern in all trials, even at higher speeds. Furthermore, they noted that the increased amplitude accompanying the faster speeds was due mainly to increased shoulder (hyper-) extension in the backward swing and increased elbow flexion in the forward swing. Maximum flexion of both the shoulder and elbow joints occurred at the moment of heel-strike of the opposite foot and maximum extension at the moment of heel-strike of the foot on the same side.[14]

In an investigation of the muscular action of the arms, Hogue found that although they appear to swing without muscular effort in walking at a normal pace on level ground, actually their pendular action was caused by a combination of muscular activity and gravity. The mid and posterior deltoid and the teres major were the muscles that he found to be most concerned, the latter two being active mainly during the backward swing. The posterior deltoid also contracted toward the end of the forward swing, leading one to suspect that it was serving as a brake to check the movement. The middle deltoid was found to be active during both flexion and extension of the arm at the shoulder joint. As this muscle is primarily an abductor, it seems that its function might be to keep the arms from brushing the sides of the body as they swing past it.[7]

Individual Variations in the Gait.   Although the basic anatomic analysis of the gait is valid for all physically normal persons, individual characteristics are present to such a degree that persons are often recognized by their gaits. These variations may be either structural or functional in origin. The structural differences include unusual body proportions, as well as differences in the limbs themselves such as knock-knees and bowlegs. Extreme variations in the angle between the neck and the shaft of the femur and in the obliquity of the femoral shaft are also responsible for atypical gaits.

Variations in the forward-back distribution of weight and in the length of stride have already been mentioned. Other variations in movement patterns which are not structural in origin are often related to characteristics of the personality. This fact was brought home forcefully to Wells when she attempted to help college students whose gaits were awkward. Almost invariably the students who walked the most awkwardly were those who were extremely shy or lacking in self-confidence. A study investigating the possible relationship between the two might be rewarding.

Anatomic Principles Applied to Walking

Principle I.   Good alignment of the lower extremities reduces friction in the joints and decreases the likelihood of strain and injury.

Principle II.   Normal flexibility of the joints (i.e., sufficiently long and flexible muscles, ligaments and fasciae) reduces internal resistance, and hence reduces the amount of force required for walking.

Principle III.   Speed of walking is increased by increasing both the length of the stride and the tempo of the gait.

Principle IV.   The longer the stride, the greater the up and down movements of the body, unless the knee is kept slightly flexed during the middle portion of the supporting phase.

Principle V.   Unnecessary lateral movements result in an ungainly and uneconomical gait.

a. Failure to keep the gluteus medius contracted when the weight is on the foot results in an exaggerated hip sway caused by the dropping of one side of the pelvis.

b. Excessive trunk rotation may be caused by an exaggerated arm swing or by restriction of the arm swing. Normally the arm swing exactly counterbalances the hip swing.[14]

c. Straight, sagittal plane action of the leg is assured by keeping the knee and the foot pointing straight forward in all phases of the gait.

d. The rotation of the pelvis should be only just enough to enable the leg to move straight forward. Too little or too much rotation tends to cause a weaving gait.

e. Minimal lateral motions occur when the feet are placed in such a way that their inner borders fall approximately along a single straight line.

Principle VI.   The tendon action of the two-joint muscles of the lower extremity contributes to economy of muscular action in walking (see p. 47).

Principle VII.   Properly functioning reflexes contribute to a well-coordinated gait.

Principle VIII.   The stability of the weight-bearing limb and the balance of the trunk over this limb are important factors in the smoothness of the gait.

Running

Easy running, like walking, is a pendulum type of movement. It is doubtful, however, whether running at top speed can be so classified. The most notable factors differentiating the run from the walk are the period of double support, characteristic of the walk but not present in the run, and the period of no support (a "sailing-through-the-air period"), characteristic of the run but not present in the walk. In the run the foot hits the ground, not in front of the body as in the walk, but almost directly under the body's center of gravity. This reduces the restraining part of the supporting phase and gives greater emphasis to the propulsive part. As the speed increases, the restraining part of the supporting phase diminishes, disappearing completely as maximum speed is attained. The use of the term "driving phase" for the supporting phase in running indicates its propulsive nature.

In running, as in walking, the force exerted to produce the movement has two components, horizontal and vertical. In running, however, because of the tremendous increase in horizontal force, the vertical component is negligible.

Whether the run is an easy jog or a full-speed sprint, economy of effort is a highly desirable objective. To achieve this it is essential that the runner, either consciously or unconsciously, observe the principles which apply to efficient running. The most noteworthy of these are listed below.

Mechanical Principles of Running

1. In accordance with the first law of motion, a body at rest remains at rest unless acted upon by a force. In running, the problem of overcoming inertia decreases as the level of speed increases. It is greatest at the take-off and least after acceleration has ceased.

a. The crouching start enables the runner to exert maximum horizontal force at the take-off by

(1) Providing a surface against which the foot can push horizontally;

(2) Putting the legs in a more horizontal position;

(3) Enabling the runner to use maximum hip, knee and ankle extension in both legs. (Figure 17–5.)

b. During acceleration the horizontal component of the leg drive gradually diminishes until a level of speed is maintained, during which period it remains uniform. The period of acceleration is characterized by a gradual decrease in the forward inclination of the trunk, a lengthening of the stride (made possible by the raising of the center of gravity as the trunk becomes more erect), and a decrease of the knee thrust, resulting from the gradual straightening of the knee at the moment of contact between the foot and the ground.

2. Also in accordance with the first law of motion, a moving body will move in a straight line unless it is acted upon by a force causing it to change its direction. In order to run in a curved pathway, as when running around a circular or oval track, an additional force is needed to overcome the body's tendency to continue in a straight line. This is achieved by leaning toward the inside as the slant of the body will introduce a lateral component to the pressure of the foot against the ground.[5] The well-banked curves of indoor tracks do this for the runner.

3. In accordance with the second law of motion, acceleration is directly proportional to the force producing it. Hence, the greater the power of the leg drive, the greater the acceleration of the runner.

4. In accordance with the third law of motion, every action has an equal and opposite reaction.

5. Since a long lever develops more speed at the end than does a short lever, the length of the leg during the driving phase of running should be as great as possible when speed is a consideration. This is achieved by full extension at the knee joint at the end of the driving phase.

6. The smaller the vertical component of force, the greater the horizontal or driving component.

a. In the most efficient run, vertical movements of the center of gravity are reduced to a minimum.

b. The vertical component of force should be just enough to counteract the downward pull of gravity but not enough to produce an unnecessary bounce in running.

7. The more completely the horizontal component of force is directed straight backward, the greater its contribution to the forward motion of the body. Lateral movements of the arms, legs and trunk detract unnecessarily from forward propulsion. To assure forward motion of the body:

Figure 17–5   Sprinting. *A*, Take-off; *B*, acceleration; *C*, full speed.

a. The knees should be lifted directly forward-upward with the entire lower extremity kept in the sagittal plane. (Unathletic girls sometimes run with a minimal knee lift and with an inward rotation of the thighs, the feet and lower legs being thrown out to the side.)

b. The arm swing should exactly counterbalance the twist of the pelvis and should not cause additional lateral motion.

8. Efficiency in running, as in any movement, requires the elimination of all unnecessary force.

a. The shorter the lever, the less the force required to move it, and the less the reaction to it. By flexing the leg at the knee and carrying the heel high up under the hip in the recovery phase, the leg is moved more rapidly, as well as more economically.

b. Internal resistance caused by the viscosity of the sarcolemma is reduced by warming-up activities.

c. Internal resistance caused by tight muscles, fasciae and ligaments is reduced by systematic stretching exercises.

d. Unnecessary force in the form of excessively rapid muscular contractions is eliminated by developing as long a stride as can be controlled.

Jumping

Jumping is a form of locomotion familiar to man from earliest childhood, whether engaged in as a simple expression of joy and exuberance, as a self-testing and competitive activity or as an integral part of a sport. Except for the jumps that start with a running approach, one of the chief problems of this motor skill is in overcoming inertia, often with a minimum of space in which to do so. Other problems are the sheer muscular strength needed for projecting oneself against the force of gravity and the coordination needed for utilizing what might be called secondary motions for the purpose of achieving maximal height or maximal distance. It is from the point of view of the constructive handling of these problems that the vertical jump and the running long jump are discussed.

Vertical Jump. If one must start from a standing position in a limited space and if the purpose is to jump as high as possible as judged by the top of the head (a variation of a familiar test), it will be necessary to get maximal power from the leg action, helped by a movement of the arms which will be in accord with the principle of transfer of momentum from a part to the whole. The feet should be pointing straight forward and either side by side or with one foot slightly in advance of the other. As the body assumes a crouch position, the knees will bend, the heels will come off the floor, and this will put the hip, knee and ankle extensor muscles on a stretch. Muscles which are stretched prior to contracting, contract with more force because they have a greater range of contraction. The depth of the crouch is governed by the individual's ability to spring from the position. This is in direct proportion to the strength of his extensor muscles. As the jumper goes into the crouch he flexes his elbows and gradually pushes them straight back. As he springs, he pushes his fists vigorously upward and stops them sharply just as he is about to leave the ground. The upward momentum of his arms is then transferred to his whole body, thus helping to give it additional height. He puts all of his force into his push-off from the ground. Obviously the magnitude of this force depends upon the strength of his lower extremity extensor muscles. Important attributes of a successful vertical jump are explosive muscular contraction and good coordination and timing of the secondary movements.

If the jump is for the purpose of reaching as high as possible with one hand, as in tipping a basketball, there are several things the jumper can do. When he is free to move his feet, even slightly, he can overcome inertia by taking a hop or short step before he jumps. This will start him moving and, even though it is horizontal rather than vertical motion, the fact of moving his body means that since he has overcome inertia he has more force available for the jump. As in the preceding vertical jump, he can swing his arms up vigorously to add momentum, but the left arm should then be brought down as this enables him to reach higher with the right arm. One explanation is that the dropping of his left shoulder permits his right shoulder to rise. The slight bending of his spine to the left aids in this motion. Another explanation is that the lowering of the left arm lowers the position of the center of gravity, not in space but relative to the body parts.[5] Since the high point of the center of gravity is determined by the force of the push-off, lowering its position in the body causes the body to go higher.

Running Long Jump.   This jump has the advantage of providing distance for overcoming inertia and for developing horizontal momentum preparatory to the take-off for the jump. Full advantage needs to be taken of this run and maximal speed should be attained three or four strides before the take-off. There must be only a slight slowing down before the spring. This requires adequate practice in order to adjust the distance of the run to the length of stride so that the jumper's foot will hit the take-off board correctly. The analysis of the jump itself is best left to the experienced coaches. Suffice it to say here the jumper should attempt to get maximal speed in his approach, to take off with a powerful spring, and to use arm swing to gain height. After reaching the height of the jump, the legs are extended forward and the trunk bent forward at the hips in a horizontal jackknife position. The jumper's dilemma in landing is the difficulty of hitting the landing pit with the heels well forward without sitting down. A vigorous forward swing with his arms shortly before the heels touch the ground helps to give him enough momentum to carry the upper part of his trunk forward as he lands.[5]

All jumps involve landing. The principles which govern this are discussed in Chapter Twenty-One, Receiving and Intercepting Impetus.

Rotatory Locomotion

The most common activities in this category are forward, backward and sideward rolls, cartwheels and handsprings. Each of these is achieved by rotating about the body's successive areas of contact with the supporting surface. In forward rolls, for instance, the body rotates about the hands, shoulders, rounded back, buttocks and feet (Fig. 17–6) and in cartwheels, about each hand followed by each foot with the body rotating laterally in a fully extended position.

The impetus for the forward roll is given by the hands and feet, the direction of their thrust being a combination of backward and downward—backward to send the body forward, and downward to resist the downward pull of gravitational force on the head and trunk. When the hands and feet are no longer pushing, the head is tucked forward and the back is rounded with the knees bent close against the body to facilitate the roll. During the foot thrust the hips are high, both for assuring a stronger backward thrust with the legs and for making greater use of the force of gravity for the roll over the back.

Principles and Their Applications to Rotatory Locomotion

Principle I.   The body moves in the direction opposite to the direction of force application.

Principle II.   Since a body at rest will remain at rest unless acted upon by a force and a body in motion will continue in motion unless acted upon by a force, it is important to keep the body moving in successive rolls and not let it come to a momentary halt following each roll. Even the briefest of interruptions necessitates the overcoming of inertia after each revolution. It takes velocity to acquire sufficient momentum to prevent these halts; therefore, each backward thrust of hands and feet against the ground should be as forceful as possible.

Principle III.   Rotatory movement is accelerated by shortening the radius. In both forward and backward rolls the radius is shortened by tucking the flexed lower extremities close to the body when the back is in contact with the floor.

In general, the factors responsible for the successful performance of rotatory locomotion are the magnitude, direction and accurate timing of the forces contributing to the desired movement of the body, including the advantageous use of the force of gravity whenever possible.

Additional Forms of Locomotion

Ascending and Descending Stairs and Inclined Planes. (Fig. 17–7.)   In walking up stairs or up a ramp the swing phase is characterized by an exaggerated knee lift and dorsiflexion of the ankle. According to Joseph and Watson, the hamstrings and tibialis anterior are the chief muscles involved.[3] In the

Figure 17–6   The body rotating around its points of contact with the supporting surface. (Redrawn from LaPorte and Renner: The Tumbler's Manual, by courtesy of Prentice-Hall, Inc.)

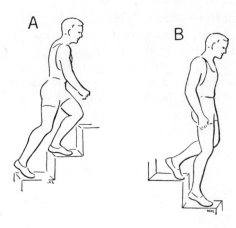

Figure 17-7   Going up and down stairs.

support phase when the action is chiefly extension of the knee and hip, with the ankle being either slightly plantar flexed or else maintained in the mid-position on the ball of the foot, they found the chief muscular action to come from the gluteus maximus, hamstrings, quadriceps femoris and soleus, with the gluteus medius helping to maintain stability at the hip joint.

The swing phase of walking down stairs starts with a slight lifting of the rear foot to clear the step. This involves slight knee flexion and dorsiflexion of the ankle. It is followed by slight hip flexion, then hip and knee extension and plantar flexion of the ankle as the foot reaches for the step below the one the supporting foot is on.

The supporting phase starts with the ankle in plantar flexion and the knee in extension. As the foot assumes the body weight, the ankle, knee and hip are approximately in their neutral positions with the knee very slightly flexed. As the other foot swings forward, the supporting leg engages in slight hip flexion, increasing knee flexion and dorsiflexion of the ankle. In the brief period of double support, the knee and ankle flexion reach their maximum. The main muscular action of the supporting limb, according to Joseph and Watson, consists of eccentric contraction of the hamstrings, quadriceps femoris and soleus, with the gluteus medius contributing to hip stability as it does in ascending.[3]

Locomotion by Specialized Steps and Jumps.   Other forms of ground-supported locomotion not involving the use of special equipment include two general categories. One of these consists of acrobatic stunts and athletic events such as walking on the hands, successive jumping and hurdling either with or without actual hurdles. The other category consists of activities used both in children's play and in forms of dance. It includes skipping, hopping, galloping, sliding, side-stepping, leaping and standard dance steps, like the polka and mazurka.

Hurdling and Skating.   Although these are not discussed in this text, they are nevertheless pictured here (Figs. 17–8 and 17–9) for the purpose of arousing interest in discussing some of the anatomic and mechanical factors involved.

Off-the-Ground Locomotion.   There are two major categories of locomotion which do not involve support on a solid surface. These are hand traveling on suspension apparatus and aquatic locomotion, which includes both swimming and boating. These are discussed in the appropriate chapters.

Figure 17–8 Hurdling. (Courtesy of Northeastern University.)

Figure 17–9 Skating. (Courtesy of Northeastern University.)

SUPPLEMENTARY MATERIAL

The following five studies are of particular interest because they represent the use of five different techniques.

Electromyographic Study of the Muscles of the Foot in Walking.[17]   Sheffield, Gersten and Mastellone investigated the action of the ankle and foot muscles used in walking. The subjects who participated in the study were ten normal adult males, and the walking was performed on the level at a rate of 60 steps per minute, one step consisting of the two phases, support and swing. The results are briefly summarized below.

TIBIALIS ANTERIOR, EXTENSOR DIGITORUM LONGUS AND EXTENSOR HAL-LUCIS LONGUS.   Active throughout both phases with two peaks of intensity, the first during the early part of the swing phase when dorsiflexion was necessary in order to clear the ground, and the second at heel-strike, apparently to lower the foot gradually instead of slapping it down.

FLEXOR DIGITORUM LONGUS, FLEXOR HALLUCIS LONGUS, PERONEUS LONGUS AND TIBIALIS POSTERIOR.   The maximum activity of these muscles commenced near the beginning of the support phase, when the metatarsal region struck the ground, and continued until this region was off the ground. There was no activity during the swing phase.

GASTROCNEMIUS AND SOLEUS.   In eight subjects the gastrocnemius became active at the time the metatarsal region touched the ground; in the other two there was slight activity beginning at the time the heel touched the ground. In all ten subjects these muscles showed a high degree of activity throughout the support phase.

On the whole the findings of these investigators substantiate those of the Advisory Committee on Artificial Limbs of the National Research Council in a similar study.[1] The latter group studied the muscular activity of six subjects as they walked at a normal pace, a rapid pace, up and down stairs and up and down a ramp. The electromyograms made during rapid walking closely resemble the muscular activity described by Sheffield and his co-workers. There are a few minor discrepancies, however. Sheffield's group appeared to find a greater degree of activity of the dorsiflexor muscles during the early part of the swing phase. They also found that the maximum activity of the second group of muscles began later than had been reported by the Research Council group. The apparent discrepancies may be due to this reviewer's interpretation, however, since she compared the electromyographic tracings of one study with the written report of another.

Analysis of the Support Phase of Walking.[2]   Barnett introduced the use of a new type of pedograph that gives quantitative results for the functions of the foot in walking. In his study, reported in 1956, he obtained records for 100 normal subjects, aged 17 to 25. These records consisted of radiographs, footprints and profile photographs of the feet and ankles taken at intervals of 1/30 second. The moments of weight-bearing over different regions of the foot were recorded by means of horizontal bands placed at intervals across the sole. On the basis of these records Barnett made the following observations:

1. HEEL PHASE. (First 10–20% of support phase.)   The initial contact is made by the posterolateral part of the heel, but the entire heel shares equally

in weight bearing almost immediately. It is this initial contact that is responsible for the wearing down of the outer posterior edge of the heel of the shoe.

2. STANDING PHASE. (Next 30–35% of support phase.) The weight is borne by the heel, the outer side of the sole and the heads of the metatarsal bones. It is during this phase that the center of gravity is directly above the foot.

3. METATARSAL PHASE. (10% or less of support phase.) Comparing his findings with Morton's observations regarding a "short first metatarsal"[10] Barnett observes that this occurs in approximately 50% of the population and he therefore considers this to be a normal variation. The more the first metatarsal protrudes beyond the second, the greater is its share of weight bearing. In feet having a so-called short first metatarsal the weight bearing is well distributed across the other metatarsals and does not exceed 4 kg. per sq. cm. beneath the second metatarsal "presumably because other factors can compensate for the normal degree of protrusion of this bone." He observes that in ordinary walking the pressure beneath the second metatarsal head can be decreased by turning the toes out and by extending the interphalangeal rather than the metatarso-phalangeal joint of the big toe. It might be of interest to check the relative length of the first and second metatarsal bones in persons who habitually walk with the toes turned out.

4. FOREFOOT PHASE. (Next 30% of support phase.) The weight is borne by the metatarsal heads and the toes with the big toe usually predominating. Barnett observes from the pedograph records that the other toes, especially the second, share a considerable part of the weight and suggests that this is due to the fact that the oblique axis of the ankle is almost parallel to the heads of the outer four metatarsals.

5. STEP-OFF PHASE. (Next 3–10% of support phase.) The weight is borne entirely by the toes, especially the big toe, but the total amount borne by this foot is small as this is the period of double support and the other foot is bearing most of the weight. Barnett comments that the fifth toe plays a greater part in the step-off than one might expect.

In discussing abnormalities, Barnett states that the majority of complaints are related to the standing phase. The most common cause of pain during the metatarsal phase, he considers, is the prolongation of this phase, usually because of a high longitudinal arch and claw foot and consequent delay in using the toes. He suggests that this lack of toe function may be the cause of metatarsalgia in the foot that appears normal in a clinical examination. (Perhaps the implication for the physical educator is that children and youths should be encouraged to use their toe muscles.)

Temporal Components of Motion in Gait.   In 1960 Smith, McDermid and Shideman developed a technique for analyzing the temporal components of motion in walking using an electrobasometer.[18] They state that this makes possible a "flexible precise analysis of both shod and unshod gait in all types, conditions, and patterns of locomotion." Based on such analyses, they developed what they termed a psycho-physiological theory of gait as contrasted to a mechanical theory.

Accelerographic Study of Gait.   In 1962 Liberson, Holmquest and Halls developed a method of recording simultaneously accelerograms, electromyograms and high speed motion pictures of normal and pathological gaits.[9] In their opinion one advantage of their technique is its application to the swing or recovery phase of the gait as well as to the stance phase. Their interest in developing this technique was in its usefulness in analyzing and correcting pathological gaits.

Electrogoniometric Study of Hip Joint Action in Walking.   In 1969 Johnston and Smidt used an electrogoniometer to measure the movements of the thighs at the hip joints in walking.[8] This provided objective evidence of the following sequence of movements:

Hip extension: From just prior to heel-strike, gradually increasing, to just prior to toe-off.

Hip flexion: From just prior to toe-off to just prior to heel-strike.

Abduction: During latter part of stance phase to just after toe-off.

Adduction: Just after toe-off to latter part of stance phase.

Outward rotation: In late stance phase through much of swing phase.

Inward rotation: Just prior to heel-strike until late stance phase.

The average motion taking place at the hip joint was 52 degrees in the sagittal plane, 12 degrees in the coronal plane, and 13 degrees in the transverse plane. A major purpose of the study was to test the use of the electrogoniometer as a method of measurement in the study of hip joint disease. The authors were favorably impressed with it as being a practical and valuable instrument for this purpose. They found the method to be "accurate, simple, and relatively inexpensive."

Additional Studies of Walking.   Extensive studies on various aspects of walking have been made by Murray and by Basmajian and their respective co-workers. For other electromyographic studies of the muscles used in walking, it is suggested that the reader refer to the current edition of Basmajian's book, *Muscles Alive.*[3]

LABORATORY EXPERIENCES

1. Try this as a class exercise, working in pairs. *A* stands with heels against a wall with the feet otherwise in a comfortable, "natural" position in readiness to walk. *B* holds a ruler across the toes of *A*'s feet and draws a line against the ruler. *A* then stands with feet parallel at right angles to the wall, and again *B* draws a line. Measure the distance between the two lines. This measurement is likely to vary from ¼ in. to 1 in. in a sizable class. *A* and *B* now change places and repeat.
   Assume that you are to engage in a walking race of 1000 yards; also assume that if you toed straight ahead, each step would be 1 yard long. It would therefore take you 1000 steps to cover the distance. But suppose you toed out so that each step was (your measurement)_____ short. How many yards short of the finish line would you be when you had taken 1000 steps? (Ans. If the difference between the two lines had been ³/₁₆ in. you would be ³/₁₆ × 1000 = 187.5 in. or 5.2 yards short.)
   Implication. If you are walking against an opponent who walks at the same rate as you, but who toes straight ahead, you would be 5.2 yards behind him when he crosses the finish line. Yet, presumably you took the same number of steps.

2. Observe the gait of people on the street or campus; detect individual character-istics; and analyze them in terms of anatomic and mechanical principles.

3. Get a subject to walk in each of the following ways. Observe and note differences in the movements of the head, shoulders, hips, etc.
   a. Placing one foot directly in front of the other.
   b. Keeping a lateral distance of 10 to 12 in. between the feet.

c. Pointing the toes out.
d. Pointing the toes in.
e. Pointing the toes straight ahead.
f. Taking a short stride.
g. Taking a long stride.

4. Select four or five individuals who are not alike in leg length. Get them to practice walking until each one finds the stride and speed that feel most comfortable to him. Compare their strides and measure the distance between footprints for each individual.

5. Observe several individuals as they run. Look for the application of the principles listed.

6. Observe other forms of locomotion and discover for yourself what principles apply to them.

REFERENCES

1. Advisory Committee on Artificial Limbs, National Research Council: The Pattern of Muscular Activity in the Lower Extremity during Walking. Berkeley, Cal.: Prosthetic Devices Research Project, Institute of Engineering Research, University of California, 1953.
2. Barnett, C. H.: The phases of human gait. Lancet, *271*:617–621, 1956.
3. Basmajian, J. V.: Muscles Alive, 3rd Ed. Baltimore: The Williams & Wilkins Company, 1974.
4. Broer, M. R.: Efficiency of Human Movement, 3rd Ed. Philadelphia: W. B. Saunders Company, 1973.
5. Bunn, J. W.: Scientific Principles of Coaching, 2nd Ed. Englewood Cliffs, New Jersey: Prentice-Hall, Inc., 1972.
6. Carlin, E. J.: Human gait. Am. J. Phys. Med., *42*:181–184, 1963.
7. Hogue, R. E.: Upper-extremity muscular activity at different cadences and inclines during normal gait. J. Am. Phys. Ther. Assn., *49*:963–972, 1969.
8. Johnston, R. C., and Smidt, G. L.: Measurement of hip-joint motion during walking. J. Bone & Joint Surg., *51A*:1083–1094, 1969.
9. Liberson, W. T., Holmquest, H. J., and Halls, A.: Accelerographic study of gait. Arch. Phys. Med. & Rehab., *43*:547–551, 1962.
10. Morton, D. J., and Fuller, D. D.: Human Locomotion and Body Form. Baltimore: The Williams & Wilkins Company, 1952.
11. Murray, M. P., Drought, A. B., and Kory, R. C.: Walking patterns of normal men. J. Bone & Joint Surg., *46A*:335–360, 1964.
12. Murray, M. P., Kory, R. C., Clarkson, B. H., and Sepic, S. B.: Comparison of free and fast speed walking patterns of normal men. Am. J. Phys. Med., *45*:8–24, 1966.
13. Murray, M. P., Kory, R. C., and Sepic, S. B.: Walking patterns of normal women. Arch. Phys. Med. & Rehab., *51*:637–650, 1970.
14. Murray, M. P., Sepic, S. B., and Barnard, E. J.: Patterns of sagittal rotation of the upper limbs in walking. J. Am. Phys. Ther. Assn., *47*:272–284, 1967.
15. Saunders, J. B. deC. M., Inman, V. T., and Eberhart, H. D.: The major determinants in normal and pathological gait. J. Bone & Joint Surg., *35A*:543–558, 1953.
16. Schwartz, R. P., Heath, A. L., Morgan, D. W., and Towns, R. C.: A quantitative analysis of recorded variables in the walking pattern of "normal" adults. J. Bone & Joint Surg., *46A*:324–334, 1964.
17. Sheffield, F. J., Gersten, J. W., and Mastellone, A. F.: Electromyographic study of the muscles of the foot in normal walking. Am. J. Phys. Med., *35*:223–236, 1956.
18. Smith, K. U., McDermid, C. D., and Shideman, F. E.: Analysis of the temporal components of motion in human gait. Am. J. Phys. Med., *39*:142–151, 1960.
19. Steindler, A.: Kinesiology of the Human Body. Springfield, Ill.: Charles C Thomas, Publisher, 1973, Lectures 37 and 38.

RECOMMENDED READINGS

Brunnstrom, S.: Clinical Kinesiology, 3rd Ed. Philadelphia: F. A. Davis Company, 1972, Chap. 11.
Elftman, H.: Biomechanics of muscle; with particular application to studies of gait. J. Bone & Joint Surg., *48A*:363–376, 1966.

Chapter Eighteen

MOVING ONE'S BODY WHEN SUSPENDED AND WHEN FREE OF SUPPORT

SUSPENSION ACTIVITIES

Climbing, hanging, swinging and other suspension activities were more commonly engaged in by our early ancestors than by members of more recent generations. The modern version of these brachial activities is seen in the trapeze activities of the aerial artist at the circus, in gymnastics events on the high bar, parallel bars, uneven bars and rings, and in various forms of hanging on ladders and ropes in the gymnasium and on the playground. Success in suspension activities depends upon considerable strength and endurance, particularly of the hand, arm and shoulder musculature, and the ability to adjust body positions to counteract or take advantage of the forces acting on the body (Fig. 18–1). Ladder or rope climbing and brachial locomotion are modifications of locomotion. Where swinging movements of a suspended body are involved the principles of a pendulum, angular motion and centrifugal force are important.

Principles Relating to Swinging Movements

Principle I. The movement of a pendulum is produced by the force of gravity. This presupposes a starting position in which potential energy is present. In other words, the pendulum must be moved from its resting position before the force of gravity can make it swing downward.

Applications

a. The initial problem of the child on the swing and of the gymnast on the flying rings is that of being given potential energy. Without the help of an accomplice, he must find a way of putting himself into a position in which he will have potential energy. He does this usually in one of three ways. He may move the apparatus to some position other than its normal position of rest before he suspends himself from it (i.e., he pulls the rings or swing as far back

434

Figure 18-1 Movement of body in suspension. This illustrates need for good muscular development in arms and shoulders. (Courtesy of Springfield College.)

as he can reach before getting on); his feet may be able to reach the supporting surface when he is on the apparatus, in which case he can push his feet against the floor or take little running steps; or he may use a pumping action to get started. For the man swinging on the rings, this involves bending the legs up in front of the body and then extending them as high as possible. The range of the arc of motion may be increased by the repetition of this procedure on the forward-upward phase of the swing. The child in the swing accomplishes the same result by inclining the trunk backward and raising the feet forward. He can start the swing even more effectively if he can pull the ropes toward his body and, at the same time, press forward against the seat.

b. Initiating a pendulum swing on the traveling rings is achieved by flexing each arm alternately. Because of the wide distance between the traveling rings, this procedure moves the body a considerable distance from its resting position and thus puts it in favorable position for the force of gravity to act on it.

Principle II. As the pendulum swings downward, gravity causes its speed to increase; as it swings upward, gravity counteracts its speed, diminishing it until the zero point is reached. Hence the pendulum's speed is greatest at the bottom of the arc and least (zero) at each end of the arc.

Application. Caution must be exercised to maintain a firm grip on the supporting surface (rings, bar or ropes) particularly at the bottom of the swing where the tendency to fly off is the greatest.

Principle III. The upward movement of a pendulum is brought about by the momentum developed in the downward movement. The swinging body moves through an arc, first in one direction, then in the reverse direction (one half the arc's distance is called the amplitude). Thus it undergoes partial rotation about a center of motion. Since this rotation takes place in a vertical plane, the influence of gravitational pull must be taken into consideration. Whereas the force of gravity *produces* the downward swing, it *opposes* the upward swing. Nevertheless it is indirectly responsible for the latter, inasmuch as the upward swing is caused by the momentum which was built up in the preceding downward swing.

Application. This is especially important in skills performed on the uneven bars when long, swinging actions are involved. The higher the position from which the downswing is initiated, the higher will be the upswing. The range of a swing depends upon the height from which the movement is initiated.

Principle IV. The height of a swing may be increased by lengthening the radius of rotation on the downswing and decreasing it on the upswing (Fig. 18-2). Shortening the radius on the upswing decreases the moment of inertia and therefore increases the angular velocity. The faster the body moves on the upswing, the more its kinetic energy is increased and the higher it goes. The increased height for the start of the downswing and the lengthened radius of rotation produce a gain in angular momentum on the downswing because gravity has a longer time to act before the body reaches the bottom of the swing. This increased momentum is conserved when the shortening of the radius occurs for the next upswing and thus another increase in angular velocity occurs (angular momentum = $I\omega$). This equation also shows that the greater the angular velocity on the downswing the less the body has to be shortened in order to reach its desired height on the upswing.

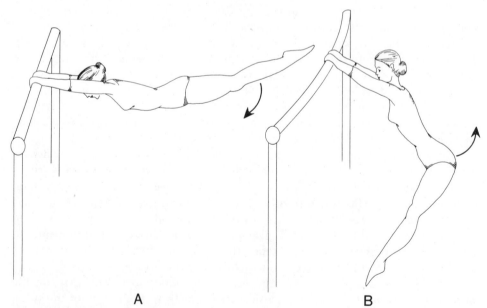

A   B

Figure 18-2 The height of a swing may be increased by lengthening the radius of rotation on the downswing and decreasing it on the upswing.

Application. A swinging performer may shorten the radius of rotation by moving body parts toward the axis of rotation. This may be done by flexing at the hips, hunching the shoulders by depressing the shoulder girdle or arching the back. A performer in the giant swing depresses the shoulder girdle and flexes at the hips on the upswing. He may also arch the back slightly. In a circle from a front uprise, the head is thrown back to shorten the radius on the upswing.

Principle V.   To increase height, the decrease in radius should be initiated at the moment that the center of gravity of the body is directly under the axis of rotation. Since, in the movement of a pendulum, speed is greatest at the bottom of the arc, shortening the radius at this point accelerates its angular velocity more than at any other position.

Application.   In the backward hip circle on the uneven parallel bars the movement is started with the body extended so that there is a long radius of rotation on the downswing. At the moment the legs pass under the hands, the hips are flexed to shorten the radius on the upswing and increase the angular velocity.

Principle VI.   The time taken by the pendulum to make a single round trip excursion (known as its *period*) is related to the length of the pendulum. The longer the pendulum, the more slowly it swings. Specifically, the period of the pendulum is proportional to the square root of its length.

Applications

a. When the hands are the axis of rotation such as in the preparatory movements for the giant swing, the period is longer than in swings about a hip axis or a knee axis.

b. When swinging on ropes, the supporting ropes should be lengthened for a slow swing and shortened for a fast swing.

Principle VII.   The period of the pendulum is not influenced by its weight. A heavy body will swing no faster than a lighter one, or vice versa. This is consistent with the behavior of freely falling bodies.

Application.   Trapeze artists take advantage of this principle. A performer swinging from one trapeze knows that a second empty trapeze of the same length swung toward him from the same height and at the same time he starts his swing, will have the same period as his. Consequently, he also knows that he may let go of his bar at the top of his swing, turn around and grasp the empty bar just at the peak of its swing.

Principle VIII.   When a pendulum reaches the end of its arc, just before it reverses its direction, it reaches a zero point in velocity. At this precise moment the force of gravity is momentarily neutralized by the upward momentum.

Application.   The performer can take advantage of this situation by using this moment to perform position changes such as changing grips, reversing direction and performing dismounts and cutaways. The underswing half-turn on the unevens is executed the best and controlled the easiest when the twist and grip change are both completed during the height of the underswing.

Principle IX.   When a body consisting of two segments reaches the vertical with the proximal segment leading on the downswing, the distal segment will accelerate relative to the other segment and precede it into the upswing. If, on the other hand, the distal segment reaches the vertical first, the reverse will occur. The distal segment will decelerate and the proximal segment will lead into the upswing (Fig. 18–3).

Application.   Action at the bottom of a swing which forces the hips through in front of the feet increases the acceleration on the upswing owing to hip flexion in shortening the radius. Such swings are called "beat" swings. "Beat" swings

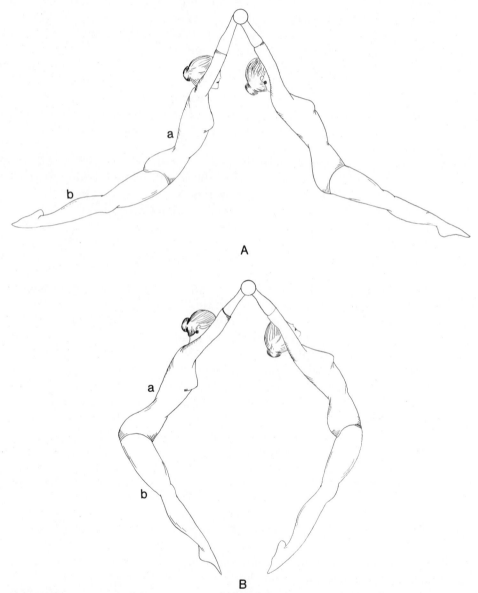

Figure 18–3   *A,* Double pendulum swing. If segment *a* precedes segment *b* to the vertical, segment *b* accelerates and precedes *a* in the upswing. *B,* When segment *b* precedes *a* to the vertical, *a* will lead into the upswing, but the whole pendulum decelerates.

are used to set up hechts and flyaways on the high or uneven bars and stutzes and somersaults on the parallel bars.

Principle X.   The rotation of a gymnast's hands about a bar is opposed by frictional forces. This accounts for some loss in swinging energy as it is converted to heat energy. Evidence of this is the appearance of friction blisters and skin irritations on the gymnast's hands. These friction forces tend to strengthen the gymnast's grip when the swing is in the direction the palms are facing and weakens it when the swing is in the reverse direction.

Application.   Gymnasts reverse their grasps when the swing is reversed. This is usually done at the peak of the swing at the point of "weightlessness" when the pressure on the hands is at a minimum. Gymnasts also sand the bar before each performance to assure its smoothness and to minimize the friction on the hands.

Principle XI.   In all mounting exercises involving swinging, the center of gravity must be brought as near as possible to the center of rotation. This is usually done when the center of gravity is directly under the bar on the down-swing.

Application.   In the glide kip on the unevens the performer swings her body forward and back alternately flexing and extending to gain momentum. At the end of the glide the gymnast flexes fully at the hips so the feet are near the bar. This sharp flexion increases the angular velocity by decreasing the moment of inertia. As the center of gravity passes under the bar on the downswing, the hips are extended vigorously. This movement raises the body and places the center of gravity close to the bar, thus further decreasing the moment of inertia and enabling the body to rotate until it is in a front support position with the center of gravity located at the fixed point of the grip.

Principle XII.   When centripetal force ceases to act on a swinging performer, his body will obey Newton's first law and fly off tangent to the arc of the swing at that instant.

Applications

a. Great care should be taken with beginners and children. The hands should be watched for indications of slippage particularly at the bottom of the swing where the centripetal force needed is maximal. Probably the safest way for children and novices to dismount is for them to stop swinging, come to a "dead stop" and then drop down.

b. Stunts requiring the release and resumption of the grasp should be executed at the peak of the swing where velocity, and hence centripetal and centrifugal forces, are zero. Dismounts and cutaways are timed to occur at that point where the tangent of the arc at the instant of release coincides with the desired line of flight.

Principle XIII.   In support swings the center of gravity should be at the point of support.

Application.   Hip circles forward or backward require the center of gravity of the body to be close to the hand supports. In this position it takes less effort to keep the body against the bar while turning because the torque between the center of gravity of the body and the axis of rotation is kept at a minimum.

Principles Related to Hand Traveling and Hanging Activities

Principle I. In hanging activities the muscles of the arm and shoulder girdle must contract to protect the joints. The pull of the body's weight puts stress on the joints by tending to separate them.

Principle II. Hand traveling is a locomotor pattern. It is governed by the principle of action and reaction. As in walking, force applied against a supporting surface in one direction causes the body to move in the opposite direction.

Application. Hand traveling sidewards on a boom or along the side of a horizontal ladder without swinging is achieved by alternately moving one hand away from the other hand, and then moving the second hand toward the first. As the first hand moves, the second hand pushes laterally against the apparatus. Both hands share the weight equally for a moment, then the second hand is released and brought toward the first hand, while at the same time the first hand is pulling laterally on the apparatus.

Principle III. The action used in hand climbing activities is essentially a chinning action.

Applications

a. In rope climbing with or without the use of the legs, the body is raised through a forceful chinning action of the arms.

b. In the back kip to support on the still rings, the performer chins forcefully from a piked inverted hang. As he rises upward, he extends his body upward and converts his chinning action to a push-up ending in a straight-arm support position.

Principle IV. In accord with Newton's law of inertia, sequential hand support movements should be continuous. The momentum of one action contributes to the next action.

Applications

a. In the kip-up on the still rings there should be no pause between the pulling phase and the pushing phase of the hands and arms.

b. Hand traveling on a horizontal bar or ladder should be a continuous hand over hand action.

NONSUPPORT ACTIVITIES

The unsupported body moves through the air along a pathway determined prior to the beginning of flight. The flight path of the body may be primarily horizontal as in a long jump, mostly vertical as in springboard diving or high jumping or somewhere in between as in vaulting and tumbling events. Principles governing the flight path of the body relate to those of the projectile. Additional principles explaining the effect of the body's lean at the moment of takeoff and the twisting movements in the air are derived from Newton's third law of action-reaction and the conservation of angular momentum.

Principles Related to Nonsupport Activities

Principle I. The path of motion of the body's center of gravity in space is determined by the angle at which it is projected into space, the force of the projection and the force of gravity.

Applications

a. Nothing a diver can do will alter the pathway of the center of gravity, once he has left the diving board. Divers who, by pulling the head down, attempt to "correct" dives they believe to be too far away from the board, merely cause additional rotation about the transverse axis. The horizontal velocity of the diver remains constant and the path of the center of gravity is not altered.

b. A trampolinist must direct his projection in a totally vertical direction in order to assure landing back in the middle of the bed. A diver must leave the board with some degree of lean to assure *not* hitting the board after takeoff.

Principle II.   The time a body remains unsupported depends upon the height of its projection, which is governed by the vertical velocity of the projection (Fig. 18–4).

Application.   The more complicated or lengthy the stunt a diver or trampolinist wishes to perform, the higher the peak of projection must be. A diver must emphasize vertical rather than horizontal distance.

Principle III.   The angular momentum ($I\omega$) of an unsupported body is conserved. It cannot be increased or decreased.

Applications

a. A performer executing a forward tuck somersault may decrease the angular velocity by increasing the moment of inertia. This is done by increasing the radius of rotation, i.e., decreasing the amount of tuck. A tuck somersault has less angular inertia than a pike somersault and a pike somersault has less than a layout.

b. If a somersault starts with a twist from the board or trampoline bed, the twist can be increased by decreasing the arch or pike of the spin and by moving

Figure 18–4   Movement of the body in the air, free of support. The height of projection is dependent upon its vertical velocity. (Judi Ford, Miss America, 1969; Junior Women's National A. A. U. Trampoline Champion, 1968. Courtesy of Mrs. Virgil Ford.)

the arms close to the body. Each of these moves decreases the moment of inertia and increases the angular velocity of the twist.

Principle IV.   Most rotatory movements are initiated before the performer leaves the supporting surface.

Applications

a. In the front somersault dive (Fig. 18–5), the diver's center of gravity must be in front of his feet at the moment of takeoff for a rotatory or torque force to exist and for the dive to be possible.

b. In a back somersault with a twist (Fig. 18–6), the diver pushes the feet sideways as well as diagonally backward against the board as the upper body leads the twist in the opposite direction. In keeping with Newton's third law the direction of the twist is opposite to the direction in which the feet push against the supporting surface.

Principle V.   When a body is free in space, movement of a part in one direction results in movement of the rest of the body in the opposite direction.

Applications

a. In a back dive in the pike position, the diver should wait until the legs have rotated past the vertical before the pike is opened. As the trunk and arms move back, the legs will react in the opposite direction and therefore move back to the vertical position.

b. A reverse dive layout with a one-half twist may be performed by initiating the twist in the air rather than from the board. By moving one arm across the chest after the body is in a layout position in the air, the diver will cause the body to twist to the opposite direction. The arm must then be moved overhead

Figure 18–5 Front somersault dive in layout position. An example of rotatory movement of the body as a whole when it is unsupported. (Courtesy of H. E. Edgerton.)

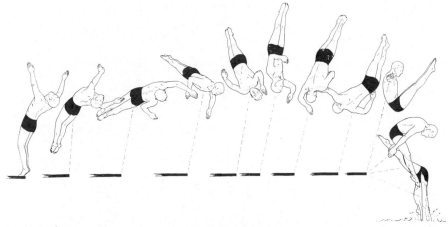

Figure 18–6 Back one and one-half somersault, one and one-half twist, free. (From Armbruster, D. A. et al.: Swimming and Diving, 5th ed. St. Louis, C. V. Mosby Co., 1968.)

keeping it close to the body so that another equal and opposite reaction does not occur. This method for initiating a twist is slow and is not usually used for more than a half twist.

Principle VI.   A performer who is rotating about a horizontal axis in the air may initiate a twist about a vertical axis by tilting the body to one side.

Application.   In any twisting somersault, a diver can tilt to the side by moving one arm from the side horizontal to a position over the head and the other arm sideward downward across the body. This happens because of action-reaction. As the arms move in one direction in the frontal plane, the body moves in the other direction. The twist will occur in the direction of the raised arm and be directly proportional to the spin. That is, the faster the performer is rotating forward or backward, the faster he will twist (Figs. 18–6 and 18–7).

ANALYSIS OF SUSPENSION AND NONSUPPORT MOVEMENTS

Movements from both categories are so numerous, particularly in gymnastics or diving, that it would be impossible to analyze them all. The movements selected for analysis here are chosen as examples to illustrate the further application of principles related either to the body suspended or to the body free of support.

The Reverse Dive Layout with One-Half Twist. (Fig. 18–8.)   A twisting dive is one in which the body makes at least one-half turn about the vertical axis. Twisting dives may be combined with somersaults in the tuck, pike or layout positions. Divers may face forward and leave the board with a forward spinning action or a backward spinning action (reverse spinning dives). They may also initiate dives from a backward stance and spin backward or forward (inward spinning dives). In the reverse dive layout with a one-half twist the diver starts the dive facing the end of the board. He performs a reverse spinning somersault about a transverse axis in a layout position completing one-half revolution. At the same time he twists one half of a revolution about the vertical axis.

In starting a reverse dive the diver must end his forward approach by

Figure 18–7   Double twisting back somersault. (Judi Ford, Miss America 1969; Junior Women's National A. A. U. Trampoline Champion, 1968. Courtesy of Mrs. Virgil Ford.)

pushing backward toward the back end of the board with his feet. The rebounding board will push back with an equal and opposite reaction causing the legs to move forward. This action of the board causes the reverse spin to develop in the body as the feet and legs move forward and the head and upper trunk rotate backward. It also causes the entire body to move forward away from the board. Because the feet push back against the board in reverse dives and force the body forward, less lean is needed on takeoff than with forward dives where the feet push forward toward the tip of the board. The amount of rotation (spin) about the transverse axis must be determined in large measure at takeoff in this dive because usual methods of controlling the rate of spin by decreasing the moment of inertia through tucking or piking are not permitted, and angular momentum of the dive is determined and conserved at takeoff and cannot be altered. Some control may be exercised by varying the arch in the back in the initial layout. An increase in the arch will increase the rate of rotation.

The twist in this dive is accomplished through the use of two methods of initiating twists. As the diver leaves the board, he not only pushes back to create the reversed spin, but he also pushes slightly to the right to initiate a twist to the left. Once the diver is in the air he uses the principle of action-reaction to complete the twist. As the diver twists to the left he brings his left arm across his chest causing his body to move in the opposite direction (left) in reaction. He continues to aid the twist by circling the arm down next to the body, close to the axis of rotation. Keeping the head in line with the body and the right arm overhead during the twist decreases the moment of inertia of the rotating body and increases the speed of the twist. Turning the head left toward the water helps in the turn and in the diver's orientation. The diver's twist is completed so that he enters the water with his back to the board and at the point where his center of gravity was predetermined to land the instant his feet left the board. In spite

Figure 18–8   The reverse dive layout with one-half twist. (From Batterman, C.: The Techniques of Springboard Diving. Cambridge, MIT Press, 1968.)

of the spin of the body about both a vertical and a horizontal axis the body's center of gravity follows a perfect parabolic curve controlled only by the velocity and angle of projection and the downward acceleration of gravity.

The entry of the dive must take into account the fact that the forward rotation of the dive will continue because of the law of conservation of momentum. The stretched position of the body with the arms overhead creates the greatest moment of inertia possible and therefore the slowest rotation, but there is still some rotation. For this reason the diver should continue to turn underwater in the same direction. The angle of entry of the dive should be a natural continuation of the parabolic path of the center of gravity of the body. For reverse dives the entry would be almost vertical.

As with all dives from a diving board this dive requires good strength, flexibility and control, particularly in the trunk and legs. Good range of motion in the ankle joint is essential as the feet contact the end of the board, dorsiflex as the board is depressed, and then ride it upward and extend until the toes leave the board. Strength in the extensors of the hip and knee are also important in lifting the body from the board and maintaining the extended position in the air. Strength of the abdominals and back extensors is of prime importance

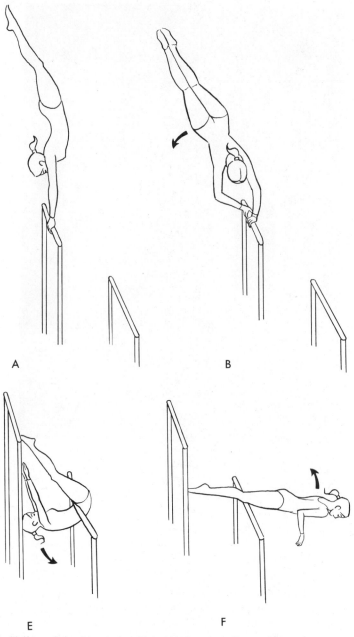

Figure 18–9 Half-turn flying hip circle with hecht dismount. (Drawn from motion picture film tracings.)

to divers. Vertical alignment in the air relies on control by these muscles as does the entry position. The abdominals also are important in the initiation and control of rotations and in the prevention of overarching of the back. Contrary to popular belief, extreme extension flexibility of the back is not desirable in dives and should be avoided. In the dive described here, overarching would decrease the height of the dive and slow the twist as it causes an increase in the

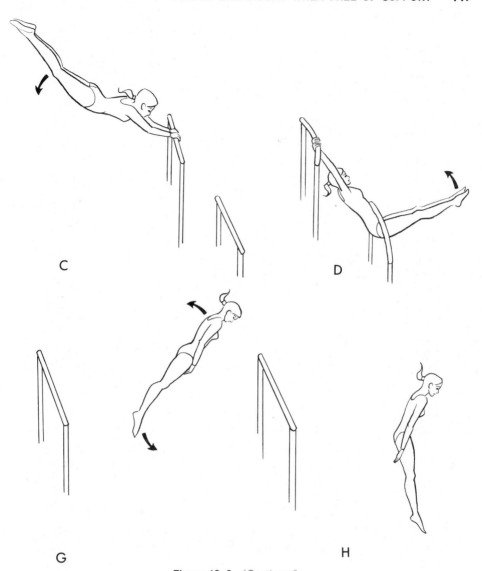

Figure 18–9   (Continued)

moment of inertia about the vertical axis. Flexibility of the back and hips for full flexion in tuck and pike positions is desirable, however.

Half-Turn Flying Hip Circle with Hecht Dismount—Uneven Parallel Bars. (Fig. 18–9.)   Gymnasts who perform on the uneven parallel bars have numerous combinations of movements from which to choose. Each routine starts with a mount and concludes with a dismount. In between the gymnast selects from a series of movements including those characterized as circling, swinging or kipping movements. Grip release and regrasps must also be incorporated. Movements are classified as being of medium or superior difficulty, and each performance should contain four medium and two superior moves in its twelve to fourteen moves. The moves shown in Figure 18–9 and described here are of medium difficulty. The gymnast starts in a handstand position on the high bar.

As she begins to swing downward she performs a half twist so that she faces in the direction of the swing. At the bottom of the swing she begins to flex at the hips in preparation for continuing in a back hip circle around the low bar. Toward the end of the hip circle she extends at the hip joint and dismounts forward over the low bar in a move called a *hecht*. The gymnast lands with the back to the bars.

In starting the downward swing from the handstand position the gymnast pushes against the bar. Because of action-reaction the bar pushes back in the opposite direction. The give or flexibility of the bar adds to the reactive force and thus increases the total energy of the system. The push of the gymnast backward and the accompanying stretch increase the distance between the center of gravity and the axis of rotation and thus increase the torque on the downward swing. The time for gravity to act on the downward swinging body is also increased. The half twist is performed at the beginning of the downswing when the forces acting on the hands are minimal and the grip change can be accomplished with ease. At the bottom of the swing the gymnast flexes at the hips, thus shortening the radius of rotation and increasing her angular velocity on the upswing. This piked position also enables her to "wrap" around the low bar as she moves into the backward hip circle. There should be no pause between one movement and the next. Any slowing down would require more energy to pick up again (law of inertia) and fluidity would be lost. As the gymnast's hands leave the high bar, she pushes up and forward causing the reactive force to add to the downward trunk rotation.

The hip circle should be accomplished with the hips close to the bar so that the center of gravity is near the axis of rotation. Otherwise, centrifugal force would tend to pull the body away from the bar. Toward the completion of the hip circle the gymnast forcefully extends by lifting the upper trunk and arms forward and upward. This action causes several things to happen. In reaction, the legs also extend so that the whole body is straight. The moment of inertia about the transverse axis is increased, and the rate of rotation decreases. The body pushes down and back against the bar causing the bar to push the body forward and up. All of this results in the body rotating up and away from the bar for the dismount. Once the body has left the bar the back should be arched to again decrease the radius slightly and aid in the rotation of the body, allowing the feet to move slightly ahead of the center of gravity at the moment of landing. The success of the hecht dismount depends upon sufficient angular momentum being developed in the downswing and hip circle and a forceful, properly timed extension of the body at the end of the hip circle.

The anatomic essentials for successful performance in this movement series are strength and flexibility. Strength of the shoulders, arms and hands is especially important for swinging movements. Grip strength is essential, and until one is sure of such strength certain swinging movements should not be attempted without the assistance of a spotter. Arm and shoulder strength can be checked by testing oneself with pushups and pullups. According to Frederick beginning gymnasts should be capable of doing at least one of each.[7] Strong abdominal and back extensor muscles are also important. These muscle groups play a significant role in maintaining and changing the trunk position in the downward swing, the hip circle and the hecht dismount as shown here. Range of motion is also needed for these movements particularly in the shoulder during the swing, and in the hip and lower back during the pike of the hip circle.

LABORATORY EXPERIENCES

1. Observe a partner perform the following moves on a trampoline. In each instance identify the underlying principles which explain the resulting action.
   a. Jump straight up and down a few times. At the peak of a jump, try to move forward so that upon landing you are six inches in front of your previous landing spot. Do *not* initiate your forward move until you are in the air.
   b. At the peak of a vertical jump, move one arm sharply across the front of the body. Observe the effect on the rest of the body.
   c. Perform a swivel hips. Observe the action of the head, arms, hips and feet. Explain how and why these actions contribute to the successful completion of the swivel hips.
   d. Initiate a 90 degree turn from the trampoline bed. Next, perform a six inch jump forward, backward and sideward. Note the direction in which the feet push against the bed of the trampoline in each move.

2. Hang motionless from a rope or a pair of rings. Now start swinging without the help of anyone else. How was the swing accomplished? Explain.

3. Swing on a pair of rings without attempting to get much height. Perform the following movements. Explain the results in terms of the underlying principles. Be sure to have mats placed under the swinging area.
   a. Reverse the grasp of one hand. At what point in the swing is this accomplished most easily?
   b. Dismount at various positions along the arc of the swing. Note the effect on the body.

4. Perform the following movements in the water and explain the actions in terms of underlying principles. (Except for the factor of increased resistance, the actions simulate those of an unsupported body.)
   a. Lie on the side and swing both legs forward vigorously, keeping the knees straight. Note the effect on the trunk.
   b. Lie on the back with the arms in a side horizontal position. Keeping the elbows straight, swing both arms in a clockwise direction across the surface of the water in a 90 degree arc as you roll to the right into a prone float. Note the direction in which the feet now point compared to the starting position.

REFERENCES

1. Batterman, C.: The Techniques of Springboard Diving. Cambridge: MIT Press, 1968.
2. Bowers, C. O., Fie, J. U., Kjeldsen, K., and Schmid, A. B.: Judging and Coaching Women's Gymnastics. Palo Alto, Cal.: National Press Books, 1972.
3. Bunn, J. W.: Scientific Principles of Coaching, 2nd Ed. Englewood Cliffs, New Jersey: Prentice-Hall, Inc., 1972.
4. Cooper, J. M., and Glassow, R. B.: Kinesiology, 3rd Ed. St. Louis: C. V. Mosby Co., 1972.
5. Dyson, G.: The Mechanics of Athletics, 5th Ed. London: University of London Press, 1970.
6. Fairbanks, A. R.: Teaching Springboard Diving. Englewood Cliffs, New Jersey: Prentice-Hall, Inc., 1963.
7. Frederick, A. B.: Gymnastics for Men. Dubuque, Iowa: William C. Brown, Co., 1969.
8. Frederick, A. B.: Women's Gymnastics. Dubuque, Iowa: William C. Brown, Co., 1966.
9. Hay, J. G.: The Biomechanics of Sports Techniques. Englewood Cliffs, New Jersey: Prentice-Hall, Inc., 1973.
10. Jensen, C. R., and Schultz, G. W.: Applied Kinesiology. New York: McGraw-Hill Book Co., Inc., 1970.

Chapter Nineteen

GIVING IMPETUS TO ONE'S OWN BODY WHEN IT IS SUPPORTED BY WATER

AQUATIC LOCOMOTION: SWIMMING

The problem of moving the body through the water is fundamentally not so different from that of moving it on land. As in walking, it is necessary to push against something in order to move the body from one place to another. The chief differences between locomotion in the water and locomotion on land are that (1) in the water the body is concerned with buoyancy rather than with the force of gravity, (2) the substance against which it pushes affords less resistance to the push, (3) the medium through which it moves affords more resistance to the body, and (4) as a means of getting the greatest benefit from the buoyancy and of reducing the resistance afforded by the water, it is customary to maintain a horizontal, rather than a vertical, position. (Review the discussion of buoyancy on pages 375 to 378.) The practical problem in swimming is not to keep from sinking, as novices are inclined to believe, but to get the mouth out of the water at rhythmic intervals in order to permit regular breathing. This is a matter of coordination, not buoyancy.

In swimming, as in all motion, the initial mechanical problem is to overcome the inertia of the body. Once the body is in motion, the problem is to overcome the forces which tend to hinder it. In terrestrial locomotion the body exerts its force against the supporting surface, i.e., the ground, in order to overcome inertia. The forces resisting the progress of the body are the force of gravity and air resistance. In aquatic locomotion the water is both the supporting medium and the source of resistance. In swimming, the hands and feet depend upon the counterpressure of the water in order that the force may be transmitted to the body. Yet, at the same time, the body must overcome the resistance afforded by the water.

Thus, the major problems in the mechanics of swimming are the minimization of resistance and the advantageous application of force. The swimmer reduces the resistance by streamlining his body position, by relaxing in the recovery phase of the stroke and by eliminating useless motions and tensions. There are

450

many different strokes in swimming, but they all involve either a pulling or a pushing motion of the arms and either a pincer or a thrusting action of the legs. In order to get maximum horizontal propulsion from the arm and leg movements, it is necessary to eliminate upward, downward and sideward components of force as much as possible. Swimming with ease, power and efficiency requires a precise coordination of arm and leg motions, of breathing and of use of the trunk muscles in maintaining an optimum position.

For a thorough coverage of the mechanical aspects of swimming, Chapter One of Counsilman's book *The Science of Swimming* is highly recommended.[2] The major principles are as follows.

Application of Force

Principle I.   The body will move in the opposite direction from that in which the force is applied. For instance, a backward thrust will send the body forward; downward pressure will lift it; pressure to the right will send it to the left.

Applications

a. In the crawl stroke, too much force at the beginning of the arc will have too great a downward component, thereby tending to lift the body. This increases resistance and is a needless expenditure of energy. In the breast stroke, the two arms balance each other; hence, too great an outward force at the beginning of the stroke or inward force at the end of the stroke does not produce lateral motion but results in a waste of energy.

b. In many aquatic stunts and lifesaving techniques the swimmer deliberately pushes himself up or down by pushing his hands and feet against the water in the direction opposite to that in which he wishes to move. No matter how complicated the movement in a synchronized swimming technique, it is brought about by observing the principle that a body moves in the opposite direction from that in which the force is applied.

Principle II.   Maximum force is attained by presenting as broad a surface as possible in the propulsive movements of the limbs and by exerting a backward pressure through as great a distance as possible, provided undesirable forces are not inadvertently introduced.

Applications

a. The full surface of the hand should be used.

b. The use of fins increases the force of the leg stroke.

c. The hand should not enter the water so soon that it shortens the stroke unduly. In the crawl stroke care must be taken not to reach too far, however, as this involves lifting the shoulder and is likely to introduce a lateral force acting on the trunk.

Reduction of Resistance

Principle III.   A rapidly moving body in the water leaves a low pressure area immediately behind it. This creates a suction effect and tends to pull the body back.

Application. Although this backward pull cannot be entirely eliminated, it can be reduced in the crawl stroke by keeping the feet close together.

Principle IV. The sudden or quick movement of a swimmer's body, or one of its parts, at the surface of the water tends to cause whirls and eddies. These create low pressure areas which have a retarding effect on the swimmer.

Application. The low pressure areas can be reduced by slicing the hand into the water and by eliminating movements which do not contribute to forward progression. In the flutter kick, movements of the feet in the air do not contribute to the propulsion of the body; hence, the feet and legs should be kept just below the surface of the water.

Principle V. The more streamlined the body, the less the resistance to progress through the water. The streamlining of the body in the crawl stroke is accomplished by four actions.

Applications

a. Carrying the head so that the water level is somewhere between the hairline and just below the eyes, depending upon the buoyancy and speed of the swimmer.

b. Carrying the body parallel with the surface of the water.

c. Carrying the buttocks just below the surface of the water.

d. Keeping the legs, ankles and feet close together.

THE SPRINT CRAWL

As an example of aquatic locomotion, the sprint crawl (Fig. 19–1) has been chosen for analysis. The technique described by Armbruster, Allen and Billingsley in their book *Swimming and Diving* is used as a basis for the analysis, not necessarily because the technique is superior but because the description is unusually clear and concise.* Their description of the position of the body demonstrates the importance of seemingly minor details in streamlining the body for minimizing the resistance of the water to forward progression.[1]

In the following analysis the position of the head and trunk and the movement of the head in breathing are described briefly. The arm and leg strokes are described in somewhat greater detail, and their propulsive phases are analyzed anatomically.

The Head and Trunk

The head and trunk have three important functions in swimming, particularly in speed swimming. These are minimizing resistance, enabling the swimmer to breathe, and providing a stable anchorage for the arm and leg muscles. The position of the body is the key to reducing resistance. The body is

---

*For an analysis of the crawl stroke for teachers of beginning swimmers, see *Basic Swimming Analyzed* by Marjorie M. Harris.[3]

almost horizontal, but not quite, because the feet and buttocks are below the surface of the water and the head and shoulders are partly above it. The head is held with the chin slightly lifted and the eyes close to the surface of the water, in some cases just below it and in some cases just above it. The exact position of the body varies with the anatomic build and the buoyancy of the individual, as well as with the speed of the stroke. A common mistake is to lift the head too much. If the head is held too high or tipped back too far, it makes the swimmer overtense and thus reduces his endurance. Armbruster et al. emphasize the importance of keeping the chin and nose in the midplane of the body in order to keep the body on an even keel. By static contraction of the rectus abdominis the spine is held in a position of slight flexion — or at least of incomplete extension — and the pelvis in a position of slightly decreased inclination.

The turning of the head for inhaling must be accomplished with the least possible interference with the rhythm of the arm and leg action and with the progress of the body through the water. It is essential not to lift the head for breathing but rather to rotate it on its longitudinal axis while at the same time tucking the chin in close to the side of the neck. In this position the face appears to be resting on the bow wave, and the mouth is just above the surface of the water. After a quick inhalation the face is again turned forward with the eyes in the horizontal plane and the nose and chin in the midsagittal plane of the body.

In order to provide a firm base of attachment for the muscles of the arms and thighs the trunk must be held steady. By the alternating action of the left and right oblique abdominals and spinal extensors the spine and pelvis are stabilized against the pull of the shoulder and hip muscles. Thus, they permit the latter to exert all their force on the limbs for the propulsive movements.

The Arm Stroke

Entry and Support. Since the arm stroke provides approximately 85 per cent of the total power, it is most important that the entry of the arm into the water should place it in the most advantageous position for exerting force which will be effective in driving the body forward. Its position on entry is with the forearm high and the elbow pointing to the side. The hand passes in front of the shoulder in preparation for the entry, and then, reaching forward with the shoulder held high, it is driven forward into the water directly in front of the shoulder. The brief moment between entry and the beginning of the chief propulsive action is known as the support phase, and its purpose is to keep the head and shoulders above the surface. The pressure of the forearm and hand is chiefly downward, passing into backward.

Catch, Pull and Push. The moment at which the chief propulsive action changes from downward to backward constitutes the catch. This occurs when the hand is five to ten inches below the surface and involves a quick inward movement of the hand and arm which serves to bring the hand to a position in front of the axis of the body in such a way that the body weight is balanced

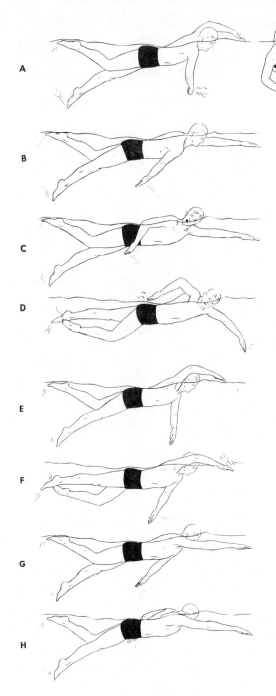

Figure 19–1 The sprint crawl. (From Armbruster, D. A. et al.: Swimming and Diving, 5th ed. St. Louis: C. V. Mosby Co., 1968.)

above the arm. The upper arm is approximately vertical, a position which favors the large muscles (sternal portion of the pectoralis major and latissimus dorsi) for their task of pulling the arm downward and backward. Since the purpose of the stroke is to drive the body forward, it is essential to apply maximum force backward. Armbruster and his co-authors state that this is best done by keeping the arm in a near vertical position during the pull and push with the hand pulling along a line below the long axis of the body. In order to keep the hand in this plane the elbow must gradually flex. They refer to the hand and forearm serving as an anchorage for the shoulder to be pulled forward over them. In order to keep the hand and forearm in the best position for pressing against the water, the elbow is flexed slightly and the hand drawn inward and slightly upward toward the chest. They give the following three reasons for flexing the elbow during the pull:

1. It permits the hand and forearm to assume a position in which they can exert their force more nearly in line with the body's long axis.

2. It shortens the lever arm and thus permits greater speed with less energy expenditure.

3. It favors the transition from pull to push.[1]

The transition from pull to push occurs as the arm passes under the shoulder. The upper arm remains nearly vertical as the forearm gradually extends until it is in front of the hip, at which time the upper arm extends and the hand gives a quick push backward.

Release and Recovery. The elbow is now near the surface with the hand slightly lower and posterior to it and the palm facing mostly upward. The pressure of the forearm and hand now being relaxed, the elbow and shoulder are raised until the hand is out of the water. As this occurs, the palm turns toward the body. The arm is then carried forward through the air with the hand moving from a position near the hip to a position in front of the shoulder, preparatory to a new entry. The movement of the arm from release to the completion of recovery is continuous. It is important that no break occur as this would mean a loss of momentum and would necessitate an additional force for overcoming inertia, or at least for regaining the lost velocity.

The movement of the arm during the recovery starts with a lift of the entire arm and shoulder from the water by raising the elbow until the hand is clear of the water. This is followed by "an outward and forward circular motion with the shoulder acting as the axis"[1] and the hand being carried forward with the palm downward and the thumb leading.

Armbruster, Allen and Billingsley state that as the elbow is brought forward it remains above the level of the hand throughout the recovery and entry, the forearm being virtually horizontal as the arm moves forward past the shoulder and the hand staying in line with the forearm. Finally, as the hand passes the head, the arm reaches forward in preparation for the entry, the shoulder girdle remains high, the tip of the elbow is above shoulder level pointing to the side and the forearm then points downward from the elbow with the wrist slightly flexed, the palm facing the water and the fingers aiming forward into the water.

Armbruster and his co-authors mention that there are various other styles of arm recovery in the crawl stroke, the chief differences being in the position of the elbow. Counsilman also discusses various forms of arm recovery and attributes the variety to variations in shoulder flexibility. He even goes so far as to express the opinion that if all swimmers had equal degrees of flexibility they might all use similar recoveries.[2]

Brief Anatomic Analysis of Propulsive Phase of Arm Stroke (Catch, Pull and Push)

Shoulder joint: Strong extension, slight inward rotation, slight "horizontal" flexion-adduction in oblique plane, followed by continued extension and possibly slight hyperextension. Muscles: Latissimus dorsi, teres major, sternal portion of pectoralis major, posterior deltoid.

Shoulder girdle: Downward rotation, adduction, slight upward tilt. Muscles: Rhomboids and pectoralis minor.

Elbow and radioulnar joints: Flexion, slight pronation; partial extension toward end. Muscles: (Flexors) brachialis, brachioradialis, probably biceps brachii because of resistance; (Pronators) pronator teres, pronator quadratus; (Extensors) triceps, anconeus.

Wrist: Held in midposition, possibly slight flexion toward end of propulsion. Muscles: Palmaris longus, flexor carpi radialis (longus and brevis), flexor carpi ulnaris.

Fingers: Held in extension and adduction. Muscles: Probably flexors and adductors in static contraction.

The Leg Stroke

Position and Nature of Movement.   The legs are relatively close together in a position of easy extension. They oscillate in an up and down movement with the feet attaining a stride of about 18 to 26 inches. In both the upstroke and downstroke the movement, described as whip-like or lashing, starts at the hip joint and progresses through the knees to the ankles and feet. The action of the latter is said to be similar to that of pedaling a bicycle but obviously with a much smaller range of motion since the ankle joints remain in varying degrees of plantar flexion throughout the entire leg stroke. Unlike the arms, whose movements alternate between propulsion and recovery, both phases of the leg stroke are propulsive. In the downstroke the water is pushed back along the front of the thigh, then the shin and finally the front of the ankle and dorsal surface of the foot. In the upstroke the water is pressed back along the posterior surface of the thigh, then the calf of the leg and finally along the sole of the foot. A quick, forceful plantar flexion at the very end of the upstroke provides a powerful backward and upward push of the sole of the foot against the water, driving the body forward.

Downstroke.   As the plantar flexors relax, the hip flexors, followed almost immediately by the knee extensors, start to contract. The thigh flexes only slightly and the knee, which was in a position of slight flexion at the completion of the upstroke, extends completely during the downstroke. The ankle and foot remain in plantar flexion, probably being held in this position by the pressure of the water against the dorsal surface of the foot. It seems likely that the dorsi-flexors contract statically to stabilize the foot against this pressure. Throughout the downstroke the foot remains in a slight toeing-in position. Armbruster warns that the heels should not be allowed to drift apart in an attempt to facilitate the in-toeing as this would involve rotation of the thigh and would cut down on the driving power of the limb.

BRIEF ANATOMIC ANALYSIS OF DOWNSTROKE

Hip joint: Partial flexion. Muscles: Iliopsoas, tensor fasciae latae, pectineus, sartorius and gracilis.

Knee joint: Strong extension. Muscles: Quadriceps femoris.

Ankle joint: Incomplete plantar flexion probably caused by pressure of water. Muscles: Tibialis anterior, peroneus tertius, extensor digitorum longus, and extensor hallucis longus may contract statically to stabilize foot against pressure of water.

Tarsal joints: Adduction and inversion. Muscles: Tibialis posterior and anterior, flexor digitorum longus and flexor hallucis longus.

Upstroke. At the completion of the downstroke the thigh is in a position of slight flexion, the knee is completely extended, the ankle is incompletely plantar flexed and the tarsal joints are probably neutral in the split second between the downstroke and the upstroke. The upstroke begins with thigh extension, and this is accompanied almost immediately by slight knee flexion. Active plantar flexion, first of the ankle and then of the tarsal joints, occurs with increasing intensity throughout the stroke and reaches a peak at the very end when the sole of the foot exerts a quick, forceful, backward and upward thrust against the water. The movements of the three major segments of the lower extremity are forceful in the upstroke but are under such good control that the foot stops just below the surface of the water. To break through the surface constitutes a major error as it causes an immediate reduction in propulsive force.

BRIEF ANATOMIC ANALYSIS OF UPSTROKE

Hip joint: Strong but incomplete extension. Muscles: Hamstrings and gluteus maximus.

Knee joint: Slight flexion against resistance. Muscles: Hamstrings, sartorius, gracilis, popliteus and gastrocnemius.

Ankle joint: Plantar flexion. Muscles: Gastrocnemius, soleus, peroneus longus and brevis, tibialis posterior, flexor digitorum longus and flexor hallucis longus.

Tarsal joints: Plantar flexion, especially in final part of stroke. Muscles: Peroneus longus and brevis, tibialis posterior, flexor digitorum longus and flexor hallucis longus.

Additional Factors. Other factors of importance to the crawl stroke swimmer and to his coach are the timing and coordination of the arm and leg strokes and of the breathing, the rhythm of the stroke as a whole, the relaxation of the body and the flexibility of the joints, particularly of the shoulders and ankles. Of these, possibly the last named is of greatest interest to the kinesiologist. The serious swimmer will want to know how to increase the range of motion in his shoulder joints and ankles; specifically, he needs to know how to stretch the pectorals and anterior ligaments of the shoulders and how to gain greater plantar flexion of the feet. Armbruster and Counsilman have both suggested a few exercises for these purposes.[1, 2] The kinesiology student should be able to originate several others.

Sample Analysis of a Common Fault in the Crawl Stroke:
Rigid Flutter Kick

A rigid flutter kick is a common fault of beginners learning the standard crawl stroke. This was analyzed by Vollmer as part of a graduate project at Wellesley College.* It is included in this text as an example of how the kinesiologist can analyze a common fault and use the analysis as a basis for making constructive suggestions in his teaching.

Description. In the rigid flutter kick the movement is one of alternate flexion and extension of the entire lower extremity, with the movement confined to the hip joint instead of being transmitted successively through the thigh to the knee joint and thence through the leg to the ankle and foot. The knee joints are fully extended throughout the kick, and the feet and ankles are held in an unchanging position of plantar flexion, the exact degree of this flexion varying with individuals. The swimmer who commits this fault finds that to cover the same distance he has to kick more times than a swimmer who kicks correctly. This results in a narrower kick. A rigid flutter kick is obviously less efficient than the correct kick. In brief, the rigid flutter kick deviates from the correct form in that there is an absence of knee and ankle flexion, an absence of relaxation at the end of the downkick or beginning of the upkick and an absence of "fishtail" action of the sole of the foot against the water.

Anatomic Analysis. In the correct downkick the upward pressure of the water against the lower leg causes flexion at the knee. In the rigid kick, however, this is prevented by the tension of the quadriceps extensors. Normally, the slight flexion at the knee is followed by extension during the course of the downstroke, but when the knee is already rigidly extended, this extension cannot take place. Similarly, the reduction of plantar flexion which should take place at the end of the downstroke fails to occur because of the continuous contraction of the plantar flexor muscles (soleus, peroneus longus and brevis, tibialis posterior, flexor digitorum longus and flexor hallucis longus).

In the upstroke the tension of the quadriceps extensors again prevents the slight knee flexion which occurs when the kick is correctly performed. (See Figs. 19–1 and 19–2.) Throughout the stroke the extensors of the lower back and the abdominal muscles contract to stabilize the pelvis against the pull of the hip flexors and extensors. Normally they relax momentarily just before the legs reverse their direction. The tension in the muscles of the lower extremities spreads to these, however, and the excess tension of these muscles causes interference with the action of the diaphragm. This, in turn, results in less efficient breathing and is an additional factor in causing fatigue.

Mechanical Analysis. The propulsive component of force which drives the body forward is that which pushes the water directly backward. In the downstroke this is provided most effectively by the instep of the foot, and in the upstroke, by the sole. The amount of propulsive force developed depends upon the angle at which the instep and the sole of the foot are held with respect to the surface of the water. In the upstroke the best angle for the sole of the foot is

---

*Used by permission of Mrs. Lola Vollmer Shepherd.

Figure 19–2 The crawl stroke. Taken through underwater window in Wellesley College swimming pool. The right arm is about to begin the pull. (Photo from files of Department of Physical Education, Wellesley College.)

possible only when the knee is slightly flexed. In the rigid kick the knee is straight, and the sole of the foot is therefore not in the best position for providing propulsive force.

In the correct form each limb acts as a series of levers—thigh, lower leg and foot—but in the rigid kick each limb acts as one long lever with the force arm extending from the distal attachments of the hip flexors and extensors to the axis of the hip joint. The resistance arm consists of the entire length of the lever from the instep or from the sole of the foot to the hip joint. The force acting on this lever comes solely from the muscles of the hip joints. The muscles of the knee and ankle do not contribute to the motion of this lever, but when the limb is used as a series of levers, they provide additional force.

Inertia must be overcome with each reversal of direction in the kick. Since, in the rigid flutter kick, the stroke is shorter and faster than it should be, the muscles of the hip joint, which have the double task of overcoming both the inertia of the limb and the resistance of the water, are overburdened. They must work harder and faster to meet the demands made on them by the frequent changes of direction and the increased resistance of the water due to the speed of movement. Ordinarily the upstroke has an advantage over the downstroke because, when the stroke is performed correctly, the sole of the foot is in a better position to push back against the water than is the instep on the downstroke. In the rigid kick this advantage is lost.

Teaching Suggestions. "The rigid crawl flutter kick is associated with undue tension of the quadriceps extensors at the knee joint, and of the plantar flexors at the ankle joint, during the changes of direction in both the downkick and the upkick. There may also be unnecessary tension of the abdominal muscles and the spinal extensors. As the kick is inefficient, it is carried on at a faster rate and through a narrower arc than would be the correct kick for the individual swimmer. Conversely, a rapid, narrow kick tends to be a rigid kick. These factors aid in its recognition. In the teaching of the kick, it would seem the best procedure to insist on a slow, deep kick in the student's first attempts, and to increase the rhythm gradually to the desired rate. Motivation should not be directed toward speed in the performance of the 'kick glide' in the teaching progression. Neither is it desirable to emphasize that the legs be held straight at the knees. The emphasis should be put on the increased action at the hips and at the ankles. Furthermore, land drills to increase ankle flexibility seem to be advisable."[4]

AQUATIC LOCOMOTION: BOATING AND CANOEING*

On the whole, the principles which apply to swimming apply also to boating and canoeing. This is particularly obvious in canoeing, for the paddle is used in much the same way as are the arms in swimming. The use of the oars in rowing is more limited, since they must be kept in the oarlocks at all times. In paddling, as in the arm movement of the crawl stroke, too much force at the beginning of the stroke has too great a downward component, and hence too great a lifting effect. Conversely, too much force at the end of the stroke has too great an upward component, and hence a depressing effect on the canoe. In order to make the canoe move smoothly in a horizontal direction without unnecessary bobbing up and down, it is essential to reduce these two components to a minimum and to emphasize the backward movement of the blade.

The techniques of steering the canoe are based on this same principle. Assuming that there is only one paddler and that he is paddling from the center of the canoe, if he wishes to move the canoe broadside to his paddling side, he would put his paddle in the water, blade parallel to the keel, directly opposite the center of the canoe, as far out as he can conveniently and safely reach, and then draw the blade squarely toward him at right angles to the keel of the canoe. If he wishes to move broadside away from his paddling side, he would slice the blade into the water opposite the center of the canoe and close to it, with the blade parallel to the keel, and then push it directly away from him at right angles to the keel. In order to turn the canoe, he would have to reach either forward or backward and press the blade toward or away from the canoe at a point as far from the canoe's center of buoyancy as he can conveniently reach. A drawing stroke nearer the bow would make the canoe turn toward the paddling side; a drawing stroke nearer the stern would make the canoe turn away from the paddling side. (The direction taken by the canoe as a whole is stated in terms of the bow. As the stern of the canoe moves toward the paddling side, the bow moves away from it.) Steering a canoe is logical and simple when one remembers the principle that movement occurs in the direction opposite to that in which the force is applied and, at the same time, re-

---

*Although it might seem that these activities should be classified with those of giving impetus to an external object, like bicycling they are forms of locomotion by self-propulsion. The primary purpose of boating and canoeing is locomotion of the self on the water, and the locomotion of the craft is of secondary importance. An additional reason for including the discussion of rowing and paddling in this chapter is that the principles of locomotion in the water are the same, regardless of whether the locomotion is caused by movement of the hands and feet or of oars and paddles.

members that a canoe tends to rotate about its center of buoyancy when force is applied at any point other than one in line with this center.

LABORATORY EXPERIENCES

1. Do the arm movement of the crawl stroke and deliberately press hard with the hand as soon as it enters the water and, at the end of the stroke, instead of taking the hand out of the water at the proper time, continue the movement of the arm until the hand has pressed upward against the water. What is the effect of these two errors on the body?

2. Observe or perform the following swimming stunts and analyze them in terms of the direction in which the body is moved and the direction of the application of force:
   a. Dolphin
   b. Side sculling
   c. Foot foremost surface dive
   d. Little man in a tub

3. Analyze any of the standard strokes, e.g., breast, side, elementary back, back crawl, etc. Either observe or practice the stroke before analyzing it.

4. Analyze other forms of aquatic locomotion, e.g., paddling and rowing. Either observe or practice each before analyzing it.

5. Analyze the following common faults kinesiologically and suggest coaching points for avoiding or correcting each fault: too wide a pull with the arms in the breast stroke; a short, choppy stroke in paddling; "catching a crab" in rowing (crew style).

REFERENCES

1. Armbruster, D. A., Allen, R. H., and Billingsley, H. S.: Swimming and Diving, 5th Ed. St. Louis: C. V. Mosby Co., 1968.
2. Counsilman, J. E.: The Science of Swimming. Englewood Cliffs, New Jersey: Prentice-Hall, Inc., 1968.
3. Harris, M. M.: Basic Swimming Analyzed. Boston: Allyn and Bacon, Inc., 1969.
4. Vollmer, L. T.: Kinesiological Analysis of Common Faults in Selected Activities. Unpublished master's study. Wellesley College, 1951.

RECOMMENDED READINGS

Bunn, J. W.: Scientific Principles of Coaching, 2nd Ed. Englewood Cliffs, New Jersey: Prentice-Hall, Inc., 1972.
Counsilman, J. E.: The Science of Swimming. Englewood Cliffs, New Jersey: Prentice-Hall, Inc., 1968.
Dyson, G. H. G.: The Mechanics of Athletics, 5th Ed. London: University of London Press, Ltd., 1970.

Chapter Twenty

GIVING IMPETUS TO EXTERNAL OBJECTS

CLASSIFICATION OF MOVEMENTS FOR GIVING IMPETUS

A baseball pitcher throws a baseball across the plate and the batter hits it to center field, a man pushes a lawnmower over the lawn, a school teacher opens the window, a traveler lifts a suitcase and places it on an overhead rack, an archer shoots an arrow from his bow, a boy pitches horseshoes and a girl practices serving tennis balls against a backboard. As widely diverse as these activities seem, they all have a common denominator. Each involves the giving of impetus to an external object either directly by some part of the body or by means of an implement held in the hand or hands.

There is an almost endless variety of ways in which an individual may give impetus to an object, and there are many factors to be considered. For instance: What is the objective in moving it; is it speed or distance, or perhaps accuracy in reaching a specified target? Is the purpose to project it into the air, to roll or slide it along the ground, or something other than either of these? What part of the body or what kind of implement is used for transmitting impetus to the object? Is it the hand, the foot, the head or some other part of the anatomy, or is it some kind of racket or stick, or perhaps scoop or basketlike structure on the end of a stick? What kind of movement is used, and within this type, what anatomic adjustments are required to meet the needs or limitations of the situation and to achieve the objective? In spite of the numerous ways in which impetus can be given, these conveniently fall into only three or four categories. This simplifies the kinesiologist's task of judging them on the bases of their effectiveness and the effect that they have on the body itself.

Throwing with Hand or Implement. This is characterized by the development of kinetic energy in a movable object which is usually held in the hand or hands, or in an implement such as a lacrosse stick, followed by the release of the object at the moment of maximum velocity (Fig. 20–1, *D*).

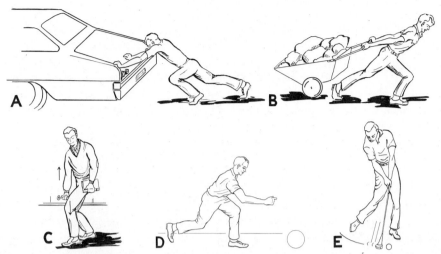

Figure 20–1   Different methods of giving impetus to an external object. *A,* Pushing; *B,* pulling; *C,* lifting; *D,* throwing; *E,* striking.

Striking, Hitting, Kicking and the Like.   Such movements are characterized by a momentary contact made with an object by a moving part of the body or by an implement held by or attached to a moving segment of the body. The object itself may be either stationary or moving. This category includes all forms of striking, such as hitting with the hand (as in handball), striking with a club or racket (as in baseball, golf and tennis) and kicking and heading (as in soccer) (Fig. 20–2, *B*).

Pushing, Pulling and Lifting.   These movements are characterized by the continuous application of force, usually by the hand or hands, but the legs may also be included. The joint actions in the upper extremities are characterized by

Figure 20–2   Giving impetus to an external object. *A,* Putting the shot (a thrusting pattern); *B,* batting a baseball (a striking pattern).

flexion or extension in the elbow while the opposite movement is occurring in the shoulder. In the lower extremities, extension occurs simultaneously in the hip, knee and ankle in both pushing and pulling movements (Fig. 20–1, *A* and *B*).

A push, pull or lift may be applied either directly or indirectly to the object. In the latter instance the push or pull pattern is used for the purpose of developing potential energy in an elastic structure such as a bow or slingshot. When the elastic structure is released, it imparts its force to the movable object, causing the arrow or shot to be projected into the air.

Three Patterns of Arm Movements in Throwing and Striking Activities. Broer was perhaps the first to call attention to the similarity of movement patterns used in seemingly dissimilar activities, such as a softball pitch, bowling, and a badminton serve.[1] Objective evidence of such similarities between throwing and striking activities within each of the three major upper extremity patterns (overhand, underhand and sidearm) was revealed by the Broer and Houtz EMG investigation of 1967.[2] The investigators also noted that representative activities from these categories showed a greater similarity in the muscular action of the lower extremities than they expected.

OVERHAND PATTERN. This kind of throw or strike is characterized by rotation at the shoulder joint. In the backswing or preparatory phase the abducted arm rotates laterally, and in the forward or force phase the arm rotates medially. Some elbow extension, wrist flexion and spinal rotation occur in the force phase. These movements are accompanied by rotation of the pelvis at the hip joint of the opposite limb, resulting in medial rotation of the thigh (Figs. 20–3 and 20–4).

UNDERHAND PATTERN. This pattern consists of a forward movement of the extended arm in the sagittal plane, usually starting from a position of hyperextension and ending in a forward reach. The basic joint action of the arm is flexion. The actions of the wrist, spine and pelvis are similar to those observed in the overhand pattern (Fig. 20–1, *D*).

SIDEARM PATTERN. In this pattern the basic movement of the upper extremities is in the horizontal or near horizontal plane, with the upper arm starting in a position of moderate shoulder abduction (side elevation); moving in horizontal flexion combined with elevation to shoulder level and ending in a position of horizontal flexion at approximately shoulder level. The elbow is maintained in extension or is extended from a slightly flexed position, depending on the nature of the skill in question (e.g., basketball throw for distance, tennis forehand drive or batting). The force is provided only in part by the upper extremity. The forward step combined with trunk rotation and medial rotation of the opposite hip, as in the overhand and underhand patterns, are important factors (Fig. 20–7).

Summary of Upper Extremity and Trunk Patterns for Giving Impetus to External Objects in Sport Activities

THROWING OR STRIKING ACTIVITIES
   Overhand Pattern
   Badminton clear
   Football pass
   Javelin throw

Overhand throw, e.g., baseball pitch
Tennis serve
Volleyball overhead serve

Underhand Pattern
Badminton serve
Bowling
Curling
Handball
Horseshoes
Polo
Underhand throw, e.g., softball pitch
Volleyball underhand serve

Sidearm Pattern
Basketball throw for distance
Batting
Tennis drives, forehand and backhand
Discus throw
Hammer throw
Volleyball sidearm serve

Modified Sidearm Pattern (Modified because of difference in plane of action. The arm pattern appears to be a combination of sidearm and underhand. It is actually an underhand movement in the frontal plane.)
Golf drive
Hockey drive (field hockey)

PUSHING, PULLING OR LIFTING ACTIVITIES
Archery (pushing with left; pulling with right)
Boat poling
Rowing and paddling strokes
Sling-shot
Weight lifting

THRUSTING AND JABBING PATTERNS
Basketball chest pass
Basketball shooting (from chest)
Boxing jab
Darts
Shot put

Giving Impetus by Parts of Body Other than Upper Extremities. Although in the majority of activities the giving of impetus is done by the hands, the occasions when another part of the body, especially the lower extremity, is responsible for this action should not be overlooked. Kicking as used in football and soccer has already been mentioned. Karate also makes use of it. However the impetus is given, whether by hand, foot, head or implement, it involves the imparting of force. And force, or effort, is described in terms of its magnitude, its direction and its point of application. These three aspects of force provide the basis for the principles that apply to the giving of impetus to external objects, the latter on occasion being other human bodies. Supplementing these aspects are the factors which relate to the stability of the body at the moment of giving impetus, and those which relate to the interaction between the body and the surface which supports it, for unless the body is stable when it is giving impetus, much of the force is wasted. The underlying mechanical principles have been presented in Part Two. Stated briefly in descriptive terms, they are as follows.

PRINCIPLES AND APPLICATIONS OF GIVING IMPETUS

PRINCIPLES

Relating to the Magnitude of Force

Principle I.   The object will move only if the force is of sufficient magnitude to overcome the object's inertia. The force must be great enough to overcome not only the mass of the object, but all restraining forces as well. These include (1) friction between the object and the supporting surface, (2) resistance of the surrounding medium (e.g., wind or water) and (3) the effect of leverage. By the latter is meant the product of the object's weight (or the resistance force) and the weight arm (or resistance arm) of the lever. Other things being equal, the shorter the weight arm of a lever, the less effort required to move it.

Relating to the Direction of Force

Principle II.   The direction in which the object moves is determined by the direction of the force applied to it. If the force consists of two or more components, the object will move in the direction of the resultant of those components.

Principle III.   If an object is free to move only along a predetermined pathway (as in the case of a window or sliding door), any component of force not in the direction of this pathway is wasted and serves to increase friction.

Relating to the Point at which the Force Is Applied

Principle IV.   Force applied in line with an object's center of gravity will result in linear motion of the object, provided the latter is freely movable.

Principle V.   If the force applied to a freely movable object is not in line with the latter's center of gravity, it will result in rotatory motion of the object.

Principle VI. If the free motion of an object is interfered with by friction or by the presence of an obstacle, rotatory motion may result, even though the force is applied in line with the object's center of gravity.

Relating to the Interaction Between the Body and the Supporting Surface

Principle VII. Force exerted by the body will be transferred to an external object in proportion to the effectiveness of the counterforce of the feet (or other parts of the body) against the ground (or other supporting surface). This effectiveness depends upon the counterpressure and the friction presented by the supporting surface. (See pages 331–333.)

Relating to the Speed, Distance and Direction of a Struck Ball

The principles relating to the speed, distance and direction of a struck ball are derived from the general principle of the conservation of momentum. (See Chapter Thirteen.) In brief, these are as follows.

Principle VIII. The greater the velocity of the approaching ball, the greater the velocity of the ball in the opposite direction after it is struck, other things being equal.

Principle IX. The greater the velocity of the striking implement at the moment of contact, the greater the velocity of the struck ball, other things being equal. Obviously, a full-powered swing will send the ball farther and faster than will a bunt. Increasing the length of the lever (Fig. 20–6) and striking with a good follow-through (Fig. 20–7) both help to increase the velocity of the striking implement, and therefore to increase the force of impact.

Principle X. The greater the mass of the ball, *up to a point,* the greater its velocity after being struck, other things being equal. A hard baseball will travel farther and faster than a softball. Nevertheless an iron ball would offer too much resistance for the average batter using an average bat.

Principle XI. The greater the mass of the striking implement, *up to a point,* the greater the striking force, and hence the greater the speed of the struck ball, other things being equal. A good baseball player usually selects a heavy bat. Too heavy a bat, however, is inadvisable because of the difficulty of swinging it with sufficient speed and control.

Principle XII. The higher the coefficient of restitution (i.e., the elasticity) of the ball and of the striking implement, the greater the speed of the struck ball, other things being equal.

Principle XIII. Other things being equal, the greater the ball's speed of departure, the greater the distance of its flight (or roll). As in the case of a thrown ball, the optimum angle of elevation is approximately 45 degrees. This angle is slightly less when back spin is imparted to the ball, and greater when top spin is imparted. (See page 350.)

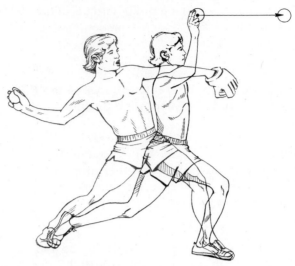

Figure 20–3   A good throw with long preparatory backswing. (Drawn from motion picture film tracing.)

Principle XIV.   The direction taken by the struck ball is determined by four factors: (1) the direction of the striking implement at the moment of contact; (2) the relation of the striking force to the ball's center of gravity (an off-center application of force causes spin, and spin affects direction); (3) degree of firmness of grip and wrist at moment of impact; and (4) the laws governing rebound. (See pages 349–351.)

APPLICATIONS

Throwing.   The efficiency of imparting force to a ball is judged in terms of the speed, distance and direction of the ball after its release. The purpose of the throw determines which of these is given the greater emphasis. Both the speed and the distance of the thrown ball are directly related to the magnitude

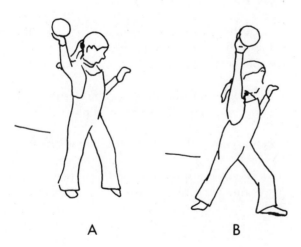

Figure 20–4   Throw of a girl aged 3 years 10 months who had not been given any directions regarding how to throw. Note elbow extension, step and weight shift. (Drawn from motion picture film tracing.)

A   B

Figure 20–5 Batting: Ready for a full-powered swing.

of the force used in throwing it and to the speed of the hand at the moment of release. The speed the hand is able to achieve depends on the distance through which it moves in the preparatory part of the act (Figs. 20–3 and 20–4). Hence, the longer the preparatory backswing and the greater the distance that can be added by means of rotating the body, shifting the weight and perhaps even taking a step, the greater the opportunity for accelerating. In order to be effective, these preparatory movements must be coordinated. Each one must be added to the preceding movement at just the right moment in order for them to contribute to maximum speed.

Greater speed and distance can be attained if internal resistance is reduced. This can be accomplished partly by a warm-up immediately preceding the throwing event and partly by a gradual increase of the range of motion in the joints involved by means of preliminary training. If distance is a major objective of the throw, the angle of projection and the effect of gravitational force must be taken into consideration. (See pages 281–85.)

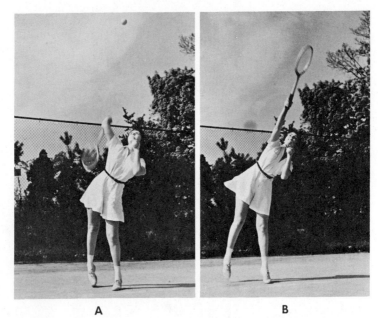

A   B

Figure 20–6 Tennis serve, an overhead pattern of striking. Note how the entire body acts as a lever to impart maximum force to the ball. (Photo by Loder.)

When the object being thrown is other than a small ball, such as a javelin, discus, bowling ball or horseshoe, the general principles are the same but must be modified according to the nature of the object and the regulations of the sport.

Striking, Hitting, Kicking and the Like. (Figs. 20–5, 20–6 and 20–7.)   As in the case of throwing, the effectiveness of striking, hitting and kicking is judged in terms of the speed, distance and direction of the struck ball. All the factors that apply to these aspects of a thrown ball apply similarly to a struck ball. There appear to be six major factors which apply to the speed of a struck ball. These are (1) the speed of the oncoming ball, (2) the mass of the ball, (3) the speed of the striking implement at the moment of contact, (4) the mass of the striking implement, (5) the coefficient of restitution (i.e., the elasticity) of the ball and (6) the coefficient of restitution of the striking implement. At least two of these factors, namely, the speed of the approaching ball and the speed of the striking implement, may be further analyzed into secondary factors. For instance, the speed of the striking implement is determined by the magnitude of the force exerted; and the magnitude of the force is dependent upon the distance of the preparatory backswing and upon the speed of muscular contraction. The distance of the preparatory backswing is further dependent upon the range of motion in the joints and upon the timing of the swing. Furthermore, the effectiveness of the force exerted by the body is completely dependent upon a strong grip and a firm wrist for transmission of the force from the body to the striking implement. (See Chapter Thirteen.)

Pushing, Pulling and Lifting. (See Figs. 20–1, *A*, *B* and *C*.)   There are relatively few sports that involve the pushing or pulling of external objects. Archery is a notable example as it consists of pulling with one hand while push-

Figure 20-7 Batting: At end of follow-through.   (Courtesy   of Northeastern University.)

ing with the other. The same is true of using a forked stick slingshot. Pushing is also used in football and both pushing and pulling in wrestling. Shot-put involves elements of both pushing and throwing. Weight lifting is the prime example of a sport activity involving lifting.

Rowing and paddling, while classified as forms of aquatic locomotion, may also be considered activities that involve external objects. Oars and paddles are both moved by pushing and pulling movements. Pole-vaulting, rope climbing and all suspension activities might also be included in the pushing and pulling category, provided one accepts activities that involve the moving of the body by means of pushing or pulling an external object, the object in such cases also serving as the means of body support. The great majority of pushing, pulling and lifting activities undoubtedly occur in everyday tasks.

The magnitude of the force used in pushing, pulling and lifting can be increased in two ways. The immediate way is by using the lower extremities and, in some instances, the body weight to supplement the force provided by the upper extremities. What might be called the long-term method is the gradual building up of muscular strength by engaging in a program of appropriate exercises.

In many, if not most, of the activities the direction and point of application of force are interrelated. They both have an important bearing on the effectiveness of the force exerted, also on the economy of effort and the avoidance of strain. Economy of effort is assured when the force is applied in line with the object's center of gravity and in the desired direction of motion: When this application of force is not feasible, the undesirable component of force should be as small as possible. For instance, if one desires to push a low trunk across the floor, it would be difficult to stoop low enough to push with the arms, or even the forearms in a horizontal position. One should stoop as low as conveniently possible, however, in order to reduce the downward component of force which would tend to increase friction. If it were necessary to move the trunk down a long corridor, it would be more efficient to tie a rope to the handle at one end and pull it. By using a long rope, the horizontal component of force would be relatively great and the vertical or lifting component relatively small. Some lifting component would be desirable, however, as it would serve to reduce friction.

When friction is a major obstacle, as when pushing a tall object like a filing cabinet across a carpeted floor, the horizontal push should be applied lower than the cabinet's center of gravity at a point found by experimentation (Fig. 20–8). When this point is found, it will be possible to push the cabinet without tipping it. When it does not seem practical to slide a heavy object along the floor, one may try "walking" it on opposite corners. This involves tipping the object until it is resting on one edge of its base and then, by a series of partial rotations, alternately pivoting it first on one corner and then on the other. This is the method often used for moving a wardrobe trunk. The arms alternate in a lever action, one hand holding the upper corner that corresponds to the lower one which is serving as the pivot, and the other hand pushing the diagonally opposite upper corner forward.

When attempting to pull an object, the same general directions apply but with this exception. As in the case of pulling the low trunk by a rope, it may be advantageous to pull in a slightly upward direction since the lifting effect would help to reduce friction. Nevertheless, unless one wishes to rotate the object, the pull should be applied in line with the object's line of gravity.

When applying a pull or a push to an object that must move on a track, such as a window or a sliding garage door, it is essential to apply the force in the direction that the track or runway permits. Force in any other direction is wasted

Figure 20–8 Using the lower extremities and body weight to supplement the upper extremities in a pushing task.

and friction is increased. Trying to open a heavy window or one that sticks can be done by standing with the right side to it, the arm close to the body, elbow fully flexed and the heel of hand placed beneath a crosspiece of the frame, and then pushing vertically upward. If more force is needed, the knees and hips should be flexed and the hands placed against a lower crosspiece. The extension of the lower extremities then supplements the force exerted by the arm. If this action is inadequate, both hands can be used by twisting the trunk to face the window. In pulling the window down one should face it, stand as close as possible and use both hands, being careful to apply the force vertically downward.

Lifting is a form of pulling; it is pulling a movable object vertically or obliquely upward (Fig. 20–9). The more nearly vertical the pull and the more in line with the object's center of gravity, the more efficient is the lift. The principle involved here is that of minimizing the resistance arm of a lever in order to reduce the amount of effort needed to lift a given weight. For instance to give an extreme example, it takes less effort to lift and hold a heavy package close to the body than it does to lift and hold it at arm's length. Likewise it takes less effort to lift a suitcase by bending the knees than by bending from the waist with the knees kept straight (Fig. 20–10). In bending, the weight arm of the lever is the horizontal distance from the center of the knee joint to the body's line of gravity; in bending from the waist the weight arm of the lever is the horizontal distance from the center of the hip joint to the body's line of gravity. There are other factors involved here too, but the relative length of the resistance arm is an important one. Also, because of the shorter resistance arm, it takes less effort to lift by bending with the trunk inclined slightly forward than with the trunk

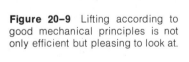

Figure 20–9 Lifting according to good mechanical principles is not only efficient but pleasing to look at.

Figure 20-10 Picking up a suitcase. *A*, Efficiently; *B*, inefficiently.

held in, or close to, a vertical position. (See the Supplementary Material on page 481.) Although it is true that more effort is required to lift the weight of the torso itself from a full stoop than from a bend at the waist, the latter method endangers the joints and muscles of the lower back (Fig. 20–11). It requires strong action of the hip and spine extensors, and the latter muscles are forced to work in a stretched condition.

If the body is used in this manner for lifting heavy objects, an additional burden is put upon the muscles of the back, one that they can ill afford to take (see Fig. 20–10, *B*). Strait, Inman and Ralston have made the interesting observation that bending from the waist to touch the floor, without flexing the knees, creates a tensile force of 450 pounds in the erector spinae muscle and a compression force of nearly 500 pounds on the fifth lumbar vertebra (see Fig. 20–11). If a 50-pound weight is held in the hands, the tensile force is increased to 750 pounds and the compressional force to 850 pounds.[5] The spinal extensors are not powerful muscles and are easily strained. It is unintelligent to expose them to the danger of strain when this can be avoided by observing the principles of good mechanics (Figs. 20–12 and 20–13).

Figure 20-11 Bending from the waist to reach the floor not only puts a strain on the back muscles but subjects the 5th lumbar vertebra to a compressional force of nearly 500 pounds.

Figure 20–12 Lifting a load with both hands at one side of the body. Note that the foot farthest from the load is placed forward. This gives better balance.

COMMON EXAMPLES OF GIVING IMPETUS TO EXTERNAL OBJECTS IN SPORTS AND IN EVERYDAY TASKS

The Forehand Drive

Although the reader is no doubt familiar with the forehand drive, a brief description is presented here in order to provide a basis for reference in the discussion that follows.

Description. (Fig. 20–14.)

Starting Position. The left side is toward the net, the feet about 18 inches apart, the knees slightly flexed and the weight on the balls of the feet. The racket is held with the eastern grip, as though shaking hands with it.

Backswing. The weight is transferred to the right foot and the trunk rotated to the right as the racket is swung back at about waist height. The elbow is kept away from the body. (It is assumed that the straight backswing is being used, rather than the circular.) There is a pause at the end of the backswing before the forward swing is begun.

Forward Swing and Follow-Through. The arm and racket swing forward and slightly upward in a continuous sweep. The racket is held with its head slightly above the level of the wrist at all times. The racket face is either flat or facing slightly upward at the moment of impact, and the grip is firm. The weight is transferred from the right to the left foot, and the body is rotated to the left so

Figure 20–13 A safe and efficient method of lifting a heavy object.

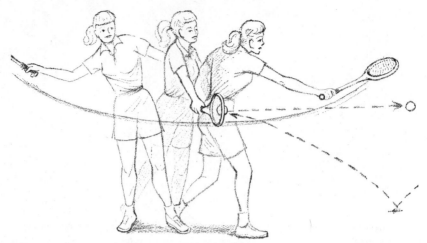

Figure 20–14 The forehand drive. (From Vannier, M., and Poindexter, H. B., Individual and Team Sports for Girls and Women, 2nd ed. Philadelphia, W. B. Saunders Company, 1968.)

that at the finish of the follow-through the right shoulder is pointing in the direction of the ball's flight. As the weight is shifted from the right to the left foot, the racket is in contact with the ball and is moving forward in a straight line, rising slightly. The racket is above shoulder height for the follow-through and may finish in a slightly closed position, that is, facing somewhat downward.

Mechanical and Anatomic Factors. The movement involved in the forehand drive is classified as "giving impetus to an object," in this instance, striking a ball with a racket. (See page 466 for the principles of giving impetus to an external object and page 470 for specific principles that apply to striking.) The action is ballistic in nature and, as such, is initiated by muscular force, continued by momentum and finally terminated by the contraction of antagonistic muscles. The chief lever participating in the movement consists of the arm and racket together with the fulcrum located at the shoulder joint, the point of force application at a point on the humerus that represents the combined forces of the muscles producing the movement (mainly the anterior deltoid and the pectoralis major), and the resistance point at the center of gravity of the arm-racket lever. At the moment of impact, however, the resistance point may be considered the point of contact of the ball with the racket face. The additional lever action due to the shift from rear to forward foot and to the rotation of the trunk from right to left should also be recognized. (Note the first two positions in Fig. 20–14.)

In considering the force that is involved in the forehand drive, it is important to distinguish between the force that is applied to the lever and the force that is applied by the lever to the ball. Whereas the force applied to the lever is muscular force, the force applied to the ball is the force of momentum. It is determined by both the mass and the velocity of the implement that makes contact with the ball. These, in turn, are related to the distance of the point of contact from the fulcrum—in other words, the length of the temporary resistance arm of the lever ("temporary" because the distance from the fulcrum to the point of contact with the ball constitutes the resistance arm of the lever only for the brief moment of impact). In addition to the angular movement of the arm-racket lever and the rotatory movement of the trunk, the linear motion produced by the forward movement of the body (due to weight shift) adds to the force which meets the ball.

The purpose of the forehand drive is to return the ball so that it will not only land within the opponent's court, but will land in such a place and manner that it will be difficult for him to return it. For the player to achieve this requires both high speed and expert placement of the ball. Hence, imparting maximum speed to the ball and, at the same time, placing it with accuracy are the two major skills that the player seeks to develop.

The force of impact is determined by the speed of the racket at the moment of contact with the ball, and maximum velocity can be obtained only when maximum distance is used for accelerating. The function of the backswing is to provide this distance. There are two types of backswing, the straight and the circular. The straight backswing has the advantage of greater ease in controlling the direction of the racket and in timing the movement, but the disadvantage of necessitating the overcoming of inertia in order to reverse the direction from the back to the forward swing. On the other hand, the circular backswing permits the arm to move in one continuous motion, thereby providing twice the distance for building up momentum. For the more skillful player who is able to control both the direction of the racket and the timing of the entire movement, it is the more efficient method.

Whichever backswing is used, two important anatomic factors are the player's range of motion at the shoulder joint and the strength of the muscles responsible for swinging the arm horizontally forward. These are the pectoralis major, anterior deltoid, subscapularis, coracobrachialis, and biceps brachii. Among the muscles that were tested by Broer and Houtz[2] and found active in the forward swing of the forehand drive were the anterior deltoid and, to a lesser degree, the middle deltoid, the trapezius (especially the middle and upper parts), the pectoralis muscles, especially the clavicular portion of the major at the end of the swing, the biceps, brachioradialis and the triceps, the latter in two short bursts, the first at the beginning of the forward swing and the second at the moment of impact. One might wonder why the trapezius, an adductor of the scapula, should be active in this forward-horizontal swing of the upper arm. It seems reasonable to assume that it stabilizes the scapula against the pull of the deltoid in order to permit the latter to exert all of its force on the humerus. A good forehand drive, however, depends upon more than just the arm movement. The shifting of the weight, the rotation of the trunk and the coordination of all these movements are a vital part of the total skill. Each movement in turn gets under way before the next one commences. If the timing is correct, the cumulative effect of these movements is to produce maximum velocity. If any of the movements is added to the preceding one either too early or too late, the potential velocity will not be realized.

Force. Other important factors that contribute to the force applied to the ball, and therefore to the speed of the ball on its return flight, are presented below.

1. The use of the arm in an almost fully extended position increases the length of the lever, thereby giving greater velocity to the racket head than would be the case if the upper arm were close to the body.

2. The concentration of mass at the level of the shoulders moving forward at the moment of impact assures maximum speed for striking.

3. A skillful player tends to use a relatively heavy racket because, other things being equal, the greater the mass of the striking implement, the greater the striking force, and hence the greater the speed of the struck ball.

4. A new ball and a well strung racket assure a good coefficient of restitution (i.e., elasticity), thereby increasing the speed of the struck ball.

5. A firm grip on the racket and the use of good wrist control assure the transmission of force from the body to the instrument, and hence to the ball.

Placement.   Placement of the ball is a matter of direction. It will be recalled that the direction taken by a struck ball is determined by four factors:

1. The direction of the striking implement at the moment of impact.

2. The relation of the striking force to the ball's center of gravity — in other words, the control of spin.

3. Firmness of grip and wrist at the moment of impact.

4. Angle of incidence.

The first of these is obvious. The beginner may be less aware of the importance of the other three factors. For successful placing of the ball, an understanding of the effect of spin and the skill of imparting the desired spin to the ball are essential. Firmness of grip is dependent upon wrist and finger strength and is closely related to the angle at which the racket face makes contact with the ball. Since the angle of rebound equals the angle of incidence (actually slightly less than this in the case of tennis balls because of their compressibility), it will be seen that firmness of grip is therefore an important factor in the direction taken by the struck ball.

Archery

Archery requires a strong pulling action, not on the object to be moved but on an elastic structure, i.e., a string stretched between the ends of a flexible bow. A notched arrow is fitted against the string and its shaft rests lightly on the index finger knuckle of the hand holding the bow. As the string is drawn back the arrow moves with it, and when it is suddenly released the string springs back, pushing the arrow forward and, in so doing, projects it into flight. Meanwhile, the hand holding the bow is engaged in what might be called a static pushing action to maintain it in correct position.

As in other impetus-giving activities, magnitude of force and direction of application are all-important. All the fine points of technique relative to stance, head and trunk alignment, and bow-arm and string-arm action are related to these factors. In archery, perhaps more than in other activities, the attempt to impart adequate force is the main cause of the difficulty in controlling direction.

The chief anatomic action of the drawing arm consists in horizontal extension of the humerus combined with adduction of the shoulder girdle. Flexion of the distal phalanges of the second, third and fourth fingers is required for exerting a steady pull on the string. In the bow-arm the triceps muscle is responsible for exerting a steady push with the elbow maintained in *incomplete* extension, as complete extension, especially hyperextension, would increase the difficulty of holding the hand and wrist properly and would almost certainly cause the rebounding string to hit against the elbow region, resulting in a painful bruise.

A common fault in archery, due to insufficient force, is creeping on the release. An analysis of this is presented below.*

Description.   The fault known as creeping may be caused by either arm. It may be due to a forward movement of the right hand prior to or at the moment of the release; or it may be due to the relaxation of the left arm at both the shoulder and the elbow joints. If the creeping is due to the right arm, the normal follow-through is omitted entirely; if it is due to the left arm, the follow-through is reduced because of the loss of tension between the bow and the string preceding the release.

Anatomic Analysis.   The arms are maintained at shoulder level by the deltoid and supraspinatus muscles and are drawn back in horizontal extension chiefly by the posterior deltoid, infraspinatus and teres minor, assisted by the latissimus dorsi. The scapulae are strongly adducted by the rhomboids and middle trapezius. Both the horizontal extension of the arm and the adduction of the scapula are stronger on the side of the drawing arm than of the bow arm. The muscles of the drawing arm are in phasic contraction, whereas those of the bow arm are in static contraction. The elbow extensors and the ulnar flexors of the wrist are in strong static contraction to resist the pressure of the bow.

When creeping is the fault of the right arm (i.e., the drawing arm), it is caused by premature relaxation or by lengthening contraction of the scapular adductors and the horizontal extensors of the shoulder joint. This results in insufficient resistance to the pull of the string. When creeping is the fault of the left, or bow, arm, it is caused by tiring and consequent relaxation of the muscles which must resist the pressure of the bow, particularly the triceps muscle.

Mechanical Analysis.   "Creeping before or during the release reduces the tension between the string and the bow, and thereby reduces the potential energy which the string has acquired. Thus the amount of force imparted to the arrow by the string is decreased. Furthermore, this fault introduces a variable factor, as the amount of creeping will tend to vary with each shot.

"A study has been made on the effect of creeping when the archer holds his anchor and aims correctly. [See Hickman.[4]] A reduced draw, or a creep, of one half inch resulted in hits 5.9 inches below the target center at forty yards, and 9.4 inches below the center at fifty yards. A creep of three quarters inch resulted in hits 8.8 inches below the center of the target at forty yards and 13.8 inches below at fifty yards."[6]

Teaching Suggestions.   The student should be instructed to keep drawing actively with the right arm and to be constantly aware of the pull between his shoulder blades until after the release. Absence of a follow-through is usually an indication of creeping. Since creeping may be caused by using too heavy a

---

*Used by permission of Mrs. Lola Vollmer Shepherd.

bow, the teacher should check to see that the bow is the right weight for the student. He should also make sure that the student has a correct anchor and that he is not holding the draw position too long. If the student has difficulty finding his aim, he should relax his draw and rest a moment before drawing again.

Working with Long-Handled Implements

Working with implements such as a hoe, rake, mop or vacuum cleaner involves a combination of pushing, pulling and, in some instances, lifting. The last is usually only for short distances, but it may occur with considerable frequency. One characteristic of working with implements such as those named is that the body must maintain a more or less fixed posture for relatively long periods of time. This causes tension and fatigue. Hence the chief problem is that of using the body in such a way that tension will be minimized and fatigue postponed for as long as possible. If the implement is used back and forth in front of the body, the tendency of the worker is to lean forward. This necessitates static contraction of the extensors of the spine in order to support the trunk against the downward pull of gravity. As implements such as the rake and hoe are lifted at the end of each stroke and carried to position for the next stroke, the force of gravity acts on the implement as well as on the worker's body. Although the implement may not weigh much in itself, its forward position means that the lever has a long weight arm, the effect of which must be balanced by the muscles. This gives an added burden to the back muscles and not infrequently causes a backache. A better method is to stand with the side turned toward the work site and the feet separated in a fairly wide stride, and work the implement from side to side. The reach can then be obtained by bending the knee of the leg on the same side as the implement and by inclining the body slightly to the same side. Those who are familiar with gymnastics will recognize this as a side lunge position. On the recovery, the knee and the trunk are both straightened. Thus there is an alternating contraction and relaxation of muscles and there is no necessity for any of the trunk muscles to remain in static contraction. Temporary relief can also be obtained by changing sides.

The use of a spade or snow shovel involves primarily the act of lifting. Because the load is taken on the end of a mechanical lever held in a more or less horizontal position, it is inevitable that the weight arm of the lever be relatively long. It can be shortened somewhat, however, by sliding one hand as far down the shaft as possible, using this hand as a fulcrum, and providing the force with the other hand by pushing down on the outer end of the handle. As a variation of this technique, when getting a particularly heavy load on a shovel, it is possible to bend one knee and brace the shaft against the thigh, thus using the thigh as a fulcrum. This is only for the initial lift, however; the hands must then be shifted to the position previously described in order to carry or throw the load.

Aside from taking and lifting the load on the spade, there is the factor of lowering the body to reach the load and of assuming the erect position for moving it. As in the case of stooping to lift a heavy object from the floor, the chief problems are economy of effort, maintenance of stability and avoidance of strain. These problems are intensified by the additional factor of taking the load on a long-handled implement instead of directly in the hand. As before, separating the feet to widen the base of support, bending at the knees instead of bending from the waist to lower the body and inclining the trunk forward only slightly will respectively increase stability, shorten the anatomic levers involved in the stooping and divide the muscular work among the knee, hip and back extensors instead of making the back muscles assume too large a share of the work. Since the lower back is easily strained by heavy shoveling, it is of great importance to protect it by observing the principles of good body mechanics.

SUPPLEMENTARY MATERIAL

In the past, some teachers of posture and body mechanics have coached their students to keep the trunk as nearly vertical as possible when performing the deep knee-bend exercise. That this is a mechanically inefficient method of stooping (and rising from a stoop) may easily be demonstrated by the use of line-of-gravity photographs. (See page 407.)

In this movement, the thigh serves as the lever, the knee joint as the fulcrum and the point at which the line of gravity intersects the thigh as the resistance point. The weight or resistance moment arm is the horizontal distance from the fulcrum to the line of gravity. Figure 20–15 is based on two line-of-gravity photographs taken by Wells of one subject, in the first, (A) attempting to keep the trunk as nearly vertical as possible, and in the other (B) inclining the trunk slightly forward from the hips in what felt to the subject like a comfortable position.

In the original photographs (3⅞ inch by 2¾ inch) the weight arm of the lever in Figure 20–15, A measured 17 mm. and in B, 14 mm. Since the 100 cm. reaction board measured 66 mm. in the photograph, the actual difference in the two weight arms was approximately 4.5 cm.

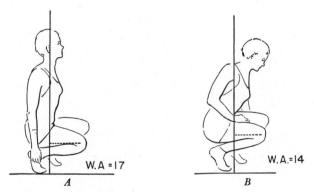

Figure 20–15 Stooping. A, Attempting to keep the trunk vertical; B, inclining the body slightly forward. (W.A. = the weight arm of the thigh lever.)

LABORATORY EXPERIENCES

1. Raise a window from the bottom:
   a. Standing at arm's length.
   b. Standing close, facing the window and using both hands.
   c. Standing close, side to the window and pushing it up with one hand with the elbow bent and the forearm in a vertical position.
      Which is the best method for a heavy window or a window that sticks? Explain in terms of components of force and the direct application of force.

2. Open (or close) a sliding door:
   a. Standing at arm's length.
   b. Standing close, facing the door.
   c. Standing close, facing in the direction that the door is to move, using a pushing motion with the forearm parallel with the door.
      Which is the best method? Explain in terms of direction of application of force and of components of force.

3. Push a heavy piece of furniture. Experiment to find the most efficient method.
   a. At what point of the object did you apply the force? Explain the underlying principles.
   b. What was the position of your arms? Explain the advantage.
   c. What was the position of your body? Explain the advantage.

4. Throw a tennis ball or baseball for distance:
   a. Standing still, facing in the direction of the throw.
   b. Standing with the left side toward the direction of the throw, with the feet apart and the weight evenly distributed, getting a full arm swing and body twist with the throw.
   c. Same as in b, except with the weight on the right foot to begin with, shifting to the left as the ball is thrown.
      Compare the three methods for distance. Explain in terms of length of backswing, speed at moment of release and total distance used in applying force to ball before releasing it.

5. If possible, observe a small child or an untrained youth and then a trained boy or girl throw a small ball as forcefully as possible at a target 20 or 30 feet away. Analyze the motions of each with reference to the pathway of the hand immediately preceding, at the moment of, and following the release. Explain the factors differentiating the good throws from the poor.

6. Observe slow motion films of throwing, striking and other forms of giving impetus. Look for the application of the principles stated in this unit or for the lack of such application.

REFERENCES

1. Broer, M. R.: Efficiency of Human Movement, 3rd Ed. Philadelphia: W. B. Saunders Company, 1973, Chaps. 16, 17, 18, 19.
2. Broer, M. R., and Houtz, S. J.: Patterns of Muscular Activity in Selected Sport Skills. Springfield, Ill.: Charles C Thomas, Publisher, 1967.
3. Dyson, G.: The Mechanics of Athletics, 5th Ed. London: University of London Press, Ltd., 1970.
4. Hickman, C. N. et al.: Archery, The Technical Side. Milwaukee: North American Press, 1947.
5. Strait, L. A., Inman, V. T., and Ralston, H. J.: Sample illustrations of physical principles selected from physiology and medicine. Am. J. Physics, 15:375–382, 1947.
6. Vollmer, L. T.: Kinesiological Analysis of Common Faults in Selected Activities. Unpublished master's study. Wellesley College, 1951.

RECOMMENDED READINGS

Bilger, A. J., and Green, E. H.: Winter's Protective Body Mechanics. N.Y.: Springer Publ. Co., 1973.
Metheny, E. R.: Body Dynamics. New York: McGraw-Hill Book Co., 1952.

Chapter Twenty-One

RECEIVING AND INTERCEPTING IMPETUS

Impetus from vertical motion is experienced by anyone who falls through space. Such motion, which occurs subsequent to a downward jump, a dive or an accidental fall, has a rapidly increasing velocity due to the effect of gravitational force. Falling bodies are known to increase their velocity at the rate of 32 feet per second, each second. When the body lands on a supporting surface, its impetus is said to have been received. Likewise, the impetus of a horizontally moving body is received when its motion is stopped as the result of contact with a resisting surface, such as a wall or other obstacle.

Examples of receiving the impetus of external objects are commonly seen in sports. Baseballs are caught or fielded with the hands; hockey balls and pucks are received with a stick; soccer balls are trapped with the feet; and blows from an opponent's fists are received by various parts of the body. Examples of receiving the impetus of external objects are also seen in industry and in daily life. Cartons and tools are tossed from one man to another; red hot rivets are tossed and caught with tongs; victims from a fire are caught in nets.

Problems and Principles

What are the particular problems involved in these diverse forms of receiving impetus, and what are the principles which enable us to solve these problems satisfactorily? Considering first the reception of the body's own impetus, the chief problems would seem to be those of *avoiding injury* and of *regaining equilibrium promptly.* It is the abrupt loss of motion resulting from collision with an unyielding surface that is likely to cause an injury. To use more technical terms, and hence more exact ones, all moving bodies have what is known as kinetic energy—the energy of motion. Like impetus and like momentum, kinetic energy is related both to the mass of the body and to its velocity. (See Chapter Twelve, especially pages 322–324.) In order to avoid injury from too abrupt a loss of kinetic energy it is necessary to find some means of losing it more gradually. This is achieved only by increasing the distance over which the kinetic energy is lost. The various devices we use for absorbing the shock of impact serve this purpose.

Another factor in injury which should not be overlooked is the *relation of the force of impact to the size of the area which bears the brunt of the impact.* A force of 100 pounds concentrated on 1 square inch of body surface, for instance, is likely to cause more serious injury than is the same amount of force spread over an area of 36 square inches. Hence the problem is to increase the size of the area which receives the force of impact. This is especially important when there is limited opportunity for increasing the distance over which the kinetic energy is lost.

The problem of regaining equilibrium is largely a problem in *controlling the placement of the limbs in preparation for landing,* for equilibrium is regained when an adequate base of support is established. This requires sufficient control to place the feet, or perhaps both the hands and the feet, in a position which will provide a favorable base. The problem of regaining equilibrium is closely related to that of avoiding injury, since establishing an adequate base is dependent upon the integrity of the bones and joints which receive the force of impact. (See Fig. 12–34.)

Various methods of falling are taught in classes in tumbling and modern dance. Perhaps one of the most effective measures for the prevention of injury in accidental falls is this kind of instruction, followed by the practice of a variety of falls until the techniques have been mastered. This helps to establish the right patterns, patterns which will be followed automatically when accidental falls occur.

The problems involved in receiving the impetus of external objects appear to be threefold: namely, *avoiding injury, maintaining equilibrium and receiving the object with accuracy and control.* As in the case of receiving the impetus of one's own body, avoidance of injury in catching or receiving external forces is achieved by increasing the distance over which the object's kinetic energy is lost. When catching a swift baseball, the experienced player will not hold his hands rigidly in front of him but will "give" with the ball. By moving his hands toward his body through a distance of 10 to 20 inches as he receives the ball, he is making it possible for the ball's kinetic energy to be lost gradually. This same principle is likewise true for the player who is reaching for a high ball with one hand. The extended arm acts as a lever, the force being applied by the impact of the ball on the palm. The moment of force is therefore the product of the force of impact and the perpendicular distance from the shoulder joint to the ball's line of flight at the instant it is caught. If this line of flight is perpendicular to the outstretched arm, the moment of force is the product of the force of impact and the length of the arm. Catching a fast ball with the arm extended can put a tremendous strain on the shoulder joint, as well as endanger the bones of the hands. To avoid injury the player should "give" by reaching somewhat forward for the ball and drawing his arm back at the moment of impact, and by rotating his body and by stepping back if the force is sufficiently great. If he lets the elbow flex slightly, he will shorten the lever of his arm and thus reduce the moment of force.

Another factor in avoiding injury when catching swift balls is the position of the hands. Beginners often reach with outstretched arms and point their fingers toward the approaching ball. This leads to many a "baseball finger." The fingers should be pointed either down or up, according to whether the ball is below or above waist level. Balls approaching at approximately waist level can be caught above the waist if the player bends his knees.

The second problem in receiving the impetus of external objects, that of *maintaining equilibrium,* is often neglected. The player should prepare for it in advance, for a swift ball or a sudden blow can easily catch him "off balance" and cause him to lose his equilibrium. There is little advantage to catching a swift ball successfully if, in the process of catching it, the player falls over backward. The stance is of great importance here. The base needs to be widened in the direction of the ball's flight, thus making it possible for the catcher to shift his weight from the forward to the rear foot at the moment of impact. This not only increases his chances of maintaining his equilibrium but also contributes to the gradual reduction of the ball's motion. Widening the stance in a direction at right angles to the flight of the approaching ball does little to increase the catcher's stability.

The third problem, that is, receiving the ball or other object with accuracy and control, is perhaps the one given the most emphasis in a game situation. As in the attempt to avoid injury, one of the key factors is the gradual loss of the object's kinetic energy. This reduces the danger of the ball's bouncing off the hands. Accurate vision, judgment and positioning of the body are of vital importance. "Keeping the eye on the ball" is essential to judging its speed and direction, and hence to adjusting the position of the body. Thus accurate judgment depends upon accurate vision, and accurate adjustment of the body depends upon both of these, as well as upon agility and smoothness of neuro-muscular response. Together, these factors make up what is known as "hand-eye and foot-eye coordination." To a certain extent this is innate, but it is also developed and improved by practice.

Intercepting a ball or puck is another illustration of receiving impetus. Ice hockey, field hockey, basketball and football are all games in which a player tries to intercept a pass. The same principles that apply to catching apply to intercepting but with this difference. Whereas in catching there is usually time to place oneself in a favorable position and to use one's arms and hands ad-vantageously, in intercepting one must take advantage of the opportunity when it comes. There is no time for preparations. The important principle to observe is to "give" with the hands or stick the moment that contact is made with the ball or puck in order to keep control of it. Otherwise it is likely to bounce off.

In receiving both the impetus of one's body and that of external objects, an important factor to be considered is the subsequent movement one expects to make. It may be the determining factor in deciding on the stance to assume. For instance, if a run is anticipated, a forward-backward stance will be more favor-able than a lateral one. Furthermore, it will be desirable to have the weight over the forward foot. If a catch is to be followed immediately by a throw, the move-ments used for "giving" may be blended into the preparatory movements of the throw. These are fine points which have much to do with the degree of one's skill in an activity.

A summary of the principles to observe in receiving impetus, both that of one's own body and that of external objects, is presented below, together with some representative applications of these principles.

PRINCIPLES OF RECEIVING IMPETUS

Principles Related to Avoiding Injury

Principle I.   The more gradually the kinetic energy of a moving body is lost, the less likely is the loss to cause injury.

Applications to receiving the impetus of one's own body

a. For landing from jumps wear rubber-soled shoes and use landing pit or gymnasium mat.

b. When landing from a fall, attempt to land on the more heavily padded parts of the body.

c. When landing from a jump, attempt to land on the balls of the feet, and immediately let the ankles, knees and hips flex, controlling the action by means of eccentric contraction of the extensor muscles of these joints (see Fig. 12–34).

d. When horizontal motion is terminated by a fall or jump, as in the case of falling off a horse, tripping and falling when running, jumping off a moving vehicle and so on, attempt to diminish the horizontal motion gradually by rolling, somersaulting, taking a few running steps or doing a series of "frog jumps."

e. When landing from a jump, if the suggestions in *c* are not adequate, attempt to transfer the downward motion of the body to horizontal motion by rolling or somersaulting.

f. When landing from a fall following horizontal motion, if the suggestions in *d* are not feasible, attempt to take some of the weight on the hands, letting the arms "give" at the wrists, elbows and shoulders. When falling forward in an extended position, attempt to arch the back as the hands take the weight, turn the face to the side, and rock down on the front of the body. This method is especially applicable to tripping and falling when running. It takes a high degree of skill, however.

Applications to receiving the impetus of external objects

a. Wear a thickly padded glove when catching fast balls. This reduces the shock of impact by effecting a slightly more gradual reduction of the ball's velocity. The greater the mass of the ball, the thicker the padding needed.

b. When catching a ball with both hands, "give" with the arms by pulling them in toward the body at the moment of impact, and, if necessary, shift the weight backward and take a backward step or two.

c. When catching a high ball with one hand, allow the arm to move horizontally backward and rotate the body in the same direction. By bending at the elbow the likelihood of straining the shoulder will be reduced. By placing oneself in a favorable position in the first place, the need for overreaching will be prevented.

d. The method of reducing kinetic energy gradually when catching a ball may be adapted in such a way that it will serve as the preparatory movement for throwing. In catching a basketball, for instance, swinging the arms down to one side and rotating the body not only assure a gradual loss of the ball's velocity but also serve to put the hands and ball in a favorable position for throwing. The transition from catching to throwing is thus made with one continuous motion.

e. The principle of "giving" when catching balls applies also to "spotting" and to receiving in apparatus work in the gymnasium. In receiving the weight of another person the "giving" is effected by a lowering and bending of the arms and bending of the knees or by taking several steps, according to whether the motion is chiefly vertical or horizontal.

Principle II. The larger the area of the body which receives the force of impact, the less will be the force per unit of surface area.

Applications to the act of landing from a fall

a. When falling forward, rocking onto the front of the body serves to increase the area which receives the force of impact, as well as to effect a gradual loss of kinetic energy.

b. When one seems to be in danger of falling on the elbow, a slight twist may make it possible to roll onto the upper arm and shoulder and thus increase the area receiving the force of impact.

c. When one seems to be in danger of falling on one knee, it may be possible to twist onto the side of the leg and rock onto the side of the thigh, perhaps using one arm to help absorb the shock.

Principles Related to Maintaining and Regaining Equilibrium

Principle III. Other things being equal, the larger the base of support and the better centered the center of gravity above this base, the greater will be the body's equilibrium.

Applications to receiving the impetus of one's own body

a. In any jump or fall the body's equilibrium is temporarily lost. In order to gain prompt control of the body upon landing, a favorable base of support can be established by adjusting the position of the feet *before landing* in such a way that they will provide a base of adequate width when the landing is made.*

b. In connection with the above, the position assumed by the feet should be such that it will facilitate the equal distribution of body weight over them.

c. External aids to making a controlled landing include a smooth landing surface and appropriate footwear. These help to prevent turned ankles and stubbed toes which might spoil an otherwise good landing.

d. When one lands with so much force that it is difficult to establish an adequate base of support with the feet alone, one or both hands should be used to establish a temporary base large enough to assure a quick recovery of equilibrium.

e. In order to provide an adequate base of support for the recovery of balance following forceful horizontal movements, the larger dimension of the base should be parallel with the direction of the horizontal movement. This will necessitate a forward-backward stance if one is facing in the direction of the horizontal motion. It will necessitate a sideward stance if one lands facing sideward with reference to the direction of motion. This adjustment of stance is particularly applicable to vaulting and tumbling activities. When one trips while running, the body automatically uses this method in its attempt to prevent a fall.

---

*The practice of teaching landing with the feet together when vaulting over gymnastic apparatus is not in keeping with this principle. This method of landing is not to be condemned for that reason, but it should be recognized as a test of skill. The skillful gymnast can regain his balance in spite of a narrow base of support. Beginners should be permitted to land with their feet separated.

Applications to receiving the impetus of external objects and forces

a. In preparation for catching a swift ball, especially a heavy one such as a medicine ball, assuming a moderately wide stance with the feet separated in the direction of the approaching ball will enable the catcher to keep his balance. It also enables him to increase the distance for stopping the ball's velocity.

b. When standing in a moving train or bus, balance is maintained more readily as the vehicle accelerates and decelerates if one takes a moderately wide stance parallel with the long axis of the vehicle, in other words, with the direction of movement.

c. If the body is subjected to pushes, pulls or blows, it can maintain and regain balance more readily if the feet are separated in a stance which is parallel with the direction of the force.

Principles Related to Accuracy and Control in Receiving External Objects

Principle IV. The more gradually the velocity of an external object is reduced, the less likely is the object to rebound when its impetus is received.

All the methods suggested for avoiding injury when receiving the impetus of external objects also apply to preventing rebound.

Principle V. "Keep the eye on the ball." Whether the object whose impetus is about to be received is a ball, a carton or a fist, keeping the eyes on it will

Figure 21–1 Lifting a suitcase down from a high shelf. *A,* Inefficiently; *B,* efficiently. In *B* she is prepared to take a step backward if necessary and to bring the suitcase down close in front of her body.

enable one to judge its speed and direction and to respond accordingly. The tendency of some novices to shut the eyes should be corrected at the outset.

Principle VI. Catching an external object with accuracy and control is dependent largely upon the position of the catcher relative to the direction of the approaching object. Putting oneself in the most favorable position possible is an essential objective for accurate catching. This applies to such everyday tasks as lifting a heavy suitcase or carton down from a high shelf, as well as to catching objects that are approaching more or less horizontally (Fig. 21–1). This is basic to the prevention of injury and to the maintenance of equilibrium.

CLASSIFICATION OF ACTIVITIES FOR RECEIVING IMPETUS IN SPORTS AND DANCE

OF BALL OR SIMILAR OBJECT
With Hand or Hands
Baseball
Basketball
Field hockey (occasionally)
Football
With Implement Held in Hand or Hands
Hockey (field and ice)
Jai-a-lai
Lacrosse
With Feet or Legs
Field hockey
Soccer
OF ANOTHER HUMAN BODY
Boxing
Spotting in gymnastics
Wrestling
OF OWN BODY, LANDING FROM A JUMP OR FALL
Baseball (sliding)
Dance (acrobatic, ballet and modern)
Football
Gymnastics (vaults and tumbling)
Ski jumping
Track and Field (high jump; long jump; hop, step and jump; pole vault)
Trampolining

LABORATORY EXPERIENCES

1. Jump from a low bench to the floor, landing on both feet.
   a. Landing with minimum "give," that is, with as little flexion at the ankles, knees and hips as possible.

    b. Landing with maximum "give," that is, allowing the ankles, knees and hips to flex to a full squat position. The head should be kept erect.

    c. Landing as in *b,* but looking down at the feet.

    Which method is preferable? Why?

2. Trip on the edge of a mat and fall forward, landing first on the knees, then on the hands.

    a. Keeping the arms rigid, elbows straight.

    b. Letting the elbows flex, arching the back, rocking down onto the abdomen and and chest, with the head turned sideways.

3. Jump down from a table or gymnasium box, using the parachute landing technique, that is, landing on the toes with the feet together, bending the knees slightly and turning sideward, rolling onto the side of the leg, thigh and hip, then onto the back of the shoulder, keeping the arms close in front of the chest and the head flexed forward.

4. Catch a medicine ball thrown straight toward your chest.

    a. With your arms rigidly outstretched.

    b. With your hands held close in front of your chest.

    c. With your arms outstretched at first, but brought in toward your chest at the moment of impact.

    Which method is preferable? Why?

5. Receive a hard drive in field hockey, (*a*) with, and (*b*) without, "giving" with the stick. Compare the results both as to control of the ball and sensation in the hands.

Chapter Twenty-Two

EXERCISES FOR SPECIAL PURPOSES

From the kinesiologic point of view the special purposes for which exercises are recommended fall into three major categories: namely, flexibility or increase of range of motion, strengthening specific muscles or muscle groups and improving postural alignment. While the objective of good body mechanics is an important one, it is not considered as a separate category because it applies to all human movement, and instruction in this area should be a basic part of instruction in all exercises, as well as in all sport skills and daily life activities.

One important category, namely, exercise for cardiovascular endurance, is mentioned here only briefly for the reason that it is related primarily to physiology rather than to kinesiology. It has been well established that a program of aerobics is more effective for this purpose than are calisthenic exercises.[2] The activities commonly recommended are jogging, swimming and rapid walking.

A word in defense of the somewhat old-fashioned term, calisthenics, may be appropriate. According to Webster's New Collegiate Dictionary, *calisthenics* means "the science of bodily exercise without apparatus, or with light hand apparatus, to promote strength and gracefulness." The Greek origins of the word are indeed apropos—kallos, meaning beauty, and sthenos, meaning strength. A balance between the two is an appropriate expression of the objectives of an exercise program.

EXERCISES FOR INCREASING THE RANGE OF MOTION

The tissues to be stretched include not only the ligaments, fasciae and other connective tissue related to the joints, but in many instances the antagonistic muscles as well, that is, the muscles that oppose the movement in which the joint is limited. For instance, the restriction in a person who is unable to bend over and touch the floor without bending the knees is even more likely due to tight tendons of the hamstring muscles than to tight knee ligaments. And the person who lacks the shoulder flexibility needed for raising the arms forward-upward and past the head is hampered at least as much, if not more, by tight pectoral muscles as by tight anterior shoulder ligaments.

Measuring the Range of Motion. In instances of unusual restriction, especially if the exercises have been prescribed by a doctor, it is desirable to measure the range of motion at the beginning and at regular intervals during the term of instruction. The reader is referred to Chapter One for the method of performing this technique. This activity is also desirable for a student who may want to increase the flexibility of a joint in order to perform better in a specific motor skill. Serious swimmers, for instance, often want to increase the plantar flexion of their ankles, and they would be interested in keeping a progress record.

Types of Exercises for Increasing the ROM. The types of exercises used for this purpose may be grouped according to the agent that provides the stretching force. These are classified as passive, active, gravity and momentum.

The *passive exercises* require the help of another person unless the part of the body is one on which the subject can use his own hands for stretching the joint. An example of the first is the passive chest lifting exercise for stretching the pectoral muscles together with other anterior structures of the shoulder joint. (This is discussed later in the chapter. See Fig. 22–13.)

A hamstring stretching exercise used in the Niels Bukh school of gymnastics in Denmark is a good example of a passive exercise in which the subject uses his own hands to do the stretching. He lies on his back with one knee bent to the chest, grasps his instep with the opposite hand and, maintaining this hold without twisting his foot, pushes against the front of his knee with the other hand, attempting to straighten his leg forcibly in a vertically upward direction.

Both of the above passive exercises also come under the heading of manual stretching exercises. An important factor in some exercises of this type is the leverage employed. In the passive chest lifting exercise, for instance, the operator can conserve his own strength and give a more forceful stretch by grasping the subject's elbows rather than his upper arms. The effort arm of the lever is then the entire length of the subject's upper arm, instead of only part of it.

Another example of this type of exercise is one that is used for stretching the hip joints in the direction of abduction and outward rotation. The subject assumes the position shown in the figure for Exercise 4–8 in Appendix G (p. 571) and rhythmically presses down on the knees.

Whatever the method of stretching used, the instructor needs to be thoroughly familiar with the structure and function of the joint in question. He must know not only the degree of limitation of motion, but also what tissues are responsible for the limitation. He should also know under what conditions the stretch reflex is likely to defeat his purposes. In the analysis of the passive chest lifting exercises it is shown how, by having the subject cooperate actively in the movement and by the operator's taking care to pull the elbows back gradually, reflex contraction of the pectorals may be avoided.

In most of the nonpassive exercises either gravity or momentum is the stretching agent, but there are a few exercises that use neither. For want of a better term these are called *active exercises*. One example of this is foot circling. The subject sits with one knee crossed over the other with the foot hanging free. The foot is circled slowly and forcefully through plantar flexion, adduction and inversion, dorsiflexion, abduction and eversion, and then plantar flexion again, and so on. Some prefer to omit the abduction and eversion as these movements are associated with weakness and poor alignment in the weight-bearing position. In each motion that is made, the subject pushes the foot to the limit of motion and, by so doing, gradually achieves a slight increase in the range.

Another exercise in the active category is bending the spine sideward as one sits astride a gymnasium bench. In an attempt to localize the bend high in the spine the subject brings one hand up under the arm pit and pushes either the fist (with wrist straight) or the heel of the hand high against the side of the ribs. The other arm is curved above the head but not touching it, and in this position the subject pushes it vigorously toward the opposite side while bending the *spine* (not the waist) to that side. This position of the two arms is called the "S" position. The movement is repeated rhythmically in a series of four. The arm swing provides a slight element of momentum but the trunk muscles should make as much effort as they can. (See Exercise 5–7 in Appendix G.)

Another, more difficult way of doing this exercise is for the subject to kneel on one knee, with the other leg extended straight to the side and the foot resting on the floor. The side bending is done to the side of the extended leg. The arms are used in the same way as in the sitting position.

There is a variety of exercises that use the *force of gravity* as the stretching agent. One of the mildest of these is another type of pectoral stretching exercise. It is called *hyperextended lying* and consists of lying on the back on a firm mat with a narrow pillow or pad (e.g., a folded towel) placed across beneath the thoracic convexity. The subject places his fingertips behind his neck, lets his elbows rest on the mat and relaxes as completely as possible. If his elbows touch the mat easily, the exercise is too elementary for him although it is always a good resting position. If they do not touch the mat easily he should not push them down but simply relax and let gravity act on them. The position is maintained for five or ten minutes, or longer if desired.

A stronger pectoral stretching exercise in which gravity does the stretching is *passive hanging* from a horizontal bar, trapeze or pair of rings. For a somewhat greater stretch, swinging on a trapeze or pair of flying rings is usually enjoyable as well as effective. A still different kind of pectoral stretching exercise using gravity calls for the individual to stand in an open doorway with the arms extended diagonally sideward and upward with the hands braced against the door frame. Keeping them in that position, the subject leans forward from the ankles. The weight of the body in that slanting position puts the pectoral muscles and the anterior joint tissues on a stretch. (See Exercise 4–1 in Appendix G.)

Gravity also provides a stretch for the ankles in two different ways. In the first, the subject stands on the bottom or next to bottom rung of the stallbars and holds the body close to the bars by grasping a bar at about shoulder or chin level. With the feet kept parallel, the heels are lowered as far as possible in a position of dorsiflexion. This stretches the Achilles tendon as well as the posterior ligaments of the ankle. (See Exercise 4–3 in Appendix G.) For increasing the range of plantar flexion (of interest to swimmers and ballet dancers), the subject assumes a kneeling position on a mat and then sits on his heels. In this position he bounces gently up and down, using his body weight to stretch the anterior ligaments of the feet and ankles.

The exercises using *momentum* for increasing flexibility include arm and leg flinging movements and bouncing movements of the trunk, the latter from both the stride standing position and from the long (straight leg) sitting position on the floor. (See the figures for Exercises 4–4 and 4–5 in Appendix G.) Momentum is the force used in many of the Danish flexibility exercises, such as double arm flinging sideward-upward and somewhat backward, done in a vigorous ballistic movement with the arms as relaxed as possible. This is repeated rhythmically, usually in a series of four. There has been some criticism in this country of the Bukh flexibility exercises because of their forcefulness and the supposed danger of stimulating the stretch reflex, thereby causing contraction of the muscles it is desired to stretch. Wells' experience with the Niels Bukh Danish exercises has not borne out this contention, however, as she found them to be effective flexibility exercises. Furthermore, as Holland has indicated, there are (or were in 1967) insufficient data for comparing the efficacy of ballistic and static methods of increasing joint mobility.[11] One Danish exercise for stretching the pectoral muscles and the anterior shoulder ligaments is described below.

The subject stands in a comfortable stride position with the arms hanging at the sides. The movement is performed in four counts as follows:

a. Swing both arms forward to the horizontal, keeping them about shoulder width apart. At the end of this movement the palms will be facing each other and the thumbs will be uppermost.

b. Keeping the body braced in a posture of good alignment, vigorously *fling* the arms sideward. The palms will now be facing forward with the thumbs still uppermost.

c. Swing the arms horizontally forward to the same position they were in at the end of *a.*

d. Let the arms swing downward and slightly past the body in a relaxed manner.

Keep the head erect and the pelvis firm throughout the exercise, and avoid hollowing (hyperextending) the lower back.

Other arm flinging exercises are (1) single arm circling forward, backward and downward, and (2) with each hand in a loose fist, arm flinging forward-upward, alternating with downward-backward, in opposition to each other and with the emphasis on the upward movement.

EXERCISES FOR STRENGTHENING MUSCLES

Three distinct concepts of exercise for this purpose have been identified. They are each based on the overload principle which has long been recognized as the essential physiologic requirement for strengthening muscles. It means that the muscles must either overcome a maximal resistance or contract at a maximal speed. It has been suggested that, although this process is commonly called "overloading," "loading to full capacity" might be a more accurate term.[10] The three types of exercise used for strengthening muscles are isotonic, isometric and isokinetic.

Isotonic exercise, as generally practiced, involves the lifting of weights, e.g., dumbbells or disk weights through a specified range of motion. The resistance to the contracting muscles is not only the actual magnitude of the weight lifted but is the product of the weight and the length of the resistance arm of the anatomic lever involved. Hence, the maximum resistance occurs only when the gravitational force is acting at right angles to the lever. The clinical value of such exercise, therefore, has been said to be "limited by its inability to impose maximum tension and work demands on a muscle throughout its range of action." Another way of expressing this is that "resistance is constant and greatest at the extremes of the range of motion."[20]

During the late forties DeLorme increased our awareness of the overload principle by his emphasis on "progressive resistance exercise" (PRE), and by designing a special exercise table for facilitating the performance of such exercises. He was in full agreement with Brouha who said that the "strength of the muscles can be developed only by exercising them against gradually increasing resistance such as pulling or pushing springs, lifting weights, or moving the body at increasing speed."[1]

Isometric exercise. Whereas "isotonic exercise involves muscular contractions against a mechanical system providing a constant load, . . . isometric exercise denotes muscular contractions against a load which is basically immovable or is simply too much to overcome."[10]

In the same decade when progressive resistance exercise was so widely publicized, the use of isometric exercise for rapid strengthening of muscles was introduced by a German physiologist.[18] The exaggerated popularity of this technique is well known to physical educators. Because of the misleading publicity it received in newspapers and popular magazines, the public tends to have a distorted interpretation of its value, as well as a total lack of appreciation of its potential harmfulness. One common misconception of the value of isometric exercise is that it is an effective method for building physical fitness, whereas its *only function is increasing muscular strength*. It does not increase cardiovascular endurance or flexibility, nor does it contribute to any objectives of physical fitness other than those related to strength.

Inasmuch as the extreme effort exerted in isometric exercises causes considerable internal pressure, especially if the breath is held, it is not wise for persons out of condition, such as the middle aged or the elderly, to engage in them. The strain might be injurious to anyone with a cardiovascular impairment or with a weakness in the abdominal wall. For persons in good health and good cardiovascular condition, isometric exercises, when given under proper supervision, have proved to be an effective and relatively quick method of increasing muscular strength. They appear to be particularly useful for strengthening muscle groups that have been weakened as the result of injuries to joints.

Isokinetic exercise stands out in contrast to both isometric and isotonic contraction, including progressive resistance exercise, in that it involves the control of speed of muscular activity instead of the control of either the distance or the amount of resistance. It is referred to as "accommodating resistance exercise."[10] The resistance varies in proportion to the changing muscular capability at every point in the range of motion, the variation being controlled so that at all times it equals the product of the muscular strength and the perpendicular distance from the application of effort to the axis of motion ($E \times EA = R \times RA$).

Awareness of the importance of the speed factor in muscle strengthening exercises is not new. What is new is the means of controlling it. This was made possible in the sixties by the development of an electromechanical device which can be preset to run at any speed between 0 and 25 revolutions per minute and which keeps the motion of a body segment at this constant, predetermined velocity[16, 17] (Fig. 22–1). It has been determined by the use of this device that in isokinetic exercise the muscle's capacity for work increases more rapidly than it does in either isotonic or isometric exercise.[17] The use of such devices has grown markedly during the seventies, the two predominant areas of use being in research and rehabilitation. Attention is called to two articles representing these two areas, namely, "Comparison of Isometric, Isotonic and Isokinetic Exercises by Electromyography" by Rosentswieg and Hinson[20] and "Isokinetic Exercise: Clinical Usage" by Coplin.[3]

MODIFICATION OF COMMON EXERCISES
TO FIT THE *PRE* CONCEPT

Although isokinetic exercise is admittedly the superior technique for building muscular strength, it requires expensive equipment and is not feasible for class use. A practical procedure is to modify familiar exercises in such a way that the resistance to be overcome can be progressively increased. This can be done by either or both of two ways: (1) by increasing the length of the resistance arm of the involved lever and (2) by increasing the magnitude of the resistance. Among some common exercises which lend themselves well to such modification are the sit-up and curl-up (actually *partial* sit-up and curl-up as the abdominal muscles are vigorously active only during the first 30 to 45 degrees of the movement, i.e., until the head and scapulae are raised from the supporting surface.

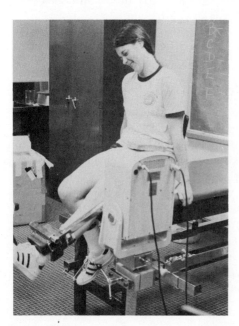

Figure 22–1 Isokinetic exercise for knee extensors.

The Partial Sit-Up and Curl-Up

Although less desirable than the curl-up, the sit-up provides a more clear-cut example of the effect of lengthening the lever arm of gravitational force (Fig. 22–2). The abdominal muscles stabilize the pelvis while the hip flexors raise the trunk.) The greater this force, the greater the muscular force needed for attaining and maintaining the position. It can also be used for demonstrating the effect of increasing the magnitude of the weight. Given the same lever arm, the greater the weight, the greater will be the muscular force required for lifting and supporting it (Fig. 22–3). If both the lever arm and the magnitude of the weight are increasing, there will be a marked increase in the demand made on the muscles.

The same principles apply to the curl-up exercise which is a more desirable form (because the abdominal muscles are acting as the chief movers), although the precise increases in muscular involvement may not be so easy to determine (Fig. 22–4). Figure 22–5 represents five stages of difficulty in the performance of the curl-up, the increased demands on the muscles being made by a combination of increased lever length and increased magnitude of weight. These variations of the curl-up are all examples of isotonic exercise. Any of them could be made isometric if adequate resistance were given manually against the chest and the position were maintained by the subject for six seconds.

The Partial Curl-Up

Starting Position.   Supine lying position with hands resting on front of thighs, elbows straight.

MOVEMENT.   The subject pulls in the chin and lifts the head and shoulders

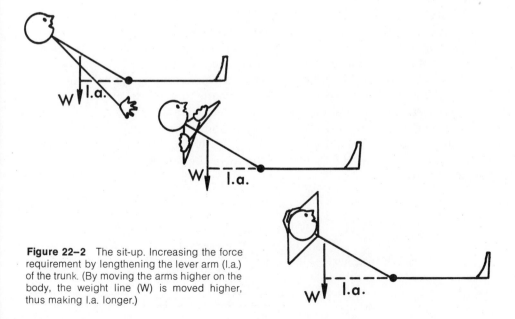

Figure 22–2 The sit-up. Increasing the force requirement by lengthening the lever arm (l.a.) of the trunk. (By moving the arms higher on the body, the weight line (W) is moved higher, thus making l.a. longer.)

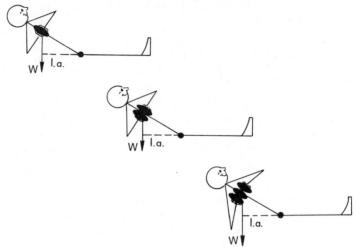

Figure 22–3 The sit-up. Increasing the force requirement by increasing the magnitude of the weight. (W, the weight line, does not change.)

until the shoulder blades are clear of the floor. He holds the position for at least six seconds. (See Figs. 22–4 and 22–5, *A*.)

Essential Joint and Muscle Analysis

Head and cervical spine

Flexion: Sternocleidomastoid, prevertebral muscles

Thoracic spine (possibly some lumbar involvement)

Flexion: Rectus abdominis; external oblique; internal oblique (upper fibers)

Hip joints

Stabilization: Iliopsoas and probably other hip flexors

Graded Exercise Series

Easier Curl-Ups

1. Hands clasped low in front of body. Assistant holds legs down with one hand or forearm and with other helps pull subject to partial curl-up position.

2. Same as basic partial curl-up but with feet supported.

3. Feet unsupported, subject's arms and hands on floor at sides of body. Subject gives slight push from elbows and hands to reach position, then with palms on thighs, holds position for one to three seconds.

4. Reverse curl-up from long sitting position. Start by flexing lumbar spine and slowly assume lying position on back with lumbar region touching floor before thoracic region. Hands may be in any of the positions suggested for the partial curl-up.

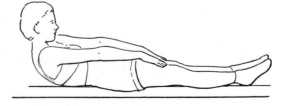

Figure 22–4 The partial curl-up.

MORE DIFFICULT PARTIAL CURL-UPS (feet unsupported)

1. Fingertips on shoulders and elbows reaching forward. (Fig. 22–5, *B*.)
2. Holding 3-pound weight against chest. (Fig. 22–5, *C*.)
3. Hands clasped on top of head. (Fig. 22–5, *D*.)
4. Holding 5-pound weight against chest.
5. Holding 7-pound weight against chest.
6. Holding 5-pound weight on top of head. (Fig. 22–5, *E*.)
7. Holding 10-pound weight against chest.
8. Holding 7-pound weight on top of head.
9. Holding 10-pound weight on top of head.

Discussion.   The most common fault in the curl-up (also found in the sit-up) is coming up or at least starting too quickly, using momentum rather than gradual muscular contraction. This nullifies the value of the exercise. Beginners are sometimes tempted to push off with the elbows, but this can be prevented if care is taken to see that the arms are in the correct position.

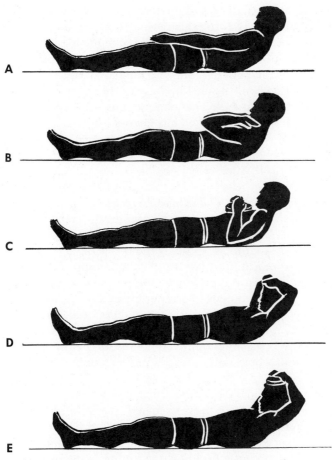

Figure 22–5 Partial curl-up series for abdominal strength.

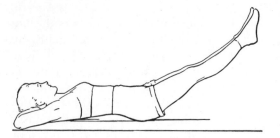

Figure 22–6   Slow leg lowering. Note the increased curve of the lumbar spine.

A fault which is common in the sit-up but less so in the curl-up is arching the lower back (hyperextending the lumbar spine) at the beginning of the movement. When this hyperextension occurs, as it frequently does not only in sit-ups, but also in slow leg raising and lowering, it indicates that the abdominal muscles do not have enough strength to prevent the hip flexors from increasing the pelvic tilt. This weakness reveals the need for a milder abdominal exercise. As Kendall has warned, this kind of exercise may cause harmful strain and may even cause a hernia.[13] It is for this reason that double leg raising and slow leg lowering from the supine position are not recommended as abdominal strengthening exercises. Only those who already have strong abdominal muscles are able to do them without hyperextending the lumbar spine (Fig. 22–6).

In the initial stage of the curl-up (also of the sit-up if the head is lifted first) the rectus abdominis and external oblique muscles are acting as movers to flex the spine; the iliopsoas and other hip flexors act as stabilizers to fix the pelvis against the pull of the abdominal muscles. In the last half or two thirds of a full sit-up or curl-up the hip flexors are acting as movers to flex the trunk as a whole on the thighs. If no further spinal flexion occurs, the abdominal muscles serve as stabilizers to fix the pelvis against the pull of the hip flexors.

Principles for Selecting Abdominal Exercises

1. The criterion for an abdominal exercise performed in the supine position is the performer's ability to prevent the tilting of the pelvis and the hyperextension of the lumbar spine. If the pelvic tilt and lumbar curve increase, it would seem to indicate the failure of the abdominal muscles to stabilize the pelvis and spine against the pull of the iliopsoas. Since the task is too great for these muscles, there is danger of straining them.

2. An objective in building a strong abdominal wall is to strengthen all four of the abdominal muscles: rectus abdominis, external oblique, internal oblique and transversus abdominis. To do this successfully requires a knowledge of the exercises in which these muscles participate and of the relative intensity of their action.

3. It seems reasonable to assume that a protruding abdomen indicates that the abdominal muscles have been stretched. It would seem to be a function of abdominal exercises, therefore, to shorten as well as to strengthen these muscles. This suggests that exercises like back bends that put the abdominal wall in a stretched position are not a desirable method for strengthening them.

Figure 22–7   The push-up. A, The starting and ending position; B, the dip.

The Push-Up

The *push-up* is an exercise for strengthening the elbow extensors and the anterior shoulder and chest muscles. The basic exercise is described and analyzed first, and then a graded series of variations of this activity is suggested.

Starting Position.   The front-leaning-rest position, i.e., semiprone with the body extended, the arms extended vertically toward the floor and the weight supported by the hands and toes. The body is in a straight line from head to heels; there is no sag at the spine nor hump at the hips. The hands are approximately shoulder width apart with the palms flat on the floor.

Movement.   With the body kept straight, the elbows are allowed to bend, and the body is lowered until the chest almost touches the floor. By pushing the hands vigorously against the floor, the body is raised until it regains the starting position. This movement is repeated slowly or rapidly, either a given number of times or as many times as the subject is able to repeat it *in correct form.*

Essential Joint and Muscle Analysis

THE DIP. (Fig. 22–7, *B*.)   Flexion at the elbow joint accompanied by a lowering of the body until it almost touches the floor.

Shoulder joints
  Horizontal extension: Pectoralis major, anterior deltoid, coracobrachialis
    and subscapularis in eccentric contraction
Shoulder girdle
  Adduction: Pectoralis minor and serratus anterior in eccentric contraction
Elbows
  Flexion: Triceps and anconeus in eccentric contraction
Wrists
  Reduction of hyperextension: Extensor carpi radialis longus and brevis
    and extensor carpi ulnaris in eccentric contraction

Maintenance of straight alignment from head to heels against the pull of gravity
    Head and neck: Cervical extensors in static contraction
    Lumbar spine: Rectus abdominis and external and internal obliques in static
       contraction
    Hips: Flexors in static contraction

    THE PUSH-UP.   Extension at the elbow joints until the body is again in the
position shown in Figure 22–7, *A.*
    Shoulder joints
      Horizontal flexion: Pectoralis major, anterior deltoid, coracobrachialis
        and subscapularis
    Shoulder girdle
     Abduction: Serratus anterior and pectoralis minor
    Elbows
      Extension: Triceps and anconeus
    Wrists
      Hyperextension: Extensor carpi radialis longus and brevis and extensor
        carpi ulnaris
Maintenance of straight alignment from head to heels: Same as above

    Graded Exercise Series.   In the push-up, the familiar form of the exercise
represents the most difficult level in the series. Starting at what might be considered the lowest level and working up, the following push-up exercises are
suggested.

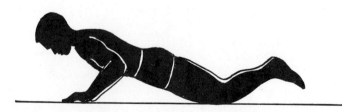

Figure 22–8   Push-up series for arm strength: Exercise 2, half dip and push-up from knees.

Figure 22–9   Push-up series for arm strength: Exercise 4, push-up from stairs with hands on fourth step.

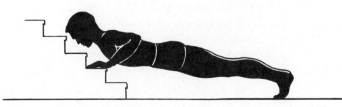

Figure 22–10   Push-up series for arm strength: Exercise 5, push-up from stairs with hands on second step.

1. Standing on hands and knees with hip and knee joints bent at right angles, dip and push up.

2. In semiprone position with hips straight and weight supported by hands and knees, perform a half dip and push-up (Fig. 22–8).

3. Same position as for 2, but complete the full dip and push-up.

4. Front-leaning-rest position, facing stairs with feet on floor and hands on fourth or fifth step, body in a straight line from head to heels, dip and push up (Fig. 22–9).

5. Continue, placing hands on lower step until able to perform regulation push-up from floor (Fig. 22–10).

Discussion.   Before a student is ready to try a full push-up in any of the elementary or intermediate positions, he may practice a reverse push-up (a slow full or half dip) or a half push-up, i.e., a push-up from a half dip position. An easy return from a reverse push-up may be achieved by first bringing one or both feet forward and perhaps kneeling on one knee. Whatever type of push-up is practiced, the student should repeat it several times in good form before being permitted to try a more advanced type.

There are two common faults that must be guarded against in the push-up. These are (1) a sagging back and (2) humped-up hips. The latter fault is usually caused by an "overcorrection" of the first one, namely maintaining a flexed position at the hips in order to prevent the back from sagging. The correction of both of these faults lies in strengthening the abdominal muscles and training them to prevent hyperextension of the lumbar spine when the body is in the extended position. Until the subject is kinesthetically aware of his position, the use of a mirror may be helpful.

The progressive lowering of the position of the hands in the staircase series of push-ups increases the strength requirement because the upper extremities are called upon to bear an increasingly larger proportion of the body weight. This can be demonstrated by placing a bathroom scale under each hand. The push-up from a half dip is easier than the push-up from a full dip in any given position because the weight of the body is lifted through a shorter distance and because the joint positions permit the muscles of the elbows and shoulders to work to better advantage. The reverse dip is easier to execute than the push-up from any given level because the muscles are performing negative rather than positive work, that is, they are engaging in eccentric (lengthening) rather than concentric (shortening) contraction.

The Pull-Up

The *pull-up* is an exercise for strengthening the elbow flexors, shoulder joint extensors, scapular adductors and downward rotators.

Starting Position.   Straight arm hanging from a horizontal bar with the hands approximately shoulder width apart, the palms facing the body and the thumb in opposition to the fingers (Fig. 22–11, *C*).

Figure 22–11 Pull-up series for arm strength. Exercise 1, reverse pull-up: *A*, bent arm hanging; *B*, half way position; *C*, straight arm hanging. (For pull-up, start with *C* and end with *A*.)

Movement.   From a "dead hang" and with a minimum of movement of the trunk and lower extremities, the subject pulls himself steadily upward until his chin is level with the bar.

Joint and Muscle Analysis

Shoulder joints

Extension: Pectoralis major (sternal portion), latissimus dorsi, teres major, posterior deltoid

Shoulder girdle

Downward rotation combined with some adduction toward end: Rhomboids, trapezius III and IV, probably pectoralis minor

Elbows

Flexion: Biceps, brachialis, brachioradialis

Radioulnar

Maintained in supination by fixed position of hands.

Wrists

Possibly slight flexion. Muscles probably stabilize wrist for action of finger and thumb muscles.

Fingers and thumb

Flexion: Static contraction of all flexors

Thumb adduction of carpometacarpal joint: Static contraction of adductor pollicis

Return movement: Reverse joint action of shoulder joints and girdle and elbows. Same muscles but contracting eccentrically instead of concentrically. Finger and thumb muscles remain in static contraction.

Graded Exercise Series

EASIER PULL-UPS

1. Reverse pull-up, that is, slow let-down from bent arm hanging position which can be reached by stepping onto a stool or by jumping (Fig. 22–11, *A*).

2. Modified pull-up from low boom or bar with body in semi-supine hanging position, arms straight, heels on floor, and body straight from heels to head.

3. Standing on bench high enough to permit subject to grasp bar (or rings) with elbows partially flexed, pull up the rest of the way.

MORE DIFFICULT PULL-UPS

Basic pull-up with weights attached to waist or ankles.

Discussion. Pull-ups are frequently taught with the forearms in pronated position, that is, with the palms facing away from the face. From the kinesiologist's point of view there is no justification for this as it is the least favorable position for both the biceps and the sternal portion of the pectoralis major muscles. The only justification appears to be the military one of developing the ability to climb over high walls. (See summaries of research in this area, pages 132ff.)

EXERCISES FOR IMPROVING THE POSTURE

The problem of posture improvement and correction is such an individual one that exercises for this purpose should be selected on an individual basis if at all possible. This presupposes a postural examination or inspection for analyzing the student's present posture and identifying his particular needs.

The following section represents one small sample from the field of posture improvement. Its purpose is to demonstrate how kinesiology may be applied to the corrective uses of exercises. No attempt is made to demonstrate its application to all the problems associated with the corrective aspects of postural education. These are far too extensive and complex to be covered in a general kinesiology text. The appropriate sources for such information are textbooks in corrective and adapted physical education. Furthermore, in addition to kinesiologic principles of posture correction, there are equally important physiologic, psychologic and pedagogic principles not ordinarily discussed in kinesiology texts.

In order to illustrate the application of kinesiology to posture problems and their treatment, one common fault and two exercises for its correction have been selected for analysis. The postural fault is the condition commonly referred to as "round shoulders," a misnomer, as the entire body is involved. The *most directly* involved aspects are protracted shoulders, forward head and rounded back. The exercises selected are specific for these conditions.

Anatomic Analysis of "Round Shoulders" (Fig. 22–12)

HEAD AND NECK. Hyperextended. The head is tipped back with the chin lifted.

THORACIC SPINE. Convexity increased. The increased thoracic curve causes a forward head. Owing to the forward head, the sternocleidomastoid and scaleni muscles, which have their upper attachments on the head and neck, no longer exert their normal lifting tension on the sternum and upper ribs. The thoracic portions of the erector spinae and other extensors are elongated because of the increased convexity.

SHOULDER GIRDLE. Abducted and tilted laterally. The rhomboids and middle trapezius are elongated, and the pectoralis minor and serratus anterior are shortened. The pectoralis minor fails to exert its usual lifting tension on the third, fourth and fifth ribs. The pectoral fascia is likely to be tight.

SHOULDER JOINTS.   Inward rotation. The abduction of the scapulae causes the arms to hang farther forward than usual and to turn slightly inward so that the palms face to the rear. Since the pectoralis major attaches to the upper part of the arm, it no longer exerts its usual lifting tension on the ribs.

CHEST. Depressed. The failure of the sternocleidomastoid, scaleni and pectoral muscles to exert their usual lifting effect on the sternum and ribs results in a lowered position of the chest. This in turn lowers the diaphragm, making it impossible for it to travel through as large an excursion as usual during respiration.

This picture does not end here because compensatory adjustments take place through the entire body. The joints mentioned, however, are the ones most directly concerned in the posture defect of round shoulders. Two typical corrective exercises have been selected for analysis, one which has for its purpose the stretching of the shortened muscles and fascia and the other, the strengthening and shortening of the muscles which have become unduly stretched.

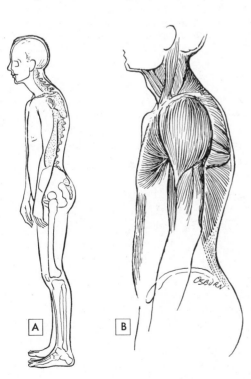

Figure 22–12 Anatomic views of forward head and round shoulders. A, Skeletal alignment; B, chief muscles affected.

Passive Chest Lifting

Description.   The subject sits on a low stool with the hands behind the neck (not clasped) and the elbows well back. The operator stands behind the subject with the toes of one foot on the edge of the stool and the knee against the subject's spine between the shoulder blades. A small pillow may be used to pad the knee, if desired. The operator grasps the subject's elbows, lifts them slightly and pulls them back with a strong steady pull. He holds the pull for several seconds, then gradually releases the tension. This is repeated from 6 to 15 times. It is essential that the pull be applied with gradually increasing intensity and never with a jerk. Care must be taken to see that the subject avoids excessive hollowing of the back. This he can do by contracting the abdominal muscles. (See Fig. 22–13.)

Purpose.   To stretch the pectoral muscles and fasciae.

Anatomic Analysis.   The upward and backward pull of the arms puts the pectoralis major and minor muscles and the pectoral fascia on a stretch. The tension on the muscles produces a pull on their attachments to the ribs and sternum and results in a lifting of the chest, expansion of the thorax and hyperextension of the thoracic spine. If the pull is applied with a quick jerk, a strong stretch reflex is likely to occur. This is an involuntary protective contraction of the pectoral muscles. It defeats the purpose of the exercise since the muscles cannot be stretched when they are contracted. When the pull is applied slowly and gradually, the reflex action is either avoided or overcome. It is also less likely to occur if the subject is told to pinch the shoulder blades together just as the operator is pulling the elbows back. According to the principle of reciprocal innervation, the scapular abductors relax when their antagonists, the adductors, are contracting. Experience has shown that an appreciably wider

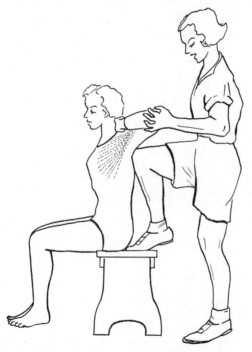

Figure 22–13 Passive chest lifting for stretching the pectoral muscles. (The dotted lines indicate the position of the pectoralis major. Pectoralis minor is beneath it.)

range of motion is possible when the movement is performed slowly and when the subject contracts the scapular adductors (see p. 69).

Mechanical Analysis.   The subject is in a stable position because of the relatively wide base of support and low position of the center of gravity.

The operator uses the subject's arms as levers. They serve as second class levers, the fulcrum being at the shoulder joint, the effort point at the elbow and the resistance point at the upper arm where the pectoralis major inserts. If the operator holds the arms at a point nearer the body, he loses leverage by shortening the length of the effort arm and either has to use more force to compensate or else be content to give a less forceful stretch.

The stretching of the pectoralis minor is caused by the transmission of the force applied to the arm through the shoulder joint (due to the ligamentous attachments) to the coracoid process of the scapula, to which the pectoralis minor is attached.

It is important to note that if the trunk were free to move, the operator's pull on the elbows would simply result in a backward inclination of the trunk. However, because of the resistance afforded by the pressure of his knee against the subject's back, movement at the hip joints is prevented. Likewise, if the spine were completely free to move, the backward pull on the arms would produce hyperextension of the entire spine. The subject himself must prevent this by contracting his abdominal muscles.

Common Faults

Of Operator

1. Pulling so suddenly that a strong reflex action of the pectoral muscles results

2. Pulling so hard that the subject hyperextends the lumbar spine rather than endure the discomfort

3. Pulling so gently that no stretch results

4. Placing the knee too low. This encourages hyperextension of the lumbar spine and detracts from the pull on the pectorals.

Of Subject

1. Failure to contract the abdominal muscles

2. Failure to hold the head in good position

3. Failure to contract the rhomboids and middle trapezius

4. Failure to relax the pectoral muscles

Front-Lying Head Raising with Palms Turning Outward

Description.   The subject lies face downward with the arms at the sides, palms down (Fig. 22–14). He raises the head from 3 to 6 inches, looking at the floor directly beneath the nose. He should attempt to stretch the top of the head forward, making the body feel as long as possible. As he raises his head, he lifts the hands from the floor, turning the thumbs up and the palms outward. At the same time that he is raising and turning his arms he should pull his shoulder blades together vigorously. After holding the position for at least five seconds he returns to the starting position and relaxes. The exercise should be repeated ten to twenty times.

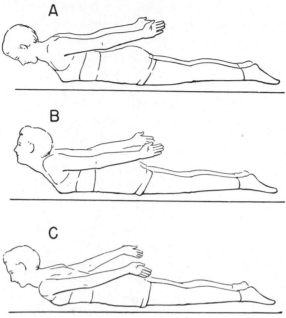

Figure 22-14 Front lying, head raising with palms turning outward. *A,* Correct form; *B,* incorrect; the head and neck are hyperextended; *C,* incorrect; the arms are rotating inward instead of outward.

A more effective but more difficult form of this exercise is to precede the head and arm movement with contraction of the abdominal and gluteal muscles, and to hold this contraction throughout the movement of the head and arms.

Purpose. To correct a forward head and round shoulders by strengthening the extensors of the thoracic spine, the adductors of the scapulae and the outward rotators of the arms.

Joint and Muscle Analysis

HEAD AND NECK. Holding in extension (but not hyperextension) against the pull of gravity

Splenius cervicis and capitis, upper portions of erector spinae, semispinalis, and so on (static contraction)

THORACIC AND LUMBAR SPINE. Extension and slight hyperextension; maintaining position against the pull of gravity

Erector spinae, semispinalis, multifidus, rotatores (concentric, followed by static contraction)

SHOULDER JOINTS. Outward rotation and hyperextension

Infraspinatus, teres minor, posterior deltoid, latissimus dorsi, teres major

SHOULDER GIRDLE. Adduction and reduction of lateral tilt

Rhomboids, middle trapezius

ELBOWS AND FOREARMS. Extension and supination

Triceps, anconeus, supinator

STABILIZATION OF PELVIS

Gluteus maximus, hamstrings

Common Faults and Their Correction

1. Hyperextending the head and neck. This can be prevented by insisting that the subject look at a spot beneath his nose.

2. Lifting the body too high, thereby hyperextending the lumbar spine. This can be prevented by telling the subject to lift his head not more than 3 inches off the floor. (Although he will probably lift his head more than this, it is not likely that he will exceed the 6-inch limit.)

3. Rotating the arms inward instead of outward. This is more likely to occur if the subject is not told to start with the palms down. If he continues to have trouble after the movement of the hands has been carefully explained, he should try turning the arms both ways several times and learn to recognize the kinesthetic "feel" of the movements of the shoulder joints and shoulder girdle. Once he can distinguish these movements, he will know when he has turned his arms the wrong way. He should aim at "pinching the shoulder blades together."

Evaluation.   This is one of the best exercises for correcting a forward head and round shoulders when it is done correctly. Unless the subject can be carefully supervised, however, it might be wise not to give it to anyone who has a tendency toward lordosis (hollow back). In such cases the exercise should be done with abdominal and gluteal contraction and the amount of lifting should be carefully regulated. Placing a small pillow beneath the abdomen is helpful.

The exercise is more strenuous than those involving the same movements in a sitting or standing position because in the horizontal position the movements are performed against the resistance of gravitational force.

The total program is likely to include approximately 8 to 15 exercises, and these are changed periodically as improvement in range of motion and strength are apparent. Although the problems in this area appear to be mostly anatomic — limited range of motion and muscular inadequacy being predominant — there are mechanical aspects that need to be considered.

THE PRACTICAL KINESIOLOGIST

If the discussions and applications of exercises which have been presented in this chapter have helped to give the student a sound basis for developing an effective exercise program, the chapter will have served its purpose. The physical educator who has a good kinesiologic background should be able to analyze and evaluate exercises, not only those with which he is already familiar but also those that are brought to his attention by his students or are seen on television or in popular magazines. He should be able to tell whether an exercise is suitable for the inexperienced performer, a performer of moderate experience and ability or an advanced performer. He should know whether it has undesirable features, such as the danger of straining ligaments, encouraging posture faults or causing excessive tension. He should also recognize the mechanical problems that may be involved, such as problems of balance, leverage or momentum. In brief, his evaluation of an exercise should be based on the answers to the following questions:

1. What is the purpose of the exercise?
2. How effectively does it accomplish its purpose?
3. Does it violate any principles of good body mechanics?

4. What are the chief joint and muscular actions involved in it?

5. What are its intensity and difficulty? (Is it suitable for a beginner, a moderately experienced performer or an advanced performer?)

6. Are there any elements of danger, injury or strain against which precautions should be taken?

7. Is it likely to call forth any undesirable or harmful responses against which the performer should be on his guard?

8. If the exercise is a difficult one, what preliminary exercise would serve to prepare the performer for it?

When the physical educator has acquired skill in answering such questions as these and in analyzing the individual needs of his students, he will have become what Huelster so aptly calls a "practical kinesiologist."[12] To assist in the achievement of this goal the student should find it profitable to analyze as many exercises as possible. Appendices D and G should prove helpful in this connection.

SUPPLEMENTARY MATERIAL

Comparisons of Effectiveness of Isometric and Isotonic Exercises

Leach, Stryker and Zohn compared the two methods in a program of rehabilitation for men who were hospitalized for knee injuries requiring surgery.[15] They divided the 169 patients into two groups which were comparable with respect to age and type of injury. One group was given DeLorme type isotonic exercises, and the other was given isometric exercises. It took an average of 14.9 treatments for the men in the isotonic exercise group to be returned to naval duty as compared to an average of 11.7 treatments for the isometric exercise group—a difference of 3.2 treatments. The authors pointed out that this difference was "statistically and clinically significant." Incidentally, neither method caused hypertrophy of the muscles exercised.

Ward and Fisk investigated the difference in response of the quadriceps femoris and the biceps brachii to isometric and isotonic exercises.[21] The isotonic exercises were based on the overload principle with a 1.5-pound increment at each session. The isometric exercises were held for six seconds each, this time corresponding to the time it took to lift and lower the weight through the range of motion in the isotonic exercises. Thus the muscles were contracting for approximately the same length of time for the two methods of exercise. As in the study by Leach et al, they found that the isometric exercises resulted in a more rapid increase of strength than the isotonic. They also noted that there was no significant muscle hypertrophy.

An Electromyographic Study of the Push-Up for Women

In 1969 Hinson completed a study the purpose of which was to investigate electromyographically the muscular activity in the performance of four types of the push-up exercise and to determine the existence of patterns of muscular contraction among them.[9] The types of push-up used were (1) the full push-up, (2) the full push-up from a 13-inch bench, (3) the knee push-up and (4) the full let-down (reverse full push-up). The subjects were divided into two groups, Group I consisting of ten women who could perform ten or more full push-ups, and Group II of ten women who were able to perform no more than five knee push-ups. The muscles that were found to be the most involved in the push-up exercises were the anterior deltoid, followed by the triceps, trapezius and clavicular portion of the pectoralis major. A similar muscular pattern was found in both groups, but Group II consistently showed greater muscular activity during the knee push-ups than the subjects in Group I. The muscular activity was essentially the same for the bench and full push-ups, and the let-down muscle action was similar but to a lesser extent than for the knee push-up.

Hinson concluded that the bench push-up did not justify the use of special equipment as the results were so similar to those of the full push-up from the floor. She also concluded that the let-down (reverse push-up) appeared to be a valid exercise for subjects whose upper arm and shoulder strength was inadequate for performing knee push-ups. A general observation was that the subjects in Group II showed greater muscular involvement than the subjects in Group I for the same task. This she interpreted as indicating a lack of efficiency or coordination on the part of those with lesser ability.

Findings from EMG Studies of Abdominal Exercises

Interesting electromyographic studies of various forms of abdominal sit-up and curl-up exercises were made during the 1955–1965 decade. Although they cannot be compared item for item because of a lack of uniformity in the methods of performing the exercise and because of different points of emphasis, the following conclusions, culled from their findings, appear to be justified.

1. Sit-ups and curl-ups elicit stronger abdominal than iliopsoas action:

a. When the feet are not held down;

b. When the legs are either straight or flexed at the knees to an angle not smaller than 110 degrees;

c. During the first 30 to 45 degrees of motion, especially if the legs are straight.

2. The lower rectus abdominis is more active than the upper when the feet are supported, and the upper rectus more active when the feet are not supported.

3. The greatest abdominal action occurs during the first 45 degrees of trunk movement. (LaBan et al found no iliopsoas action during the first 30 degrees of trunk movement when the legs were straight.[14] Flint found the iliopsoas to be unaffected by extension or flexion of the knees.[6])

4. The sit-up requires more total muscular effort than the curl-up (because the curl-up shortens the lever arm),[4] but the initial stage of the curl-up, until the shoulder blades are off the floor, is more effective for strengthening the abdominal muscles (especially if the position is held for several seconds) than the complete sit-up or curl-up movement. When the position is held the exercise is isometric in nature.

Recommended Abdominal Exercises.

The following exercises have been suggested by various investigators as effective ones for strengthening the abdominal muscles.[4, 6, 7, 8, 19]

1. Partial curl position (supine lying or hook lying with knees at 110 degree angle) held for two to three seconds.

Figure 22–15   Lying on side with legs supported, trunk lifting sideward; a strong exercise for abdominal and spinal muscles. (From Wells, K. F.: Posture Exercise Handbook—A Progressive Sequence Approach. Copyright © 1963, The Ronald Press Company, New York.)

2. Curl-up with a twist (touching hand to outer surface of opposite knee).

3. Basket hang (double knee bending to chest from hanging position).

4. Side lying with legs supported, trunk lifting sideward (Fig. 22–15).

5. Kneeling with hips and spine extended, i.e., with trunk and thighs vertical, leaning backward to a 60 to 45 degree angle.

6. The "V" sit-up (from hook lying, trunk raising and double leg extending upward at the same time).

LABORATORY EXPERIENCES

1. Turn to Appendix G. State the purpose and give the essential joint and muscle analysis for as many of the exercises as possible.

2. Find a subject who has an increased lumbar curve and increased pelvic tilt. Analyze his posture, select two or three appropriate exercises, and suggest a sport which might be beneficial, also one which might be harmful to his posture.

3. Do the same for a subject who has weak lower back muscles.

4. Do the same for a subject who has severely pronated feet.

5. Select from three to ten exercises seen in popular magazines, in newspapers or on television. Using the examples in this chapter as guides, analyze and evaluate these exercises and answer the eight questions on pages 511 and 512.

6. Observe someone doing a conditioning exercise. Analyze the exercise, using the examples in this chapter as guides.

7. Originate an exercise for stretching the hamstring muscles which will not tend to accentuate a round upper back.

8. In the straight leg lowering exercise from supine lying, identify the resistance moment arm of the lever; also the rotatory component of the resistance. (See page 500.)

9. Devise an exercise for a swimmer who wants to increase his ankle flexibility, especially his plantar flexion. (Note: Merely plantar flexing the feet volitionally is not forceful enough to increase the range of motion.)

10. Devise an exercise for a girl who is unable to lift herself onto the deck at the deep end of a pool.

REFERENCES

1. Brouha, L., and Radford, E. P., Jr.: The cardiovascular system in muscular activity. *In* Johnson, W. R., and Buskirk, E.: Science and Medicine of Exercise and Sports, 2nd Ed. New York: Harper & Row, Pubs., Inc., 1973.
2. Cooper, K. H.: Aerobics. New York: Bantom Books, Inc., 1972.
3. Coplin, T. H.: Isokinetic exercise: Clinical usage. J. Nat. Athletic Trainers Assn., (Fall), 1971.
4. Crowe, P., O'Connell, A. L., and Gardner, E. B.: An Electromyographic Study of the Abdominal Muscles and Certain Hip Flexors during Selected Sit-ups. Part I. Report presented at National Convention of the American Association for Health, Physical Education and Recreation, 1963.
5. DeLorme, T. L., and Watkins, A. L.: Progressive Resistance Exercise. New York: Appleton-Century-Crofts, Inc., 1951.
6. Flint, M. M.: An electromyographic comparison of the function of the iliacus and the rectus abdominis muscles. J. Am. Phys. Ther. Assn., *45*:248–253, 1965.
7. _____. Abdominal muscle involvement during the performance of various forms of sit-up exercises. Am. J. Phys. Med., *44*:224–234, 1965.
8. Flint, M. M., and Gudgell, J.: Electromyographic study of abdominal muscular activity during exercise. Res. Quart. Am. Assn. Health, Phys. Ed. & Recrn., *36*:29–37, 1965.
9. Hinson, M. M.: An electromyographic study of the push-up for women. Res. Quart. Am. Assn. Health, Phys. Ed. & Recrn., *40*:305–311, 1969.
10. Hislop, H. J., and Perrine, J. J.: The isokinetic concept of exercise. J. Am. Phys. Ther. Assn., *47*:114–117, 1967.
11. Holland, G. J.: The physiology of flexibility; a review of the literature. *In* Kinesiology Review 1968. Washington, D.C.: Am. Assn. Health, Phys. Ed. & Recrn., 1968, pp. 49–62.
12. Huelster, L. J.: Learning to analyze performance. J. Health & Phys. Ed., *10*:84, 120–121, 1939.
13. Kendall, F. P.: A criticism of current tests and exercises for physical fitness. J. Am. Phys. Ther. Assn., *45*:187–197, 1965.
14. LaBan, M. M., Raptou, A. D., and Johnson, E. W.: Electromyographic study of function of iliopsoas muscle. Arch. Phys. Med. & Rehab., *46*:676–679, 1965.
15. Leach, R. E., Stryker, W. S., and Zohn, D. A.: A comparative study of isometric and isotonic quadriceps exercise programs. J. Bone & Joint Surg., *47A*:1421–1426, 1965.
16. Moffroid, M. T., and Whipple, R. H.: Specificity of speed exercise. J. Am. Phys. Ther. Assn. *50*: 1699–1704, 1970.
17. Moffroid, M., Whipple, R., Hofkosh, J., Lowman, E., and Thistle, H.: A study of isokinetic exercise. J. Am. Phys. Ther. Assn., *49*:735–746, 1969.
18. Muller, E. A., and Hettinger, T. W.: Die Bedeutung des Trainingerlaufes für die Trainingsfestigkeit von Muskeln. Arbeitsphysiol., *15*:452, 1954.
19. Partridge, M. J., and Walters, C. E.: Participation of the abdominal muscles in various movements of the trunk in man; an electromyographic study. Phys. Ther. Rev., *39*:791–800, 1959.
20. Rosentswieg, J., and Hinson, M. M.: Comparison of isometric, isotonic and isokinetic exercises by electromyography. Arch. Phys. Med. & Rehab., *53*:249–260, 1972.
21. Ward, J., and Fisk, G. H.: The difference in response of the quadriceps and the biceps brachii muscles to isometric and isotonic exercise. Arch. Phys. Med. & Rehab., *45*:614–620, 1964.

Chapter Twenty-Three

IMPLICATIONS FOR TEACHING

CHARACTERISTICS OF SKILLFUL PERFORMANCE

Now that we have this fund of knowledge about human motion, what are we going to do with it? What use are we going to make of it in our teaching careers? There can be no one single answer. Much depends upon the abilities, experience and attitudes of the students we are teaching; much also depends upon the nature of the material to be taught and upon us, ourselves—our experience, our convictions, our philosophy, even our own personalities. The purpose of this concluding chapter is to direct the reader's attention to ways in which the study of kinesiology can contribute meaningfully to effective teaching of physical education.

Looking back on the course that we are now completing, we realize that we have learned something about the mechanism of human movement. We see the body as a living machine functioning in accordance with the universal laws of motion and mechanical principles. We see it as an intricate structure of bones, joints, ligaments and muscles capable of amazing versatility in the movements it can perform. Yet the muscles themselves are only able to pull. Nevertheless, by means of the coordinated action of related segments, each being pulled by the muscles acting upon it, the body as a whole has an almost limitless repertoire of movement patterns. It can not only pull; it can also push, lift, strike, throw, kick, walk, run, jump and swim, to name but a few of its amazing capabilities. Note the ways in which these diverse movement patterns can be organized into sports and games, such as tennis, football or obstacle relay races; gymnastic activities, such as the face vault, the cartwheel or rope climbing; and the dance, e.g., modern, folk or tap. These movement patterns are performed with many gradations of skill depending upon the experience and ability of the performer.

The physical education teacher must be prepared to teach a great variety of motor skills. Furthermore, he must teach the ways in which these are modified and combined in order to adapt to the requirements of a particular sport, dance or gymnastic activity. He hopes that his teaching will be such that his students will become proficient both in the individual motor skills and in each total activity of which they form a part. He is vitally concerned, therefore, with knowing the characteristics of skillful performance.

Efficient motion is one of the most important of these. Efficiency refers to the relationship between the amount of work accomplished and the force or energy expended. In mechanics we have seen that efficiency is expressed as the ratio of output to input. In human motion it is the ratio of the external work accomplished to the muscular energy expended. Whereas one of the greatest hindrances to mechanical efficiency is friction, in human motion it is unproductive muscular effort. The poorly coordinated person and the novice tend to make superfluous movements or to tense the muscles unnecessarily. The characteristic of efficient bodily motion is the absence of wasted movements, the use of the correct muscles with no more than the needed amount of force, and the relaxation of all muscles which do not contribute either directly or indirectly to the task. It results in smoothness and grace, in what is commonly called well-coordinated movement. In relaxation terminology the same quality is known as "differential relaxation." This means simply the ability to relax the unneeded muscles while performing a motor skill. It is an important characteristic of skillful performance, since wasted movements and unnecessary tensions not only make for awkward performance, but also hasten the onset of fatigue and increase its intensity. As Steindler has said, ". . . skillful or perfect motion always involves the least expenditure of effort . . ." for the work accomplished.[11] In rapid movements efficiency is characterized by a ballistic type of motion.

Another characteristic of skillful performance is *accuracy*. One may shoot at a basket with a beautifully coordinated and efficient movement, but unless the ball goes into the basket, the player is not considered skillful. Accuracy is based on a combination of factors, namely good judgment of direction, distance and force, proper timing and good muscular control. It is needed in simple acts such as lifting a forkful of food to the mouth, as well as in more complicated skills such as pole vaulting and pitching a baseball.

Closely related to the characteristics already mentioned are those of *adequate strength, speed* and *power*. Power implies the speed with which force is exerted. It is an important characteristic of skillful performance in such activities as high jumping, broad jumping, throwing, striking and kicking, and in speed events such as sprinting and swimming.

Judgment has already been mentioned as a factor in accuracy. It is more than that, however. In dual and team games and in boxing and wrestling, good judgment is one of the most important characteristics of skillful performance. It implies a sizing up of the situation and choosing wisely between several possible responses. It marks the difference between using one's head and acting blindly, between intelligent and unintelligent participation.

The general characteristics of skillful performance may therefore be summed up as *efficiency, accuracy, good judgment* and *adequate speed, strength* and *power* for the task. Of course motivation is an all-important factor, and there are also the various individual factors of *special aptitudes* which make one person a potential sprinter and another a potential high jumper. These are related to build, to constitution and to temperament. It is a matter of common observation that greater skillfulness is achieved by individuals who happen to be endowed with greater aptitudes or innate capacities for certain kinds of accomplishments. Great individual differences are seen with respect to the various factors of motor ability such as hand-eye coordination, agility, reaction time and finger dexterity. To be sure, all these can be developed by practice, but not everyone can develop them to the same degree, for there is a wide range in native capacity.

The truly skillful performer is one who habitually obeys the principles of both the anatomic and the mechanical aspects of human motion. His neuromuscular coordination is at peak performance; his muscular function is highly efficient; his kinesthetic sense is well developed; his flexor and extensor reflexes are dependable; the movements of his joints are commensurate with his individual structure; and his techniques of motion are in accord with the laws of his physical environment. In short, he has learned how and has made it his practice to observe the principles of skillful motion.

The mechanical principles that apply to specific motor skills have already been emphasized. The anatomic principles are more general in nature. Most of them have been mentioned elsewhere in the text, but it may be helpful to bring them together here.

PRINCIPLES

Relating to the Structure and Function of Joints

Principle I.   Since the range of motion may be limited by tight muscles, fasciae or ligaments, it may be increased by the stretching of these tissues.

Principle II.   The stretching of tight muscles, fasciae or ligaments should be done gradually and should be preceded by warm-up activities. The danger of rupturing soft tissues is minimized when they have been adequately "warmed-up."

Principle III.   Increase gained in the range of motion will be lost unless it is deliberately retained by means of continued exercise.

Principle IV.   Flexibility of weight-bearing joints should not exceed the ability of the muscles to maintain the body segments in good alignment.

Relating to the Muscular System and to Neuromuscular Function

Principle I.   Muscles contract more forcefully if they are first put on a stretch, provided they are not overstretched. This principle suggests the function of the "wind-up" in pitching and of the preliminary movements in other sport skills.

Principle II.   Increase in muscular strength is brought about by increasing the demands made on muscles. This is known as the overload principle. It means that a muscle must be loaded beyond its customary load if strength is to be increased. This principle forms the basis for conditioning exercises and is the principle on which the system of "progressive resistance exercise" is based. *Strength will not be progressively developed by the mere repetition of exercises of the same intensity.*

Principle III.   Unnecessary movements and tensions in the performance of a motor skill mean both awkwardness and unnecessary fatigue; hence they should be eliminated. This is achieved by first developing kinesthetic awareness of muscular tension and then by learning how to relax unneeded muscles.

Principle IV. Skillful, efficient performance in a particular technique can be developed only by practice of that technique. Only in this way can the necessary adjustments in the neuromuscular mechanism be made to assure a well coordinated movement.

Principle V. Fatigue from overpractice diminishes skillful performance. It can be avoided by introducing properly spaced rest periods in the practice period.

Principle VI. The most efficient type of movement in throwing and striking skills is ballistic movement. Skills which are primarily ballistic should be practiced ballistically even in the earliest learning stages. This means that from the beginning the emphasis should be placed on form rather than on aim. Accuracy of aim will develop with practice. If the emphasis is placed on accuracy in the learning stages, the beginner tends to perform the skill as a "moving fixation" or slow, tense movement. Once this pattern of movement is established, it is extremely difficult to change it later to a ballistic movement.

Principle VII. An important factor in the learning and perfecting of a motor skill is kinesthetic perception. There is no evidence of a general kinesthetic sense, however. Kinesthetic perception appears to be specific for the skill in question.

Principle VIII. Reflex responses of the neuromuscular system should be recognized and should be utilized when such utilization is clearly indicated. (This statement is intentionally general because much more needs to be learned about some of the physiologic reflexes before specific principles can be derived from them.) Of the more familiar reflexes, the extensor reflex is closely related to postural adjustments, and reciprocal innervation is closely related to ballistic motion.

Principle IX. When there is a choice of anatomic leverage, the lever appropriate for the task should be used, i.e., a lever with a long resistance arm for movements requiring range or speed, and a lever with a long effort arm for movements requiring strength. For example, kicking is an effective way of imparting force to a football because the leg provides a lever with a long resistance arm, but, for the same reason, it is a poor way of moving a heavy suitcase along the floor.

Dual Purpose of Kinesiology. In the Introduction to the Study of Kinesiology it was stated that such study had a dual purpose for the physical educator, namely, perfecting of performance in motor skills as well as perfecting the performer himself. (See page ii.) This brings us to a more specific consideration of ways and means. As we look back over the two kinds of basic information that have been represented in the study of kinesiology, we realize that we have received two sets of tools. One set has to do with the mechanical aspects of motor skills, and the other is involved with the anatomic and neurophysiologic aspects. Both sets of tools are related to the human structure and its movements, but their uses differ as widely as do those of woodworking tools and metalworking tools. They serve two totally different purposes. The purpose previously referred to as "perfecting performance" includes presenting the skill and its purpose with such clarity that the students will learn it with a minimum of difficulty. This is what Lawther means when he advocates giving the student a "gross-framework-idea" of the skill.[6] It also includes analyzing the student's performance, diagnosing his difficulties and making effective suggestions for correcting them.

A student's difficulty may be due to the violation of a mechanical principle, in which case the teacher should make the appropriate suggestion, or it may be due to some physical inadequacy such as lack of strength in a particular group of muscles or limited flexibility in some joint. In these cases it might be desirable to give the student a series of strengthening or flexibility exercises. This would be an example of "perfecting the performer." The entire exercise program — physical fitness, conditioning and posture correction — belongs in this category. It involves the ability to identify the needs of the individual, to evaluate the exercises from the point of view of their effect on the human structure, and to judge their appropriateness for the age, ability and specific requirements of the individual.

The usefulness of a kinesiology course should now be fully apparent. The more knowledgeable and perceptive the instructor is concerning the role of mechanics in performance, the better equipped he will be to become an effective teacher of motor skills. Likewise, the better his understanding of the proper functioning of muscles and joints and of the effects of specific exercises, the more skillful he will be in prescribing and teaching physical fitness, conditioning and postural exercises. In short, unless the study of kinesiology stimulates the student to put theory into practice it is of academic interest only and has no practical value.

There arises another question concerning these two major areas of activity; to what extent does a knowledge of mechanical and anatomic principles *on the part of the nonprofessional student* contribute to the effectiveness of his learning? This embodies two different questions which should be considered separately.

STUDENT UTILIZATION OF KNOWLEDGE OF MECHANICAL AND ANATOMIC PRINCIPLES

Knowledge of Mechanical Principles.   Whether the learning of motor skills is facilitated by an understanding of the mechanical principles that apply to them is a question of prime interest to physical education teachers and athletic coaches. Of three studies with which the authors are familiar, two indicated that a knowledge of mechanical principles was beneficial. Daugherty found that the junior high school boys who were taught certain principles demonstrated greater accuracy and force in selected skills than did the boys who were unfamiliar with the principles.[4] Mohr and Barrett had similar results with college women who were taught the mechanical principles of certain swimming strokes in conjunction with the usual swimming instruction.[9]

The approach of the third investigator, Colville, was somewhat different.[3] She selected three mechanical principles and devised experiments which involved the application of these. The principles investigated and the skills used were as follows:

FIRST PRINCIPLE: The angle of incidence is approximately equal to the angle of reflection.

Skill: Rolling a ball against a surface or surfaces from which it would rebound.

SECOND PRINCIPLE: In stopping a moving object, the force opposing the momentum must be equal to the force of the momentum and if the object is to be caught, this momentum must be dissipated by reducing the resistance of the catching surface.

Skill: Catching a tennis ball in a lacrosse stick and catching a badminton bird on a tennis racket.

THIRD PRINCIPLE: An object set in forward motion through the air by an external force is acted upon by gravitational acceleration.

Skill: Archery.

(For the details of each test the reader should consult the article.)

For all three tests the results gave no indication of a significant difference in performance level between the experimental and control groups. Both methods (instruction with and without using part of the time for learning the principles) resulted in a significant amount of learning which was similar in pattern as well as in amount.

Without having full information about the study one cannot help but have certain questions and comments, for instance: (1) Was instruction given regarding the application of the principles? (2) Might not the first and second tests, because of their artificial nature, have been comparable to nonsense syllables in verbal tests and therefore lacking in motivation for the subjects? (3) It would seem that a better choice of principles might have been made, for instance, principles that were more directly related to the quality of performance.

Lawther has reported several additional studies which are listed below.[6]

1. Hendrickson and Schroeder: Transfer of Training in Learning to Hit a Submerged Target. (This has to do with the principle of light refraction as it affects success in hitting underwater targets.)

2. Frey: A Study of Teaching Procedures in Selected Physical Education Activities for College Women of Low Motor Ability. (This investigates the effect of giving detailed reasons for specific forms used in teaching tennis, volleyball and rhythmic activities.)

3. Cobane: A Comparison of Two Methods of Teaching Selected Motor Skills. (This is somewhat similar to Colville's study but is applied to the teaching of tennis.)

4. Nessler: An Experimental Study of Methods Adapted to Teaching Low Skilled Freshman Women in Physical Education. (There was no report of the methods used, but the implication seemed to be that a knowledge of mechanical principles was one of the factors included.)

5. Broer: Effectiveness of General Basic Skills Curriculum for Junior High School Girls. (This included the factor of instruction in simplified mechanics prior to the teaching of volleyball, basketball and softball.)

6. Halverson: A Comparison of Three Methods of Teaching Motor Skills. (Knowledge of mechanical principles constituted one factor in this study. The skill was one-handed shooting in basketball.)

Of the nine studies, five reported either negative or negligible results, and four reported positive results. The latter were the studies by Daugherty,[4] Mohr and Barrett,[9] Hendrickson and Schroeder,[6] and Broer.[6] Lawther observed that most of the studies used beginners as subjects. He suggested that a knowledge of the appropriate mechanical principles might be of greater value at the higher skill levels than at the early stages of learning.

The lack of agreement shown by the results of the studies concerning the value to the learner of a knowledge of mechanical principles is also evident in the opinions of physical education instructors. Those who take the negative side may do so for a number of reasons. They may have had poor results in their own teaching experience and assumed that the procedure itself was ineffective without considering the fact that their own presentation may have been at fault. They may have talked too much in their explanation of the mechanical principles (a fault guaranteed to bore the class if not actually cause resentment); they may have failed to make their explanations clear; they may not have been convinced of the value of such explanations in the first place, and consequently they may have lacked enthusiasm in their presentation; they may have been influenced by some of the research studies which reported negative results.

It is significant that instructors who teach kinesiology tend to use this teaching technique in their sports classes and their coaching. McCloy asserted that one of the best ways to be sure that the students would attain the correct objectives was to teach the activities in such a way that the mechanics of each type of skill would be clear to the student. He advocated using simplified vocabulary and explanations so that the student would understand how the skill was to be performed and why the method taught was effective. Furthermore, based on his own experience, he claimed that this technique of teaching could be used successfully with children as young as 10 or 12 years of age.[8]

Broer,[1] Bunn,[2] Dyson,[5] and Rasch and Burke[10] are also among those who advocate giving instruction in mechanical principles when teaching or coaching athletic skills.

Knowledge of Anatomy and Anatomic Principles. Wells knows of no research in this area and therefore offers her own opinion which is based upon her teaching experience in the field of corrective physical education. This has included all grades from first grade through college. As a result of this experience, she is convinced of the value of giving brief, simple anatomic explanations accompanied by the use of such visual aids as muscle charts, a human skeleton, various anatomic models and drawings on the chalkboard. These explanations and demonstrations have been found to arouse the intelligent interest of pupils from about the fourth or fifth grade on. Obviously they must be geared to the age. Whether the students actually perform the exercises with greater energy and zest may be open to question, but there is no question that they tend to perform them with a greater degree of accuracy and precision.

Teaching for Understanding. Any teacher of physical education who has a good knowledge of motor skills can probably teach them to his students. If, in addition, he has a good understanding of kinesiology he will be in a better position to select effective techniques and methods and to diagnose and remedy individual difficulties. He will thus be improving his method of teaching his students how to learn new skills and how to improve their performance. This is desirable but it does not go far enough. Some students may be satisfied with it but the more intelligent student wants to know the *why* of the directions given by the instructor or coach. He wants to understand the reasons for what he does and why one approach is more effective than another.

For the majority of students, greater understanding leads to greater interest, and greater interest leads not only to greater effort but also to more productive effort. This constitutes genuine motivation, and finding effective motivation for his students has always been one of the major challenges faced by the instructor.

It is the conviction of this text that the solution to the quest for motivation is to *teach for understanding,* and that an effective way of doing this is to instruct the students in regard to mechanical and anatomic principles and to supplement this with simple demonstrations. If the explanations and the demonstrations are to be meaningful to the student, they must be geared to his intellectual and educational level. They should drive home essential points vividly and succinctly if they are to make a lasting impression. An example of a simple and meaningful demonstration may be found in Exercise 1 on page 432. Often such a demonstration will be more effective than a meticulously accurate scientific explanation.

As an aid to the beginning teacher who is interested in explaining the appropriate mechanical and anatomic principles, the following guidelines are suggested.

1. Only those instructors who are convinced of the value of this technique or who are at least open-minded about it should use it.

2. The explanations should be kept brief. Preferably, they should not take over five minutes, or possibly ten at the most, out of a 45- to 50-minute period. It is well to remember Lockhart's warning about keeping oral instructions at a minimum.[7] As she says, most physical education teachers talk too much. This has the unfortunate effect of defeating their purpose. Making oneself understood is desirable, but overexplaining to the point of boring or antagonizing one's listeners may be disastrous.

3. Whenever feasible, visual aids and demonstrations should be used in conjuction with explanations.

4. The explanatory talks on mechanical principles and anatomy should be given only occasionally, not as a part of every lesson.

5. Explain only those aspects of a subject that you consider of vital importance to learning the skill in question and which you believe cannot be taught effectively during the activity practice.

6. Avoid any but the simplest mechanical principles unless you know that your students are familiar with physics.

7. In general, save the finer points of instruction in mechanical principles for intermediate and advanced classes.

8. Do not be surprised to discover that adequate preparation for a brief, effective explanation may take as long as preparation for an hour's lecture. It takes time to select, condense and simplify.

Finally, the whole purpose of kinesiology can be summed up in three phrases. It is (1) to provide the physical education instructor with the tools he needs in order to TEACH FOR UNDERSTANDING, (2) to guide his students in acquiring proficiency in motor skills and (3) to aid his students in improving their own physiques when such a need is indicated.

REFERENCES

1. Broer, M. R.: Efficiency of Human Movement, 3rd Ed. Philadelphia: W. B. Saunders Company, 1973.
2. Bunn, J. W.: Scientific Principles of Coaching, 2nd Ed. Englewood Cliffs, New Jersey: Prentice-Hall, Inc., 1972.
3. Colville, F. M.: The learning of motor skills as influenced by knowledge of mechanical principles. J. Ed. Psych., 48:321–327, 1957.
4. Daugherty, G.: The effects of kinesiological teaching on the performance of junior high school boys. Res. Quart. Am. Assn. Health, Phys. Ed. & Recrn., 16:26–33, 1945.
5. Dyson, G. H. G.: The Mechanics of Athletics, 5th Ed. London: University of London Press Ltd., 1970.
6. Lawther, J. D.: The Learning of Physical Skills. Englewood Cliffs, New Jersey: Prentice-Hall, Inc., 1968.
7. Lockhart, A.: Communicating with the learner. Quest. VI:57–67, 1966.
8. McCloy, C. H.: The mechanical analysis of motor skills. In Johnson, W. R. (Ed.): Science and Medicine of Exercise and Sports. New York: Harper & Row, 1960, Chap. 4.
9. Mohr, D. R., and Barrett, M. E.: Effect of knowledge of mechanical principles in learning to perform intermediate swimming skills. Res. Quart. Am. Assn. Health, Phys. Ed. & Recrn., 33:574–580, 1962.
10. Rasch, P. J., and Burke, R. K.: Kinesiology and Applied Anatomy, 5th Ed. Philadelphia: Lea & Febiger, 1974.
11. Steindler, A.: Mechanics of Normal and Pathological Locomotion in Man. Springfield, Ill.: Charles C Thomas, Publisher, 1973.

RECOMMENDED READINGS

Lawther, J. D.: The Learning of Physical Skills. Englewood Cliffs, New Jersey: Prentice-Hall, Inc., 1968.
Lockhart, A.: Communicating with the learner. Quest, VI:57–67, 1966.
McCloy, C. H.: The mechanical analysis of motor skills. In Johnson, W. R. (Ed.): Science and Medicine of Exercise and Sports. New York: Harper and Row, 1960, Chap. 4.
Quest, Monograph VI, A Symposium on Motor Learning. A publication of the National Association for Physical Education of College Women and the National College Physical Education Association for Men, 1966. The entire issue.

APPENDIX A*

OUTLINE FOR STUDYING THE JOINTS AND THEIR MOVEMENTS

Name of joint_____ Bones involved_____

Type of Joint, Movement and Number of Axes of Motion (Check below.)

____Diarthrodial

    ____Irregular
    ____Hinge
    ____Pivot
    ____Condyloid (ovoid)
    ____Saddle
    ____Ball-and-socket

____Synarthrodial

    ____Cartilaginous
    ____Ligamentous
    ____Fibrous

Type of Movement

    ____Gliding
    ____Axial or rotatory

Axis of Motion

    ____Nonaxial
    ____Uniaxial
    ____Biaxial
    ____Triaxial

Name or describe briefly:

Articulating processes and surfaces_____

_____

_____

_____

Ligaments and cartilages_____

_____

_____

_____

_____

_____

---

*The check lists in Appendices A and D may be reproduced for class use without specific permission.

Movements (check)   Comments

____Flexion and extension   _____

____Hyperextension   _____

____Abduction and ad-
duction or lateral
flexion   _____

____Rotation   _____

____Outward (lat.) and
inward (med.)   _____

Movements (check)

____Upward and downward   _____

____Right and left   _____

____Supination and
pronation   _____

Other: _____

_____   _____

_____   _____

_____   _____

_____   _____

APPENDIX B

CLASSIFICATION OF JOINTS AND THEIR MOVEMENTS

Type	Articulation	Movement
	Diarthrodial: Nonaxial	
	Shoulder Girdle	
	Sternoclavicular	Limited motion of outer end of clavicle in all three planes
		Elevation – Depression
		Forward – Backward
		Rotation: Forward-downward – Backward-upward
	Acromioclavicular	Movements of scapula (including motion in both joints)
Irregular;		Elevation – Depression
Arthrodial;		Rotation: Upward – Downward
Plane		Abduction – Adduction
		Upward Tilt – Reduction of same
	Intercarpal	Slight gliding movements in cooperation with movements of wrist and metacarpals
	Intertarsal	Slight gliding movements in cooperation with movements of talonavicular and ankle joints
	Diarthrodial: Uniaxial	
	Elbow	
	Humero-ulnar	Flexion – Extension – Hyperextension (slight)
	Knee	
	Tibiofemoral	Flexion – Extension – Hyperextension (slight)
Hinge;	Ankle	
Ginglymus	Talotibial and talofibular	Dorsiflexion – Plantar flexion (Extension)
	Fingers and thumb	Flexion – Extension
	Interphalangeal	
	Toes	
	Interphalangeal	Flexion – Extension
	Forearm	
Pivot;	Proximal and distal radioulnar	Supination – Pronation
Screw;	Neck	
Trochoid	Atlantoaxial (1st and 2nd cervical)	Rotation: Right – Left

Diarthrodial: Biaxial

	Wrist	
	Radiocarpal	Flexion – Extension – Hyperextension
		Abduction – Adduction
	Fingers	
Condyloid;	Metacarpophalangeal	Flexion – Extension
Ovoid;		Abduction – Adduction
Ellipsoidal	Toes	
	Metatarsophalangeal	Flexion – Extension – Hyperextension
	Head	
	Occipito-atlantal	Flexion – Extension – Hyperextension
		Lateral flexion: Right – Left
Saddle;		
Seller;	Thumb	
Reciprocal	Carpometacarpal	Flexion – Extension – Hyperextension
reception		Abduction – Adduction
		Opposition (combination of abduction, hyperflexion, and possibly slight inward rotation)*

Diarthrodial: Triaxial

	Shoulder	
	Glenohumeral	Flexion – Extension – Hyperextension
Ball-and-socket;		Abduction – Adduction
Enarthrodial		Rotation: Outward – Inward
		Horizontal flexion (from abduction)
		Horizontal extension (from flexion)
	Hip	
	Femoro-acetabular	Flexion – Extension – Hyperextension
		Abduction – Adduction
		Rotation: Outward – Inward
		Horizontal flexion (from abduction)
		Horizontal extension (from flexion)
Shallow ball-	Foot	
and-socket	Talonavicular	Dorsiflexion – Plantar flexion (very slight)
		Abduction – Adduction (slight)
		Inversion – Eversion (very slight)

Combination Diarthrodial Nonaxial and Fibrocartilaginous Synarthrodial

Triaxial simulated ball-and-socket	Vertebral bodies Intervertebral cartilages	Flexion
		Extension
		Hyperextension
Nonaxial irregular	Vertebral arches	Lateral flexion: Right – Left
		Rotation: Right – Left

*Opinions differ with respect to inward rotation.

APPENDIX C

MUSCULAR ATTACHMENTS

The Upper Extremity*

MUSCLE	PROXIMAL ATTACHMENTS	DISTAL ATTACHMENTS
Shoulder Joint		
Coracobrachialis	Coracoid process of scapula	Inner surface of humerus opposite deltoid attachment
Deltoid	Anterior: Anterior border of outer third of clavicle Middle: Acromion process and outer end of clavicle Posterior: Lower margin of spine of scapula	Lateral aspect of humerus, near midpoint
Infraspinatus & Teres Minor	Axillary border and posterior surface of scapula below scapular spine	Posterior aspect of greater tuberosity of humerus
Latissimus Dorsi	Spinous processes of lower six thoracic and all lumbar vertebrae; posterior surface of sacrum; crest of ilium; lower three ribs	Anterior surface of humerus below head by flat tendon just anterior to, and parallel with, tendon of pectoralis major
Pectoralis Major	Medial two thirds of clavicle; anterior surface of sternum; cartilages of first six ribs; slip from aponeurosis of external oblique abdominal muscle	Lateral surface of humerus just below head by flat tendon two to three inches wide
Subscapularis	Entire anterior surface of scapula	Lesser tuberosity of humerus
Supraspinatus	Medial two thirds of supraspinatus fossa above scapular spine	Top of greater tuberosity of humerus
Teres Major	Posterior surface of inferior angle of scapula	Anterior surface of humerus below head, just medial to latissimus dorsi tendon
Shoulder Girdle		
Levator Scapulae	Transverse processes of first four cervical vertebrae	Vertebral border of scapula between medial angle and scapular spine
Pectoralis Minor	Anterior surface of third, fourth and fifth ribs near cartilages	Tip of coracoid process of scapula

*See Chapters Four and Five.

The Upper Extremity (*Continued*)

MUSCLE	PROXIMAL ATTACHMENTS	DISTAL ATTACHMENTS
Rhomboids: Major and Minor	Spinous processes of seventh cervical and first five thoracic vertebrae	Vertebral border of scapula from spine to inferior angle
Trapezius	Occipital bone; ligamentum nuchae; spinous processes of seventh cervical and all thoracic vertebrae	Part 1: Posterior border of lateral third of clavicle Part 2: Top of acromium process Part 3: Upper border of scapular spine Part 4: Root of scapular spine
Elbow and Forearm		
Anconeus	Posterior surface of lateral epicondyle of humerus	Lateral side of olecranon process and posterior surface of upper part of ulna
Biceps Brachii	Long head: upper margin of glenoid fossa Short head: apex of coracoid process of scapula	Bicipital tuberosity of radius
Brachialis	Anterior surface of lower half of humerus	Anterior surface of coronoid process of ulna
Brachioradialis	Upper two thirds of lateral supracondylar ridge of humerus	Lateral side of base of styloid process of radius
Pronator Teres	Medial epicondyle of humerus and medial side of coronoid process of ulna	Lateral surface of radius near middle
Pronator Quadratus	Anterior surface of lower one fourth of ulna	Anterior surface of lower one fourth of radius
Supinator	Lateral condyle of humerus; adjacent portion of ulna; radial collateral and annular ligaments	Lateral surface of upper third of radius
Triceps Brachii	Long head: Infraglenoid tuberosity Lateral head: Posterior surface of upper half of humerus Medial head: Posterior surface of lower two thirds of humerus	Olecranon process of ulna
Wrist		
Extensor Carpi Radialis Brevis	Lateral condyle of humerus	Posterior surface of base of third metacarpal
Extensor Carpi Radialis Longus	Lateral epicondyle of humerus and supracondylar ridge above	Posterior surface of base of second metacarpal
Extensor Carpi Ulnaris	By two heads from lateral epicondyle of humerus and middle third of posterior ridge of ulna	Posterior surface of base of fifth metacarpal
Flexor Carpi Radialis	Medial epicondyle of humerus	Anterior surface of base of second metacarpal
Flexor Carpi Ulnaris	By two heads from medial condyle of humerus and medial border of olecranon process of ulna	Palmar surface of pisiform and hamate carpal bones, and base of fifth metacarpal
Palmaris Longus	Medial epicondyle of humerus	Transverse carpal ligament and palmar aponeurosis

The Upper Extremity (*Continued*)

MUSCLE	PROXIMAL ATTACHMENTS	DISTAL ATTACHMENTS
Thumb and Fingers		
Abductor Pollicis Longus	Dorsolateral surface of ulna below anconeus, dorsal surface of radius near center and intervening interosseous membrane	Lateral surface of base of first metacarpal
Extensor Digiti Minimi	Proximal tendon of extensor digitorum	Fifth finger's extensor digitorum tendon
Extensor Digitorum	Lateral epicondyle of humerus	By four tendons, one to each finger, each tendon dividing into three slips, the middle one attaching to dorsal surface of second phalanx and the other two uniting to attach to dorsal surface of base of distal phalanx
Extensor Indicis	Dorsal surface of lower half of ulna	Index finger's extensor digitorum tendon
Extensor Pollicis Brevis	Dorsal surface of radius below abductor pollicis longus	Dorsal surface of base of first phalanx
Extensor Pollicis Longus	Dorsal surface of middle third of ulna	Dorsal surface of base of distal phalanx
Flexor Digitorum Profundus	Upper two thirds of anterior and medial surfaces of ulna	By four tendons (one to each finger) to base of distal phalanx, after passing through tendon of flexor digitorum superficialis
Flexor Digitorum Superficialis	Humero-ulnar head: Medial epicondyle of humerus, ulnar collateral ligament, medial margin of coronoid process Radial head: Oblique line on anterior surface of radial shaft	By four tendons to the four fingers, each tendon splitting to attach to either side of base of middle phalanx
Flexor Pollicis Longus	Anterior surface of middle half of radius	Anterior surface of base of distal phalanx of thumb
Abductor Digiti Minimi	Pisiform bone and tendon of flexor carpi ulnaris	Ulnar side of base of first phalanx of fifth finger and ulnar border of aponeurosis of extensor digiti minimi
Abductor Pollicis Brevis	Anterior surface of transverse carpal ligament, greater multangular and navicular bones	Radial side of base of first phalanx of thumb
Adductor Pollicis	Carpal (oblique) head: Deep carpal ligaments, capitate bone and bases of second and third metacarpals Metacarpal (transverse) head: Lower two thirds of anterior surface of third metacarpal	Ulnar side of base of proximal phalanx of thumb
Flexor Digiti Minimi Brevis	Hook of hamate bone and adjacent parts of transverse carpal ligament	Ulnar side of base of first phalanx of fifth finger
Flexor Pollicis Brevis	Superficial head: Greater multangular bone and adjacent part of transverse carpal ligament Deep head: Ulnar side of first metacarpal	Superficial head: Radial side of base of first phalanx of thumb Deep head: Ulnar side of base of first phalanx of thumb

The Upper Extremity (Continued)

MUSCLE	PROXIMAL ATTACHMENTS	DISTAL ATTACHMENTS
Interossei Dorsales	By two heads from adjacent sides of metacarpals in each interspace	Base of proximal phalanx and aponeurosis of extensor muscles on each side of middle finger, on thumb side of index finger and on ulnar side of fourth finger
Interossei Palmares	1st: Ulnar side of second metacarpal	1st: Ulnar side of base of first phalanx of index finger and expansion of extensor digitorum tendon
	2nd: Radial side of fourth metacarpal	2nd: Radial side of base of first phalanx of fourth finger and expansion of extensor digitorum tendon
	3rd: Radial side of fifth metacarpal	3rd: Radial side of base of first phalanx of fifth finger and expansion of extensor digitorum tendon
Lumbricales	Tendons of flexor digitorum profundus in center of palm	Extensor aponeuroses on radial side of proximal phalanges
Opponens Digiti Minimi	Hook of hamate bone and adjacent parts of transverse carpal ligament	Entire length of ulnar border of fifth metacarpal
Opponens Pollicis	Anterior surface of greater multangular bone and transverse carpal ligament	Entire radial border of anterior surface of first metacarpal

The Lower Extremity*

MUSCLE	PROXIMAL ATTACHMENTS	DISTAL ATTACHMENTS
Hip Joint		
Adductor Brevis	Outer surface of body and inferior ramus of pubis	Line from lesser trochanter to linea aspera and upper fourth of linea aspera
Adductor Longus	Anterior surface of pubis	Medial lip of middle half of linea aspera
Adductor Magnus	Inferior rami of pubis and ischium and lateral border of inferior surface of ischial tuberosity	Linea aspera, medial supracondylar line and adductor tubercle on medial condyle of femur
Biceps Femoris, Long Head	Lower and medial impression on tuberosity of ischium	Lateral side of head of fibula and lateral condyle of tibia
Gluteus Maximus	Posterior gluteal line of ilium and adjacent portion of crest; posterior surface of lower part of sacrum and side of coccyx	Posterior surface of femur on ridge below greater trochanter; iliotibial tract of fascia lata
Gluteus Medius	Posterior surface of ilium between crest, posterior gluteal line and anterior gluteal line	Oblique ridge on lateral surface of greater trochanter
Gluteus Minimus	Posterior surface of ilium between anterior and inferior gluteal lines	Anterior border to greater trochanter
Gracilis	Anterior aspect of lower half of symphysis pubis and upper half of pubic arch	Medial surface of tibia just below condyle

*See Chapters Six and Seven.

The Lower Extremity (*Continued*)

MUSCLE	PROXIMAL ATTACHMENTS	DISTAL ATTACHMENTS
Iliopsoas	Psoas major: Sides of bodies and intervertebral cartilages of last thoracic and all lumbar vertebrae; front and lower borders of transverse processes of lumbar vertebrae Iliacus: Anterior surface of ilium and base of sacrum	Both: Lesser trochanter of femur and for a short distance below along medial border of shaft
Pectineus	Pectineal line between iliopectineal eminence and tubercle of pubis	Pectineal line of femur, between lesser trochanter and linea aspera
Rectus Femoris	Anterior inferior iliac spine and groove above brim of acetabulum	Base of patella, as part of quadriceps femoris tendon; by means of patellar ligament it attaches to the tibial tuberosity
Sartorius	Anterior superior iliac spine and upper half of notch below it	Anterior and medial surface of tibia just below condyle
Semimembranosus	Upper and lateral impression on tuberosity of ischium	Horizontal groove on posterior surface of medial condyle of tibia
Semitendinosus	Lower and medial impression on tuberosity of ischium with biceps femoris	Upper part of medial surface of shaft of tibia
Six Deep Outward Rotators	Outer and inner surfaces of sacrum and of pelvis in region of obturator foramen	Posterior and medial aspects of greater trochanter
Tensor Fasiae Latae	Anterior part of outer lip of iliac crest and outer surface of anterior superior iliac spine	Iliotibial tract of fascia lata on latero-anterior aspect of thigh, about one third of the way down

Knee Joint

MUSCLE	PROXIMAL ATTACHMENTS	DISTAL ATTACHMENTS
Biceps Femoris	Long head: Lower and medial impression on tuberosity of ischium Short head: Lateral lip of linea aspera	Lateral side of head of fibula and lateral condyle of tibia
Gracilis	See hip joint	
Popliteus	Lateral surface of lateral condyle of femur	Posterior surface of tibia, above popliteal line
Rectus Femoris Sartorius, Semimembranosus, Semitendinosus	See hip joint	
The Three Vasti	V. Lateralis: Upper part of intertrochanteric line; anterior and lower borders of greater trochanter; lateral lip of gluteal tuberosity; upper half of linea aspera V. Intermedius: Anterior and lateral surfaces of upper two thirds of shaft of femur V. Medialis: Lower half of intertrochanteric line; medial lip of linea aspera; upper part of medial supracondylar line	The tendons of the three vasti muscles unite with that of rectus femoris to form the quadriceps femoris tendon; this attaches to the base of the patella, and indirectly, by means of the patellar ligament, to the tuberosity of the tibia

The Lower Extremity (Continued)

MUSCLE	PROXIMAL ATTACHMENTS	DISTAL ATTACHMENTS
Ankle Joint, Foot and Toes		
Extensor Digitorum Longus	Lateral condyle of tibia and upper three fourths of anterior surface of fibula	Dorsal surface of second and third phalanges of four lesser toes
Extensor Hallucis Longus	Middle half of anterior surface of fibula	Dorsal surface of base of distal phalanx of hallux (great toe)
Flexor Digitorum Longus	Posterior surface of middle three fifths of tibia	Plantar surface of base of distal phalanx of each of the four lesser toes
Flexor Hallucis Longus	Posterior surface of lower two thirds of fibula	Plantar surface of base of distal phalanx of hallux (great toe)
Gastrocnemius	Posterior surface of each femoral condyle and adjacent parts, by two separate heads	Posterior surface of calcaneus by means of calcaneal tendon (tendon of Achilles)
Peroneus Brevis	Lateral surface of lateral two thirds of fibula	Tuberosity on lateral side of base of fifth metatarsal
Peroneus Longus	Lateral condyle of tibia; lateral surface of head and upper two thirds of fibula	Lateral margin of plantar surface of first cuneiform and base of first metatarsal
Peroneus Tertius	Anterior surface of lower third of fibula	Dorsal surface of base of fifth metatarsal
Soleus	Posterior surface of head of fibula and upper two thirds of shaft; popliteal line and medial border of middle third of tibia	Posterior surface of calcaneus by means of calcaneal tendon (tendon of Achilles)
Tibialis Anterior	Lateral condyle and upper two thirds of lateral surface of tibia	Plantar surface of base of first metatarsal and medial surface of first cuneiform
Tibialis Posterior	Posterior surface of upper two thirds of tibia beginning at popliteal line; medial surface of upper two thirds of fibula	Tuberosity of navicular bone with branches to sustentaculum tali of calcaneus, to the three cuneiforms, to cuboid and to the bases of the three middle metatarsal bones

The Spinal Column*

MUSCLE	LOWER ATTACHMENTS	UPPER ATTACHMENTS
Deep Posterior Spinal Muscles	Posterior surface of sacrum and posterior processes of all the vertebrae	Spinous and transverse processes and laminae of vertebrae slightly higher than lower attachments
Erector Spinae	Thoracolumbar fascia; posterior portions of lumbar, thoracic and lower cervical vertebrae; angles of ribs	Angles of ribs; posterior portions of cervical and thoracic vertebrae; mastoid process of temporal bone
Hyoid Muscles	Suprahyoid: Hyoid bone Infrahyoid: Sternum, clavicle and scapula	Temporal bone and mandible Hyoid bone
Levator Scapula	See shoulder girdle	
Obliquus Externus Abdominis	Anterior half of crest of ilium; aponeurosis from ribs to crest of pubis	Lower border of lower eight ribs by tendinous slips which interdigitate with those of serratus anterior

*See Chapter Eight.

The Spinal Column (*Continued*)

MUSCLE	LOWER ATTACHMENTS	UPPER ATTACHMENTS
Obliquus Internus Abdominis	Inguinal ligament; crest of ilium; thoracolumbar fascia	Anterior and middle fibers into crest of pubis, linea alba and aponeurosis on front of body; posterior fibers, by three separate slips, into cartilages of lower three ribs
Prevertebral Muscles	Anterior surfaces of various parts of cervical vertebrae and of upper three thoracic vertebrae	Anterior portions of occipital bone and of cervical vertebrae
Psoas	See hip joint	
Quadratus Lumborum	Crest of ilium and iliolumbar ligament	Lower border of twelfth rib and tips of transverse processes of upper four lumbar vertebrae
Rectus Abdominis	Crest of pubis	Cartilages of fifth, sixth and seventh ribs
Scalenes (three)	First two ribs	Transverse processes of cervical vertebrae
Semispinalis Thoracis, Cervicis and Capitis	Transverse processes of all thoracic and seventh cervical vertebrae; articular processes of lower four cervical vertebrae	Spinous process of upper four thoracic and lower five cervical vertebrae; occipital bone
Splenius Capitis and Cervicis	Lower half of ligamentum nuchae; spinous processes of seventh cervical and upper six thoracic vertebrae	Mastoid process of temporal bone and adjacent part of occipital bone; transverse processes of upper three cervical vertebrae
Sternocleidomastoid	By two heads from top of sternum and medial third of clavicle	Mastoid process of temporal bone and adjacent portion of occipital bone
Suboccipitals	Posterior portions of atlas and axis	Occipital bone and transverse process of atlas

Major Respiratory Muscles*

MUSCLE	PERIPHERAL ATTACHMENT	CENTRAL ATTACHMENT
Diaphragm	Circumference of thoracic outlet	Central tendon, a cloverleaf-shaped aponeurosis

	UPPER ATTACHMENTS	LOWER ATTACHMENTS
Intercostales Externi	Lower border of each rib but last	Upper border of rib immediately below
Intercostales Interni	Inner surface and costal cartilage of each rib but last	Upper border of rib immediately below
Levatores Costarum	Transverse processes of seventh cervical and upper eleven thoracic vertebrae	Upper eight: Each to rib immediately below, between tubercle and angle Lower four: By two bands each, one to rib immediately below and other to second rib below
Serratus Posterior Inferior	Lower borders of lower four ribs	Spinous processes and ligaments of lower two thoracic and upper two or three lumbar vertebrae
Serratus Posterior Superior	Spinous processes and ligaments of lower two or three cervical and upper two thoracic vertebrae	Upper borders of second, third, fourth and fifth ribs

	LATERAL ATTACHMENTS	MEDIAL ATTACHMENTS
Transversus Abominis	Inguinal ligament, crest of ilium, thoracolumbar fascia and cartilages of lower six ribs	Linea alba and crest of pubis
Transversus Thoracis	Lower borders and inner surfaces of costal cartilages of second, third, fourth, fifth and sixth ribs	Lower half of inner surface of sternum and adjoining costal cartilages

*See Chapter Nine.

Additional Muscles Which Participate in Respiration

Muscles of Shoulder Joint or Shoulder Girdle
    Pectoralis Major
    Pectoralis Minor
    Trapezius I and II
Muscles of the Spinal Column
    Quadratus Lumborum
    Scalenes: Anterior, posterior, medialis
    Sternocleidomastoid

APPENDIX D

CHECK LISTS FOR THE MUSCULAR ANALYSIS OF MOVEMENTS OF THE MAJOR BODY SEGMENTS

These check lists were originally devised for the recording of the muscular actions identified in the palpation experiments described in the section headed Laboratory Experiences at the ends of Chapters Four through Nine. For the most part only the basic movements of individual body segments were used in these exercises. Although it is recognized that the palpation method is not as accurate as the electromyographic method for ascertaining muscular actions, the palpation method is invaluable as a method for studying muscular activity and for supplementing book study.

In addition to their use in identifying the actions of muscles in basic movements, the check lists are useful for the recording of the muscular analyses of postural and conditioning exercises and of the typical motor skills of familiar sports, gymnastic and tumbling events, dance techniques, and so on. For this purpose an ample number of duplicate copies of the lists should be available inasmuch as a complete set may be needed *for each phase* of a movement that involves the entire body. It would be helpful if spaces were provided on these for the student's name and the name of the motor skill being analyzed.

For developing skill in analyzing movements anatomically, much practice is needed. It is therefore suggested that the student start as soon as feasible to make such analyses and that he progress from the basic movements to more complex motor skills as rapidly as he is able. The following suggestions may prove helpful.

Procedure for Making an Anatomic Analysis of a Movement*

1. Have someone demonstrate the movement to be analyzed both before and at frequent intervals throughout the analysis. In lieu of this, motion pictures (preferably slow motion films shown on a projector which can be stopped at will) are an excellent substitute. If these are not available, a series of still shots or even a single photograph or sketch is helpful.

2. Divide the movement into logical phases, such as
   - a. Essential act or propulsive phase; b. return movement or recovery phase. Appropriate for calisthenic exercises, swimming strokes and other two-part movements.
   - a. Preparatory movement; b. essential act; c. follow through or recovery. Appropriate for throwing, striking and kicking activities.

3. Consider the starting position of the body (vertical, horizontal—prone, supine, side, or other) and the means of its support (ground, water, suspension apparatus, none). In this connection consider the effect of gravity on the muscular action.

4. Consider the nature of the movement, whether fast or slow, ballistic or non-ballistic, against or not against resistance, and so on. Consider the effect of this on the muscular action.

---

*See Appendix G for illustrations of conditioning and postural exercises, sport movements and gymnastic techniques which serve as material for practice in making kinesiologic analyses.

5. Identify the movement of each body segment and analyze the joint actions. These may be recorded on the check lists by placing a check in the appropriate spaces across the top of the check list.

6. Considering all of the essential factors, analyze the muscular action and record on the check list.

Elementary method.   Place a check mark in the appropriate space for each muscle that contributes positively to the movement.

Advanced method

(1) To differentiate between principal and assistant muscles use P and A.

(2) To differentiate between concentric (shortening), eccentric (lengthening), and static contraction, use different colored pencils.

7. After completing the muscular analysis consider the following questions:

a. Are there any clear-cut examples of the neutralizing or of the mutually neutralizing action of muscles? If so, identify and explain.

b. Are there any clear-cut examples of stabilization of a segment of the body by muscular action? If so, identify and explain.

c. Are there any pertinent mechanical aspects or principles which should be taken into consideration in this exercise? If so, identify and explain.

Check lists follow

*Check List for Muscular Analysis of Movements of the Arm on the Body**

	Sideward Elev. of Arm	Sideward Depr. of Arm	Fwd. Elev. of Arm	Fwd. Depr. of Arm	Bkwd. Elev. of Arm	Hor. Bkwd. Swing of Arm	Hor. Sideward Fwd. Swing	Outwd. Rot'n of Arm	Inwd. Rot'n of Arm	Elev. of Shoul. Gird.	Depr. of Shoul. Gird.	Abd. of Scap.	Add. of Scap.
SHOULDER GIRDLE													
Subclavius													
Pectoralis minor													
Serratus anterior													
Levator scapulae													
Trapezius I													
Trapezius II													
Trapezius III													
Trapezius IV													
Rhomboids													

*The check lists in Appendices A and D may be reproduced for class use without specific permission.

Check List for Muscular Analysis of Movements of the Arm on the Body (Continued)

	Side-ward Elev. of Arm	Side-ward Depr. of Arm	Fwd. Elev. of Arm	Fwd. Depr. of Arm	Bkwd. Elev. of Arm	Hor. Bkwd. Swing of Arm	Hor. Side-ward Fwd. Swing	Outwd. Rot'n of Arm	Inwd. Rot'n of Arm	Elev. of Shoul. Gird.	Depr. of Shoul. Gird.	Abd. of Scap.	Add. of Scap.
SHOULDER JOINT													
Deltoid: middle													
Deltoid: anterior													
Deltoid: posterior													
Supraspinatus													
Pect. major: clavicular													
Pect. major: sternal													
Coracobrachialis													
Subscapularis													
Latissimus dorsi													
Teres major													
Infrasp. & teres minor													

Check List for Muscular Analysis of Movements of Forearm at Elbow and Radioulnar Joints

	Flexion	Extension	Supination	Pronation
MUSCLES OF ELBOW AND FOREARM:				
Biceps				
Brachialis				
Brachioradialis				
Pronator teres				
Pronator quadratus				
Supinator				
Triceps				
Anconeus				
MUSCLES OF WRIST:				
Flexor carpi radialis				
Flexor carpi ulnaris				
Palmaris longus				
Extensor carpi radialis longus				
Extensor carpi radialis brevis				
Extensor carpi ulnaris				

Check List for Muscular Analysis of Movements of the Hand at the Wrist

	Flexion	*Extension*	*Ulnar Flexion*	*Radial Flexion*
MUSCLES OF WRIST				
Flexor carpi radialis				
Flexor carpi ulnaris				
Palmaris longus				
Extensor carpi radialis longus				
Extensor carpi radialis brevis				
Extensor carpi ulnaris				
MUSCLES OF THUMB AND FINGERS				
Flexor digitorum superficialis				
Flexor digitorum profundus				
Extensor digitorum				
Extensor indicis				
Extensor digiti minimi				
Flexor pollicis longus				
Extensor pollicis longus				
Extensor pollicis brevis				
Abductor pollicis longus				

Check List for Muscular Analysis of Movements of the Fingers

	Metacarpophalangeal				Interphalangeal	
	Flex.	Ext.	Abd.	Add.	Flex.	Ext.
ON FOREARM						
Flexor digitorum superficialis						
Flexor digitorum profundus						
Extensor digitorum						
Extensor indicis						
Extensor digiti minimi						
IN HAND						
Lumbricales						
Palmar interossei						
Dorsal interossei						
Abductor digiti minimi						
Flex. dig. minimi brev.						
Opponens digiti minimi						

Check List for Muscular Analysis of Movements of the Thumb

	Carpometacarpal					Metacarpophalangeal		Interphalangeal	
	Flex.	Ext. & Hyp. Ex.	Abd.	Add. & Hyp. Add.	Opp.	Flex.	Ext.	Flex.	Ext.
ON FOREARM									
Fl. pol. long.									
Ext. pol. long.									
Ext. pol. brev.									
Abd. pol. long.									
IN HAND									
Fl. pol. brev.									
Abd. pol. brev.									
Opponens pol.									
Adductor pol.									

Check List for Muscular Analysis of Movements of the Pelvic Girdle

	Increased Inclination	Decreased Inclination	Lateral Tilt*	Rotation*
Rectus abdominis				
External oblique				
Internal oblique				
Erector spinae				
Quadratus lumborum				
Psoas				
Gluteus maximus				
Gluteus medius and minimus				
Tensor fasciae latae				
Others:				

Note: Because of the numerous two-joint muscles found in the lower extremity, the check list for the muscular analysis of movements of the hip is combined with that for the knee. See following page.

*Indicate left (L) or right (R).

*Check List for Muscular Analysis of Movements
of the Thigh and Leg*

	Hip						Knee			
	Flex.	*Ext.*	*Abd.*	*Add.*	*Out. Rot.*	*Inwd. Rot.*	*Flex.*	*Ext.*	*Out. Rot.*	*Inwd. Rot.*
Iliopsoas										
Sartorius										
Pectineus										
Tensor fasciae latae										
Gluteus maximus										
Gluteus medius										
Gluteus minimus										
Six deep rotators										
Adductor magnus										
Adductor longus										
Adductor brevis										
Gracilis										
Biceps femoris										
Semitendinosus										
Semimembranosus										
Rectus femoris										
Vastus intermedius										
Vastus lateralis										
Vastus medialis										
Popliteus										
Gastrocnemius										

Check List for Muscular Analysis of Movements
of Ankle, Foot and Toes

	Ankle		Foot				Toes	
	Dorsi-flex.	Plant Flex.	Dorsi-flex.	Plant. Flex.	Inv. & Adduc.	Evers. & Abd.	Flex.	Ext.
Tibialis anterior								
Ext. halluc. long.								
Ext. digit. longus								
Peroneus tertius								
Peroneus longus								
Peroneus brevis								
Tibialis posterior								
Gastrocnemius								
Soleus								
Flexor hal. long.								
Flex. digit. long.								

Check List for the Muscular Analysis of Movements of the Head and Neck

	Flexion	Extension	Lateral Flexion	Rotation Same Side*	Rotation Opposite Side*
ANTERIOR:					
Prevertebral muscles					
Hyoid muscles					
LATERAL:					
Three scalenes					
Sternocleidomastoid					
Levator scapulae					
POSTERIOR:					
Splenius					
Suboccipitals					
Erector spinae					
Semispinalis					
Deep poster. muscles					
OTHER:					

*Indicate left (L) or right (R).

*Check List for the Muscular Analysis of Movements
of the Thoracic and Lumbar Spine*

	Flexion	Extension	Lateral Flexion	Rotation Same Side*	Rotation Opposite Side*
ANTERIOR:					
Rectus abdominis					
Ext. oblique abd.					
Int. oblique abd.					
LATERAL:					
Quad. lumborum					
POSTERIOR:					
Erector spinae					
Semispinalis thoracis					
Deep. post. muscles					
OTHER:					

*Indicate left (L) or right (R).

*Check List for the Muscular Analysis of the Movements
Involved in Respiration*

	Normal Inhalation	Vigorous Inhalation	Vigorous Exhalation
MUSCLES OF RESPIRATION:			
Diaphragm			
External intercostals			
Internal intercostals, anterior			
Internal intercostals, posterior and lateral			
Levatores costarum			
Serratus posterior superior			
Serratus posterior inferior			
Transversus thoracis			
Transversus abdominis			
MUSCLES OF THE SPINE:			
Sternocleidomastoid			
Three scalenes			
Thoracic extensors			
Rectus abdominis			
External oblique			
Internal oblique			
MUSCLES OF THE SHOULDER GIRDLE AND JOINT:			
Pectoralis minor			
Trapezius I			
Levator scapulae			
OTHERS:			

APPENDIX E

MATHEMATICS REVIEW

1. **Order of Arithmetic Operations:**
   Certain arithmetic operations take precedence over others. In completing problems with a series of operations the following guidelines apply:

   a. Addition or subtraction may occur in any order.

   example: $4 + 8 - 7 + 3 = 8$ or $8 + 3 + 4 - 7 = 8$

   b. Multiplication or division must be completed before addition or subtraction.

   example: $48 \div 6 + 2 = 10$ example: $4 + (2/3)(1/2) = 4\ 1/3$

   c. Any quantity above a division line, under a division line or a radical sign

   ($\sqrt{}$) or within parentheses or brackets must be treated as one number.

   example: $\sqrt{36 - 25} = \sqrt{11}$ example: $2(5 + 3 - 4) = 8$

   example: $\dfrac{9 + 2}{3} = \dfrac{11}{3}$

2. **Fractions, Decimals and Per Cents:**

   a. To add (or subtract) fractions, the denominator in each term must be the same. (Choose the lowest common denominator for each term. Multiply each term by the common denominator and then add [or subtract].)

   example: $\dfrac{3}{4} + \dfrac{5}{3} = \dfrac{29}{12} = 2\dfrac{5}{12}$ (lowest common denominator = 12)

   solution:

   $$\dfrac{\left(\dfrac{3}{4} \times 12\right)}{12} + \dfrac{\left(\dfrac{5}{3} \times 12\right)}{12} = \dfrac{9}{12} + \dfrac{20}{12} = \dfrac{29}{12} = 2\dfrac{5}{12}$$

   example: $\dfrac{cd}{x} + \dfrac{x}{c} = \dfrac{c^2 d + x^2}{xc}$ (lowest common denominator = xc)

   solution:

   $$\dfrac{\left(\dfrac{cd}{x} \cdot xc\right)}{xc} + \dfrac{\left(\dfrac{x}{c} \cdot xc\right)}{xc} = \dfrac{c^2 d}{xc} + \dfrac{x^2}{xc} = \dfrac{c^2 d + x^2}{xc}$$

   b. To multiply fractions, multiply the numerators by each other and the denominators by each other.

   example: $\dfrac{3}{8} \cdot \dfrac{2}{3} = \dfrac{6}{24} = \dfrac{1}{4}$

   example: $pq\left(\dfrac{p}{q}\right) = \dfrac{p^2 q}{q} = p^2$

c. To divide fractions, invert the divisor and multiply.

example: $\dfrac{3}{8} \div \dfrac{9}{2} = \dfrac{3}{8} \times \dfrac{2}{9} = \dfrac{6}{72} = \dfrac{1}{12}$

example: $\dfrac{n}{r} \div \dfrac{s}{t} = \dfrac{n}{r} \times \dfrac{t}{s} = \dfrac{nt}{rs}$

example: $\left(\dfrac{1}{a} + \dfrac{1}{b}\right) \div \left(\dfrac{1}{a} - \dfrac{1}{b}\right) = \dfrac{b+a}{ab} \cdot \dfrac{ab}{b-a} = \dfrac{b+a}{b-a}$

d. To convert a fraction to a per cent, divide the numerator by the denominator and multiply by 100.

example: $\dfrac{3}{8} = .375 \times 100 = 37.5\%$

Note: To convert a per cent to a decimal move the decimal point two places to the left.

e. When *dividing* by a decimal divide by the integer and add sufficient zeros to move the decimal point the appropriate number of digits to the *right*.

example: $36 \div .04 = 900$ or $36 \div 4 = 9$ plus 00. $= 900$
appropriate number of digits to right $= 2$

When *multiplying* by a decimal multiply the integer and add enough zeros to move the decimal point the appropriate number of digits to the *left*.

example: $6 \times .012 = .072$ or $6 \times 12 = 72$ plus 0 to left $= .072$
appropriate number of digits to left $= 3$

f. Decimals may be expressed as positive or negative powers of 10:

$$10^0 = 1 \qquad\qquad 10^{-1} = 0.1$$
$$10^1 = 10 \qquad\qquad 10^{-2} = 0.01$$
$$10^2 = 100 \qquad\qquad 10^{-3} = 0.001$$
$$10^3 = 100 \qquad\qquad 10^{-4} = 0.0001$$
$$\text{etc.} \qquad\qquad\qquad \text{etc.}$$

example: $5624 = 56.24 \times 10^2$ example: $.0379 = 3.79 \times 10^{-2}$
$\qquad\qquad = 5.624 \times 10^3 \qquad\qquad\qquad\qquad = 37.9 \times 10^{-3}$
$\qquad\qquad = .5624 \times 10^4 \qquad\qquad\qquad\qquad = 379 \ \times 10^{-4}$

3. **Proportions, Formulas and Equations**
The location of values in proportions, equations or formulas may be shifted provided that whatever addition, subtraction, multiplication or division is performed on one side of the equation is also performed on the other side.

example: $\dfrac{a}{b} = \dfrac{c}{d}$

solve for d: $d \cdot \dfrac{a}{b} = \dfrac{c}{d} \cdot d$

$d \cdot \dfrac{a}{b} \cdot \dfrac{b}{a} = c \cdot \dfrac{b}{a}$

$d = c \cdot \dfrac{b}{a}$

example: $v^2 = u^2 + 2as$

solve for s: $2as = v^2 - u^2$

$s = \dfrac{v^2 - u^2}{2a}$

4. *Right Triangles and Trigonometric Functions:*

    a.   In a right triangle one angle always equals 90°. The other two angles will always be acute angles and the sum of these two angles will be 90° since the sum of the angles in any triangle is 180°.

    b.   In a right triangle the *sides* are related to each other so that the square of the longest side or hypotenuse (c) is equal to the sum of the squares of the other two sides: $c^2 = a^2 + b^2$. This is the Pythagorean Theorem.

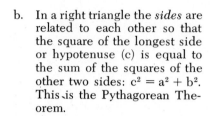

    c.   In triangle ABC, side a is called the side opposite angle A, side b is opposite angle B and the hypotenuse, c, is opposite the right angle. Side b is named the side *adjacent* to angle A and side a is the side adjacent to angle B.

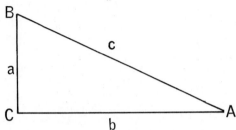

    d.   *Trigonometric functions* are ratios between the sides of a right triangle and are determined by the value of one of the acute angles. There are six trigonometric functions, the sine, cosine, tangent, cotangent, secant and cosecant, but it will be necessary to consider only four of them here.

In △ ABC the ratio between the side opposite and the hypotenuse is called the sine of the angle. For angle A it would be written sine $\angle A = \dfrac{a}{c}$ or $\sin A = \dfrac{a}{c}$; the sine $\angle B = \dfrac{b}{c}$ or $\sin B = \dfrac{b}{c}$.

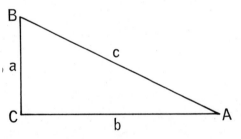

The cosine expresses the ratio between the side adjacent and the hypotenuse. For angle A, $\cos A = \dfrac{b}{c}$; for angle B, $\cos B = \dfrac{a}{c}$. The tangent and cotangent represent ratios between the two sides of the triangle. For angle A, $\tan A = \dfrac{a}{b}$ and $\cot A = \dfrac{b}{a}$; for angle B, $\tan B = \dfrac{b}{a}$ and $\cot B = \dfrac{a}{b}$. A glance at these values shows that the $\sin A = \cos B$, and that the $\tan A = \cot B$.

    e.   A table of trigonometric functions appears in Appendix F.

        example: sin 60° = .8660
                  cos 30° = .8660
                  tan 22° = .4040
                  cot 68° = .4040

Tables of trigonometric functions usually go up to 90°. Angles greater than 90° may be handled as follows:

Functions of angles greater than 90° but less than 180° are the same as functions of an angle equal to 180° minus the angle in question. All functions are negative except the sine.

example: sin 120° = sin 60°
tan 150° = −tan 30°

Functions of angles greater than 180° but less than 270° are the same as functions of an angle equal to 270° minus the angle in question. Functions are negative except for the tan and cot.

example: cos 220° = −cos 50°
tan 195° = tan 75°

Functions of angles greater than 270° but less than 360° are the same as functions of an angle equal to 360° minus the angle in question. All functions are negative except the cosine.

example: cot 300° = −cot 60°
sin 330° = −sin 30°

f. Through the use of trigonometric functions, it is possible to determine the values of all components of a triangle when the values of *one side and one angle* or the values of *two sides* are known.

example: In triangle ABC, angle A = 25° and the length of the hypotenuse is 15 ft. Find the length of the other two sides.

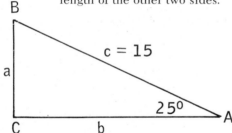

solution:

1. $\sin 25° = \dfrac{a}{c} = \dfrac{a}{15}$

   $a = 15 \sin 25°$

   $a = (15)(.4226)$

   $\boxed{a = 6.34 \text{ ft.}}$

2. $\cos 25° = \dfrac{b}{c} = \dfrac{b}{15}$

   $b = 15 \cos 25°$

   $b = (15)(.9063)$

   $\boxed{b = 13.59 \text{ ft.}}$

example: In triangle ABC the length of the sides are 3 in. and 5 in. What is the length of the hypotenuse and the size of both acute angles?

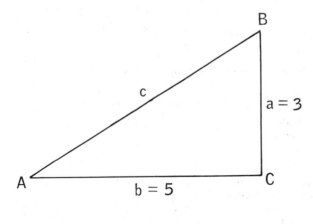

solution:

1. $\tan A = \dfrac{a}{b} = \dfrac{3}{5}$

   $A = \arctan .600$
   (i.e. A = angle whose tan is .600)

   $\boxed{A = 31°}$

2. $B = 90 - A;\ \boxed{B = 59°}$

3. $\sin A = \dfrac{a}{c} = \dfrac{3}{c}$

   $C = \dfrac{3}{\sin A} = \dfrac{3}{\sin 31°}$

   $C = \dfrac{3}{.5150} = \boxed{5.83 \text{ in.}}$

Note: C may also be found using the Pythagorean Theorem
$C^2 = a^2 + b^2$

5. Geometry of Circles

a. The circumference of a circle is calculated using the formula $C = 2\pi r$, where C is the circumference, r is the radius and π (pi) is a constant value of 3.1416. Pi is the ratio which exists between the diameter of a circle and its circumference.

b. In making one complete turn about a circle the radius goes through one revolution, 360° or 2π radians. A radian is the angle subtended by an arc of a circle equal in length to the radius. One radian equals $\frac{360°}{2\pi}$ or 57.3°. Some equivalents for these angular units of measure are as follows:

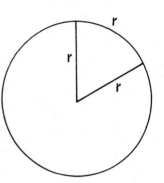

Revolutions	Radians	Degrees
1	2π or 6.28	360°
0.5	1π or 3.14	180°
0.25	0.5π or 1.57	90°
2	4π or 12.56	720°

To convert degrees to revolutions divide by 360

Example: 1260° = 3.50 rev.

To convert radians to revolutions divide by 6.28

Example: 15.75 radians = 2.51 rev.

To convert degrees to radians divide by 57.3

Example: 360° = 6.28 radians

To convert revolutions to radians multiply by 6.28

Example: 2.3 rev. = 14.44 radians

To convert revolutions to degrees multiply by 360

Example: 2.3 rev. = 828°

To convert radians to degrees multiply by 57.3

Example: 7.6 radians = 435.5°

APPENDIX F

TABLE OF TRIGONOMETRIC FUNCTIONS

DEGREES	SINES	COSINES	TANGENTS	COTANGENTS	
0	.0000	1.0000	.0000		90
1	.0175	.9998	.0175	57.290	89
2	.0349	.9994	.0349	28.636	88
3	.0523	.9986	.0524	19.081	87
4	.0698	.9976	.0699	14.301	86
5	.0872	.9962	.0875	11.430	85
6	.1045	.9945	.1051	9.5144	84
7	.1219	.9925	.1228	8.1443	83
8	.1392	.9903	.1405	7.1154	82
9	.1564	.9877	.1584	6.3138	81
10	.1736	.9848	.1763	5.6713	80
11	.1908	.9816	.1944	5.1446	79
12	.2079	.9781	.2126	4.7046	78
13	.2250	.9744	.2309	4.3315	77
14	.2419	.9703	.2493	4.0108	76
15	.2588	.9659	.2679	3.7321	75
16	.2756	.9613	.2867	3.4874	74
17	.2924	.9563	.3057	3.2709	73
18	.3090	.9511	.3249	3.0777	72
19	.3256	.9455	.3443	2.9042	71
20	.3420	.9397	.3640	2.7475	70
21	.3584	.9336	.3839	2.6051	69
22	.3746	.9272	.4040	2.4751	68
23	.3907	.9205	.4245	2.3559	67
24	.4067	.9135	.4452	2.2460	66
25	.4226	.9063	.4663	2.1445	65
26	.4384	.8988	.4877	2.0503	64
27	.4540	.8910	.5095	1.9626	63
28	.4695	.8829	.5317	1.8807	62
29	.4848	.8746	.5543	1.8040	61
30	.5000	.8660	.5774	1.7321	60
31	.5150	.8572	.6009	1.6643	59
32	.5299	.8480	.6249	1.6003	58
33	.5446	.8387	.6494	1.5399	57
34	.5592	.8290	.6745	1.4826	56
35	.5736	.8192	.7002	1.4281	55
36	.5878	.8090	.7265	1.3765	54
37	.6018	.7986	.7536	1.3270	53
38	.6157	.7880	.7813	1.2799	52
39	.6293	.7771	.8098	1.2349	51
40	.6428	.7660	.8391	1.1918	50
41	.6561	.7547	.8693	1.1504	49
42	.6691	.7431	.9004	1.1106	48
43	.6820	.7314	.9325	1.0724	47
44	.6947	.7193	.9657	1.0355	46
45	.7071	.7071	1.0000	1.0000	45
	COSINES	SINES	COTANGENTS	TANGENTS	DEGREES

NOTE: With angles above 45° be sure to use the headings that appear at the *bottom* of the columns.

APPENDIX G

EXERCISES FOR KINESIOLOGIC ANALYSIS

These exercises and techniques, intended as laboratory material for the student, are presented for analysis (major joint and muscle action) of movements. Many are commonly used to develop strength, increase flexibility and improve posture. In most instances they are organized according to the major body segments (the upper and lower extremities and the trunk-head-neck). Many of the exercises are illustrated by three views: (1) the starting position, (2) the movement and (3) the return to the starting position. The calisthenic and gymnastic exercises were selected on the basis of their use in (1) physical fitness and posture programs, in (2) conditioning programs for improving athletic performance and in (3) tests for assessing strength and muscular endurance. The sports and gymnastics techniques are representative of movements involving the giving of impetus to one's own body and to external objects. The exercises are organized in the following series:

Series 1 Weight Training Exercises (barbells and weighted pulleys)
Series 2 Calisthenic and Gymnastic Exercises
Series 3 Isometric Tension Exercises (singly and with partners)
Series 4 Flexibility Exercises
Series 5 Posture Exercises
Series 6 Selected Sports and Gymnastics Techniques

The exercises within each series are numbered consecutively in the following manner: The first exercise in Series 1 is numbered 1–1, the second, 1–2. The first exercise in Series 2 is numbered 2–1, followed by 2–2, and so on in similar fashion.

Series 1. Weight Training Exercises.
The Upper Extremity

Starting Position   Movement   Return to Starting Position

Exercise 1–1.

Exercise 1–2.

Exercise 1–3.

Series 1. Weight Training Exercises.

The Upper Extremity

Starting Position *Movement* *Return to Starting Position*

Exercise 1–4.

Exercise 1–5.

Exercise 1–6.

Series 1. Weight Training Exercises.
The Upper Extremity

Starting Position   *Movement*   *Return to Starting Position*

Series 1. Weight Training Exercises.
The Lower Extremity

Starting Position *Movement* *Return to Starting Position*

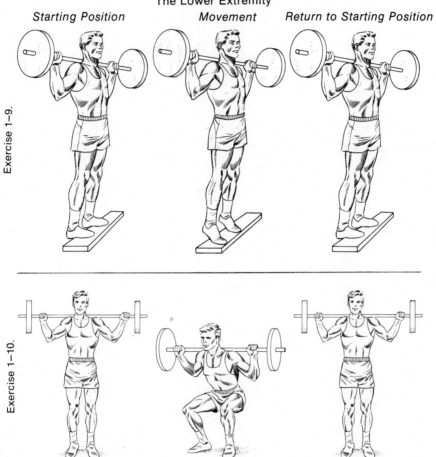

Exercise 1–9.

Exercise 1–10.

Series 1. Weight Training Exercises.
The Lower Extremity

Starting Position

Movement

Return to Starting Position

The Upper Extremity

Exercise 1–11.

Exercise 1–12.

Exercise 1–13.

Exercise 1–14.

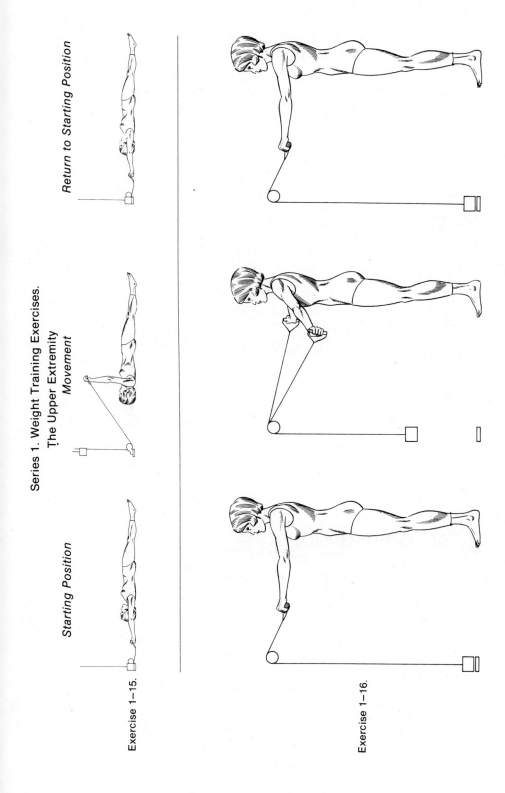

Series 1. Weight Training Exercises.
The Upper Extremity

Starting Position   *Movement*   *Return to Starting Position*

Exercise 1–15.

Exercise 1–16.

Series 1. Weight Training Exercises.
The Upper Extremity

Starting Position

Movement

Return to Starting Position

Exercise 1–17.

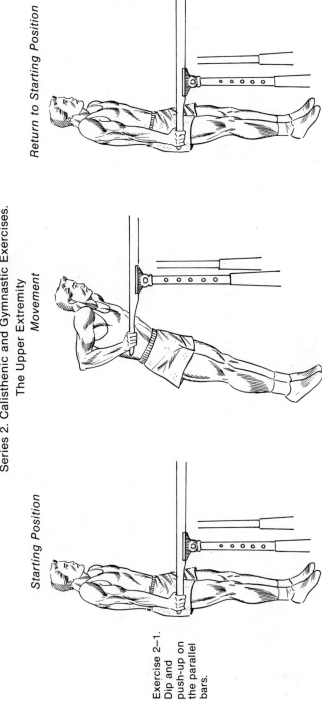

Series 2. Calisthenic and Gymnastic Exercises. The Upper Extremity

Starting Position

Movement

Return to Starting Position

Exercise 2–1. Dip and push-up on the parallel bars.

Series 2. Calisthenic and Gymnastic Exercises.
The Trunk

Starting Position

Movement

Return to Starting Position

Exercise 2–2.
Twist sit-up
with legs
extended.

Exercise 2–3.
Sit-up with
knees
flexed.

Exercise 2–4.
Sit-up with
double leg
lift.

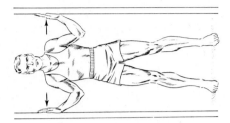

Exercise 3–3.
Push Out

Series 3. Isometric Tension Exercises.
The Upper Extremity

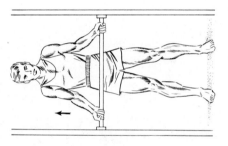

Exercise 3–2.
Pull Up

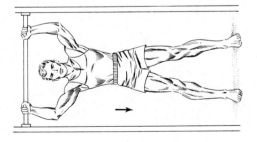

Exercise 3–1.
Pull Down

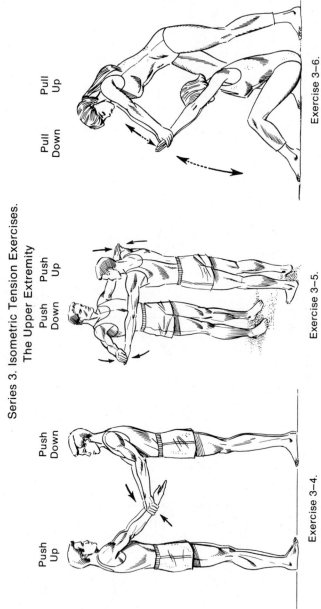

Series 3. Isometric Tension Exercises.
The Upper Extremity

Push Down   Push Up   Exercise 3–5.

Push Down   Push Up   Exercise 3–4.

Pull Down   Pull Up

Exercise 3–6.

Series 3. Isometric Tension Exercises.
The Lower Extremity and Trunk

Push Up

Exercise 3–7.

Hold

Exercise 3–8.

Pull Leg Down

Exercise 3–9.

Press Lumbar
Spine Back

Exercise 3–10.

The Trunk—Head—Neck

Push Down   Pull Up

Exercise 3–11.

Pull Up   Push Down

Exercise 3–12.

Exercise 3–13.
Pull neck
backward.

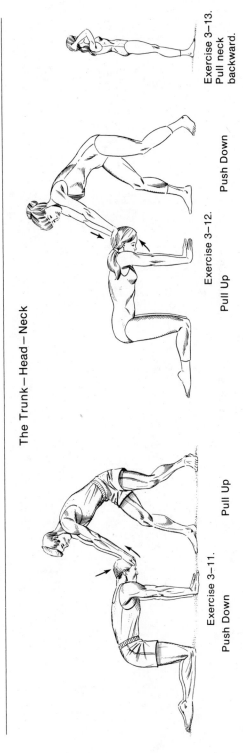

Series 4. Flexibility Exercises for Major Joints.

Exercise 4–1.

Exercise 4–2.

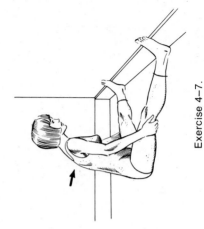

Exercise 4–3.

Exercise 4–4.

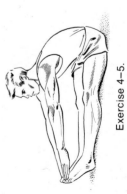

Exercise 4–5.

Exercise 4–6.

Exercise 4–7.

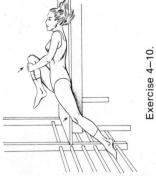

Exercise 4–10.

Series 4. Flexibility Exercises for Major Joints.

Exercise 4–9.

Exercise 4–8.

Series 5. Posture Exercises.

Exercise 5–1.
(Photographs taken from Wells, K. F.: Posture Exercise Handbook: A Progressive Sequence Approach. The Ronald Press Company, New York, 1963.)

Series 5. Posture Exercises.

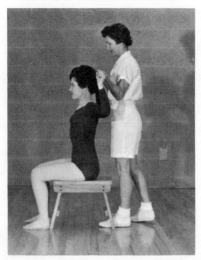

Exercise 5–2.

Exercise 5–3.

Series 5. Posture Exercises.

Exercise 5–4.

Exercise 5–5.

Exercise 5–6.

Series 5. Posture Exercises.

Exercise 5–7.

Exercise 5–8.

Series 6. Sports and Gymnastics Techniques.

A   B   C   D

Figure 6–1   Volleyball serve.

A   B   C

Figure 6–2   Soccer throw-in.

Series 6. Sports and Gymnastics Techniques.

Figure 6-3 Baseball swing.

Series 6. Sports and Gymnastics Techniques.

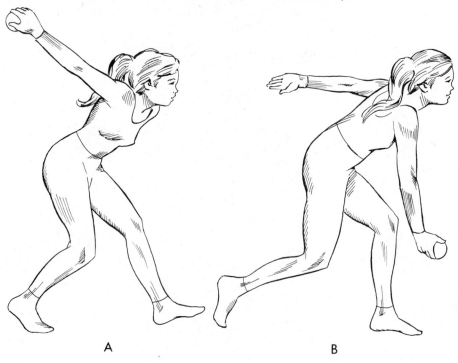

A   B

C

Figure 6–4 Underarm softball throw.

Series 6. Sports and Gymnastics Techniques.

A   B   C

Figure 6-5 Leap.

Series 6. Sports and Gymnastics Techniques.

Figure 6-6   Backward somersault.

Figure 6–7 Back walkover.

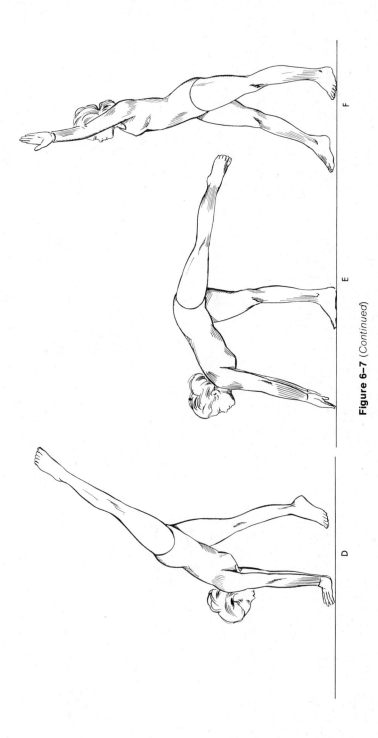

Figure 6–7 (*Continued*)

INDEX

Note: Page numbers in *italics* denote illustrations.
Page numbers followed by (t) denote tables.